W9-CEN-285

(continued on back endpaper)

Companion volumes prepared by
EDWIN MANSFIELD

MICROECONOMIC PROBLEMS:
CASE STUDIES AND EXERCISES FOR REVIEW
Seventh Edition

MICROECONOMICS: SELECTED READINGS
Fifth Edition

Microeconomics

THEORY/APPLICATIONS

SEVENTH EDITION

EDWIN MANSFIELD

DIRECTOR, CENTER FOR ECONOMICS
AND TECHNOLOGY
UNIVERSITY OF PENNSYLVANIA

W.W. NORTON & COMPANY NEW YORK · LONDON

TO DIXIE
who once again asked that this dedication be
as short as possible

Copyright © 1991 by W.W. Norton & Company, Inc.

Printed in the United States of America.

The text of this book is composed in Galliard,
with the display set in Univers 59.
Composition by TSI Graphics.
Manufacturing by The Maple-Vail Book Group.
Book design by Suzanne Bennett.

Library of Congress Cataloging-in-Publication Data

Mansfield, Edwin.
    Microeconomics: theory, applications/Edwin Mansfield.—7th ed.
        p.   cm.
    Includes bibliographical references.
    1. Microeconomics.   I. Title.
HB172.M36   1991
338.5—dc20   90-31462

ISBN 0-393-96036-6
W.W. Norton & Company, Inc., 500 Fifth Avenue, New York, N.Y. 10110
W.W. Norton & Company, Ltd., 10 Coptic Street, London WC1A 1PU

1 2 3 4 5 6 7 8 9 0

CONTENTS

Part One
Introduction

Part Two
Consumer Behavior and Market Demand

Chapter 5 Market Demand   108

Part Three
The Firm: Its Technology and Costs

Chapter 6 The Firm and Its Technology   137

Chapter 7 Optimal Input Combinations and Cost Functions   167

Part Four
Market Structure, Price and Output

Chapter 10 Monopolistic Competition and Oligopoly   294

Chapter 11 Game Theory and Strategic Behavior   323

Part Five
Markets for Inputs

Part Six
General Equilibrium, Economic Efficiency, Externalities, and Public Goods

Part Seven
Intertemporal Choice and Decision-Making Involving Risk

PREFACE

In the last decade or so, a new generation of economists has advanced micro-economic theory in important new directions. Most notably, these economists have worked to understand the role of strategy in competitive rivalries, the effects of the information available to market participants on the outcomes of the markets in which they take part, and the ways in which economic models can be used to analyze financial markets. Their work has not changed the underlying structure of our discipline, but it has brought to us significant new insights, which all too frequently are omitted from intermediate microeconomic texts. Since I believe that it is high time that students are introduced to these exciting new developments and insights, I have made a particular effort in preparing this edition to provide clear, effective, and interesting discussions of the many important developments in microeconomic theory that have occurred in recent years. The result is the most extensive revision to date of this book.

In particular, the chapters on oligopoly and monopolistic competition have been completely rewritten. There is now a new chapter on Game Theory and Strategic Behavior, which discusses such topics as Nash equilibrium, the prisoners' dilemma, strategic moves, threats, entry deterrence, limit pricing, first-mover advantages, and preemptive strategies. This discussion of game theory, while pitched at a basic level, is more complete and up-to-date than in competing texts.

Further, the pervasive effects of asymmetric and imperfect information are emphasized at appropriate places throughout the text. Beginning in Chapter 2, the possibility of a "winner's curse" in auctions where information is imperfect and the effects of asymmetric information on the market for used cars are described. In Chapter 12, both market signaling in labor markets (and the role of education in this regard) and efficiency wage theory are taken up. In Chapter 15, the effect of imperfect information on the efficiency of competitive markets is discussed, and in Chapter 18 the problem of moral hazard is described. In contrast to other texts, which either ignore these topics or lump them together in a chapter at the end of the book, the present text weaves them into the main thread of the discussion.

In addition, this edition explores a variety of influential and useful modern developments in the theory of the firm. In Chapter 6, for instance, there is a new section called "Firm Owners and Managers: A Principal-Agent Problem"; and in Chapter 12, there is a new section on "Employers and Workers: A Principal-Agent Problem." Still more examples appear in the treatment of monopoly pricing in Chapter 9, which has been enriched by the addition of new sections on two-part tariffs, tying, and bundling.

Several other additions deserve mention here. One is the new coverage of the capital asset pricing model in Chapter 18. This powerful tool helped to link microeconomic theory with the day-to-day operation of the financial markets, a topic of great interest to students (and many others). There are also new sections on economies of scope in Chapter 7 and on internal rates of return and bond yields in Chapter 17. The discussion of public goods in Chapter 16, as well as the entire treatment of economic efficiency in Chapter 15, has been revised and updated. Finally, the sections dealing with the Consumer Price Index and the optimal combinations of fertilizers in corn production have been simplified and clarified.

Given the host of new topics included in this edition, I have had no choice but to purge all passages that seemed out-of-date or extraneous. Chapter 3 provides a case in point. It has been rewritten extensively with some material dropped. In the case of two topics, however—cardinal utility and the kinked demand curve—I decided to keep them in the book, because many instructors find them useful. But since their coverage is optional, I put these discussions in chapter appendices.

While teachers, who are familiar with the foregoing developments in our field, are likely to be particularly interested in these aspects of the revision, students may be more impressed with the many new applications and examples that have been added. I have always felt that it is crucial to show how microeconomics can illuminate pressing problems of public and private policy. This is particularly important as the American and world economies move into the 1990s. Almost half of the boxed examples—22 of them, to be precise—are new. They deal with the following topics: (1) Is the War on Drugs Being Won? (2) Should Bovine Growth Hormone Be Banned? (3) Rent-Control California-Style: Mobile Home Owners vs. Park Owners, (4) Sickness and Health Insurance, (5) Calculating a Cost-of-Living Index, (6) Residential Demand for Water, (7) Should Two New York Dairy Farms Merge? (8) The Effects of Biotechnology on an Antibiotic's Production Costs, (9) What Would Be the Effects of National Dental Insurance? (10) Why Should the Price of Bananas Be So Much Higher in Denmark Than in Ireland? (11) A Two-Part Tariff at Disneyland, (12) The Rejection of the Santa Fe-Southern Pacific Merger, (13) A Cartel in the Orange Groves, (14) Should Amherst Buy All Its Steel from Duquesne? (15) How Government Can Tilt the Outcome of Oligopoly, (16) The Value of the Marginal Product of Irrigation Water, (17) How Much Effect Would a Wage Increase Have on the Nursing Shortage? (18) The Effect of Voting Rules, (19) Should Refuse Collection Be Privatized? (20) Should the Carborundum Corporation Expand Its Capacity? (21) Did Proposition 13 Result in Lower Housing Prices? and (22) The Growth of Labor Productivity at General Motors and Toyota.

The well-received cross-chapter cases have also been reworked. In Parts Two and Four, there are new ones; both of them are concerned with the application of microeconomics to international topics and issues. The new case in Part Two deals with "The Demand for Airline Travel: The North Atlantic Market"; the new case in Part Four deals with "The Economics of 1992." These topics were selected by the same criteria used in choosing the other cross-chapter cases: to show how the material in several related chapters can be woven together to help illuminate a topic or issue of interest to both students and teachers. Indeed, given the importance of helping students to see that the world economy is becoming increasingly interdependent, it is worth noting that practically all of the cross-chapter cases now deal with international issues.

Finally, a number of new end-of-chapter questions have been added, and a host of small alterations have been inserted to make the discussion more current. From the first chapter to the last, a wide variety of changes have been made in tables, figures, text, and footnotes. Each sentence has been gone over with an eye toward improvement.

As with previous editions, a workbook and reader accompany the text. *Microeconomic Problems: Case Studies and Exercises for Review,* Seventh Edition, has been revised very substantially, making it more effective in guiding students toward an understanding of the theories comprising and underlying microeconomics. In particular, the organization of the book has been changed, problems have been segregated from review questions, and there is a more orderly transition from simpler to more difficult items. Also, new problems and questions have been added that test students' skills in applying microeconomic theory to real-world situations. *Microeconomic Problems* now contains about 1,100 questions and problems, together with their solutions.

Microeconomics: Selected Readings, Fifth Edition, includes papers on topics such as the demand for lemons, market signaling, laboratory experimentation in economics, recent antitrust cases, predatory behavior, and the economic implications of robots, among many others. In my opinion, this reader continues to be broader and more varied than other books of readings at the intermediate level.

An *Instructor's Manual* is available for the text. In addition to teaching suggestions for each chapter, it includes a test bank of multiple-choice questions and problem sets which not only reflects the decision-making emphasis of the text, but also develops theory as a set of principles that yields insights into everyday problems. William Gunther and Paul Sommers, the authors of the *Instructor's Manual,* have created a freshly varied diet of teaching materials for this new edition, and this is the place to record my thanks to them.

Test questions also are available to instructors on floppy disks for use with a personal computer. Information on obtaining these disks can be obtained from the publisher.

Since it would be impossible to list all of the many instructors and reviewers who have contributed in important ways to this and the previous editions, I must be content with thanking only a sample: Charles A. Berry, University of Cincinnati; Allan Braff, University of New Hampshire; Stephen R. Brenner,

Grinnell College; Byron Brown, Michigan State University; Eleanor Brown, Pomona College; Neil Bruce, Queen's University; James Cairns, Royal Military College of Canada; Joseph Cammarosano, Fordham University; Alvin Cohen, Lehigh University; Marshall Colberg, Florida State University; James Dana, Dartmouth College; Avinash Dixit, Princeton University; James Dolan, Regis College; Robert Dorfman, Harvard University; Catherine Eckel, Virginia Polytechnic Institute; Allan Feldman, Brown University; Alan Fisher, California State University at Fullerton; J. Fred Giertz, Miami University; Ellen Goldstein, California State University at Fullerton; Warren Gramm, Washington State University; William Gunther, University of Alabama; Kanji Haitani, State University of New York, Fredonia; Simon Hakim, Temple University; Richard Harmstone, Pennsylvania State University; William Holohan, University of Wisconsin at Milwaukee; Theodore E. Keeler, University of California, Berkeley; Elizabeth Sawyer Kelley, University of Wisconsin at Madison; Jonathan Kesselman, University of British Columbia; Charles Knoeber, North Carolina State University; Steven Kohlhagen, University of California, Berkeley; Shou-Eng Koo, Indiana University and Purdue University; John Laitner, University of Michigan; Richard Levin, Yale University; J. Patrick Lewis, Otterbein College; C. Richard Long, Georgia State University; Paul Malatesta, Colgate University; Lawrence Martin, Michigan State University; M. R. Metzger, George Washington University; Edwin Mills, Princeton University; Hajime Miyazaki, Stanford University; David Molina, North Texas State University; John Murphy, Canisius College; Richard Musgrave, Harvard University; K. R. Nair, West Virginia Wesleyan College; John Neufeld, University of North Carolina; Mancur Olson, University of Maryland; John Palmer, University of Western Ontario; R. D. Peterson, Colorado State University; Charles Plourde, York University; Robert Pollak, University of Pennsylvania; Richard Porter, University of Michigan; Charles Ratliff, Davidson College; David J. Ravenscraft, University of North Carolina, Chapel Hill; Thomas Riddell, Bucknell University; Ray Roberts, Jr., Furman University; Anthony Romeo, University of Connecticut; Robert E. Rosenman, Washington State University; Anthony Rufolo, Federal Reserve Bank of Philadelphia; Sol S. Shalit, University of Wisconsin at Milwaukee; Barry Siegel, University of Oregon; N. J. Simler, University of Minnesota; A. Michael Spence, Harvard University; James Stephenson, Iowa State University; Daniel Sullivan, Northwestern University; Richard Sylla, North Carolina State University; W. James Truitt, Baylor University; Gordon Tullock, Virgina Polytechnic Institute; Hal Varian, University of Michigan; David Vrooman, St. Lawrence University; Donal Walker, Indiana University of Pennsylvania; Joan Werner, University of Michigan; A. R. Whitaker, U.S. Naval Academy; Bronislaw Wojtun, Lemoyne-Owen College; Gary Yohe, Wesleyan University; and Richard Zeckhauser, Harvard University. Further, I would like to thank W. Drake McFeely of Norton for doing a fine job with the publishing end of the work. And special thanks go to my wife, who again helped in countless ways.

E.M.

Philadelphia, 1991

PART ONE

INTRODUCTION

THE NATURE OF
MICROECONOMICS

INTRODUCTION

Winston Churchill, Britain's great prime minister, was not well versed in economics. Indeed, according to his critics, he was "without a deep appreciation of decimal points." While he could succeed without much knowledge of economics, you may not be so fortunate. Economics helps us to understand the nature and organization of our society, the arguments underlying many of the great public issues of the day, and the operation and behavior of business firms and other economic decision-making units. To perform effectively and responsibly as citizens, administrators, workers, or consumers, most people need to know some economics.

Precisely what does economics deal with? According to one standard definition, economics is concerned with the way in which resources are allocated among alternative uses to satisfy human wants. It is customary to divide eco-

Microeconomics   nomics into two parts: microeconomics and macroeconomics. *Microeconomics* deals with the economic behavior of individual units such as consumers, firms, and resource owners; macroeconomics deals with the behavior of economic aggregates such as gross national product and the level of employment.

This book is concerned with microeconomics. A general definition of microeconomics fraught with vague words like *resources* and *human wants* is unlikely to communicate the power of microeconomic theory or its usefulness in solving major problems in the real world. So we begin our discussion by giving four examples of the kinds of problems that microeconomics can help to solve. (Each of these examples is considered in detail in subsequent chapters.) Although these four examples cover only a small sample of the questions to which microeconomics is relevant, they give you a reasonable first impression of the nature of microeconomics and its relevance to the real world.

OPTIMAL PRODUCTION DECISIONS

Business firms are constantly faced with the problem of choosing among alternative ways of manufacturing their products. Consider firms that produce ethanol, a chemical made from corn and used for fuel. The federal government, which has encouraged ethanol production to help meet the nation's fuel needs, favored the establishment of many small ethanol plants, but this has not occurred. As shown in Table 1.1, the cost of producing a gallon of ethanol is much higher for a small plant than for a large one. Thus firms have tended to build big plants, not small ones.

But how big should a plant be? And how many workers should be hired to run it? And how much output should it produce per day? These are examples of one type of problem that microeconomics is designed to solve. They are questions faced by an individual firm that is trying to maximize its profit or attain some other set of objectives of its owners and managers. Microeconomics serves as the basis for, and is helpful in promoting an understanding of, the powerful modern tools of managerial decision-making that help to solve such problems.

TABLE 1.1 Cost Per Gallon of Producing Ethanol in Plants of Various Sizes

Size of plant (millions of gallons per year)	Cost of production (per gallon)
10	$0.82
50	0.42
100	0.33

Source: A. Hacking, *Economic Aspects of Biotechnology* (Cambridge: Cambridge University Press, 1986), p. 202.

These analytical tools are as applicable in Tokyo or Singapore as in New York or Toronto, and woe to the firm that ignores or misapplies them in this era of intense international competition. Gone are the days when firms in a handful of nations in North America and Europe were the only ones that used them in a sophisticated way. Now the Japanese and others set the standard with regard to production decisions of this sort in industries like steel and consumer electronics. Besides being useful throughout the world, these analytical tools are applicable to government as well as business. The techniques introduced in recent decades in many government agencies to promote better decision-making are fundamentally applications of microeconomics.[1]

1. For answers to the kinds of problems posed in this section, see Chapters 8–13.

PRICING POLICY

Most firms are also faced with the problem of pricing their products. For example, consider a firm manufacturing telephone systems. If it sells in a variety of countries, it must decide whether to set a lower price in some countries than in others. In fact, according to the American Telephone and Telegraph Company, Japanese, Korean, and Taiwanese producers of telephone systems often set a much lower price in the United States than in their home markets. Is this sensible? And if so, how large should the international price differential be?

This type of problem faces many, many firms. For example, as shown in Table 1.2, the price of the same type of car of the same quality has been about 43 percent higher in the United Kingdom than in Belgium. It is important that firms know whether such price differentials are in their best interests—or whether they are too high or too low. Microeconomics provides a basis for analyzing and solving such problems. When a management consultant is hired to help solve a problem of this sort, his or her recommendations, if sound, will rely on the application of well-established principles of microeconomics.[2]

TABLE 1.2 Percentage Difference Between the Price of an Automobile in Selected European Countries and in Belgium, 1983

Country	Percentage difference in price
Belgium	0
France	+15
Germany	+17
Italy	+29
United Kingdom	+43

Source: M. Emerson, et al, *The Economics of 1992* (Oxford: Oxford University Press, 1988), p. 78. These prices exclude taxes and pertain to Japanese cars, but the results for European cars are very similar.

EFFICIENT ALLOCATION OF A SOCIETY'S RESOURCES

In the previous two sections we were concerned with problems facing individual business firms. Although such problems are important and interesting, they are by no means the only type dealt with by microeconomics. On the contrary, much of microeconomics is concerned with problems that face us all as citizens. Together we must somehow decide how we want to organize the production and marketing of goods and services in our country. We must also decide how

2. For a description of the way in which a pricing problem like that described in this section can be solved, see Chapter 9.

these goods and services are to be distributed among the people. Some of the subtlest and most significant applications of microeconomics are in this area.

In recent years, there has been a great deal of talk concerning the restructuring of various aspects of the economy. Some people charge that many basic American industries like steel and automobiles are unable to compete with their foreign rivals, and that fundamental changes should be made in government policy concerning taxes, education, foreign trade, and a host of other topics influencing the competitiveness of American firms in world markets. Suppose that we ask the following basic question: If we could restructure the entire economic system and if we agreed that the goal was to make anyone better off (in terms of his or her own tastes) as long as this did not make someone else worse off (in terms of the latter's tastes), what sorts of changes would we be justified in making? More specifically, suppose that we could take resources away from some sectors of the economy and provide them to other sectors, or that we could prohibit consumers from consuming certain goods, or that we could prohibit firms from laying off workers or charging certain prices. What actions of this sort (if any) would we be justified in taking?

Students sometimes complain that they are not confronted with significant or revelant questions. Surely such complaints cannot be lodged legitimately against this question! Having said this, it is important to add that microeconomics has progressed far enough to be able to provide at least partial answers to this kind of question, which is fortunate since the value of a field lies more in its power to answer questions than in the audacity with which it poses them. Nonetheless, one should not be encouraged to believe that microeconomics is the key that by itself will unlock the answers to the great social problems of the day. Microeconomics provides a way of thinking about many of these problems that is valuable, as indicated perhaps by the formidable number of economists appointed by both Democratic and Republican administrations to positions of great responsibility. But microeconomics, although valuable, is only one of many disciplines that have important roles to play in this area.[3]

PUBLIC POLICY CONCERNING MARKET STRUCTURE

Another problem that faces us all as citizens is the way that industries are structured. Suppose for simplicity that all industries sell to a large number of independent buyers, none of which is in a position to influence the price of the product. Suppose that we have three choices: to allow each industry to be taken over by a single firm, to allow each industry to become dominated by a few firms (but prevent a single firm from taking over), or to make sure that each industry is composed of a large number of independent firms. Which choice should we make?

This is a very important problem—and one that continues to be the center of considerable controversy. In the United States, the antitrust laws are designed to promote competition and to control monopoly. For example, the Sherman

3. For a discussion of the problem described in this section, see Chapter 15.

Act of 1890, the first major federal legislation directed against monopoly, outlaws conspiracies or combinations in restraint of trade and forbids the monopolizing of trade or commerce. This seems to indicate that we as a nation have decided not to allow industries to be taken over by a single firm. But is this policy justified? To what extent has it been outmoded by developments in the years that have elapsed since the passage of the Sherman Act?

According to some prominent observers, a policy designed to insure that each industry be composed of a large number of independent firms would be a mistake. They claim that very large firms are required in many industries to insure efficiency and promote progress. How can their arguments be evaluated? What criteria can be used to judge the relative advantages of alternative ways that industries can be structured? In various discussions, one often hears of the advantages of a competitive system in which industries are composed of many small firms. In what sense can such a system be shown to be optimal? Is it always optimal, or just under certain special conditions?

This problem is of the utmost importance, since it concerns the basic framework within which the nation's business activity is carried out. It is one of the most fundamental questions of public policy. Compared with the production and pricing problems of individual firms, it—like the problem in the previous section—is certainly more difficult to formulate and to solve, if for no other reason than that it is harder to decide what benefits the entire country than it is to decide what benefits a particular firm. By the same token, this problem is much broader than the problems of the individual firms discussed above. Whereas our interest there was to find policies that would benefit a particular firm, our interest here is to find policies that will benefit the nation as a whole.

This is another example of a problem that microeconomics is aimed at helping to solve. Although it is not possible to solve this problem in as neat or as simple a fashion as one might solve a less complicated problem, it is possible to throw considerable light on the issues involved—and microeconomists have labored for generations to see to it that problems of this sort are analyzed as dispassionately and as scientifically as possible. Moreover, the results have been put to use in the world of action as well as in the world of speculation and study. The lawyer who argues an antitrust case, and the judge who decides one, must both rely on and use the principles of microeconomics.[4]

MICROECONOMICS: PROBLEM-SOLVING AND SCIENCE

The previous four sections have provided some examples of problems that microeconomics can help solve. These examples are useful in indicating the relevance of microeconomics, but they may be misleading if they suggest that microeconomics is wholly a bag of techniques to solve practical problems. On the contrary, *microeconomics, like any branch of the natural or social sciences, is concerned with the explanation and prediction of observed phenomena regardless of*

4. For discussion of the problem described in this section, see Chapters 8–11, 15, and 17.

whether these explanations or predictions have any immediate applications to practical problems. As indicated in the previous sections, it has turned out that many parts of microeconomics have been relevant and useful in solving practical problems, but this does not mean that all of microeconomics *has* found an application of this sort or that all of microeconomics *should* find an application of this sort.

For example, one of the principal objectives of microeconomics is to answer questions like the following: What determines the price of various commodities? (Why is filet mignon more expensive than hot dogs?) What determines the amount that a worker makes? (Why are surgeons paid more than librarians?) What determines the way that a consumer allocates his or her income among various commodities? (How will an increase in the price of butter affect the amount of margarine purchased by the Thompson family?) What determines how much of a particular commodity will be produced? (What accounts for the woeful decrease in the number of cigar-store Indians produced?) What determines the number and size of firms in a particular industry? (Why are there so many producers of milk and so few producers of computers?)

None of these questions, as it stands, is in the form of a practical problem. Yet to understand the world about us and to perform effectively as citizens, administrators, or workers, it is obvious that we must have at least a minimal understanding of the answers to these questions. The situation is something like that of mathematics. Although pure mathematics is not concerned with the solution of particular problems, it has turned out that various branches of mathematics are of great value in solving practical problems. And a minimal knowledge of mathematics is extremely important as a basis for understanding the world around us and for further professional and technical training.

HUMAN WANTS AND RESOURCES

At the beginning of this chapter, we gave a very brief definition of economics which must now be expanded and explained. We said that economics focuses on the way in which resources are allocated among alternative uses to satisfy human wants. This is a perfectly satisfactory definition, but it does not mean much unless we define what is meant by *human wants* and by *resources*. What do these terms mean?

Human wants

Human wants are the things, services, goods, and circumstances that people desire. Wants vary greatly among individuals and over time for the same individual. Some people like sports, others like books; some want to travel, others want to putter in the yard. An individual's desire for a particular good during a particular period of time is not infinite, but in the aggregate human wants seem to be insatiable. Besides the basic desires for food, shelter, and clothing, which must be fulfilled to some extent if the human organism is to maintain its existence, wants arise from cultural factors. For example, society, often helped along by advertising and other devices to modify tastes, promotes certain images of the "full, rich life," which frequently entail the possession and consumption of certain types of automobiles, houses, appliances, and other goods and services.

Resources are the things or services used to produce goods which can be used to satisfy wants. Economic resources are scarce, while free resources, such as air, are so abundant that they can be obtained without charge. The test of whether a resource is an economic resource or a free resource is price: Economic resources command a nonzero price but free resources do not. In a world where all resources were free, there would be no economic problem since all wants could be satisfied.

An economic resource that is used in the production of a particular good is called an input. In the example in Table 1.1, the inputs in the manufacture of ethanol are labor, corn (and other materials), energy, and manufacturing equipment. Economic resources have alternative uses. A particular resource generally can be used in the production of many types of goods. For example, the labor used by the ethanol manufacturer could be used by many other kinds of firms and in many other kinds of work. Of course, as resources become more specialized, there generally are fewer alternative jobs for them—but there are still some. Even the equipment used to make the ethanol can probably be adapted for somewhat different uses.

Economic resources are of a variety of types. In the nineteenth century it was customary for economists to classify economic resources into three categories: land, labor, and capital. In recent years this sort of classification has tended to go out of style in part because each category contains such an enormous variety of resources. Nevertheless, it is worthwhile defining each of these general types of resources. Land is a shorthand expression for natural resources. Labor is human effort, both physical and mental. Capital includes equipment, buildings, inventories, raw materials, and other nonhuman producible resources that contribute to the production, marketing, and distribution of goods and services. Note that the economist's definition of capital is different from that of the man in the street who employs the word to mean money. For example, a man with a hot dog stand who has $200 in his pocket may say that he has $200 in capital; but his definition is different from that of the economist who would include in the man's capital the value of his stand, the value of his equipment, the value of his inventory of hot dogs and mustard, and the value of other nonlabor resources (other than land) that he uses.

Technology

TECHNOLOGY

Another term that must be defined at this point is *technology*. Technology is society's pool of knowledge regarding the industrial and agricultural arts. Technology consists of knowledge used in industry and agriculture concerning the principles of physical and social phenomena (such as the laws of motion and the properties of fluids), knowledge regarding the application of these principles to production (such as the application of various aspects of genetic theory to the breeding of new plants), and knowledge regarding the day-to-day operation of production (such as the rules of thumb of the skilled craftsman). Note that technology is different from the techniques in use, since not all that is known is likely to be in use. Also, technology is different from pure science, although the distinction is not very precise. Pure science is directed toward understanding, whereas technology is directed toward use.

The important thing about technology is that it sets limits on the amount and types of goods that can be derived from a given amount of resources. Put differently, it sets limits on the extent to which human wants can be satisfied by a given amount of resources. For instance, consider the manufacturer of ethanol, discussed above. Suppose that, with the existing technology, one bushel of corn will yield approximately 2.5 gallons of ethanol. There is no way to produce more than this amount of ethanol from a bushel of corn. This is beyond the current state of the art. Engineers and craftsmen do not yet know how to accomplish this. It is obvious that this limitation of existing knowledge results in a corresponding limitation on how much ethanol can be produced from corn. If, for example, 100 million bushels of corn are devoted to ethanol production, the maximum amount of ethanol that can be produced is 250 million gallons.

THE TASKS PERFORMED BY AN ECONOMIC SYSTEM

Economics, of course, deals with the functioning of economic systems—just as, for example, biology deals with the functioning of biological systems. Perhaps the best way to define the economic system is to describe what it does. A society's economic system must allocate its resources among competing uses, combine and process these resources in such a way as to produce goods and services, determine the amount of various goods and services that will be produced, distribute these goods and services among the society's members, and determine what provision is to be made for the future growth of the society's per capita income. Put in a single sentence, these tasks do not seem quite as awesome as in fact they are. To do justice to each of these tasks, a fuller explanation is needed.

How should resources be used?

First, the economic system must allocate its resources among competing uses and combine and process these resources to produce the desired level and composition of output. Suppose that the desired level and composition of output is known. There usually are many ways of producing a commodity, and it is not easy to decide which way is best. For example, a plant can use different types and quantities of equipment, different amounts and qualities of raw materials, different amounts and qualities of labor, different locations, different means of transporting and distributing its product, and different ways of informing potential customers of the product's existence. Of the many combinations of resources that could be used, which should be used? Or looking at the problem from a somewhat different point of view, there is an enormous quantity and variety of resources in any society: How should each of these resources be used?

Even if some smart Philadelphia lawyer, or some other type of philosopher-king, could tell us which combination of resources is best for the production of each good, this would not be a complete solution to the problem. We would also have to find a way to insure that this combination would in fact be used.

The difficulty of solving this aspect of the problem should not be under-estimated. Even in highly disciplined organizations like armies, it is not unusual for a general's plan of action to be executed improperly or distorted considerably.

*What should be
produced?*

Second, an economic system must determine the level and composition of output. To what extent should society's resources be used to produce weapons systems? To what extent should they be used to build medical laboratories? To what extent should they be used to produce cotton and wool cloth? To what extent should they be used to produce artificial fibers like nylon? To what extent should they be used to produce neckties? To what extent should they be used to produce Levis? What is the proper combination of goods—weapons systems, medical laboratories, natural fibers, artificial fibers, neckties, Levis, and so on—that should be produced? The enormous complexity of this question, as well as its importance, should be obvious. If you feel a bit overwhelmed by it, this is precisely the message we wish to convey.

*How should output
be distributed?*

Third, the economic system must also determine how the goods and services that are produced are distributed among the members of society. How much of each type of good and service is each person to receive? This is a subject that has generated, and continues to generate, heated controversy. Some people are in favor of a relatively egalitarian society where the amount received by one family varies little from that received by another family of the same size. Other people favor a less egalitarian society where the amount that a family or person receives varies a great deal. Few people favor a thoroughly egalitarian society, if for no other reason than that some differences in income are required to stimulate workers to do certain types of work.

*What provision for
growth?*

Fourth, another task of an economic system is to provide for whatever rate of growth of per capita income the society desires and can achieve. The goal of economic growth is a relatively new one; most past societies have had economies that were unprogressive. Regardless of its newness, however, it has come to be regarded as an extremely important task, particularly in the less-developed countries of Africa, Asia, and South America. There is very strong pressure in these countries for changes in technology, the adoption of superior techniques, increases in the stock of capital resources, and better and more extensive education and training of the labor force. These are viewed as some of the major ways to promote the growth of per capita income. In the industrialized nations, the goal of rapid economic growth has become more controversial in recent years. This has been due in part to the fact that some observers have questioned the extent to which economic growth is worth its costs in social dislocation, pollution, and so forth. But there is no indication that most industrialized nations have lost interest in further economic growth.

OUR MIXED CAPITALIST SYSTEM

The previous section described the four basic functions that any economic system must perform. How does our economic system in the United States perform each of these functions? Let's begin with the determination of the level and composition of output in the society. How is this decided? In a substantially free-enterprise economy, such as ours, consumers choose the amount of each good that they want, and producers act in accord with these decisions. The importance that consumers attach to a good is indicated by the price they are willing to pay for it.

However, consumer sovereignty does not extend to all areas of our society. For example, with regard to the consumption of commodities like drugs, society imposes limits on the decisions of individuals. Moreover, some goods cannot be bought and sold in the marketplace, or even if they could be, it would be inefficient to do so. Such goods, called public goods, will not be provided in the right amounts by private industry, so the government tends to intervene. Examples of public goods are national defense and a healthful environment. Decisions regarding the provision of these goods tend to be made in the political arena.

Going back to the first function described in the previous section, how does our economic system allocate its resources among competing uses, and how does it process these resources to obtain the desired level and composition of

Price system

output? Basically, the *price system* does the job by indicating the desires of workers and the relative value of various types of materials and equipment as well as the desires of consumers. For example, if industrial psychologists are scarce relative to the uses for them, their price in the labor market—their wage—will be bid up and they will tend to be used only in the places where they are most productive. The forces that push firms in the direction of actually carrying out the proper decisions take the form principally of profits or losses. Profits are the carrot, and losses are the stick which are used to eliminate the less efficient and the less alert firms and to increase the more efficient and the more alert.

Although decentralized decision-making based on the price system is used to organize production in most areas of our economy, there are notable exceptions. For example, in the acquisition of new weapons by the Department of Defense, the price system, in anything like its customary form, has not been applied. Instead, the government has exercised control over sellers through the auditing of costs and through the intimate involvement of its agents in the managerial and operating structure of the sellers. Moreover, there is extensive government ownership of the seller's facilities; the government decides what weapons are to be created through its program decisions; and it often decides how they are to be created and produced.

Turning to the next function, how does our economic system determine how much in the way of goods and services each member of the society is to receive? In general, the income of individuals depends largely on the quantities of resources of various kinds that they own and the prices they get for them. For example, if a person both works and rents out houses he or she owns, the person's total income is the number of hours worked per year multiplied by his or her hourly wage rate plus the number of houses owned times the annual rental per house. Thus the distribution of income depends on the way that resource ownership is distributed. Some individuals own higher-priced labor resources than others, because of greater intelligence or superior training. Some individuals own a much greater amount of capital and land than others. However, this is only part of the story. The government modifies the resulting distribution of income by imposing income taxes and by welfare programs such as aid to dependent children. In this way, an attempt is made to reduce income differentials somewhat.

Finally, how does our economic system determine our nation's rate of growth of per capita income? A nation's rate of growth of per capita income depends on the rate of growth of its resources and the rate of increase of the efficiency with which they are used. In our economy, the rate at which labor and capital resources are increased is motivated, at least in part, through the price system. Higher wages for more highly skilled work are an incentive for an individual to undergo further training and education. Capital accumulation occurs in response to expectations of profit. Increases in efficiency, due in considerable measure to the advance of technology, are also stimulated by the price system, but it must be recognized that the government plays an extremely significant role in supporting research and development. In areas like defense, space, and many aspects of agriculture and medicine, the government plays a dominant role in research and development.

THE PRICE SYSTEM AND MICROECONOMICS

From the discussion in the previous section it is clear that the price system plays a major role in the way our economy goes about performing the four principal functions that any economic system must perform. It is not the only means by which our economy goes about performing these tasks, but its role is very important. A person who wants to understand the way in which our economic system functions must therefore have at least a basic knowledge of how the price system works. Microeconomics—or at least a major part of it—is often called price theory because so much of it is concerned so directly with the workings of the price system.

At this point, we are in a position to bring together various strands of the preceding discussion in order to describe more fully the nature and purpose of microeconomics. Economics, it will be recalled, deals with the way in which scarce resources are allocated among alternative uses to satisfy human wants. Microeconomics is the branch of economics that is concerned with the economic behavior of individual consumers, firms, and resource owners, not with the aggregate changes of the economy. As pointed out in the previous paragraph, one of the principal purposes of microeconomics is to provide an understanding of the workings and effects of the price system, which plays an important role in the way our economy functions.

In the course of providing such an understanding, microeconomics helps to answer questions like: What determines the price of various commodities? What determines the amount that a worker makes? What determines the way that a consumer allocates his or her income among various commodities? What determines how much of a particular commodity will be produced? What determines the number and size of firms in a particular industry? Moreover, in the course of investigating these and related questions, microeconomics has shed considerable light on the kinds of problems discussed at the beginning of this chapter: How should a firm choose among alternative manufacturing processes if it wants to maximize its profits? What sort of pricing policy should it adopt? What kinds of social changes can be made if it is agreed that the goal is to make anyone better off if it does not make someone else worse off? What are the advantages and disadvantages of various ways in which industries might be organized?

MODEL-BUILDING AND THE ROLE OF MODELS

Before concluding this introductory chapter, it is important that we describe briefly the basic methodology used in microeconomics to answer the kinds of questions cited above. This methodology is much the same as that used in any other type of scientific analysis. The basic procedure is the formulation of mod-*Model* els. A *model* is composed of a number of assumptions from which conclu-sions—or predictions—are deduced. For example, suppose that we want to formulate a model of the solar system. We might represent each of the planets by a point in space, and we might make the assumption that each would change position in accord with certain mathematical equations. Based on this model, we might predict when an eclipse would occur.

To be useful, a model must in general simplify and abstract from the real situation. Although the assumptions that are made obviously must bear some relationship to the type of situation to which the model is applicable (since randomly chosen assumptions are unlikely, for example, to predict eclipses very well), it is very important to understand that the assumptions need not be exact replicas of reality. Thus, in the example above, the fact that planets are in fact not points makes little or no difference. Moreover, even if the equations rep-resenting their movements are somewhat in error, this may make little differ-ence since, despite these errors, the model may predict well enough to be useful. In both the natural and social sciences, models based on simplified and idealized circumstances have found many, many uses. Also, some assumptions may refer to things that are not directly measurable, like utility in economic theory. The fact that they are not directly measurable does not mean that they are useless: Their usefulness depends on whether or not they result in models that are more powerful and accurate.

There are a number of important reasons why economists, like other scien-tists, use models. One is that the real world is so complex that it is necessary to simplify and abstract if any progress is to be made. Another is that a simple model may be the cheapest way of obtaining needed information. Of course, although the use of models is well accepted throughout the various branches of the scientific community, this does not mean that all models are good or useful. A model may be so oversimplified and distorted that it is utterly useless. The trick is to construct a model in such a way that irrelevant and unimportant considerations and variables are neglected, but the important factors—those that have an important effect on the phenomena the model is designed to predict—are included.

THE EVALUATION OF A MODEL

The purpose of a model is to make predictions concerning phenomena in the real world, and in many respects the most important test of a model is how well

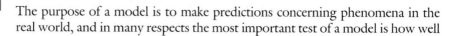

it predicts these phenomena. In this sense, a model that predicts the price of hamburger within plus or minus 1 cent a pound is better than a model that predicts the price of hamburger within plus or minus 2 cents a pound. Of course, this does not mean that a model is useless if it cannot predict very accurately. Under some circumstances, one does not need a very accurate prediction. For some purposes, it is sufficient that a model's predictions be accurate to within a mile; for other purposes, its predictions must be accurate to within a gnat's whisker. Also, for some purposes, a model's predictions must describe various aspects and dimensions of reality; for other purposes, only one aspect or dimension is important.

A model's predictions are derived by applying the rules of logic to the assumptions. For example, in the model of the solar system described above, we see at what point in time an eclipse will occur according to the model by making computations based on the model's assumptions and employing the rules of logic. One elementary test of a model's predictions is whether or not they really do flow logically from the model's assumptions. Sometimes errors of logic and computation creep in to mar a prediction. More fundamentally, another test of a model is whether its assumptions are logically consistent, one with another. Sometimes the natural or social scientist, in building a model, makes assumptions that are not really compatible.

Range of application

Another important consideration in judging a model is the range of phenomena to which it applies. In any science, there is a great and understandable attempt to formulate models that are as general as possible. A model that can predict the behavior of any consumer in the economy is more valuable than one that can predict only the behavior of Martin Smith. Hence the economist is much more interested in a model that is relevant to many consumers in the economy than in one that is relevant to only one consumer. However, the more general a model is meant to be, the more difficult it is to attain a given degree of accuracy. It is relatively easy to construct empirically valid models with little or no generality. For example, if one wanted to go to the trouble of studying a particular person's eating habits, it is likely that one could formulate a model that would predict his or her choice of breakfast food cereals pretty well. But it would be much more difficult to find a model that would be equally accurate in predicting the choice of any type of food by any consumer in the economy. If a theory is to be general, it must ignore many details (and sometimes some variables that are considerably more important than details); the result is that its predictions are likely to fall short—perhaps considerably short—of a high degree of accuracy.

It is important to add another point that is frequently misunderstood: If one is interested in predicting the outcome of a particular event, one will be forced to use the model that predicts best, even if this model does not predict very well. The choice is not between a model and no model; it is between one type of model and another. After all, if one must make a forecast, one will use the most accurate device available to make such a forecast. And any such device is a model of some sort. Consequently, when economists make simplifying assumptions and derive conclusions that are only approximately true, it is somewhat beside the point to complain that the assumptions are simpler than reality or that the predictions are not always accurate. All of this may be true, but if the predictions are better than those obtained on the basis of other models, this model must be used until something better comes along. Thus, if a model can predict the price of hamburger to within plus or minus 1 cent a pound and no other model can do better, this model will be used even if those interested in predicting the price of hamburger bewail the model's limitations and wish it could be improved.

The basic point can perhaps be illustrated by the story of the man whose weakness was games of chance and whose wife told him one day that the local casino was dishonest and asked him to stop visiting it. He replied "It's a darned shame and I'd like to stop going . . . but it's the only game in town." Similarly, if a model is the best that is available, it will—and should—be used until a better model appears.

The best models in town

At this point, a final word should be added concerning the microeconomic models discussed in subsequent chapters. No claim is made that these models are sufficiently accurate or powerful to solve all—or most—of the problems that face firms, governments, or others. Some of these models have been used to predict reasonably well; others have not been nearly so successful. Still others have not really been tested, and no one knows how well they would predict. Moreover, no claim is made that the models discussed in subsequent chapters are the last word on the subject. Undoubtedly they will be improved. All that we do claim is that, according to a consensus of the economics profession, they are the best models we have. Like the local casino they may have their imperfections (although dishonesty is not among them), but they are the best in town.

Summary

1. Economics deals with the way in which resources are allocated among alternative uses to satisfy human wants. Economic activity is directed toward the satisfaction of human wants. Resources are the things and services used to produce goods that can satisfy wants. Economic resources are scarce and have a nonzero price; free resources are not scarce and can be obtained free of charge.
2. Technology is society's pool of knowledge regarding the industrial and agricultural arts. It sets limits on the amount and types of goods and services that can be derived from a given set of resources.
3. Any economic system must accomplish four tasks: It must allocate resources, determine the composition of output, distribute the product, and provide for growth. In our society, individual consumers have great power in determining the composition of output; the prices they are willing to pay for a good indicate how much importance they attach to it. The price system also is an important determinant of how resources are allocated and how the product is distributed.
4. Government also plays a very important role in these tasks. In some areas, the composition of output and the allocation of resources are determined by political decisions. Moreover, the government modifies the distribution of income, and it plays an important role in stimulating and maintaining growth.
5. The methodology used by economists is much the same as that used in any other type of scientific analysis; the basic procedure is the formulation of models.
6. Economic theory is divided into two parts: microeconomics and macroeconomics. Microeconomics is concerned with the economic behavior of individual economic units like consumers, firms, and resource owners.
7. One of the most important purposes of microeconomics is to provide an un-

derstanding of the working and effects of the price system. In the course of providing such an understanding, microeconomics helps to answer many practical problems of businesses and governments and throws important light on many fundamental issues that confront responsible citizens and elected representatives.

1. In 1973, Harley-Davidson, headquartered in Milwaukee, Wisconsin, had 78 percent of the U.S. market for super-heavyweight motorcycles. In 1981, its share had fallen to 30 percent, because of intense competition from Japanese firms like Honda and Yamaha. Between 1981 and 1986, Harley-Davidson accomplished a dramatic turnaround, increasing its market share and raising its profits by about $60 million. One important reason for this turnaround was that Harley-Davidson increased the amount of output produced per employee by about 50 percent.[5] If you were asked to construct a model to explain changes over time in the amount of output produced per employee at Harley-Davidson, what variables would you include? In other words, what variables determine how much output is produced per employee?

2. In 1985, President Ronald Reagan's Commission on Industrial Competitiveness concluded: "Perhaps the most glaring deficiency in America's technological capabilities has been our failure to devote enough attention to manufacturing or 'process' technology. It does us little good to design state-of-the-art products, if within a short time our foreign competitors can manufacture them more cheaply." How can one tell whether too little attention is being devoted to manufacturing technology? What factors might induce firms to devote too little attention to it?

3. Cigarette bootleggers take cigarettes from states with low cigarette taxes and sell them in states with high cigarette taxes. Such smuggling results in a loss in tax revenue to the latter states. The Advisory Commission on Intergovernmental Relations estimated that this loss in 1979 and 1975 was as follows:

Loss from cigarette-tax evasion

	1975	1979
	(millions of dollars)	
All states	337	280
Florida	36	43

(a) If you had to construct a model to predict the amount of cigarettes bootlegged, what factors would you include? (b) Based on the above figures, do you think that Florida's cigarette-tax rate was lower than that of neighboring states? Why or why not? (c) Between 1975 and 1979, Florida changed its tax on a pack of cigarettes by 3 cents per pack. Do you think that it increased or decreased the tax? Why? (d) Could the change in the total loss from cigarette-tax evasion have been due in part to the great increase in the price of gasoline in the late 1970s? Why or why not?

4. According to the principle of Occam's razor, if two models predict equally well, the one that is less complicated should be chosen. Do you agree? How can you tell how complicated a model is?

5. On most questions of policy one can find disagreements among economists. Thus the economic advisers of Republican presidents have tended to have views somewhat different from those of Democratic presidents. Does this prove that economics is not a science?

5. P. Reid, *Well Made in America* (New York: McGraw-Hill, 1990).

6. The median salary of teachers of economics has generally been higher than that of teachers of physics, chemistry, mathematics, or biology. Is this a powerful argument that economics is a science? Why or why not?

7. If a certain proposition holds true for a part of a system, must it hold true for the whole system? For example, suppose that a farmer will benefit from producing a larger crop. Does it follow that all farmers will benefit from producing a larger crop? Explain.

8. One purpose of microeconomics is to determine how we can achieve an optimal allocation of resources. Describe some of the problems involved in defining an "optimal" allocation. Do you think that there is an optimal allocation of resources in the United States at present? Why or why not?

9. In evaluating the accuracy of their statements, should you distinguish between (1) economists' descriptive statements, propositions, and predictions about the world, and (2) their statements about what policies should be adopted? Explain.

10. Suppose that you were given the task of constructing a model to predict the IBM Corporation's total sales next year. How would you go about it? What variables would you include?

11. Medicare is a compulsory hospitalization insurance plan plus a voluntary insurance plan covering doctors' fees for people over 65 years old. The hospitalization insurance pays for practically all the hospital costs of the first 90 days of each spell of illness, as well as some additional costs. Medicaid is a subsidy for medical care received by the poor. In the first few years after the enactment of Medicare and Medicaid, the price of medical care rose about 9 percentage points more than consumer prices generally. Suppose that you are an adviser to the Secretary of Health and Human Services, who is interested in why this price increase occurred. In particular, he asks you whether the enactment of Medicare and Medicaid could have been responsible for it. What sort of a model might you construct to help answer this question?

2

DEMAND AND SUPPLY

INTRODUCTION

Because so much of microeconomics is concerned with the workings of the price system, it is important to understand the mechanism at the center of that system: the market. We begin by discussing the basic concepts of demand and supply, as well as the price elasticity of demand and the price elasticity of supply. Then we describe briefly how price is determined, and we see how our results can be used to throw important light on some major present-day policy issues. Finally, we show that the workings of a market are affected if buyers and/or sellers have imperfect information. This chapter provides a brief, initial look at these central concepts, not an exhaustive treatment. In later chapters, each of these topics will be discussed in much more detail.[1]

MARKETS

Since this chapter is concerned with the behavior of markets, it is necessary to describe at the outset what we mean by a market. This is not quite as straightforward as it may seem, because most markets are not well defined in a geographical or physical sense. (For example, the New York Stock Exchange is an atypical market in the sense that it is located principally in a particular building.) *Market* What is a *market*? A good working definition is that it is a group of firms and individuals in touch with each other in order to buy or sell some good. Of

1. Readers familiar with these concepts can use this chapter for review, or go directly to Chapter 3 without loss of continuity.

course, not every person in a market has to be in contact with every other person in the market; a person or firm is part of a market even if in contact with only a subset of the other persons or firms in the market.

Markets vary enormously in their size, arrangements, and procedures. For some houshold goods, all of the consumers west of the Rocky Mountains may be members of the same market. For other goods, like Rembrandt paintings, only a few collectors, dealers, and museums scattered around the world are members of the market. Basically, however, all markets consist primarily of buyers and sellers, although third parties like brokers and agents may be present as well. In most markets, the sellers suggest the price, but this is not always the case. In this chapter, we generally assume that a market contains many small buyers and sellers so that none of them individually exerts a significant influence on the price.[2] We will relax that assumption in later chapters.

THE DEMAND SIDE OF THE MARKET

The Market Demand Curve

According to Thomas Carlyle, the famous nineteenth-century historian and essayist, "it is easy to train an economist; teach a parrot to say Demand and Supply." Although he may have exaggerated the susceptibility of parrots to an economics education, Carlyle certainly was right about the central role played by demand and supply in economics. The market for every good has a demand side and a supply side. The demand side can be represented by a *market demand schedule*, a table which shows the quantity of the good that would be purchased at each price. (The price of the good is, of course, the amount of money that must be paid for a unit of it.) For example, suppose that the market demand schedule for coal is as shown in Table 2.1.[3] According to this table, 665 million tons of coal will be demanded per year if its price is $46 per ton, 670 million tons of coal will be demanded if its price is $45 per ton, and so on. Another way of presenting the data in Table 2.1 is by a *market demand curve*, which is a plot of the market demand schedule on a graph. The vertical axis of the graph measures the price per unit of the good, and the horizontal axis measures the quantity of the good demanded per unit of time. Figure 2.1 shows the market demand curve for coal, based on the figures in Table 2.1.

Market demand curve

Two things should be noted concerning Figure 2.1. First, the market demand curve for coal *slopes downward to the right*. In other words, the quantity of coal demanded increases as the price falls. This is true of the demand curve for most goods: They almost always slope downward to the right. In subsequent chapters, we shall learn why this is not always the case, but these reasons

2. More accurately, we generally assume in this chapter that markets are perfectly competitive. A perfectly competitive market exists when no buyer or seller can influence price, output is homogeneous, resources are mobile, and knowledge is perfect. A fuller definition of a perfectly competitive market is given in Chapter 8. (At the end of this chapter, we focus on some cases where information is imperfect.)

3. These figures are hypothetical, but adequate for present purposes. In subsequent chapters, we shall provide data describing the actual relationship between the price and quantity demanded of various goods. At this point, the emphasis is on the concept of a market demand schedule, not on the detailed accuracy of these figures.

TABLE 2.1 Market Demand Schedule for Coal, 1991

Price per ton (dollars)	Quantity demanded per year (millions of tons)
46	665
45	670
44	680
43	690
42	700
41	710
40	730

need not concern us at present. Second, the market demand curve in Figure 2.1 pertains to a *particular period of time:* 1991. It is important to recognize that any demand curve pertains to some period of time, and that its shape and position depend on the length and other characteristics of this period. For example, if we were to estimate the market demand curve for coal for the first week in 1991, it would be a different curve than the one in Figure 2.1, which pertains to the whole year. The difference arises partly because consumers can adapt their purchases more fully to changes in the price of coal in a year than in a week.

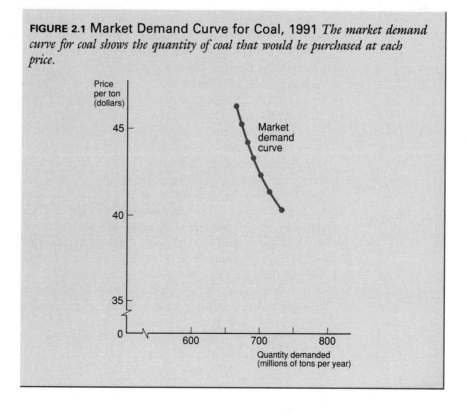

FIGURE 2.1 Market Demand Curve for Coal, 1991 *The market demand curve for coal shows the quantity of coal that would be purchased at each price.*

FIGURE 2.2 Effect of Increased Energy-Consciousness on Market Demand Curve for Electricity *If people take pride in reducing the unnecessary use of electricity, the demand curve for electricity may shift to the left.*

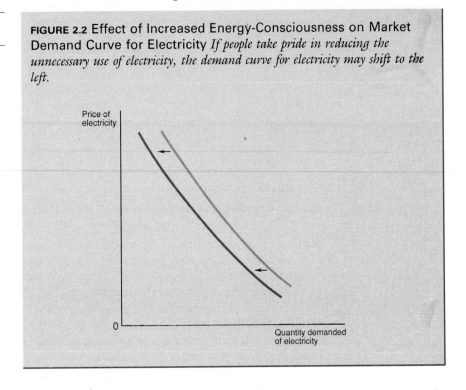

Besides the length of the time period, what other factors determine the position and shape of the market demand curve for a good? One important factor is the *tastes of consumers*. If consumers show an increasing preference for a product, the demand curve will shift to the right: That is, at each price, consumers will desire to buy more than previously. On the other hand, if consumers show a decreasing preference for a product, the demand curve will shift to the left, since, at each price, consumers will desire to buy less than previously. For example, let's turn from coal to the case of electricity. If consumers become more energy-conscious, and begin to take more pride in cutting back on the unnecessary use of electricity, the demand curve for electricity may shift to the left, as shown in Figure 2.2. The greater the shift in preferences, the larger the shift in the demand curve.

Another factor that influences the position and shape of a good's market demand curve is *the level of consumer incomes*. For some types of products, the demand curve shifts to the right if per capita income increases; whereas for other types of commodities, the demand curve shifts to the left if per capita income rises. In subsequent chapters, we shall analyze why some goods fall into one category and other goods fall into the other, but, at present, this need not concern us. All that is important here is that changes in per capita income affect the demand curve. In the case of electricity, all the available studies indicate that an increase in per capita income would shift the demand curve to the right, as shown in Figure 2.3.

Still another factor that influences the position and shape of a good's market demand curve is the *level of other prices*. For example, since natural gas can be substituted to some extent for electricity, the quantity of electricity demanded

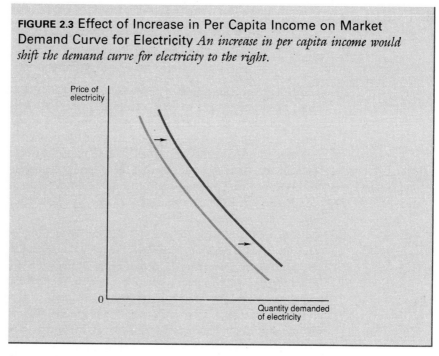

FIGURE 2.3 Effect of Increase in Per Capita Income on Market Demand Curve for Electricity *An increase in per capita income would shift the demand curve for electricity to the right.*

depends on the price of natural gas. If the price of gas is high, more electricity will be demanded than if the price of gas is low, because people and firms will be stimulated to substitute electricity for the high-priced gas. Thus, as shown in Figure 2.4, increases in the price of gas will shift the market demand curve for

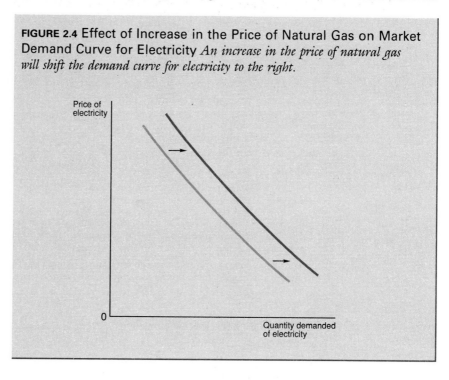

FIGURE 2.4 Effect of Increase in the Price of Natural Gas on Market Demand Curve for Electricity *An increase in the price of natural gas will shift the demand curve for electricity to the right.*

electricity to the right (and decreases in the price of gas will shift it to the left).[4]

The Price Elasticity of Demand

The shape of a good's market demand curve varies from one good to another and from one market to another. In particular, market demand curves vary in the sensitivity of quantity demanded to price. For some goods, a small change in price results in a large change in quantity demanded; for other goods, a large change in price results in a small change in quantity demanded. To gauge the sensitivity, or responsiveness, of the quantity demanded to changes in price, *Price elasticity of* economists use a measure called the *price elasticity of demand*. The price elasticity *demand* of demand is defined to be *the percentage change in quantity demanded resulting from a 1 percent change in price.*[5]

For example, suppose that a 1 percent reduction in the price of electricity results in a 1.2 percent increase in the quantity demanded in the United States. If so, the price elasticity of demand for electricity is 1.2. Convention dictates that we give the elasticity a positive sign despite the fact that the change in price is negative and the change in quantity demanded is positive. Clearly, the price elasticity of demand will generally vary from one point to another on a demand curve. For example, the price elasticity of demand may be higher when the price of electricity is high than when it is low. Similarly, the price elasticity of demand will vary from market to market. For example, Japan may have a different price elasticity of demand for electricity than does the United States. (More is said about the demand curve for electricity in Problem 1 in Chapter 5.)

Alfred Marshall, the great English economist who lived about a century ago, was one of the first economists to give a clear formulation of the concept of the price elasticity of demand. It is a very important concept and one that will be used repeatedly throughout this book. One thing to note at the outset is that the price elasticity of demand is expressed in terms of *relative* changes in price and quantity demanded, not *absolute* changes in price and quantity demanded. This is because absolute changes are difficult to interpret. For example, suppose that a price goes up by a dime. This is a lot for a subway ride but little for a house. Similarly, it is a lot for a bottle of beer but little for a fifty-gallon keg. A

---

4. Let the quantity demanded of a good per unit of time equal Q_D. In general,

$$Q_D = f(P, T, I, R, N)$$

where P is the price of the good, T stands for the tastes of consumers, I is the level of consumer income, R is the price of related goods, and N is the number of consumers in the market. The demand curve shows the relationship between Q_D and P when the other variables are held constant. In general, changes in the values at which these other variables are held constant will affect the relationship between Q_D and P, which is another way of saying that these other variables will generally influence the position and shape of the market demand curve.

5. For readers with a knowledge of calculus, it is worth noting that, if Q_D is the quantity demanded and P is the price, a more precise definition of the price elasticity of demand is

$$\eta = \frac{-dQ_D}{dP} \cdot \frac{P}{Q_D}.$$

Much more will be said about the measurement, effects, and determinants of the price elasticity of demand in Chapter 5.

frequent error is to confuse the price elasticity of demand with the slope of the demand curve. They are by no means the same thing.[6]

Suppose that we have a market demand schedule showing the quantity of a commodity demanded in the market at various prices. How can we estimate the price elasticity of market demand? Let ΔP be a change in the price of the good and ΔQ_D be the resulting change in its quantity demanded. If ΔP is very small, we can compute the *point elasticity of demand*:

Point elasticity

$$\eta = -\frac{\Delta Q_D}{Q_D} \div \frac{\Delta P}{P}. \qquad [2.1]$$

For example, consider Table 2.2 where data are given for very small increments in the price of a commodity. If we want to estimate the price elasticity of demand when the price is between 99.95 cents and $1, we obtain the following result:

$$\eta = -\frac{40{,}002 - 40{,}000}{40{,}000} \div \frac{99.95 - 100}{100} = .1.$$

TABLE 2.2 Quantity Demanded at Various Prices (Small Increments in Price)

Price (cents per unit of commodity)	Quantity demanded per unit of time (units of commodity)
99.95	40,002
100.00	40,000
100.05	39,998

Note that we used $1 as P and 40,000 as Q_D. We could have used 99.95 cents as P and 40,002 as Q_D, but it would have made no real difference to the answer. (Try it and see.)

However, if we have data concerning only large changes in price (that is, if ΔP and ΔQ_D are large), the answer may vary considerably depending on which value of P and Q_D is used in Equation 2.1. For example, take the case in Table 2.3. Suppose that we want to estimate the price elasticity of demand in the price range between $4 and $5. Then, depending on which value of P and Q_D is used, the answer will be

$$\eta = -\frac{20 - 3}{3} \div \frac{4 - 5}{5} = 28.33$$

$$\eta = -\frac{3 - 20}{20} \div \frac{5 - 4}{4} = 3.40.$$

6. The slope of the demand curve is dP/dQ_D. A glance at footnote 5 will show that this slope is not equal to the price elasticity of demand. Sometimes the price elasticity of demand is also confused with dQ_D/dP. This too is an error since they are by no means the same thing.

TABLE 2.3 Quantity Demanded at Various Prices (Large Increments in Price)

Price (dollars per unit of commodity)	Quantity demanded per unit of time (units of commodity)
3	40
4	20
5	3

Arc elasticity

The difference between these two results is enormous. In a case of this sort, it is advisable to compute the *arc elasticity of demand*, which uses the average value of P and Q_D:

$$\eta = -\frac{\Delta Q_D}{(Q_{D1} + Q_{D2})/2} \div \frac{\Delta P}{(P_1 + P_2)/2}$$

$$= -\frac{\Delta Q_D (P_1 + P_2)}{\Delta P (Q_{D1} + Q_{D2})} \qquad [2.2]$$

where P_1 and Q_{D1} are the first values of price and quantity demanded, and P_2 and Q_{D2} are the second set. Thus, in Table 2.3,

$$\eta = -\frac{20 - 3}{(20 + 3)/2} \div \frac{4 - 5}{(4 + 5)/2} = 6.65.$$

This is the arc elasticity of demand when price is between $4 and $5.

Price Elasticity and Total Expenditure

The demand for a commodity is said to be *price elastic* if the elasticity of demand exceeds 1. The demand for a commodity is said to be *price inelastic* if the elasticity of demand is less than 1. And the demand for a commodity is said to be of *unitary elasticity* if the price elasticity of demand is equal to 1. Many important decisions hinge on the price elasticity of demand for a commodity. One reason why this is so is that the price elasticity of demand determines whether a given change in price will increase or decrease the amount of money spent on a commodity—often a matter of basic importance to firms and government agencies.

Elastic vs. inelastic

To illustrate, suppose that the demand for a commodity is elastic, that is, the price elasticity of demand exceeds 1. In this situation, if the price is reduced, the percentage increase in the quantity consumed is greater than the percentage reduction in price. (That this is the case follows from the definition of the price elasticity of demand.) Consequently, a price *reduction* must lead to an *increase* in the expenditure on the product, and a price *increase* must lead to a *decrease* in the expenditure on the product.

On the other hand, suppose that the demand for a commodity is inelastic, that is, the price elasticity of demand is less than 1. In this situation, if the price is reduced, the percentage increase in the quantity consumed is less than the percentage reduction in price. (This follows from the definition of the price elasticity.) Thus a price *reduction* must lead to a *decrease* in the expenditure on the product, and a price *increase* must lead to an *increase* in the expenditure on the product. Finally, if the demand for a product is of unitary elasticity, price increases or decreases do not affect the expenditure on the product.

THE SUPPLY SIDE OF THE MARKET

The Market Supply Curve

Each market has a supply side as well as a demand side. The supply side can be represented by a *market supply schedule*, a table which shows the quantity of the good that would be supplied at various prices. For example, suppose that the market supply schedule for coal is shown in Table 2.4.[7] Then 600 million tons of coal will be supplied if its price is $40 per ton, 650 million tons of coal will be supplied if its price is $41 per ton, and so on. Another way of presenting the data in Table 2.4 is by a *supply curve*, which is a plot of the market supply schedule on a graph. The vertical axis of the graph measures the price per unit of the good, and the horizontal axis measures the quantity of the good supplied per unit of time. Figure 2.5 shows the market supply curve for coal, based on the figures in Table 2.4.[8]

Market supply curve

TABLE 2.4 Market Supply Schedule for Coal, 1991

Price per ton (dollars)	Quantity supplied per year (millions of tons)
40	600
41	650
42	700
43	750
44	775
45	800
46	825

Two things should be noted concerning Figure 2.5. First, the market supply curve for coal *slopes upward to the right*. In other words, the quantity of coal supplied increases as the price increases. This is because increases in its price give the makers of coal a greater incentive to produce it and offer it for sale. Empirical studies indicate that the market supply curves for a great many commodities share this characteristic of sloping upward to the right. In subsequent chapters, we will analyze in detail the factors responsible for the shape of a

---

7. These figures are hypothetical, but adequate for present purposes. In subsequent chapters, we shall provide data describing the actual relationship between the price and quantity supplied of various goods. At this point, the emphasis is on the concept of a market supply schedule, not on the detailed accuracy of these figures.

8. Note once more that we assume that the market for coal is perfectly competitive. (See footnote 2.) This simplification is adopted throughout most of this chapter. In subsequent chapters we relax the assumption that markets are perfectly competitive.

FIGURE 2.5 Market Supply Curve for Coal, 1991 *The market supply curve for coal shows the quantity of coal that would be supplied at each price.*

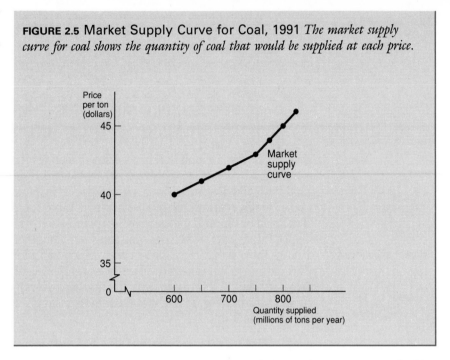

particular good's market supply curve. Second, the market supply curve in Figure 2.5 pertains to a *particular period of time*: 1991. Any supply curve pertains to some period of time, and its shape and position depend on the length and other characteristics of this period. For example, if we were to estimate the market supply curve for coal for the first week in 1991, it would be a different curve than the one in Figure 2.5, which pertains to the whole year. In part, the difference arises because coal producers can adapt their output rate more fully to changes in coal's price in a year than in a week.

Besides the length of the time period, what other factors determine the position and shape of the market supply curve for a good? One important factor is *technological change*. Recall that technology was defined in Chapter 1 as society's pool of knowledge concerning the industrial arts. As technology progresses, it becomes possible to produce commodities more cheaply, so that firms often are willing to supply a given amount at a lower price than formerly. Thus technological change often causes the supply curve to shift to the right. For example, this certainly has occurred in the case of coal, as indicated in Figure 2.6. There have been many important technological changes in coal production in the past fifty years, including the invention and improvement of continuous mining machinery, trackless mobile loaders, and shuttle cars.

Another factor that influences the position and shape of a good's market supply curve is the *level of input prices*. The supply curve for a commodity is affected by the prices of the resources (labor, capital, and land) used to produce it. Decreases in the prices of these inputs make it possible to produce commodities more cheaply, so that firms may be willing to supply a given amount at a lower price than they formerly would. Thus decreases in the price of inputs may cause the supply curve to shift to the right. On the other hand, increases in the

FIGURE 2.6 Effect of Technological Change on the Market Supply
Curve for Coal *Improvements in technology shift the supply curve to the
right.*

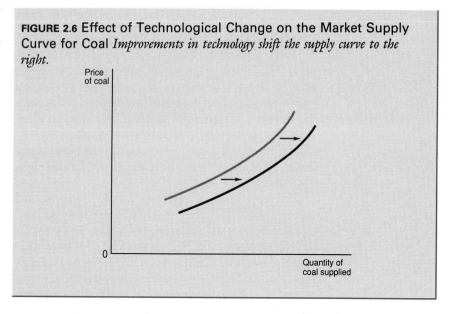

price of inputs may cause it to shift to the left. For example, if the wage rates of
coal miners increase (as they did in 1990), the supply curve for coal may shift to
the left, as shown in Figure 2.7.[9]

FIGURE 2.7 Effect of Increase in Wages of Coal Miners on Market
Supply Curve for Coal *Increases in wage rates shift the supply curve to the
left.*

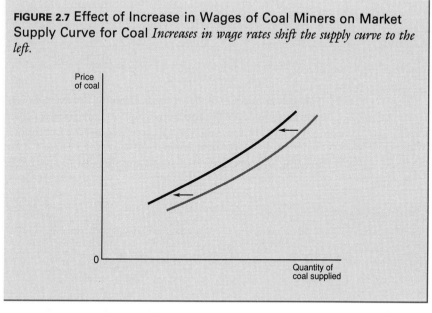

9. Let the quantity supplied of a good per unit of time equal Q_S. In general, $Q_S = g(P, M, V)$
where P is the price of the good, M is the level of input prices, and V stands for the level of
technology. The supply curve shows the relationship between Q_S and P when the other variables
are held constant. In general, changes in the values at which these other variables are held
constant will affect the relationship between Q_S and P, which is another way of saying that these
other variables will generally influence the position and shape of the market supply curve.

Price elasticity of supply

Like market demand curves, market supply curves vary in shape. In particular, they vary with respect to the sensitivity of quantity supplied to price. For some goods, a small change in price results in a large change in quantity supplied; for other goods, a large change in price results in a small change in quantity supplied. To gauge the sensitivity of the quantity supplied to changes in price, economists use a measure called the *price elasticity of supply*, which is defined to be *the percentage change in quantity supplied resulting from a 1 percent change in price*.[10] Thus, if a 1 percent increase in the price of natural gas results in a 0.5 percent increase in the quantity supplied, the price elasticity of supply of natural gas is 0.5.

Clearly, the price elasticity of supply is analogous to the price elasticity of demand. Like the latter, it is expressed in terms of relative, not absolute, changes in price and quantity, and it should not be confused with the slope of the supply curve. Its value is likely to vary from one point to another on a supply curve. For example, the price elasticity of supply of natural gas may be higher when the price is low than when it is high. In general, the price elasticity of supply would be expected to increase with the length of the period to which the supply curve pertains. Why? Because, as noted in the previous section, manufacturers of the good will be able to adapt their output rates more fully to changes in its price if the period is long rather than short.

Point and arc elasticities

If we have a market supply schedule showing the quantity of a commodity supplied at various prices, we can readily estimate the price elasticity of supply. Let ΔP be the change in the price of the good and ΔQ_S be the resulting change in its quantity supplied. If ΔP is very small, we can compute the *point elasticity of supply:*

$$\eta_S = \frac{\Delta Q_S}{Q_S} \div \frac{\Delta P}{P}. \qquad [2.3]$$

If ΔP is not so small, we can compute the *arc elasticity of supply* by using the average value of Q_S and P in Equation 2.3. These calculations are similar to (but not exactly the same as[11]) those required to compute the price elasticity of demand. To illustrate them, take the case in Table 2.4. Suppose that we want to compute the price elasticity of supply between $40 and $41. The arc elasticity

---

10. More accurately, if Q_S is the quantity supplied of the good and P is the price, the price elasticity of supply is

$$\eta_S = \frac{dQ_S}{dP} \cdot \frac{P}{Q_S}.$$

More will be said about the measurement of the price elasticity of supply in Chapter 8.

11. In calculating the price elasticity of demand, we multiply the relative change in quantity demanded resulting from a 1 percent change in price by -1, so that the result will be a positive number. In calculating the price elasticity of supply, we do *not* have to multiply the relative change in quantity supplied resulting from a 1 percent change in price by -1, because it already is positive in the typical case. This is because, as we have already stressed, supply curves generally slope *upward* to the right, whereas demand curves generally slope *downward* to the right.

of supply is

$$\eta_S = \frac{\Delta Q_S}{(Q_{S1} + Q_{S2})/2} \div \frac{\Delta P}{(P_1 + P_2)/2}$$

$$= \frac{650 - 600}{(650 + 600)/2} \div \frac{41 - 40}{(41 + 40)/2}$$

$$= 3.24.$$

DETERMINANTS OF PRICE

The Equilibrium Price

Recall from the previous chapter that prices in a free-enterprise economy are important determinants of what is produced, how it is produced, who receives it, and how rapidly per capita income grows. It behooves us, therefore, to look carefully at how prices themselves are determined in a free-enterprise economy. As a first step toward describing this process, we must define the equilibrium price of a good. At various points in this book, you will encounter the concept of an equilibrium, which is very important in economics, as in many other scientific fields.

Equilibrium

An equilibrium is *a situation where there is no tendency for change*; in other words, it is a situation that can persist. Thus *an equilibrium price is a price that can be maintained*. Any price that is not an equilibrium price cannot be maintained for long, since there are basic forces at work to stimulate a change in price. The best way to understand what we mean by an equilibrium price is to take a particular case, such as the market for coal. Let's put both the demand curve for coal (in Figure 2.1) and the supply curve for coal (in Figure 2.5) together in the same diagram. The result, shown in Figure 2.8, will help us determine the equilibrium price of coal.

We begin by seeing what would happen if various prices were established in the market. For example, if the price were $44 a ton, the demand curve indicates that 680 million tons of coal would be demanded, while the supply curve indicates that 775 million tons would be supplied. Thus, if the price were $44 a ton, there would be a mismatch between the quantity supplied and the quantity demanded per year, since the rate at which coal is supplied would be greater than the rate at which it is demanded. Specifically, as shown in Figure 2.8, there would be an *excess supply* of 95 million tons. Under these circumstances, some of the coal supplied by producers could not be sold, and as inventories of coal built up, suppliers would tend to cut their prices in order to get rid of unwanted inventories. Thus a price of $44 per ton would not be maintained for long— and for this reason, $44 per ton is not an equilibrium price.

If the price were $40 per ton, on the other hand, the demand curve indicates that 730 million tons of coal would be demanded, while the supply curve indicates that 600 million tons would be supplied. Again we find a mismatch between the quantity supplied and the quantity demanded per year, since the rate at which coal is supplied would be less than the rate at which it is demanded. Specifically, as shown in Figure 2.8, there would be an *excess demand* of 130 million tons. Under these circumstances, some of the consumers

FIGURE 2.8 Equilibrium Price and Quantity of Coal, 1991 *The equilibrium price is $42 per ton; the equilibrium quantity is 700 million tons per year.*

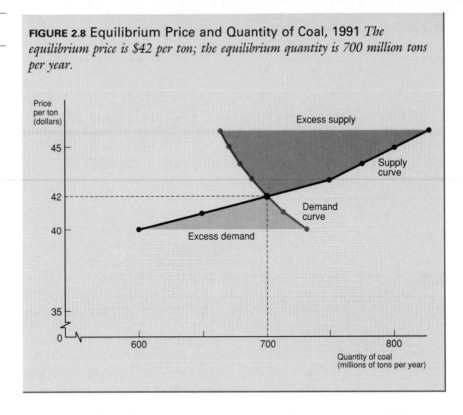

who want coal at this price would have to be turned away empty-handed. There would be a shortage. And given this shortage, suppliers would find it profitable to increase the price, and competition among buyers would bid the price up. Thus a price of $40 per ton could not be maintained for long—so $40 per ton is not an equilibrium price.

Equilibrium price

The equilibrium price must be the price where the quantity demanded equals the quantity supplied. Obviously this is the only price at which there is no mismatch between the quantity demanded and the quantity supplied, and consequently the only price that can be maintained for long. In Figure 2.8, the price at which the quantity supplied equals the quantity demanded is $42 per ton, the price where the demand curve intersects the supply curve. Thus $42 per ton is the equilibrium price of coal under the circumstances visualized in Figure 2.8, and 700 million tons is the equilibrium quantity.[12]

The Actual Price

What we set out to explain was the actual price, not the equilibrium price—since the actual price is all that is observed in the real world. In general, economists simply assume that the actual price will approximate the equilibrium

---

12. If $P = D(Q)$ is the demand curve and $P = S(Q)$ is the supply curve, we have two equations in two unknowns—price (P) and quantity (Q). To determine the equilibrium price, we can solve these equations simultaneously for P and Q.

price, which seems reasonable enough, since the basic forces at work tend to push the actual price toward the equilibrium price. Thus, if the demand and supply curves remain fairly stable for a time, the actual price should move toward the equilibrium price.

To see that this is the case, consider the market for coal, as described by Figure 2.8. What if the price somehow is set at $44 per ton? As we saw in the previous section, there is downward pressure on the price of coal under these conditions. Suppose the price, responding to this pressure, falls to $43. Comparing the quantity demanded with the quantity supplied at $43, we find that there is still downward pressure on price, since the quantity supplied exceeds the quantity demanded at $43. The price, responding to this pressure, may fall to $42.50, but comparing the quantity demanded with the quantity supplied at this price, we find that there is still a downward pressure on price, since the quantity supplied exceeds the quantity demanded at $42.50.

So long as the actual price exceeds the equilibrium price, there will be a downward pressure on price. Similarly, so long as the actual price is less than the equilibrium price, there will be an upward pressure on price. Thus there is always a tendency for the actual price to move toward the equilibrium price. But it should not be assumed that this movement is always rapid. Sometimes it takes a long time for the actual price to get close to the equilibrium price. Sometimes the actual price never gets to the equilibrium price because by the time it gets close, the equilibrium price changes. All that safely can be said is that the actual price will move toward the equilibrium price. But of course this information is of great value, both theoretically and practically. For many purposes, all that is required is predicting if the price will move up or down.

Effects on Price of Shifts in the Demand Curve

We have already seen that demand curves shift in response to changes in tastes, income, and prices of other products. Any supply-and-demand diagram like Figure 2.8 is essentially a snapshot of the situation during a particular period of time. The results in Figure 2.8 are limited to a particular period because the demand and supply curves in the figure pertain only to that period. What happens to the equilibrium price of a product (which we shall call good X) when its demand curve changes?

Suppose that consumer tastes shift in favor of good X, causing the demand curve for good X to shift to the right. This state of affairs is shown in Figure 2.9, where the demand curve shifts from D to D_1. It is not hard to see the effect on the equilibrium price of good X. When D is the demand curve, the equilibrium price is OP. But when the demand curve shifts to D_1, a shortage of $(OQ_2 - OQ)$ develops at this price. That is, the quantity demanded exceeds the quantity supplied at this price by $(OQ_2 - OQ)$. Consequently, suppliers raise their prices. After some testing of market reactions and trial-and-error adjustments, the price will tend to settle at OP_1, the new equilibrium price, and quantity will tend to settle at OQ_1.

On the other hand, suppose that consumer demand for good X falls off, perhaps because of a great drop in the price of a product that is an effective substitute for good X. The demand for good X now shifts to the left. Specifically, as shown in Figure 2.9, it shifts from D to D_2. What will be the effect on

FIGURE 2.9 Effects of Shifts in Demand Curve on Equilibrium Price
A rightward shift of the demand curve tends to increase price; a leftward shift tends to reduce price.

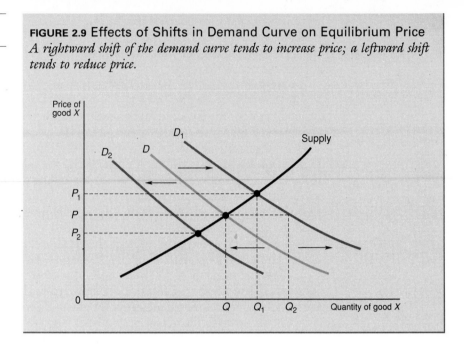

the equilibrium price of good X? Clearly, the new equilibrium price will be OP_2, where the new demand curve intersects the supply curve.

To illustrate the usefulness of this model, consider the market for heating oil. In December 1989, there was an unusual spell of sustained cold weather in the northeastern United States, which caused the demand curve for heating oil to shift markedly to the right. What happened to the price of heating oil? In accord with our model, it rose to $1.30 a gallon, which was almost 50 percent higher than in the warmer days a month before.[13]

In general, a shift to the right in the demand curve results in an increase in the equilibrium price, and a shift to the left in the demand curve results in a decrease in the equilibrium price. This is the lesson of Figure 2.9. Of course, this conclusion depends on the assumption that the supply curve slopes upward to the right, but, as we noted in a previous section, this is generally the case.

Effects on Price of Shifts in the Supply Curve

Supply curves, like demand curves, shift over time. What happens to the equilibrium price of a good when its supply curve shifts? Suppose that, because of technological advances, producers of good X are willing and able to supply more of good X at a given price than they used to. Specifically, suppose that the supply curve shifts from S to S_1 in Figure 2.10. What will be the effect on the equilibrium price? Clearly, it will fall from OP (where the S supply curve intersects the demand curve) to OP_3 (where the S_1 supply curve intersects the demand curve). On the other hand, suppose that input prices rise, with the result that the supply curve shifts from S to S_2 in Figure 2.10. Clearly, the

13. "Heating Oil Stockpiles Grow Tight," *New York Times*, December 23, 1989.

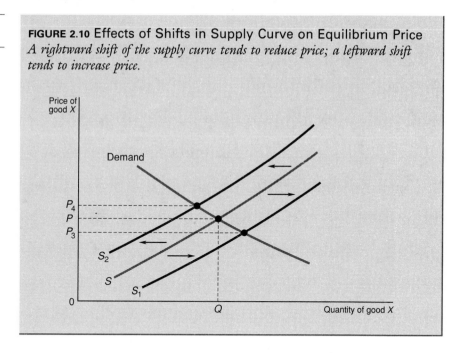

FIGURE 2.10 Effects of Shifts in Supply Curve on Equilibrium Price
*A rightward shift of the supply curve tends to reduce price; a leftward shift
tends to increase price.*

equilibrium price will increase from OP (where the S supply curve intersects
the demand curve) to OP_4 (where the S_2 supply curve intersects the demand
curve).

Lovers of turkey were shown in the late 1980s what a shift to the right in the
supply curve of a commodity will do. Because of declines in the price of fuel oil,
which made turkey coops cheaper to heat, and a drop in the price of the grain
that turkeys eat, there was a shift to the right in the supply curve for turkeys. As
our theory would predict, the wholesale price of a turkey fell—from 93 cents a
pound in 1985 to 88 cents in 1986 to 51 cents in 1987.

In general, a shift to the right in the supply curve results in a decrease in the
equilibrium price, and a shift to the left in the supply curve results in an increase
in the equilibrium price. Of course, this conclusion depends on the assumption
that the demand curve slopes downward to the right, but, as we noted in a
previous section, this is generally the case.

ANALYZING THE EFFECTS OF AN EXCISE TAX

To illustrate how basic demand-and-supply models can be used to throw light
on the effects of various public-policy measures, we discuss in this section the
effects on price of an excise tax. Suppose that such a tax is imposed on a particular good, say cigarettes.[14] In Figure 2.11, we show the demand and supply
curves, D and S, for cigarettes before the imposition of the tax. Obviously, the
equilibrium price of a pack of cigarettes is $1.40, and the equilibrium quantity

14. For simplicity, we assume that the market for cigarettes is perfectly competitive. In later chapters, we present models that pertain to cases where there are relatively few producers.

FIGURE 2.11 Effect of Excise Tax on Price and Output of Cigarettes
A 20 cent excise tax shifts the supply curve upward by 20 cents, and increases the equilibrium price from $1.40 to $1.50 per pack.

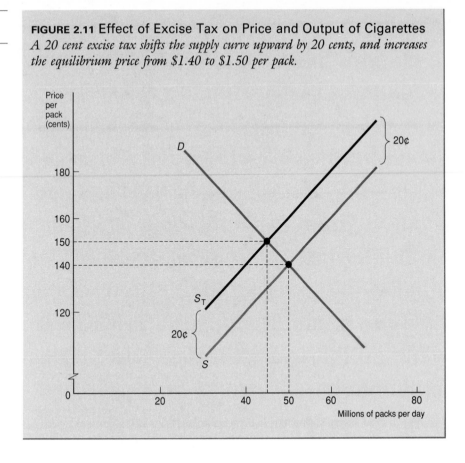

is 50 million packs. If a tax of 20 cents is imposed on each pack produced, what is the effect on the price of each pack? Or to see it from the smoker's perspective, how much of the tax is passed on to the consumer in the form of a higher price?

Since the tax is collected from the sellers, the supply curve is shifted upward by the amount of the tax. In Figure 2.11, the posttax supply curve is S_T. For example, if the pretax price had to be $1.20 a pack to induce sellers to supply 40 million packs of cigarettes, the posttax price would have to be 20 cents higher—or $1.40 a pack—to induce the same supply. Similarly, if the pretax price had to be $1.40 a pack to induce sellers to supply 50 million packs of cigarettes, the posttax price would have to be 20 cents higher—or $1.60 a pack—to induce the same supply. The reason why the sellers require 20 cents more per pack to supply the pretax amount is that they must pay the 20 cents per pack to the government. Thus to wind up with the same amount as before (after paying the tax), they require the extra 20 cents per pack.

Figure 2.11 shows that, after the tax is imposed, the equilibrium price of cigarettes is $1.50, an increase of 10 cents over its pretax level. Consequently, in this case, half of the tax is passed on to consumers, who pay 10 cents more for cigarettes. And half of the tax is swallowed by the sellers, who receive (after they pay the tax) 10 cents per pack less for cigarettes. But it is not always true that sellers pass half of the tax on to consumers and absorb the rest themselves. On

Effects of excise tax

EXAMPLE 2.1

IS THE WAR ON DRUGS BEING WON?

In 1989, President Bush announced a war on drugs. In many respects, this war was not new. The United States has been engaged for many years in a number of programs to reduce the consumption of illicit drugs like cocaine and heroin. Between 1981 and 1987, federal expenditures on drug enforcement more than tripled—from less than $1 billion per year to about $3 billion. By arresting drug users and emphasizing the hazards of drug use, these programs have attempted to push the demand curve for drugs to the left, as shown below. By trying to seize drugs entering the country and by trying to make it more costly for drug smugglers and producers to avoid arrest, they have attempted to push the supply curve to the left, as also shown below. In this way, the government has tried to reduce drug consumption (from OQ_1 to OQ_2).

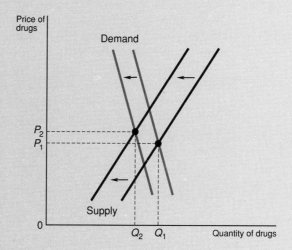

(a) Between 1981 and 1989, the retail price of cocaine fell from $115 to $88 a gram. Does this mean that these government programs have been failing? (b) Between 1981 and 1989, the amount of cocaine seized by the government increased from about 1.7 tons to about 85 tons. Does this mean that these programs have been working? (c) According to a study carried out by the RAND Corporation, it is relatively inexpensive for people to produce and smuggle cocaine into the United States, and federal attempts to keep it out result in only minor increases in these people's costs. Does this suggest that these programs are likely to shift the supply curve for cocaine far to the left? (d) The RAND study suggests that the supply curve for cocaine has shifted to the right, because smugglers have become more adept at their trade. Would this help to explain the fall in the price of cocaine? If true, what does it indicate about the success of existing government programs?

Drug Enforcement Agency

SOLUTION

(a) Not necessarily. If the leftward shift of the demand curve were greater than the leftward shift of the supply curve, both the price and the quantity consumed of cocaine would decrease. Thus the fact that the price fell does not prove that there was no decrease in the quantity consumed. (b) Not necessarily. An increase in the amount seized does not imply that less has been entering the United States. In fact, according to the RAND study cited in part (c), more cocaine has been entering the United States. (c) No. It suggests that federal programs of this sort are likely to have little effect on the supply curve. (d) A rightward shift of the supply curve would help to explain the fall in the price of cocaine. If true, it would indicate that government programs are not making great progress, since one of their principal aims is to shift this supply curve to the left.*

*For further discussion, see Peter Reuter, "Can the Borders Be Sealed?" *The Public Interest*, Summer 1988; and "The Supply-Side Scourge," *Time*, November 13, 1989.

the contrary, in some cases, consumers may bear almost all of the tax (and sellers may bear practically none of it), while in other cases consumers may bear almost none of the tax (and sellers may bear practically all of it). The result will depend on how sensitive the quantity demanded and the quantity supplied are to the price of the good.

In particular, holding the supply curve constant, the less sensitive the quantity demanded is to the price of the good, the bigger the portion of the tax that is shifted to consumers. To illustrate this, consider panel A of Figure 2.12, which shows the effect of a 20 cents per pack tax on cigarettes in two markets, one where the quantity demanded (D_1) is much more sensitive to price than in the other case (D_2). Before the tax, the equilibrium price is OP_0, regardless of whether D_1 or D_2 is the demand curve. After the tax, the equilibrium price is OP_1 if the demand curve is D_1, or OP_2 if the demand curve is D_2. Clearly, the increase in the price to the consumer is greater if the quantity demanded is less sensitive to price (D_2) than if it is more sensitive (D_1).

Also, holding the demand curve constant, the less sensitive the quantity supplied is to the price of the good, the bigger the portion of the tax that is absorbed by producers. To illustrate this, consider panel B of Figure 2.12,

FIGURE 2.12 Effect of Excise Tax on Price of Cigarettes, Under Alternative Assumptions Concerning Sensitivity of Quantity Demanded and Quantity Supplied to Price *The tax results in a larger increase in price if the quantity demanded is less sensitive to price than if it is more sensitive, and if the quantity supplied is more sensitive to price than if it is less sensitive.*

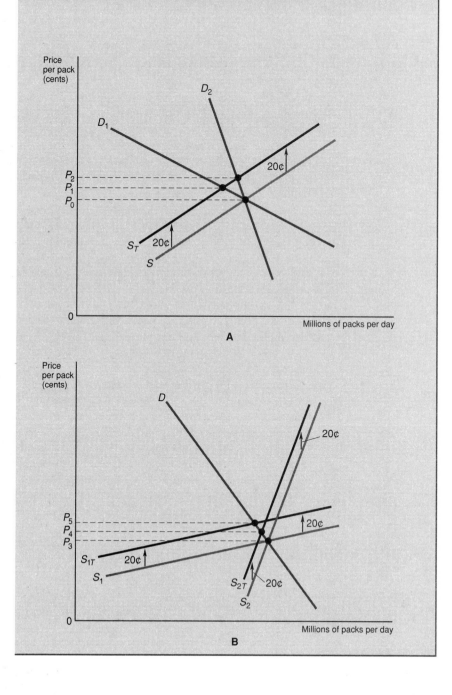

which shows the effect of a 20 cents per pack tax on cigarettes in two markets, one where the quantity supplied (S_1) is much more sensitive to price than in the other case (S_2). Before the tax, the equilibrium price is OP_3, regardless of whether S_1 or S_2 is the pretax supply curve. After the tax, the equilibrium price is OP_4 if the (pretax) supply curve is S_2, or OP_5 if the (pretax) supply curve is S_1. Clearly, the increase in price to the consumer is greater if the quantity supplied is more sensitive to price (S_1) than if it is less sensitive (S_2).

PRICE FLOORS AND CEILINGS

As a further illustration of how the simple models taken up in this chapter can help to illuminate public-policy issues, consider the case of price floors or price ceilings. As is well known, governments often intervene in markets to prop up the price of a particular good or to see to it that its price does not exceed a certain level. At this point we will sketch only roughly the effects of such price floors or price ceilings. More details on this subject will be added in later chapters.

Price floor

The effects of a price floor are shown in Figure 2.13. As is evident, the equilibrium price of the good is OP. Nonetheless, because the government feels that this price is not equitable, it sets a minimum price of OP_m. At this minimum price, the quantity supplied (OQ_S) exceeds the quantity demanded (OQ_D), and the government is faced with the problem of disposing of the surplus or of limiting production so that the quantity supplied is no more than OQ_D. One important area where price floors have been adopted in the United States has been agriculture. For major farm commodities like wheat and corn, there long have been minimum prices established by the government. As our model predicts, a major problem stemming from these price floors has been the disposal and limitation of farm surpluses.[15]

Price ceiling

The effects of a price ceiling are shown in Figure 2.14. Although the equilibrium price is OP, the government sets a maximum price of OP_n, because it does not want the price of the good to rise to its equilibrium level. At this maximum price, the quantity demanded (OQ_D) exceeds the quantity supplied (OQ_S); in other words, there is a shortage of the good. To allocate the limited supply among the many buyers who want to purchase the good, the government may resort to some form of rationing. For example, in World War II when price controls were in effect, families were issued ration coupons which determined how much they could buy of various commodities. Frequently, *black markets* develop under these circumstances, where the good is sold illegally at a price higher than the legal maximum. As our model predicts, a major problem stemming from price ceilings has been the resolution of the shortages that ensue.

---

15. In Chapters 8 and 15, we discuss these agricultural price floors and their effects in much more detail.

FIGURE 2.13 Effects of a Price Floor *If the government sets a minimum
price of* OP$_m$, *the quantity supplied exceeds the quantity demanded, and
there is the problem of disposing of the surplus.*

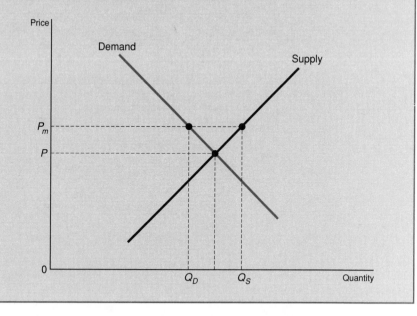

FIGURE 2.14 Effects of a Price Ceiling *If the government sets a ceiling
price of* OP$_n$, *the quantity demanded exceeds the quantity supplied, and
there is a shortage of the good.*

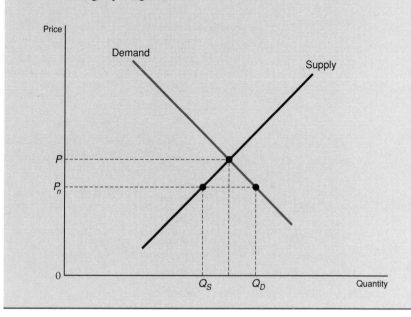

EXAMPLE 2.2

SHOULD BOVINE GROWTH HORMONE BE BANNED?

Bovine growth hormone, a drug that is produced by the new techniques of genetic engineering, may have a major impact on milk production. In tests in the Midwest and other regions, it has been shown to increase milk production by 10 to 20 percent when administered to cows. The Food and Drug Administration has decided that it poses no health hazards to people. According to many observers, it is the first economically important product of agricultural biotechnology ready to be marketed, the producers being American Cyanamid, Eli Lilly, Monsanto, and Upjohn. Yet the National Farmers Union (with 300,000 members) and other farm groups were fighting hard in 1990 to convince state legislatures to ban its use.

(a) If the government did not intervene in the market for milk, what effect would bovine growth hormone have on the price of milk? (b) If the government were to buy enough milk to prevent the price from falling below *OP* (in the graph below) and if bovine growth hormone shifts the supply curve for milk (as shown below), what would be the effect on the amount that the government would have to pay farmers for milk? (c) According to the *New York Times*, "Lower milk prices will . . . benefit consumers even if taxpayers have to keep paying more in dairy price supports. Under present law the . . . [price paid by the government] can be lowered each year, a flexibility Congress should resist impairing. . . . [But as] many as 10 percent of the country's 150,000 dairy farmers might be forced out of business."* Why might they be forced out of business?

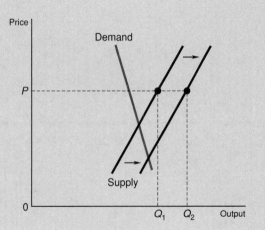

SOLUTION

(a) The price of milk would fall because the use of bovine growth hormone would shift the supply curve for milk to the right. The supply curve would shift because this hormone would increase the amount of milk produced from a given amount of resources. (b) The amount that the government would pay farmers for milk would increase by OP times $(OQ_2 - OQ_1)$. (c) Because if the price of milk was lowered, these dairy farmers would not be able to avoid unacceptable losses.

*"Hiding Behind Hormones in Milk," *New York Times*, May 5, 1989. Also see "Market Sours on Milk Hormone," *Science*, November 17, 1989.

Rent Control in New York City: Illustration of a Price Ceiling

Price floors and ceilings can and do affect our everyday lives. Since 1943, New York City has had a system of rent control which imposes ceilings on rents. The purpose is, of course, to establish a rent (that is, the price of using an apartment for a month) that is below the equilibrium level. One important justification that proponents of rent control give for such price ceilings is that they help the poor. In the short run, rent control is likely to transfer income from landlords to tenants.

But as time goes on, rent control can have some very undesirable effects. As shown in Figure 2.14, a price ceiling results in a shortage. That is, the quantity demanded of apartments will exceed the quantity supplied. According to some observers, New York City has a shortage of about $3 billion worth of new rental housing despite a loss in population of about 1 million people in the 1970s and the nation's largest government-assisted middle-income and low-rent public housing programs. In 1986, the *New York Times* reported that some people had to look for a year or more to obtain an apartment.

Because the quantity demanded exceeds the quantity supplied, the available apartments have to be rationed by some device other than price. This, of course, may allow landlords to engage in many forms of subtle and not-so-subtle discrimination in choosing tenants. Also, landlords will have an incentive to accept side payments or bribes from those looking for housing. They will curtail maintenance of their properties in many cases; because there is a shortage, renters are willing to accept poorer service and do more things for themselves. To the extent possible, landlords may try to subdivide apartments, since the ceiling on the rents from the subdivisions may exceed that of the original apartment. In all these ways, landlords may try to adjust to, and to some extent evade, the price ceilings.

In New York, according to estimates made by the RAND Corporation, rent increases have fallen far short of cost increases because of the rent-control laws. For housing units built before 1943, the average increase in rents was about 2 percent per year, whereas the average increase in landlords' costs was about 6 percent per year. Thus it is not surprising that more new housing has not been built, and that existing housing often has been poorly maintained.

In 1989, the *New York Times* argued that the city should end "rent regulation for apartments as they become vacant. . . . It would increase housing supply for the benefit of most people." Most economists certainly would agree that the continuation of a price ceiling is not a policy that is likely to resolve a serious shortage. But our purpose here is not to decide whether the opponents of rent controls are right or wrong; instead, it is to indicate the central role played by the microeconomic concepts discussed in this chapter in understanding the issue. Even though this chapter deals only with the basic concepts of demand and supply, the results are of importance in illuminating this and many other major policy issues.

EXAMPLE 2.3

RENT CONTROL CALIFORNIA-STYLE: MOBILE HOME OWNERS VS. PARK OWNERS

Rent control laws covering mobile home parks are common in California. A mobile home park is a tract of land on which there are pads which are rented to residents who live in mobile homes that they own, but which are placed on the pads they rent. Once placed on a pad, very few mobile homes are ever moved. The rent control laws have prevented the owners of mobile home parks from raising rents in accord with the increases in their costs. In a case involving the city of Santa Barbara, the United States Court of Appeals expressed its concern that these laws have "eviscerated" the property rights of the park owners, and have given "a windfall to current park tenants at the expense of current mobile park owners."*

(a) Do you think that these laws have had an effect on the price of a mobile home? (b) If so, is this due to their effect on the demand curve for mobile homes, the supply curve for them, or both? (c) Why have they had this effect on the demand and/or supply curve? (d) In what sense, if any, have they given a windfall to current park tenants at the expense of current mobile park owners?

SOLUTION

(a) Yes. According to studies by UCLA's Werner Hirsch, the price of a mobile home tends to be about 32 percent higher in communities that have enacted these laws than in those without them. (b) As shown on p. 43, this price increase (from OP_1 to OP_2) is due to a rightward shift in the demand for mobile homes in communities with these laws. (c) The demand curve for mobile homes has been pushed to the right by these laws because they lower the costs of mobile home owners, thus raising the value of a mobile home. All other things being equal, a potential buyer is willing to pay more for a mobile home located in an area where rents paid to park owners are lower than elsewhere. (d) Mobile home owners in rent-controlled areas have seen the value of their mobile homes rise. This is due to the reduction in the rents (current and prospective) they must pay to the park owners.**

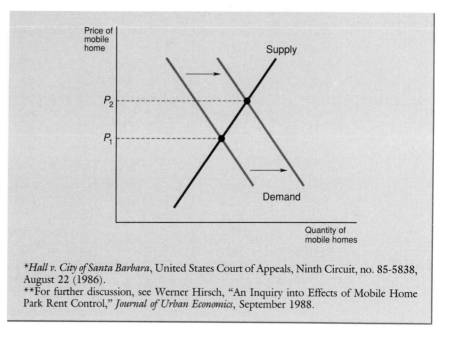

Hall v. City of Santa Barbara, United States Court of Appeals, Ninth Circuit, no. 85-5838, August 22 (1986).
**For further discussion, see Werner Hirsch, "An Inquiry into Effects of Mobile Home Park Rent Control," *Journal of Urban Economics*, September 1988.

IMPERFECT INFORMATION, AUCTIONS, AND THE WINNER'S CURSE

Throughout this chapter we have assumed that both buyers and sellers have reliable information concerning the nature and quality of the goods traded in the markets under consideration, as well as the prices at which they are sold. For many purposes, this is a reasonable first approximation to reality. But in some cases, it misses the essence of the situation. For example, suppose that a piece of land is auctioned off. This piece of land appears to have valuable oil and mineral deposits, but no one knows exactly what they are worth. (Until a variety of complex and expensive tests are performed, it is impossible to tell whether oil is present, and if so, in what amounts.) *If each bidder bids what he or she thinks the land is worth*, how much will the highest bidder be willing to pay for this land?

Without knowing more about the particular piece of land, it is impossible to provide a numerical answer to this question. Nonetheless, economists have shown that the following remarkable proposition is true: If each bidder behaves in the assumed way, *the highest bidder is likely to pay more for the land than it is worth*. To see why, suppose that each bidder makes an estimate of what the land is worth, and that *on the average, the bidders' estimates are approximately correct*. Since each bidder is assumed to submit a bid that equals his or her estimate of the land's worth, the highest bidder is likely to pay more for the land than it is worth because his or her estimate of the land's value must exceed the average estimate, which is approximately equal to the land's true value. (If his or her

TABLE 2.5 Estimates of Value of a Piece of Land, Ten Oil Firms

Firm	Estimate of value of land	Firm	Estimate of value of land
American Petrofina	$15,000	Exxon	$20,000
Amoco	16,000	Occidental	17,000
Ashland	17,000	Phillips	16,000
Atlantic Richfield	18,000	Texaco	19,000
Chevron	16,000	Unocal	16,000
		Average	17,000

estimate did not exceed the average estimate, he or she would not be the highest bidder.)[16]

Winner's curse

To illustrate this so-called "winner's curse," suppose that ten oil firms make bids for a particular piece of land, and that each firm's estimate of its value is shown in Table 2.5. Because each firm is assumed to bid what it thinks the land is worth, the winning bid ($20,000) is made by Exxon. But if, on the average, the firms' evaluations are approximately correct, then the true value of the piece of land is about $17,000, since this was their average estimate. Thus Exxon is likely to have paid too much for it.

Can the winner's curse be avoided? The answer is yes. To avoid it, sophisticated bidders make bids that are *below* their estimates of what the land is really worth. Thus the ten oil firms, recognizing the existence of the winner's curse, may submit bids that are several thousand dollars less than their estimates of the land's true value. In this way, they try to insure that, if they are the highest bidder, they will not have paid too much for the land.

ASYMMETRIC INFORMATION AND THE MARKET FOR USED CARS

Asymmetric information

In some markets, buyers and sellers do not have the same information. For example, consider the market for used cars. The seller of a used car generally knows a great deal more about its performance and weaknesses than does the buyer. This *asymmetry of information* will influence how the market works. To see why, suppose that all new cars are good or defective, that after a person buys a new car, he or she finds out whether it is good or defective, and that, if this car is offered for sale (as a used car), a potential buyer will not be able to determine (before buying it) whether it is good or defective.

16. For discussions of this and related points, see P. Milgrom, "Auctions and Bidding: A Primer," *Journal of Economic Perspectives*, Summer 1989; J. Kagel and D. Levin, "The Winner's Curse and Public Information in Common Value Auctions," *American Economic Review*, December 1986; and S. Thiel, "Some Evidence on the Winner's Curse," *American Economic Review*, 1988.

Under these circumstances, the equilibrium price of a used car will be less than the price of a new car. Since the buyer of a used car cannot tell the difference between a good and a defective car, both good and defective used cars must sell for the same price. Clearly, this price must be less than the price of a new car. Otherwise, it would pay to buy a new car, determine whether it is defective, and (if it proves to be defective) sell it and buy another new car. Unless the price of a used car is less than the price of a new one, there would be no demand for used cars.

Lemons

"Lemons"—that is, defective cars—are likely to constitute a large number of the used cars offered for sale. Owners of good used cars are likely to find the equilibrium price of a used car so low that they are not motivated to offer many of their cars for sale. On the other hand, defective used cars may constitute a large number of the used cars offered for sale, and this makes potential buyers even more inclined to offer relatively low prices for used cars.

The buyer of a used car would be willing to pay more than the equilibrium price if he or she were sure of getting a good one, and the seller of a good used car would be delighted to agree to such a transaction. However, the asymmetry of information—the fact that the seller knows whether the used car is good or defective, but the buyer does not—makes it difficult for such trades to occur. Faced with this situation, sellers of used cars try in various ways to *signal* buyers that their car is good. They cite relevant facts concerning the car, they encourage the buyer to have his or her experts inspect it before purchase, and they offer money-back guarantees or free service contracts.[17]

In subsequent chapters, we will discuss many other cases of asymmetric information. For example, Chapter 11 considers cases where firms do not know their rivals' costs as well as they know their own costs. Chapter 12 takes up cases where employers do not know as much about job applicants' productivity as do the applicants themselves, and Chapter 18 discusses cases where insurance companies cannot monitor the behavior of people they insure, with the result that the latter may not take reasonable precautions to avoid the catastrophes that trigger payment of the insurance. In recent years, economists have devoted considerable attention to the effects of asymmetric information on markets.

Summary

1. The market demand curve for a good almost always slopes downward to the right; that is, the quantity demanded increases as the price falls. The position and shape of the market demand curve for a good depend on the tastes of consumers, the level of consumer incomes, the prices of other goods, and the length of the time period to which the demand curve pertains.
2. The price elasticity of demand, defined as the percentage change in the quantity demanded resulting from a 1 percent change in price, is a measure of the responsiveness of quantity demanded to changes in price. The price elasticity of

17. For a seminal article in this area, see G. Akerlof, "The Market for Lemons," *Quarterly Journal of Economics*, August 1970, reprinted in E. Mansfield, *Microeconomics: Selected Readings*, 5th ed. (New York: Norton, 1985), pp. 55–66.

demand will generally vary from one point to another on a demand curve. Estimated price elasticities are of two different types: point elasticities and arc elasticities.

3. The market supply curve for a good generally slopes upward to the right; that is, the quantity supplied increases as the price rises. The position and shape of the market supply curve for a good depends on the state of technology, input prices, and the length of the time interval to which the market supply curve pertains.

4. The price elasticity of supply, defined as the percentage change in the quantity supplied resulting from a 1 percent change in price, is a measure of the responsiveness of quantity supplied to changes in price. The price elasticity of supply will generally vary from one point to another on a supply curve.

5. An equilibrium price is a price that can be maintained. In a competitive market, it is the price where the quantity demanded equals the quantity supplied. In other words, it is the price where the demand curve intersects the supply curve. If the actual price exceeds the equilibrium price, there will be an excess supply of the good, and the actual price will tend to fall. If the actual price is less than the equilibrium price, there will be an excess demand for the good, and the actual price will tend to rise.

6. In general, a shift to the right in the demand curve results in an increase in the equilibrium price, and a shift to the left in the demand curve results in a decrease in the equilibrium price. In general, a shift to the right in the supply curve results in a decrease in the equilibrium price, and a shift to the left in the supply curve results in an increase in the equilibrium price.

7. Demand-and-supply analysis can be used to predict the effect of an excise tax. Since the tax is collected from the sellers, the supply curve of the good on which the tax is imposed is shifted upward by the amount of the tax. How much the price of the good is increased by the tax depends on how sensitive the quantity demanded and quantity supplied are to changes in the price of the good.

8. Models of this type can also be used to analyze the effects of price floors and price ceilings imposed by the government. Price floors tend to result in surpluses, and price ceilings tend to result in shortages.

9. In some markets, it is important to recognize that buyers and sellers have imperfect information. Under certain circumstances, the winning bid in an auction is likely to be too high if it equals what the bidder believes to be the value of the auctioned item. This is the "winner's curse."

10. Buyers and sellers sometimes do not have the same information. For example, the seller of a used car generally knows far more about its performance and weaknesses than does the buyer. This asymmetry of information can have an important influence on how a market functions.

**Questions/
Problems**

1. There is a considerable amount of air travel between Los Angeles and New York City; it is one of the most intensively traveled routes in the country. According to P. Verleger, the price elasticity of demand for air travel between Los Angeles and New York City is about 0.67. (a) Suppose that an economic consultant says that the demand curve for air travel between Los Angeles and New York City is as shown on the next page.

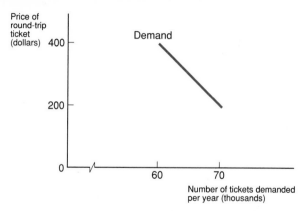

Is this graph in accord with Verleger's findings? Why or why not? (b) Suppose that the airlines double the price of a ticket between Los Angeles and New York City. Will this price increase affect the demand curve for air travel between these two cities? If so, in what way? (c) Suppose that a severe recession occurs. Will this affect the demand curve for air travel between these two cities? If so, in what way? (d) Because of the marked increase in the price of jet fuel (and other things), the cost of providing air transportation between Los Angeles and New York City has changed appreciably in recent decades. Does such a change in costs affect the demand curve for air travel between these two cities? If so, in what way?

2. In July 1986, there was a major drought in the southeastern United States. As a result, beef prices fell by 5 percent. Why? (Hint: The drought reduced hay and feed production, and farmers moved their cattle much earlier to slaughterhouses.)

3. Suppose that the demand curve for cantaloupes is

$$P = 120 - 3Q_D$$

where P is the price per pound (in cents) of a cantaloupe and Q_D is the quantity demanded per year (in millions of pounds). Suppose that the supply curve for cantaloupes is

$$P = 5Q_S$$

where Q_S is the quantity supplied per year (in millions of pounds). What is the equilibrium price per pound of a cantaloupe? What is the equilibrium quantity of cantaloupes produced?

4. The market supply curve for good Y is a straight line through the origin. Does the price elasticity of supply vary with good Y's price? What is good Y's price elasticity of supply?

5. Suppose that the number of cameras demanded in the United States at various prices is as follows:

Price of a camera (dollars)	Quantity demanded per year (millions of cameras)
80	20
100	18
120	16

Draw three points on the demand curve for cameras. Calculate the arc price elasticity of demand when (a) the price is between $80 and $100, and (b) the price is between $100 and $120.

6. Suppose that the relationship between the quantity of cameras supplied per year in the United States and the price per camera is as follows:

Price of a camera (dollars)	Quantity supplied per year (millions of cameras)
60	14
80	16
100	18
120	19

Draw four points on the supply curve for cameras, and estimate the price elasticity of supply when the price is between $80 and $100.

7. Based on the data presented in Questions 5 and 6, what is the equilibrium price of a camera in the United States? If the price is $80, will there be an excess demand? An excess supply? If the price is $120, will there be an excess demand? An excess supply?

8. Suppose that an excise tax of $40 is imposed on each camera. What will be the posttax equilibrium price of a camera? What will be the posttax equilibrium quantity? How does it compare with the pretax equilibrium quantity?

9. After the government imposes the tax in Question 8, it decides to set a price ceiling of $100 on the price of a camera. Will there be a surplus of cameras? A shortage? If so, how big a surplus or shortage?

10. According to Richard Titmuss of the London School of Economics, no Englishman pays even a shilling for all the blood his physicians prescribe for him, and no blood donor is paid for his blood. Yet blood is more readily available for patients there than in the United States where we pay for the donation of blood. What hypotheses can be advanced to account for this?

11. Suppose that the government puts a price floor of 80 cents per pound on cantaloupes. How big will be the resulting surplus of cantaloupes, based on the data in Question 3? What measures can the government adopt to cut down on this surplus?

12. Indicate whether each of the following will shift the demand curve for cantaloupes to the left, to the right, or have no effect on it: (a) a report by the U.S. Surgeon-General that cantaloupes cause cancer; (b) a 10 percent increase in the price of honeydew melons; (c) a 20 percent increase in per capita income; (d) a 10 percent increase in the wages of workers producing cantaloupes.

PART TWO

CONSUMER BEHAVIOR AND MARKET DEMAND

3

THE TASTES AND PREFERENCES OF THE CONSUMER

INTRODUCTION

Microeconomics is the branch of economics that deals with the behavior of individual decision-making units, one of the most important of which is the consumer. For many purposes the consumer is not an individual but a household; the decisions regarding the purchase of a house or car, for example, often are household rather than individual decisions. In other cases, however, the individual person is the consumer, as, for example, when he or she buys a meal at a restaurant. Regardless of the precise way in which the consumer is defined, there are millions of consumers in the United States—and they spend a great deal of money. In recent years, the American consumer has spent over $3 trillion per year on final goods and services. About 70 percent of the final goods and services produced by the American economy go directly to consumers. (The rest are sold to business firms, to the government, and in export markets.) Moreover, the importance of consumers is not a purely American phenomenon. For example, in our neighbor to the north, Canada, about two-thirds of the final goods and services produced by the Canadian economy go directly to consumers. Similar figures could be cited for many other countries.

In this chapter we present a simple model to represent the consumer's tastes and to help predict how much of various commodities he or she will buy. Besides being of interest for its own sake, this model is a first step toward analyzing the forces underlying the market demand curve, the importance of which was stressed in the previous chapter. Some of the major concepts that are introduced in this model are indifference curves, the marginal rate of substitution, utility, and the budget line. Finally, we show how this body of theory has been applied to help solve very important practical problems of budget allocation by government agencies.

THE NATURE OF THE CONSUMER'S PREFERENCES

Our purpose in this chapter is to present a simple model of consumer behavior that will enable us to predict how much of a particular commodity—hot dogs, paint, housing—a consumer buys during a particular period of time. Clearly, one of the most important determinants of a consumer's behavior is his or her tastes or preferences. After all, some consumers like Joseph Conrad while others like comic books; some like Mozart and others like the Rolling Stones. And it is obvious that these differences in tastes result in quite different decisions by consumers as to what commodities they buy. In this section we present three basic assumptions that the economist makes about the nature of the consumer's tastes.

To begin with, suppose that the consumer is confronted with any two market baskets, each containing various quantities of commodities. For example, one market basket might contain 1 ticket to a basketball game and 3 chocolate bars, while the other might contain 4 bottles of soda and a bus ticket. The first assumption that the economist makes is that consumers can decide whether they prefer the first market basket to the second, whether they prefer the second to the first, or whether they are indifferent between them.[1] This certainly seems to be a plausible assumption.

Transitivity   Second, we assume that the consumer's preferences are transitive. For example, if a man prefers Budweiser to Heineken and Heineken to Coors, he must also prefer Budweiser to Coors. Otherwise his preferences would not be transitive, which would mean that his preferences would be contradictory or inconsistent. Similarly, if he is indifferent between mince pie and pumpkin pie and between pumpkin pie and apple pie, he must also be indifferent between mince pie and apple pie. His tastes may be judged to be shallow or deep, lofty or mean, selfish or generous. This makes no difference to the theory. But his preferences must be transitive. Although not all consumers may exhibit preferences that are transitive, this assumption certainly seems to be a plausible basis for a model of consumer behavior.

Third, we assume that the consumer always prefers more of a commodity to less. For example, if one market basket (a very big one) contains 15 harmonicas and 2 gallons of gasoline, whereas another market basket (also big) contains 15 harmonicas and 1 gallon of gasoline, we assume that the first market basket, which unambiguously contains more commodities, is preferred. Also, we assume that, by adding a certain amount of harmonicas to the second market basket, we can make it equally desirable in the eyes of the consumer to the first market basket; that is, we can make the consumer indifferent between them. These assumptions, like the previous two, seem quite plausible.

INDIFFERENCE CURVES

If the assumptions in the previous section hold, we can represent the consumer's tastes or preferences by a set of indifference curves. *An* indifference

---

1. One way of telling whether the consumer prefers one market basket to another is to set equivalent prices for them and ask which one the consumer wants.

TABLE 3.1 Alternative Market Baskets

Market basket	Meat (pounds)	Potatoes (pounds)
	(per unit of time)	
1	1	4
2	1	6
3	2	3
4	2	4
5	3	2
6	3	3
7	4	1
8	4	2
9	5	0
10	5	1

Indifference curve

curve *is the locus of points representing market baskets among which the consumer is indifferent.* For example, suppose we confine our attention to the ten market baskets in Table 3.1, in which the first market basket contains 1 pound of meat and 4 pounds of potatoes, the second market basket contains 1 pound of meat and 6 pounds of potatoes, and so on. Suppose the consumer is asked to choose between various pairs of these market baskets and that he or she is indifferent between some of these market baskets. For example, the consumer may not care whether he or she consumes 4 pounds of meat plus 2 pounds of potatoes or 2 pounds of meat plus 3 pounds of potatoes. Suppose that we enlarge the number of market baskets (containing various quantities of meat and potatoes) under consideration, so that we include all market baskets in which from 1 to 8 pounds of meat are combined with from 1 to 8 pounds of potatoes. Then suppose we plot each of the market baskets on a diagram like Figure 3.1 and that *curve A is the set of points representing market baskets among which the consumer is indifferent.* For example, this curve includes all of the market baskets that the consumer regards as being equivalent (in terms of his or her satisfaction) to 4 pounds of meat plus 2 pounds of potatoes.

Curve *A* is an *indifference curve.* Of course there are many such indifference curves, each pertaining to a different level of satisfaction. For example, indifference curve *B* in Figure 3.1 represents a higher level of satisfaction than indifference curve *A,* since it includes market baskets with more of both meat and potatoes than the market baskets represented by indifference curve *A.* One can visualize a series of indifference curves—one showing all market baskets that are equivalent (in the eyes—or belly—of the consumer) to 1 pound of potatoes and 2 pounds of meat, one showing all market baskets that are equivalent to 2 pounds of potatoes and 2 pounds of meat, and so on. The resulting series of indifference curves is called an indifference map.

A consumer's indifference map lies at the heart of the theory of consumer behavior, since such a map provides a representation of the consumer's tastes. To illustrate how a consumer's indifference map mirrors his or her tastes, con-

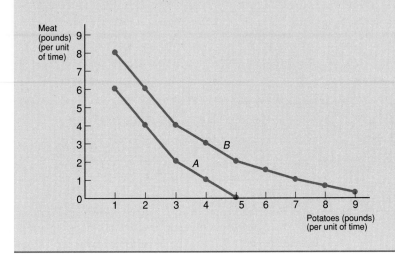

FIGURE 3.1 Indifference Curves *The consumer is indifferent among the market baskets represented by points on indifference curve A. Market baskets represented by points on indifference curve B are preferred over those represented by points on indifference curve A.*

sider the various indifference maps in Figure 3.2. Consumer *A*'s indifference curves are relatively steep, whereas consumer *B*'s indifference curves are relatively flat. What does this mean? Apparently consumer *A* needs several extra units of good *Y* to compensate for the loss of a single unit of good *X*. Thus, in this sense, good *Y* is less important (relative to good *X*) to consumer *A* than to consumer *B*.

What about consumers *C* and *D* in Figure 3.2? Apparently consumer *C* regards good *X* as useless, since he does not care whether he has more or less of it. Consumer *D* seems to regard good *X* as a nuisance, since she is willing to reduce the amount of good *Y* she consumes in order to get rid of some good *X*. But situations of this sort are ruled out by the assumption (discussed on p. 50) that the consumer prefers more of a commodity to less. This does not mean that some things are not a nuisance. It means only that in the case of consumer *D* we would define a commodity as the lack of good *X*, not the consumption of good *X*. Using this simple, legitimate trick, we no longer violate this assumption, since more of all commodities is now preferred to less.[2]

2. As explained in detail on pp. 56–57, economists often attach a number, known as a *utility*, to each market basket, this number being a measure of how much satisfaction the consumer gets from this market basket. Market baskets with higher utilities are preferred by the consumer over market baskets with lower utilities. Let *U* represent the consumer's utility, and let the consumer consume x_1 units of good 1, x_2 units of good 2, and so on. The *utility function* is the relationship between *U* and $x_1, x_2, \cdots, x_n$. It is

$$U = U(x_1, x_2, \cdots, x_n).$$

Using this utility function, one can define an indifference curve very simply. An indifference curve is given by the equation

$$U(x_1, x_2, \cdots, x_n) = a$$

where *a* is a constant.

FIGURE 3.2 Indifference Maps of Various Consumers *The shape of a consumer's indifference curves may vary greatly, depending on his or her tastes. However, consumer D's positively sloped indifference curves are ruled out by the assumption that the consumer prefers more of a commodity to less.*

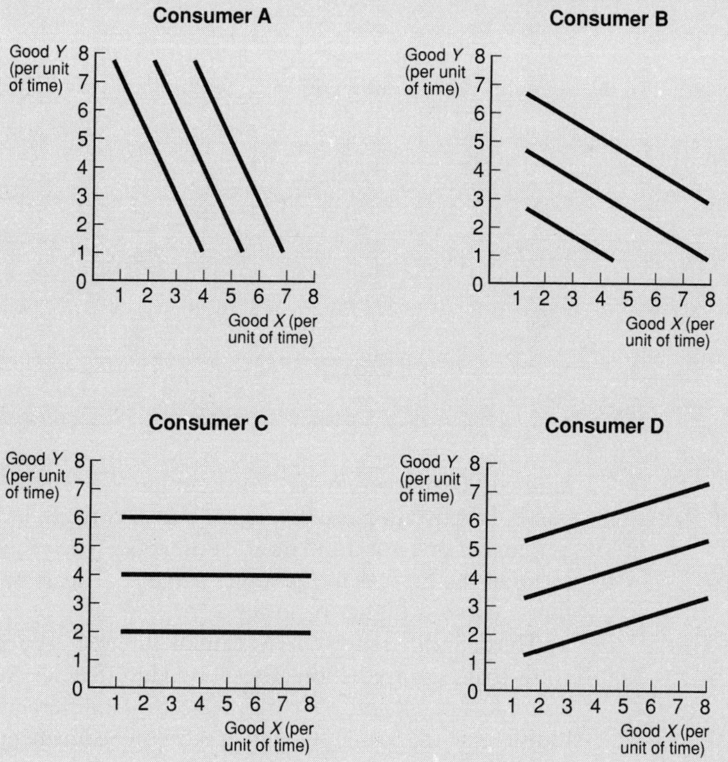

Consumer A

Good Y (per unit of time)

Good X (per unit of time)

Consumer B

Good Y (per unit of time)

Good X (per unit of time)

Consumer C

Good Y (per unit of time)

Good X (per unit of time)

Consumer D

Good Y (per unit of time)

Good X (per unit of time)

Characteristics of Indifference Curves

All indifference curves have certain characteristics that should be noted. First, given the fact (noted in the last section) that every commodity is defined so that more of it is preferred to less, it follows that indifference curves must have a negative slope. If more of both commodities is desirable, and if one market basket has more of good *Y*, it must have less of good *X* than another market basket if the two market baskets are to be equivalent in the eyes of the consumer. If the two market baskets are equivalent, and if one market basket contains more of both commodities—which would be the case if an indifference curve had a positive slope—it would mean that one or the other of the commodities is not defined so that more of it is preferred to less.

Second, given the fact that every commodity is defined so that more of it is preferred to less, it also follows that indifference curves that are higher in graphs like Figure 3.1 represent greater levels of consumer satisfaction than indiffer-

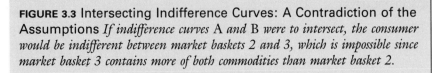

FIGURE 3.3 Intersecting Indifference Curves: A Contradiction of the
Assumptions *If indifference curves* A *and* B *were to intersect, the consumer
would be indifferent between market baskets 2 and 3, which is impossible since
market basket 3 contains more of both commodities than market basket 2.*

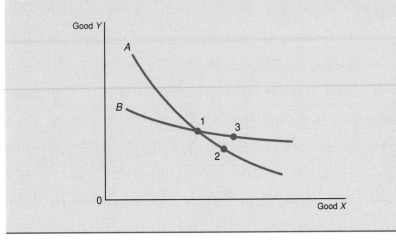

ence curves that are lower. For example, curve *B* in Figure 3.1 is preferred to
curve *A*. Why? Because the higher curve, curve *B*, includes market baskets with
as much of one good and more of the other (or as much of the second good and
more of the first) than the lower curve *A*. This is what we mean when we say
that a curve is higher or lower.

Third, indifference curves cannot intersect. To prove this statement, let's
show that a contradiction arises if two indifference curves were to intersect. For
example, take the case of two intersecting indifference curves in Figure 3.3. On
indifference curve *A,* market basket 1 is equivalent to market basket 2. On
indifference curve *B,* market basket 1 is equivalent to market basket 3. Hence, if
the indifference curves intersect, market basket 2 must be equivalent to market
basket 3. But this cannot be, since market basket 3 contains more of both
commodities than market basket 2, and commodities are defined so that more
of them is preferred to less. If the consumer's tastes are transitive, as we assume
in this model, there cannot be an intersection of indifference curves.

The Marginal Rate of Substitution

In the section before last, we pointed out that consumers differ in the importance that they attach to an extra unit of a particular good. Of course, this is
hardly news. For example, it is well known that an alcoholic will sometimes
trade a valuable item like a watch for an extra drink of whiskey, whereas the
president of the Temperance Union will not give a cent for an extra (presumably the first) dose of Demon Rum. However, news or not, it is useful to have a
measure of the relative importance attached by the consumer to the acquisition
of another unit of a particular good. The measure that economists have devised
is called the *marginal rate of substitution,* a term indicative of the economist's
talent for elegant and graceful phrase-making.

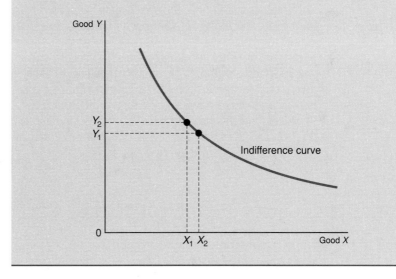

FIGURE 3.4 The Marginal Rate of Substitution *The marginal rate of substitution of good* X *for good* Y *is* $(OY_2 - OY_1)/(OX_2 - OX_1)$, *which is the number of units of good* Y *that must be given up—per unit of good* X *received—to maintain a constant level of satisfaction.*

Marginal rate of substitution

The *marginal rate of substitution* is defined as the number of units of good Y that must be given up if the consumer, after receiving an extra unit of good X, is to maintain a constant level of satisfaction. For example, in Figure 3.4, the consumer can give up $(OY_2 - OY_1)$ units of good Y to receive $(OX_2 - OX_1)$ extra units of good X, and this trade will leave him or her no better or no worse off. Thus the marginal rate of substitution of good X for good Y is $(OY_2 - OY_1)/(OX_2 - OX_1)$. This is the number of units of good Y that must be given up—per unit of good X received—to maintain a constant level of satisfaction.

More precisely, the marginal rate of substitution is equal to -1 times the slope of the indifference curve.[3] Thus the marginal rate of substitution of good X for good Y is higher for consumer A (whose indifference curve on p. 53 is steeper) than for consumer B (whose indifference curve is flatter). In general, the marginal rate of substitution will vary from point to point on a given

---

3. The definition in the previous paragraph is an approximation that is quite adequate when good X is measured in small units. Suppose that there are only two commodities and that an indifference curve is $U((x_1, x_2) = a$. (Recall the discussion in footnote 2.) Taking the total differential, we obtain

$$\frac{\partial U}{\partial x_1}dx_1 + \frac{\partial U}{\partial x_2}dx_2 = 0.$$

Thus the slope of the indifference curve is

$$\frac{dx_2}{dx_1} = -\frac{\partial U}{\partial x_1} \div \frac{\partial U}{\partial x_2},$$

which equals -1 times the marginal rate of substitution of the first good for the second good.

indifference curve, since the indifference curve's slope will vary from point to point. For example, on indifference curve *A* (or curve *B*) in Figure 3.1, the marginal rate of substitution of potatoes for meat gets smaller as the consumer has more potatoes and less meat.

In the economist's model of consumer behavior it is generally assumed that indifference curves have the sort of shape exhibited by curves *A* and *B* in Figure 3.1. More specifically, it is assumed that they show that the more the consumer has of a particular good, the less will be the marginal rate of substitution of this good for any other good. Put somewhat crudely, this amounts to assuming that the more the consumer has of a particular good, the less important to him or her (relative to other goods) is an extra unit of this good. In mathematical *Convexity* terms, this assumption means that indifference curves are *convex*. In other words, an indifference curve lies above its tangent, as illustrated in panel A of Figure 3.5. This contrasts with the case presented in panel B of Figure 3.5 where the indifference curve is not convex.[4]

THE CONCEPT OF UTILITY

In previous sections, we have stressed that the consumer's indifference map is a representation of his or her tastes. This certainly is true, since the consumer's indifference map shows each and every one of his or her indifference curves. Given the indifference map of a particular consumer, we can attach a number, a *Utility* *utility,* to each of the market baskets that might confront this consumer. *This utility indicates the level of enjoyment or preference attached by this consumer to this market basket.* Since all market baskets on a given indifference curve yield the same amount of satisfaction, they would have the same utility. Market baskets on higher indifference curves would have higher utilities than market baskets on lower indifference curves.

The purpose of attaching these utilities to market baskets is that, once this is done, we can tell at a glance which market baskets the consumer would prefer over other market baskets. If the utility attached to one market basket is higher than that attached to another market basket, he or she will prefer the first over the second market basket. If the utility attached to the first market basket is lower than the second, he or she will prefer the second over the first market basket. If the utility attached to the first market basket equals the second, he or she will be indifferent between the two market baskets.

How should we choose these utilities? Any way will do as long as market baskets on the same indifference curve receive the same utility and market baskets on higher indifference curves receive higher utilities than market baskets on lower indifference curves. For example, if the consumer prefers market basket 1 to market basket 2, and market basket 2 to market basket 3, the utility of market basket 1 must be higher than the utility of market basket 2, and the utility of

4. The assumption of convexity may not always hold, but a discussion of cases where it fails belongs in a more advanced book.

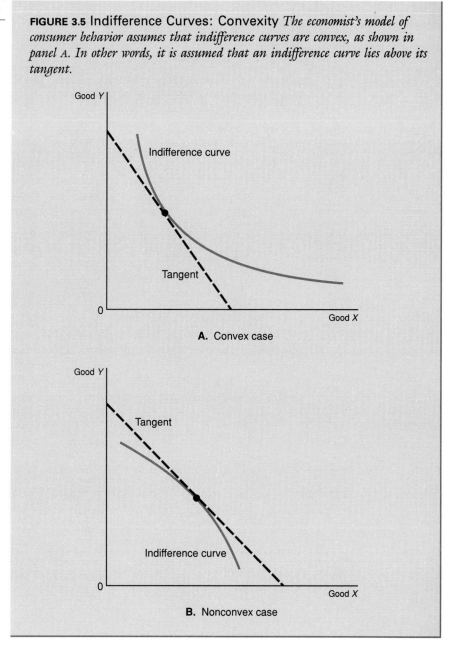

FIGURE 3.5 Indifference Curves: Convexity *The economist's model of consumer behavior assumes that indifference curves are convex, as shown in panel A. In other words, it is assumed that an indifference curve lies above its tangent.*

Good Y

Indifference curve

Tangent

0   Good X

A. Convex case

Good Y

Tangent

Indifference curve

0   Good X

B. Nonconvex case

market basket 2 must be higher than the utility of market basket 3. But any set of numbers conforming to these requirements is an adequate measure of utility. Thus the utility of market baskets 1, 2, and 3 may be 50, 40, and 30, or 10, 9, 8. Both are adequate utility measures, since all that counts is that the utility of market basket 1 be higher than that of market basket 2, which in turn should be higher than that of market basket 3.

EXAMPLE 3.1

THE EXPERIMENTAL DETERMINATION OF INDIFFERENCE CURVES

K. MacCrimmon and M. Toda published an experimental study in which they asked a group of college students to choose among market baskets containing various amounts of money and pens. One of the students said she was indifferent among market baskets A to E below. MacCrimmon and Toda also asked the students to choose among market baskets containing various quantities of money and French pastries (to be eaten on the spot). The same student said she was indifferent among market baskets F to J below.

Market basket	Number of pens	Amount of money (dollars)	Market basket	Number of French pastries	Amount of money (dollars)
A	0	20.00	F	0	6.00
B	50	17.50	G	3	5.50
C	100	15.00	H	6	5.00
D	130	14.00	I	8	6.00
E	160	13.00	J	10	7.00

(a) Draw the student's indifference curve for money and pens. (Assume that the points given in the table can be connected with straight lines.) (b) Draw her indifference curve for money and French pastries. (c) Do these indifference curves represent the same level of utility? (d) Are French pastries always a good? (e) If the French pastries could be taken home and eaten later, would the indifference curve for money and French pastries be the same as that given above?

SOLUTION

(a) and (b) The indifference curves are shown below.

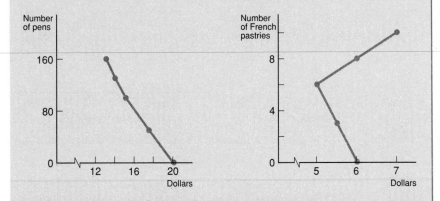

(c) No, since one indifference curve includes market basket A, which contains $20 alone, while the other indifference curve includes market basket F, which contains $6 alone. So long as more money is preferred to less, the former indifference curve must represent a higher level of utility than the latter. (d) No. For more than 6 French pastries, the indifference curve is upward sloped to the right because the student was willing to consume more French pastries only if she received more money. (e) No. The student would probably have not required more money to make her willing to consume more than 6 French pastries, if she did not have to eat them on the spot.*

*For further discussion, see K. MacCrimmon and M. Toda, "The Experimental Determination of Indifference Curves," *Review of Economic Studies,* October 1969.

THE BUDGET LINE

Given his or her tastes, we assume that the consumer is rational, in the sense that he or she tries to get on the highest possible indifference curve. In other words, the consumer tries to maximize utility. To do so, the consumer must consider factors other than his or her own tastes. Account must be taken of the prices of various commodities and the level of the consumer's income, since both of these factors limit, or constrain, the nature and size of the market basket that he or she can buy.

Money income　　The consumer's money income is the amount of money that he or she can spend per unit of time.[5] If William Smith had an infinite money income, he would not have to worry about certain market baskets' being too expensive for him to purchase. He could simply buy the market basket he liked best—the market basket on his highest indifference curve. But no one has an unlimited money income. Even the Rockefellers and Mellons cannot get on their highest indifference curve, since this would mean the expenditure of more than even they have. For us poorer folk, the problem is much more difficult still, since our incomes are much smaller. What we can buy is much more severely constrained by our incomes.

Besides his or her money income, the consumer must also take account of the prices of all relevant commodities. The price of a commodity is the amount of money that the consumer must pay for a unit of the commodity. The higher prices are, the fewer units of a commodity can be bought with a given money income. For example, an income of $50,000 went a lot further when movies were 50 cents and sodas were 5 cents a bottle than it does now when movies are often $7 and sodas are 60 cents or more a can.

To show how the consumer's money income and the level of commodity prices influence the nature and size of the market baskets available to the consumer, it simplifies matters without distorting the essentials of the situation if we assume that there are only two commodities that the consumer can buy, good X and good Y. Since the consumer must spend all of his or her money income on one or the other of these two commodities, it is evident that

$$Q_x P_x + Q_y P_y = I \qquad [3.1]$$

---

5. To the extent that the consumer can borrow, the amount he or she can borrow can, for some purposes, also be included as income, since it increases the amount the consumer can spend during the period.

where Q_x is the amount the consumer buys of good X, Q_y is the amount the consumer buys of good Y, P_x is the price of good X, P_y is the price of good Y, and I is the consumer's money income.[6] For example, if the price of good X is $1 a unit and the price of good Y is $2 a unit and the consumer's income is $100, it must be true that $Q_x + 2Q_y = 100$. Note that we assume that the consumer takes prices as given. This, of course, is generally quite realistic.

It is possible to plot the combinations of quantities of goods X and Y that the consumer can buy on the same sort of graph as the indifference map. Solving Equation 3.1 for Q_y, we have

$$Q_y = \frac{1}{P_y}I - \frac{P_x}{P_y}Q_x. \qquad [3.2]$$

Equation 3.2, which is a straight line, is plotted in Figure 3.6. The first term on the right-hand side of Equation 3.2 is the intercept of the line on the vertical axis: It is the amount of good Y that could be bought by the consumer if he or she spent all of his or her income on good Y. The slope of the line is equal to the negative of the price ratio, P_x/P_y.

Budget line

The straight line in Equation 3.2 is called the *budget line*. It shows all of the combinations of quantities of good X and good Y that the consumer can buy. In subsequent sections, we shall be interested in the effects of changes in product prices and money income on consumer behavior. These changes are reflected by changes in the budget line. Equation 3.2 shows that increases in

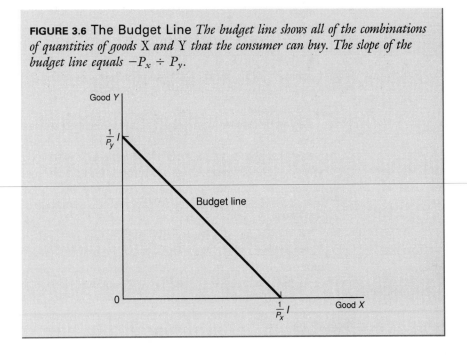

FIGURE 3.6 The Budget Line *The budget line shows all of the combinations of quantities of goods* X *and* Y *that the consumer can buy. The slope of the budget line equals* $-P_x \div P_y$.

6. Of course, the consumer can also save some of his or her income, but, from the point of view of this model, savings can be viewed as a commodity like any other. Thus, with this amendment, Equation 3.1 can easily encompass saving.

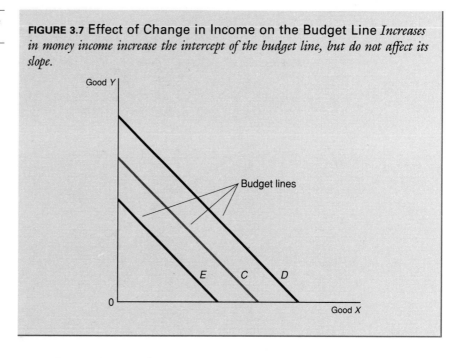

FIGURE 3.7 Effect of Change in Income on the Budget Line *Increases in money income increase the intercept of the budget line, but do not affect its slope.*

money income increase the intercept of the budget line, but leave unaffected the slope of the budget line. For example, Figure 3.7 shows the effect of an increase in income, with C the original budget line and D the budget line after the increase in income. Conversely, decreases in income lower the intercept of the budget line. In Figure 3.7, E is the budget line after a decrease in income, with C once again the original budget line.

Equation 3.2 also shows what happens to the budget line if the price of good X changes. Increases in P_x increase the absolute value of the slope of the budget line; decreases in P_x decrease the absolute value of the slope. The vertical intercept of the line is unaffected. Figure 3.8 shows the effect of changes in P_x on the budget line. Suppose that the original budget line is F. If P_x increases, the budget line becomes G. If P_x decreases, the budget line becomes H. Intuitively, it is easy to see why an increase (decrease) in the price of good X results in the budget line's cutting the X axis at a point closer to (farther from) the origin. The point where the budget line cuts the X axis equals the maximum number of units of good X that the consumer can buy with his or her fixed money income, and this number obviously is inversely related to the price of good X.

THE EQUILIBRIUM OF THE CONSUMER

Given that the consumer is constrained to purchase one of the market baskets that lies on the budget line, which one will he or she choose? To answer this question, we assume, as noted in the previous section, that the consumer tries to maximize utility. This assumption is so general and so reasonable that most people would accept it as a good approximation to reality. Of course, this is not

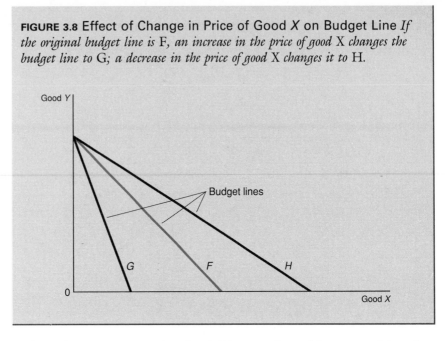

FIGURE 3.8 Effect of Change in Price of Good *X* on Budget Line *If the original budget line is* F, *an increase in the price of good* X *changes the budget line to* G; *a decrease in the price of good* X *changes it to* H.

to deny that some acts are irrational. However, by and large, people's actions seem to be such that they promote, not frustrate, the achievement of their goals. Even the ascetic, although his actions may seem irrational at first glance, can be regarded as attempting to maximize utility, if we recognize the very peculiar nature of his or her tastes.

Going a step further, we note that, although the consumer may attempt to maximize utility, he or she may not succeed in doing so because of miscalculation or for other reasons. The problem of maximizing utility may not be as simple as it looks. For example, how many people know how much their cars really cost them? It is not that they do not know how to do the arithmetic, although even the brightest people have been known to have lapses in this regard. More important is the fact that what should or should not be regarded as a cost in a particular situation is not always straightforward. More will be said on this score in subsequent chapters. For the moment, all we want to point out is that consumers may not be able to achieve the maximization of utility, at least right away.

However, if the consumer is allowed some time to adapt and to learn, it seems likely that he or she will eventually find the market basket that maximizes his or her utility. Let us define the consumer's equilibrium behavior as a course of action that will not be changed by him or her in favor of some other course of action, if the consumer's money income, tastes, and the prices he or she faces remain the same. Then the consumer's equilibrium behavior will be to choose the market basket that maximizes his or her utility. And eventually one would expect the consumer to come very close to acting in accord with this equilibrium behavior.

More precisely, what market basket will maximize the consumer's utility? Figure 3.9 brings together the consumer's indifference map and his or her

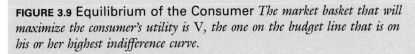

FIGURE 3.9 Equilibrium of the Consumer *The market basket that will maximize the consumer's utility is* V, *the one on the budget line that is on his or her highest indifference curve.*

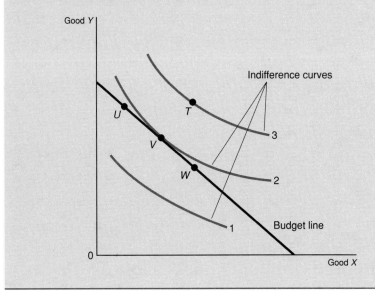

budget line. All of the relevant information needed to answer this question is contained in Figure 3.9. *The indifference map shows what the consumer's preferences are.* For example, any market basket on indifference curve 3 is preferred to any on indifference curve 2; and any market basket on indifference curve 2 is preferred to any on indifference curve 1. The consumer would like to choose a market basket on the highest possible indifference curve. This is the way to maximize his or her utility.

But not all market baskets are within reach. *The budget line shows what the consumer can do.* He or she can choose any market basket such as *U, V,* or *W* on the budget line, but he or she cannot obtain a market basket like *T* which is above the budget line. (Of course, the consumer can also buy any market basket below the budget line, but any such market basket lies on a lower indifference curve than a market basket on the budget line.) Since this is the case, *the market basket that will maximize the consumer's utility is the one on the budget line that is on his or her highest indifference curve*—which is *V* in Figure 3.9. It can readily be seen that this market basket is at a point where the budget line is tangent to an indifference curve. This market basket, *V,* is the one that the rational consumer would, according to our model, be predicted to buy in equilibrium.[7]

Maximizing utility

7. Mathematically, one can state the conditions for equilibrium as follows: Suppose that the consumer's utility function is

$$U = U(x_1, x_2 \cdots, x_n).$$

Then he or she maximizes U subject to the constraint that

$$x_1p_1 + x_2p_2 + \cdots + x_np_n = I$$

(cont'd.)

EXAMPLE 3.2

SICKNESS AND HEALTH INSURANCE

Americans spend over $350 billion per year on medical care. John Jones, a Chicago stockbroker, was very sick last year, but is in good health this year. He belongs to a health insurance plan which stipulates that the patient must pay the first $200 of medical expenses that he or she incurs per year and that the insurance company will pay 80 percent of the patient's medical expenses above $200 (which is called the "deductible"). Mr. Jones's budget line and indifference curves are shown below, for this year and last year:

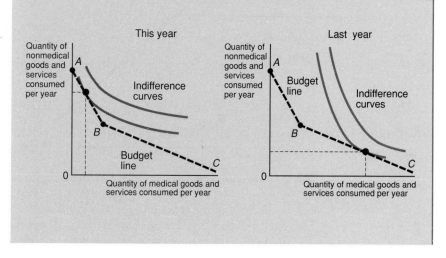

where p_i is the price of the ith good. To maximize U subject to the constraint, we construct the function

$$L = U(x_1, x_2 \cdots, x_n) - \lambda(x_1 p_1 + \cdots + x_n p_n - I)$$

where λ is a Lagrangian multiplier. The first-order conditions for a maximum are

$$\frac{\partial L}{\partial x_1} = \frac{\partial U}{\partial x_1} - \lambda p_1 = 0$$

$$\frac{\partial L}{\partial x_2} = \frac{\partial U}{\partial x_2} - \lambda p_2 = 0$$

....

$$\frac{\partial L}{\partial x_n} = \frac{\partial U}{\partial x_n} - \lambda p_n = 0$$

$$\frac{\partial L}{\partial \lambda} = x_1 p_1 + x_2 p_2 + \cdots + x_n p_n - I = 0.$$

From these equations it follows that

$$\frac{\partial U}{\partial x_1} \div p_1 = \frac{\partial U}{\partial x_2} \div p_2 = \cdots = \frac{\partial U}{\partial x_n} \div p_n$$

$$x_1 p_1 + x_2 p_2 + \cdots + x_n p_n - I = 0.$$

If utility is cardinally measurable, this result is equivalent to the budget allocation rule in Equation 3.3 in the chapter appendix. We ignore the possibility of corner solutions where the optimal value of x_1, x_2, $\cdots$, or x_n is zero. This possibility is taken up in our discussion of Figure 3.10.

(a) Why are his indifference curves so much flatter this year than last year? (b) His budget line is *ABC*. Why isn't it a straight line? (c) Suppose that Mr. Jones could pay a fixed fee of $800 per year for health insurance, and that the insurance company would reimburse him for any and all health expenses. What would be the shape of his budget line? (d) Under the circumstances described in part (c), what incentive would Mr. Jones have to restrict his consumption of medical goods and services? (For example, why not waste medicine?) (e) If his budget line is *ABC,* does he have any incentive to restrict his consumption of medical goods and services?

New York Hospital

SOLUTION

(a) Last year, he was very sick; thus, if the amount of medical goods and services he received went down by one unit, it took a considerable extra amount of nonmedical goods and services to offset the loss. This year, he is in good health; thus, if the amount of medical goods and services he receives goes down by one unit, it takes only a relatively small extra amount of non-medical goods and services to offset the loss. (b) The budget line is not a straight line because, if he spends less than $200 on medical goods and services, he pays the full amount, whereas for expenses above $200, he pays only 20 cents for each dollar's worth of medical goods and services. (The insurance company pays the remaining 80 cents.) (c) His budget line would be a horizontal line because, once he pays the fixed fee, the price of an extra unit of medical goods and services is zero. (d) There is little or no incentive to restrict consumption, since he pays nothing (at least in money) for extra medical goods and services. (e) Yes, since even for expenses above $200, he must pay 20 cents for every extra dollar of medical goods and services.*

*For further discussion, see the *Economic Report of the President* (Washington, D.C.: Government Printing Office, 1985).

CORNER SOLUTIONS

Although we have just stated that the consumer will choose the market basket where the budget line is tangent to an indifference curve (market basket *V* in Figure 3.9), there are exceptions. In particular, the consumer may consume

FIGURE 3.10 Corner Solution *The market basket that maximizes the consumer's utility is* M, *which lies on the vertical axis.*

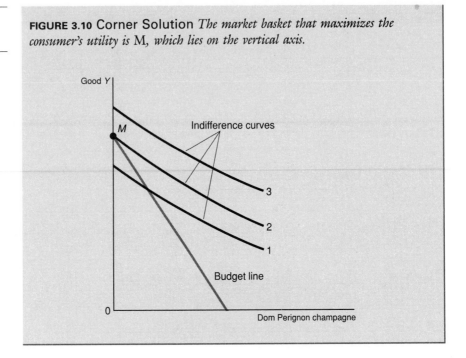

none of some goods because even tiny amounts of them (or the minimum amount of them that can be bought) are worth less to the consumer than they cost. For example, although your money income may permit you to buy some Dom Perignon champagne (which you would enjoy), you may not purchase any because even a swallow would be worth less to you than it would cost.

Figure 3.10 shows the situation graphically. For simplicity, we suppose that there are only two goods, Dom Perignon champagne and good *Y*. Given the position of the consumer's indifference curves, he or she will maximize utility by choosing market basket *M*, which contains all good *Y* and no Dom Perignon champagne at all. This market basket maximizes the consumer's utility because it is on a higher indifference curve than any other market basket on the budget line. It is a *corner solution,* in which the budget line reaches the highest achievable indifference curve along an axis (in this case, the vertical axis).

DETERMINANTS OF CONSUMER TASTES AND PREFERENCES

In previous sections of this chapter, we have discussed how the consumer's tastes can be represented and the way his or her tastes influence the market basket that is chosen. But we have said nothing about the factors that determine his or her tastes. Clearly, the consumer's tastes can be changed by various forms of experience. The child whose widest grins of satisfaction are reserved for candy and other sweets grows into the woman who politely declines a sweet drink in favor of dry white wine. The boy who regards the ballet as sissy stuff grows to be the man who pays $100 for a ticket to the Royal Ballet and gives

EXAMPLE 3.3

THE FOOD-STAMP PROGRAM

In 1986 the food-stamp program in the United States included about 19 million individuals, and cost about $11 billion. Suppose that if a family is eligible for food stamps, it pays $80 per month to obtain $150 worth of food. (a) If the family's cash income is $250 and it is not eligible for food stamps, draw its budget line on a graph where the quantity of food consumed per month is measured along the horizontal axis and the quantity of nonfood items consumed per month is measured along the vertical axis. (b) Draw the family's budget line on this graph if it is eligible for food stamps. (c) Show that if the family were given $70 in cash (rather than in food), it might achieve a higher level of satisfaction.

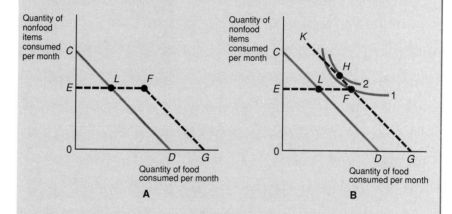

A

B

SOLUTION

(a) Without food stamps, the family's budget line is *CD* in panel A. In this panel, *OC* is the quantity of nonfood items the family can obtain with its entire income ($250) and *OD* is the quantity of food it can obtain with it. (b) With food stamps, the family's budget line is *CLFG* in panel A. *EC* is the quantity of nonfood items the family can buy with $80. If the family buys food stamps, *OE* is the maximum quantity of nonfood items it can obtain once it pays for the food stamps. *EF* is the $150 worth of food it receives with the food stamps, and *DG* (= *LF*) is the $70 worth of food that it can obtain with food stamps that it couldn't otherwise obtain, when the quantity of nonfood items is held constant. If the quantity of nonfood items consumed by the family exceeds *OE*, it does not have enough money left for food to buy food stamps, so the budget line is the same as without food stamps. (That is, it is *CL*.) If the quantity of nonfood items consumed by the family does not exceed *OE*, it can buy food stamps, and consume an extra amount of food equal to *DG*, so the budget line is *FG*. (c) If the family were given $70 in cash (rather than in food), its budget line would be *GK* in panel B. Because its money income increases by $70, the budget line is higher, but parallel to, the old budget line, *CD*. With this budget line, the family can reach point *H* on indifference curve 2, whereas with budget line *CLFG,* the best it can do is reach point *F* on indifference curve 1. Since indifference curve 2 is higher than indifference curve 1, the family achieves a higher level of satisfaction if it receives the cash rather than the food. Of course, not all families have indifference curves of this sort; some have indifference curves such that they achieve as high a level of satisfaction with the food as with the cash. This is the case for families with indifference curves tangent to the budget line between *F* and *G.**

*For further discussion, see K. Clarkson. "Welfare Benefits of the Food Stamp Program." *Southern Economic Journal,* July 1976; and M. MacDonald, *Food, Stamps, and Income Maintenance* (New York: Academic Press, 1977).

away complimentary ringside tickets to the fights. Age has a great effect on a person's tastes; so does education. Indeed, one of the benefits of education is that it allows people to appreciate and enjoy various forms of experience more keenly than they otherwise would.

Demonstration effects   Another factor influencing a consumer's tastes is his or her observation of what other consumers have. These effects are sometimes called demonstration effects. For example, if the Joneses have a Cadillac, their neighbors, the Smiths, may feel that they should have one, too. Or if the Jones's daughter can buy expensive clothes, the Smiths may feel that their daughter should have them, too. (Whether their daughter feels this way is another matter—which shows the importance of asking in each case what individuals are regarded as the "consumer," and how decisions are made.) Sometimes an opposite kind of effect is at work: If many consumers have a certain commodity, others may not want it. For example, the snobbish Crandalls may take pride in having tastes that are different from the common herd of mankind.

Advertising   Another important determinant of a consumer's tastes is the advertising and selling expenses incurred by manufacturers and sellers of various goods and services. There can be no doubt that advertising influences consumers, although the extent of its influence varies greatly from one product to another, and from one consumer to another. For goods where quality is hard for the consumer to measure, and where the relative advantages of a particular good or brand are not very great, advertising may play a very important role. Of course, advertising also plays a significant role merely by informing the consumer of the existence and characteristics of new products. Much more will be said about the effects of advertising in subsequent chapters.

Finally, we have assumed in previous sections that a consumer's tastes (that is, his or her indifference map) are independent of the structure of prices. For example, changes in the prices of meat and potatoes are not supposed to affect the indifference map in Figure 3.1. This rules out cases in which goods are consumed because they are expensive—conspicuous consumption—and cases in which quality is judged by price. This assumption is a reasonable first approximation but it obviously does not hold for all cases. It is possible to extend our model to allow for violations of this assumption, but a discussion of such extensions properly belongs in a more advanced text.

BUDGET ALLOCATION BY A GOVERNMENT AGENCY: AN APPLICATION

In Chapter 1 we said that microeconomics has turned out to be useful in helping to solve many important practical problems; yet in this chapter we have provided no evidence so far to support that statement. The material provided in previous sections of the present chapter must be understood if the reader is to understand the theory of consumer behavior. But it is by no means obvious how it would enable anyone to solve any kind of a practical problem. Appearances, however, can be deceiving. The kind of analysis discussed in this chapter can be useful in many contexts. The purpose of this section is to show how the model described in previous sections has been used to solve problems of budget allocation by government agencies.

*Highways vs.
mass transit*

For concreteness' sake, let's consider a particular agency, the Department of Transportation. And let's consider the decision that it (and Congress) must make with regard to the allocation of funds between urban highways and urban mass transit (buses and rail lines), both of which can be used to meet the transportation needs of our urban population. Suppose that the Department of Transportation has $2 billion to spend on urban highways and/or mass transit. How should it allocate this sum between them? In other words, how much should it spend on highways, and how much should it spend on mass transit? This is an important decision, one that involves huge sums of money and the time, comfort, and convenience of many people.

What has this problem got to do with the theory of consumer preferences we discussed in previous sections of this chapter? Strange as it may seem, economists have used the theory discussed above to help solve this kind of problem. The way in which they have dealt with the problem is instructive in many respects, one being that it illustrates how simple models can be adapted to throw light on very complicated problems.

In effect, the economists have said, "Let's view the Department of Transportation as a consumer. Let's regard highways and mass transit as two goods that the department can buy, with each good having a price and the total amount that can be spent on them both being fixed. Assuming that the department is interested in maximizing the effectiveness of the nation's transportation system, let's use as indifference curves for the department the combinations of extra miles of highway and extra miles of mass transit that will result in a certain expected addition to the nation's total transportation capability. Clearly, the bigger the expected addition to this capability, the higher the indifference curve. Then let's find the point on the budget line (which can be derived from the price of a mile of highway, the price of a mile of mass transit, and the total budget to be allocated) that lies on the highest indifference curve. This point will indicate the optimal allocation of the budget."

To actually attack the problem in this way, the first step, of course, is to determine various "indifference curves" of the "consumer," the Department of Transportation. Figure 3.11 shows what they might look like. As in Figure 3.4, each indifference curve slopes downward, since highways can be substituted for mass transit, and vice versa. Moreover, they are likely to be convex. What exactly does each of these indifference curves mean? Consider indifference curve 1. Each point on this indifference curve represents a combination of highways and mass transit that results in the same addition to transportation capability, that is, the same expected addition to our ability to transport people quickly and safely. The Department of Transportation is viewed as being interested in maximizing the nation's transportation capability. In other words, transportation capability (measured in this way) is a measure of this consumer's "utility." Thus the consumer is indifferent among all of the points on curve 1. And the consumer clearly prefers indifference curve 2 to indifference curve 1, because points on indifference curve 2 result in more transportation capability than those on indifference curve 1.

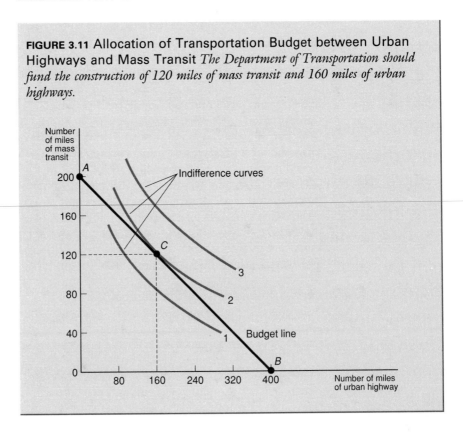

FIGURE 3.11 Allocation of Transportation Budget between Urban Highways and Mass Transit *The Department of Transportation should fund the construction of 120 miles of mass transit and 160 miles of urban highways.*

Having constructed the indifference curves, the next step is to construct the appropriate budget line. If the Department of Transportation has $2 billion to spend, if each mile of mass transit costs $10 million, and if each mile of highway costs $5 million, the budget line is *AB* in Figure 3.11. Based on our discussion on pp. 59–61, this should be clear enough. Given this budget line and the indifference map, the problem boils down to finding the point on the budget line that lies on the highest indifference curve. A careful inspection of Figure 3.11 shows that this optimal point is point *C*, where the Department of Transportation funds the construction of 120 miles of mass transit and 160 miles of urban highways.

In recent years, economic analysis of this kind has played an important role in policy-making in many government agencies. In practice, of course, the measurement of "transportation capability" or "social worth" often presents extremely difficult problems, with the result that it is not possible to draw curves like 1, 2, and 3 with great accuracy. Nevertheless, this does not mean that this type of analysis is not useful. On the contrary, it has proved very useful, since it provides a correct way of thinking about the problem. It focuses attention on the relevant factors, and puts them in their proper place.[8]

This example also illustrates the fact that most aspects of microeconomics are concerned with means to achieve specified ends, not with the choice of ends. Thus economists in this case were interested in increasing the transportation capability to be obtained from a given budget. But they took as given the hypothesis that it was a good thing to increase transportation capability. In other words, they took as given the fact that the "utility" of the "consumer" should be increased. In certain circumstances, this hypothesis could perhaps be wrong. For example, suppose that the department wants to maximize its power and influence in the federal government, or to maximize the political fortunes of its top officials, rather than the nation's transportation capability. The same techniques could be used; all that would be required is a reinterpretation of the indifference curves.[9] Of course, this does not mean that it is not valuable to have techniques like those discussed here. They are obviously of great value. What it does mean is that one cannot expect them to do more than they are designed to do. They cannot tell us what our goals or ends should be.

Summary

1. We assume that, when confronted with two market baskets, a consumer can say which one is preferred, or whether he or she is indifferent between them. Also, we assume that the consumer's tastes are transitive and that a commodity is defined in such a way that more is preferred to less.
2. An indifference curve is the locus of points representing market baskets among which the consumer is indifferent. A consumer's tastes can be represented by a

8. It should be emphasized, however, that the particular example presented in this section is highly simplified. For one thing, costs incurred by parties other than the federal government are ignored. Also, the indifference curves may not always have the shape shown in Figure 3.11. Further, miles of highway or mass transit are rather crude units of measurement. Despite these and other limitations, this example communicates the spirit of this sort of analysis.

9. Under these circumstances, each indifference curve would show the combinations of highways and mass transit that result in the same level of power for the department or the same level of political fortunes for the department's top officials.

set of indifference curves. An indifference curve must have a negative slope, and two indifference curves cannot intersect. Market baskets on higher indifference curves provide more satisfaction than those on lower indifference curves.

3. The slope of an indifference curve (multiplied by −1) is called the marginal rate of substitution. The marginal rate of substitution shows approximately how many units of one good must be given up if the consumer, after receiving an extra unit of another good, is to maintain a constant level of satisfaction.

4. Utility is a number that indexes the level of satisfaction derived from a particular market basket. Market baskets with higher utilities are preferred over market baskets with lower utilities. The consumer is assumed to be rational in the sense that he or she tries to maximize utility.

5. The budget line indicates all of the combinations of quantities of goods—all of the market baskets—that the consumer can buy, given his or her money income and the level of each price. In equilibrium, we would expect the consumer to attain the highest level of satisfaction that is compatible with the budget line, which means that the consumer will choose the market basket on the budget line that is on the highest indifference curve. This market basket is at a point where the budget line is tangent to an indifference curve (unless there is a corner solution).

6. The model of consumer behavior presented in this chapter has been used to solve problems of budget allocation by government agencies. To illustrate its use, we took up a case study involving expenditures on urban transportation.

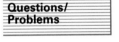

**Questions/
Problems**

1. In the diagram below, we show one of Ellen White's indifference curves and her budget line. If the price of good A is $50, what is Ms. White's income? What is the equation for her budget line? What is the slope of the budget line? What is the price of good B? What is her marginal rate of substitution in equilibrium?

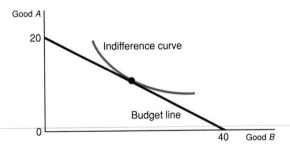

2. "A survey shows that most people prefer Cadillacs to Chevrolets." What exactly does this mean? If this is true, why do more people drive Chevrolets than Cadillacs?

3. One of Ms. Jones's indifference curves includes the following market baskets. Each of these market baskets gives her equal satisfaction.

Market basket	Meat (pounds)	Potatoes (pounds)
1	2	8
2	3	7
3	4	6
4	5	5
5	6	4

(cont'd.)

Market basket	Meat (pounds)	Potatoes (pounds)
6	7	3
7	8	2
8	9	1

In her case, what is the marginal rate of substitution of potatoes for meat? How does the marginal rate of substitution vary as she consumes more meat and less potatoes? Is this realistic?

4. "As a society becomes increasingly affluent, wants are increasingly created by the process by which they are satisfied." Do you agree? Why or why not? Assuming that this is true, what would be the implications of this for the theory of consumer behavior?

5. Martin Cole purchases 100 loaves of bread per year when the price is $1 per loaf. The price increases to $1.50. To offset the harm to Martin, his father gives him $50 a year. Will Martin be better or worse off after the price increase plus the gift than he was before? Will his consumption of bread increase or decrease?

*6. "Whether or not utility is some kind of glow or warmth, or happiness, is here irrelevant; all that counts is that we can assign numbers to entities or conditions which a person can strive to realize." Comment on this statement. Do you agree with it? Why or why not?

7. Suppose that consumers in San Francisco pay twice as much for apples as for pears, whereas consumers in Los Angeles pay 50 percent more for apples than for pears. If consumers in both cities maximize utility, will the marginal rate of substitution of pears for apples be the same in San Francisco as in Los Angeles? If not, in which city will it be higher?

8. A consumer is willing to trade one pound of steak for three pounds of hamburger. He currently is purchasing as much steak as hamburger per month. The price of steak is twice that of hamburger. Should he increase his consumption of hamburger and reduce his consumption of steak? Or should he reduce his consumption of hamburger and increase his consumption of steak?

*9. Suppose that James Gray spends his entire income on goods X and Y. The marginal utility of each good (shown below) is independent of the amount consumed of the other good. The price of X is $100 and the price of Y is $500.

Number of units of good consumed	Mr. Gray's marginal utility (utils)	
	Good X	Good Y
1	20	50
2	18	45
3	16	40
4	13	35
5	10	30
6	6	25
7	4	20
8	2	15

If Mr. Gray has an income of $1,000 per month, how many units of each good should he purchase?

10. Steve Walcott spends a total of $4,000 per month on goods A and B. The price of A is $200 per unit, and the price of B is $800 per unit. Draw Mr. Walcott's budget line. At what point does it cut the axis along which the quantity of A is measured? At what point does it cut the axis along which the quantity of B is measured? What is its slope?

*This question pertains to the chapter appendix.

ORDINAL AND CARDINAL UTILITY

Economists, as we have seen, assume that the amount of satisfaction a consumer gets from a particular market basket can be measured by its utility. Following the lead of E. Slutsky, Vilfredo Pareto, John Hicks, and others, they generally assume that utility is measurable in an *ordinal* sense, which means that a consumer can only *rank* market baskets with regard to the satisfaction they give him or her.[10] For example, you may be able to say with assurance that you prefer two tickets to the Super Bowl to two tickets to the San Francisco Opera, but you may not be able to say how much more satisfaction you get from the former than the latter. For an ordinal measurement of utility, this is adequate, since all that is needed is a ranking.

Ordinal utility

In contrast, according to such great nineteenth-century economists as William Stanley Jevons of England, Karl Menger of Austria, and Leon Walras of France, utility was measurable in a *cardinal* sense, which means that the difference between two measurements is itself numerically significant. For example, if I weigh 185 pounds and you weigh 170 pounds, the difference between these measurements has numerical significance: It says that I weigh 15 pounds more than you do. Moreover, if the difference between Ed McMahon's weight and Johnny Carson's weight is 60 pounds, it follows that the difference between my weight and yours is less than the difference between Ed McMahon's weight and Johnny Carson's. According to most nineteenth-century economists, utility was measurable in the same sense.

Cardinal utility

Our discussion in this chapter was based on the modern assumption that utility is ordinally measurable, which is less restrictive than the older assumption that utility is cardinally measurable. That is, we need not assume that a consumer can answer questions like: How much extra satisfaction will you get from a second helping of mashed potatoes? However, if one is willing to assume that the consumer is able to characterize his or her preferences by attaching a cardinal utility to each market basket, it is possible to obtain some additional results, presented in this appendix. To focus on the important factors at work here, let's assume that there are only two goods, food and medicine.

Consider a consumer making choices concerning how much of each good to buy. In contrast to our earlier discussion in this chapter, suppose that it is possible to measure the amount of satisfaction that the consumer gets from each market basket by its cardinal utility. For example, the utility attached to the market basket containing 2 pounds of food and 1 ounce of medicine may be 13 utils, and the utility attached to the market basket containing 1 pound of food and 1 ounce of medicine may be 8 utils. (A util is the traditional unit in which utility is expressed.)

10. For example, see J. Hicks, *Value and Capital* (New York: Oxford University Press, 1946); H. Hotelling, "Demand Functions with Limited Budgets," *Econometrica*, 1935; and P. Samuelson, *Foundations of Economic Analysis* (Cambridge, Mass: Harvard University Press, 1947).

MARGINAL UTILITY

It is important to distinguish between total utility and marginal utility. The total utility of a market basket is the number described in the previous paragraph, whereas *the* marginal utility *measures the additional satisfaction derived from an additional unit of a commodity (when the levels of consumption of all other commodities are held constant)*. To see how marginal utility is obtained, let's take a close look at Table 3.2. The total utility the consumer derives from the consumption of various amounts of food is given in the middle column of this table. (For simplicity, we assume for the moment that only food is consumed.) The marginal utility, shown in the right-hand column, is the extra utility derived from each amount of food over and above the utility derived from 1 less pound of food. Thus it equals the difference between the total utility of a certain amount of food and the total utility of 1 less pound of food.

TABLE 3.2 Consumer's Total and Marginal Utility from Consuming Various Amounts of Food per Day

Pounds of food	Total utility	Marginal utility*
0	0	—
1	4	4(= 4 − 0)
2	9	5(= 9 − 4)
3	13	4(= 13 − 9)
4	16	3(= 16 − 13)
5	18	2(= 18 − 16)

*These figures pertain to the interval between the indicated number of pounds of food and one pound less than the indicated number. This table assumes that no medicine is consumed.

For example, as shown in Table 3.2, the *total* utility of 3 pounds of food is 13 utils, which is a measure of the total amount of satisfaction that the consumer gets from this much food. In contrast, the *marginal* utility of 3 pounds of food is the extra utility obtained from the third pound of food—that is, the total utility of 3 pounds of food less the total utility of 2 pounds of food. Specifically, as shown in Table 3.2, it is 4 utils. Similarly, the *total* utility of 2 pounds of food is 9 utils, which is a measure of the total amount of satisfaction that the consumer gets from this much food. In contrast, the *marginal* utility of 2 pounds of food is the extra utility from the second pound of food—that is, the total utility of 2 pounds of food less the total utility of 1 pound of food. Specifically, as shown in Table 3.2, it is 5 utils.

The Law of Diminishing Marginal Utility

It seems reasonable to believe that, as a person consumes more and more of a particular commodity, there is, beyond some point, a decline in the extra satisfaction derived from the last unit of the commodity consumed. For example, if a person consumes 2 pounds of food in a particular period of time, it may be just what the doctor ordered. If he or she consumes 3 pounds of food in the same period of time, the third pound of food is likely to yield less satisfaction than the second. If he or she consumes 4 pounds of food in the same period of time, the fourth pound of food is likely to yield less satisfaction than the third. And so on.

This assumption or hypothesis is often called the law of diminishing marginal utility. This law states that, *as a person consumes more and more of a given commodity (the consumption of other commodities being held constant), the marginal utility of the commodity eventually will tend to decline.* In other words, it states that the relationship between the marginal utility of a commodity and the amount consumed will be like that shown in Table 3.2. Beyond some point (2 pounds of food in Table 3.2), the marginal utility declines as the amount consumed increases.

Law of diminishing marginal utility

THE BUDGET ALLOCATION RULE

If the law of diminishing marginal utility holds true, *the consumer, if he or she maximizes utility, will allocate his or her expenditures among commodities so that, for every commodity purchased, the marginal utility of the commodity is proportional to its price.* Thus, in the case of the consumer whose choices are limited to food and medicine, the optimal market basket is the one where

$$\frac{MU_F}{P_F} = \frac{MU_M}{P_M} \qquad [3.3]$$

where MU_F is the marginal utility of food, MU_M is the marginal utility of medicine, P_F is the price of a pound of food, and P_M is the price of an ounce of medicine. This is a famous result. In the rest of this appendix, we will explain why it is true.

Budget allocation rule

To understand why the budget allocation rule in Equation 3.3 is correct, it is convenient to begin by pointing out that $MU_F \div P_F$ is the marginal utility of the *last dollar's worth* of food and that $MU_M \div P_M$ is the marginal utility of the *last dollar's worth* of medicine. To see why this is so, take the case of food. Since MU_F is the extra utility of the *last pound* of food bought, and since P_F is the price of this *last pound,* the extra utility of the *last dollar's worth* of food must be $MU_F \div P_F$. For example, if the last pound of food results in an extra utility of 4 utils and this pound costs $2, then the extra utility from the last dollar's worth of food must be $4 \div 2$, or 2 utils. In other words, the marginal utility of the last dollar's worth of food is 2 utils.

Since $MU_F \div P_F$ is the marginal utility of the last dollar's worth of food and $MU_M \div P_M$ is the marginal utility of the last dollar's worth of medicine, what Equation 3.3 really says is that *the rational consumer will choose a market basket where the marginal utility of the last dollar spent on all commodities purchased is the same.* To see why this must be so, consider the numerical example in Table 3.3, which shows the marginal utility the consumer derives from various amounts of food and medicine. Rather than measuring food and medicine in physical units, we measure them in Table 3.3 in terms of the amount of money spent on them.

TABLE 3.3 Consumer's Marginal Utility from Consuming Various
Amounts of Food and Medicine per Day

Dollars worth of each commodity	Food	Medicine
1	9	4
2	7	3
3	4	2
4	3	1
5	2	0

Given the information in Table 3.3, how much of each commodity should the consumer buy if his or her money income is only \$4 (a ridiculous assumption but one that will help to make our point)? Clearly, the first dollar the consumer spends should be on food since it will yield him or her a marginal utility of 9. The second dollar he or she spends should also be on food since a second dollar's worth of food has a marginal utility of 7. (Thus the total utility derived from the \$2 of expenditure is $9 + 7 = 16$.[11]) The marginal utility of the third dollar is 4 if it is spent on more food—and 4 too if it is spent on medicine. Suppose that he or she chooses more food. (The total utility derived from the \$3 of expenditure is $9 + 7 + 4 = 20$.) What about the final dollar? Its marginal utility is 3 if it is spent on more food and 4 if it is spent on medicine; thus he or she will spend it on medicine. (The total utility derived from all \$4 of expenditure is $9 + 7 + 4 + 4 = 24$.)

Clearly, the consumer, if rational, will allocate \$3 of his or her income to food and \$1 to medicine. This is the equilibrium market basket, the market basket that maximizes consumer satisfaction. The important thing to note is that this market basket conforms to the budget allocation rule in Equation 3.3. As shown in Table 3.3, the marginal utility derived from the last dollar spent on food is equal to the marginal utility derived from the last dollar spent on medicine. (Both are 4.) Thus this market basket has the characteristic described in the paragraph before last. The marginal utility of the last dollar spent on all commodities purchased is the same.

In general, one can prove mathematically that the budget allocation rule in Equation 3.3 is correct. (Such a proof is given in footnote 7 on page 63–64.) Since this rule provides valuable insight into rational decision making, it should be understood. However, its applicability is limited by the fact that utility ordinarily is not cardinally measurable.

11. Since the marginal utility is the extra utility obtained from each dollar spent, the total utility from the total expenditure must be the sum of the marginal utilities of the individual dollars of expenditure.

4

CONSUMER BEHAVIOR AND INDIVIDUAL DEMAND

THE EQUILIBRIUM OF THE CONSUMER: REVIEW AND ANOTHER VIEWPOINT

In this chapter, we proceed further with the development of a model of consumer behavior. Building on the results of the previous chapter, we show how the consumer responds to changes in his or her money income and to changes in the prices of commodities. In addition, we present some illustrations of how this theory has been applied to help solve important problems of public policy. Specifically, we describe how it has been applied to the evaluation of the effects of sugar import quotas and to the interpretation and construction of price indexes.

To begin with, it is useful to review briefly the conditions under which the consumer is in equilibrium. However, rather than merely parrot what has already been said in the previous chapter, we look at these conditions from a somewhat different point of view. We said in the previous chapter that the consumer's equilibrium market basket is at a point where the budget line is tangent to an indifference curve: This is the market basket that maximizes the consumer's utility.[1] Since the slope of the indifference curve equals -1 times the marginal rate of substitution of good X for good Y (see p. 55) and since the slope of the budget line is $-P_x/P_y$ (see p. 60), it follows that the rational consumer will choose in equilibrium to allocate his or her income between good X and good Y so that the marginal rate of substitution of good X for good Y equals P_x/P_y.

---

1. For simplicity, we assume here that the optimal market basket is not a corner solution. (See pages 65–66.)

This is a famous result—and a very useful one that should be understood fully. It is easier to agree that it is true than it is to see what it really means and why it is true. Perhaps the best way to understand this result is to define once again the marginal rate of substitution: The marginal rate of substitution is the rate at which the consumer is *willing* to substitute good X for good Y, holding his or her total level of satisfaction constant. Thus, if the marginal rate of substitution is 3, the consumer is willing to give up three units of good Y in order to get one more unit of good X.

Marginal rate of substitution

On the other hand, the price ratio, P_x/P_y, is the rate at which the consumer is *able* to substitute good X for good Y. Thus, if P_x/P_y is 2, he or she *must* give up two units of good Y to get one more unit of good X. What the result described in this section is really saying is: The rate at which the consumer is willing to substitute good X for good Y (holding satisfaction constant) must equal the rate at which he or she is able to substitute good X for good Y. Otherwise it is always possible to find another market basket that will increase the consumer's satisfaction. And this means, of course, that the present market basket is not the equilibrium one that maximizes consumer satisfaction.

Price ratio

To see that this must be the case, suppose that the consumer has chosen a market basket in which the marginal rate of substitution of good X for good Y is 3. Suppose that the ratio, P_x/P_y, is 2. If this is the case, the consumer can trade two units of good Y for an extra unit of good X in the market, since the price ratio is 2. But this extra unit of good X is worth three units of good Y to the consumer, since the marginal rate of substitution is 3. Consequently, he or she can increase satisfaction by trading good Y for good X—and this will continue to be the case as long as the marginal rate of substitution exceeds the price ratio. Conversely, if the marginal rate of substitution is less than the price ratio, the consumer can increase satisfaction by trading good X for good Y. Only when the marginal rate of substitution equals the price ratio does the consumer's market basket maximize his or her utility.

EFFECTS OF CHANGES IN CONSUMER MONEY INCOME

With this review in mind, let us turn to new territory and consider the effect of changes in money income on the amounts of good X and good Y purchased by the consumer. For example, suppose that the consumer is a student and that the amount of money he earns and receives from home increases from $6,000 to $8,500 a year. What effect will this have on his purchases? How much of the extra money will he spend on books? Entertainment? Clothes? Food?

In the previous chapter, we saw that an increase in money income results in an increase in the intercept of the budget line, but leaves unaffected the slope of the budget line (as long as the prices of commodities remain constant). Similarly, a decrease in money income results in a decrease in the intercept of the budget line, but leaves unaffected the slope of the budget line (as long as the prices of commodities remain constant). To determine the effect of a change in money income on the market basket chosen by the consumer, one can compare the equilibrium position based on the budget line corresponding to the old

FIGURE 4.1 Effects of Changes in Money Income on Consumer Equilibrium *The income-consumption curve connects points (like* U, V, *and* W) *representing equilibrium market baskets corresponding to all possible levels of money income.*

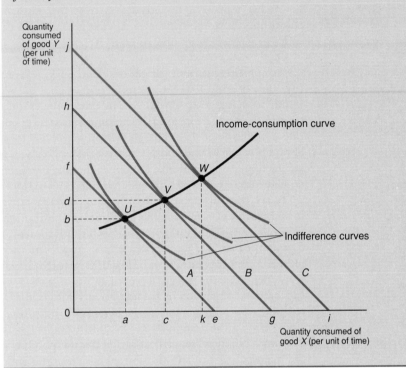

level of money income with the equilibrium position based on the budget line corresponding to the new level of money income.

For example, suppose that the budget line corresponding to the old level of income—$6,000 in the case of the student—is *A* in Figure 4.1. Given the consumer's indifference map, the market basket that maximizes his utility is comprised of *Oa* units of good *X* and *Ob* units of good *Y*, if his income is at the old level. Now suppose that his income rises—to $8,500 in the case of the student—and that the new budget line is *B* in Figure 4.1. With these new conditions, the market basket that maximizes his utility is comprised of *Oc* units of good *X* and *Od* units of good *Y*.

Clearly, the way in which an increase in money income influences a consumer's purchases depends on his or her tastes. In other words, the nature of the market basket chosen at the old income, the nature of the market basket chosen at the new income, and consequently the nature of the difference between these two market baskets is influenced by the shape of the consumer's indifference curves. Also, the way in which an increase in money income influences a consumer's purchases depends on the price ratio, P_x/P_y. Of course, this price ratio is held constant when we analyze the effects of changes in money income on consumer behavior, but the level at which the price ratio is held constant will influence the results.

Holding commodity prices constant, we find that each level of money income results in an equilibrium market basket for the consumer. That is, corresponding to each level of money income is an equilibrium market basket for a particular consumer. For example, the equilibrium market baskets corresponding to three income levels are represented by points U, V, and W in Figure 4.1. If we connect all of the points representing equilibrium market baskets corresponding to all possible levels of money income, the resulting curve is called the *income-consumption curve*. Figure 4.1 shows such a curve.

Income-consumption curve

The income-consumption curve can be used to derive Engel curves, which are important for studies of family expenditure patterns. An *Engel curve* is the relationship between the equilibrium quantity purchased of a good and the level of income.[2] Ernst Engel was a nineteenth-century German statistician who did pioneering work related to such curves, named after him by economists.

Engel curve

It is easy to see how an Engel curve can be derived from the income-consumption curve. Take the case in Figure 4.1 as an example. When money income equals P_x times Oe (or P_y times Of, since they are equal), the income-consumption curve shows that the consumer buys Oa units of good X. When

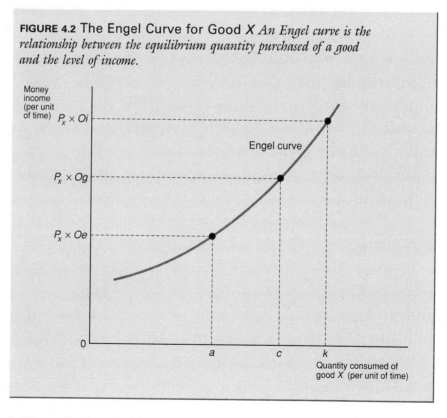

FIGURE 4.2 The Engel Curve for Good X *An Engel curve is the relationship between the equilibrium quantity purchased of a good and the level of income.*

2. Often an Engel curve is defined to be the relationship between the consumer's *expenditure* on a commodity and his or her money income. But since the commodity prices are held constant, the consumer's expenditure on the product is proportional to the number of units of the commodity that he or she consumes. So it makes no real difference for present purposes whether we use expenditure or quantity demanded of the commodity as the relevant variable.

money income equals P_x times Og (or P_y times Oh), the income-consumption curve shows that the consumer buys Oc units of good X. When money income is P_x times Oi (or P_y times Oj), the income-consumption curve shows that the consumer buys Ok units of good X. These are three points on the Engel curve for good X for this consumer. Each of these points shows the equilibrium amount of good X that he or she purchases at a certain level of money income. As more and more points are included, all of the points on the Engel curve for good X for this consumer are traced out. The result is shown in Figure 4.2.

Shape of Engel curve   Of course, the shape of a consumer's Engel curve for a particular good will depend on the nature of the good, the nature of the consumer's tastes, and the level at which commodity prices are held constant. For example, Engel curves

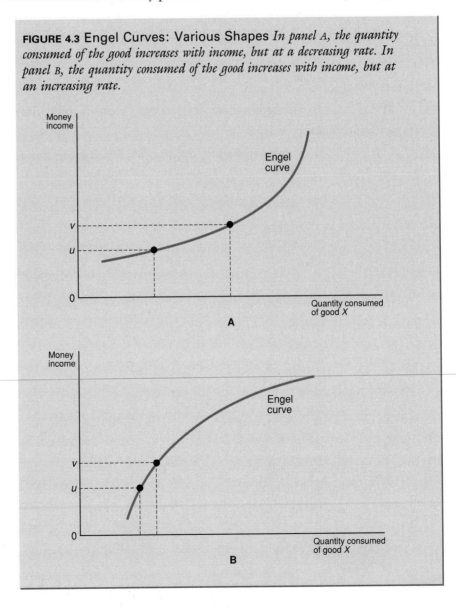

FIGURE 4.3 Engel Curves: Various Shapes *In panel A, the quantity consumed of the good increases with income, but at a decreasing rate. In panel B, the quantity consumed of the good increases with income, but at an increasing rate.*

with quite different shapes are shown in panels A and B of Figure 4.3. According to the Engel curve in panel A, the quantity consumed of the good increases with income, but at a *decreasing* rate. According to the Engel curve in panel B the quantity consumed of the good increases with income, but at an *increasing* rate. A comparison of panel A with panel B shows that a change in income from *Ou* to *Ov* does not have as great an effect on consumption of the good in panel B as on consumption of the good in panel A.

In general, one would expect that Engel curves for goods like salt and shoelaces would show that the consumption of these commodities does not change very much in response to changes in income. For example, only a rather unusual type of person would respond to a large increase in income by gorging himself or herself with salt and shoelaces—singly or in combination. On the other hand, goods like caviar and filet mignon might be expected to have Engel curves showing that their consumption increases considerably with increases in income. In general, this is probably so. But one should be careful about such generalizations. For example, if the consumer were a vegetarian, this would not hold true for filet mignon.

EFFECTS OF CHANGES IN COMMODITY PRICE

In the previous two sections we have been concerned with the effect of changes in money income on the market basket that, in equilibrium, will be chosen by the consumer. Another important question is: Holding the consumer's money income constant, what will be the effect of a change in the price of a certain commodity on the amount of this commodity that the consumer will purchase? For example, take the case of the college student mentioned in the section before last. Suppose that his income remains constant at $6,000 and that the prices of all commodities other than food are held constant. Suppose that the price of food is allowed to vary and that we watch how the quantity of food that he consumes (per unit of time) varies in response to changes in the price of food. What sort of relationship exists between the price of food and the quantity of food that he consumes (per unit of time)?

This case is unnecessarily specific. Let's pose the question more generally. Let's assume that there are only two commodities, good *X* and good *Y*. Suppose that the price of good *Y* and the money income of the consumer are held constant, but the price of good *X* is allowed to vary from one level to another. Suppose that the budget line corresponding to the original price of good *X* is *B* in Figure 4.4. If the price of good *X* is increased and the new budget line is *C*, the new equilibrium market basket for the consumer will be *T*, rather than the original equilibrium market basket of *S*. (In the previous chapter, we saw that an increase in the price of good *X* increases the absolute value of the slope of the budget line but does not affect the vertical intercept of the line.) Thus the increase in the price of good *X* will result in the consumer's buying *Ou* units of good *X* and *Ov* units of good *Y*, rather than the original market basket composed of *Or* units of good *X* and *Os* units of good *Y*.

Corresponding to each price of good *X* is an equilibrium market basket that can be determined in this way. The curve that connects the various equilibrium

FIGURE 4.4 Effects of Changes in Price of Good *X* on Consumer Equilibrium *The price-consumption curve connects points (like* R, S, *and* T) *representing equilibrium market baskets corresponding to all possible levels of the price of good* X.

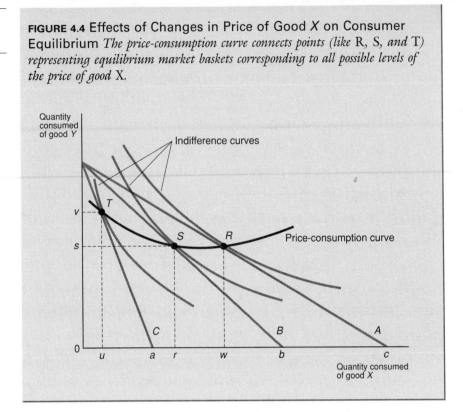

*Price-consumption
curve*

points is called the *price-consumption curve*. Figure 4.4 shows the price-consumption curve for this consumer, given the level of his or her money income and the price of good *Y*. One reason why the price-consumption curve is of interest is that it can be used to derive the consumer's individual demand curve for the commodity in question. The individual demand curve shows how much of a given commodity the consumer would purchase (per unit of time) at various prices of the commodity, holding constant the consumer's money income, his or her tastes, and the prices of other commodities. The individual demand curve is a central concept in the theory of consumer behavior.

How can the individual demand curve be derived from the price-consumption curve? To illustrate the procedure, consider the case in Figure 4.4. When the price of good *X* is *I/Oa* (where *I* is the money income of the consumer), the price-consumption curve shows that the consumer buys *Ou* units of good *X*.[3] When the price of good *X* is *I/Ob*, the price-consumption curve shows that the consumer buys *Or* units of good *X*. When the price of good *X* is *I/Oc*, the price-consumption curve shows that the consumer buys *Ow* units of good *X*. These are three points on the individual demand curve. By deriving more and more points in this way, one can obtain the entire individual demand curve for good *X*. The result, curve *D*, is shown in Figure 4.5.

3. From Figure 4.4, we know that the price of good *X* must be *I/Oa* when the budget line is *C* because, if the consumer devotes all of his or her money income, *I*, to good *X*, he or she can get *Oa* units of good *X*.

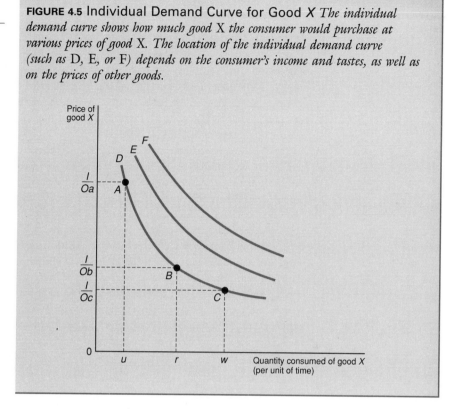

FIGURE 4.5 Individual Demand Curve for Good X *The individual demand curve shows how much good* X *the consumer would purchase at various prices of good* X. *The location of the individual demand curve (such as D, E, or F) depends on the consumer's income and tastes, as well as on the prices of other goods.*

The Individual Demand Curve: Location and Shape

The location and shape of an individual demand curve will depend on the level of money income and the level at which the prices of other goods are held constant, as well as on the nature of the commodity and the tastes of the consumer. For example, suppose that we consider the demand curve for good X of the consumer represented in Figure 4.5. If his or her income were to be held constant at a level higher than I, a different demand curve would result. Rather than D it might be E in Figure 4.5. Also, if the price of good Y were higher than that assumed in Figure 4.4, a different demand curve would result. Rather than D, it might be F in Figure 4.5. An important point to remember about a demand curve is that it is always drawn with certain assumptions about the level of the consumer's money income and the level of other prices in mind. In general it is only valid if these assumptions are correct.

It is important to differentiate between shifts in a consumer's demand curve for a particular commodity and changes in the amount of the commodity that he or she consumes. As we have seen, a consumer's demand curve may shift because of changes in his or her income or tastes, as well as because of changes in the prices of other goods. Such shifts in the consumer's demand curve are likely to result in changes in the amount of the commodity that he or she consumes, but they are not the only reason for such changes. In addition,

EXAMPLE 4.1

MEDICAL INSURANCE AND THE DEMAND FOR MEDICAL CARE

Many employees receive medical insurance as a fringe benefit from their employers. Since employees have not had to pay income taxes on this fringe benefit, some economists, such as Martin Feldstein (former chairman of President Reagan's Council of Economic Advisers), argue that too much medical insurance has been provided by employers, and that the resulting economic waste runs into the billions of dollars.

(a) Why would an employee (who pays 30 cents in taxes for every extra dollar earned) prefer an additional dollar of nontaxed medical insurance rather than another dollar of wages, even if the dollar's worth of insurance is worth only 80 or 90 cents to him or her? (b) Why are employers led to provide medical insurance which is worth less to their employees than it costs? (c) If less medical insurance were provided tax free, what would be the effect on the price paid by an employee for medical care? (d) Suppose that an employee's demand curve for medical care is as shown below. If the cost of a patient-day of care is OP_0, but if (because of the insurance) the employee pays a price of only OP_2, will the employee demand some medical care that is worth less to him or her than it costs? (e) In 1989, the *New York Times* proposed that the federal government "tax health benefits that exceed a certain basic level. . . ." Why might this help reduce excess health costs?

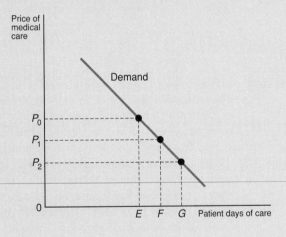

SOLUTION

(a) Another dollar of wages, if the tax rate is 30 percent, is worth 70 cents. Thus, even if a dollar's worth of medical insurance is worth only 80 or 90 cents, it is worth more than an extra dollar of wages. (b) Employers are competing among themselves to obtain and keep good workers. If workers prefer a dollar's worth of medical insurance to an extra dollar's worth of wages, employers will act accordingly. (c) If less medical insurance were provided tax free, this employee would have to pay more of the full costs of medical care. In other words, the price to him or her of medical care would increase. (d) Yes. The maximum amount that the employee would pay for an extra unit of medical care can be determined from the demand curve. For example, the maximum amount that the employee would pay for the OF^{th} day of care is OP_1. (Why? Because if the price were any higher than OP_1, the employee would demand less than OF days of care.) If the employee pays a price of only OP_2, he or she demands OG days of care. But the maximum amount that the employee would pay exceeds the cost (OP_0) only for the first OE days of care. (This is obvious because the demand curve lies above OP_0 only for quantities demanded that are less than OE.) For the remaining EG days of care, the maximum amount that the employee would pay is less than the cost. (e) It would give the worker more incentive to restrict his or her health costs.*

*For further discussion, see Martin Feldstein, "The Welfare Loss of Excess Health Insurance." *Journal of Political Economy*, March 1973; and "The Health Crisis and Baby Bells," *New York Times*, August 10, 1989.

changes in the price of the good will result in changes in the amount of the commodity that he or she consumes. We must be careful to distinguish between cases where the demand curve remains the same and changes in the consumption of the commodity occur because of changes in the commodity's price, and those cases where the demand curve shifts. The movement from point A to point B in Figure 4.5 is an example of the former; the shift of the demand curve from D to E is an example of the latter.

SUBSTITUTION AND INCOME EFFECTS

When the price of a good changes, the consumer is affected in two ways: First, he or she attains a different level of satisfaction, and second, he or she is likely to substitute now cheaper goods for more expensive goods. The total effect of a price change is illustrated in Figure 4.6. The original price ratio is given by the slope of the budget line A. Given this price ratio, the consumer chooses point U on indifference curve 1, and consumes Ox_1 units of good X. Now suppose that the price of good X is increased and B is the new budget line. Given the new price ratio, the consumer chooses point V on indifference curve 2, and consumes Ox_2 units of good X. The total effect of the price change on the quantity demanded of good X is a reduction of $Ox_1 - Ox_2$ units.

The total effect of this—or any—price change can be divided conceptually into two parts: the substitution effect and the income effect. First, consider the substitution effect. In Figure 4.6, when the price of good X increases, it is clear that a decrease occurs in the consumer's level of satisfaction: He or she winds up on indifference curve 2 rather than indifference curve 1. Suppose that, when the price goes up, we could increase the consumer's money income by an amount sufficient to keep him or her on the old indifference curve. If this could be done, it would mean that the budget line would be parallel to the budget line B, but that it would be tangent to indifference curve 1. This hypothetical budget line is labeled C in Figure 4.6. The *substitution effect* is defined to be the movement

FIGURE 4.6 Substitution and Income Effects for a Normal Good *If the price of good* X *increases (and the budget line shifts from A to B), the total effect of this price change on the quantity demanded of good* X *is a reduction of* $Ox_1 - Ox_2$ *units. This total effect can be divided into two parts: the substitution effect (a reduction of the quantity consumed from* Ox_1 *to* Ox_3 *units) and the income effect (a reduction of the quantity consumed from* Ox_3 *to* Ox_2 *units).*

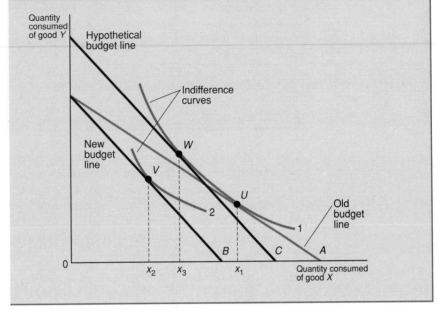

from the original equilibrium point U to the imaginary equilibrium point W, which corresponds to the hypothetical budget line C. The substitution effect is the reduction of the quantity consumed from Ox_1 to Ox_3 units of good X. Put differently, it is the change in quantity demanded of good X resulting from a price change when the level of satisfaction is held constant.

Substitution effect

Next, consider the income effect. The movement from the imaginary equilibrium point W to the actual new equilibrium point V is the income effect. This movement does not involve any change in prices; the price ratio is the same in budget line C as in budget line B. It is due to a change in total satisfaction; such a change is a movement from one indifference curve to another. If we define the consumer's real income as his or her level of satisfaction (or utility), the *income effect* is the change in quantity demanded of good X due entirely to a change in real income, *all prices being held constant*. In Figure 4.6, it is the reduction from Ox_3 to Ox_2 units. The total effect of a change in price is obviously the sum of the income effect and the substitution effect.[4]

Income effect

4. For an explanation of substitution and income effects in elementary mathematical terms, see J. Henderson and R. Quandt, *Microeconomic Theory*, 3d ed. (New York: McGraw-Hill, 1980), and H. Varian, *Microeconomic Analysis*, 2d ed. (New York: Norton, 1984).

The substitution effect is always negative. That is, if the price of good X increases and real income is held constant, there will always be a decrease in the consumption of good X; and if the price of good X decreases and real income is held constant, there will always be an increase in the consumption of good X. This result follows from the fact that indifference curves are convex (see Chapter 3). However, the income effect is not predictable from the theory alone. In most cases, one would expect that increases in real income will result in increases in consumption of a good and that decreases in real income will result in decreases in consumption of a good. This is the case for so-called *normal* goods. But not all goods are normal. Some goods are called *inferior goods* because the income effect is the opposite (of that of a normal good) for them. An illustration of an inferior good is given in Figure 4.7, where real income is assumed to increase from indifference curve 1 to indifference curve 2. Prices are assumed to be the same before and after the increase in real income; the original budget line is A and the subsequent budget line is B. Figure 4.7 shows that, because of the shapes of the indifference curves, the consumer purchases ($OX_2 - OX_3$) fewer units of good X after the increase in real income than he or she originally did.

Ordinarily, the substitution effect of a price change is strong enough to offset an inferior good's income effect, with the consequence that the quantity demanded of a good is inversely related to its price. However, it is possible for an inferior good to have an income effect that is so strong that it offsets the

Normal vs. inferior goods

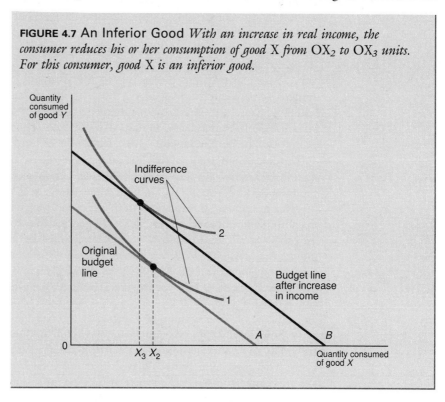

FIGURE 4.7 An Inferior Good *With an increase in real income, the consumer reduces his or her consumption of good* X *from* OX_2 *to* OX_3 *units. For this consumer, good* X *is an inferior good.*

substitution effect, with the result that the quantity demanded is directly related to the price, at least over some range of variation of price. A case of this sort is known as *Giffen's paradox*. For Giffen's paradox to occur, a good must be an inferior good, but not all inferior goods exhibit Giffen's paradox.

Oleomargarine is likely to be an inferior good for many consumers. Increases in real income are likely to lead to a substitution of butter for oleomargarine. Many other examples of inferior goods could be put forth, although, as stated above, inferior goods are in the minority. Giffen's paradox is a much, much rarer phenomenon. In the rest of this book, we shall assume that goods do not exhibit Giffen's paradox. That is, all demand curves are assumed to have a negative slope.

CONSUMER'S SURPLUS

Previous sections have presented a model of how consumers respond to changes in price and money income. But no attempt has been made to indicate how this model can be used to help solve practical problems. In the balance of this chapter, we discuss some applications of this model. Let's start with the very simple case where a consumer receives an additional amount of some good. For example, suppose that the consumer receives three pounds of sugar from a kindly (and not particularly calorie-conscious) neighbor. How much is this sugar worth to the consumer? This example, while trivial and homely in the extreme, will enable us to derive some results that will be used in the next section to throw light on an important problem of public policy.

To determine how much the additional three pounds of sugar are worth to this consumer, the proper question to ask is: What is the maximum amount that he or she would be willing to pay for the extra sugar? The consumer's demand curve for sugar provides the answer to this question. Suppose that the consumer's demand curve for sugar is as shown in the left-hand panel of Figure 4.8, and that he or she is presently consuming no sugar. For simplicity, suppose that sugar can only be purchased in units of a pound; in other words, fractions of a pound cannot be purchased. (This assumption will be relaxed later.)

The maximum amount that the consumer will pay for the first pound of sugar is 60 cents. As shown by the demand curve in the left-hand panel of Figure 4.8, the consumer would not buy any sugar at all if the price were above 60 cents per pound, but at a price of 60 cents he or she will buy one pound. The maximum amount that the consumer will pay for the second pound of sugar is 45 cents. As shown in Figure 4.8, the price must be lowered to 45 cents to induce the consumer to buy a second pound. Finally, the maximum amount that the consumer will pay for the third pound of sugar is 30 cents. As shown in Figure 4.8, the price must be lowered to 30 cents to induce the consumer to buy a third pound.

Adding up the maximum amounts that the consumer would pay for each pound of sugar, we find that the total maximum amount that he or she would be willing to pay for all three additional pounds of sugar is 60 + 45 + 30 = 135 cents. The important thing to note is that this total maximum amount equals the area under the demand curve from zero to three pounds of sugar. In other words, it equals the shaded area in the left-hand panel of Figure 4.8. To see this,

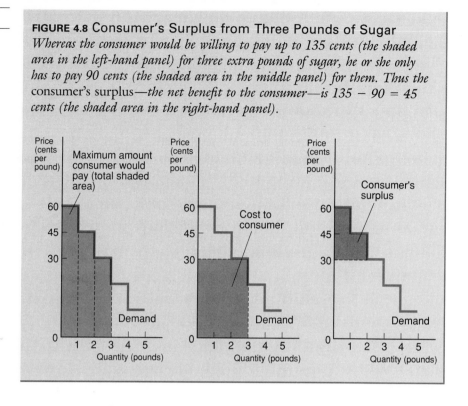

FIGURE 4.8 Consumer's Surplus from Three Pounds of Sugar
Whereas the consumer would be willing to pay up to 135 cents (the shaded area in the left-hand panel) for three extra pounds of sugar, he or she only has to pay 90 cents (the shaded area in the middle panel) for them. Thus the consumer's surplus—the net benefit to the consumer—is 135 − 90 = 45 cents (the shaded area in the right-hand panel).

note that this shaded area equals the sum of three rectangles shown in this panel. The area of the tallest shaded rectangle equals 60 cents; the area of the next tallest rectangle equals 45 cents; and the area of the shortest rectangle equals 30 cents; thus the total shaded area equals 60 + 45 + 30 = 135 cents.

Having determined the value of the additional three pounds of sugar to the consumer, let's suppose that he or she no longer receives sugar from a kindly neighbor. Instead, the consumer must pay 30 cents per pound for sugar. At this price, the consumer's demand curve in Figure 4.8 shows that he or she will buy three pounds of sugar, and pay 3 × 30 = 90 cents for them. Since the total cost of the three pounds of sugar equals the price per pound (30 cents) times the quantity purchased (three pounds), it equals the shaded area in the middle panel of Figure 4.8. (This shaded area is a rectangle with length equal to the price per pound and width equal to the quantity purchased.)

Whereas the three pounds of sugar are worth 135 cents to the consumer, he or she only has to pay 90 cents for them. The difference between what the consumer would be willing to pay (135 cents) and what the consumer actually has to pay (90 cents) is called *consumer's surplus*. Consumer's surplus is a measure of the net benefit received by the consumer. Since the consumer receives sugar worth 135 cents (to him or her) for 90 cents, he or she receives a net benefit of 45 cents. Geometrically, consumer's surplus can be represented by the shaded area in the right-hand panel of Figure 4.8. To see why this is the case, note that, to obtain consumer's surplus, we must deduct the shaded area in

Consumer's surplus

the middle panel (which equals the cost of the sugar) from the shaded area in the left-hand panel (which equals the maximum amount the consumer would pay for the sugar). The result is, of course, the shaded area in the right-hand panel.

Finally, we must relax the assumption that sugar can only be purchased in units of a pound. If fractions of a pound can be purchased, the demand curve is a smooth line, as in Figure 4.9 (rather than a series of steps, as in Figure 4.8). But regardless of whether the demand curve is smooth or a series of steps, the maximum amount that the consumer will pay for the three pounds of sugar is the area under the demand curve from zero to three pounds of sugar. In Figure 4.9, this area equals *OABC*. Since the price of a pound of sugar is *OP* in Figure 4.9, the amount that the consumer actually pays for the three pounds of sugar is equal to the area of rectangle *OPBC*. Since consumer's surplus equals the maximum amount that the consumer would pay (area *OABC*) minus the amount he or she actually pays (area *OPBC*), the shaded area in Figure 4.9 equals consumer's surplus.

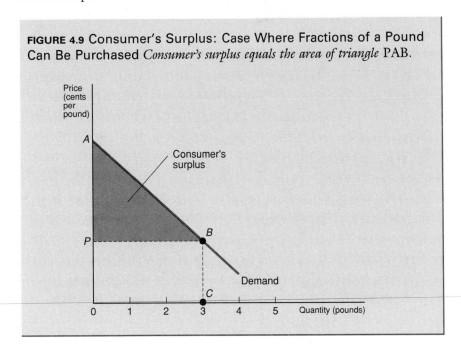

FIGURE 4.9 Consumer's Surplus: Case Where Fractions of a Pound Can Be Purchased *Consumer's surplus equals the area of triangle* PAB.

Consumer's Surplus and Restrictions on Sugar Imports

The concept of consumer's surplus is of practical importance. To illustrate how it has been used, let's consider American restrictions on sugar imports, a subject that has stimulated plenty of controversy. Because their costs are relatively high, American sugar producers find it difficult to compete with Central American and other foreign producers. To protect the American sugar industry from foreign competition, the U.S. government has imposed restrictions on how much foreign-produced sugar can be imported into the United States. (In 1990, only 1.6 million tons could be imported.) One of the major questions concerning such restrictions is: How much of a loss do they impose on U.S. consumers?

To see how the theory introduced in the previous section can be of use in dealing with this question, suppose that, in the absence of government restrictions on sugar imports, the price of sugar in the United States would be OP_0 in Figure 4.10. Based on the consumer's demand curve in the left-hand panel of this graph, the consumer would purchase OQ_0 pounds of sugar per year, the total cost of the sugar being $OP_0 \times OQ_0$. However, this total cost is an underestimate of what the sugar is really worth to the consumer. As stressed in the previous section, the consumer receives a consumer's surplus equal to the shaded area in the left-hand panel of Figure 4.10.

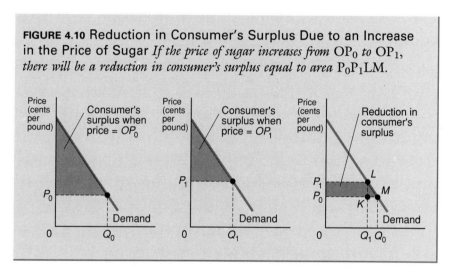

FIGURE 4.10 Reduction in Consumer's Surplus Due to an Increase in the Price of Sugar *If the price of sugar increases from* OP_0 *to* OP_1, *there will be a reduction in consumer's surplus equal to area* P_0P_1LM.

If the government imposes restrictions on sugar imports into the United States, the price of sugar will rise (because the import restrictions push the supply curve for sugar upward and to the left). Suppose that the price goes up to OP_1, as shown in the middle panel of Figure 4.10. Because of the higher price, the consumer will purchase somewhat less sugar (OQ_1 rather than OQ_0 pounds per year). The total amount spent on sugar will increase from $OP_0 \times OQ_0$ to $OP_1 \times OQ_1$. More important, the price increase results in a reduction in consumer's surplus. If price equals OP_1, the consumer's surplus equals the shaded area in the middle panel of Figure 4.10. Thus the increase in price from OP_0 to OP_1 results in a reduction in consumer's surplus equal to the shaded area in the right-hand panel of Figure 4.10. (Clearly, this shaded area equals the shaded area in the left-hand panel minus that in the middle panel.) As shown there, the loss in consumer's surplus equals the area to the left of the demand curve from the original price to the increased price.[5]

The loss to the consumer from the price increase can be measured by the shaded area in the right-hand panel of Figure 4.10. To understand more clearly

5. The shaded area in the right-hand panel of Figure 4.10 also measures the *gain* in consumer's surplus if price is *lowered* from OP_1 to OP_0. Based on our discussion in this and the previous section, the reader should be able to demonstrate that this is true.

why this measure is a sensible one, note that this shaded area is composed of two parts: rectangle P_0P_1LK and triangle KLM. The first part (rectangle P_0P_1LK) shows the extra amount that the consumer has to pay for the amount of sugar he or she consumes (after the price increase). Clearly, this extra amount equals $(OP_1 - OP_0)OQ_1$, and is equal to the area of rectangle P_0P_1LK. The second part (triangle KLM) shows the net loss to the consumer because he or she consumes less sugar (OQ_1 rather than OQ_0 pounds) due to the higher price. As we saw in the previous section, the value to the consumer of the forgone ($OQ_0 - OQ_1$) pounds of sugar (that is, the maximum amount that he or she would pay for them) is equal to area Q_1LMQ_0. If we subtract area Q_1KMQ_0, which equals the amount that the consumer would have had to pay for these ($OQ_0 - OQ_1$) pounds, the net loss to the consumer is triangle KLM.

Ilse Mintz, in a study published by the American Enterprise Institute, applied this technique to estimate the loss to consumers due to the restrictions on sugar imports.[6] According to her estimates, the demand curve for sugar in the United States was as shown in Figure 4.11. The restrictions raised the price of sugar by 2.57 cents, as shown in Figure 4.11. Without the restrictions, U.S. consumers would have purchased 23.2 billion pounds of sugar; with them, they purchased 22.4 billion pounds. As indicated in the right-hand panel of Figure 4.10, the reduction in consumer's surplus due to the price increase equals the

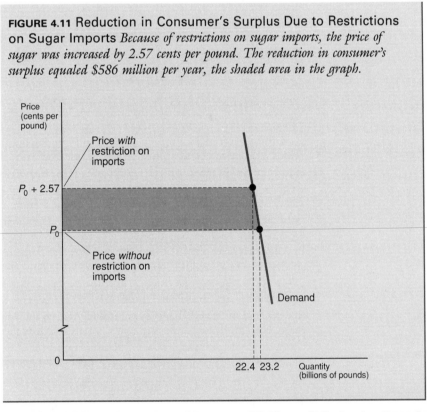

FIGURE 4.11 Reduction in Consumer's Surplus Due to Restrictions on Sugar Imports *Because of restrictions on sugar imports, the price of sugar was increased by 2.57 cents per pound. The reduction in consumer's surplus equaled $586 million per year, the shaded area in the graph.*

6. I. Mintz, *U.S. Import Quotas, Costs and Consequences* (Washington, D.C.: American Enterprise Institute, February 1973).

area to the left of the demand curve from the original price to the increased price. This area, which is shaded in Figure 4.11, equals ½(2.57 cents) (22.4 billion pounds + 23.2 billion pounds) = $586 million per year.

Thus Mintz's results indicated that American consumers were worse off by about $586 million per year because of restrictions on sugar imports. Subsequent studies, based on the same technique, have borne out her conclusion that these restrictions have imposed considerable losses on American consumers.[7] (According to some estimates, these losses have reached about $1 billion per year.) It is not our intention to take up the pros and cons of such restrictions at this point. (Much more will be said on this score in the cross-chapter case dealing with steel import quotas at the end of Part VI.) For present purposes, all that we want to do is illustrate how the concept of consumer's surplus has been used to shed light on important questions of public policy.[8]

INDEXES OF THE COST OF LIVING

Another area where the theory described in previous sections has proved useful is in the construction of index numbers of the cost of living. The phrase *cost of living* means the cost of living at a constant level of satisfaction. Cost-of-living indexes have always been closely associated with the issue of inflation. For example, labor unions want to know whether wages are keeping pace with the cost of living. Automatic adjustments in wages based on changes in cost-of-living indexes have been incorporated in many wage contracts. And cost-of-living indexes are used to measure changes in the purchasing power of the dollar for a variety of purposes, including the adjustment of pensions and welfare payments (and even alimony payments).

The most famous index of the cost of living is the Consumer Price Index, which the Bureau of Labor Statistics has been calculating for over fifty years. This index includes the prices of practically everything people buy for living— food, clothing, homes, automobiles, household supplies, house furnishings, fuel, drugs, doctors' fees, rent, transportation, and so forth. It pertains to urban consumers, and is based on data concerning the spending habits and prices paid

7. For example, see M. Morkre and D. Tarr, *Staff Report on Effects of Restrictions on U.S. Imports*, Federal Trade Commission, June 1980. According to the 1987 Annual Report of the Council of Economic Advisers, the import quota is imposed to maintain price supports for sugar at three to four times the world price. See *Economic Report of the President* (Washington, D.C.: Government Printing Office, 1987).

8. One further point needs to be made concerning the concept of consumer's surplus. When we use this concept, we assume that the consumer's indifference curves are of a particular type. Suppose that we plot the consumer's indifference curves where the amount of sugar consumed per day is the good on the horizontal axis and the amount of money that the consumer can spend on all goods other than sugar is the good on the vertical axis. (See problem 1 on page 103 for a discussion of goods of the latter kind.) When we use the concept of consumer's surplus, we assume that these indifference curves are parallel; that is, the vertical distance between any two indifference curves is the same regardless of where along the horizontal axis one measures this distance. This is a very restrictive assumption, but according to some economists it may be a reasonable approximation for commodities, like sugar, on which the consumer spends only a small amount of his or her income. Fortunately, for many applications, this approximation is good enough for practical purposes. See R. Willig, "Consumer Surplus Without Apology," *American Economic Review*, September 1976.

by such consumers. Prices are obtained by personal visits to a sample of about twenty-five thousand retail stores and service establishments in the United States. Prices are collected at intervals ranging from once every month to once every three months. Based on these data, the Bureau of Labor Statistics publishes each month the Consumer Price Index for the urban population as a whole and for each of twenty-eight metropolitan areas.

In the following sections, we describe briefly how the Consumer Price Index is constructed, and point out that it is not an ideal price index. Ideally, a cost-of-living index is constructed so that, if the index goes up more rapidly than a family's money income, we can be sure that the family is worse off, whereas if the index goes up less rapidly than the family's money income, we can be sure that the family is better off. Thus, if the ideal price index increases by 15 percent between 1990 and 1993, we can be sure that a family is worse off in 1993 than in 1990 if its money income increases by less than 15 percent, and that it is better off if its money income increases by more than 15 percent. As you might expect, ideal price indexes are not easy to come by in the real world.

THE CONSUMER PRICE INDEX

To see how the Consumer Price Index is constructed, suppose for simplicity that there are only two goods, hamburgers and coffee, and that in 1990 the typical household bought 500 units of hamburger and 400 units of coffee per month. Since the price in 1990 was $3 per unit for hamburger and $1.25 per unit for coffee, the total amount that this household spent in 1990 on this market basket of goods and services—500 units of hamburger and 400 units of coffee—was 500($3) + 400($1.25) = $2,000 per month.

In 1993, suppose that the price of hamburger rises to $4 per unit and that the price of coffee rises to $2 per unit. The Consumer Price Index attempts to summarize or describe these price increases from 1990 to 1993 in a single number. The first step in calculating this index is to determine what the 1990 market basket—500 units of hamburger and 400 units of coffee—would cost in 1993. Since the 1993 price of hamburger is $4 per unit and the 1993 price of coffee is $2 per unit, the answer is 500($4) + 400($2) = $2,800. The next step is to divide this figure ($2,800) by the 1990 cost of this market basket ($2,000), the result being 1.40, which means that the cost increased by 40 percent from 1990 to 1993. Thus the Consumer Price Index rose by 40 percent during this period; if it was 100 in 1990, it was 140 in 1993.

More generally, suppose that the typical household buys H_1 units of hamburger and C_1 units of coffee in year 1, the price of hamburger then being P_1^H per unit and the price of coffee being P_1^C per unit. The money income, I, required to buy this market basket is

$$I = H_1 P_1^H + C_1 P_1^C. \qquad [4.1]$$

Thus, since the typical household buys this market basket in year 1, its money income must equal I. In year 2 (subsequent to year 1), the money income, I', required to buy this market basket is

$$I' = H_1 P_2^H + C_1 P_2^C, \qquad [4.2]$$

EXAMPLE 4.2

NEW YORK CITY'S WATER CRISIS

On January 7, 1986, Mayor Koch of New York City proposed that water meters be installed in all buildings in the city. This was not a new idea. When New York City experienced a water crisis a number of years ago (because the average rate of use of water exceeded the yield of the water system), the mayor's Committee on Management Survey recommended the use of universal metering. Many consumers paid only a flat fee for water and were not metered. With metering, consumers would be charged 2 cents per hundred gallons of water. The cost of installing and operating the meters was estimated to be about $50 per million gallons of water saved per day. But this was only part of the cost of metering, since it did not include the loss to consumers arising from the fact that they would be led to consume less water. To make a fair comparison of the cost of metering with the cost of other ways of meeting the crisis, it was obvious that such losses should be taken into account.

(a) If a consumer's demand curve for water was approximately linear, as shown below, how large was the monetary value of his or her loss due to the consumption of less water? (b) How much was the monetary value of such losses per million gallons of water saved? (c) Including such losses as well as the cost of installing and operating the meters, what was the total cost of each million gallons of water saved by metering? (d) The cost of providing water with a new dam was estimated to be about $1,000 per million gallons per day. Was building a new dam (which in fact was done) the right solution?

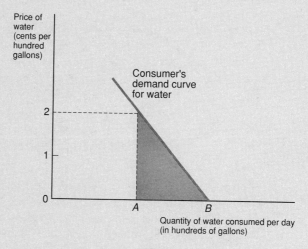

SOLUTION

(a) Without metering, the consumer would consume OB hundreds of gallons of water per day (since the price of an extra hundred gallons was zero). With metering, the consumer would consume OA hundreds of gallons of water per day (since the price of an extra hundred gallons was 2 cents). The consumer would be willing to pay an amount equal to the shaded area under the demand curve for the (OB − OA) hundreds of gallons per day that he or she forgoes because of metering. Since the demand curve is assumed to be linear, this equals $\frac{1}{2} \times$ (2 cents) $\times$ the quantity of water saved per day (in hundreds of gallons). In other words, it equals 1 cent per hundred gallons saved per day. (b) Since 1 cent per hundred gallons is equivalent to $100 per million gallons, the monetary value of such losses was $100 per million gallons saved. (c) $100 + $50 = $150. (d) It appears that metering would have been cheaper than building the dam. (However, it should be recognized that this kind of analysis is subject to limitations described in Chapter 15.)*

*For further discussion of this case, see J. Hirschleifer, J. Milliman, and J. DeHaven, *Water Supply* (Chicago: University of Chicago Press, 1960).

where P_2^H is the price per unit of hamburger and P_2^C is the price per unit of coffee in year 2. Thus, if the price index is 100 in year 1, its value in year 2 equals

$$p^* = 100\frac{I'}{I} = 100\left(\frac{H_1 P_2^H + C_1 P_2^C}{H_1 P_1^H + C_1 P_1^C}\right). \qquad [4.3]$$

Graphical Representation of the Price Index

To relate our discussion of the Consumer Price Index to the previous material on consumer behavior, let's consider three different budget lines for the average household. *The first budget line is the one that describes this household's situation in year 1.* Because this household had a money income of I in year 1, and because the price of a unit of hamburger was P_1^H and the price of a unit of coffee was P_1^C in year 1, the equation for this budget line is

$$H = \frac{I}{P_1^H} - \frac{P_1^C}{P_1^H}C. \qquad [4.4]$$

This budget line—labeled "Year 1 budget line"—is shown in Figure 4.12.

The second budget line is the one that describes this household's situation in year 2, assuming that its money income is the same in year 2 as in year 1. Recalling that the price of a unit of hamburger is P_2^H and the price of a unit of coffee is P_2^C in year

FIGURE 4.12 Graphical Representation of Consumer Price Index *If
the price index equals 100 in year 1, it equals 100 times* OR′ ÷ OR *in
year 2.*

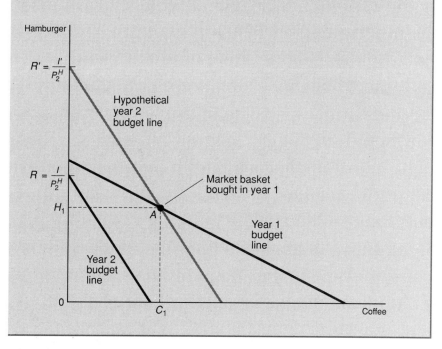

2, the equation for this budget line is

$$H = \frac{I}{P_2^H} - \frac{P_2^C}{P_2^H}C. \qquad [4.5]$$

This budget line—labeled "Year 2 budget line"—is shown in Figure 4.12.

*The third budget line is a hypothetical budget line that describes this household's
situation in year 2 if it had just enough money income (no more, no less) to buy the
market basket it bought in year 1.* Given that this household purchased H_1 units
of hamburger and C_1 units of coffee in year 1, the market basket it purchased in
year 1 can be represented by point A in Figure 4.12. And since this hypothetical
budget line assumes that this household has just enough income to purchase
this market basket, it follows that this hypothetical budget line must pass
through point A. Moreover, because this hypothetical budget line assumes that
the prices of hamburger and coffee are at their year 2 levels, it must have the
same slope as the actual budget line in year 2. (Why? Because the slope of a
budget line equals the price ratio, as emphasized on page 60.) Thus this hypothetical budget line must be parallel to the actual budget line in year 2—and it
must pass through point A. In other words, it must be the "Hypothetical year 2
budget line" shown in Figure 4.12.

Assuming for simplicity that the price index in year 1 equals 100, it is easy to
calculate the price index in year 2. The first step is to divide the vertical intercept
of the "Hypothetical year 2 budget line" by the vertical intercept of the "Year 2

*Hypothetical budget
line*

budget line." That is, we must divide OR' by OR in Figure 4.12. The reason why we divide OR' by OR is that the result equals I'/I. To see why, note that OR' equals I'/P_2^H and that $OR = I/P_2^H$, as indicated in Figure 4.12. (Of course, this follows from the fact that the vertical intercept of a budget line equals money income divided by the price of the good on the vertical axis.) The second step is to multiply $OR' \div OR$ by 100. Since $OR' \div OR$ equals I'/I, it follows from Equation 4.3 that if the price index is 100 in year 1, its value in year 2 is 100 times $OR' \div OR$. In this way, we can represent the price index graphically.

PROBLEMS WITH THE PRICE INDEX

As pointed out in a previous section, an ideal price index would tell us the extent to which a family's money income would have to increase (or decrease) in a certain period of time to offset price changes and maintain the family's well-being at a constant level. In practice, cost-of living indexes, like most things in life, are not ideal. In fact, as we shall show in this section, a household that bought H_1 units of hamburger and C_1 units of coffee in year 1 would not maintain the same level of well-being in year 2 if its income was increased to

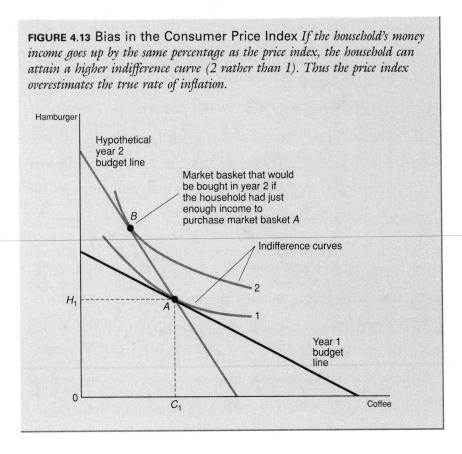

FIGURE 4.13 Bias in the Consumer Price Index *If the household's money income goes up by the same percentage as the price index, the household can attain a higher indifference curve (2 rather than 1). Thus the price index overestimates the true rate of inflation.*

keep pace with the Consumer Price Index. Instead, its level of well-being would be higher in year 2 than in year 1.

To see that this is true, consider Figure 4.13, which reproduces the "Year 1 budget line" and the "Hypothetical year 2 budget line" we drew in Figure 4.12. In addition, two of the household's indifference curves are included. Indifference curve 1 is the highest indifference curve that this household could reach in year 1. It is tangent to the "Year 1 budget line" at point A, which is what would be expected given that this household in fact bought the market basket represented by point A in year 1.

As we know from the previous section, the Consumer Price Index rose from 100 in year 1 to 100 times I'/I in year 2. If this household's money income rose by this same percentage, its budget line in year 2 would be the "Hypothetical year 2 budget line." Indifference curve 2 is the highest indifference curve that this household could attain under these circumstances. (The market basket the household would choose is at point B.) Since indifference curve 2 is higher than indifference curve 1, this household would be better off in year 2 than in year 1 if its money income increased by the same percentage as the Consumer Price Index went up.

Upward bias

In other words, the Consumer Price Index overestimates the rate of inflation. To understand why, it is important to recognize that this index takes no account of the fact that households adapt their purchases to changes in prices. For example, if the price of coffee goes up a lot more than the price of hamburger, households are likely to cut back on their consumption of coffee and beef up their consumption of hamburger. The Consumer Price Index ignores such changes in the household's market basket. It compares the household's cost of purchasing a *fixed* market basket (the market basket purchased in year 1) in year 2 with that in year 1.[9]

In addition, there are other problems in the Consumer Price Index. For one thing, the quality of a product often changes over time, and it is difficult to know how to adjust the change in the product's price for the quality change. For example, suppose that the price of a refrigerator goes up by 10 percent between 1990 and 1993, but the quality of the refrigerator also increases. How much of the 10 percent price increase is really offset by the quality increase? This is a very tricky question. Although the Bureau of Labor Statistics tries to adjust price changes for changes in quality, the available evidence seems to indicate that the adjustments sometimes are crude at best.[10]

9. A price index of this sort (that is, one calculated according to Equation 4.3) is often called a *Laspeyres price index*. If C_2 were substituted for C_1 and if H_2 were substituted for H_1 in Equation 4.3, the result would be a so-called *Paasche price index*. In other words, a Paasche index is based on the market basket purchased in year 2. (C_2 and H_2 are the numbers of units of coffee and hamburger bought in year 2.)

10. This discussion of the Consumer Price Index is simplified in many regards. For more complete accounts, see R. Pollak, *The Theory of the Cost-of-Living Index* (New York: Oxford University Press, 1989); W. E. Diewert, "The Economic Theory of Index Numbers: A Survey," Discussion paper 79-09, Department of Economics, University of British Columbia, March 1979; S. Braithwait, "The Substitution Bias of the Laspeyres Price Index: An Analysis Using Estimated Cost of Living Indexes," *American Economic Review*, March 1980; and R. Gordon, "The Consumer Price Index: Measuring Inflation and Causing It," *The Public Interest*, 1981.

EXAMPLE 4.3

CALCULATING A COST-OF-LIVING INDEX

According to the Bureau of Labor Statistics, the price of food was 5.8 percent higher in the United States in 1989 than in 1988, and the price of shelter was 4.5 percent higher in 1989 than in 1988.[*] Suppose that a family spent half of its 1988 money income on food and half on shelter. (a) For this family, calculate a price index for 1989, given that the index's value in 1988 was 100. (b) If prices increased more rapidly in the city where this family lives than in the nation as a whole, is the result in part (a) correct? (c) Is there likely to be a bias in this price index?

SOLUTION

(a) From Equation 4.3, we see that the value of the price index in 1989 is:

$$100\left(\frac{F_1 P_2{}^F + S_1 P_2{}^S}{F_1 P_1{}^F + S_1 P_1{}^S}\right),$$

where F_1 is the number of units of food bought in 1988 and S_1 is the number of units of shelter bought in 1988. The price of a unit of food is $P_1{}^F$ in 1988 and $P_2{}^F$ in 1989, and the price of a unit of shelter is $P_1{}^S$ in 1988 and $P_2{}^S$ in 1989. The above formula is exactly the same as the expression in Equation 4.3. However, since the goods now are food and shelter rather than hamburgers and coffee, F_1 and S_1 are used in place of H_1 and C_1—and $P_1{}^F$, $P_2{}^F$, $P_1{}^S$, and $P_2{}^S$ are used in place of $P_1{}^H$, $P_2{}^H$, $P_1{}^C$, and $P_2{}^C$, respectively. We can rewrite the above formula as:

$$100 \times \frac{F_1 P_1{}^F\left(\dfrac{P_2{}^F}{P_1{}^F}\right) + S_1 P_1{}^S\left(\dfrac{P_2{}^S}{P_1{}^S}\right)}{F_1 P_1{}^F + S_1 P_1{}^S} =$$

$$100\left(\frac{F_1 P_1{}^F}{F_1 P_1{}^F + S_1 P_1{}^S}\right)\left(\frac{P_2{}^F}{P_1{}^F}\right) + 100\left(\frac{S_1 P_1{}^S}{F_1 P_1{}^F + S_1 P_1{}^S}\right)\left(\frac{P_2{}^S}{P_1{}^S}\right).$$

Since $F_1 P_1{}^F + S_1 P_1{}^S$ equals the family's money income in 1988, $F_1 P_1{}^F \div (F_1 P_1{}^F + S_1 P_1{}^S)$ equals the proportion of its 1988 money income spent on food, which equals ½. Similarly, $S_1 P_1{}^S \div (F_1 P_1{}^F + S_1 P_1{}^S)$ equals the proportion of its 1988 money income spent on shelter, which equals ½. Thus since $P_2{}^F/P_1{}^F = 1.058$ and $P_2{}^S/P_1{}^S = 1.045$, the above formula equals

$$100\left(\frac{1}{2}\right)(1.058) + 100\left(\frac{1}{2}\right)(1.045) = 105.2.$$

The value of the price index in 1989 is 105.2, which indicates that the price level rose by 5.2 percent from 1988 to 1989. (b) No. The calculations in part (a) assume that the prices paid by the family increased at the same rate as in the nation as a whole. If they increased more rapidly, the price index for the family exceeded 105.2. (c) This price index may overestimate the true rate of inflation for the reasons cited on page 101.

[*]The figures for both 1989 and 1988 come from the *1990 Annual Report of the Council of Economic Advisors*, p. 360.

Summary

1. Another way of expressing the conditions for consumer equilibrium is as follows: The rational consumer will choose in equilibrium to allocate his or her income between good X and good Y in such a way that the marginal rate of substitution of good X for good Y equals the ratio of the price of good X to the price of good Y.

2. If we hold commodity prices constant, each level of money income results in an equilibrium market basket for the consumer, and the curve that connects the points representing all of these equilibrium market baskets is called the income-consumption curve. The income-consumption curve can be used to derive the Engel curve, which is the relationship between the equilibrium amount of a good purchased by a consumer and the level of the consumer's money income. Engel curves play an important role in family expenditure studies.

3. Holding constant the consumer's money income as well as the prices of other goods, we can determine the relationship between the price of a good and the amount of this good that a consumer will consume. This relationship is called the consumer's individual demand curve for the good in question. The individual demand curve, one of the central concepts in the theory of consumer behavior, can be derived from the price-consumption curve, which includes all of the equilibrium market baskets corresponding to various prices of the good.

4. The location and shape of an individual demand curve will depend on the level of money income and the level at which the prices of other goods are held constant, as well as on the nature of the good and the tastes of the consumer. It is important to differentiate between shifts in a consumer's demand curve for a particular commodity and changes in the amount of the commodity that he or she consumes.

5. The total effect of a price change on the quantity demanded can be divided into two parts: the substitution effect and the income effect. The substitution effect is the change in quantity demanded of a good resulting from a price change when the level of satisfaction, or real income, is held constant. The income effect shows the effect of the change in real income that is due to the price change. The substitution effect is always negative. The income effect is not predictable from the theory alone: Its sign is different for normal goods than for inferior goods.

6. An illustration of how this model of consumer behavior has been used to help solve practical problems is provided by the study of the effects of sugar import quotas. An important question in this case was: How can one estimate the monetary value of the loss to consumers arising from the fact that import quotas raise the price of sugar and lower sugar consumption? If certain assumptions are made, this question can be answered, at least approximately, based on the concept of consumer's surplus.

7. Another type of problem where this sort of model has proved useful is in the construction of index numbers of the cost of living. The methods used to calculate the Consumer Price Index, as well as its limitations, have been discussed.

Questions/ Problems

1. As shown on p. 104, the price-consumption curve for good X is upward sloping when good Y is the money spent by the consumer on goods other than good X. Of course, good Y is a peculiar sort of good, but there is nothing to prevent us from defining a good in this way. In weighing every purchase the consumer must decide whether to give up

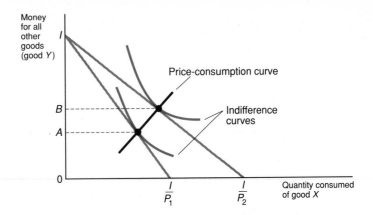

money he or she can spend on goods other than good X in exchange for good X. Since good Y is money, its price is always 1. (For example, it takes a quarter to buy a quarter.)

(a) Prove that the consumer's demand curve for good X is price inelastic. (Hint: Recall from Chapter 2 that, if the demand for a good is price inelastic, a decrease in its price results in a decrease in the amount spent on it.) (b) Prove that, if this price-consumption curve were downward sloping, the consumer's demand curve for good X would be price elastic.

2. In late 1985, New York City's Department of Consumer Affairs published the results of an eleven-month study of prescription drug prices charged by ninety-two pharmacies in New York. The survey reported that thirty tablets of Dyazide (prescribed for high blood pressure) cost $16.95 at one pharmacy and $6.95 at another pharmacy about three miles away. What factors may be responsible for this discrepancy? Will it persist over time? According to a spokesman for the department, "in low-income areas with no competition, they can charge pretty high prices, and there is no pressure to bring those prices down."[11] Why is there no such pressure?

3. Lewis and Clark Lake is a large reservoir in South Dakota created on the Missouri River by the Gavins Point Dam. It is located in an area where there are few natural bodies of water, and it has become very popular as a recreational area. Suppose that 10,000 families are potential users of the lake for recreational purposes and that each family's demand curve for recreational trips to the lake is as follows:

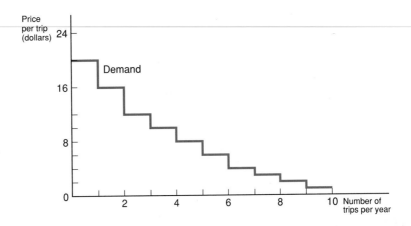

11. *New York Times*, December 28, 1985, p. 48.

(a) If an ordinance were passed which limited each family to no more than 5 trips per year to the lake, what is the loss (in money terms) to each family? (b) If an ordinance were passed which allowed a family to use the lake for recreational purposes only if it purchased a permit for $75 a year, would it be worthwhile for each family to buy the permit, if it could not use the lake without the permit (and it could use the lake as much as it liked with one)? (c) Suppose that we consider two goods: trips to the lake and money that can be spent on things other than trips to the lake. In answering questions (a) and (b), what assumption are you making regarding each family's indifference curves concerning these two goods?

4. In the previous question, how much is the consumer's surplus from each family's utilization of the lake if there is a charge of $8 for each trip to the lake?

5. Suppose that all consumers pay 25 cents for a telephone call and 25 cents for a newspaper (and that all consumers purchase some of both goods). (a) If all consumers are maximizing utility, is it possible to determine each consumer's marginal rate of substitution of telephone calls for newspapers? (b) Suppose that a local economist applies for a grant to estimate this marginal rate of substitution; his proposed procedure is to ask a sample of consumers. Can you suggest a simpler procedure? (c) Based on these facts alone, can you estimate this marginal rate of substitution? If so, what is it?

6. A representative of the dairy industry asserts that, as income increases, the proportion of income spent on food tends to rise. (a) Do you think this proposition is true? Why or why not? (b) Indicate the general shape of the Engel curve for food, based on this proposition.

7. According to some observers, the typical Irish peasant in the nineteenth century was so poor he spent almost all his income for potatoes. When the price of potatoes fell, he could get the same amount of nutrition for a smaller expenditure on potatoes, so some of his income was diverted to vegetables and meat. Since the latter also provided calories, he could even reduce his consumption of potatoes under these circumstances. If this is true, were potatoes (a) a normal good? (b) an inferior good? (c) a good exhibiting Giffen's paradox?

8. Suppose that a family consumes a quite different set of commodities in a later period than in an earlier one, and that many of the goods it consumes in the later period were not available in the earlier one. What difficulties does this cause the economist who would like to construct a cost-of-living index?

9. Suppose that a 1 percent increase in the price of pork chops results in Ms. Smith's buying 3 percent fewer pork chops per week. What is the price elasticity of demand for pork chops on the part of Ms. Smith? Is her demand for pork chops price elastic or price inelastic? Will an increase in the price of pork chops result in an increase, or a decrease, in the total amount of money that she spends on pork chops?

10. Calculate a cost-of-living index for a family that consumes the following amounts of bread and clothing (and no other goods) in 1990 and 1993:

	1990	1993
Amount consumed of bread	100	140
Amount consumed of clothing	120	130
Price of bread (dollars)	0.30	0.50
Price of clothing (dollars)	30.00	40.00

11. In the 1970s and early 1980s, government policy-makers, responding to OPEC's massive increases in oil prices in the 1970s, were intent on reducing the amount of gasoline consumed by the American public. One major proposal was that a new tax should be imposed on gasoline, thus raising the price of gasoline; but many observers objected that such a tax would hit many families harder than was equitable (or politically feasible). To counter this objection, it was suggested that the revenue the government received from

the new gasoline tax should be returned to the public. The amount that each family would receive would be the same, regardless of how much gasoline it consumed.

(a) If the gasoline tax alone had been enacted, would this have changed the slope of a consumer's budget line? If so, how? (For simplicity, assume that there were only two goods: gasoline and some item other than gasoline.) (b) After the gasoline tax had been enacted, suppose that the tax rebate described above was instituted. Would this tax rebate have shifted a consumer's budget line? If so, how?

THE INCOME-COMPENSATED DEMAND CURVE

Besides the ordinary demand curve discussed in this chapter, economists are interested in income-compensated demand curves. In Figure 4.6, we showed how (in principle) the effects of a price change can be divided into a substitution effect and a price effect. To carry out this decomposition, when the price of a good changes, we adjust the consumer's money income so that he or she remains on the same indifference curve. This is not the only procedure that could be adopted. Instead, we could change the consumer's money income so that he or she could still buy the market basket (no more, no less) that was purchased before the price change.[12]

Income-compensated
demand curve

If this latter procedure is used, we can construct an income-compensated demand curve for the good in question (say good X) by seeing how much the consumer demands of good X at each level of price, *when his or her money income is adjusted so that, regardless of the price of good* X, *the original market basket can be purchased*. The results are shown in Figure 4.14, together with the ordinary demand curve for good X. Both the income-compensated demand curve and the ordinary demand curve show the relationship between the price of good X and the amount of this good demanded by the consumer. The difference between them reflects the fact that the ordinary demand curve assumes that the consumer's money income is *held constant*, whereas the income-compensated demand curve assumes the consumer's money income is *adjusted to allow him or her to purchase the original market basket*.

In Figure 4.14, the ordinary demand curve is flatter than the income-compensated demand curve. This will always be the case for a normal good. When price falls, the income effect is positive for a normal good. Whereas the ordinary demand curve includes this income effect, the income-compensated demand curve does not. Thus, when price falls, the quantity demanded increases by a greater amount based on the ordinary demand curve than it does based on the income-compensated demand curve.

12. The procedure used in Figure 4.6 to carry out the decomposition is due to Sir John Hicks; the alternative procedure discussed in this appendix is due to the late Russian economist, Eugen Slutsky.

FIGURE 4.14 Income-Compensated and Ordinary Demand Curve for Good *X* *For normal goods, the ordinary demand curve is flatter than the income-compensated demand curve.*

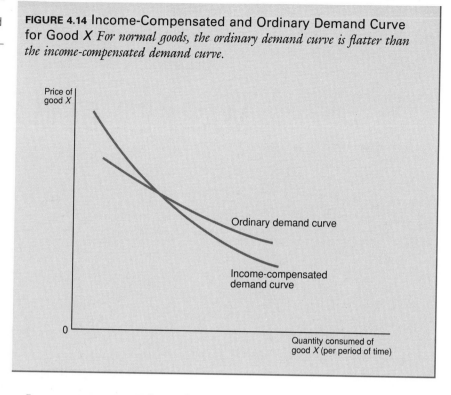

Income-compensated demand curves are of practical importance because the empirical relationships between price and quantity obtained in statistical investigations are often really demand curves of this type. In their calculations, statisticians and econometricians generally hold constant the effects of real income, which means that the results often approximate income-compensated demand curves. More will be said about these empirical relationships in Chapter 5.

5

MARKET DEMAND

INTRODUCTION

The previous chapter was concerned with the determinants of the quantity of a good demanded by an individual consumer. For many purposes, it is not so much the quantity demanded by a particular consumer that counts; instead it is the quantity demanded by all the consumers in a market. For example, the auto industry is much more concerned with the quantity of cars that will be demanded by the entire national market than with the quantity of cars that you or I will purchase next year. Economists, too, when confronted with many problems, are much more interested in the quantity of a good demanded in a market than in the quantity of a good demanded by a particular individual. For example, as we saw in Chapter 2, it is the market demand curve, not the individual demand curve, that (together with the market supply curve) determines the equilibrium price of a good.

In this chapter we are concerned with market demand. After showing how the market demand curve is related to the demand curves of the individual consumers in the market, we discuss some major determinants of the price elasticity of market demand. Then we take up the effects of two other factors, besides the good's price, on the quantity of the good that is demanded in the market—aggregate money income and the prices of other commodities. Next, we look at market demand from the seller's side of the market, placing emphasis on the concept of marginal revenue and the differences between the demand curve for the industry and the demand curve for the firm. Finally, we discuss the measurement of market demand curves, and we describe two cases where such measurements were used to help guide public and private decision-makers.

DERIVATION OF THE MARKET DEMAND CURVE

In Chapter 4, we showed how an individual demand curve can be derived from a consumer's indifference map. This demand curve is of course the relationship between the quantity of the good demanded by the consumer (per unit of time) and the good's price, when the money income of the consumer and the prices of other goods are held constant. The shape and level of the individual demand curve obviously depend on the consumer's tastes, as reflected in his or her indifference map. They also depend on the level of the consumer's money income and the level of the prices of other goods.

Market demand curve

The *market demand curve* for a commodity is simply the *horizontal* summation of the individual demand curves of all the consumers in the market. Put differently, to find the market quantity demanded at each price, we add up the individual quantities demanded at that price. For example, Table 5.1 shows the

TABLE 5.1 Individual and Market Demand Schedules

Price (cents per unit of the commodity)	Quantity demanded (per unit of time)				Quantity demanded in market (per unit of time)
	Individual A	Individual B	Individual C	Individual D	
	(units of the commodity)				
1	50	40	30	20	140
2	40	30	25	19	114
3	30	20	18	18	86
4	25	15	13	17	70
5	20	14	13	16	63
6	15	13	11	15	54
7	10	12	9	14	45
8	8	11	7	13	39
9	6	10	5	12	33
10	5	9	3	11	28

individual demand schedules[1] for four consumers. If these four consumers comprise the entire market, the market demand schedule is given in the last column of Table 5.1. Figure 5.1 shows the individual demand curves based on these same data, as well as the resulting market demand curve.

The market demand curve for a commodity is one of the most important concepts in microeconomics. The market demand curve shows how much of the commodity will be purchased (per unit of time) by the consumers in the market at each possible price (given that the level of money income of the consumers and the prices of other commodities are held constant). Information

---

1. Recall from Chapter 2 that a demand schedule is a table showing the quantity demanded at various prices.

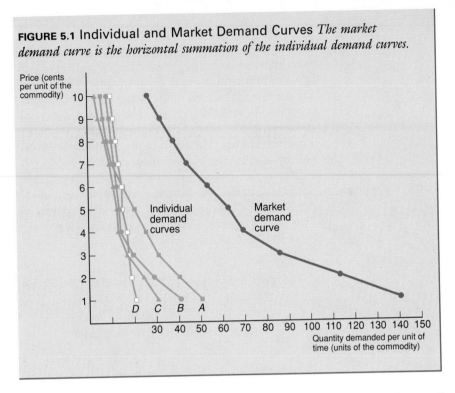

FIGURE 5.1 Individual and Market Demand Curves *The market demand curve is the horizontal summation of the individual demand curves.*

regarding the market demand curve is of the utmost importance to producers of the commodity. Obviously, they need to know how much can be sold at various prices. The market demand curve is also of great importance to economists because, as pointed out in Chapter 2, it plays an important role in determining the price of the commodity.

THE PRICE ELASTICITY OF DEMAND

At each point on the market demand curve, the price elasticity of demand, defined as the percentage change in the quantity demanded resulting from a 1 percent change in price, gauges the sensitivity of the quantity demanded to changes in price. Chapter 2 pointed out the significance of the price elasticity of demand, but nothing has been said about its determinants. What determines whether the demand for a commodity is price elastic or price inelastic in a certain price range? Why does the price elasticity of demand for one commodity equal 3.0 and the price elasticity of demand for another commodity equal 1.5? This is a very important question, and the one to which we turn our attention in this section.

The role of substitutes First, and foremost, the price elasticity of demand for a commodity depends on the number and closeness of the *substitutes* that are available. If a commodity has many close substitutes, its demand is likely to be price elastic. If increases occur in the price of the product, a large proportion of its buyers will turn to the close substitutes that are available; if decreases occur in its price, a great many buyers of substitutes will switch to this product.

Of course, the extent to which a commodity has close substitutes depends on how narrowly it is defined. In general, one would expect that, as the definition of the product becomes narrower and more specific, the product has more close substitutes and its demand becomes more price elastic. Thus the demand for a particular brand of cigarettes is likely to be more price elastic than the overall demand for cigarettes and the demand for cigarettes is likely to be more price elastic than the demand for tobacco products as a whole. If a commodity is defined so that it has perfect substitutes, its price elasticity of demand is infinite. Thus, if the cotton produced by Farmer Jones is exactly the same as the cotton produced by other farmers and if he increases his price slightly (to a point above the market level), his sales would be reduced to nothing.

Second, it is sometimes asserted that the price elasticity of demand for a commodity is likely to depend on the importance of the commodity in consumers' budgets. For example, the demand for commodities like thumbtacks, pepper, and salt may be quite inelastic. The typical consumer spends only a very small fraction of his income on such goods. On the other hand, for commodities that bulk larger in the typical consumer's budget, like major appliances, the elasticity of demand may tend to be higher. Consumers may be more conscious of, and influenced by, price changes in the case of goods that require larger outlays. However, although a tendency of this sort is sometimes hypothesized, there is no guarantee that it exists. As some economists have pointed out, the link between a commodity's price elasticity of demand and its importance in consumer's budgets may in fact be much weaker than that which is implied by this hypothesis.

Third, the price elasticity of demand for a commodity is likely to depend on the length of the period to which the demand curve pertains. (Every market demand curve—like every individual demand curve—pertains, of course, to a certain time interval.) In many cases, demand is likely to be more elastic, or less inelastic, over a long period of time than over a short period of time. The longer the period of time, the easier it is for consumers and business firms to substitute one good for another. If, for example, the price of natural gas should decline relative to other fuels, the consumption of natural gas in the week after the price decline would probably increase very little. But over a period of several years, people would have an opportunity to take account of the price decline in choosing the type of fuel to be used in new houses and renovated old houses. In the longer period of several years, the price decline would have a greater effect on the consumption of natural gas than it would have in the shorter period of one week.[2]

2. For durable goods like cars, the price elasticity of demand may be lower in the long run than in the short run. If the price of cars increases, the quantity demanded is likely to go down considerably because many potential buyers will put off purchasing a new automobile. However, with the passage of time, the quantity of cars demanded will tend to go up as old cars wear out.

EXAMPLE 5.1

RESIDENTIAL DEMAND FOR WATER

Water is obviously of fundamental importance to human beings, no matter where they live. However, this does not mean that the residential demand for water is the same in one region as in another. Henry Foster and Bruce Beattie have estimated the demand curve for water in six regions of the United States. The results, shown below, pertain to New England and the Northern Atlantic region, the Midwest, the Southeast, the Plains and Rocky Mountain region, the Southwest, and the Pacific Northwest.

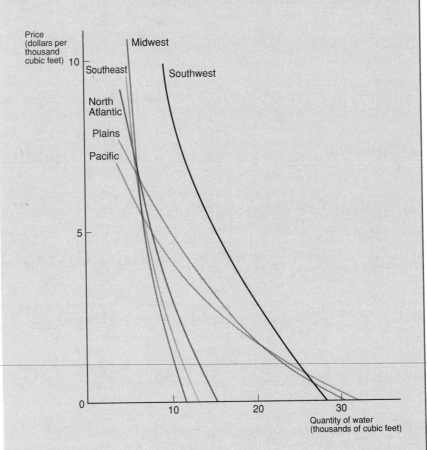

(a) If the price of water is $5 per thousand cubic feet, in which region is the consumption of water highest? (b) According to their findings, the price elasticity of demand for water in all regions is between .39 and .69. Why do you think the demand for water is price inelastic? (c) In those regions where outdoor use comprises a relatively large fraction of total water use, the price elasticity of demand tends to be relatively high. Why? (d) The demand curve for water in the summer tends to be to the right of the demand curve in the winter, and it tends to be more price elastic than the demand curve in the winter. Why?

SOLUTION

(a) Southwest. (b) Because there are few good substitutes for water. (c) Outdoor use of water is less essential than the use of water for drinking, cooking, and bathing purposes. Thus the quantity of water demanded for outdoor use is more sensitive to price than is the quantity of water demanded for drinking, cooking, and bathing purposes. (d) Because more water for outdoor use is demanded in the summer, and because this demand is relatively price elastic for the reason given in the answer to part (c).[*]

[*]For further discussion, see D. Gibbons, *The Economic Value of Water* (Washington, D.C.: Resources for the Future, 1986).

THE INCOME ELASTICITY OF DEMAND

Up to this point, we have been concerned solely with the effect of price on the quantity of the commodity demanded in the market. Yet price is not the only factor that influences the quantity demanded in the market. Another important factor is the level of money income among the consumers in the market. For example, if consumers have plenty of money to spend, the quantity demanded of beef is likely to be greater than if they are poverty-stricken. Or if incomes in a particular community are high, the quantity demanded of caviar is likely to be greater than if incomes are low.

For an individual consumer, we saw in Chapter 4 that the relationship between money income (per period of time) and the amount consumed of a particular commodity (per period of time) can be represented by an Engel curve. Recall that this curve is based on the condition that the prices of all commodities remain constant. At any point on the Engel curve, one can characterize the sensitivity of the amount consumed to changes in the consumer's money income by the *income elasticity of demand*, which is defined as

Income elasticity of demand

$$\eta_I = \frac{\Delta Q}{Q} \div \frac{\Delta I}{I} \qquad [5.1]$$

where ΔQ is the change in quantity consumed that results from a small change in the consumer's money income ΔI, Q is the original quantity consumed, and I is the original money income of the consumer.[3]

Some goods have positive income elasticities, indicating that increases in the consumer's money income result in increases in the amount of the good con-

---

3. More precisely, the income elasticity of demand is

$$\frac{dQ}{dI} \div \frac{Q}{I}.$$

The text definition is the same except that finite differences are substituted for derivatives.

sumed. For example, one would generally expect steak and caviar to have positive income elasticities. Other goods have negative income elasticities, indicating that increases in the consumer's money income result in decreases in the amount of the good consumed. For example, margarine and poor grades of vegetables and other types of food might have negative income elasticities.[4] However, one must be careful to point out that the income elasticity of demand for a good is likely to vary considerably, depending on the level of the consumer's money income. Thus, in some ranges of income, the income elasticity may be positive; in other ranges of income, it may be negative.

The concept of income elasticity of demand can be applied to an entire market as well as to a single consumer, the only change in Equation 5.1 being that we must interpret Q as the total quantity demanded in the market, I as the aggregate money income of all consumers in the market, and ΔQ and ΔI as the changes in total quantity demanded and in aggregate money income. As in the case of the individual consumer, it is assumed that the prices of all commodities are held constant. Figure 5.2 shows a variety of possible relationships between the total quantity demanded in the market and the aggregate money income of the consumers. In one case, the income elasticity is greater than 1, which means that a 1 percent increase in money income results in more than a 1 percent increase in the total quantity demanded. In another case, the income elasticity is less than 1 (but greater than zero), which means that a 1 percent increase in money income results in less than a 1 percent increase in the total quantity demanded. In still another case, the income elasticity is negative, indicating that

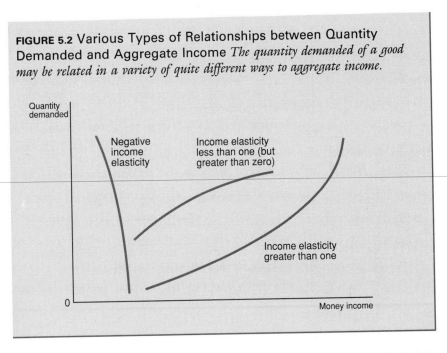

FIGURE 5.2 Various Types of Relationships between Quantity Demanded and Aggregate Income *The quantity demanded of a good may be related in a variety of quite different ways to aggregate income.*

---

4. The similarity between goods with a negative income elasticity and inferior goods should be obvious.

increases in aggregate money income result in decreases in the total quantity demanded.[5]

There are, of course, enormous differences among goods with respect to their income elasticity of demand. No refined statistical surveys are needed to tell us that the income elasticity of demand for high-quality food and clothes is generally higher than the income elasticity of demand for salt and Kleenex. *Luxuries* and *necessities* Luxury items are generally assumed to have high income elasticities of demand. Indeed, one way to define *luxuries* and *necessities* is to say that luxuries are goods with high income elasticities of demand, and necessities are goods with low income elasticities of demand.

Engel's law An empirical law of consumption, *Engel's law*, was developed in the nineteenth century by Ernst Engel (whose work was noted in Chapter 4). Based on data concerning the budgets and expenditures of a large number of families, Engel found that the income elasticity of demand for food was quite low. He concluded from this result that the proportion of its income spent on food by a nation (or a family) was a good index of its welfare, with the better-off nations spending a smaller proportion on food than the poorer ones. This generalization is crude, but still serviceable within limits.[6]

EXAMPLE 5.2

GOVERNMENT POLICY-MAKING IN THE 1973 FUEL CRISIS

Top government policy-makers confronted a now-famous energy crisis at the end of 1973 when the Arab oil-producing countries announced a cutback of exports of oil to the United States. The first official estimates were that American consumers would have to reduce their consumption of gasoline by 20 or 30 percent. William E. Simon, the newly appointed federal "energy czar," stated repeatedly that he wanted to avoid rationing gasoline, if possible. So did other government officials, on the grounds that rationing would lead to black markets and create a large bureaucracy.

(a) How could gasoline consumption be cut by 20 or 30 percent without rationing? (b) Many economists pointed out to Simon and other government policy-makers that the short-term demand for gasoline is quite inelastic. Among the estimates of the price elasticity of demand for gasoline that were presented were the following:

Source of estimate	Estimate
Hendrik Houthakker	0.3
Phillip Verleger	0.3
Alan Greenspan	0.4
U.S. Department of Transportation	0.2

---

5. Of course, the quantity demanded may be influenced by the distribution of money income among consumers as well as the aggregate money income. We assume that the income distribution is held constant.

6. A number of economists, including H. Houthakker, have made excellent empirical studies of Engel's law and its validity.

If the arc elasticity of demand for gasoline equaled 0.3, how big a price increase was required to cut consumption by 25 percent? (c) Was rationing avoided? If so, how was the problem solved?

SOLUTION

(a) By increasing the price of gasoline. This, of course, is what would happen in a free market. (b) Increases in price of about 182 percent would be required. To see this, let Q_{D2} be the quantity demanded after the increase in price (from P_1 to P_2), Q_{D1} be the quantity demanded before the increase in price, η be the price elasticity of demand, $\Delta P = P_2 - P_1$, and $\Delta Q_D = Q_{D2} - Q_{D1}$. It follows from Equation 2.2 that $-\Delta Q_D(P_1 + P_2) \div \Delta P(Q_{D1} + Q_{D2}) = \eta$. If consumption is to be cut by 25 percent, Q_{D2} equals $0.75Q_{D1}$, and $\Delta Q_D = -.25Q_{D1}$. Thus $.25Q_{D1}(P_1 + P_2) \div 1.75Q_{D1}\Delta P = \eta$, or

$$\frac{\Delta P}{P_1 + P_2} = \frac{.25}{1.75\eta} = \frac{1}{7\eta}.$$

Consequently, if $\eta = 0.3$,

$$\frac{\Delta P}{P_1 + P_2} = \frac{1}{7 \times .3} = \frac{1}{2.1} = 0.476,$$

and (since $\Delta P = P_2 - P_1$),

$$\frac{P_2 - P_1}{P_1 + P_2} = 0.476.$$

Solving* for P_2 in terms of P_1,

$$P_2 = 2.82P_1.$$

That is, the price must increase by 182 percent. (c) Fortunately, subsequent analysis indicated that gasoline consumption did not have to be cut so severely, and it was possible to avoid both rationing and the enormous price increase set forth in the answer to (b). However, there were substantial price increases.

*Since $\dfrac{P_2 - P_1}{P_1 + P_2} = 0.476$, it follows that $P_2 - P_1 = 0.476(P_1 + P_2)$, which means that $0.524P_2 = 1.476P_1$, or $P_2 = 2.82P_1$.

CROSS ELASTICITIES OF DEMAND

In previous sections we have discussed the effects of two factors—the price of the commodity and the level of aggregate money income—on the quantity of the commodity demanded in the market. These two factors are not the only important ones; another important factor is the price of other commodities. Holding constant the commodity's own price (as well as the level of money incomes) and allowing the price of another commodity to vary, there may be important effects on the quantity demanded in the market for the commodity in question. By observing these effects, we can classify pairs of commodities as *substitutes* or *complements*, and we can measure how close the relationship (either substitute or complementary) is.

Consider two commodities, good X and good Y. Suppose that good Y's price goes up. What is the effect on the quantity of good X that is bought (per unit of time)? The *cross elasticity of demand* is defined as

$$\eta_{xy} = \frac{\Delta Q_x}{Q_x} \div \frac{\Delta P_y}{P_y} \qquad [5.2]$$

where ΔP_y is the change in the price of good Y, P_y is the original price of good Y, ΔQ_x is the resulting change in the quantity demanded of good X, and Q_x is the original quantity demanded of good X. Thus the cross elasticity of demand is the relative change in the quantity of good X resulting from a 1 percent change in the price of good Y.[7]

Whether goods X and Y are classified as *substitutes* or *complements* depends on whether the cross elasticity of demand is positive or negative. For example, an increase in the price of lamb, when the price of pork remains constant, will tend to increase the quantity of pork demanded; thus η_{xy} is positive, and lamb and pork are classified as substitutes. On the other hand, an increase in the price of fishing licenses may tend to decrease the purchase of fishing poles, when the price of fishing poles remains constant; thus η_{xy} is negative, and fishing licenses and fishing poles are classified as complements. Figure 5.3 shows the relationship between the consumption of good X and the price of good Y, given that they are substitutes or complements.

The cross elasticity of demand looks at the change in quantity demanded that results from a change in price *without* compensating for the change in the level of real income. This is the only feasible procedure because we seldom have data concerning the indifference maps of individual consumers. Moreover, we are generally interested in the relationship between commodities in the whole market rather than the relationship for a particular consumer.[8]

Finally, one other point should be noted. Whether goods X and Y are substitutes or complements can be determined by looking at the relative change in the quantity demanded of good X divided by the relative change in the price of good Y, that is, η_{xy}. It can also be determined by looking at the relative change in the quantity demanded of good Y divided by the relative change in the price of good X, η_{yx}. However, it should not be expected that the two elasticities will

7. More precisely, the cross elasticity of demand is

$$\frac{dQ_x}{dP_y} \div \frac{Q_x}{P_y}.$$

The definition in the text is the same except that finite differences are substituted for derivatives.

In subsequent discussions of marginal revenue, marginal product, marginal cost, and other such terms, we shall use finite differences and not bother to repeat each time the alternate definition based on the use of derivatives (since the alternative definition is obvious in each case).

8. For a single individual, goods can be classified as substitutes or complements more accurately on the basis of his or her utility function. Good Y is a substitute (complement) for good X if the marginal rate of substitution of good Y for money is reduced (increased) when good X is substituted for money in such a way as to leave the consumer no better or worse off than before.

FIGURE 5.3 Relationship between Consumption of Good *X* and Price of Good *Y*, Given That They Are Substitutes or Complements *If goods* X *and* Y *are substitutes, the quantity demanded of* X *is directly related to the price of good* Y. *If they are complements, the relationship is inverse.*

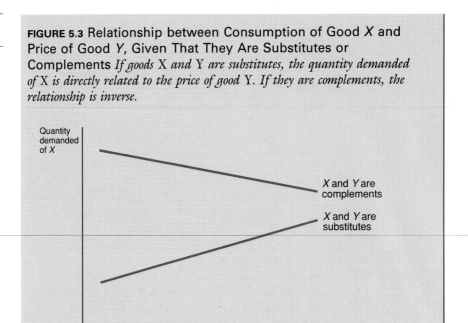

have the same numerical value. For example, goods *X* and *Y* may be substitutes, but the consumption of good *X* may be more sensitive to changes in the price of good *Y* than the consumption of good *Y* is to price changes of good *X*.

THE SELLERS' SIDE OF THE MARKET AND MARGINAL REVENUE

Up to this point, we have looked at the subject of demand chiefly from the point of view of consumers. But, as we have already noted, the expenditures of the consumers are the receipts of the sellers. In the next three sections, we look at demand from the other side of the market—the seller's side. We begin by defining marginal revenue. Then, in the following section, we show how marginal revenue can be estimated from the demand curve. Next, we discuss the differences between the demand curve for the industry and the demand curve for the firm. Finally, we discuss the relationship between marginal revenue and the price elasticity of demand. These results are of great importance and they form a bridge to the theory of the firm, which is presented in succeeding chapters.

Total revenue   The sellers of a commodity are interested, of course, in the total amount of money spent by consumers on the commodity. This amount is called *total revenue* by economists. From the market demand curve, one can easily determine the total revenue of the sellers at each price, since total revenue is, by

TABLE 5.2 Quantity Demanded, Total Revenue, and Marginal
Revenue

Price (dollars per unit of the commodity)	Quantity demanded (units of the commodity)	Total revenue (dollars)	Marginal revenue (dollars per unit of the commodity)
13	0	0	
12	1	12	12
11	2	22	10
10	3	30	8
9	4	36	6
8	5	40	4
7	6	42	2
6	7	42	0
5	8	40	-2
4	9	36	-4
3	10	30	-6

definition, price times quantity. Thus, in Table 5.2, total revenue is $36 at a
price of $9. The value of total revenue at various prices is shown in the third
column of Table 5.2.

Marginal revenue   Economists and firms are also concerned with *marginal revenue,* which is
defined as the addition to total revenue attributable to the addition of 1 unit to
sales. Thus, if $R(q)$ is total revenue when q units are sold and $R(q - 1)$ is total
revenue when $(q - 1)$ units are sold, the marginal revenue between q units and
$(q - 1)$ units is $R(q) - R(q - 1)$. This is illustrated in Table 5.2. For example,
when only 1 unit is sold, it is possible to charge a price of $12 and the total
revenue is $12. The marginal revenue between 1 unit of output and zero units
of output is total revenue at 1 unit of output minus total revenue at zero units of
output. Since the latter is zero, the marginal revenue between 1 unit of output
and zero units of output is $12.

It is evident from Table 5.2 that total revenue from a given number of units
of output—say n units—is equal to the sum of marginal revenue between zero
and 1 units of output, marginal revenue between 1 and 2 units of output,
marginal revenue between 2 and 3 units of output, and so on up to marginal
revenue between $(n - 1)$ and n units of output. For example, total revenue for
2 units of output is $22, which equals the sum of marginal revenue between
zero and 1 units of output ($12) and marginal revenue between 1 and 2 units of
output ($10). It is easy to prove that this will always be true. By the definition
of marginal revenue, the sum of the marginal revenue between zero and 1 units
of output, 1 and 2 units of output, and so on up to $(n - 1)$ and n units of
output is

$$[R(1) - R(0)] + [R(2) - R(1)] + [R(3) - R(2)] + \cdots + [R(n) - R(n - 1)].$$

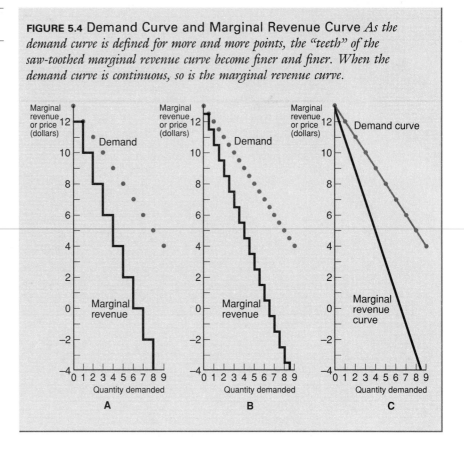

FIGURE 5.4 Demand Curve and Marginal Revenue Curve *As the demand curve is defined for more and more points, the "teeth" of the saw-toothed marginal revenue curve become finer and finer. When the demand curve is continuous, so is the marginal revenue curve.*

Since $R(1), R(2), \cdots, R(n-1)$ appear with both positive and negative signs, they cancel out; and since $R(0) = 0$, this sum must equal $R(n)$.

The *marginal revenue curve* shows marginal revenue at various levels of output of a commodity. For example, panel A of Figure 5.4 shows the marginal revenue curve for the situation in Table 5.2. Note that the marginal revenue curve lies above zero when total revenue is increasing, that it lies below zero when total revenue is decreasing, and that it equals zero when total revenue is at a maximum. For example, in panel A of Figure 5.4, the marginal revenue curve is zero between 6 and 7 units of output, and inspection of Table 5.2 confirms that they are the output levels where total revenue is maximized. Also, marginal revenue is shown to be positive for output levels of less than 6 units and negative for output levels of greater than 7 units; inspection of Table 5.2 confirms that total revenue is increasing up to 6 units of output and is decreasing beyond 7 units of output.

The marginal revenue curve consists of a number of "steps" when the demand curve is defined for only a relatively few points. For example, this is the case in panel A of Figure 5.4. However, as the demand curve is defined for more and more points, the "teeth" of the saw-toothed marginal revenue curve become finer and finer. For example, they are finer in panel B than in panel A.

Marginal revenue curve

Finally, when the demand curve is continuous, as in panel C, the marginal revenue curve becomes continuous, too.[9]

INDUSTRY AND FIRM DEMAND CURVES

Throughout this chapter we have been concerned with the market demand curve for a commodity. It is important to distinguish between the market demand curve for a commodity and the market demand curve for the output of a single firm producing the commodity. Of course, if only one firm produces the commodity (in which case the industry in question is a *monopoly*) there is no difference between these demand curves. But if there is more than one firm producing the commodity, as is usually the case, the demand curve for the output of each firm will generally be quite different from the demand curve for the commodity. In particular, the firm's demand curve will generally be more price elastic than that facing the industry as a whole, since the products of other firms are close substitutes for the products of any one firm.

A perfectly competitive firm's demand curve

Suppose that there are a great many sellers of the product in question, say 50,000 sellers of the same size, and that the conditions in the industry are close to *perfectly competitive*. (In perfect competition, the number of firms is large and their products are homogeneous, and for simplicity it is assumed that the firms have full knowledge of the market. Much more will be said about perfect competition in subsequent chapters.) In a case of this sort, if any one firm were to triple its output and sales, the total industry output would increase by only .004 percent. Since this change in total output is too small to have any noticeable effect on the price of the commodity, each seller can act as if variations in its own output will have no real effect on market price. Put differently, it appears to each firm that it can sell all it wants—within the range that is within its capabilities—without influencing the price. Thus the demand curve facing the individual firm in perfect competition is *horizontal*.

The firm in a perfectly competitive market can increase its sales rate without shading its price to get the extra business. Its demand curve, shown in Figure 5.5, is infinitely elastic: A very small decrease in price would result in an indefinitely large increase in the quantity it could sell, and a very small increase in price would result in its selling nothing. Moreover, since price remains constant, each additional unit sold increases total revenue by the amount of the price, the consequence being that price and marginal revenue are always equal.

---

9. Let the demand curve be

$$P = a - bQ.$$

Then the total revenue curve is

$$R = PQ = aQ - bQ^2,$$

and the marginal revenue curve is

$$\frac{dR}{dQ} = \frac{d(PQ)}{dQ} = a - 2bQ.$$

Thus the marginal revenue curve is a straight line and it has the same intercept on the y axis (that is, a) as the demand curve. (P is price, and Q is quantity demanded.)

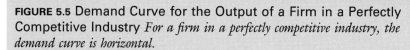

FIGURE 5.5 Demand Curve for the Output of a Firm in a Perfectly Competitive Industry *For a firm in a perfectly competitive industry, the demand curve is horizontal.*

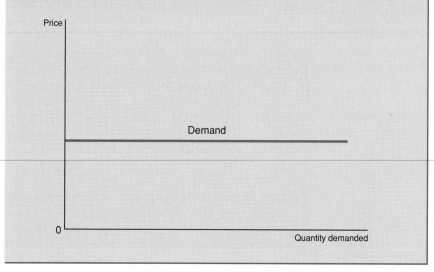

Thus, in the case of perfect competition, the demand curve facing a particular firm and the marginal revenue curve facing that firm are one and the same.

In a situation where the industry is not perfectly competitive, the demand curve for the output of a particular firm will not be horizontal, but it is likely to be more elastic than the demand curve for the commodity. If competition is not perfect, marginal revenue will not equal price, as it does in perfect competition. Instead, it will be less than price because demand is less than infinitely elastic.

Finally, it is important to note that marginal revenue at a certain output level is related in the following way to price and the price elasticity of demand at that output level:

$$MR = P\left[1 - \frac{1}{\eta}\right] \qquad [5.3]$$

where MR is marginal revenue, P is price, and η is the price elasticity of demand.[10] For example, if the price of a good is \$10 and if its price elasticity of demand is 2, marginal revenue equals \$10 $[1 - \frac{1}{2}]$ = \$5. Equation 5.3 is a very famous result which will be discussed further in subsequent chapters.

---

10. Let p be price and q be quantity demanded. If the demand curve is $p = f(q)$, marginal revenue is

$$MR = \frac{d(pq)}{dq} = f(q) + q\frac{df(q)}{dq} = p + q\frac{dp}{dq}.$$

Thus marginal revenue must be less than price as long as $dp/dq < 0$. It follows from this equation that

$$MR = p\left(1 + \frac{qdp}{pdq}\right)$$

$$= p\left(1 - \frac{1}{\eta}\right).$$

EXAMPLE 5.3

ANIMAL EXPERIMENTS AND THE THEORY OF DEMAND

Experimental psychologists like B. F. Skinner have long studied the behavior of rats and other animals. During the early 1980s, some microeconomists began to carry out similar sorts of research. In one well-known experiment, white rats were put in cages containing levers to activate dipper cups. When its lever was pushed down by a rat, one dipper cup provided a certain amount of collins mix; the other provided a certain amount of root beer. A rat was allotted a fixed "income" of so many pushes per day on the levers, and the experimental economists established the "price" per unit of collins mix and root beer as the number of pushes the rat had to "spend" to procure a unit.

(a) One rat was given an income of 300 pushes per day, and both liquids were priced at 20 pushes per day, with the result that the rat drank about 11 units of root beer and about 4 units of collins mix per day. Then the experimenters increased the price of root beer to 40 pushes and reduced the price of collins mix to 10 pushes, while adjusting the rat's income so that it could purchase its old "market basket" if it wanted. Did this mean that the rat's budget line was unchanged? (b) After the changes in prices and income described in part (a), the rat changed its "market basket" to 17 units of collins mix and 8 units of root beer per day. Was this in accord with the theory of consumer behavior? (c) In another experiment, a rat was able to obtain either standard laboratory food or water by pushing down the levers. No alternative food or liquid was available. Based on the rat's behavior when the "prices" of food and water were varied, its price elasticity of demand for food was 0.20. Why is this price elasticity so low? (d) In the same experiment, the cross elasticities of demand were:

Commodity	Cross elasticity of demand (percentage change in quantity demanded of this good due to a 1 percent change in the price of the other good)
Food	−0.55
Water	−0.32

Why are the cross elasticities of demand negative?

SOLUTION

(a) No. The slope of the budget line is −1 times the price ratio. When both liquids were priced at 20 pushes per day, the slope was −1. After the price changes, the ratio of the price of root beer to the price of collins mix was 4; thus, the slope was −4. Since its slope changed, it is obvious that the budget line must have changed. (b) Yes. Since root beer became more expensive relative to collins mix, one would expect anyone (rat or human being) to reduce the consumption of root beer and to increase the consumption of collins mix. (c) Goods that have few good substitutes tend to have low price elasticities of demand. There obviously are few, if any, good substitutes for food. (d) Food and water are complements because there are physiological limits on the amount that animals can increase their food consumption without increasing their intake of fluids.*

*For further discussion, see J. Kagel, R. Battalio, H. Rachlin, and L. Green, "Demand Curves for Animal Consumers," *Quarterly Journal of Economics,* February 1981; and J. Kagel, R. Battalio, H. Rachlin, L. Green, R. Basmann, and W. Klemm, "Experimental Studies of Consumer Demand Behavior," *Economic Inquiry,* March 1975.

MEASUREMENT OF DEMAND CURVES

The market demand curve plays a very important role in microeconomics, and there have been literally hundreds of published studies—and many more unpublished ones—that attempt to measure the market demand curves for particular commodities. This section describes briefly various ways in which such empirical studies have been carried out. The following two sections provide examples of the ways in which the results of such studies have been used to help solve important practical problems.

Market experiments

One technique that is frequently used to estimate the demand curve for a particular commodity is the direct market experiment. The idea is to vary the price of the product while attempting to keep other market conditions fairly stable (or to take changes in other market conditions into account). For example, the Parker Pen Company conducted an experiment some years ago to determine the price elasticity of demand for its product, Quink. They raised the price from 15 cents to 25 cents in four cities and found that demand was quite inelastic. Also, in some stores, the old package selling at 15 cents was put next to a package marked "New Quink, 25 cents"; the heavy sales of New Quink also indicated that demand was quite inelastic. Attempts were also made to estimate the cross elasticity of demand with other brands.

Consumer interviews

Another technique that is sometimes employed is to interview consumers and administer questionnaires concerning their buying habits, motives, and intentions. Unfortunately, the direct approach of simply asking people how much they would buy of a particular commodity at particular prices does not seem to work very well in most cases. The snap judgments of consumers in response to such a hypothetical question do not seem to be very accurate. However, more subtle approaches can be of value. For example, interviews indicated that most buyers of a certain baby food selected it on their doctor's recommendation, and that most of them knew very little about prices or substitutes. This information, together with other data, led the manufacturer to the conclusion that the price elasticity of demand was quite low.

Statistical techniques

Still another very popular technique is the use of statistical methods to extract information from data regarding sales, prices, incomes, and other variables in the past. Basically, what is involved is a comparison of various points in time or various sectors of the market; the point of this comparison is to see what effect the observed variation in price, income, and other relevant variables, had on the quantity demanded. For example, to estimate the price elasticity of demand, one might plot the quantity demanded in 1991 versus the 1991 price,

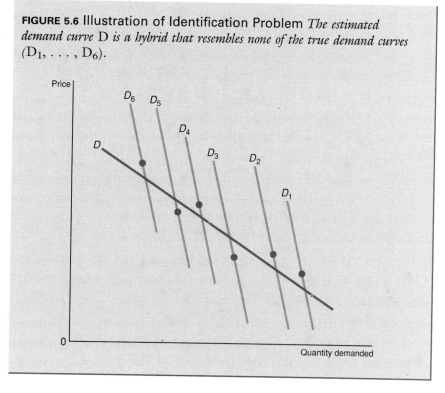

FIGURE 5.6 Illustration of Identification Problem *The estimated demand curve* D *is a hybrid that resembles none of the true demand curves* $(D_1, \ldots, D_6)$.

the quantity demanded in 1990 versus the 1990 price, and so on. If the results were as shown by the points in Figure 5.6, one might construct a curve like D as an estimate of the demand curve.

Although this example provides some understanding of the type of analysis that is involved, it makes the naïve assumption that the demand curve has remained constant over the period. Suppose that the 1991 demand curve was D_1, that the 1990 demand curve was D_2, and so on. Then the estimated demand curve D is a hybrid that resembles none of the true demand curves. Sophisticated econometric techniques have been developed for dealing with this so-called *identification problem*. Econometric techniques have also been devised to measure at the same time the effect of money income and the prices of other commodities on the quantity demanded; thus estimates can be made of the relationship between a commodity's price and the quantity demanded, when these other factors are held constant. However, even an elementary description of these econometric techniques lies outside the scope of this book.[11]

Each of the approaches to the measurement of demand curves has its disadvantages. Direct experimentation can be expensive or risky because customers may be lost and profits cut by the experiment. Also, since they are seldom really controlled experiments and since they are often of relatively brief duration and

11. For a description of these techniques, see J. Johnston, *Econometric Methods*, 3d ed. (New York: McGraw-Hill, 1984).

the number of observations is small, experiments often cannot produce all of the information that is needed. Interviews and questionnaires suffer from a great many disadvantages, some of which are noted above. So do consumer clinics where consumers are placed in simulated market conditions and changes in their behavior are observed as the conditions of the experiment are changed; consumer clinics are expensive and they cannot avoid the distortion due to the consumers' realizing that they are in an experimental situation.[12]

The difficulties involved in the application of statistical and econometric techniques are also very considerable. Unreliable and biased results can be obtained if important variables are unwittingly (or wittingly) omitted from the analysis. If some of the variables influencing the quantity demanded are highly correlated among themselves, it may not be possible to obtain reliable estimates of the separate effects of each of them. Also, the demand function is likely to be only one of a number of equations that connect the relevant variables, and it may be difficult to unscramble these equations adequately from the available statistics.

There are no easy remedies for these problems. Nevertheless, these problems, although sometimes formidable, are not insolvable. Many interesting and important studies have been made of the demand curves for particular commodities. And many interesting estimates have been made of the price elasticity, the income elasticity, and the cross elasticity of demand of various commodities. A sample of the results are presented in Tables 5.3, 5.4, and 5.5. The reader should study these tables carefully.

TABLE 5.3 Estimated Price Elasticity of Demand for Selected Commodities, United States

Commodity	Price elasticity	Commodity	Price elasticity
Electricity	1.20	Potatoes	0.31
Beef	0.92	Oats	0.56
Women's hats	3.00	Barley	0.39
Sugar	0.31	Buckwheat	0.99
Corn	0.49	Haddock	2.20
Cotton	0.12	Tires	1.20
Wheat	0.08	Movies	3.70

Source: H. Schultz, *Theory and Measurement of Demand*, (Chicago: University of Chicago Press, 1938); M. Spencer and L. Siegelman, *Managerial Economics* (Homewood, Ill.: Irwin, 1959); F. Bell, "The Pope and the Price of Fish," *American Economics Review*, December 1968; L. Taylor, "The Demand for Electricity: A Survey," *Bell Journal of Economics*, Spring 1975; and H. Houthakker and L. Taylor, *Consumer Demand in the United States* (Cambridge, Mass.: Harvard, 1970).

12. W. Baumol, "The Empirical Determination of Demand Relationships," reprinted in E. Mansfield, *Microeconomics: Selected Readings*, 5th ed.

TABLE 5.4 Estimated Cross Elasticities of Demand for Selected Commodities

Commodity	Cross elasticity with respect to price of:	Cross elasticity
Beef	Pork	+0.28
Butter	Margarine	+0.67
Margarine	Butter	+0.81
Pork	Beef	+0.14
Electricity	Natural gas	+0.20
Natural gas	Fuel oil	+0.44

Source: H. Wold, *Demand Analysis*; R. Halvorsen, "Energy Substitution in U.S. Manufacturing," *Review of Economics and Statistics*, November 1977.

TABLE 5.5 Estimated Income Elasticity of Demand for Selected Commodities

Commodity	Income elasticity	Commodity	Income elasticity
Butter	0.42	Meat	0.35
Cheese	0.34	Milk	0.07
Cream	0.56	Restaurant	
Eggs	0.37	consumption	1.48
Fruits and berries	0.70	Tobacco	1.02
Flour	−0.36	Haddock	0.46
Electricity	0.20	Dentists' services	1.41
Liquor	1.00	Furniture	1.48
Margarine	−0.20	Books	1.44

Source: H. Wold, *Demand Analysis*, p. 265; F. Bell, "The Pope and the Price of Fish"; H. Houthakker and L. Taylor, *Consumer Demand in the United States*; and L. Taylor, "The Demand for Electricity."

APPLICATIONS

Free Public Transit

The concepts of price elasticity, income elasticity, and cross elasticity of demand have many practical uses. For example, consider the proposals that have been made to provide free public transit service in our metropolitan areas. Proponents of free public transit point out that there is considerable concern in our cities over traffic congestion, and they argue that, if public transit were free, many commuters would use public transit rather than their cars, thus alleviating traffic problems, decreasing air pollution, and reducing the demand for parking facilities.

Whether or not public transit should be free is an important and complex issue of public policy. To evaluate this proposal, decision-makers have to consider a host of questions, including how the public transit agencies would be financed in the absence of fares. Two of the most fundamental questions are: To what extent would free transit fares increase the use of public transit? To what extent would it reduce the use of automobiles in the city? Clearly, these questions must be answered if one is to forecast the consequences of free public transit.

Faced with these questions, the U.S. Department of Transportation asked a team of economists at Charles River Associates to study them.[13] With respect to the effect of free fares on the use of public transit, the economists pointed out that the answer depends on the price elasticity of demand for public transit service. If this price elasticity is high, the reduction of the price of public transit from its current level to zero will result in a considerable increase in the number of trips made on public transit. On the other hand, if it is very low, such a price reduction would result in little increase in the number of such trips. In fact, according to estimates made by the economists, this price elasticity is about 0.17. Thus free transit fares would result in about a 40 percent increase in the number of trips made on public transit.[14]

With respect to the effects of free public transit on the use of automobiles in the city, the economists pointed out that the answer depends on the cross elasticity of demand for auto travel (in the city) with respect to transit fares. This cross elasticity is positive because auto travel and public transit are substitutes. If this cross elasticity is high, the reduction of transit fares to zero will result in a considerable drop in the use of autos in the city. On the other hand, if this cross elasticity is low, such a fare reduction would have little effect on the number of auto trips in the city. In fact, according to the economists' estimates, the value of this cross elasticity is such that free transit would reduce auto trips in the city by only about 7 percent.[15]

These results have been of use to federal, local, and other officials, as well as to other groups, in their treatment of this important issue. Based on these results, it appears that free transit would not stimulate huge increases in transit usage, and "that it will be very difficult to divert auto travelers to transit by lowering fares. . . ."[16] While these facts alone cannot resolve the issue, they certainly are of great relevance. Without question, the concepts of the price elasticity and cross elasticity of demand have played an important role in illuminating this major policy issue.

---

13. T. Domencich and G. Kraft, *Free Transit* (Lexington, Mass.: Heath, 1970).

14. To obtain this figure, note that it follows from Equation 2.2 that, if P_2 equals zero (and thus if $\Delta P = P_2 - P_1 = -P_1$), η equals $\Delta Q_D \div (Q_{D1} + Q_{D2}) = (Q_{D2}/Q_{D1} - 1) \div (1 + Q_{D2}/Q_{D1})$. Thus $Q_{D2}/Q_{D1} = (1 + \eta) \div (1 - \eta)$. Since η is approximately 0.17, Q_{D2}/Q_{D1} is approximately $(1 + .17) \div (1 - .17) = 1.41$.

     The elasticity figure used here pertains to work travel. For a more complete discussion, see ibid.

15. Ibid., p. 102.

16. Ibid., p. 98.

The concepts discussed in this chapter are obviously of fundamental importance in the formulation of business policy, as well as public policy. To illustrate the use of the concept of price elasticity by business, let's go back over fifty years and consider a famous case involving Columbia Records. In 1938, the Columbia Broadcasting Company purchased the American Record Company and changed its name to Columbia Records. When the new company began operations, classical records were sold by the industry at about $1.50, semiclassical and well-established popular records were sold at $0.75, and popular records were sold at $0.35. Among classical records, a sale of 5,000 was considered good; although extremely popular releases might reach a sales volume of 50,000, some records might not sell more than 200.

In November 1938, a New York newspaper began a promotion scheme whereby it offered classical albums to its readers at prices averaging about $0.50 a record. The results were very impressive; more than 50,000 records of a single symphony were sold in a few weeks. Observing this fact, and the enthusiastic reception of the radio broadcasts of symphonic and operatic performances, the executives of the Columbia Broadcasting System concluded that there was a very good opportunity to increase the market for classical records by price reductions. However, during the first couple of years, the new company maintained the high level of prices on classical records while it improved the mechanical quality of its records and the skill and reputation of the artists it recorded.

Before instituting a price reduction, Columbia obviously had to estimate more precisely what the effect of a price reduction would be on its revenues and costs. The answers to these questions clearly depended upon the price elasticity of demand for classical records, as well as on the way in which the firm's costs varied with the quantity of records it produced (a subject that is discussed at length in Chapter 7). Edward Wallerstein, president of Columbia Records, began by trying to estimate the public's reaction to lower prices. He asked a number of dealers to keep detailed records of their customary sales and then for one month to offer all people who entered their stores regular classical and semiclassical records at two-thirds of list price. These dealers found that the unannounced price reduction of 33⅓ percent more than doubled the number of records sold. Thus the apparent price elasticity of demand, based on this crude experiment, was well above 1. This evidence, in addition to the other indications, convinced Wallerstein that Columbia should go further in analyzing the pros and cons of a price reduction of substantial magnitude.

Based on the estimated price elasticity of demand, it was possible to estimate the effect of a price cut on the firm's total revenue. In addition, a close examination was made of the firm's cost structure to determine the effect of a price cut on the firm's total costs. Since many costs were fixed, total costs would not increase in proportion to the increased volume resulting from the price cut. After considerable study, it was decided to reduce the price of 10-inch classical records from about $1.25 to $0.75 and to reduce the price of 12-inch classical records from about $1.75 to $1.00. Presumably a price reduction of this extent was chosen because it was felt to be the most profitable one. The response was overwhelming. Other firms followed Columbia's lead. To the surprise of much of the industry, total expenditure on classical records rose greatly.

Summary

1. The market demand curve for a commodity is simply the horizontal summation of the individual demand curves of all the consumers in the market. Since individual demand curves almost always slope downward to the right, it follows that market demand curves will do so, too.
2. The price elasticity of demand for a commodity depends on the number and closeness of substitutes that are available. If a commodity has many close substitutes, its demand is likely to be elastic. Of course, the extent to which a commodity has close substitutes depends on how narrowly it is defined.
3. The income elasticity of demand is the percentage change in quantity demanded resulting from a 1 percent change in money income. Commodities differ greatly in their income elasticities. Goods that people regard as luxuries are generally assumed to have high income elasticities of demand. Indeed, one way to define luxuries and necessities is to say that luxuries are goods with high income elasticities of demand, and necessities are goods with low income elasticities of demand.
4. The cross elasticity of demand is the relative change in the quantity demanded of good X divided by the relative change in the price of good Y. Whether commodities are classified as substitutes or complements depends on whether the cross elasticity is positive or negative.
5. Marginal revenue is the addition to total revenue attributable to the addition of the last unit of sales. Obviously, total revenue from n units of output is equal to the sum of marginal revenue in the intervals between zero and 1 unit of output, 1 and 2 units of output, and so on up to $(n - 1)$ to n units of output.
6. It is important to distinguish between the market demand curve for a commodity and the market demand curve for the output of a single firm producing the commodity. In a perfectly competitive industry, the firm's demand curve will be horizontal. If the industry contains more than one firm but is not perfectly competitive, the firm's demand curve will not be horizontal, but it is likely to be more elastic than the demand curve for the commodity.
7. One technique used to estimate the market demand curve is direct market experimentation. Another technique is to interview consumers and administer questionnaires concerning their habits, motives, and intentions. Still another technique is the use of statistical and econometric techniques to extract information from data regarding sales, prices, incomes, and other variables in the past.
8. Each of these approaches has its disadvantages, and there is no easy remedy to the estimation problem. Nevertheless, the difficulties generally are not insurmountable. Many interesting and important estimates have been made of the demand curves for various goods.

Questions/ Problems

1. D. Chapman, T. Tyrell, and T. Mount estimated that the long-run price elasticity of demand for electricity by all U.S. residential consumers is 1.2, that the income elasticity of demand for electricity by such consumers is 0.2, and that the cross elasticity of demand for electricity with respect to the price of natural gas is 0.2. (a) If the price of electricity is expected to rise by 1 percent in the long run, by how much would the price of natural gas have to change to offset the effect of this increase in electricity's price on the quantity of electricity consumed? (b) Among residential consumers in a Chicago

suburb, holding other factors constant, there was the following relationship between their aggregate money income and the amount of electricity they consumed:

Aggregate income (millions of dollars)	Quantity of electricity consumed
100	300
110	303
121	306

Is this evidence consistent with the results presented by Chapman, Tyrell, and Mount? If not, what factors might account for the discrepancy? (c) Would you expect the income elasticity of demand and the cross elasticity of demand to be higher or lower in the short run than in the long run? Why?

2. A business analyst says that the demand curve for videocassette recorders has shifted to the right, and that at the same time the price elasticity of demand for videocassette recorders has increased from 3 to 4. Is this possible? Can the new demand curve be entirely above and to the right of the old demand curve, if the new price elasticity is 4 whereas the old price elasticity was 3?

3. The steel industry has long maintained that the demand for steel is price inelastic. According to a well-known study by T. Yntema, the price elasticity of demand for steel is no more than 0.4. (a) Are there any major substitutes for steel? If so, what are some of them? (b) Some years ago the chief executive officer of Bethlehem Steel testified before a Senate committee that the price elasticity of demand for steel was much less than 1. If so, can we deduce that the demand for Bethlehem's steel is price inelastic? (c) If the demand for Bethlehem's steel is inelastic at the price it is charging, is it maximizing its profits? (d) Is the cross elasticity of demand between Bethlehem's steel and imported Japanese steel positive or negative? Why?

4. The cross elasticity of demand can be used to determine which products belong to the same market. For example, in a famous antitrust case, the U.S. Department of Justice brought suit against the Du Pont Company for having monopolized the sale of cellophane. In its defense, Du Pont claimed that cellophane had many close substitutes, such as aluminum foil, waxed paper, and polyethylene. Can you guess how Du Pont used cross elasticities of demand in this case? (Incidentally, the Supreme Court accepted Du Pont's argument in its landmark decision handed down in 1953.)

5. Suppose that a consumer considers Geritol of supreme importance and that he spends all of his income on Geritol. To this consumer, what is the price elasticity of demand for Geritol? What is the income elasticity of demand for Geritol? What is the cross elasticity of demand between Geritol and any other good?

6. In the aluminum industry, is the demand curve for the output of each firm horizontal? (Why or why not?) Is it less elastic than the demand curve for aluminum as a whole? (Why or why not?) Is the price of aluminum less than, equal to, or greater than marginal revenue?

7. Which of the following are likely to have a positive cross elasticity of demand: (a) automobiles and oil, (b) wood tennis rackets and metal tennis rackets, (c) gin and tonic, (d) fishing poles and fishing licenses, (e) a Harvard education and a Stanford education.

8. The demand for refined sugar in the United States has declined greatly since 1975, due in part to reports that it causes tooth decay, reduces the nutritional value of the diet, and leads to obesity. Given that per capita consumption of refined sugar has declined, can we be sure that the price elasticity of demand for refined sugar is (a) less than 1, (b) greater than 1, (c) greater than zero?

9. Suppose the mayor of New York asked you to advise him concerning the proper fare that should be charged by the New York City subway. In what way might information concerning the price elasticity of demand be useful?

10. According to the Senate Subcommittee on Antitrust and Monopoly, the income elasticity of demand for automobiles in the United States is between 2.5 and 3.9. What does this mean? If incomes rise by 5 percent, what effect will this have on the quantity of autos demanded? How might this fact be used by General Motors?

11. Suppose you are a trustee of a major university. At a meeting of the board of trustees, one university official argues that the demand for places at this university is completely inelastic. As evidence, he cites the fact that, although the university has doubled its tuition in the last decade, there has been no appreciable decrease in the number of students enrolled. Do you agree? Comment on his argument.

12. According to William Baumol, "Some mail-order houses have employed systematic programs in which a few experimental pages were bound inconspicuously into the catalogues distributed to customers within restricted geographical regions, thus permitting observation of the effects of price, product, or even catalogue display variations." Comment on the accuracy of this technique. What might be some of the problems in estimating a product's price elasticity of demand in this way? What techniques might be better than this one?

13. Show that, if the Engel curve for a good is a straight line through the origin, the income elasticity of demand for the good is 1.

14. E. Lewit and D. Coate estimated the price elasticity of demand for cigarettes among adults to be about 0.42 and the income elasticity to be about 0.08. (a) Among adults in a Texas community, holding other factors constant, there is the following relationship between their aggregate money income and the amount of cigarettes they consume:

Aggregate income (millions of dollars)	Quantity of cigarettes consumed
100	1,000
110	1,001
121	1,002

Is this evidence consistent with the results presented by Lewit and Coate? (b) Does your answer to question (a) depend on the units in which the quantity of cigarettes consumed is measured in the table above? (c) During 1967 to 1970, the Federal Communications Commission required that one anti-smoking television commercial be aired for every four pro-smoking advertisements, under the Fairness Doctrine. What effect did this have on the demand curve for cigarettes? (d) Would you expect changes in price to have as much effect on how many cigarettes existing smokers consume as on whether or not people begin to smoke?

THE DEMAND FOR AIRLINE TRAVEL: THE NORTH ATLANTIC MARKET

Air travel between North America and Europe is a very big business, as reflected by the fact that about 12 percent of all international air passengers travel between these two continents. The North Atlantic market (as airline specialists call the market for air travel between North America and Europe) is marked by at least two noteworthy characteristics. First, the bulk of the travelers are non-business travelers. About 46 percent of all passengers are vacation travelers, 34 percent are visiting relatives and friends, and the rest are business travelers. Second, there is considerable seasonal variation in the demand for air travel in this market, the peak season being the summer. About 37 percent of all traffic in this market occurs in the third quarter of the year.

Many major international airlines, such as TWA, American, Pan Am, British Airways, Lufthansa, Air France, and SAS fly between North America and Europe. They, as well as a host of industry and government analysts, are vitally interested in the demand for air travel in this market. In particular, they are interested in the price elasticity and income elasticity of demand for such air travel. In 1980, J. M. Cigliano of the Lockheed-California Company published the results of a study in which he estimated these elasticities.[1] His findings have been used in a variety of contexts, as we shall see below.

Table 1 shows the estimated elasticities of demand for air travel between the United States and Europe, as well as between Canada and Europe. For the U.S.–Europe route, the price elasticity of demand is about 1.2, which means that a 1-percent reduction in price would increase the quantity of air tickets demanded by about 1.2 percent. The income elasticity of demand is about 1.9, which means that a 1-percent increase in consumer incomes would increase the quantity demanded by about 1.9 percent.

For the Canada–Europe route, the income elasticity (1.8) is much the same as between the United States and Europe, but the price elasticity (0.8) is much lower. In part, this may reflect a different mix of air travelers. Compared with the U.S.–Europe route, a relatively large proportion of the travelers between

1. J. M. Cigliano, "Price and Income Elasticities for Airline Travel: The North Atlantic Market," *Business Economics,* September 1980.

TABLE 1 Price and Income Elasticities of Demand for Air Travel in the North Atlantic Market

Route	Price elasticity	Income elasticity
United States to (or from) Europe	1.2	1.9
Canada to (or from) Europe	0.8	1.8

Source: J. M. Cigliano, "Price and Income Elasticities."

Canada and Europe may be business travelers, whose travel plans are relatively insensitive to the price of air travel. Whatever the reasons for the difference between the Canada–Europe and U.S.–Europe routes in the price elasticity of demand, this difference is of considerable interest to the airlines. It indicates that increases in air fares would reduce the total amount of money spent on air travel between the United States and Europe, but increase the amount spent on travel between Canada and Europe.

Table 2 shows the estimated elasticities of demand for each of three fare categories of air travel between the United States and Europe. These fare categories are (1) first class, (2) regular economy, and (3) excursion. As would be expected, the price elasticity of demand is much lower for first-class travel than for regular-economy travel—and lower for regular-economy travel than for excursion travel. This reflects the fact that the proportion of all travelers that are business travelers is highest for first-class travel and lowest for excursion travel. Indeed, only about 15 percent of excursion passengers are business travelers.

If an airline believes that the demand for its first-class tickets is much less price elastic than the demand for its excursion tickets, it may be able to increase its revenues and profits by setting the price of a first-class ticket much higher than that of an excursion ticket. While a rigorous proof of this statement must be postponed to Chapter 9, it seems intuitively obvious that the airline should consider setting a higher price for the first-class traveler (who is less sensitive to price) than for the excursion traveler (who is more price-sensitive). What is less obvious is that a knowledge of the price elasticities of demand may enable us to

TABLE 2 Price and Income Elasticities of Demand for Air Travel between the United States and Europe

Fare category	Price elasticity	Income elasticity
First class	0.4	1.5
Regular economy	1.3	1.4
Excursion[a]	1.8	2.4

Source: See Table 1.
[a] This is the category that Cigliano calls "long excursion."

estimate *how big* the difference between the prices should be, if profits are to be maximized. More will be said on this score in Chapter 9.

Finally, note once again that the income elasticities of demand for air travel in the North Atlantic market are about 1.8 or 1.9. From the point of view of forecasting the demand for air travel in this market, this means that recessions (periods when consumer incomes drop) can hit air travel pretty hard. (A 1-percent reduction in income will result in a 1.8 or 1.9 percent cut in air travel.) According to Cigliano, this helps to explain the dramatic drop in air traffic in this market in some recent recessions.

Analytical Questions

1. According to these results, the income elasticity of demand is much higher for excursion tickets than for first-class tickets. Why do you think that this is true?

2. Why can we be sure that "increases in air fares would reduce the total amount of money spent on air travel between the United States and Europe, but increase the amount spent on travel between Canada and Europe"?

3. Between the United States and Europe, is marginal revenue positive or negative for first-class travel? For regular-economy travel? For excursion travel? Why is this important?

4. Do you think that the amount of air travel from the United States to Europe is influenced by the prices of hotel rooms and meals in Europe? If so, what sort of effects do these prices have on the amount of air travel? Are hotel rooms and meals in Europe complements to air travel? Why or why not?

5. Would you expect the cross elasticity of demand between air travel from Europe to the United States and ground transportation in the United States to be positive or negative? Why?

PART THREE

THE FIRM: ITS TECHNOLOGY AND COSTS

6

THE FIRM AND ITS TECHNOLOGY

THE ASSUMPTION OF PROFIT MAXIMIZATION

Both General Electric and the Ford Foundation have assets that run into the billions of dollars. Both are large, powerful organizations, but only one of them is a firm. What is a firm? Put briefly, it is a unit that produces a good or service for sale. In contrast to not-for-profit institutions like the Ford Foundation, firms attempt to make a profit. There are literally millions of firms in the United States: Some are proprietorships (owned by a single person), some partnerships (owned by two or more people), and some corporations (which are fictitious legal persons). About six-sevenths of the goods and services produced in the United States are produced by firms; the rest are provided by government and not-for-profit institutions. It is obvious that an economy like ours revolves around the activities of firms.

Economic profit   As a first approximation, economists generally assume that firms attempt to maximize profits. However, the economist's definition of profits does not coincide with the accountant's. The economist does not assume that the firm attempts to maximize the current, short-run profits measured by the accountant. Instead he or she assumes that the firm will attempt to maximize the sum of profits over a long period of time, these profits being properly discounted to the present. Also, when the economist speaks of profits, he or she means profit after taking account of the capital and labor provided by the owners. More will be said on this score in the next chapter.

Although the assumption of profit maximization serves as a reasonable first approximation, it has obvious limitations. For one thing, the making of profits generally requires time and energy, and if the owners of the firm are the managers as well, they may decide that it is preferable to sacrifice profits for leisure. (Profit-maximizers in Miami Beach and the Virgin Islands encourage this type of thinking.) In a case of this sort, it is more accurate to assume that the owner-manager, like the consumer, is maximizing utility, since utility is a function of his or her profits and the amount of leisure he or she enjoys. Using the kind of analysis described in Chapter 3, we can determine how much money the owner-manager will give up for leisure (see Example 6.1).

It should also be noted that, in an uncertain world, the concept of maximum profit is not clearly defined. Since any particular course of action will not result in a unique, certain level of profit, but in a variety of possible levels of profit, each with a certain probability of occurrence, it makes no sense to speak about the maximization of profits. However, if the firm is able, explicitly or implicitly, to attach a probability to each level of profit that could result from each course of action, it is meaningful to assume that the firm attempts to maximize expected profits.[1] For simplicity, we shall assume in the following pages that the firm has full knowledge of the relevant variables, and that there is no uncertainty.

Observers of the modern corporation often state that profits are not the sole objective of these firms. Industry spokesmen often claim that the following objectives are also of importance: achieving better social conditions in the firm's community, increasing (or at least maintaining) its market share, creating an image as a good employer and a useful part of the community, and so forth. For example, oil firms often stress their concern over the environment and over the reduction of wasteful uses of fuel. Besides the question of how seriously one should take such self-proclaimed goals, the important question is how distinct these goals are from the goal of profit maximization. To the extent that many of these goals are simply means to achieve profits *in the long run,* there may be less inaccuracy in the profit maximization assumption than might appear at first glance.

In addition, economists are interested in the theory of the profit-maximizing firm because it provides rules of behavior for firms that do want to maximize profits. The theory of the profit-maximizing firm suggests how a firm should operate if it wants to make as much money as possible. Even if a firm does not want to maximize profit, the theory can be useful. For example, it can show how much the firm is losing by taking certain courses of action. In recent years the theory of the profit-maximizing firm has been studied more and more for the sake of determining rules of business behavior.

---

1. Expected profit is defined as the long-term average value of profit—the sum of the various possible levels of profit, after each level is weighted by the probability of its occurrence. The firm may be interested in the variance, as well as the expected value of profits, in which case it will maximize some function of both the expected value and the variance. For further discussion of this and related topics, see Chapter 18, which deals with decision-making under conditions of risk.

EXAMPLE 6.1

PROFITS VERSUS LEISURE

In a famous article, Tibor Scitovsky suggested that the entrepreneur (that is, the owner-manager of the firm) maximizes utility, which is a function of the firm's profits and the amount of leisure the entrepreneur enjoys. Suppose that a particular entrepreneur's indifference curves between profit and leisure are as shown in the graph below. Also, suppose that the amount of work that the entrepreneur must do is proportional to his or her firm's output. If this is the case, the relationship between leisure and profit is given by the curved line *ABCD*.

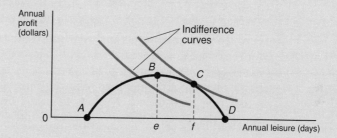

(a) Why does the relationship between leisure and profit have the shape indicated by *ABCD*? (b) Will the entrepreneur maximize profit? (c) If the entrepreneur's indifference curves were horizontal lines, would he or she maximize profit?

SOLUTION

(a) Up to some point, increases in the firm's output result in increases in profit; beyond this point, they result in decreases in profit. Thus, since the entrepreneur's days of work are assumed to be proportional to the firm's output, up to some point, increases in the number of days he or she works result in increases in profit; beyond this point, they result in decreases in profit. Finally, since the entrepreneur's number of days of leisure equals the total time during the year minus his or her number of days of work, it follows that, up to some point, increases in his or her number of days of leisure are associated with increases in profit; beyond that point (indicated by *e* in the graph) they are associated with decreases in profit. (b) No. He or she maximizes utility by choosing point *C*, where there are *Of* days of leisure, and profit is below the maximum that could be achieved. (c) Yes. He or she would choose point *B*, where profits are a maximum.*

*For further discussion, see T. Scitovsky, "A Note on Profit Maximization and Its Implications." *Review of Economic Studies,* Winter 1943.

FIRM OWNERS AND MANAGERS:
A PRINCIPAL-AGENT PROBLEM

In the previous section, we pointed out that economists generally regard the assumption of profit maximization as only a first approximation.[2] One factor that can stand in the way of the maximization of profit is the separation of ownership from control in the large corporation. The owners of the firm—the stockholders—usually have little detailed knowledge of the firm's operations. Even if the board of directors is made up largely of people other than top management, top management usually has a great deal of freedom as long as it seems to be performing reasonably well. Under these circumstances, one might suppose that the behavior of the firm often will be dictated in part by the interests of the management group, the result being larger salaries, more perquisites, and a bigger staff than otherwise would be the case.

This is a so-called *principal-agent problem*. An *agency relationship* exists between the firm's owners and its managers: the managers are *agents* who work for the owners, who are the *principals*. The principal-agent problem is that the managers may pursue their own objectives, even though this reduces the profits of the owners.[3] Consider Joan Johnson, a manager (and part owner) who gets satisfaction both from her profits from the firm she manages and from the benefits (large staff, company-paid travel, and so on) that she receives from this firm. If were the sole owner of her firm, an extra dollar of benefits she receives would reduce her profits by one dollar. In other words, the cost of these benefits would come entirely out of her own pocket. On the other hand, if she were to own only one-quarter of her firm (and if Japanese investors own the rest), an extra dollar of benefits would reduce her profits by only 25 cents. Thus only one-quarter of the cost of these benefits would come out of her pocket.

Clearly, Joan Johnson is likely to increase the amount of benefits she receives if the cost to her of a dollar's worth of benefits is 25 cents rather than a dollar. Since the other owners pick up three-quarters of the tab, why not take an extra "business" trip to Paris (and get a good meal at Tour D'Argent)? If she had to pay the full cost, she would forgo the Paris trip (and eat at McDonald's); but since she only pays 25 percent of the full cost, she finds it worthwhile to go to Paris.

If a manager like Joan Johnson is not an owner of the firm, this problem becomes even more severe. Since the cost of the benefits she receives is borne

---

2. For discussions of models of the firm based on assumptions other than profit maximization, see H. Simon, "Theories of Decision-Making in Economics and Behavioral Science," reprinted in E. Mansfield, *Microeconomics: Selected Readings,* 5th ed.; R. Cyert and J. March, *A Behavioral Theory of the Firm* (Englewood Cliffs, N.J.: Prentice-Hall, 1963); and H. Leibenstein, "Allocative Efficiency vs. X-Efficiency," reprinted in E. Mansfield, *Microeconomics: Selected Readings,* 5th ed.

3. See M. Jensen and W. Meckling, "Theory of the Firm: Managerial Behavior, Agency Costs, and Ownership Structure," *Journal of Financial Economics,* 1976; J. Pratt and R. Zeckhauser (eds.), *Principals and Agents: The Structure of Business* (Boston: Harvard Business School, 1985); and E. Fama, "Agency Problems and the Theory of the Firm," *Journal of Political Economy,* 1980. Also, see O. Williamson, *The Economics of Discretionary Behavior* (Englewood Cliffs, N.J.: Prentice-Hall, 1964), as well as his *Markets and Hierarchies: Analysis and Antitrust Implications* (New York: Free Press, 1975) and *The Economic Institutions of Capitalism* (New York: Free Press, 1985).

entirely by the owners, she has an incentive to increase these benefits very substantially. Because the owners of the firm find it difficult to distinguish between those benefits that promote profits and those that do not do so, she has a certain amount of leeway. But the owners are unlikely to put up with this kind of behavior if it becomes too serious or blatant. After all, the cost of these additional benefits comes entirely out of their pockets!

What can the owners do? To begin with, they can avoid investing in a firm where the managers behave in this way. If no owners are willing to invest, and if the managers have to put up their own funds to finance the business, the situation is the same as when Joan Johnson was the sole owner of her firm. As we saw above, the benefits she received were constrained by her having to pay their full costs. If the managers do not finance the business themselves, they must formulate a contractual agreement that would be attractive to potential owners. One possibility might be to establish a contract making the managers responsible for paying for the benefits that they receive; but such a contract would be very difficult, if not impossible, to enforce, since the owners would have to monitor the managers' activities in minute detail.

A more feasible procedure might be to establish a contract that gives the managers an incentive to reduce benefits and to pursue objectives that are reasonably close to profit maximization. For example, the firm's owners might give the managers a financial stake in the success of the firm. Many corporations have stock purchase plans, whereby managers can purchase shares of common stock at less than market price. These plans provide managers with an incentive to promote the firm's profits and to act in accord with the interests of the firm's owners. Recent empirical research suggests that, if managers own between 5 and 20 percent of a firm, the firm is likely to perform better (in terms of profitability) than if they own less than 5 percent.[4]

If a firm is poorly managed and if its owners are unable to exert proper control over its management, it may be taken over by other owners who are tougher and more adept in this regard. Sometimes the takeover is relatively cut-and-dried; the old owners are happy to sell out to the new owners. But in other cases, the old management may go to great lengths to avoid being taken over by new owners. The firms that are targets of hostile takeovers tend to be poorly performing companies; one way that the performance of such companies may be improved is through takeovers.[5]

Principal-agent problems exist between owners and workers, as well as between owners and managers. Workers, like managers, may pursue their own interests, not those of their employers. In Chapter 12, we describe how a firm can establish incentives for workers to act so as to increase the firm's profits. As we shall see, firms often pay their workers bonuses to reward the outcomes of high levels of effort, and profit-sharing arrangements are frequently used for this purpose.

---

4. R. Morck, A. Shleifer, and R. Vishny, "Management Ownership and Corporate Performance: An Empirical Analysis," *Journal of Financial Economics,* March 1988.

5. R. Morck, A. Shleifer, and R. Vishny, "Characteristics of Hostile and Friendly Takeover Targets," in A. Auerbach (ed.), *Takeovers: Causes and Consequences* (Chicago: University of Chicago Press, 1988).

TECHNOLOGY AND INPUTS

One of the fundamental determinants of a firm's behavior is the state of technology. Whether a firm produces textiles or locomotives, whether a firm is big or small, whether a firm is run by a genius or a moron (or even your brother-in-law), the firm cannot do more than is permitted by existing technology. Technology, as we defined it in Chapter 1, is the sum total of society's pool of knowledge concerning the industrial and agricultural arts. Although this definition is accurate, it is not very useful in indicating how we can represent the state of technology in a model of the firm. The purpose of the rest of this chapter is to show how economists represent the state of technology.

To begin with, an *input* is defined as anything that a firm uses in its production process. Most firms require a wide variety of inputs. For example, some of the inputs in the iron and steel industry are iron ore, coal, oxygen, skilled labor of various types, the services of blast furnaces, open hearths, electric furnaces, and rolling mills, as well as the services of the people managing the companies. To give a more humble example, the inputs in the production and sale of hot dogs by a street vendor are the hot dogs, the rolls, the stove, the truck, and the services of the vendor.

In representing and analyzing production processes, we assume that all inputs can be divided into two categories: fixed inputs and variable inputs. A **Fixed input** *fixed input* is an input whose quantity cannot be changed during the period of time under consideration. This period will vary from problem to problem. Of course, the amount of most inputs can be varied to some extent, no matter how brief the time interval. But for some inputs, the cost of quick variation in their amount is so large as to make such variation impractical. For simplicity, we regard these inputs as being fixed. The firm's plant and equipment are examples of inputs that often are included in this category.

On the other hand, a *variable input* is an input whose quantity can be **Variable input** changed during the relevant period. For example, the number of workers hired to perform a job like construction can often be increased or decreased on short notice. The amount of raw material used in the production of a commodity like dresses can often be increased or decreased by using up or building up the firm's inventories. The amount of water used in the production of a service like a car wash can sometimes be varied within limits simply by turning the relevant knobs.

THE SHORT RUN AND THE LONG RUN

Whether or not an input is regarded as variable or fixed depends on the length of the period under consideration. The longer the period, the more inputs are variable, not fixed. Although the length of the relevant period varies from problem to problem, economists have found it useful to focus special attention **Short run vs. long run** on two time periods: the short run and the long run. The *short run* is defined to be that period of time in which some of the firm's inputs are fixed. More specifically, since the firm's plant and equipment are among the most difficult inputs to change quickly, the short run is generally understood to mean the length of time during which the firm's plant and equipment are fixed. On the other hand, the *long run* is that period of time in which all inputs are variable. In the long run, the firm can make a complete adjustment to any change in its environment.

In both the short run and the long run, a firm's productive processes ordinarily permit substantial variation in the proportions in which inputs are used. In the long run, there can be no question but that input proportions can be varied considerably. For example, an automobile die can be made on conventional machine tools with more labor and less expensive equipment, or it can be made on numerically controlled machine tools with less labor and more expensive equipment. Similarly, an airplane can be almost handmade or it can be made using much equipment and relatively little labor. In the short run, there are also considerable opportunities for changes in input proportions. For one thing, the ratio between fixed and variable inputs can vary greatly.

Production processes with fixed, not variable, proportions are ones where there is one, and only one, ratio of inputs that can be used. For example, to produce a certain product, 2 hours of labor must be combined with a certain amount of capital. Consequently, if output is increased or decreased, the quantity of all inputs must be varied in proportion to output. There seem to be very few cases where all inputs must be combined in fixed proportions. However, there are cases where the amount of a *certain* input can be varied only within narrow limits. For example, a particular drug may have to contain a certain amount of aspirin per ounce of the drug. Thus it is not unusual for some inputs to be required in relatively fixed proportions but it is very unusual for this to be the case for all, or most inputs.

Production function

THE PRODUCTION FUNCTION

For any commodity, the *production function* is the relationship between the quantities of various inputs used per period of time and the maximum quantity of the commodity that can be produced per period of time. More specifically, the production function is a table, a graph, or an equation showing the maximum output rate that can be achieved from any specified set of usage rates of inputs. The production function summarizes the characteristics of existing technology at a given point in time; it shows the technological constraints that the firm must reckon with. In most of this book, we assume that the firm takes the production function as given; in Chapter 17, when we analyze the process of technological change, we study the firm's attempts to change the production function.

To illustrate the production function, consider the simplest case—when there is one fixed input and one variable input. Suppose that the fixed input is the service of an acre of land, the variable input is labor (in units per year), and the output is corn (in bushels). Suppose that a scientifically inclined farmer decides to find out what the effect on annual output will be if he or she applies various numbers of units of labor during the year to the acre of land. (The farmer can vary the number of units of labor by hiring fewer or more laborers.) If he or she obtains the results in Table 6.1, then these results might be regarded

TABLE 6.1 Output of Corn When Various Amounts of Labor Are
Applied to an Acre of Land

Amount of labor (units per year)	Output of corn (bushels per year)
1	6
2	13.5
3	21
4	28
5	34
6	38
7	38
8	37

as the production function in this situation. Alternatively, the curve in Figure
6.1, which presents exactly the same results, might be regarded as the production function.

The production function is an important starting point for the analysis of the
firm's technology: It gives us the maximum *total output* that can be realized by
using each combination of quantities of inputs. But there is more that we need

FIGURE 6.1 Relationship between Total Output and Amount of
Labor Used on One Acre of Land *The production function shows the
relationship between output (in this case, bushels of corn) and input (in this
case, units of labor).*

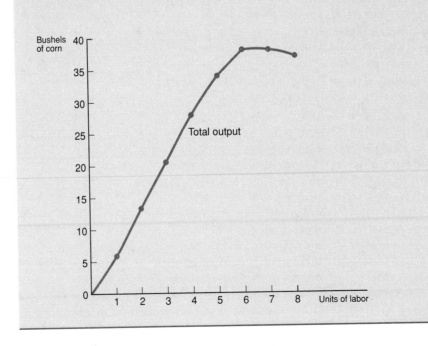

to know about the production process. In particular, two other important concepts are the average product and the marginal product of an input. The *average product* of an input is total product (that is, total output) divided by the amount of the input used to produce this amount of output. The *marginal product* of an input is the addition to total output due to the addition of the last unit of the input, when the amounts of other inputs used are held constant.

To illustrate these concepts, let us go back to the farmer in Table 6.1. On the basis of the production function shown in this table, we can compute the average product and marginal product of labor. Both the average product and the marginal product of labor will vary, of course, depending on how much labor is used. If $Q(L)$ is the total output rate when L units of labor are used per year, the average product of labor when L units of labor are used per year is $Q(L)/L$. And the marginal product of labor when between L and $(L - 1)$ units of labor are used per year is

$$[Q(L) - Q(L - 1)].$$

Thus the average product of labor is 6 bushels of corn per unit of labor when 1 unit of labor is used, and the marginal product of labor is 7.5 bushels of corn per unit of labor when between 1 and 2 units of labor are used. The results for other levels of utilization of labor are shown in Table 6.2.

TABLE 6.2 Average and Marginal Products of Labor

Amount of labor	Total output	Average product of labor	Marginal product of labor*
0	0	—	—
1	6.0	6.00	6.0
2	13.5	6.75	7.5
3	21.0	7.00	7.5
4	28.0	7.00	7.0
5	34.0	6.80	6.0
6	38.0	6.33	4.0
7	38.0	5.43	0.0
8	37.0	4.62	−1.0

*These figures pertain to the interval between the indicated amount of labor and one unit less than the indicated amount of labor.

Panel A of Figure 6.2 shows the average product curve for labor. The numbers are taken from Table 6.2. As is typically the case for production processes, the average product of labor (which is the only variable input in this case) rises, reaches a maximum, and then falls. Panel B of Figure 6.2 shows the marginal product curve for labor. (These numbers also are taken from Table 6.2.) The marginal product of labor also rises, reaches a maximum, and then falls. This, too, is typical of many production processes.[6] Finally, panel C of Figure 6.2

6. Sometimes, however, an input's marginal product decreases throughout the entire range of its utilization.

FIGURE 6.2 Average and Marginal Product Curves for Labor
*Marginal product exceeds average product when the latter is increasing, and
is less than average product when the latter is decreasing.*

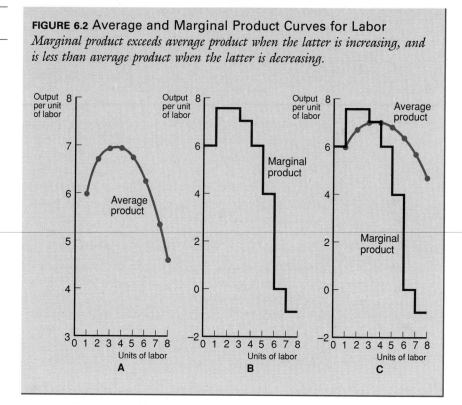

shows both the average product curve and the marginal product curve for
labor. As is always the case, marginal product exceeds average product when the
latter is increasing, equals average product when the latter reaches a maximum,
and is less than average product when the latter is decreasing. This is simply a
matter of arithmetic: If the addition to a total is greater (less) than the average,
the average is bound to increase (decrease).[7]

Tables 6.1 and 6.2 are constructed on the assumption that land, the fixed
input, is equal to one acre. Suppose that we could increase the amount of land
to two acres. What effect would this have on total output and on the average
and marginal products of labor? Generally, over the relevant range of production, an increase in the fixed input will result in an increase in all of them. For
example, the result might be like that shown in Figure 6.3.

7. If x is the amount of the variable input that is used and

$$Q = f(x)$$

where Q is the output rate, then the average product of the variable input is $Q \div x = f(x) \div x$,
and the marginal product of the variable input is $dQ/dx = df(x)/dx$.
   Thus average product is a maximum when

$$\frac{d(Q/x)}{dx} = \left(\frac{dQ}{dx} - \frac{Q}{x} \right) \frac{1}{x} = 0,$$

which means that dQ/dx must equal Q/x when the average product is a maximum. But since
dQ/dx is the marginal product and Q/x is the average product, this proves the proposition in
the text: When the average product is a maximum, the average product equals the marginal
product.

FIGURE 6.3 Total Output, Average Product, and Marginal Product
Curves for Labor, with One and Two Acres of Land *An increase in
the amount of land results in a shift in all three of these curves. (Note that
only part of each of these curves is shown; the region where average or
marginal product is increasing is omitted.)*

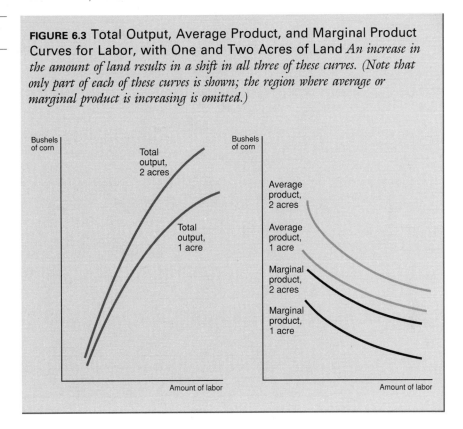

THE LAW OF DIMINISHING MARGINAL RETURNS AND THE GEOMETRY OF AVERAGE AND MARGINAL PRODUCT CURVES

Previous sections have defined the production function and the average and
marginal products of an input. We are now in a position to discuss one of the
most famous laws of microeconomics—the law of diminishing marginal
returns. The law of diminishing marginal returns, like the Scriptures, is often
quoted and frequently misinterpreted. Put very briefly, this law states that *if
equal increments of an input are added, the quantities of other inputs held constant,
the resulting increments of product will decrease beyond some point; that is, the marginal product of the input will diminish.* This law is illustrated by Table 6.2;
beyond 3 units of labor, the marginal product of labor decreases.

Several things should be noted concerning this law. First, the law of diminishing marginal returns is an empirical generalization, not a deduction from
physical or biological laws. In fact, it seems to hold for most production functions in the real world. Second, it is assumed that technology remains fixed. The
law of diminishing marginal returns cannot predict the effect of an additional
unit of input when technology is allowed to change. Third, it is assumed that
there is at least one input whose quantity is being held constant. The law of

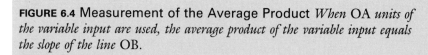

FIGURE 6.4 Measurement of the Average Product *When* OA *units of the variable input are used, the average product of the variable input equals the slope of the line* OB.

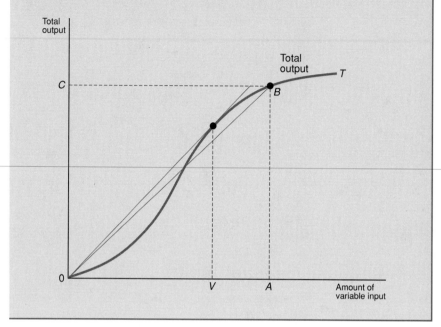

diminishing marginal returns does not apply to cases where there is a proportional increase in all inputs. Fourth, it must be possible, of course, to vary the proportions in which the various inputs are used.

If there is a fixed input and only one variable input, the typical form of the relationship between the amount of the variable input and the total output is given by *OT* in Figure 6.4.[8] Given such a graph, how can we determine the average product and the marginal product of the variable input? To make the analysis more concrete, suppose that Figure 6.4 refers to another farm like the one in Table 6.1, that the output is corn, and that the variable input is labor. First, consider the average product of the variable input, labor. Since average product equals total output divided by the amount of variable input, the average product of any amount of variable input, *OA*, equals *AB*(= *OC*) divided by *OA*. And *AB/OA* is obviously the slope of the line, *OB,* which joins the origin and the point on the total output curve corresponding to this amount of variable input. Thus the slope of the line joining the origin and the relevant point on the total output curve is equal to the average product of the variable input, labor.

Second, consider the marginal product of the variable input, labor. Given the total output curve in Figure 6.5 (which is the same as that in Figure 6.4), how can we determine the marginal product? If the amount of variable input

---

8. In Figure 6.4, we assume that the amount of the variable input is varied continuously, with the result that the total output, the average product, and the marginal product curves are continuous.

FIGURE 6.5 Measurement of Marginal Product *The marginal product of the variable input equals the slope of line* NN' *when* OG *units of variable input are used.*

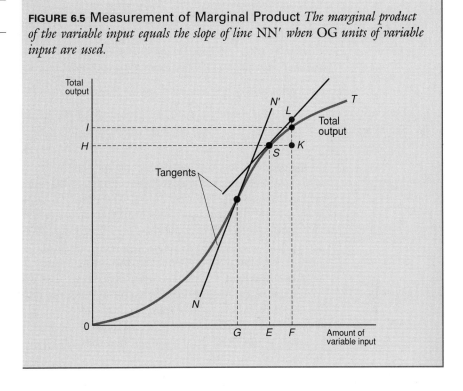

increases from *OE* to *OF,* total output increases from *OH* to *OI.* Clearly, as the increment in the amount of variable input becomes smaller and smaller, the extra output divided by the extra variable input, *HI/EF,* approaches the slope of the total output curve at *S.* (Even if the increment is *EF,* the approximation is not too bad: The slope of the total output curve is *KL/SK = KL/EF,* which is fairly close to *HI/EF.*) Thus, since the slope of a curve at any point equals the slope of its tangent at that point, we can determine the marginal product of any amount of variable input by drawing the tangent to the total output curve at that amount of variable input and measuring its slope. For example, the slope of *NN'* is the marginal product of variable input when *OG* units of variable input are used.

Using these results, it is possible to prove a number of interesting results concerning the average product curve (the curve showing the relationship between average product and the amount of variable input used) and the marginal product curve (the curve showing the relationship between marginal product and the amount of variable input used). To begin with, in Figure 6.4, since a line joining the origin and a point on the total output curve is bound to be steepest (that is, has the maximum slope) when the line is tangent to the total output curve, it follows that the average product must be a maximum if *OV* units of variable input are used. Moreover, since the tangent to the total output curve is exactly the same as the line joining the origin and the total output curve when *OV* units of the variable input are used, the slope of the tangent must equal the slope of this line, and marginal product must equal average product.

Thus *marginal product must equal average product when the latter is a maximum.*[9] Also, since the marginal product is a maximum at *OG* (Figure 6.5), where the slope of the tangent to the total output curve is greatest, and since *OG* is less than *OV*, it follows that *the maximum marginal product occurs at a lower level of variable input than the maximum average product.*

THE PRODUCTION FUNCTION: TWO VARIABLE INPUTS

In the previous sections, we were concerned with the case in which there is only one variable input. In the next four sections, we take up the more general case in which there are two variable inputs. These variable inputs can be thought of as working with one or more fixed inputs, or they may be thought of as the only two inputs (in which case the situation is the long run). In either case, it is easy to extend the results to as many inputs as one likes. This section takes up the production function, and the next two sections are concerned with its representation through a system of geometric constructs called isoquants.

If we increase the number of variable inputs from one to two, the production function becomes slightly more complicated, but it is still the relationship between various combinations of inputs and the maximum amount of output that can be obtained from them. Really, the only change is that the output is a function of two variables rather than one. For example, suppose in our agricultural example that we allow both land and labor to vary; the results might be given by Table 6.3. This is the production function in tabular form. Note that we can obtain the marginal product of each input by holding the other input constant. For example, the marginal product of land when 4 units of labor are used and when between 1 and 2 acres of land are used is 51 bushels per acre; the marginal product of labor when 2 acres are used and when between 3 and 4 units of labor are used is 20 bushels per unit. Similarly, the average product of

TABLE 6.3 Hypothetical Production Function for Corn, Two Variable Inputs

Amount of labor (units)	Number of acres			
	1	2	3	4
	(bushels of corn produced per year)			
1	5	11	18	24
2	14	30	50	72
3	22	60	80	99
4	29	80	115	125
5	34	84	140	145

9. Of course this is precisely the same result as that stated on p. 146.

FIGURE 6.6 Production Function, Two Variable Inputs *The production surface,* OAQB, *shows the amount of total output that can be obtained from various combinations of quantities of land and labor.*

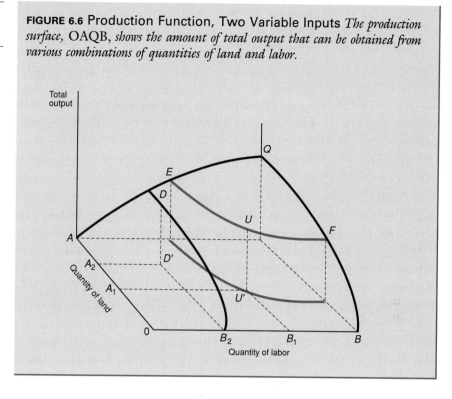

either land or labor can be computed simply by dividing the total output by the amount of either land or labor that is used.[10]

Another way to present the production function is by a surface, like that in Figure 6.6.[11] The production surface is $OAQB$. The height of a point on this surface denotes the quantity of output. Dropping a perpendicular down from a point on the production surface to the "floor" and seeing how far the resulting point is from the labor and land axes indicates how much of each input is required to produce this much output. For example, to produce $U'U$ units of output requires OB_1 $(= A_1U')$ units of labor and OA_1 $(= B_1U')$ acres of land. Conversely, one can take any amounts of land and labor, say OA_2 acres of land and OB_2 units of labor, and find out how much output they will produce by measuring the height of the production surface at D', the point where labor input is OB_2 and land input is OA_2. According to Figure 6.6, the answer equals $D'D$.

Note that this hypothetical production function illustrates the fact that a

---

10. If x_1 is the amount of the first input and x_2 is the amount of the second input, the production function is

$$Q = f(x_1, x_2)$$

where Q is the output rate. The marginal product of the first input is $\partial Q/\partial x_1$; the marginal product of the second input is $\partial Q/\partial x_2$.

11. Note that this surface is not meant to represent the numerical values in Table 6.3 but is a general representation of how a production surface of this sort is likely to appear.

given amount of output can be produced in quite different ways. For example, in Table 6.3, 80 bushels of corn can be produced with either 4 units of labor and 2 acres of land or with 3 units of labor and 3 acres of land. (Moreover, the production function does not include many of the different ways in which a given output can be produced because it includes only efficient combinations of inputs.)[12] Generally there is a variety of ways to produce a given output and a variety of efficient input combinations; thus it is possible for the firm to substitute one input for another in producing a specified amount of output.

ISOQUANTS

Isoquant

An *isoquant* is a curve showing all possible (efficient) combinations of inputs that are capable of producing a certain quantity of output. Given the production function, one can readily derive the isoquant pertaining to any level of output. For example, in Figure 6.6, suppose that we want to find the isoquant corresponding to an output of $U'U$. All that we need to do is to cut the production surface at the height of $U'U$ parallel to the base plane, the result being *EUF,* and to drop perpendiculars from *EUF* to the base. Clearly, this results in a curve that includes all efficient combinations of land and labor that can produce $U'U$ bushels of corn.[13]

Several isoquants, each pertaining to a different output rate, are shown in Figure 6.7. The two axes measure the quantities of inputs that are used. In contrast to the previous diagrams, we assume that labor and capital—not labor and land—are the relevant inputs in this case. The curves show the various combinations of inputs that can produce 50, 100, and 150 units of output. For example, consider the isoquant pertaining to 50 units of output per period of time. According to this isoquant, it is possible to attain this output rate if OL_0 units of labor and OK_0 units of capital are used per period of time. Alternatively, this output rate can be attained if OL_1 units of labor and OK_1 units of capital—or OL_2 units of labor and OK_2 units of capital—are used per period of time.

A *ray* is a line that starts from some point and goes off into space. A ray from the origin, such as *OBDE,* describes all input combinations where the capital-labor ratio is constant, with the slope of the ray being equal to the constant capital-labor ratio. For example, at points D and E, 100 and 150 units of output are produced with a capital-labor ratio of $OK_3/OL_3 = OK_4/OL_4$. Moving out from the origin along any ray, such as *OBDE,* we see that various output levels can be produced with the same ratio of one input to another. Of course, the absolute amount of each input increases as we move out to higher and higher output levels, but the ratio of one input to the other remains constant. It is

12. For example, if 2 units of labor and 3 units of capital can produce 1 unit of output, this combination of inputs and output will not be included in the production function if it is also possible to produce 1 unit of output with 2 units of labor and 2 units of capital. The former input combination is clearly inefficient, since it is possible to obtain the result with the same amount of labor and less capital.

13. Using the notation in footnote 10, an isoquant shows all combinations of x_1 and x_2 such that $f(x_1, x_2)$ equals a certain output rate.

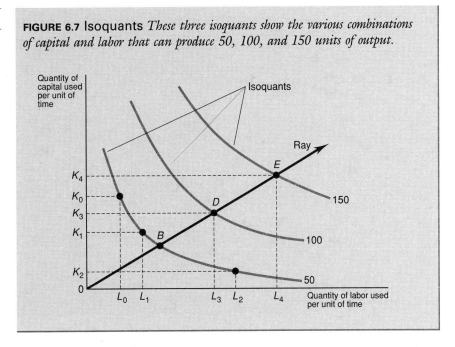

FIGURE 6.7 Isoquants *These three isoquants show the various combinations of capital and labor that can produce 50, 100, and 150 units of output.*

important to understand the difference between such a ray and an isoquant; an isoquant pertains to a fixed, not a changing, output rate and a changing, not a fixed, ratio of inputs.

An isoquant plays much the same kind of role in production theory that an indifference curve plays in demand theory. An indifference curve shows the various combinations of two commodities that provide equal satisfaction to the consumer; an isoquant shows the various combinations of two inputs that result in an equal output for the firm. It is obvious that, like indifference curves, two isoquants cannot intersect. If an intersection were to occur, it would mean that two different output rates are the maximum obtainable from a given combination of resources; this is obviously absurd.

Isoquants can be used to illustrate the case in which inputs must be used in fixed proportions. Figure 6.8 shows a case of this sort; the necessary ratio of capital to labor is the slope of the ray *OP*. The isoquants are right angles, indicating that, if one input is changed while the other input is held constant, there is no increase in the output rate. In other words, the marginal product of either input is zero if the other input is held constant. Sometimes there are a number of processes that can be used to produce a given commodity, each utilizing the inputs in fixed proportions (but with the proportions fixed at different levels). This case is discussed at length in the Appendix to this book, where we take up linear programming.

The Economic Region of Production

In some cases, isoquants may have positively sloped segments, or bend back upon themselves, as shown in Figure 6.9. Above *OA* and below *OB*, the slope of the isoquants is positive, which implies that increases in both capital and

FIGURE 6.8 Isoquants in the Case of Fixed Proportions *If inputs must be used in fixed proportions, the isoquants are right angles.*

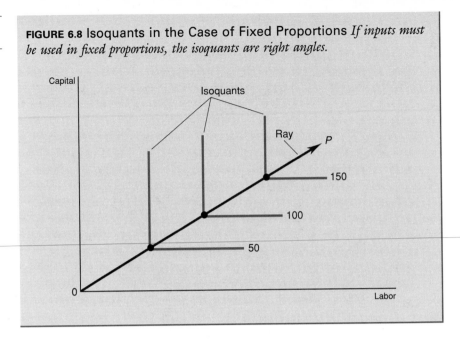

labor are required to maintain a certain output rate. If this is the case, the marginal product of one or the other input must be negative. Above *OA,* the marginal product of capital is negative; thus output will increase if less capital is used, while the amount of labor is held constant. Below *OB,* the marginal product of labor is negative; thus output will increase if less labor is used, while the amount of capital is held constant. The lines *OA* and *OB* are called *ridge lines.*

Clearly, no profit-maximizing firm will operate at a point outside the ridge lines, since it can produce the same output with less of both inputs, which must be cheaper. To illustrate this, consider point *C* in Figure 6.9. Because this is a point where the isoquant is positively sloped—and thus outside the ridge lines—it requires a greater amount of both labor and capital than some other point (for example, point *D*) on the same isoquant. Since both capital and labor have positive prices, it must be cheaper to operate at point *D* than at point *C.* In general, it is always possible to find a cheaper way to produce a given quantity of output than to operate at a point outside the ridge lines. Thus the shaded area between the ridge lines is often called the *economic region of production.* For example, in Figure 6.9, the economic region of production is the area between *OA* and *OB.* No rational firm will venture outside this region.

Substitution among Inputs

From both a practical and a theoretical point of view, it is important to study the rate at which one input must be substituted for another to maintain a constant output rate. Consider the isoquant, *Z,* in Figure 6.10. The relevant output rate can be produced with OL_0 units of labor and OK_0 units of capital. However, if the amount of labor is increased to OL_1, the same output rate can

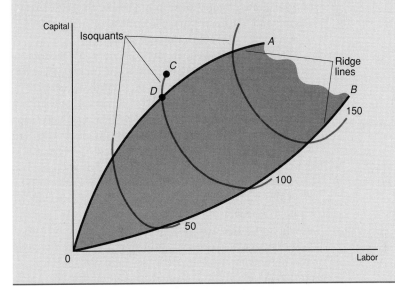

FIGURE 6.9 The Economic Region of Production *No profit-maximizing firm will operate at a point outside the ridge lines,* OA *and* OB.

be attained with less capital: OK_1 units rather than OK_0. Thus, in the relevant range, the rate at which labor can be substituted for capital is $- (OK_0 - OK_1)/(OL_0 - OL_1) = BA/BC$; the minus sign is added to make the result a positive number. If we consider a very small increase in labor (OL_1 being very

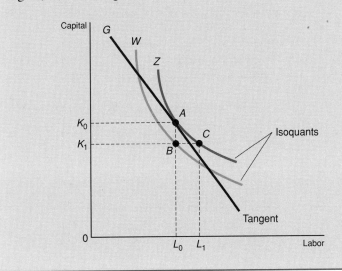

FIGURE 6.10 The Marginal Rate of Technical Substitution *The marginal rate of technical substitution equals minus one times the slope of the tangent,* G, *to the isoquant.*

close to OL_0), BA/BC equals -1 times the slope of the tangent, G, to the isoquant at A, which is called the *marginal rate of technical substitution*. It measures, for small changes in labor, the change in capital required per unit change in labor. The reader will note that, as its name indicates, it is analogous to the marginal rate of substitution in demand theory. (Economists, having found an elegant and felicitous phrase like the marginal rate of substitution, did not want to abandon it for anything cumbersome.)

Using the diagram in Figure 6.10, it is easy to demonstrate that the marginal rate of technical substitution of labor for capital is equal to the ratio of the marginal product of labor to the marginal product of capital. Suppose that labor input is held at the OL_0 level, while capital is increased from OK_1 to OK_0. Output would increase from the level (say Q_1) corresponding to isoquant W to the level (say Q_0) corresponding to isoquant Z. The marginal product of capital is $(Q_0 - Q_1) \div (OK_0 - OK_1) = (Q_0 - Q_1) \div BA$. On the other hand, suppose that capital is held at OK_1 while labor is increased from OL_0 to OL_1. The marginal product of labor is $(Q_0 - Q_1) \div (OL_1 - OL_0) = (Q_0 - Q_1) \div BC$. Thus the ratio of the marginal product of labor to the marginal product of capital equals $BA \div BC$, which (in the limit for small changes in the amount of labor) equals the marginal rate of technical substitution.[14]

It is also easy to show that the marginal rate of technical substitution of labor for capital tends to decrease as an increasing amount of labor is substituted for capital. As labor is substituted for capital, the marginal product of labor tends to fall. Increases in labor, holding capital constant, result in a decrease in the marginal product of labor in the economic region of production. When capital is decreased, even more of a decrease occurs in the marginal product of labor, since a decrease in capital results in a downward shift in the marginal product curve for labor. At the same time, the marginal product of capital rises (for the same kinds of reasons) as more labor is substituted for capital. Thus, since the marginal rate of technical substitution equals the marginal product of labor (which is falling) divided by the marginal product of capital (which is rising), it must be falling as labor is substituted for capital.

Since the marginal rate of technical substitution falls as labor is substituted for capital, it follows that isoquants must be convex. (See p. 56.) Because the marginal rate of technical substitution equals -1 times the slope of the isoquant and because the marginal rate of technical substitution falls as we move to the right along an isoquant, the absolute value of the slope of the isoquant must be

14. Using the notation in footnote 10, the total differential of the production function is

$$dQ = \frac{\partial f}{\partial x_1} dx_1 + \frac{\partial f}{\partial x_2} dx_2.$$

Since output remains constant along an isoquant, $dQ = 0$ along an isoquant. Thus

$$\frac{\partial f}{\partial x_1} dx_1 + \frac{\partial f}{\partial x_2} dx_2 = 0,$$

and the marginal rate of technical substitution, defined as $-dx_2/dx_1$, is

$$\frac{\partial f}{\partial x_1} \div \frac{\partial f}{\partial x_2},$$

which is the ratio of the marginal product of the first input to the marginal product of the second input. This is another proof of the proposition in the text.

EXAMPLE 6.2

MILK PRODUCTION
Based on data obtained by the U.S. Department of Agriculture, 8,500 pounds of milk can be produced during a specified time period by a cow fed the following combinations of quantities of hay and grain:

Quantity of hay (pounds)	Quantity of grain (pounds)
5,000	6,154
5,500	5,454
6,000	4,892
6,500	4,423
7,000	4,029
7,500	3,694

(a) Plot these data as an isoquant. (b) Calculate the marginal rate of technical substitution at all points along this isoquant. (c) Is this isoquant convex? (d) If the price of a pound of hay equals the price of a pound of grain, should a cow be fed 5,000 pounds of hay and 6,154 pounds of grain?

SOLUTION

(a) The isoquant is as follows:

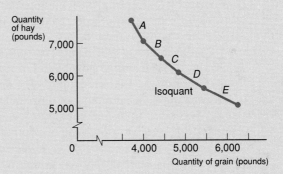

(b) For each segment (A, B, . . . , E) of the isoquant, the marginal rate of technical substitution is as follows:

Segment	Marginal rate of technical substitution
A	$-(7,500 - 7,000) \div (3,694 - 4,029) = 1.49$
B	$-(7,000 - 6,500) \div (4,029 - 4,423) = 1.27$
C	$-(6,500 - 6,000) \div (4,423 - 4,892) = 1.07$
D	$-(6,000 - 5,500) \div (4,892 - 5,454) = 0.89$
E	$-(5,500 - 5,000) \div (5,454 - 6,154) = 0.71$

(c) Yes, since the marginal rate of technical substitution falls as more grain is substituted for hay. (d) No, because other combinations of quantities of hay and grain are cheaper. If P equals the price of a pound of either hay or grain, the cost of 5,000 pounds of hay and 6,154 pounds of grain is $11,154P$. In contrast, the cost of 6,000 pounds of hay and 4,892 pounds of grain is $10,892P$, which is lower.*

*For further discussion, see E. Heady's classic work, *Economics of Agricultural Production and Resource Use* (New York: Prentice-Hall, 1952).

getting smaller as we move to the right along an isoquant. But if the absolute value of the slope is getting smaller as we move to the right, the isoquant must be convex.

THE LONG RUN AND RETURNS TO SCALE

Previous sections have shown how a firm's technology can be represented by a production function and have described the characteristics of production functions (and of related concepts like the marginal and average product) that seem to hold in general for production processes. However, one important characteristic of production functions has not been described: how output responds in the long run to changes in the *scale* of the firm. In other words, suppose that we consider a long-run situation in which all inputs are variable, and suppose that the firm increases the amount of all inputs by the same proportion. What will happen to output? This is an important question, the answer to which (as we shall see in subsequent chapters) helps to determine whether firms of certain sizes can survive in the industry.

Increasing, decreasing, and constant returns to scale

To repeat, what will happen to output under the assumed conditions? Clearly, there are three possibilities: First, output may increase by a larger proportion than each of the inputs. For example, a doubling of all inputs may lead to more than a doubling of output. This is the case of *increasing returns to scale*. Second, output may increase by a smaller proportion than each of the inputs. For example, a doubling of all inputs may lead to less than a doubling of output. This is the case of *decreasing returns to scale*. Third, output may increase by exactly the same proportion as the inputs. For example, a doubling of all inputs may lead to a doubling of output. This is the case of *constant returns to scale*.

At first glance it may seem that production functions must necessarily exhibit constant returns to scale. After all, if two factories are built with the same plant and the same types of workers, it would seem obvious that twice as much output will result. Unfortunately (or fortunately, depending on your point of view), it is not as simple as that. For instance, if a firm doubles its scale, it may be able to use techniques that could not be used at the smaller scale. Thus, although one could double a firm's size by simply building two small factories, this may be inefficient. One large factory may be more efficient than two smaller factories of the same total capacity because it is large enough to use certain techniques that the smaller factories cannot use.

Another reason for increasing returns to scale stems from certain geometrical relations. For example, since the volume of a box that is $4 \times 4 \times 4$ feet is 64 times as great as the volume of a box that is $1 \times 1 \times 1$ foot, the former box can carry 64 times as much as the latter box. But since the area of the six sides of the $4 \times 4 \times 4$-foot box is 96 square feet and the area of the six sides of the $1 \times 1 \times 1$-foot box is 6 square feet, the former box only requires 16 times as much wood as the latter. Greater specialization also can result in increasing returns to scale: As more men and machines are used, it is possible to subdivide tasks and allow various inputs to specialize. Also economies of scale may arise because of probabilistic considerations: For example, because the aggregate behavior of a bigger number of customers tends to be more stable, a firm's inventory may not have to increase in proportion to its sales.

Decreasing returns to scale can also occur; the most frequently cited reason is the difficulty of coordinating a large enterprise. It can be difficult even in a small firm to obtain the information required to make important decisions; in a large firm, the difficulties tend to be greater. It can be difficult even in a small firm to be certain that management's wishes are being carried out; in a larger firm these difficulties too tend to be greater. Although the advantages of a large organization seem to have captured the public fancy, there are often very great disadvantages. For example, in certain kinds of research and development, there is evidence that large engineering teams tend to be less effective than smaller ones and that large firms tend to be less effective than small ones.

Diagrams like those in Figure 6.11 can be used to analyze and describe the situation in a particular firm. Panel A describes a case in which there are constant returns to scale. Examination of the isoquants for outputs of 50, 100, and 150 units shows that they intersect any ray from the origin, like OA, at equal distances. (That is, $OD = DC = CB$.) In other words, twice as much of both inputs are needed to produce 100 units of output than to produce 50 units of

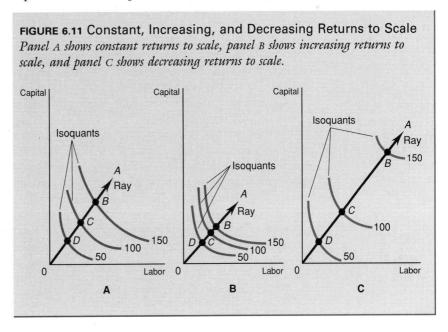

FIGURE 6.11 Constant, Increasing, and Decreasing Returns to Scale
Panel A shows constant returns to scale, panel B shows increasing returns to scale, and panel C shows decreasing returns to scale.

output, and three times as much of both inputs are needed to produce 150 units of output than to produce 50 units of output. Panel B describes a case in which there are increasing returns to scale. In this case, successive isoquants, as one moves out from the origin, become closer and closer together. For example, $OD > DC > CB$. Panel C describes a case in which there are decreasing returns to scale. In this case, successive isoquants become farther and farther apart as we move out from the origin. For example, $OD < DC < CB$.

Whether or not there are constant, increasing, or decreasing returns to scale in a particular situation is an empirical question that must be settled case by case. There is no simple, all-encompassing answer.[15] In some industries the available evidence may indicate that increasing returns are present over a certain range of output. In other industries, decreasing or constant returns may be present. In the next section, we turn to a discussion of empirical studies.

MEASUREMENT OF PRODUCTION FUNCTIONS

Economists and statisticians have devoted a great deal of time and effort, particularly in the past forty years, to the measurement of production functions. Three methods have been used in most of these studies. The first method is

Time-series data   based on the statistical analysis of time-series data concerning the amount of various inputs used in various periods in the past and the amount of output produced in each period. For example, one might obtain data concerning the amount of labor, the amount of capital, and the amount of various raw materials used in the aluminum industry during each year from 1961 to 1991. On the basis of such data and information concerning the annual output of aluminum during 1961 to 1991, one might estimate the relationship between the amounts of the inputs and the resulting output.

The second method is based on the statistical analysis of cross-section data

Cross-section data   concerning the amount of various inputs used and output produced in various firms or sectors of the industry at a given point in time. For example, one might obtain data concerning the amount of labor, the amount of capital, and the amount of various raw materials used in various firms in the aluminum industry in 1991. On the basis of such data and information concerning the 1991 output of each firm, one might estimate the relationship between the amounts of the inputs and the resulting output.

The third method is based on technical information supplied by the engineer

Engineering data   or the agricultural scientist. This information is collected by experiment or from experience with the day-to-day workings of the technical process. There are considerable advantages to be gained from approaching the measurement of the production function from this angle because the range of applicability of the data is known, and, unlike time-series and cross-section studies, we are not restricted to the narrow range of actual observations. However, there are also some difficult problems in this approach, which are discussed in the following paragraphs.

15. Also, it is important to note that the answer is likely to depend on the level of output that is considered. There may be increasing returns to scale at small output levels and constant or decreasing returns to scale at larger output levels.

EXAMPLE 6.3

SHOULD TWO NEW YORK DAIRY FARMS MERGE?

Agricultural economists have estimated the production function for many
types of farms, here and abroad. Suppose that a study came up with the
following result for a particular type of New York dairy farm:

$$Q = KA^{.1}L^{.1}E^{.1}S^{.7}R^{.1}, \qquad [6.1]$$

where Q is output per period, A is the amount of land used, L is the amount of
labor used, E is the amount of equipment used, S is the amount of livestock
and feed used, R is the amount of other resources used, and K is a
constant.

The owner of a New York dairy farm of this type is concerned that his farm
may be too small to compete effectively with larger dairy farms. His farm is of
below-average size, and he is troubled by the possibility that larger farms may
be more efficient than farms like his. He is considering the merger of his farm
with a neighboring farm that is essentially the same (in size and other characteristics) as his own, and he hires you to advise him on this score. What's the
answer?

SOLUTION

According to the estimate of the production function in Equation 6.1, there
are increasing returns to scale in dairy farming of this type. To see that this is
true, if the amount of every input is doubled, Equation 6.1 states that output
will equal Q', where

$$\begin{aligned}
Q' &= K(2A)^{.1}(2L)^{.1}(2E)^{.1}(2S)^{.7}(2R)^{.1} \\
&= 2^{(.1 + .1 + .1 + .7 + .1)}[KA^{.1}L^{.1}E^{.1}S^{.7}R^{.1}] \\
&= 2^{1.1}Q \\
&= 2.14Q.
\end{aligned}$$

Consequently, a 100 percent increase in all inputs leads to a 114 percent
increase in output.

If this production function is a reliable representation of the technology of
New York dairy farms of this type, it appears that the proposed merger would
increase productivity (since doubling all inputs would more than double output). But before making a final decision, the farmer should make sure that the

production function is based on accurate data that really do pertain to farms like his own. (For example, if the data pertain entirely to farms that are much smaller than his, the results may be quite misleading.) Also, to determine whether such a merger would be worthwhile, there are many other factors to consider besides the effects on productivity. (For example, would the merger result in the farmer's exposure to additional financial risk?) All that can be said on the basis of the evidence presented here is that the proposed merger might well increase productivity.

All three approaches are handicapped by the fact that the data may not always represent technically efficient combinations of inputs and output. For example, because of errors or constraints, the amount of inputs used by the aluminum industry in 1991 may not have been the minimum required to produce the 1991 output of the aluminum industry. Since the production function theoretically includes only efficient input combinations, a case of this sort should be excluded, if our measurements are to be pristine pure. In practice, however, such cases are not always excluded (or recognized) and the resulting estimate of the production function is in error for this reason.

Another important problem is the measurement of capital input. The principal difficulty stems from the fact that the stock of capital is composed of various types and ages of machines, buildings, and inventories. Combining them into a single measure—or a few measures—is a formidable problem. In addition, errors can arise in the first two techniques because various data points, which are assumed to be on the same production function, are in fact on different ones. Moreover, biases can occur because of identification problems somewhat similar to those discussed on page 125.

With regard to the third method, it is difficult to combine the results for the processes for which engineers have data into an overall plant or firm production function. Since engineering data generally pertain to only a part of the firm's activities, this is often a very hard job. For example, engineering data tell us little or nothing about the firm's marketing or financial activities. Moreover, engineering data are generally available for only parts of the firm's fabricating activities.

Despite these difficulties, estimates of production functions have proved of considerable interest and value. Many of these estimates have been based on the assumption that the production function is a so-called Cobb-Douglas function, which is

$$Q = AL^{\alpha_1}K^{\alpha_2}M^{\alpha_3} \qquad [6.2]$$

Cobb-Douglas function

where Q is the output rate; L is the quantity of labor; K is the quantity of capital; and M is the quantity of raw materials; and A, α_1, α_2, and α_3 are parameters that vary from case to case. Ordinarily it is assumed that the value of each α is less than 1, which ensures that the marginal product of each input (which equals its α times its average product) decreases with increases in its utilization. Increasing returns to scale occur if $\alpha_1 + \alpha_2 + \alpha_3 > 1$; decreasing returns to scale occur if $\alpha_1 + \alpha_2 + \alpha_3 < 1$.[16]

16. In Equation 6.2, there are three inputs. In other Cobb-Douglas production functions, there may be more or less than three inputs. On page 161, there are five inputs in the Cobb-Douglas

TABLE 6.4 Estimates of α_1, α_2, and α_3 for Selected Industries

Industry	Country	α_1	α_2	α_3	$\alpha_1+\alpha_2+\alpha_3$
Gas	France	.83	.10	—	0.93
Railroads	United States	.89	.12	.28	1.29
Coal	United Kingdom	.79	.29	—	1.08
Food	United States	.72	.35	—	1.07
Metals and machinery	United States	.71	.26	—	0.97
Communications	Soviet Union	.80	.38	—	1.18
Cotton	India	.92	.12	—	1.04
Jute	India	.84	.14	—	0.98
Sugar	India	.59	.33	—	0.92
Coal	India	.71	.44	—	1.15
Paper	India	.64	.45	—	1.09
Chemicals	India	.80	.37	—	1.17
Electricity	India	.20	.67	—	0.87
Food*	United States	.63	.44	—	1.07
Paper*	United States	.62	.37	—	0.98
Telephone	Canada	.70	.41	—	1.11
Chemicals†	United States	.54	.38	.11	1.03
Aircraft†	United States	.79	.18	.04	1.01

*The figure for α_1 is the sum of the figures given for production workers and nonproduction workers.

†In these cases, M is cumulated past expenditure on research and development, not the quantity of raw materials, and K is the quantity of capital services.

Source: A. A. Walters, "Production and Cost Functions." *Econometrica,* January 1963: J. Moroney, "Cobb-Douglas Production Functions and Returns to Scale in U.S. Manufacturing," *Western Economic Journal,* 1967; A. Dobell, L. Taylor, L. Waverman, T. Liu, and M. Copeland, "Communications in Canada," *Bell Journal of Economics and Management Science,* 1972; J. P. Lewis, "Postwar Economic Growth and Productivity in the Soviet Communications Industry," *Bell Journal of Economics and Management Sciences.* Autumn 1975; and Z. Griliches, "Returns to Research and Development Expenditures in the Private Sector," in J. Kendrick and B. Vaccara, *New Developments in Productivity Measurement and Analysis* (Chicago: National Bureau of Economic Research, 1980).

Table 6.4 shows the estimates of α_1, α_2, and α_3 for a number of industries in the United States and abroad. They provide interesting information concerning production relations in these industries. To see more clearly the implications of these results, note that α_1 is the percentage increase in output resulting from a 1 percent increase in labor, holding the quantities of the other inputs constant. For example, in the Canadian telephone industry in about 1972, a 1 percent increase in labor would have resulted in a 0.70 percent increase in output. Similarly, α_2 is the percentage increase in output resulting from a 1 percent increase in capital, holding the quantities of other inputs constant.

The results also cast light on returns to scale. In 6 of the 18 cases, there seem

production function in Equation 6.1. Since the sum of the exponents in Equation 6.1 is greater than 1 (in fact, it is 1.1), this production function exhibits increasing returns to scale, as we prove on page 161.

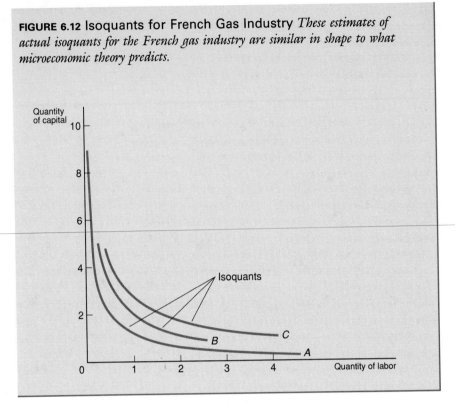

FIGURE 6.12 Isoquants for French Gas Industry *These estimates of actual isoquants for the French gas industry are similar in shape to what microeconomic theory predicts.*

to be decreasing returns; in 12 of the 18 cases there seem to be increasing returns to scale. Finally, it is possible to construct isoquants from the results in Table 6.4. For example, Figure 6.12 shows some isoquants for the French gas industry. Note that these isoquants (*A, B,* and *C*) are similar in shape to the hypothetical isoquants introduced earlier in this chapter.[17]

Summary

1. As a first approximation, economists generally assume that firms attempt to maximize profits. This is the standard assumption in economics, because it is a close enough approximation for many important purposes and because it provides rules of behavior for firms that do want to make as much money as possible.
2. The production function is used by economists to represent the technology available to the firm. For any commodity, the production function is the relationship between the quantities of various inputs used per period of time and the maximum quantity of the commodity produced per period of time.
3. In analyzing production processes, we generally assume that all inputs can be

17. For further discussion, see M. Brown, *The Theory and Empirical Analysis of Production* (New York: National Bureau of Economic Research, 1967). There has also been much use made of the transcendental logarithmic production function described in L. Christenson, D. Jorgenson, and L. Lau, "Conjugate Duality and the Transcendental Logarithmic Production Function," *Econometrica,* July 1971. The French data in Figure 6.12 come from studies by M. Verhulst of the gas industry.

divided into two categories: fixed and variable. In the short run, the firm's plant and equipment are fixed; in the long run, all inputs are variable. Both in the short run and in the long run, a firm's production processes ordinarily permit substantial variation in input proportions.

4. The law of diminishing marginal returns states that as equal increments of one input are added, the quantities of other inputs held constant, the resulting increments of product will decrease beyond some point; that is, the marginal product of the input will diminish.

5. An input's marginal product must equal its average product when the latter is a maximum. The maximum marginal product occurs at a lower level of variable input than the maximum average product.

6. An isoquant is a curve that shows all possible combinations of inputs that are capable of producing a certain quantity of output. We can construct ridge lines so that all points where the isoquants are positively sloped lie outside the ridge lines. No rational firm will operate outside the ridge lines because the marginal product of one or the other input is negative in this region.

7. If the firm increases all inputs by the same proportion and output increases by more (less) than this proportion, there are increasing (decreasing) returns to scale. Whether or not there are constant, increasing, or decreasing returns to scale is an empirical question that must be settled case by case.

8. Economists and statisticians have devoted a great deal of time and effort to the measurement of production functions. Three methods have been used in most of these studies: statistical analysis based on time series of inputs and output, statistical analysis based on cross-section data, and analysis based on engineering data. Although there are a great many difficulties in existing measurement techniques, estimates of production functions have proved of considerable interest and value.

1. Fill in the blanks in the following table:

Number of units of variable input	Total output (number of units)	Marginal product* of variable input	Average product of variable input
3	—	Unknown	30
4	—	20	—
5	130	—	—
6	—	5	—
7	—	—	$19\frac{1}{2}$

*These figures pertain to the interval between the indicated amount of the variable input and one unit less than the indicated amount of the variable input.

2. In Question 1, does the production function exhibit diminishing marginal returns? If so, at what number of units of variable input do diminishing marginal returns begin to set in? Can you tell on the basis of the table in Question 1?

3. As the quantity of a variable input increases, explain why the point where *marginal* product begins to decline is encountered before the point where *average* product begins to decline. Explain, too, why the point where *average* product begins to decline is encountered before the point where *total* output begins to decline.

4. Suppose that a good is produced with two inputs, labor and capital, and that the production function is

$$Q = 10 \sqrt{L} \sqrt{K}$$

where Q is the quantity of output, L is the quantity of labor, and K is the quantity of capital. Does this production function exhibit increasing returns to scale? Decreasing returns to scale? Constant returns to scale? Explain.

5. Econometric studies of the cotton industry in India indicate that the Cobb-Douglas production function can be applied, and that the exponent of labor is .92 and the exponent of capital is .12. Suppose that both capital and labor were increased by 1 percent. By what percent would output increase?

6. In an article published by the Federal Reserve Bank of Philadelphia in 1989, it is suggested that bank managers "be encouraged to own stock in the companies they manage. In this way, they would directly benefit from the decisions they make that increase the market value of the bank."[18] Is this suggestion aimed at solving the principal-agent problem? If so, how effective do you think it would be?

7. (Advanced) Suppose you are assured by the owner of an aircraft factory that his firm is subject to constant returns to scale, with labor and capital the only inputs. He claims that output per worker is a function of capital per worker only. Is he right?

8. Laserex, a manufacturer of lasers, reports that the marginal product of labor is 10 units of output per hour of labor and that the marginal rate of technical substitution of labor for capital is 5. What is the marginal product of capital?

9. The following graph shows the combinations of quantities of grain and protein that must be used to produce 150 pounds of pork. Curve A assumes that no Aureomycin is added, while curve B assumes that some of it is added.

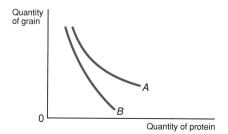

(a) If Aureomycin can be obtained free, should pork producers add it? (b) Does the addition of Aureomycin affect the marginal rate of technical substitution? If so, how?

10. Suppose that an entrepreneur's utility depends on the size of his or her firm (as measured by its output) and its profits. In particular, the indifference curves are as follows:

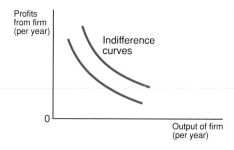

(a) Will the entrepreneur maximize profit? (b) If not, will he or she produce more or less than the profit-maximizing output? (c) Draw a graph to indicate the point he or she will choose. (Hint: Reread Example 6.1.)

18. L. Mester, "Owners Versus Managers: Who Controls the Bank?", *Business Review*, May 1989.

OPTIMAL INPUT COMBINATIONS AND COST FUNCTIONS

DECISIONS REGARDING INPUT COMBINATIONS

In the previous chapter we were concerned with the motivation of the firm and the way in which the technology available to the firm can be represented. We decided to assume, as a first approximation, that firms attempt to maximize profit. We also decided that the technology available to the firm can be represented by a production function, which conforms to certain rules like the law of diminishing marginal returns. These decisions take us part way—but only part way—toward a model of the firm. The next step is to determine how a profit-maximizing firm will combine inputs to produce a given quantity of output. That is the purpose of this chapter.

To be specific, suppose that a producer of electronic computers decides for some reason to produce 100,000 computers next year. Suppose that, in accord with the conclusions of the previous chapter, we assume that the firm is an out-and-out profit maximizer, and that we are given its production function, derived largely through engineering studies and statistical analysis. On the basis of this information, can we predict what combination of inputs the firm will use to produce 100,000 computers next year and how much it will cost to produce this amount? Or putting the problem somewhat differently, suppose that we are hired by the firm to help with this decision. Can we tell the firm what combination of inputs it *should* use and how much it *should* cost to produce this amount?

In this chapter, we begin by determining which combination of inputs a firm will choose if it minimizes the cost of producing a given amount of output.

Then we discuss the nature of costs—what is meant by a cost and how various concepts of cost differ from one another. Finally, we show how the short-run and long-run cost functions of the firm can be derived theoretically, and we provide a brief discussion of the measurement of cost functions.

THE OPTIMAL COMBINATION OF INPUTS

For the sake of generality, let's consider a firm of any sort, not just the computer firm noted previously. If the firm maximizes profit, it will minimize the cost of producing a given output or maximize the output derived from a given level of cost.[1] This seems obvious. Suppose that the firm is a perfect competitor in the input markets, which means that it takes input prices as given. (The case in which the firm can influence input prices is taken up in Chapter 13.) Suppose that there are two inputs, capital and labor, that are variable in the relevant time period. What combination of capital and labor should the firm choose if it wants to maximize the quantity of output derived from the given level of cost?

As a first step toward answering this question, let's determine the various combinations of inputs that the firm can obtain for a given expenditure. For example, if capital and labor are the inputs and the price of labor is P_L per unit and the price of capital is P_K per unit, the input combinations that can be obtained for a total outlay of R are such that

$$P_L L + P_K K = R \qquad [7.1]$$

where L is the amount of the labor input and K is the amount of the capital input. Given P_L, P_K, and R, it follows that

$$K = \frac{R}{P_K} - \frac{P_L}{P_K} L. \qquad [7.2]$$

Isocost curve Thus the various combinations of capital and labor that can be purchased, given P_L, P_K, and R, can be represented by a straight line like that shown in Figure 7.1. (Capital is plotted on the vertical axis, labor is plotted on the horizontal.) This line, which has an intercept on the vertical axis equal to R/P_K and a slope of $- P_L/P_K$, is called an *isocost curve*.

If we superimpose the relevant isocost curve on the firm's isoquant map, we can readily determine graphically which combination of inputs will maximize the output for the given expenditure. Obviously, the firm should pick that point on the isocost curve that is on the highest isoquant, for example, P in Figure 7.2. This clearly is a point where the isocost curve is tangent to the isoquant. Thus, since the slope of the isocost curve is the negative of P_L/P_K and the slope of the isoquant is the negative of the marginal rate of technical substitution, it follows that the optimal combination of inputs must be such that the ratio of input prices, P_L/P_K, equals the marginal rate of technical substitution. And since it will be recalled that the marginal rate of technical substitution

1. The conditions for minimizing the cost of producing a given output are the same as those for maximizing the output from a given cost. This is shown in the present section. Thus we can view the firm's problem in either way.

FIGURE 7.1 Isocost Curve *The isocost curve shows the combinations of inputs that can be obtained for a total outlay of* R.

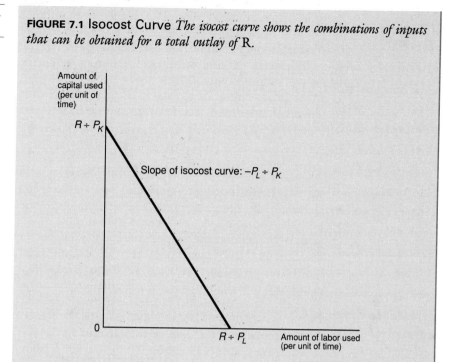

FIGURE 7.2 Maximization of Output for Given Cost *To maximize output for a given cost, the firm should choose the input combination at point* P.

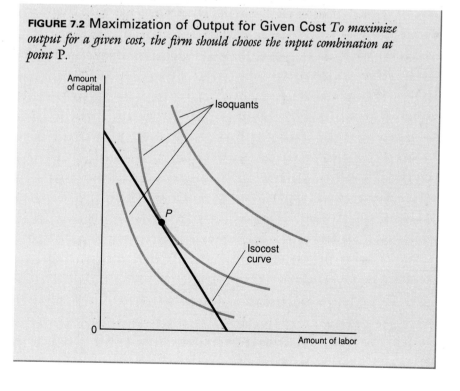

of labor for capital is MP_L/MP_K, it follows that the optimal combination of inputs is one where $MP_L/MP_K = P_L/P_K$. Or, put differently, the firm should choose an input combination where $MP_L/P_L = MP_K/P_K$.

In general, the firm will maximize output by distributing its expenditures among various inputs in such a way that the marginal product of a dollar's worth of any one input is equal to the marginal product of a dollar's worth of any other input used. The firm will choose an input combination such that

$$\frac{MP_a}{P_a} = \frac{MP_b}{P_b} = \cdots = \frac{MP_m}{P_m} \qquad [7.3]$$

where $MP_a, MP_b, \cdots MP_m$ are the marginal product of inputs $a, b, \cdots m$, and $P_a, P_b, \cdots P_m$ are the prices of inputs $a, b, \cdots m$.

Returning to the case where labor and capital are the only two inputs, suppose that a firm decides to spend $200 on these inputs and that the price of labor is $10 per unit and the price of capital is $20 per unit. Table 7.1 shows the marginal product of each input when various combinations of inputs (the total cost of each combination being $200) are used. What combination is best? According to Equation 7.3, the marginal product of capital should be set at twice the marginal product of labor, since the price of a unit of capital is twice the price of a unit of labor. This occurs at 14 units of labor and 3 units of capital; thus this is the optimal combination.

To prove that this allocation of cost ($140 to labor and $60 to capital) is optimal, suppose that we shift $20 from labor to capital (with the result that $120 is devoted to labor and $80 to capital). Since the marginal product of the extra unit of capital that is gained is 14 units of output and the marginal product of the 2 units of labor given up is 2 times 8 units of product,[2] this change

TABLE 7.1 Marginal Products of Capital and Labor

Amount of input used		Marginal product*	
Labor	Capital	Labor	Capital
2	9	20	4
4	8	18	6
6	7	16	8
8	6	14	10
10	5	12	12
12	4	10	14
14	3	8	16
16	2	6	18
18	1	4	20

*The marginal products are defined for the interval between the indicated amount of labor or capital and one unit (capital) or two units (labor) less than this amount.

2. The marginal product of labor between 12 and 14 units of labor is 8 units of output per unit of labor. The marginal product of capital between 3 and 4 units of capital is 14 units of output per unit of capital.

will reduce output by 2 units. Similarly, the transfer of $20 from capital to labor
will reduce output.

A graph similar to Figure 7.2 can be used to determine the input combination that will minimize the cost of producing a given output. Moving along the
isoquant corresponding to the stipulated output level, we must find that point
on the isoquant that lies on the lowest isocost curve, for example, W in Figure
7.3. Input combinations on isocost curves like C_0 that lie below W are cheaper
than W, but they cannot produce the desired output. Input combinations on
isocost curves like C_2 that lie above W will produce the desired output but at a
higher cost than W. It is obvious that the optimal point, W, is a point where the
isocost curve is tangent to the isoquant. Thus, to minimize the cost of producing a given output or to maximize the output from a given cost outlay, the firm
must equate the marginal rate of technical substitution and the input-price
ratio.[3]

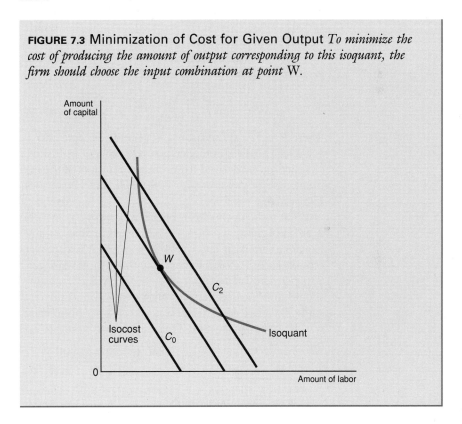

FIGURE 7.3 Minimization of Cost for Given Output *To minimize the
cost of producing the amount of output corresponding to this isoquant, the
firm should choose the input combination at point* W.

3. Suppose that Q is the output rate and that the production function is $Q = f(x_1, x_2)$ where x_1 and
    x_2 are the amounts of the two inputs used. If we want to find the values of x_1, and x_2 that
    maximize Q for the given cost, C_0, we set up the Lagrangian function:

    $$L = f(x_1, x_2) - \lambda(P_1x_1 + P_2x_2 - C_0)$$

    where P_1 is the price of the first input, P_2 is the price of the second input, and λ is the
    Lagrangian multiplier. Some first-order conditions are

    $$\frac{\partial L}{\partial x_1} = \frac{\partial f}{\partial x_1} - \lambda P_1 = 0; \quad \frac{\partial L}{\partial x_2} = \frac{\partial f}{\partial x_2} - \lambda P_2 = 0,$$

(cont'd.)

Note that this tells us how to solve the problem posed at the beginning of the chapter—the problem of the computer firm that decides for some reason to produce 100,000 computers next year and wants to know what combination of inputs to use. All that we need to do is to estimate the isoquant that pertains to an output by the firm of 100,000 computers per year. (If we are given the firm's production function, this is simple enough.) Then using data concerning the prices of the inputs, we can draw isocost curves, as in Figure 7.3, and determine the point, like W, where the isoquant is tangent to an isocost curve. This point represents the optimal combination of inputs.

THE PRODUCTION OF CORN: AN APPLICATION

To show how the theory presented in previous sections can be applied to help improve decision-making, this section describes how Earl Heady, a prominent agricultural economist, helped to determine the optimal combination of fertilizers in the production of Iowa corn.[4] He carried out experiments to determine the effect of various quantities of nitrogen (N) and phosphate (P) on corn yield per acre (Y), and found that

$$Y = -5.682 - .316N - .417P$$
$$+ 6.3512 \sqrt{N} + 8.5155 \sqrt{P} + .3410 \sqrt{PN} \qquad [7.4]$$

where P and N are measured in pounds per acre and Y is measured in bushels per acre. This equation is a production function: It shows the amount of output (Y) that can be derived from various amounts of the inputs (N and P). Various isoquants (for yields of 40, 60, 80, 104, and 120 bushels per acre) are shown in Figure 7.4.

What is the optimal combination of nitrogen and phosphate fertilizers? This is an important question, both to farm managers and to the general public. Corn is a very large and valuable crop, and it is important that it be produced as economically as possible. Suppose that a farm manager is thinking of spending $30 per acre on fertilizer and that he wants to know how this expenditure should be allocated between nitrogen and phosphate. At the time of Heady's study, the price of nitrogen was 18 cents per pound and the price of phosphate was 12 cents per pound. Thus, since he is going to spend $30,

$$18N + 12P = 3,000.$$

which imply that $\partial f/\partial x_1 \div P_1 = \partial f/\partial x_2 \div P_2 = \lambda$, the condition in Equation 7.3.

If we want to minimize the cost for the given input, Q_0, we set up the Lagrangian function:

$$P_1 x_1 + P_2 x_2 - M[f(x_1, x_2) - Q_0]$$

where M is the Lagrangian multiplier. Some first-order conditions are

$$P_1 - \frac{M \partial f}{\partial x_1} = 0; \quad P_2 - \frac{M \partial f}{\partial x_2} = 0,$$

which imply that $\partial f/\partial x_1 \div P_1 = \partial f/\partial x_2 \div P_2 = 1/M$, the condition in Equation 7.3. If the output level is the same, the values of x_1 and x_2 that are chosen must be the same, regardless of whether the output is maximized for the given cost or the cost is minimized for the given output.

4. See E. Heady, "An Econometric Investigation of the Technology of Agricultural Production Functions," *Econometrica*, April 1957.

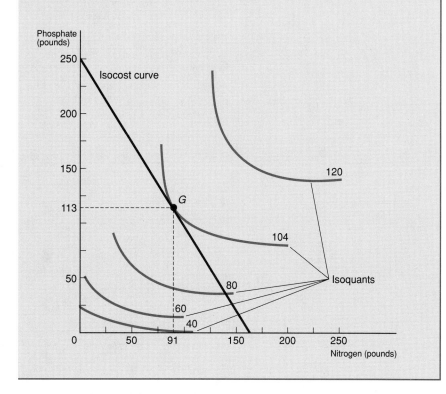

FIGURE 7.4 Optimal Combination of Nitrogen and Phosphate Fertilizers *Based on these actual isoquants for Iowa corn, the optimal point is G, where about 91 pounds of nitrogen and about 113 pounds of phosphate are used per acre.*

Solving for P, we find that

$$P = 250 - 1.5N. \qquad [7.5]$$

This is the formula for the isocost curve in this case, which is plotted in Figure 7.4.

To maximize the amount of corn that can be produced with this $30 expenditure on fertilizer, the farm manager should find the point on this isocost curve that is on the highest isoquant. As shown in Figure 7.4, this optimal point is G, where about 91 pounds of nitrogen per acre and about 113 pounds of phosphate per acre are used. This is the optimal input combination. Of course, the figure of $30 was chosed arbitrarily, but regardless of the total expenditure that is chosen, this method will provide the optimal allocation.

THE NATURE OF COSTS

The costs incurred by a firm are often thought to include only the money outlays the firm must make to obtain the use of resources. However, the firm's money outlays are only part of the cost picture. In many cases, economists are

EXAMPLE 7.1

RICE MILLING IN INDONESIA

Indonesia had a study performed by a team of American engineers to determine what sorts of facilities it should adopt for the milling of rice. Four types of facilities were evaluated: (1) husker-polishers, (2) integrated rice mills, (3) bulk satellites, (4) bulk terminals. In its initial report, the team recommended that Indonesia devote the bulk of its funds to the last three types. Soon after this report was submitted, C. Peter Timmer, a Harvard economist, constructed an isoquant for milling rice (corresponding to the relevant quantity of rice to be produced), the inputs being labor and capital.

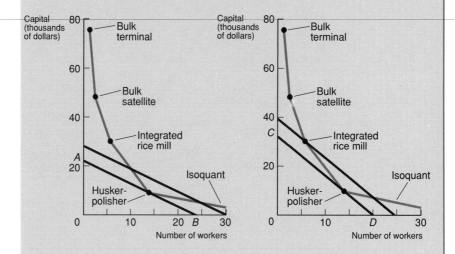

This isoquant is shown in both of the panels above. The point on the isoquant corresponding to each type of facility is indicated. For example, the bulk terminal requires about $78,000 in capital inputs and about one worker to produce this amount of output.

(a) If the isocost curves were straight lines parallel to *AB* (as in the left-hand panel of the figure), what type of facility was optimal? (b) If the isocost curves were straight lines parallel to *CD* (as in the right-hand panel of the figure), what type of facility was optimal? (c) Timmer was not sure what the ratio of the price of labor to the price of capital would be, but he was reasonably sure that it would be between that underlying isocost curve *AB* and that underlying isocost curve *CD*. If this is true, can we be reasonably certain of what type of facility was optimal? (d) Was the set of isocost curves that was parallel to *AB* based on a higher or a lower ratio of the price of labor to the price of capital than that underlying isocost curve *CD*? (e) The engineering team recommended the use of bulk terminals and bulk satellites because they were necessary to *modernize* (their term) Indonesian rice marketing. Is this a persuasive argument?

SOLUTION

(a) Husker-polishers, since the point on the isoquant corresponding to this type of facility was on the lowest isocost curve (this curve being *AB*). (b) Husker-polishers, since the point on the isoquant corresponding to this type of facility was on the lowest isocost curve (this curve being *CD*). (c) Yes. Husker-polishers will be optimal. (d) It was based on a lower ratio. We know that this is true because the slope of *AB* is closer to zero than the slope of *CD*. (*AB* is closer to being horizontal than *CD*.) As pointed out previously, the slope of an isocost curve equals $-P_L \div P_K$. Thus, if *AB*'s slope is closer to zero than *CD*'s, it must be based on a lower ratio of P_L to P_K. (e) No. Policymakers generally are interested in minimizing the cost of producing a given output, not obtaining the most modern type of equipment (for its own sake).*

*See C. P. Timmer, J. Thomas, L. Wells, and D. Morawetz, *The Choice of Technology in Developing Countries* (Cambridge, Mass.: Harvard University Press, 1975).

interested in the social costs of production, the costs to society when its resources are employed to make a given commodity. Since economic resources are, by definition, limited, when resources are used to produce a certain product, less can be produced of some other product that can be made with those resources. For example, aluminum can be used to produce airplanes, cooking utensils, outdoor furniture, and cans, among other things. Thus, when aluminum is used in the making of airplanes, some value of alternative products is given up.

Alternative cost, or opportunity cost

According to the economist's definition, the *cost* of producing a certain product is the value of the other products that the resources used in its production could have produced instead. For example, the cost of producing airplanes is the value of the goods and services that could be obtained from the manpower, equipment, and materials used currently in aircraft production. The costs of inputs to a firm are their values in their most valuable alternative uses. These costs, together with the firm's production function (which indicates how much of each input is required to produce various amounts of the product), determine the cost of producing the product. This is called the *alternative cost doctrine* or the *opportunity cost doctrine*.

Historical cost

It is important to note that the alternative cost of an input may not equal its *historical cost*, which is defined to be the amount the firm actually paid for it. For example, if some gullible soul buys the Brooklyn Bridge for $1,000, this does not mean that its value, either to the buyer or to society, is $1,000. Similarly, if a firm invests $1 million in a piece of equipment that is quickly outmoded and is too inefficient relative to new equipment to be worth operating, its value is clearly not $1 million. Although conventional accounting rules place great emphasis on historical costs, the economist—and the sophisticated accountant and manager—stresses that historical costs should not necessarily be accepted uncritically.

Of course, the alternative cost of an input depends on the use for which the cost is being determined. For example, the cost of a pound of aluminum to transportation uses is the amount the aluminum is worth in nontransportation uses; the cost of a pound of aluminum to the aircraft industry is the amount the aluminum is worth to other transportation industries as well as in nontransportation uses; and the cost of a pound of aluminum to Boeing is the amount the aluminum is worth to other aircraft manufacturers as well as in all nonaircraft uses. If all aluminum were homogeneous in all relevant respects, all three of these alternative costs would tend to be the same, because aluminum would be transferred from low-value uses to high-value uses until the yields in all uses were the same. However, if aluminum is not homogeneous, it is not necessary that these alternative costs be equal.

The alternative uses of a resource will often be different in the long run than in the short run. For example, in the short run, a plumber generally cannot enter fields requiring specialized skills unrelated to plumbing. But given time he or she can acquire other skills and become a programmer or a machinist. In the long run, alternatives tend to be greater and more varied than in the short run. Frequently, the alternative cost of an input is underestimated because people look only at its alternative uses in the short run.

The Enforcement of the Laws: An Application

Many of the concepts of microeconomics are useful for the formulation of public policy, as well as for business decision-making. To illustrate this point, let's consider how the concept of alternative costs can be used to shed light on the optimal enforcement of the laws. The question here is: What proportion of the people who commit crimes of a certain kind should society try to apprehend and convict? Your first reaction may be that they all should be caught and convicted; but, if so, it is easy to show that you ought to reconsider.

Costs from crime

To answer this question properly, let's begin by looking at how the costs to society from crime depend on the level of law enforcement. Clearly, the damage to the victims will tend to increase as the laws are enforced more leniently because people will be encouraged to engage in criminal activities. In other words, as the chance of getting caught decreases, more people will be willing to take the chance, with the result that criminal activity will increase, and the damage to crime victims will increase. Thus, as shown in Figure 7.5, the costs to society from crime will increase if society permits a decrease in the probability that a criminal will be apprehended and convicted. For example, in Figure 7.5, these costs will be OC_1 if the probability is 0.4, but OC_2 if the probability is 0.6.

Costs of apprehension

Looking only at the costs to society from crime, it appears that the optimal level of this probability is 1.00; that is, that the optimal policy is to catch and convict all criminals. But this ignores another important type of cost—the cost to society of apprehending and convicting criminals. After all, the services of policemen, detectives, prosecutors, judges, and wardens, as well as other resources used to apprehend and convict criminals, are not free. On the contrary, these resources all have alternative costs—since they can be used in other activities. For example, the policeman who tries to nail a purse snatcher could be working in industry or in some other part of government.[5]

5. Even the conscription of juries results in social costs, since the jurors could be performing other services.

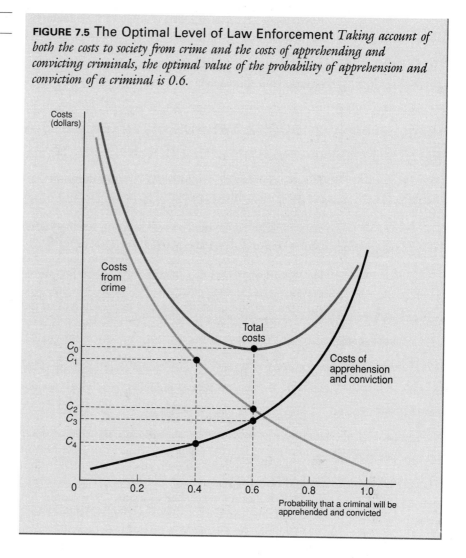

FIGURE 7.5 The Optimal Level of Law Enforcement *Taking account of both the costs to society from crime and the costs of apprehending and convicting criminals, the optimal value of the probability of apprehension and conviction of a criminal is 0.6.*

How do the social costs of apprehending and convicting criminals depend on the level of law enforcement? Clearly, they go up as the laws are enforced more stringently because more people and nonhuman resources are required to ferret out and convict criminals. Thus, as shown in Figure 7.5, the costs to society of apprehending and convicting criminals will increase with increases in the probability that a criminal will be apprehended and convicted. For example, these costs will be OC_4 if the probability is 0.4, but OC_3 if it is 0.6.

Recognizing that both of these costs must be taken into account, it is clear that the optimal level of law enforcement is at the point where the sum of both costs is a minimum. Thus, under the circumstances shown in Figure 7.5, the optimal value of the probability of apprehension and conviction is 0.6. To increase it beyond 0.6 would not be socially desirable because the extra cost of apprehension and conviction would exceed the resulting reduction in the cost to society from crime. Among others, Gary Becker, George Stigler, and Simon

Rottenberg have carried out a number of illuminating studies of the economics of crime and punishment. Of course, economics is only one of many disciplines that have a role to play here. But as illustrated by Figure 7.5, relatively simple microeconomic concepts can throw a great deal of light on many fundamental questions in this area.[6]

SOCIAL VERSUS PRIVATE COSTS AND EXPLICIT VERSUS IMPLICIT COSTS

The social costs of producing a given commodity do not always equal the private costs, which are defined to be the costs to the individual producer. For example, a steel plant may discharge waste products into a river located near the plant. To the plant, the cost of disposing of the wastes is simply the amount paid to pump the wastes to the river. However, if the river becomes polluted and if its recreational uses are destroyed and the water becomes unfit for drinking, additional costs are incurred by other people. Differences of this sort between private and social costs occur frequently; in Chapters 15 and 16 we shall see that such differences may call for remedial public-policy measures.

Explicit costs   Turning to the private costs of production, it is important to recognize that there are two types of costs, both of which are generally important. The first type is explicit costs, which are the ordinary expenses that accountants include as the firm's expenses. They are the firm's payroll, payments for raw materials, and so. The second type is implicit costs, which include the costs of resources owned and used by the firm's owner. The second type of costs is often omitted in calculating the costs of the firm.

Implicit costs   Implicit costs arise because the alternative cost doctrine must be applied to the firm as well as to society as a whole. Consider Martin Moran, the proprietor of a firm who invests his own labor and capital in the business. These inputs should be valued at the amount he would have received if he had used these inputs in another way. For example, if he could have received a salary of $50,000 if he worked for someone else, and if he could have received dividends of $10,000 if he invested his money in someone else's firm, he should value his labor and his capital at these rates. It is important that these implicit costs be included in a firm's total costs. Their exclusion can result in serious error.

THE PROPER COMPARISON OF ALTERNATIVES

It is also important to note that, in making decisions, costs incurred in the past often are irrelevant. Suppose that you are going to make a trip and that you want to determine whether it will be cheaper to drive your car or to go by bus.

---

6. See G. Becker, "Crime and Punishment: An Economic Approach," *Journal of Political Economy*, March 1968; S. Rottenberg, "The Clandestine Distribution of Heroin, Its Discovery and Suppression," *Journal of Political Economy*, January 1968; and G. Stigler, "The Optimum Enforcement of Laws," *Journal of Political Economy*, May 1970.
    Note that the kind of model utilized in this section will be discussed further and in more detail when we discuss environmental pollution in Chapter 16.

What costs should be included if you drive your car? Since the only *extra* costs that will be incurred will be the gas and oil (and a certain amount of wear and tear on tires, engine, etc.), they are the only costs that should be included. Costs incurred in the past, such as the original price of the car, and costs that will be the same regardless of whether you make the trip by car or bus, such as your auto insurance, should not be included. On the other hand, if you are thinking about buying a car to make this and many other trips, these costs should be included.[7]

As an illustration, consider the case of Continental Air Lines, which deliberately runs extra flights that do no more than return a little more than their out-of-pocket costs. Suppose that Continental is faced with the decision of whether or not to run an extra flight between city X and city Y. Suppose that the fully allocated costs—the out-of-pocket costs plus a certain percent of overhead, depreciation, insurance, and other such costs—is $4,500 for the flight. Suppose that the out-of-pocket costs—the actual sum that Continental has to disburse to run the flight—are $2,000 and the expected revenue from the flight is $3,100. In a case of this sort, Continental will run the flight. This is the correct decision, since the flight will add $1,100 to profit. It will increase revenue by $3,100 and costs by $2,000. Overhead, depreciation, and insurance would be the same whether the flight is run or not. In this decision, the correct concept of cost is out-of-pocket, not fully allocated costs. Fully allocated costs are irrelevant and misleading here. The importance of this way of looking at costs cannot be overemphasized.[8]

COST FUNCTIONS IN THE SHORT RUN

At the beginning of this chapter, we showed how the profit-maximizing firm will choose the combination of inputs to produce any given level of output. (Recall that this input combination is the one that minimizes the firm's cost of producing this level of output.) Given this optimal input combination, it is a simple matter to determine the profit-maximizing firm's cost of producing any level of output, since this cost is the sum of the amount of each input used by the firm multiplied by the price of the input. Given the firm's cost of producing each level of output, we can define the firm's *cost functions*, which play a very important role in the theory of the firm. A firm's cost functions show various relationships between its costs and its output rate. The firm's production function and the prices it pays for inputs determine the firm's cost functions. Since the production function can pertain to the short run or the long run, it follows that the cost functions can also pertain to the short run or the long run. In the next four sections, we discuss the short-run cost functions; then we turn to the long-run cost functions.

7. This example is worked out in more detail in the paper by E. Grant and W. Ireson in E. Mansfield, *Managerial Economics and Operations Research*, 5th ed. (New York: Norton, 1987).

8. It is very important in applied work to recognize what are the relevant alternatives and their effects. In this connection, it may be worthwhile to cite the case of the well-known actor, Maurice Chevalier, who, when asked how it felt to have reached his advanced age, is said to have replied, "Fine, relative to the alternative."

The short run is a time period so brief that the firm cannot change the quantity of some of its inputs. As the length of the time period increases, the quantities of more and more inputs become variable. Any time interval between one where the quantity of no input is variable and one where the quantity of all inputs is variable could reasonably be called the short run. However, as we pointed out in Chapter 6, we use a more restrictive definition: We say that the short run is the time period so brief that the firm cannot vary the quantities of plant and equipment. These are the firm's *fixed inputs*, and they determine the firm's *scale of plant*. Inputs like labor, which the firm can vary in quantity in the short run, are the firm's *variable inputs*.

The amount of calendar time corresponding to the short run will be longer in some industries than in others. In industries where the amount of fixed inputs are small and relatively easily modified, the short run may be very short. For example, this may be the case in cotton textiles. On the other hand, in other industries the short run may be measured in years. For example, in the steel industry, it takes a long time to expand a firm's basic productive capacity.

Three concepts of total cost in the short run are important: total fixed cost, total variable cost, and total cost. *Total fixed costs* are the total obligations per period of time incurred by the firm for fixed inputs. Since the quantity of the fixed inputs is fixed (by definition), the total fixed cost will be the same regardless of the firm's output rate. Examples of fixed costs are depreciation of buildings and equipment and property taxes. In Table 7.2, the firm's total fixed costs are assumed to be $1,000; the firm's total fixed cost function is shown graphically in Figure 7.6A.

Total variable costs are the total costs incurred by the firm for variable inputs. They increase as the firm's output rate increases, since larger output rates require larger variable input rates, which mean higher variable costs. For exam-

Total fixed costs

Total variable costs

TABLE 7.2 Fixed, Variable, and Total Costs

Units of output	Total fixed cost (dollars)	Total variable cost (dollars)	Total cost (dollars)
0	1,000	0	1,000
1	1,000	50	1,050
2	1,000	90	1,090
3	1,000	140	1,140
4	1,000	196	1,196
5	1,000	255	1,255
6	1,000	325	1,325
7	1,000	400	1,400
8	1,000	480	1,480
9	1,000	570	1,570
10	1,000	670	1,670
11	1,000	780	1,780
12	1,000	1,080	2,080

FIGURE 7.6 Total Fixed and Total Variable Costs *The total fixed cost
function is a horizontal line. Total variable costs increase as output rises.*

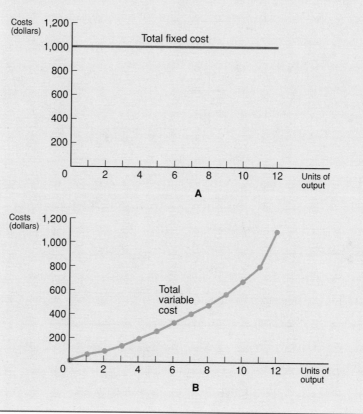

ple, the larger the product of a cotton mill, the larger the quantity of cotton that
must be used, and the higher the total cost of the cotton. A hypothetical total
variable cost schedule is shown in Table 7.2; Figure 7.6B shows the corresponding total variable cost function. Up to a certain output rate (2 units of output),
total variable costs are shown to increase at a decreasing rate; beyond that
output level, total variable costs increase at an increasing rate. *This latter characteristic of the total variable cost function follows from the law of diminishing marginal returns.* At small levels of output, increases in the variable inputs may
result in increases in their productivity, with the result that total variable costs
increase with output, but at a decreasing rate. More will be said on this score in
the next section.

Total costs   Finally, *total costs* are the sum of total fixed costs and total variable
costs. To derive the total cost column in Table 7.2, add total fixed cost and total variable
cost at each output. The corresponding total cost function is shown in Figure
7.7. The total cost function and the total variable cost function have the same
shape, since they differ by only a constant amount. All of the total cost functions are shown together in Figure 7.8.

FIGURE 7.7 Total Costs *Because total variable costs increase with output, so do total costs.*

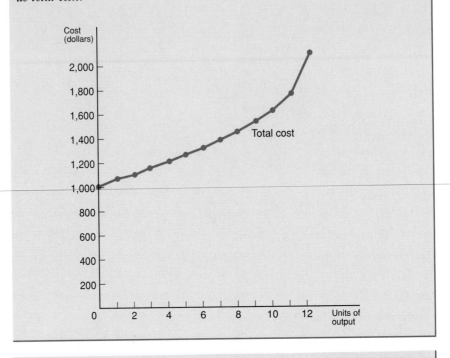

FIGURE 7.8 Fixed, Variable, and Total Costs *The total cost function and the total variable cost function have the same shape, since they differ by only a constant amount, which is total fixed cost.*

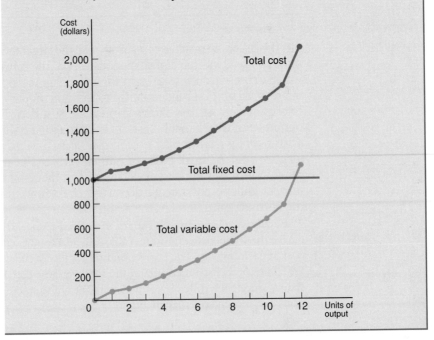

TABLE 7.3 Average and Marginal Costs

Units of output	Average fixed cost (dollars)	Average variable cost (dollars)	Average total cost (dollars)	Marginal cost* (dollars)
1	1,000.00 (=1,000÷1)	50.00 (=50÷1)	1,050.00 (=1,050÷1)	50 (=1,050−1,000)
2	500.00 (=1,000÷2)	45.00 (=90÷2)	545.00 (=1,090÷2)	40 (=1,090−1,050)
3	333.33 (=1,000÷3)	46.67 (=140÷3)	380.00 (=1,140÷3)	50 (=1,140−1,090)
4	250.00 (=1,000÷4)	49.00 (=196÷4)	299.00 (=1,196÷4)	56 (=1,196−1,140)
5	200.00 (=1,000÷5)	51.00 (=255÷5)	251.00 (=1,255÷5)	59 (=1,255−1,196)
6	166.67 (=1,000÷6)	54.17 (=325÷6)	220.83 (=1,325÷6)	70 (=1,325−1,255)
7	142.86 (=1,000÷7)	57.14 (=400÷7)	200.00 (=1,400÷7)	75 (=1,400−1,325)
8	125.00 (=1,000÷8)	60.00 (=480÷8)	185.00 (=1,480÷8)	80 (=1,480−1,400)
9	111.11 (=1,000÷9)	63.33 (=570÷9)	174.44 (=1,570÷9)	90 (=1,570−1,480)
10	100.00 (=1,000÷10)	67.00 (=670÷10)	167.00 (=1,670÷10)	100 (=1,670−1,570)
11	90.91 (=1,000÷11)	70.91 (=780÷11)	161.82 (=1,780÷11)	110 (=1,780−1,670)
12	83.33 (=1,000÷12)	90.00 (=1,080÷12)	173.33 (=2,080÷12)	300 (=2,080−1,780)

*Note that marginal cost pertains to the interval between the indicated output level and one unit less than this output level.

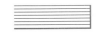

Average and Marginal Costs

Average fixed cost

The total cost functions are of great importance, but it is possible to get a better understanding of the behavior of cost by looking at the average cost functions and the marginal cost function as well. There are three average cost functions, corresponding to the three total cost functions. The *average fixed cost* is total fixed cost divided by output. Table 7.3 and Figure 7.9 show the average fixed

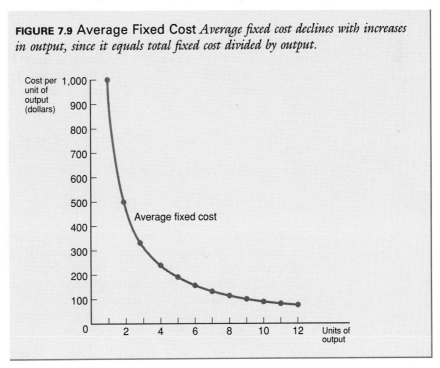

FIGURE 7.9 Average Fixed Cost *Average fixed cost declines with increases in output, since it equals total fixed cost divided by output.*

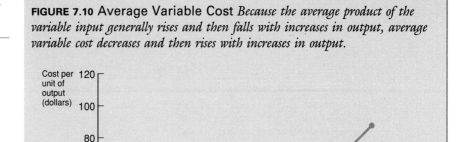

FIGURE 7.10 Average Variable Cost *Because the average product of the variable input generally rises and then falls with increases in output, average variable cost decreases and then rises with increases in output.*

cost function in the example given in the previous section. The average fixed cost declines with increases in output; mathematically, the average fixed cost function is a rectangular hyperbola.

Average variable cost

The *average variable cost* is total variable cost divided by output. For the example in the previous section, the average variable cost function is shown in Table 7.3 and Figure 7.10. At first, increases in output result in decreases in average variable cost, but beyond a point, they result in higher average variable cost. The results of the theory of production in Chapter 6 lead us to expect this curvature of the average variable cost function. If AVC is the average variable cost, TVC is the total variable cost, Q is the quantity of output, V is the quantity of the variable input, and P is the price of the variable input, it is obvious that

$$AVC = \frac{TVC}{Q} = P\frac{V}{Q}.$$

Thus, since Q/V is the average product of the variable input (AVP),

$$AVC = P\frac{1}{AVP}. \qquad [7.6]$$

Consequently, since AVP generally rises and then falls with increases in output (see Figure 6.2, p. 146) and since P is constant, AVC must decrease and then rise with increases in output. The fact that the shape of the average variable cost curve follows in this way from the characteristics of the production function is important and should be fully understood.

The *average total cost* is total cost divided by output. For the example in the previous section, the average total cost function is shown in Table 7.3 and

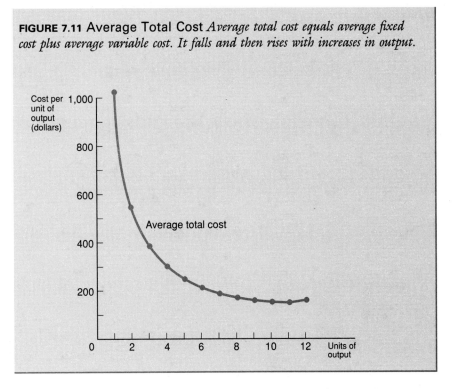

FIGURE 7.11 Average Total Cost *Average total cost equals average fixed cost plus average variable cost. It falls and then rises with increases in output.*

Average total cost Figure 7.11. The average total cost equals the sum of average fixed cost and average variable cost, which helps to explain the shape of the average total cost function. For those levels of output where both average fixed cost and average variable cost decrease, average total cost must decrease too. However, average total cost achieves its minimum after average variable cost, because the increases in average variable cost are for a time more than offset by decreases in average fixed cost. (All of the average cost curves are shown in Figure 7.13.)

The *marginal cost* is the addition to total cost resulting from the addition of

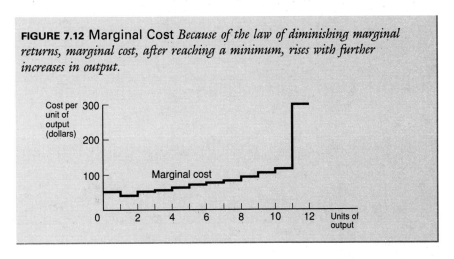

FIGURE 7.12 Marginal Cost *Because of the law of diminishing marginal returns, marginal cost, after reaching a minimum, rises with further increases in output.*

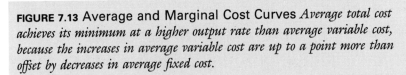

FIGURE 7.13 Average and Marginal Cost Curves *Average total cost achieves its minimum at a higher output rate than average variable cost, because the increases in average variable cost are up to a point more than offset by decreases in average fixed cost.*

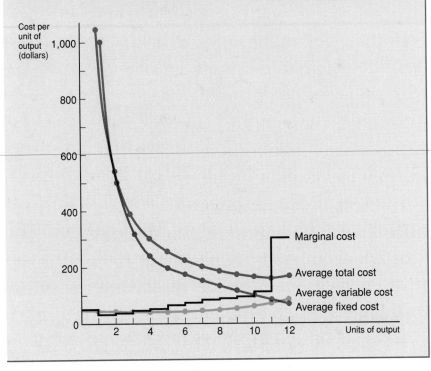

Marginal cost

the last unit of output. That is, if $C(Q)$ is the total cost of producing Q units of output, the marginal cost between Q and $(Q - 1)$ units of output is $C(Q) - C(Q - 1)$. For the example in the previous section, the marginal cost function is shown in Table 7.3 and Figure 7.12. At low output levels, marginal cost may decrease (as it does in Figure 7.12) with increases in output, but after reaching a minimum, it increases with further increases in output. The reason for this behavior is found in the law of diminishing marginal returns. If ΔTVC is the change in total variable costs resulting from a change in output of ΔQ and if ΔTFC is the change in total fixed costs resulting from a change in output of ΔQ, marginal cost equals

$$\frac{\Delta TVC + \Delta TFC}{\Delta Q}.$$

But since ΔTFC is zero (fixed costs being fixed), marginal cost equals

$$\frac{\Delta TVC}{\Delta Q}.$$

Moreover, if the price of the variable input is taken as given by the firm, $\Delta TVC = P(\Delta V)$, where ΔV is the change in the quantity of the variable input resulting from the increase of ΔQ in output. Thus the marginal cost equals

$$MC = P\frac{\Delta V}{\Delta Q} = P\frac{1}{MP} \qquad [7.7]$$

where MP is the marginal product of the variable input. Since MP generally increases, attains a maximum, and declines with increases in output (see Figure 6.2, p. 146), marginal cost normally decreases, attains a minimum, and then increases.[9] The fact that the shape of the marginal cost function depends in this way on the law of diminishing marginal returns is important and should be fully understood.

Geometry of Average and Marginal Cost Functions

Given the total cost function, we frequently want to derive the average and marginal cost functions. The purpose of this section is to show how this can be done graphically. The procedures are quite similar to those used in Chapter 6 to derive average and marginal product curves. Figure 7.14 shows how the average cost function can be derived from the total cost function, OTT', which is shown in panel A. (Note that, when we refer to average cost, we mean average *total* cost.) The average cost at any output level is given by the slope of the ray from the origin to the relevant point on the total cost function. For example, the average cost at an output OQ_0 is the slope of OR. We plot this slope, which equals OU, against OQ_0 in panel B. For each output, we plot in panel B the slope of the ray (from the origin to the relevant point on the total cost function) against the output, which results in AA', the average cost function. Beginning with a very small output, it is clear from Figure 7.14 that increases in output result in decreases in average cost, since the slope of such rays decreases with increases in output. However, it is also clear that average cost reaches a minimum at OQ_1, since beyond OQ_1 the slope of these rays increases with increases in output.

Figure 7.15 illustrates the derivation of the marginal cost function. As output increases from OQ_2 to OQ_3, total cost (OTT' in panel A) increases from OC_2 to OC_3. Thus the extra cost per unit of output is

$$\frac{OC_3 - OC_2}{OQ_3 - OQ_2} = \frac{BA}{CB}.$$

9. If C is total cost, $C = F + V(Q)$, where F is the total fixed costs and $V(Q)$ is total variable costs. Thus average fixed cost is F/Q, average variable cost is $V(Q)/Q$, and average total cost is $F/Q + V(Q)/Q$. The marginal cost equals $dC/dQ = dV(Q)/dQ$.

It is easy to show that marginal cost equals average variable cost when average variable cost is a minimum. If average variable cost is a minimum,

$$\frac{d[V(Q)/Q]}{dQ} = \left[\frac{dV(Q)}{dQ} - \frac{V(Q)}{Q}\right]\frac{1}{Q} = 0,$$

which means that $dV(Q)/dQ = V(Q)/Q$, which means that marginal cost equals average variable cost. It is also easy to show that marginal cost equals average total cost when average total cost is a minimum. When average total cost is a minimum,

$$\frac{d[F/Q + V(Q)/Q]}{dQ} = \left\{\frac{dV(Q)}{dQ} - \left[\frac{F}{Q} + \frac{V(Q)}{Q}\right]\right\}\frac{1}{Q} = 0,$$

which means that $dV(Q)/dQ = F/Q + V(Q)/Q$, which means that marginal cost equals average total cost.

FIGURE 7.14 Construction of the Average Cost Function *The average cost at output* OQ_0, *is* OU, *which is the slope of* OR. *The average cost at output* OQ_1 *is* OW, *which is the slope of* OS.

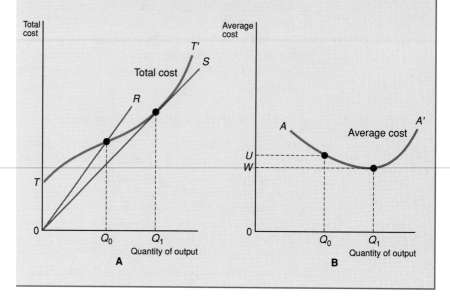

FIGURE 7.15 Construction of the Marginal Cost Function *The marginal cost at output* OQ_3 *is the slope of the tangent,* UU'. *When average cost is a minimum (at output* OQ_1), *marginal cost equals average cost* (= OW).

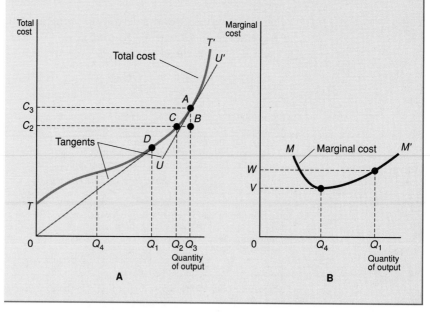

If we increase OQ_2 until the distance between OQ_2 and OQ_3 is extremely small, the slope of the tangent (UU') at A becomes a very good estimate of BA/CB. In the limit, for changes in output in a very small neighborhood around OQ_3, the slope of the tangent to the total cost function at OQ_3 is marginal cost. In panel B, MM' shows the slope of the tangent to the total cost curve at each output; this is the marginal cost function. It is evident from Figure 7.15 that, at small output rates, marginal cost decreases with increases in output, since the slope of the tangent to the total cost function decreases with increases in output. However, it is also evident that marginal cost reaches a minimum, OV, at OQ_4 and increases thereafter, since the slope of the tangent to the total cost function is a minimum at OQ_4 and increases thereafter.

It should also be noted that when average cost is a minimum (at output OQ_1), the slope of the ray OD equals the slope of the tangent to the total cost function, since OD is the tangent to the total cost function. Thus, since average cost equals the slope of the ray OD and marginal cost equals the slope of the tangent to the total cost function, it follows that *average cost must equal marginal cost at the output level where average cost is a minimum.* In Figures 7.14 and 7.15, both equal OW.

EXAMPLE 7.2

SHORT-RUN COSTS OF A BOEING 747

The Boeing 747 is an airplane that carries many of the world's travelers. According to data provided by Boeing to a Senate committee in 1975, the cost (in cents) per passenger-mile of operating such an airplane on a flight of 1,200 and 2,500 miles with 250, 300, and 350 passengers aboard was as follows:

Number of	Number of miles	
passengers	1,200	2,500
	(cents per passenger-mile)	
250	4.3	3.4
300	3.8	3.0
350	3.5	2.7

(a) If the number of passengers is between 250 and 300, what is the marginal cost of carrying an extra passenger on a 1,200-mile flight? (b) If the number of passengers is 300 and if the flight is between 1,200 and 2,500 miles, what is the marginal cost of flying an additional mile? (c) In 1975, the economy fare for a 2,500-mile flight was $156.60. If a Boeing 747 carried 300 passengers on such a flight, would it cover its operating costs? (d) Do you think that the above table can be applied to 1991? Why or why not?

SOLUTION

(a) If 250 passengers were carried, total operating costs were $1,200 \times 250 \times 4.3$ cents, or $12,900. If 300 passengers were carried, total operating costs were $1,200 \times 300 \times 3.8$ cents, or $13,680. Thus, since 50 extra passengers cost an extra $13,680 − $12,900, or $780, one extra passenger costs (approximately) an extra $780 ÷ 50, or $15.60. (b) For a 1,200-mile flight, total operating costs were 1,200 × 300 × 3.8 cents, or $13,680. For a 2,500-mile flight, total operating costs were 2,500 × 300 × 3.0 cents, or $22,500. Since 1,300 extra miles cost an extra $22,500 − $13,680, or $8,820, one extra mile cost (approximately) an extra $8,820 ÷ 1,300, or $6.78. (c) Yes. The total operating cost per passenger equaled 2,500 × 3.0 cents, or $75, which is less than $156.60. (d) No. Input prices are different in 1991 than in 1975. For example, fuel prices increased greatly in the late 1970s. Also, wage rates of airline personnel are different in 1991 than in 1975.*

*See S. Breyer, *Regulation and Its Reform* (Cambridge, Mass.: Harvard University Press, 1982); and U.S. Senate Committee on the Judiciary, *Civil Aeronautics Board Practices and Procedures,* 1975. Note that these data pertain only to an airplane's operating costs.

The Break-Even Chart: An Application

A standard tool used by economists to help solve certain kinds of managerial problems is the break-even chart, which is an important practical application of cost functions. Typically, a break-even chart assumes that the firm's average variable costs are constant in the relevant output range. Thus the firm's total cost function is assumed to be a straight line, as shown in Figure 7.16. In Figure 7.16, we assume that the firm's fixed costs are $300 per month and that its variable costs are $1 per unit of output per month. Since average variable cost is constant, the extra cost of an extra unit—marginal cost—must be constant, too, and equal to average variable cost.

To construct a break-even chart, the firm's total revenue curve must be plotted on the same chart with its total cost function. It is generally assumed that the price the firm receives for its product will not be affected by the amount it sells, with the result that total revenue is proportional to output and the total revenue curve is a straight line through the origin. Figure 7.16 shows the total revenue curve, assuming that the price of the product will be $1.50 per unit. The break-even chart, which combines the total cost function and the total revenue curve, shows the monthly profit or loss resulting from each sales level. For example, Figure 7.16 shows that, if the firm sells 300 units per month, it will make a loss of $150 per month. The chart also shows the break-even point, the output level that must be reached if the firm is to avoid losses; in Figure 7.16, the break-even point is 600 units of output per month.

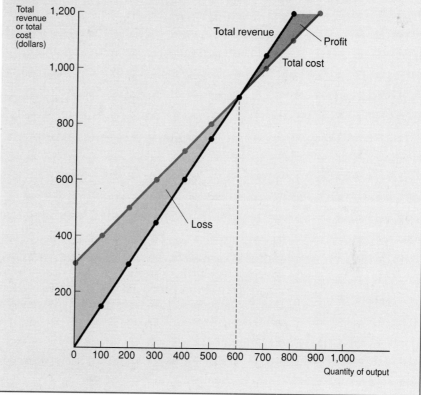

FIGURE 7.16 Break-Even Chart *The break-even point, the output level that the firm must reach to avoid losses, is 600 units of output per month.*

In recent years, break-even charts have been used extensively by company executives, government agencies, and other groups. Under the proper circumstances, break-even charts can produce useful projections of the effect of the output rate on costs, receipts, and profits. For example, a firm may use a break-even chart to determine the effect of a projected decline in sales on profits. Or it may use it to determine how many units of a particular product it must sell in order to break even. However, break-even charts must be used with caution, since the assumptions underlying them may be inappropriate. If the product price is highly variable or costs are difficult to predict, the estimated total cost function and the estimated total revenue curve may be subject to considerable error.

Although the total cost function generally is assumed to be a straight line in break-even charts, this assumption can easily be dropped and a curvilinear total cost function can be used instead. However, for fairly small changes in output, a linear approximation is probably good enough in many cases. As we shall see (later in this chapter), empirical studies suggest that the total cost function is often close to linear, as long as the firm is not operating at capacity.[10]

10. Note, however, that the results of some of these studies have been subjected to criticism of various sorts. See page 207.

EXAMPLE 7.3

THE EFFECTS OF BIOTECHNOLOGY ON AN ANTIBIOTIC'S PRODUCTION COSTS

One of the most exciting areas of technology in the 1990s is biotechnology. The following actual comparison has been made of the cost per pound of producing an antibiotic drug using conventional methods and using new methods based on biotechnology:*

	Conventional	Biotechnology
Raw materials	$ 5.12	$2.47
Labor	1.24	0.95
Utilities	2.73	0.71
Plant and equipment	3.49	1.44
Overhead	.75	0.56
Total	$13.32	$6.14

This comparison assumes that 5.9 million pounds per period are produced with each method. Suppose that a conventional plant and a plant based on biotechnology are in existence, and that a major chemical firm would like to know what the cost per pound would be if each plant produced 5.5 (rather than 5.9) million pounds per period. It hires you as an adviser. What's the answer?

SOLUTION

Assuming that overhead and plant and equipment costs are fixed costs, the total fixed costs are $5.9 \times (3.49 + .75) = 25.0$ millions of dollars at the conventional plant and $5.9 \times (1.44 + .56) = 11.8$ millions of dollars at the plant based on biotechnology. If average variable cost for each plant is constant for outputs ranging from 5.5 to 5.9 million pounds, and if output equals Q millions of pounds per period, the total variable costs (in millions of dollars) are $(5.12 + 1.24 + 2.73)Q = 9.09Q$ at the conventional plant and $(2.47 + .95 + .71)Q = 4.13Q$ at the plant based on biotechnology.

Adding the total fixed and total variable costs, we get the total costs, which equal (in millions of dollars)

$$TC_c = 25.0 + 9.09Q$$

at the conventional plant. Thus, if $Q = 5.5$, total costs are $25.0 + 9.09(5.5) = 75.0$ millions of dollars, and cost per pound is \$75 million divided by 5.5 million pounds, or \$13.64. At the plant based on biotechnology, total costs (in millions of dollars) are

$$TC_b = 11.8 + 4.13Q,$$

so, if $Q = 5.5$, total costs are $11.8 + 4.13(5.5) = 34.5$ millions of dollars, and cost per pound is \$34.5 million divided by 5.5 million pounds, or \$6.27.

To sum up, if each plant produced 5.5 (rather than 5.9) million pounds per period, it appears that cost per pound would be \$6.27 at the plant based on biotechnology, as compared with \$13.64 at the conventional plant. However, before accepting these results, you should make sure that overhead and plant and equipment costs are fixed costs, while the costs of raw materials, labor, and utilities are variable costs. Further, you should see whether average variable cost really is close to constant for outputs ranging from 5.5 to 5.9 million pounds.

*A. Hacking, *Economic Aspects of Biotechnology* (Cambridge: Cambridge University Press, 1986), p. 267. Because of rounding errors, the figures in the table do not sum to the totals.

COST FUNCTIONS IN THE LONG RUN

In the long run, the firm can build any scale or type of plant that it wants. All inputs are variable; the firm can alter the amounts of land, buildings, equipment, and other inputs per period of time. There are no fixed cost functions (total or average) in the long run, since no inputs are fixed. A useful way to look at the long run is to consider it a *planning horizon*. While operating in the short run, the firm must continually be planning ahead and deciding its strategy in the long run. Its decisions concerning the long run determine the sort of short-run position the firm will occupy in the future. For example, before a firm makes the decision to add a new type of product to its line, the firm is in a long-run situation, since it can choose among a wide variety of types and sizes of equipment to produce the new product. But once the investment is made, the firm is confronted with a short-run situation, since the type and size of equipment is, to a considerable extent, frozen.

Suppose that it is possible for a firm to construct only three alternative scales of plant; the short-run average cost function for each scale of plant is represented by S_1S_1', S_2S_2', and S_3S_3', in Figure 7.17. In the long run, the firm can build (or convert to) any one of these possible scales of plant. Which scale is most profitable? Obviously, the answer depends on the long-run output rate to be produced, since the firm will want to produce this output at a minimum average cost. For example, if the anticipated output rate is OQ, the firm should choose the smallest plant, since it will produce OQ units of output per period of time at a cost per unit, OC, which is smaller than what the medium-sized plant

FIGURE 7.17 Short-Run Average Cost Functions for Various Scales of Plant *The long-run average cost function is the solid portion of the short-run average cost functions,* S_1DES_3'.

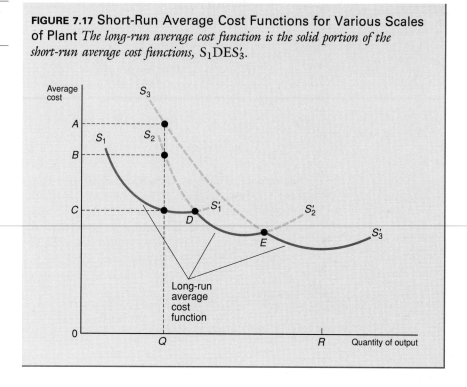

(its cost per unit being OB) or the large plant (its cost per unit being OA) can do. However, if the anticipated output rate is OR, the firm should choose the largest plant.

Long-run average cost function

The *long-run average cost function* shows the minimum cost per unit of producing each output level when any desired scale of plant can be built. In Figure 7.17, the long-run average cost function is the solid portion of the short-run average cost functions, S_1DES_3'. The broken-line segments of the short-run functions are not included because they are not the lowest average costs, as is evident from the figure.

At this point, we must abandon the simplifying assumption that there are only three alternative scales of plant. In fact, there are a great many alternative scales, with the result that the firm is confronted with a host of short-run average cost functions, as shown in Figure 7.18. The minimum cost per unit of producing each output level is given by the long-run average cost function, LL'. The long-run average cost function is tangent to each of the short-run average cost functions at the output where the plant corresponding to the short-run average cost function is optimal. Mathematically, the long-run average cost function is the envelope of the short-run functions.

Note, however, that the long-run average cost function (LL') is not tangent to the short-run functions at their minimum points, unless the LL' curve is horizontal. When the LL' curve is decreasing, it is tangent to the short-run functions to the left of their minimum points. When the LL' curve is increasing,

FIGURE 7.18 Long-Run Average Cost Function *The long-run average cost function, which shows the minimum long-run cost per unit of producing each output level, is the envelope of the short-run functions.*

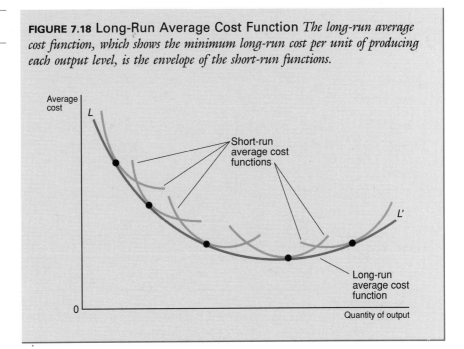

it is tangent to the short-run functions to the right of their minimum points. A famous mistake was made by the well-known Princeton economist, Jacob Viner, in his pathbreaking 1931 article regarding cost functions. He tried to get the *LL'* curve to be tangent to the short-run functions at their minimum points. As noted above, this in general cannot be done.

In terms of least-cost input combinations, the long-run average cost function can be interpreted in the following way: For any specified output, the total cost—and the average cost—is the smallest in the long run when all inputs (not just those that were variable in the short run) are combined in such a way that the marginal product of a dollar's worth of one input equals the marginal product of a dollar's worth of any other input used. Only if the firm uses the least-cost combination of all inputs to produce each level of output can the levels of cost shown by the long-run average cost function be reached.

Given the long-run average cost of producing a given output, it is easy to derive the long-run total cost of the output, since the latter is simply the product of long-run average cost and output. Figure 7.19 shows the relationship between long-run total cost and output; this relationship is called the *long-run total cost function*. Given the long-run total cost function, it is easy to derive the *long-run marginal cost function*, which shows the relationship between output and the cost resulting from the production of the last unit of output, if the firm has plenty of time to make the optimal changes in the quantities of all inputs used. Of course, long-run marginal cost must be less than long-run average cost when the latter is decreasing, equal to long-run average cost when the latter is a minimum, and greater than long-run average cost when the latter is increasing. It can also be shown that, when the firm has built the optimal scale of plant for

Long-run total cost function

Long-run marginal cost function

FIGURE 7.19 Long-Run Total Cost Function *The long-run total cost of a given output equals the long-run average cost (given in Figure 7.18) times output.*

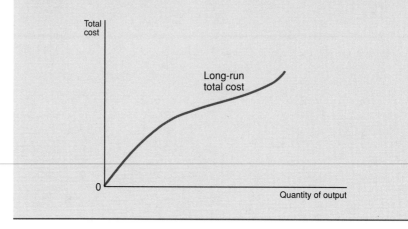

producing a given level of output, long-run marginal cost and short-run marginal cost will be equal at that output.[11]

Expansion path

The Expansion Path and Long-Run Total Costs

At this point, it is also worthwhile to show how a firm's long-run total cost function can be derived from its isoquants. Figure 7.20 shows a firm's isoquants corresponding to output levels of 50, 100, and 150. The least-cost combination of inputs to produce 50 units of output is represented by point E_0, where the isoquant is tangent to the relevant isocost curve. Similarly, the least-cost combination of inputs to produce 100 units of output is represented by point E_1, and the least-cost combination of inputs to produce 150 units of output is represented by point E_2. These tangency points (E_0, E_1, E_2), as well as those representing the least-cost combinations of inputs to produce other quan-

11. Suppose that the long-run average cost of producing an output rate of Q is $L(Q)$ and that the short-run average cost of producing this output with the ith scale of plant is $A_i(Q)$. Let $M(Q)$ be the long-run marginal cost and $R_i(Q)$ be the short-run marginal cost with the ith scale of plant. If the firm is maximizing profit, it is operating where short-run and long-run average costs are equal; in other words, $L(Q) = A_i(Q)$. Also, the long-run average cost function is tangent to the short-run average cost function, which means that

$$\frac{dL(Q)}{dQ} = \frac{dA_i(Q)}{dQ} \text{ and } Q\frac{dL(Q)}{dQ} = Q\frac{dA_i(Q)}{dQ}.$$

From these conditions, it is easy to prove that the long-run marginal cost, $M(Q)$, equals the short-run marginal cost, $R_i(Q)$.

$$M(Q) = \frac{d[QL(Q)]}{dQ} = L(Q) + \frac{QdL(Q)}{dQ}$$

$$R_i(Q) = \frac{d[QA_i(Q)]}{dQ} = A_i(Q) + \frac{QdA_i(Q)}{dQ}.$$

Since we know from the previous paragraph that $L(Q) = A_i(Q)$ and that $QdL(Q)/dQ = QdA_i(Q)/dQ$, it follows that $R_i(Q)$ must equal $M(Q)$.

FIGURE 7.20 The Expansion Path *The expansion path indicates how, as output changes from 50 to 100 to 150 units (but input prices remain fixed), the quantity that is used of each input changes.*

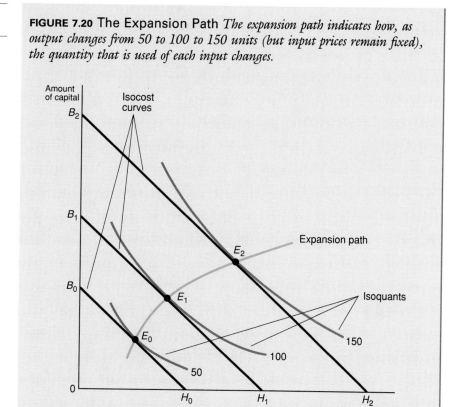

tities of output, lie along a curve known as the *expansion path,* shown in Figure 7.20. The expansion path indicates how, as the output rate changes (but input prices remain fixed), the quantity of each input changes.

If capital and labor are the only inputs, it is a simple matter to derive the long-run total cost function from the expansion path. Each point on the expansion path represents the least-cost combination of inputs to produce a certain output in the long run (since neither input is fixed). Consider point E_0, which corresponds to an output of 50 units. The total cost of the combination of inputs represented by E_0 is OH_0 times P_L, the price of a unit of labor. Why? Because point E_0 is on isocost curve B_0H_0, which means that the input combination at point E_0 costs the same as that at point H_0. And the cost of the input combination at point H_0 equals OH_0 times P_L.

Consequently, to obtain one point on the long-run total cost function, we plot OH_0 times P_L against 50 units of output, shown in Figure 7.21. To obtain a second such point, consider point E_1 on the expansion path, which corresponds to an output of 100 units. Using the same reasoning as in the previous paragraph, the total cost of the combination of inputs represented by E_1 is OH_1 times P_L. Thus the minimum cost of producing 100 units of output in the long run is OH_1 times P_L, which means that the point on the long-run total cost

FIGURE 7.21 Derivation of Long-Run Total Cost Function *The total cost of input combinations* E_0, E_1, *and* E_2 *in Figure 7.20 are* $OH_0 \times P_L$, $OH_1 \times P_L$, *and* $OH_2 \times P_L$, *respectively. Thus the minimum cost of producing 50 units is* $OH_0 \times P_L$, *the minimum cost of producing 100 units is* $OH_1 \times P_L$, *and the minimum cost of producing 150 units is* $OH_2 \times P_L$.

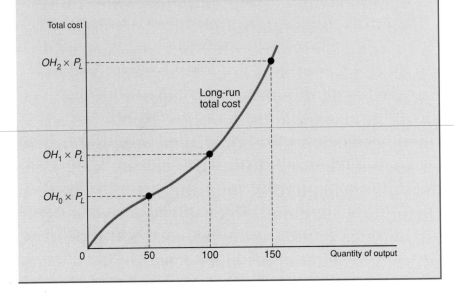

function corresponding to an output of 100 units is OH_1 times P_L. Consequently, OH_1 times P_L is plotted against 100 units of output in Figure 7.21. Repeating this procedure for each of a number of different output levels, we obtain the long-run total cost function shown in Figure 7.21.

The Shape of the Long-Run Average Cost Function

The long-run average cost function in Figure 7.18 is drawn with much the same sort of shape as the short-run average cost function. Both decrease with increases in output up to a certain point, reach a minimum, and increase with further increases in output. However, the factors responsible for this shape are not the same in the two cases. In the case of the short-run average cost function, the theory of diminishing marginal returns is operating behind the scenes. The short-run average cost function turns upward because decreases in average fixed costs are eventually counterbalanced by increases in average variable costs due to decreases in the average product of the variable input. However, the law of diminishing marginal returns is not responsible for the shape of the long-run average cost function, since there are no fixed inputs in the long run.

The shape of the long-run average cost function is determined in part by economies and diseconomies of scale. As pointed out in Chapter 6, increases in scale often result in important economies, at least up to some point. Because larger scale permits the introduction of different kinds of techniques, because larger productive units are more efficient, and because larger plants permit greater specialization and division of labor, the long-run average cost function declines, up to some point, with increases in output. Of course, the range of output over which the average cost function declines varies from industry to industry. (Moreover, in a given industry, this range varies over a period of time, particularly in response to changes in technology.)

Why does the long-run average cost function turn upward? The answer that is generally given is that, beyond a point, increases in scale result in inefficiencies in management. More and more responsibility and power must be given by top management to lower-level employees. Coordination becomes more difficult, red tape increases, and flexibility is reduced. It is not easy to determine just when these diseconomies of scale begin to offset the economies of scale already cited. In many industries, the available empirical studies seem to indicate that after an initial decline, long-run average cost is constant over a considerable range of output. The situation is like that shown in Figure 7.22. Eventually, however, one would expect the long-run average cost function to rise.

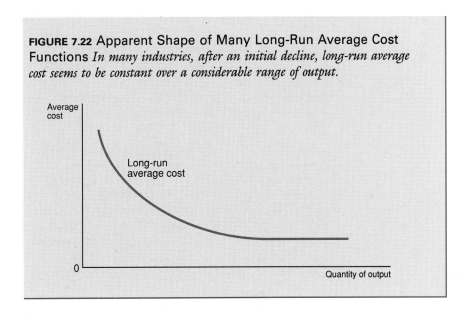

FIGURE 7.22 Apparent Shape of Many Long-Run Average Cost Functions *In many industries, after an initial decline, long-run average cost seems to be constant over a considerable range of output.*

It is important to note that the shape of the long-run average cost function is of great significance from the viewpoint of public policy. If the long-run average cost function decreases markedly up to a level of output that corresponds to all, or practically all, that the market demands of the commodity, it makes little sense to force competition in this industry, since costs would be higher if the output were divided among a number of firms than if it were produced by only one firm. In this case, the industry is a natural monopoly, and government agencies like the Federal Energy Regulatory Commission and the Federal Communications Commission, rather than competition, often are relied on to regulate the industry's performance. (This topic will be discussed further in Chapter 9.)

EXAMPLE 7.4

LONG-RUN COSTS AT IBM

The IBM Corporation is the leading manufacturer of electronic computers in the world. Based on its internal memoranda, IBM's long-run total cost of producing various quantities of its Pisces (370/168) machines was as shown below.

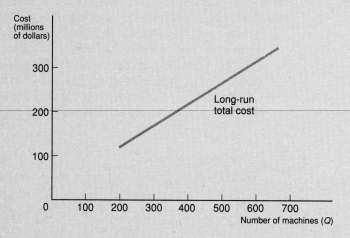

For output levels in the relevant range, the equation for this total cost function is

$$C = 28,303,800 + 460,800Q$$

where C is total cost (in dollars) and Q is the number of machines.

(a) If the entire market for this type of machine is 1,000 machines, and if all firms have the same long-run total cost function, to what extent would a firm with 50 percent of the market have a cost advantage over a firm with 20 percent of the market? (b) What is the long-run marginal cost of producing such a machine? Does marginal cost depend on output? (c) Do there appear to be economies of scale? (d) The data presented above are forecasts of costs based largely on engineering data, not an historical record of actual costs. Why would IBM make such forecasts? What factors might result in errors in these forecasts?

SOLUTION

(a) If Q equals 500, average cost equals $[28,303,800 + 460,800(500)] \div 500 = \$517,408$. If Q equals 200, average cost equals $[28,303,800 + 460,800(200)] \div 200 = \$602,319$. Thus a firm with 50 percent of the market has an average cost that is about 14 percent below that of a firm with 20 percent of the market. (b) \$460,800. (It is clear from the above equation that, if Q increases by 1, C increases by \$460,800.) In the output range covered by the data (about 200 to 700 units, according to the graph above), marginal cost does not vary. (c) Yes. Since long-run average cost equals $460,800 + 28,303,800/Q$, long-run average cost declines with increases in Q. (d) Since profits equal revenues minus costs, such forecasts are very useful in estimating the profits (or losses) that will accrue to the firm if it sells various quantities of output. However, such forecasts can be in error if input prices (such as wage rates) differ from the assumptions on which the forecasts are based, or if the productivity of inputs differs from what is expected.*

*See G. Brock, *The U.S. Computer Industry* (Cambridge, Mass.: Ballinger, 1975); and IBM, "Poughkeepsie SDD Cost Estimating," *Telex v. IBM,* Plaintiff's Exhibit 213.

ECONOMIES OF SCOPE

In previous sections of this chapter we have assumed that the firm produced only one product. While this is true for some firms, it is not true for others, like IBM Corporation or Exxon Corporation. If a firm produces more than one product, it may experience *economies or diseconomies of scope*. Economies of scope exist when a single firm producing various products jointly can produce them more cheaply than if each product is produced by a separate firm. For example, suppose that the Monarch Manufacturing Company produces 1,000 tons of lumber and 2,000 tons of paper, the total cost being \$120,000. If a firm producing 1,000 tons of lumber would incur costs of \$50,000, and if a firm producing 2,000 tons of paper would incur costs of \$90,000, Monarch experiences economies of scope because its cost of producing both lumber and paper (\$120,000) is less than the cost of producing them separately (\$50,000 + \$90,000 = \$140,000).

A measure of the degree of economies of scope is the following:

$$\frac{TC(Q_1) + TC(Q_2) - TC(Q_1 + Q_2)}{TC(Q_1 + Q_2)}, \qquad [7.8]$$

where $TC(Q_1)$ is the total cost of producing Q_1 units of the first good only, $TC(Q_2)$ is the total cost of producing Q_2 units of the second good only, and $TC(Q_1 + Q_2)$ is the cost of jointly producing Q_1 units of the first good and Q_2 units of the second good. Thus, in the case of Monarch, this measure of the degree of economies of scope equals

$$\frac{\$50,000 + \$90,000 - \$120,000}{\$120,000} = 0.17.$$

If this measure is negative, there are diseconomies of scope, which means that the cost of jointly producing the goods is greater than if they are produced separately.

Economies of scope often occur because the production of various products uses common production facilities or other inputs. For example, the production of cars and trucks may use the same sheet metal or engine assembly facilities. In other cases, economies of scope occur because the production of one product produces by-products that the producer can sell. For example, a cattle producer may sell the hides of its cattle which are raised for beef. Regardless of the reason for their existence, it is important to recognize that economies of scope can be important.[12]

MEASUREMENT OF COST FUNCTIONS

Economists have made a great many studies to estimate cost functions—or *cost curves,* as they are often called—in particular firms and industries. Typically, these studies have been based on the statistical analysis of historical data regarding cost and output. Some studies have relied primarily on time-series data, in which the output level of a firm is related to its costs. For example, Figure 7.23

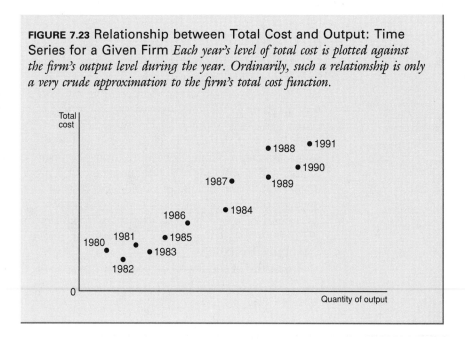

FIGURE 7.23 Relationship between Total Cost and Output: Time Series for a Given Firm *Each year's level of total cost is plotted against the firm's output level during the year. Ordinarily, such a relationship is only a very crude approximation to the firm's total cost function.*

plots the output level of a hypothetical firm against its costs in various years in the past. Other studies have relied primarily on cross-section data, in which the output levels of various firms at a given point in time are related to their costs.

12. For further discussion, see J. Panzar and R. Willig, "Economies of Scope," *American Economic Review,* May 1981; and E. Bailey and A. Friedlander, "Market Structure and Multiproduct Industries: A Review Article," *Journal of Economic Literature,* September 1982.

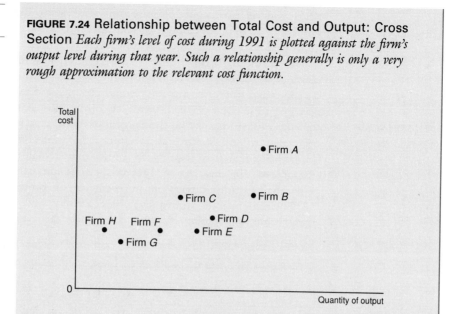

FIGURE 7.24 Relationship between Total Cost and Output: Cross Section *Each firm's level of cost during 1991 is plotted against the firm's output level during that year. Such a relationship generally is only a very rough approximation to the relevant cost function.*

For example, Figure 7.24 plots the 1991 output of eight firms in a given industry against their 1991 costs. Using data of this sort, as well as engineering data, economists have attempted to estimate the relationship between cost and output.

There are a number of important difficulties in estimating cost functions in this way. First, accounting data, which are generally the only cost data available, suffer from a number of deficiencies, when used for this purpose. The time period used for accounting purposes generally is longer than the economist's short run. The depreciation of an asset over a period of time is determined largely by the tax laws rather than economic criteria. Many inputs are valued at historical, rather than alternative, cost. Moreover, accountants often use arbitrary allocations of overhead and joint costs.

Second, engineering data also suffer from important limitations. Engineering data, like cost accounting data, relate to processes within the firm. One difficulty in using them to estimate cost functions for an entire firm is that the costs of various processes may affect one another and may not be additive. Also, there is the inevitable arbitrariness involved in allocating costs that are jointly attached to the production of more than one commodity in multiproduct firms.

Third, an important criticism of cross-section studies is that they are subject to the so-called regression fallacy. It is often argued that the output produced and sold by the firm is only partly under the control of the firm and that actual and expected output will differ. When firms are classified by actual output, firms with very high output levels are likely to be producing at an unusually high level, and firms with very low output levels are likely to be producing at an unusually low level. Since firms producing at an unusually high level of output are likely to be producing at lower unit costs than firms producing at an unusually low level of output, cross-section studies are likely to be biased, the observed cost of producing various output levels being different from the minimum cost of producing these output levels.

Despite these and other problems, estimates of cost functions have proved of considerable use, both to economists interested in promoting better managerial decisions and to economists interested in testing and extending economic theory. From the latter point of view, one of the most interesting conclusions of the empirical studies is that the long-run average cost function in most industries seems to be L-shaped (as in Figure 7.22), not U-shaped. That is, there is no evidence that it turns upward, rather than remaining horizontal, at high output levels (in the range of observed data). A summary of the results of some of the major studies carried out in recent years is presented in Tables 7.4 and 7.5. The reader should study these tables carefully, since they summarize a great many interesting results.

L-shaped long-run average cost function

TABLE 7.4 Results of Studies of Cost Functions: General Industry*

Author	Industry	Type	Period	Result
Bain	Manufacturing	Q	L	Small economies of scale of multiplant firms.
Eiteman and Guthrie	Manufacturing	Q	S	MC below AC at all outputs below "capacity."
Hall and Hitch	Manufacturing	Q	S	Majority have MC decreasing.
Lester	Manufacturing	Q	S	Decreasing average variable cost to capacity.
Moore	Manufacturing	E	L	Economies of scale generally.
T.N.E.C. Monograph 13	Various industries	CS	L	Small- or medium-size plants usually have lowest costs. Blair draws different conclusions.
Alpert	Metal	E	L	Economies of scale to 80,000 pounds/month; then constant returns.
Johnston	Multiple product	TS	S	"Direct" cost is linearly related to output. MC is constant.
Dean	Leather belts	TS	S	Significantly increasing MC rejected by Dean.
Dean	Hosiery	TS	S	MC constant. SRAC "failed to rise."
Dean and James	Shoe stores	CS	L	LRAC is U-shaped (interpreted as not due to diseconomies of scale).
Holton	Retailing (Puerto Rico)	E	L	LRAC is L-shaped. But Holton argues that inputs of management may be undervalued at high outputs.
Ezekiel and Wyiie	Steel	TS	S	MC declining, but large sampling errors.

Yntema	Steel	TS	S	MC constant.
Ehrke	Cement	TS	S	Ehrke interprets as constant MC. Apel argues that MC is increasing.
Nordin	Light plant	TS	S	MC is increasing.
Gupta	29 manufacturing industries (India)	CS	L	LRAC is L-shaped in 18 industries, U-shaped in 5, and linear in the rest.
Jansson and Schneerson	Shipping	CS	L	Economies of scale in hauling, but not in handling.
Norman	Cement	CS,E	L	Substantial economies of scale.
Zagouris, Caouris, and Kantsos	Solar desalinization	E	L	Economies of scale.

*The following abbreviations are used: MC = marginal cost, AC = average cost, SRAC = short-run average cost, LRAC = long-run average cost, S = short run, and L = long run, Q = questionnaire, E = engineering data, CS = cross section, and TS = time series.

Source: A. A. Walters, "Production and Cost Functions," *Econometrica,* January 1963; V. Gupta, "Cost Functions, Concentration, and Barriers to Entry in 29 Manufacturing Industries in India," *Journal of Industrial Economics,* 1968; J. Jansson and D. Schneerson, "Economies of Scale of General Cargo Ships," *Review of Economies and Statistics,* May 1978; G. Norman, "Economies of Scale in the Cement Industry," *Journal of Industrial Economics,* June 1979; and N. Zagouris, Y. Caouris, and E. Kantsos, "Production and Cost Functions of Water Low-Temperature Solar Desalinization," *Applied Economics,* September 1989.

TABLE 7.5 Results of Studies of Cost Functions: Public Utilities

Author	Industry	Type*	Result†
Lomax	Gas (U.K.)	CS	LRAC of production declines (no analysis of distribution).
Gribbin	Gas (U.K.)	CS	LRAC of production declines (no analysis of distribution).
Lomax	Electricity (U.K.)	CS	LRAC of production declines (no analysis of distribution).
Johnston	Electricity (U.K.)	CS	LRAC of production declines (no analysis of distribution).
Johnston	Electricity (U.K.)	TS	SRAC falls, then flattens tending toward constant MC up to capacity.
McNulty	Electricity (U.S.A.)	CS	Average costs of administration are constant.
Nerlove	Electricity (U.S.A.)	CS	LRAC excluding transmission costs declines, then shows signs of increasing.
Johnston	Coal (U.K.)	CS	Wide dispersion of costs per ton.
Johnston	Road passenger transport (U.K.)	CS	LRAC either falling or constant.
Johnston	Life assurance	CS	LRAC declines.

Dhrymes and Kurz	Electricity (U.S.A.)	CS, TS	Substantial economies of scale.
Eads, Nerlove, and Raduchel	Airlines (U.S.A.)	CS, TS	No evidence of substantial economies of scale.
Knapp	Sewage purification (U.K.)	CS	Significant economies of scale up to 10 million gallons daily.
Stevens	Refuse collection (U.S.A.)	CS	Considerable economies of scale in cities up to 20,000 population.

Railways

Borts	U.S.A.	CS	LRAC increasing in East, decreasing in South and West.
Broster	U.K.	TS	Operating cost per unit of output falls.
Mansfield and Wein	U.S.A.	TS	MC is constant.
Griliches	U.S.A.	CS	No significant economies of scale to an indiscriminate expansion of traffic.
Caves, Christensen, and Swanson	U.S.A.	CS	Economies of scale.
Friedlander and Spady	U.S.A.	CS	Economies of scale.
Harmatuck	U.S.A.	CS	Economies of scale.
Harris	U.S.A.	CS	Economies of scale.
Keeler	U.S.A.	CS	Economies of scale.
Sidhu, Charney, and Due	U.S.A.	CS	Economies of scale.

*CS means cross-section; TS means time series.
†LRAC means long-run average cost; SRAC means short-run average cost; MC means marginal cost.
Source: A. A. Walters, "Production and Cost Functions," *Econometrica*, January 1963; P. Dhrymes and M. Kurz, "Technology and Scale in Electricity Generation," *Econometrica*, July 1964; G. Eads, M. Nerlove, and W. Raduchel, "A Long-Run Cost Function for the Local Service Airline Industry," *Review of Economics and Statistics*, August 1969; Z. Griliches, "Railroad Cost Analysis," *Bell Journal of Economics and Management Science*, 1972; M. Knapp, "Economies of Scale in Sewage Purification and Disposal," *Journal of Industrial Economics*, December 1978; B. Stevens, "Scale, Market Structure, and the Cost of Refuse Collection," *Review of Economics and Statistics*, August 1978; D. Caves, L. Christensen, and J. Swanson, "Productivity Growth, Scale Economies and Capacity Utilization in U.S. Railroads, 1955–74," *American Economic Review*, December 1981; A. Friedlander and R. Spady, *Freight Transport Regulation*, MIT Press, 1981; D. Harmatuck, "A Policy-Sensitive Railway Cost Function," *Logistics and Transportation Review*, May 1979; R. Harris, "Rationalizing the Rail Freight Industry," University of California, Berkeley, 1977; T. Keeler, "Railroad Costs, Returns to Scale, and Excess Capacity," *Review of Economics and Statistics*, May 1974; N. Sidhu, A. Charney, and J. Due, "Cost Functions of Class II Railroads and the Viability of Light Traffic Density Railway Lines," *Quarterly Review of Economics and Business*, Autumn 1977; R. Braeutigam, A Daughety, and M. Turnquist, "The Estimation of a Hybrid Cost Function for a Railroad Firm," *Review of Economics and Statistics*, August 1982; S. Jara-Diaz and C. Winston, "Multiproduct Transportation Cost Functions: Scale and Scope in Railroad Operations," Massachusetts Institute of Technology, 1981; and T. Keeler, *Railroads, Freight, and Public Policy* (Washington, D.C.: Brookings Institution, 1983).

Another interesting conclusion of the empirical studies is that marginal cost in the short run tends to be constant in the relevant output range. As shown in Tables 7.4 and 7.5, this is a frequent result of these studies. This result seems to be at variance with the theory presented earlier (pp. 185–87), which says that marginal cost curves should be U-shaped. To explain this variance, critics have asserted that the empirical studies are biased toward constant marginal cost by the nature of accounting data and the statistical methods used. Another reason why marginal costs appear constant is that the data used in these studies often do not cover periods when the firm was operating at the peak of its capacity. Although marginal costs may well be relatively constant over a wide range, it is inconceivable that they do not eventually increase with increases in output.

An illustration of the sort of empirical work that has been done in this area is Joel Dean's pioneering study of the short-run cost functions in a hosiery mill. This study, published in 1941, was one of the first attempts by an economist to measure a firm's cost function. Dean found that the total cost function was linear within the range of observation, marginal cost being constant. His estimate of the total cost function is shown in Figure 7.25.[13]

Another illustration of studies of this kind is Martin Feldstein's study of cost functions in British hospitals. Among other things, he found that the long-run average cost function "is a shallow U-shaped curve with a minimum at the current average size (310 beds), [which indicates] . . . that the medium size hospital of 300 to 500 beds is at least as efficient at providing general ward care

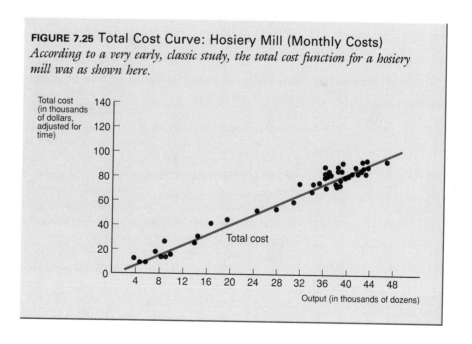

FIGURE 7.25 Total Cost Curve: Hosiery Mill (Monthly Costs)
According to a very early, classic study, the total cost function for a hosiery mill was as shown here.

13. See J. Dean, "Statistical Cost Functions of a Hosiery Mill," *Studies in Business Administration* 14 (no. 3), University of Chicago Press, 1941. See also A. A. Walters, "Production and Cost Functions," *Econometrica*, January 1963.

as are larger hospitals."[14] Figure 7.26 shows the average cost function he estimated. His study illustrates the fact that microeconomic concepts are useful for
nonprofit (and government) organizations as well as for firms.

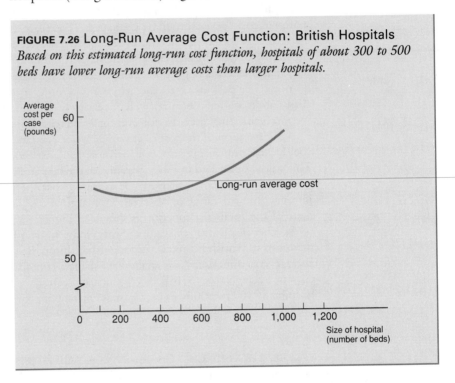

FIGURE 7.26 Long-Run Average Cost Function: British Hospitals
*Based on this estimated long-run cost function, hospitals of about 300 to 500
beds have lower long-run average costs than larger hospitals.*

Summary

1. To minimize the cost of producing a given output, a firm must combine inputs
   so that the marginal product of a dollar's worth of any one input is equal to the
   marginal product of a dollar's worth of any other input used. The optimal combination of inputs can be determined graphically by superimposing the relevant
   isocost curves on the firm's isoquant map, and by determining the point at
   which the relevant isoquant touches the lowest isocost curve.
2. The cost of producing a certain product is the value of the other products that
   the resources used in its production could have produced instead. This is the
   alternative cost doctrine. The alternative cost of an input may not be equal to its
   historical cost, and it is likely to be smaller in the short run than in the long run.
   (Opportunity cost is another name for alternative cost.)
3. The social costs of producing a given commodity do not always equal the private
   costs, as in the case of a steel mill that discharges wastes into a river. In making
   decisions, costs incurred in the past and costs that are the same for all alternative
   courses of action are irrelevant.
4. A cost function is a relation between a firm's costs and its output rate. The firm's
   production function and the prices it pays for inputs determine a firm's cost
   function.
5. Three concepts of total cost are important in the short run: total fixed costs, total

14. M. Feldstein, *Economic Analysis for Health Service Efficiency* (Chicago: Markham, 1968),
    p. 86.

variable costs, and total costs. The average fixed costs, average variable costs, average costs, and marginal costs are also important.

6. The short-run average cost function decreases at first, but eventually it turns up because of the law of diminishing marginal returns. Similarly, the marginal cost curve eventually turns up for the same reason.

7. A useful way to look at the long run is to view it as a planning horizon. Economies and diseconomies of scale affect the shape of the long-run average cost function. Because of economies of scale, the long-run average cost curve is likely to decrease, up to some point, with increases in output. As output becomes greater and greater, it is often stated that diseconomies of scale will result, with the consequence that the long-run average cost curve will turn upward. The shape of the long-run average cost curve in a particular industry is of great importance from the viewpoint of public policy.

8. Economists have made a great many studies to estimate the cost functions of particular firms and industries. Typically, these studies have been based on historical data regarding cost and output, although accounting data, which are generally the only cost data available, suffer from a number of deficiencies when used for this purpose.

9. One of the most interesting conclusions of these studies is that the long-run average cost curve seems to be L-shaped. However, the evidence is limited. Another interesting conclusion is that the short-run marginal cost function often seems to be horizontal, not U-shaped. But this may be due in considerable part to the limited range of the observations.

1. In October 1986, about nine months after the crash of the space shuttle *Challenger*, the Congressional Budget Office published a study indicating that the marginal cost of a 1989 flight by a space shuttle would be about $48 million. (a) What kinds of expenses are included in this figure? (b) Should the entire cost of the shuttle be included? Why or why not? (c) According to the study, the "Challenger accident will increase the marginal cost of shuttle operations . . ."[15] Why was this likely?

2. According to the National Academy of Engineering, the long-run average total cost of producing an aircraft increases by about 35 percent if 350, rather than 700, of the aircraft are produced. Since the end of World War II, the number of prime free-world manufacturers of large commercial air transports has decreased from 22 to 5.[16] Are these two facts related? If so, how?

3. Fill in the blanks in the table below.

Output	Total cost (dollars)	Total fixed cost (dollars)	Total variable cost (dollars)	Average fixed cost (dollars)	Average variable cost (dollars)
0	50	—	—	—	—
1	70	—	—	—	—
2	100	—	—	—	—
3	120	—	—	—	—
4	135	—	—	—	—
5	150	—	—	—	—
6	160	—	—	—	—
7	165	—	—	—	—

15. Congressional Budget Office, *Setting Space Transportation Policy for the 1990s* (Washington, D.C.: Government Printing Office, 1986), p. 25.

16. National Academy of Engineering, *The Competitive Status of the U.S. Civil Aviation Manufacturing Industry* (Washington, D.C.: National Academy Press, 1985).

Suppose that the price of an important input increased greatly, with the result that each of the figures concerning total cost rose by 50 percent. What effect would this have on the value of marginal cost?

4. As we saw in Example 6.2, 8,500 pounds of milk can be produced by a cow fed the following combinations of quantities of hay and grain:

Quantity of hay (pounds)	Quantity of grain (pounds)
5,000	6,154
5,500	5,454
6,000	4,892
6,500	4,423
7,000	4,029
7,500	3,694

(a) If the price of hay equals one-half the price of a pound of grain (which equals P), what is the cost of each combination? What is the minimum-cost combination (of those shown above)? (b) Plot the isocost curves and the isoquant. Use this graph to determine the minimum-cost combination. Compare your results with those obtained in part (a).

5. Economist T. Yntema estimated the short-run total cost function of the United States Steel Corporation (now USX Corporation) in the 1930s to be as follows:

$$C = 182.1 + 55.73Q$$

where C is total annual cost (in millions of dollars) and Q is millions of tons of steel produced. (a) What was U.S. Steel's fixed cost? (b) If U.S. Steel produced 10 million tons of steel, what was its average variable cost? (c) What was U.S. Steel's marginal cost? (d) Do you think that this equation provided a faithful representation of U.S. Steel's short-run total cost function, regardless of the value of Q? (e) If you needed to estimate this firm's marginal cost in 1992, would you use this equation? (f) In recent years, there have been charges that Japanese steel makers have been "dumping" steel in the United States—that is, selling here below cost. Can this equation be used to tell whether this is so?

6. According to Frederick Moore, "The '.6 rule' derived by engineers is a rough method of measuring increases in capital cost as capacity is expanded. Briefly stated the rule says that the increase in cost is given by the increase in capacity raised to the .6 power." Give some reasons why this rule holds for tanks, columns, compressors, and similar types of equipment. (Hint: Capacity of a container is related to volume, whereas cost is related to surface area.)

7. The graph on page 211 shows the average total cost of producing a ton of ammonia using the partial oxidation process and the steam reforming process, with plants of various sizes (as measured by daily capacities). In particular, curve C pertains to the partial oxidation process when naptha is used as a raw material, curve D pertains to the steam reforming process when naptha is used as a raw material, and curve E pertains to the steam reforming process when natural gas is used as a raw material. (a) Can the short-run cost function for ammonia be derived from this graph? (b) This graph assumes that naptha costs $0.008 per pound and natural gas costs $0.20 per mcf; if this assumption is true, which process should be used? (c) Does this graph suggest that there are economies of scale in ammonia production? (d) The graph on p. 211 pertains to conditions in the early 1960s. In the late 1960s, a new process for producing ammonia was introduced. Using this new process, a plant with a capacity of 1,400 tons per day had an average cost of about $16 per ton. Did the long-run cost function for the production of ammonia shift between the early and late 1960s?

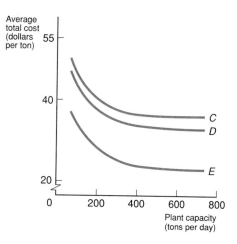

8. A plant producing a component of the space shuttle can produce any number of these components (up to 100 per week) at a total cost of $100, but it cannot produce more than 100 per week, regardless of how much its costs are. Graph its marginal cost curve. Indicate why few (if any) plants in the real world have a marginal cost curve of this sort.

9. Suppose that you are a consultant to a firm that publishes books. Suppose that the firm is about to publish a book that will sell for $10 a copy. The fixed costs of publishing the book are $5,000; the variable cost is $5 a copy. What is the break-even point for this book?

10. Suppose that a semiconductor plant's production function is $Q = 5LK$, where Q is its output rate, L is the amount of labor it uses per period of time, and K is the amount of capital it uses per period of time. Suppose that the price of labor is $1 a unit and the price of capital is $2 a unit. The firm's vice-president for manufacturing hires you to figure out what combination of inputs the plant should use to produce 20 units of output per period. What advice would you give?

OPTIMAL LOT SIZE AND JAPANESE MANUFACTURING METHODS

In recent years, American firms have been trying to learn about, and in some cases catch up with, the manufacturing techniques used by the Japanese. One of the hallmarks of Japanese manufacturers is that products are made in small batches or lots, whereas in the United States they have been made in relatively large batches or lots. There are many advantages in small lot sizes. Less inventories must be held. Also, there may be less scrap and better quality of workmanship. If a worker makes a single part and passes it to the next worker immediately (rather than making a large batch of the parts and then passing them on all at once), the first worker will be informed very soon if the next worker finds it defective. Thus the causes of defects tend to be nipped in the bud, and the production of large lots containing many defective items is avoided.

Why have American firms produced relatively large lot sizes? To answer this question, we must discuss the factors determining the most economical lot size. Suppose that a firm needs to produce 100,000 identical parts of a particular type per year. For example, a manufacturer of outboard motors may have to produce 100,000 parts of a particular type, since each of its outboard motors requires such a part. Each time that the firm begins to produce this type of part, it incurs a setup cost of S dollars. For example, the outboard motor manufacturer may have to devote considerable labor time to setting up the equipment that produces this part.

The advantage of producing large lots is that this cuts the total setup costs incurred during the year. If the firm were to produce its annual requirement of 100,000 parts in one huge lot, it would only have to set up the equipment once, the result being that its total setup costs for the year would be S dollars. If it produced its annual requirement of 100,000 parts in two lots (each of 50,000), it would have to set up the equipment twice, the result being that the total setup costs for the year would be $2S$ dollars. The relationship between the size of a lot and the annual total setup costs is shown in Figure 1.

The disadvantage of producing large lots is that they result in large inventories that are expensive to maintain and finance. If, for example, the firm

FIGURE 1 Relationship Between the Size of Lot and the Annual Setup Costs *The larger the lot size, the lower the annual setup costs.*

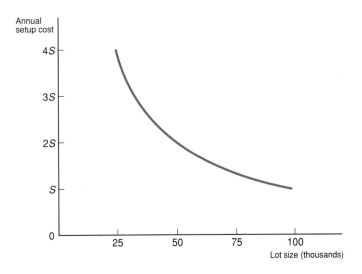

produces all 100,000 of the parts in one huge lot at the beginning of the year, its inventory equals 100,000 parts at the beginning of the year and zero parts at the end of the year. Its average inventory is 50,000 parts, as shown in the left-hand panel of Figure 2. On the other hand, if the firm produces the annual requirement of 100,000 parts in two lots (each of 50,000 units), its inventory

FIGURE 2 Size of Inventory During the Year, Given that Lot Size Equals 100,000 and 50,000 *Average inventory is 50,000 parts if the lot size equals 100,000 and 25,000 parts if the lot size equals 50,000.*

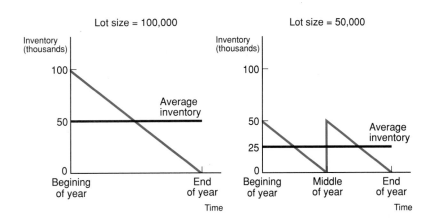

FIGURE 3 Relationship between Size of Lot and Total Annual Costs
Total cost is the sum of the cost of carrying inventory and the setup cost. Thus the "Total cost" curve is the vertical sum of the "Cost of carrying inventory" curve and the "Setup cost" curve. For example, if the lot size is 70,711, annual setup cost equals OA, *annual inventory cost equals* OB, *and annual total cost equals* OA + OB = OE.

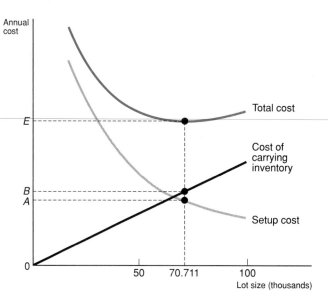

equals 50,000 parts at the beginning of the year and zero parts at the end of six months; then after the second lot is produced, its inventory jumps back up to 50,000 parts, after which it declines once again to zero parts at the end of the year. Thus its average inventory is 25,000 parts, as shown in the right-hand panel of Figure 2.

Assuming that the annual cost of holding inventory is proportional to the average inventory, the relationship between the size of a lot and the annual cost of holding inventory is shown in Figure 3. Adding the annual setup costs for each lot size (taken from Figure 1 and reproduced in Figure 3) to the inventory costs, we obtain the total annual cost for each lot size. Under the conditions shown in Figure 3, the optimal lot size is 70,711, where the total annual costs are a minimum.[1]

---

1. In general, total annual setup costs equal SQ/L, where S is the cost per setup, Q is the total annual requirement of the relevant part, and L is the number of identical parts of this sort produced in a lot. Since $L/2$ is the average inventory, the annual cost of holding inventory equals $bL/2$, where b is the annual cost of holding each identical part of this sort in inventory for a year. Adding the annual setup costs and the annual costs of holding inventory, we obtain the following expression for the total annual costs:

$$C = bL/2 + SQ/L.$$

The value of the optimal lot size depends on the cost of setting up the equipment each time. If this cost is high, the optimal lot size tends to be large; if it is low, the optimal lot size tends to be small. This fact is shown in Figure 4. In the upper panel, the cost of each setup is large, which means that the curve showing the annual setup costs is higher than in the lower panel where the cost of each setup is small. Consequently, the optimal lot size, *OL,* is bigger in the case shown in the upper panel than in the case shown in the lower panel.

At this point, it is easy to understand why American firms have produced larger lot sizes than Japanese firms. The Japanese, using ingenuity and determination, have succeeded in lowering the cost of each setup. In other words, the Japanese have managed to get themselves into the situation shown in the lower panel of Figure 4, whereas American firms have tended to be in the situation shown in the top panel. The importance of this factor has been pointed out in the following way by Robert Hall:

> When the Japanese explain in detail how they achieved their big increases in productivity, the biggest "war stories" from the plant floor involve hard-fought battles to reduce setup times on a piece of equipment which at first was regarded as an insurmountable obstacle. Accounts of these battles detail changing the design of bolts, and the fit of pieces together on the machine. They describe the building of special tools to speed changeover, and practice sessions to learn how to perform changeovers quickly.[2]

To illustrate more specifically how the Japanese have gone about this, consider Toyota, a major auto producer. In 1971, it took Toyota's workers about an hour to set up the 800-ton presses used in forming auto hoods and fenders. After five years of intensive effort, the setup time was reduced to 12 minutes (as contrasted with about 6 hours in the United States), and the aim was to reduce it to under 10 minutes. To accomplish this, "The press was modified to allow the old dies to quickly slide out of the press onto a waiting table while new dies are pushed in from the other side. The workers performing the changeover 'dry

---

To minimize total annual costs, we set

$$\frac{dC}{dL} = \frac{b}{2} - SQ/L^2 = 0.$$

Solving for L, we find that, to minimize total annual costs, L should equal

$$\sqrt{\frac{2SQ}{b}}$$

In the particular case in Figure 3, Q equals 100,000 and b equals $S \div 25,000$. Thus, to minimize total annual costs, L should equal $\sqrt{2S(100,000) \div (S/25,000)} = \sqrt{5 \text{ billion}} = 70,711$. In other words the optimal lot size is 70,711, which means that 70,711 identical parts of this sort should be produced in each lot. (Of course, there is no reason for the number of setups per year to be an integer number. For example, one could have 5 setups during each two-year period, or 2½ setups per year.)

2. See R. Schonberger, *Japanese Manufacturing Techniques* (New York: Free Press, 1982), p. 20.

FIGURE 4 Effects of Cost per Setup on Optimal Lot Size *If the cost per setup is relatively high (as in panel A), the optimal lot size tends to be relatively large.*

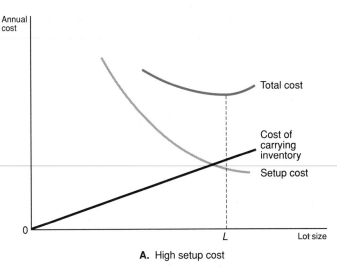

A. High setup cost

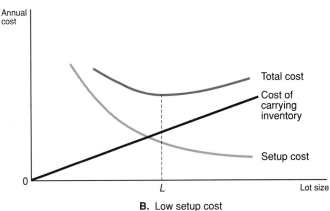

B. Low setup cost

ran' the procedure so that it worked like kicking the extra point after a touchdown in football."[3]

Recognizing the importance of this factor, American firms have been devoting considerable effort to making similar reductions in setup costs. Because the Japanese industrial climate differs in many respects from that in the United States, it would be simplistic to think that what works in Japan will necessarily work in the United States. But there can be no doubt about the American interest in Japanese manufacturing techniques.[4]

3. Ibid., p. 21.
4. See ibid., and R. Hayes, "Why Japanese Factories Work," in A. Kantrow (ed.), *Survival Strategies for American Industry* (New York: Wiley, 1983).

**Analytical
Questions**

1. When Toyota reduced the time required to set up its presses, did it change its production function? If so, how?

2. If the manufacturer of outboard motors incurs a setup cost of $100,000 each time that it begins to produce a particular type of part, how much are its total setup costs per year if it produces 50,000 parts of this type each year and if the lot size is 10,000?

3. Under the conditions described in the previous question, what is the average level of inventory for this part? Why is it likely that the cost to the firm of carrying this inventory will increase as the inventory gets bigger?

4. Under the conditions described in Question 2, if the annual cost to the firm of holding each identical part of this sort in the inventory is $2, what is the total annual cost of holding inventory? What is the sum of the annual setup cost and the annual cost of holding inventory?

5. Under the conditions described in Questions 2 and 4, is the firm producing the optimal lot size? If not, what is the optimal lot size?

6. The firm's managers ask you to estimate how sensitive the firm's total cost (of setup and holding inventory) is to variations in the lot size from its optimal level. Why is this question important, and how would you answer it?

7. A government official asks you whether American firms should invest whatever resources are required to reduce their setup costs to the Japanese level. How would you answer this question?

PART FOUR

MARKET STRUCTURE, PRICE, AND OUTPUT

8

PRICE AND OUTPUT UNDER PERFECT COMPETITION

MARKET STRUCTURE: AN INTRODUCTION

Previous chapters have provided models of the behavior of consumers and firms. In Chapters 8 to 11 we turn to the analysis of markets; our principal purpose is to explain the behavior of price and output. We will be concerned with questions of the following sort: What determines the price of a product? What determines how much of a product is produced? How are resources allocated among alternative uses? These are some of the most basic—and most important—questions in economics. In Chapter 2, we provided some preliminary answers to these questions. In Chapters 8 to 11, we discuss them in much more detail.

To begin with, we must distinguish between various types of markets. Economists have found it useful to classify markets into four general types: perfect competition, monopoly, monopolistic competition, and oligopoly. This classification is based largely on the number of firms in the industry that supplies the product. In perfect competition and monopolistic competition, there are many sellers, each of which produces only a small part of the industry's output. In monopoly, on the other hand, the industry consists of only a single firm. Oligopoly is an intermediate case where there are few sellers.

In this chapter we investigate how price and output are determined in perfectly competitive markets. Monopoly, monopolistic competition, and oligopoly are taken up in subsequent chapters. The analysis in this chapter brings together, and builds on, the topics discussed in previous chapters. In Chapter 2, we emphasized the important role played by the market demand and market supply curves. In Chapter 5, we used the tools devised in Chapters 3 and 4 to show how a product's market demand curve can be derived. In the present chapter, we use the tools devised in Chapters 6 and 7 to show how a product's market supply curve can be derived. Then we discuss in detail the way in which the demand and supply sides of the market interact to determine the equilibrium price and output of the firm and the industry in the short run and the long run.

PERFECT COMPETITION

What do economists mean by perfect competition? When first exposed to this concept, students sometimes find it difficult to grasp because it is quite different from the concept of competition used by their relatives and friends in the business world. When business executives speak of a highly competitive market, they generally mean a market where each firm is keenly aware of its rivalry with a few others and where advertising, packaging, styling, and other competitive weapons are used to attract business away from them. In contrast, the basic feature of the economist's definition of perfect competition is its impersonality. Because there are so many firms in the industry, no firm views another as a competitor, any more than one small wheat farmer views another small wheat farmer as a competitor.

Perfect competition　　More specifically, *perfect competition* is defined by four conditions. First, perfect competition requires that the product of any one seller be the same as the product of any other seller. This is an important condition because it makes sure that buyers do not care whether they purchase the product from one seller or another, as long as the price is the same. Note that the *product* may be defined by a great deal more than the physical characteristics of the good. Although the various English pubs may serve the same beer, their products may not be identical because the atmosphere may be friendlier in one place than another, the location may be better, and so forth.

Second, perfect competition requires each participant in the market, whether buyer or seller, to be so small, in relation to the entire market, that he or she cannot affect the product's price. No buyer can be large enough to wangle a better price from the sellers than some other buyer. No seller can be large enough to influence the price by altering his or her output rate. Of course, if all producers act together, changes in output will certainly affect price, but any producer acting alone cannot do so. It will be recalled from Chapter 5 that this means that the firm's demand curve is horizontal.

Third, perfect competition requires that all resources be completely mobile. In other words, each resource must be able to enter or leave the market, and switch from one use to another, very readily.[1] More specifically, it means that labor must be able to move from region to region and from job to job; it means that raw materials must not be monopolized; and it means that new firms can enter and leave an industry. Needless to say, this condition is often not fulfilled in a world where considerable retraining is required to allow a worker to move

---

1. Of course, this does not mean that such movements of resources do not take time. In the short run, many resources cannot be transferred from one use to another.

from one job to another and where patents, large investment requirements, and economies of scale make difficult the entry of new firms.

Fourth, perfect competition requires that consumers, firms, and resource owners have perfect knowledge of the relevant economic and technological data. Consumers must be aware of all prices. Laborers and owners of capital must be aware of how much their resources will bring in all possible uses. Firms must know the prices of all inputs and the characteristics of all relevant technologies. Moreover, in its purest sense, perfect competition requires that all of these economic decision-making units have an accurate knowledge of the future together with the past and present.

Having described these four requirements, it is obvious that no industry is perfectly competitive. Some agricultural markets may be reasonably close, since the first three requirements are frequently met; but even they do not meet all of the requirements.[2] Nevertheless, this does not mean that the study of the behavior of perfectly competitive markets is useless. Recall from Chapter 1 that a model may be quite useful even though some of its assumptions are unrealistic. The conclusions derived from the model of perfect competition have proved very useful in explaining and predicting behavior in the real world. They have permitted a reasonably accurate view of resource allocation in important segments of our economy.

PRICE DETERMINATION IN THE SHORT RUN

The Output of the Firm

Having described perfect competition, we proceed to the determination of price and output. The first question we take up is: How much output will the firm produce in the short run? In the short run, the firm can expand or contract its output rate by increasing or decreasing the rate at which it employs variable inputs. Since the market is perfectly competitive, the firm cannot affect the price of its product and, like any perfectly competitive firm, it can sell any amount of its product that it wants at the prevailing price. Also, assume, as in previous chapters, that the firm maximizes its profits. To illustrate the firm's situation, consider the example in Table 8.1. The market price is $10 a unit, and the firm can produce as much as it chooses. Thus the firm's total revenue at various output rates is given in column 3 of Table 8.1. The firm's total fixed cost, total variable cost, and total cost are given in columns 4, 5, and 6 of Table 8.1. Finally, the last column shows the firm's total profit, the difference between total revenue and total cost, at various output rates.

Figure 8.1 provides a graphical description of the relationship between total revenue and total cost, on the one hand, and output, on the other. Of course, the vertical distance between the total revenue curve and the total cost curve is the profit at the corresponding output rate. (Note once again that cost curves are another name for cost functions. Both terms are in common use.) Below 2 units of output and above 7 units of output, this distance is negative.

---

2. Some agricultural markets in which the conditions would otherwise be reasonably close to perfect competition are heavily affected by government programs. See pp. 245–48.

TABLE 8.1 Cost and Revenue of a Firm: Prices Taken as Given by the Firm

Output per period	Price (dollars)	Total revenue (dollars)	Total fixed cost (dollars)	Total variable cost (dollars)	Total cost (dollars)	Total profit (dollars)
0	10	0	12	0	12	−12
1	10	10	12	2	14	− 4
2	10	20	12	3	15	5
3	10	30	12	5	17	13
4	10	40	12	8	20	20
5	10	50	12	13	25	25
6	10	60	12	23	35	25
7	10	70	12	38	50	20
8	10	80	12	69	81	− 1

Since the firm can sell either large or small volumes of output at the same price per unit, the total revenue curve will be a straight line through the origin. This is always the case when the firm takes the price as given. The total cost

FIGURE 8.1 Relationship between Total Cost and Total Revenue: Prices Taken as Given by the Firm *The output rate that will maximize the firm's profits is either 5 or 6 units per time period. At either of these output rates, profit (total revenue minus total cost) equals $25.*

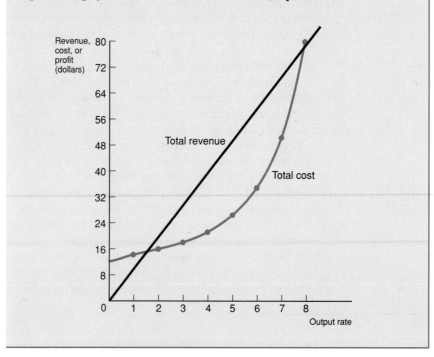

TABLE 8.2 Marginal Revenue and Marginal Cost: Prices Taken as Given by the Firm

Output per period	Marginal revenue (dollars)	Marginal cost* (dollars)
1	10	2
2	10	1
3	10	2
4	10	3
5	10	5
6	10	10
7	10	15
8	10	31

*This is the marginal cost between the indicated output level and one unit less than this output level.

curve has the kind of shape we would expect, on the basis of Chapter 7, of a short-run total cost curve.

Optimal output rate   Based on an examination of either Table 8.1 or Figure 8.1, the output rate that will maximize the firm's profits is either 5 or 6 units per time period. These are the output rates where the profit figure in the last column of Table 8.1 is the largest and where the vertical distance between the total revenue and total cost curves in Figure 8.1 is the greatest.

For many purposes it is convenient to present the marginal revenue and marginal cost curves, as well as the total revenues and total cost curves. Table 8.2 shows marginal revenue and marginal cost at each output rate. These figures were derived in the way shown in Chapters 5 and 7. Figure 8.2 shows the resulting marginal revenue and marginal cost curves. Since the firm takes the price as given, marginal revenue equals price, since the change in total revenue resulting from a 1-unit change in sales necessarily equals the price.

The important thing to note is that the maximum profit is achieved at the output rate where price (= marginal revenue) equals marginal cost. Both the figures in Table 8.2 and the curves in Figure 8.2 indicate that price equals marginal cost at an output rate between 5 and 6 units, which we know from Table 8.1 or Figure 8.1 to be the profit-maximizing output. Is this merely a chance occurrence, or will it usually be true that price will equal marginal cost at the profit-maximizing output rate?

Price Equals Marginal Cost

The fact that price equals marginal cost at the optimal output rate is not merely a chance occurrence; it will usually be true if the firm takes as given the price of the product. To prove that this is the case, consider Figure 8.3, which shows a typical short-run marginal cost curve. Suppose that the price is OP_0. At any output rate (after perhaps an irrelevant range in which marginal cost is falling)

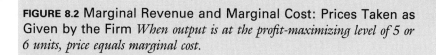

FIGURE 8.2 Marginal Revenue and Marginal Cost: Prices Taken as Given by the Firm *When output is at the profit-maximizing level of 5 or 6 units, price equals marginal cost.*

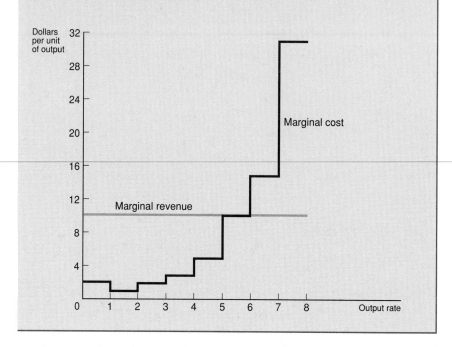

FIGURE 8.3 Short-Run Average and Marginal Cost Curves *If price is* OP_0, *the firm will produce an output of OX; if price is* OP_2, *it will produce an output of OY; and if price is less than* OP_3, *it will produce nothing.*

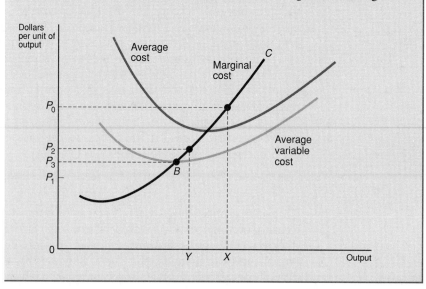

less than *OX*, price exceeds marginal cost; thus increases in output will increase profit since they will add more to total revenues than to total costs. At any output rate above *OX*, price is less than marginal cost; thus decreases in output will increase profits, since they will reduce total cost more than total revenue. Since increases in output up to *OX* result in increases in profit and further increases in output result in decreases in profit, *OX* must be the profit-maximizing output.

Even if the firm is doing the best it can, it may not be able to earn a profit. For example, if the price is OP_2 in Figure 8.3, short-run average costs exceed the price at all possible outputs. Since the short run is too short to allow the firm to alter the scale of its plant, it cannot liquidate its plant in the short run. All that the firm can do is to produce at a loss or discontinue production. The firm's decision will depend on whether the price of the product will cover average variable costs. If there exists an output rate where price exceeds average variable costs, it will pay the firm to produce, even though price does not cover average total costs. If there does not exist an output rate where price exceeds average variable costs, the firm is better off to produce nothing at all. Thus, if the average variable cost curve is as shown in Figure 8.3, the firm will produce if the price is OP_2, but not if it is OP_1.

Discontinuing production
The reasoning behind this conclusion is as follows: If the firm produces nothing, it must still pay its fixed costs. Consequently, if the loss resulting from production is less than the firm's fixed costs, it is more profitable (in the sense that losses are smaller) to produce than not to produce. On a per unit basis, this means that it is better to produce than to discontinue production if the loss per unit of production is less than average fixed costs, that is, if $ATC - P < AFC$, where *ATC* is average total costs, *P* is price, and *AFC* is average fixed cost. But this will be so if $ATC < AFC + P$, since *P* has merely been added to both sides of the inequality. Subtracting *AFC* from both sides, this will be so if $ATC - AFC < P$. But $ATC - AFC$ is average variable costs, which means that we have proved what we set out to prove: that it is better to produce than to discontinue production if price exceeds average variable costs.

Thus, if the firm maximizes profit or minimizes losses, it sets its output rate so that short-run marginal cost equals price.[3] But this rule, like most others, has an exception: If the market price is too low to cover the firm's average variable costs at any conceivable output rate, the firm will minimize losses by discontinuing production.

Finally, it is a simple matter to derive the firm's short-run supply curve. Suppose that the firm's short-run cost curves are those in Figure 8.3. If the price of the product is below OP_3, the firm will produce nothing, because there is no

---

3. Let the total cost be $C(Q)$, where Q is the output rate. The total profit per period is

$$\pi = PQ - C(Q)$$

where P is the price of the product. If π is a maximum,

$$P - \frac{dC(Q)}{dQ} = 0,$$

or price must equal marginal cost. The second-order condition for a maximum is

$$\frac{d^2C(Q)}{dQ^2} > 0.$$

output level where price exceeds average variable cost. If the price of the product exceeds OP_3, the firm will set its output rate at the point at which price equals marginal cost. This is the output rate that maximizes profit. Thus, if the price is OP_0, the firm will produce OX; if the price is OP_2, the firm will produce OY, and so forth. The resulting supply curve is that shown in Figure 8.4 as OP_3BC. *Given the way it was constructed, this curve is exactly the same as the firm's short-run marginal cost curve for prices above OP_3; at or below OP_3, the supply curve coincides with the price axis.*

FIGURE 8.4 The Supply Curve of the Perfectly Competitive Firm *The supply curve of the perfectly competitive firm equals* OP_3BC.

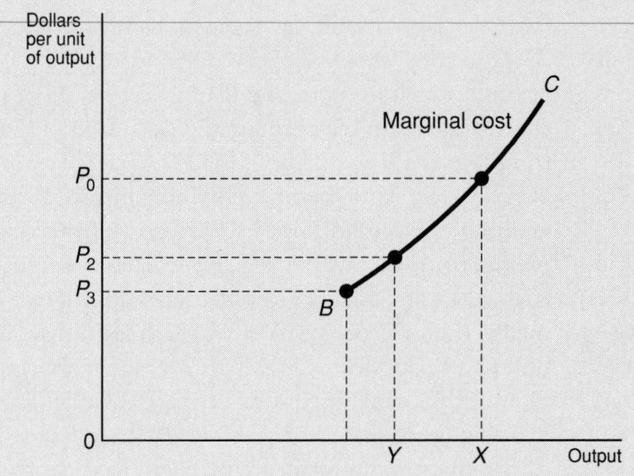

Short-Run Supply Curve of the Industry

The price of the industry's product in the short run was given to us in the previous section. What we want to do is to see how it is determined. This price is influenced both by the consumers that demand the good and the firms that supply it. The determinants of the industry demand curve (that is, the market demand curve) have been discussed in previous chapters, particularly in Chapter 5. In this section, we discuss the determinants of the short-run industry supply curve (that is, the short-run market supply curve), and in the next section, we combine the demand and supply curves to determine the industry's price and output in the short run.

Rough approximation   As a rough approximation, the industry's short-run supply curve can be regarded as the horizontal summation of the short-run supply curves of all of the firms in the industry. For example, if there were three firms in the industry and if their supply curves were OSS_1S_1', OSS_2S_2', OSS_3S_3' in Figure 8.5, the industry's supply curve would be $OSS'S''$, since $OSS'S''$ shows the amounts of the product that all of the firms together would supply at various prices. Of course, if there were only three firms, the industry would not be perfectly

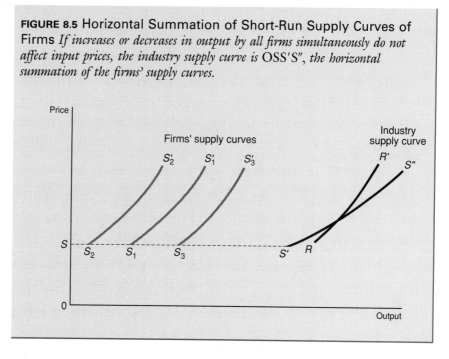

FIGURE 8.5 Horizontal Summation of Short-Run Supply Curves of
Firms *If increases or decreases in output by all firms simultaneously do not
affect input prices, the industry supply curve is OSS'S", the horizontal
summation of the firms' supply curves.*

competitive, but we can ignore this inconsistency. The point of Figure 8.5 is to
illustrate the fact that the industry supply curve is the horizontal summation of
the firm supply curves, at least under one important assumption.

The assumption underlying this construction of the short-run industry supply curve is that supplies of inputs to the industry as a whole are perfectly
elastic. In other words, it is assumed that increases or decreases in output by all
firms simultaneously do not affect input prices. This is a strong assumption.
Although changes in the output of one firm alone often cannot affect input
prices, the simultaneous expansion or contraction of output by all firms may
well alter input prices, with the result that the individual firm's cost curves—
and supply curve—will shift. For example, an expansion of the whole industry
may bid up the price of certain inputs, with the result that the cost curves of the
industrial firms will be pushed upward.[4]

If, contrary to the assumption underlying Figure 8.5, input prices are influenced in this way by expansion of the industry, what will be the effect on the
short-run industry supply curve? It will make the short-run industry supply
curve less elastic than *OSS'S"*. In the relevant price range, the curve might be
more like *RR'*. To see this, note that expansion of the industry causes the
short-run average cost curve and the short-run marginal cost curve to move
upward, because of the resulting increase in input prices. But if the marginal
cost curve moves upward, price will equal marginal cost at a lower output than
would have been the case if the marginal cost curve had not moved.

In summary, the shape of the short-run supply curve is determined by the

---

4. More will be said about the effect of industry output on individual cost curves in subsequent
   sections of this chapter.

number of firms in the industry, the size of the plant and other factors determining the shape of the marginal cost curve of each firm, and the effect of changes in industry output on input prices.

Short-Run Equilibrium Price and Output for the Industry

Equilibrium price and output

As we know from Chapter 2, the short-run equilibrium price level is the price at which the quantity demanded and the quantity supplied of the product in the short run are equal. For example, if the demand curve is D and the supply curve is as shown in Figure 8.6, the equilibrium price is OP and the equilibrium industry output is OQ, this point being the intersection of the demand and supply curves. Once enough time has elapsed for firms to adjust their utilization of the variable inputs, the price will tend to equal this equilibrium level. If the price is above this equilibrium level, the quantity supplied will tend to exceed the quantity demanded, with the result that the price will tend to fall. If the price is below this equilibrium level, the quantity demanded will tend to exceed the quantity supplied, with the result that the price will tend to rise. There is no tendency for the price to move in one direction or the other if and only if it is at the equilibrium level.

At the equilibrium price, price will equal marginal cost for all firms that choose to produce, rather than shut down their plants. Price may be above or below average total cost, since there is no necessity that profits be zero or that fixed costs be covered in the short run. An increase in demand will increase equilibrium price and output in the short run. For example, suppose that demand shifts from D to E in Figure 8.6. The shift in the demand curve will

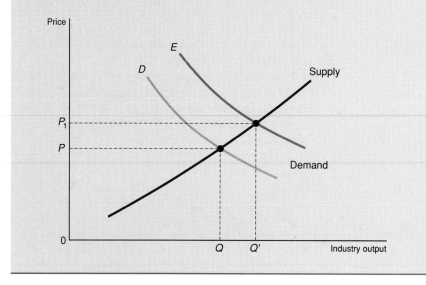

FIGURE 8.6 Determination of Price and Output in the Short Run *If the demand curve shifts from* D *to* E, *the price will eventually rise to* OP_1, *and each firm (that produces) will adjust its output rate upward so its marginal cost equals the higher price.*

cause a shortage at the old price, *OP,* with the result that the price will eventually be pushed up to OP_1. At the same time, each firm will adjust its output rate upward so that its marginal cost will equal the higher price, with the result that industry output will grow to OQ'.

EXAMPLE 8.1

AUCTIONS AND EXPERIMENTAL ECONOMICS

In the 1980s and 1990s, Charles Plott of Caltech, Vernon Smith of the University of Arizona, and others have carried out a variety of interesting experiments to study how markets work in relatively simple situations. The subjects (often college students) trade a commodity with no intrinsic value. Buyers make a profit by purchasing the commodity from sellers and reselling it to the experimenter. Sellers make a profit by buying units from the experimenter and selling them to buyers. The terms on which the experimenter will buy or sell the commodity are spelled out to the subjects (and determine the demand and supply curves).

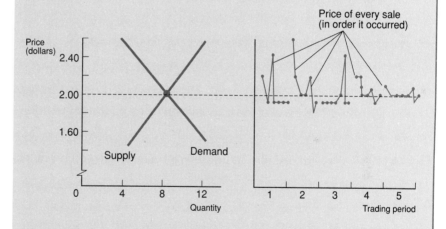

In one of Smith's experiments, an auction occurred in which public bids or offers were made to buy or sell units of the good in question. There were five trading periods. Each participant was free to accept whatever terms he or she chose. The market demand and supply curves were as shown in the left-hand panel in the above figure. The right-hand panel shows the price of every sale in the order in which it occurred.

(a) In this experiment, did the actual price converge on the competitive equilibrium price? (b) How many trading periods were required before the actual prices all were within about 10 percent of the competitive equilibrium price? (c) Did this experiment incorporate all of the characteristics of perfect competition? (d) Did this experiment prove that actual price always converges on the competitive equilibrium price?

SOLUTION

(a) Yes. The competitive equilibrium price is $2, and it is clear from the right-hand panel of the graph that the actual price tended to converge on it as time went on. (b) By the fourth trading period, all of the actual prices at which sales were made were within about 10 percent of $2, the competitive equilibrium price. (c) No. According to the customary definition, a perfectly competitive market contains a great many buyers and sellers, whereas only a few existed in this experiment. It is noteworthy that the competitive equilibrium price is a good approximation to the outcome of this auction even though the number of buyers and sellers is not very large. (d) No. The results of experiments vary depending on the number of buyers and sellers and the way the market is organized. For example, if there is only one seller, the price tends to depart from the competitive equilibrium price. (More will be said on this score in Chapter 9.)*

*For further discussion, see C. Plott, "Theories of Industrial Organization as Explanation of Experimental Market Behavior," reprinted in E. Mansfield, *Microeconomics: Selected Readings,* 5th ed.; and V. Smith, A. Williams, W. K. Bratton, and M. Vannoni, "Competitive Market Institutions: Double Auctions vs. Sealed Bid-Offer Auctions," *American Economic Review,* March 1982.

PRICE DETERMINATION IN THE LONG RUN

The Long-Run Adjustment Process

In the long run, the firm can change its plant size. This means that established firms may leave an industry if the industry has below-average profits, or that new firms may enter an industry if the industry has above-average profits. The next two sections are concerned with the long-run equilibrium of a perfectly competitive industry. We begin in this section by describing the adjustment process for an established firm.

Suppose that the firm has a plant with short-run average and marginal cost curves of A_0A_0' and M_0M_0', shown in Figure 8.7. Suppose that the price of the product is OP. With its existing plant the firm makes a small profit on each unit of output. However, in the long run, the firm is not limited to this plant. The firm could build a plant corresponding to any of the short-run cost curves in Figure 8.7. For example, it could build a medium-sized plant corresponding to the short-run cost curves of A_1A_1' and M_1M_1', or it could build a large plant corresponding to the short-run cost curves of A_2A_2' and M_2M_2'. What will the firm do in the long run? If it attempts to maximize profit it will choose to build the plant corresponding to short-run cost curves of A_2A_2' and M_2M_2'. The maximum attainable profit under the postulated circumstances will be earned by using this plant and producing OQ_2 units of output per period of time.

In general, maximum profit will be obtained by producing at an output rate and with a plant such that the *long-run marginal cost is equal to price at the point where the short-run marginal cost of the plant is equal to price*. This, of course, is true at the output of OQ_2 units and with the plant corresponding to short-run cost curves A_2A_2' and M_2M_2' in Figure 8.7. The plant will be chosen so that long-run marginal cost equals price, since this clearly is a condition for profit

FIGURE 8.7 Initial Change of Plant Size in the Long Run *To maximize profit in the long run, the firm will choose an output level* (OQ$_2$) *and plant size so that the long-run marginal cost is equal to price* (OP) *at the point where the short-run marginal cost* (M$_2$M$_2'$) *of the plant is equal to price.*

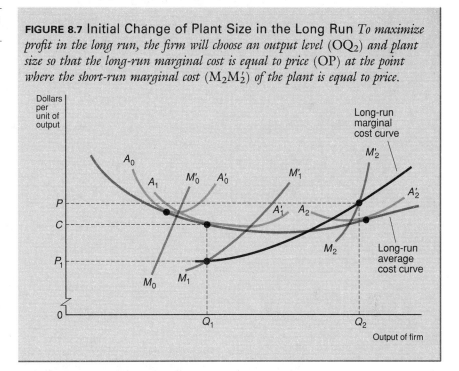

maximization in the long run. To maximize profit, the firm will operate this plant at the point where short-run marginal cost equals price. Thus the equality of long-run marginal cost, short-run marginal cost, and price follows from the assumption of profit maximization. (See footnote 11, Chapter 7.)

If all firms in the industry except this one had plants of optimal size, the expansion of this one firm would have no significant influence on price. Con-

Economic profit sequently, since OP is greater than the average cost of producing OQ$_2$ units, all firms would be earning a profit. Recall from Chapter 7 that costs, as reckoned by economists (but not accountants), include the returns that could be gotten from the most lucrative alternative use of the firm's resources. Consequently, an *economic profit* means that the firm is making more than it could make with its resources in other industries. Of course, the existence of above-average profits in this industry attracts new entrants; when these new firms enter the industry, the adjustment process must go on.

The arrival of new entrants shifts the industry supply curve to the right. That is, more will be supplied at a given price than before. For example, suppose that the industry supply curve shifts from S to S_1 in Figure 8.8, with the result that the price drops from OP to OP_1 and industry output increases from OQ to OQ_3. Although total industry output increases (because of the new entrants), the output of each of the firms is smaller. Given that the price is now OP_1 the optimal output of each firm is OQ_1, rather than OQ_2 (see Figure 8.7). And the optimal plant is the one corresponding to the short-run cost curves A_1A_1' and M_1M_1'. Firms that have built plants corresponding to the short-run cost curves A_2A_2' and M_2M_2' will lose a great deal of money. But even those firms that have plants of optimal size (corresponding to the short-run curves A_1A_1' and M_1M_1') will lose P_1C dollars per unit.

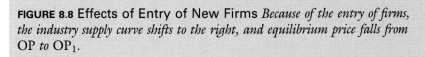

FIGURE 8.8 Effects of Entry of New Firms *Because of the entry of firms, the industry supply curve shifts to the right, and equilibrium price falls from* OP *to* OP_1.

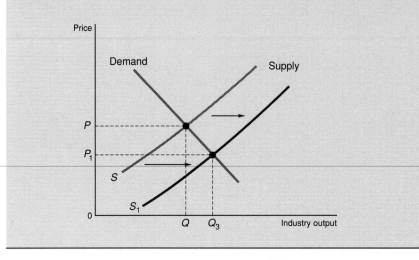

This does not mean that firms with plants of optimal size are not maximizing profits. On the contrary, it is evident from Figure 8.7 that, with the price at OP_1, long-run marginal cost equals short-run marginal cost equals price when the firm produces OQ_1 units of output with the plant corresponding to the short-run cost curves A_1A_1' and M_1M_1'. Thus this is the profit-maximizing solution for the firm. The trouble is that, even if the firm does the best it can, it cannot make an economic profit. The result will be an out-migration of firms from the industry. Since the returns that could be obtained from the firm's resources are greater in other industries, entrepreneurs will transfer these resources to other industries. In this way, the adjustment process will go on, since the exit of firms will shift the industry's supply curve to the left.

Long-Run Equilibrium of the Firm

When and where will this adjustment process end? Eventually, enough firms will leave the industry so that economic losses are eliminated, but profits are avoided, too. At this point the remaining firms will be in equilibrium. In other words, the long-run equilibrium position of the firm is at the point at which its long-run average total costs equal price. If price is in excess of average total costs for any firm, economic profits are being earned and new firms will enter the industry. If price is less than average total costs for any firm, that firm will eventually leave the industry.

Going a step further, we can show that price must be equal to the *lowest value* of long-run average total costs. In other words, firms must be producing at the minimum point on their long-run average cost curves. The reason for this is as follows: To maximize their profits, firms must operate where price equals long-run marginal cost. Also, we have just seen that they must operate where price equals long-run average cost. But if both of these conditions are satisfied, it

Price = marginal cost = average cost

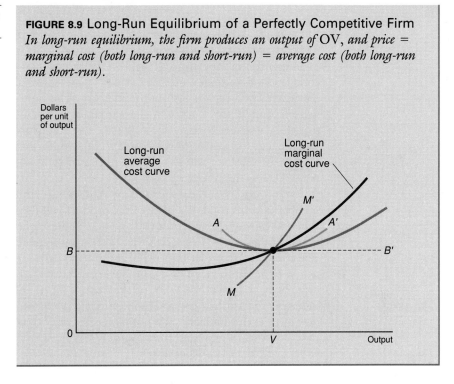

FIGURE 8.9 Long-Run Equilibrium of a Perfectly Competitive Firm
*In long-run equilibrium, the firm produces an output of OV, and price =
marginal cost (both long-run and short-run) = average cost (both long-run
and short-run).*

follows that long-run marginal cost must equal long-run average cost. And we
know from Chapter 7 that long-run marginal cost is equal to long-run average
cost only at the point at which long-run average cost is a minimum. Thus this
must be the equilibrium position of the firm.

This equilibrium position is illustrated in Figure 8.9. When all adjustments
are made, price equals *OB*. Since the demand curve is horizontal, the marginal
revenue curve is the same as the demand curve, both being *BB'*. The equilibrium output of the firm is *OV,* and its plant corresponds to short-run average
and marginal cost curves *AA'* and *MM'*. At this output and with this plant,
long-run marginal cost equals short-run marginal cost equals price: This insures
that the firm is maximizing profit. Also, long-run average cost equals short-run
average cost equals price. This insures that economic profits are zero. Since the
long-run marginal cost and long-run average cost must be equal, the equilibrium point is at the bottom of the long-run average cost curve.

Since price must be the same for all firms in the industry, this implies that the
minimum of the long-run average cost curve must be the same for all firms.
However, this is not as unrealistic as it appears at first glance. Firms that appear
to have lower costs than others in the industry often have unusually good
resources or particularly able managements. The owners of superior resources
(including management ability) can obtain a higher price for them if they are
put to alternative uses than more ordinary resources. Consequently, the alternative costs, or implicit costs, of one's using superior resources are higher than
those of using ordinary resources. If this is taken into account, and if these
superior resources are costed properly, the firms with apparently lower costs
have no lower costs at all.

In the previous two sections, it was assumed implicitly that the industry exhibited constant costs, which means that expansion of the industry does not result in an increase in input prices. Figure 8.10 shows long-run equilibrium under conditions of constant cost. The left-hand panel shows the short- and long-run cost curves of a typical firm in the industry. The right-hand panel shows the demand and supply curves in the market as a whole, D being the original demand curve and S being the original short-run supply curve. It is assumed that the industry is in long-run equilibrium, with the result that the price line is tangent to the long-run (and short-run) average cost curve at its minimum point. (OP is the price.)

Assume now that the demand curve shifts to D_1. In the short run, with the number of firms fixed, the price of the product will rise from OP to OP_1; each firm will expand output from OQ to OQ_1; and each firm will be making economic profits since OP_1 exceeds the short-run average costs of the firm at OQ_1. The consequence is that firms will enter the industry and shift the supply curve to the right. In the case of a constant-cost industry, the entrance of the new firms does not affect the costs of the existing firms. The inputs used by this industry are used by many other industries as well, and the appearance of the new firms in this industry does not bid up the price of inputs and consequently raise the costs of existing firms. Neither does the appearance of the new firms lower the costs of existing firms.

FIGURE 8.10 Long-Run Equilibrium: Constant-Cost Industry *A constant-cost industry has a horizontal long-run supply curve, as shown in panel B. If demand shifts upward from D to D₁, the resulting increase in price (to OP₁) results in the entry of firms, which shifts the supply curve to the right (to S₁), thus pushing the price back to its original level (OP).*

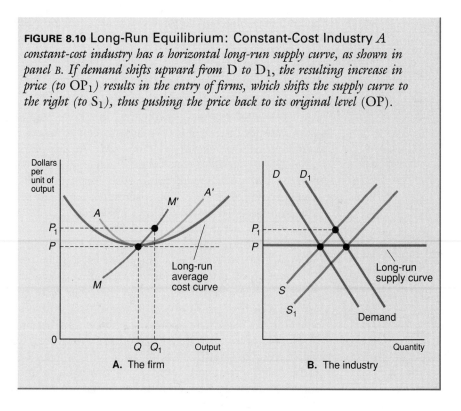

A. The firm

B. The industry

Consequently, *a constant cost industry has a horizontal long-run supply curve.* Since output can be increased by increasing the number of firms producing *OQ* units at an average cost of *OP,* the long-run supply curve is horizontal at *OP.* So long as the industry remains in a state of constant costs, its output can be increased indefinitely. If price exceeds *OP,* firms would enter the industry; if price were less than *OP,* firms would leave the industry. Thus long-run equilibrium can only occur in this industry when price is *OP.* And industry output can be expanded or contracted, in accord with demand conditions, without altering this long-run equilibrium price.

Increasing- and Decreasing-Cost Industries

An increasing-cost industry is shown in Figure 8.11. The original conditions are the same as in Figure 8.10, *D* being the original demand curve, *S* being the original supply curve, *OP* being the equilibrium price, and the long-run and short-run average cost curves of each firm being *LL'* and *AA'* in the left panel. As in Figure 8.10, the original position is one of long-run equilibrium, since the price line is tangent to the average cost curves at their minima.

Now suppose that the demand curve shifts to D_1, with the result that the price of the product increases and firms earn economic profits, thus attracting new entrants. More and more inputs are required by the industry, and in an increasing-cost industry, the price of inputs increases with the amount used by the industry. Consequently, the cost of inputs increases for the established firms as well as the new entrants and the average cost curves are pushed up to L_1L_1' and A_1A_1'.

FIGURE 8.11 Long-Run Equilibrium: Increasing-Cost Industry *An increasing-cost industry has a positively sloped long-run supply curve, as shown in panel B. After long-run equilibrium is achieved, increases in output require increases in the price of the product.*

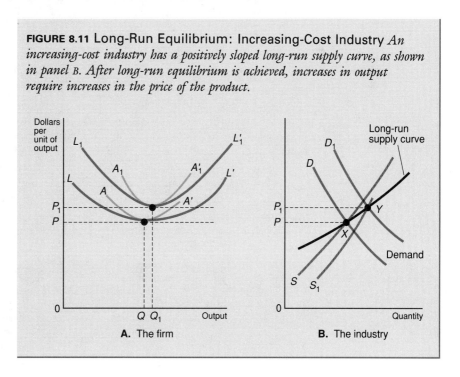

A. The firm   **B.** The industry

EXAMPLE 8.2

WHAT WOULD BE THE EFFECTS OF NATIONAL DENTAL INSURANCE?

Many countries, such as Sweden and the United Kingdom, have national health insurance covering dental services. In the United States, there have been proposals for such dental insurance. A number of questions arise concerning the effects of these proposed insurance schemes, one of the most important being: How much more dental care would be demanded if these plans were implemented? Economists at the RAND Corporation* have estimated that the demand curves for dental care for adult males, adult females, and children in the United States are as follows:

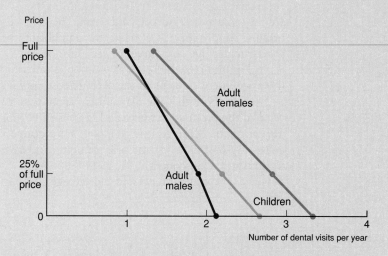

(a) According to some proposals, national dental insurance would pay for three-quarters of the price of dental care. About how much of an increase in the quantity demanded of dental care would result if these proposals were adopted? (b) Based on the above diagram, can you determine whether it would be possible to meet the resulting increase in demand with the current number of dentists? If not, what additional curve do you need? (c) Do you think that the quantity of dental services supplied would be the same, regardless of the price of dental care? Why or why not? (d) What would be the effect of the above proposals on the market demand curve for dental care? Why? (e) Would the price of dental care tend to rise? (f) Many economists suggest that, if the above proposals for a national dental insurance plan were adopted, they should be phased in slowly and gradually, as in Sweden in 1974. Why?

SOLUTION

(a) Based on the demand curves shown above, the quantity demanded of dental care would more than double if people were to pay 25 percent of the full price. (b) No. If the market for dental services were perfectly competitive, the supply curve for dental care would be needed to tell us how much dental

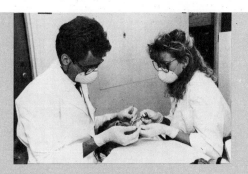

care would be supplied at each price. (c) No. As the price of dental care increases (at least up to some point), it seems likely that more dental services will be supplied. (d) The market demand curve for dental care would tend to shift to the right. At a particular price, people would demand more dental care than in the past because they would have to pay only 25 percent of this price. (e) If the demand curve for dental services were to shift to the right, and if the supply curve were not to shift (and if it were to slope upward to the right), the price would tend to rise. (f) It would take considerable time for the supply of dental services to adjust to the increase in demand.**

*W. Manning and C. Phelps, "The Demand for Dental Care," *Bell Journal of Economics*, Autumn 1979.
**For further discussion, see Manning and Phelps, *op. cit.*

If the marginal cost curve of each firm is shifted to the left by the increase in input prices, the industry supply curve will tend to shift to the left. However, this tendency is more than counterbalanced by the effects of the increase in the number of firms, which shifts the industry supply curve to the right. The latter effect must more than offset the former effect because otherwise there would be no expansion in total industry output. (No new resources would have been attracted to the industry.) The process of adjustment must go on until a new point of long-run equilibrium is reached. In Figure 8.11, this point is where the price of the product is OP_1 and each firm produces OQ_1 units;[5] the new short-run supply curve is S_1.

Increasing-cost industry

An increasing-cost industry *has a positively sloped long-run supply curve.* That is, after long-run equilibrium is achieved, increases in output require increases in the price of the product. For example, points X and Y in Figure 8.11 are both on the long-run supply curve for the industry. The difference between constant-cost and increasing-cost industries is as follows: In constant-cost industries, new firms enter in response to an increase in demand until price returns to its original level; whereas in increasing-cost industries, new firms enter until the

5. We cannot be sure that OQ_1 exceeds OQ, as shown in Figure 8.11. It is possible for OQ_1 to be less than or equal to OQ.

FIGURE 8.12 Long-Run Equilibrium: Decreasing-Cost Industry

A decreasing-cost industry has a negatively sloped long-run supply curve, as shown in panel B. After long-run equilibrium is achieved, increases in output are accompanied by decreases in price.

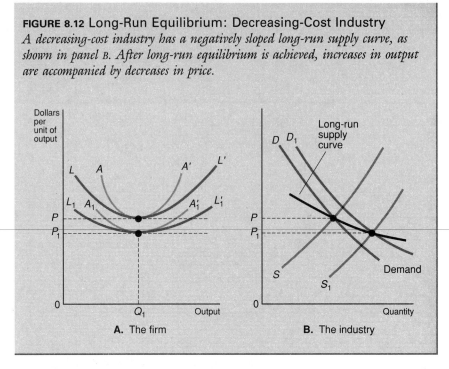

A. The firm

B. The industry

minimum point on the long-run average cost curve has increased to the point where it equals the new price.[6]

A decreasing-cost industry is shown in Figure 8.12. Once again, we begin with an industry in long-run equilibrium, the demand curve being D, the short-run supply curve being S, price being OP, and the long-run and short-run average cost curves of each firm being LL' and AA'. As before, we postulate an increase in demand to D_1, the result being economic profit for established firms and the entry of new firms. However, in the case of a decreasing-cost industry, the expansion of the industry results in a decrease in the costs of the established firms. Thus the new long-run equilibrium is at a price of OP_1, the equilibrium output of each firm being OQ_1, and the new long-run and short-run average cost curves being L_1L_1' and A_1A_1'.

A decreasing-cost industry has a negatively sloped long-run supply curve. That is, after long-run equilibrium is reached, increases in output are accompanied by decreases in price. *External economies,* which are cost reductions that occur when the industry expands, may be responsible for the existence of decreasing-cost industries. An example of an external economy is an improvement in transportation that is due to the expansion of an industry and that reduces the costs of each firm in the industry. If there are important external economies, an industry may be subject to decreasing costs. Note that the external economies are quite different from economies of scale: The individual firm has no control over external economies.

Decreasing-cost industry

6. This is only one way in which equilibrium can be achieved in increasing-cost industries. It is also possible that the increase in input prices (due to the expansion of industry output) raises average cost more than the increase in demand raises average revenue. Thus firms may experience losses, some may leave the industry, and the remaining firms may produce at a larger scale.

Most economists seem to regard increasing-cost industries as being the most frequently encountered of the three types. Decreasing-cost industries are the most unusual situation, although quite young industries may fall into this category. Later in this chapter, we present estimates of the shape of the long-run supply curve in various industries.

THE ALLOCATION PROCESS: SHORT AND LONG RUN

At this point, it is instructive to describe the process by which a perfectly competitive economy—an economy composed of perfectly competitive industries—would allocate resources. In Chapter 1, we noted that the allocation of resources among alternative uses is one of the major functions of an economic system. Equipped with the concepts of this and previous chapters, we can now go much farther than we could in Chapter 1 in describing how a perfectly competitive economy goes about shifting resources in accord with changes in consumer demand.

Shift in tastes

To be specific, suppose that a change occurs in tastes, with the result that consumers are more favorably disposed toward corn and less favorably disposed toward potatoes than in the past. What will happen in the short run? The increase in the demand for corn increases the price of corn, and results in some increase in the output of corn. However, the output of corn cannot be increased very substantially because the capacity of the industry cannot be expanded in the short run. Similarly, the fall in the demand for potatoes reduces the price of potatoes, and results in some reduction in the output of potatoes. But the output of potatoes will not be curtailed greatly because firms will continue to produce as long as they can cover variable costs.

The change in the relative prices of corn and potatoes tells producers that a reallocation of resources is called for. Because of the increase in the price of corn and the decrease in the price of potatoes, corn producers are earning economic profits and potato producers are showing economic losses. This will trigger a redeployment of resources. If some variable inputs in the production of potatoes can be used as effectively in the production of corn, these variable inputs may be withdrawn from potato production and switched to corn production. Even if there are no variable inputs that are used in both corn and potato production, adjustment can occur in various interrelated markets, with the result that corn production gains resources and potato production loses resources.

Short-run effects

When short-run equilibrium is attained in both the corn and potato industries, the reallocation of resources is not yet complete since there has not been enough time for producers to build new capacity or liquidate old capacity. In particular, neither industry is operating at minimum average cost. The corn producers may be operating at greater than the output level where average cost is a minimum; and the potato producers may be operating at less than the output level where average cost is a minimum.

What will happen in the long run? The shift in consumer demand from potatoes to corn will result in greater adjustments in production and smaller adjustments in price than in the short run. In the long run, existing firms can leave potato production and new firms can enter corn production. Because of short-run economic losses in potato production, some potato land and related equipment will be allowed to run down, and some firms engaged in potato production will be liquidated. As firms leave potato production, the supply curve shifts to the left, causing the price to rise above its short-run level. The transfer of resources out of potato production will stop when the price has increased, and costs have decreased, to the point where losses are avoided.

While potato production is losing resources, corn production is gaining them. The short-run economic profits in corn production will result in the entry of new firms. The increased demand for inputs will raise input prices and cost curves in corn production, and the price of corn will be depressed by the movement to the right of the supply curve because of the entry of new firms. Entry ceases when economic profits are no longer being earned. At that point, when long-run equilibrium is achieved, there will be more firms and more resources used in the corn industry than in the short run.

Long-run effects   Finally, long-run equilibrium is established in both industries, and the re-allocation of resources is complete. It is important to note that this reallocation can affect industries other than corn and potatoes. If potato land and equipment can be easily adapted to the production of corn, which seems unlikely, potato producers can simply change to the production of corn. If not, the resources used in potato production are converted to some use other than corn, and the resources that enter corn production come from some use other than potato production. The full repercussions can be analyzed by general equilibrium analysis, which is discussed in Chapter 14.

ESTIMATES OF PRICE ELASTICITY OF SUPPLY

Previous sections of this chapter have dealt at length with the role of demand curves and supply curves, both short-run and long-run, in the determination of price. Chapter 5 presented the results of various empirical studies of the demand curve for selected commodities. In this section we present the results of various empirical studies of the supply curve for selected commodities. The econometric techniques used to estimate the supply curve are much like those used to estimate the demand curve, which were discussed in Chapter 5.

To illustrate the kind of studies that have been carried out, consider the investigation sponsored by the Environmental Protection Agency of the elasticity of supply of construction services in the United States.[7] Studies made for EPA estimated that a 1 percent increase in the price of construction leads to an increase of 6.5 percent in the supply of construction services. EPA was extremely interested in the price elasticity of supply of construction services because it wanted to know how much construction prices had to rise in order to bring forth the extra construction services required to build the treatment plants and other equipment needed to meet new environmental protection standards.

7. The Environmental Protection Agency has sponsored a variety of studies of this and related topics, including *The Economics of Clean Water.*

EXAMPLE 8.3

SPECULATION AND THE COFFEE MARKET

Speculators frequently try to buy up commodities when they are cheap and sell them in subsequent periods when they are dear. For example, in 1986 the Brazilian coffee crop was poor because of a severe drought. Suppose that the market supply curve for coffee was as shown below in 1986 and 1985, and that the market demand curve for coffee, also shown below, was the same in both periods.

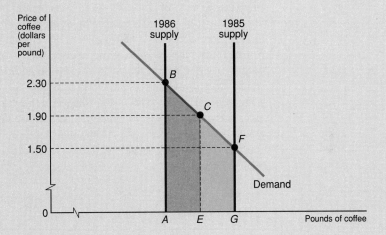

(a) Suppose that in 1985 speculators forecasted the poor 1986 coffee crop. How much money would they have made by buying a pound of coffee in 1985 and selling it in 1986? (Assume that storage costs are zero.) (b) As they bought more and more 1985 coffee for sale in 1986, what would happen to the price of coffee in 1985? What would happen to the 1986 price? (c) At what point would it no longer be profitable for speculators to buy more coffee in 1985 for sale in 1986? (d) If speculators bought *EG* pounds in 1985 and sold them in 1986, would society gain? (e) If speculators had forecasted a poor coffee crop in 1986, and bought large amounts of coffee in 1985 for sale in 1986, would society have gained by their actions if the 1986 coffee crop turned out to be larger than that in 1985?

*Coffee, Sugar, and
Cocoa Exchange, Inc.*

SOLUTION

(a) Since the 1985 price was $1.50 per pound and the 1986 price was $2.30 per pound, they would have made $2.30 − $1.50 = $0.80. (b) As they bought more and more coffee in 1985, the price of coffee would have risen then. As they sold more and more coffee in 1986, the price of coffee would have fallen then. (c) If they took *EG* pounds off the market in 1985, the remaining supply would be *OE* pounds, and the price would be $1.90 per pound, as shown in the graph. When these *EG*(= *AE*) pounds were added to the 1986 supply, it would mean that the total supply would be *OE* pounds (the same as in 1985), and the 1986 price would be $1.90 per pound. Since the price would be the same in 1986 as in 1985, there would be no profit in buying more coffee in 1985 for sale in 1986. (d) If we use the area under the demand curve as a measure of the value to society of an additional amount of output (recall Chapter 4), the value of the additional *AE* pounds in 1986 equals shaded area *ABCE* in the graph, and the value of the *EG*(= *AE*) pounds given up in 1985 equals shaded area *ECFG*. Since the former area exceeds the latter, society would gain, at least by this criterion. (e) No. They would have withdrawn coffee from use in 1985 (when relative to 1986 it was scarce) and made it available in 1986 (when relative to 1985 it was plentiful).[*]

[*]For further discussion, see "Coffee Price Boom Stirs Fear in Brazil," *New York Times*, February 17, 1986.

Of course, there is a considerable difference between short-run and long-run elasticities of supply. Turning to agriculture, Marc Nerlove and William Addison have estimated short-run and long-run elasticities of supply for a number of vegetables produced for fresh market in the United States. The short-run elasticity is defined to be the elasticity over one production period. The results are shown in Table 8.3.[8] Note that the short-run elasticities are considerably lower than the long-run elasticities, as would be expected. For example, the short-run elasticity of supply for cabbage is estimated to be 0.36, whereas the long-run elasticity is estimated to be 1.2. According to these estimates the long-run elasticity of supply is greater for cucumbers, green peas, and spinach than for the other commodities. Although these estimates are based on quite sophisticated techniques, Nerlove and Addison caution that they are tentative and presented mainly for purposes of illustration.

AGRICULTURAL PRICES AND OUTPUT: AN APPLICATION

Perhaps the most important sector of the American economy that contains industries that are reasonably close to perfect competition is agriculture. Farm-

8. For those who want to review the definition of the price elasticity of supply, see page 28.

TABLE 8.3 Estimated Price Elasticities of Supply

	Price elasticity	
Commodity	Short run	Long run
Green lima beans	0.10	1.70
Green snap beans	0.15	∞*
Cabbage	0.36	1.20
Carrots	0.14	1.00
Cucumbers	0.29	2.20
Lettuce	0.03	0.16
Onions	0.34	1.00
Green peas	0.31	4.40
Green peppers	0.07	0.26
Tomatoes	0.16	0.90
Watermelons	0.23	0.48
Beets	0.13	1.00
Cantaloupes	0.02	0.04
Cauliflower	0.14	1.10
Celery	0.14	0.95
Eggplant	0.16	0.34
Kale (Va. only)	0.20	0.23
Spinach	0.20	4.70
Shallots (La. only)	0.12	0.31

*According to Nerlove and Addison, this estimate holds only for a limited range of output.
Source: M. Nerlove and W. Addison, op. cit.

ing is still our most important single industry, although it includes a much smaller percentage of our people than it once did. One of the most important points to note about American agriculture is that agricultural prices generally fell, relative to other prices, from World War I to the early 1970s. That is, if we correct for changes in the general price level resulting from overall inflation, there was a declining trend in farm prices. Another important fact is that farm incomes vary between good times and bad to a much greater extent than non-farm incomes, whereas farm output is more stable than industrial output.

The theory presented in this and previous chapters is useful in explaining the reasons for these characteristics of American agriculture. Figure 8.13 shows the demand and supply curves for farm products at various points in time. Since we know from Chapter 5 that the demand for food does not grow very rapidly in this country, we would expect the demand curve to shift relatively slowly to the right, from D in the first period to D_1 in the second period to D_2 in the third period. On the other hand, because of very great technological improvements in agriculture, the supply curve has been shifting relatively rapidly to the right, from S in the first period to S_1 in the second period to S_2 in the third period. The consequence is that agricultural prices fell (relative to other prices) from OP to OP_1 to OP_2.

FIGURE 8.13 Shifts in Demand and Supply: Agriculture *Agricultural prices have fallen (relative to other prices) because the demand curve has shifted slowly to the right, whereas the supply curve has shifted rapidly to the right.*

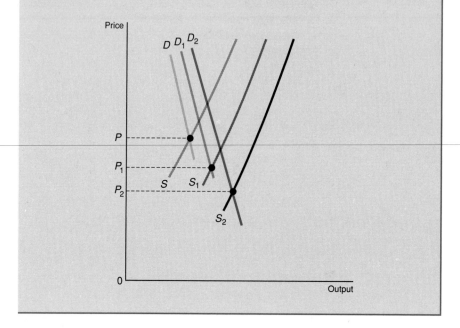

It is also easy to see why farm incomes are so unstable. We know from Chapter 5 that the demand curve for basic farm products is relatively inelastic. Also, the supply curve for basic farm products is relatively inelastic in the short run. Since both the demand curve and the supply curve are inelastic, a small shift (to the right or left) in either curve, or both, results in a large change in price. To illustrate, consider Figure 8.14. In panel A, the demand and supply curves are much less elastic than in panel B, with the result that a small shift in the demand curve results in a much bigger change in price in panel A than in panel B.[9]

9. For simplicity, suppose that the demand and supply curves exhibit the same elasticity at each point, in which case

$$Q_D = \alpha_0 P^{-\beta_0} \qquad [8.1]$$

$$Q_S = \alpha_1 P^{\beta_1} \qquad [8.2]$$

where P is price, Q_D the quantity demanded, and Q_S the quantity supplied. Equation 8.1 is the demand function in which β_0 is the price elasticity of demand. Equation 8.2 is the supply function in which β_1 is the price elasticity of supply. Suppose that the demand curve shifted slightly, with α_0 increasing or decreasing by a small amount. What would be the effect on the equilibrium price? Suppose that the supply curve shifted slightly, with α_1 increasing or decreasing by a small amount. What would be the effect on the equilibrium price?

Since $Q_D = Q_S \, (= Q)$ in equilibrium, it follows from Equations 8.1 and 8.2 that

$$\log P = \frac{\log \alpha_0 - \log \alpha_1}{\beta_0 + \beta_1}.$$

FIGURE 8.14 Relationship between Elasticity of Supply and Demand and Instability of Price *Because the demand and supply curves are much less elastic in panel A than in panel B, a small shift in the demand curve (from D to D₁) results in a much bigger change in price in panel A than in panel B.*

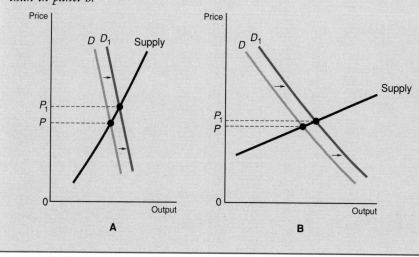

Although agricultural prices have generally fallen (relative to industrial prices) over the past sixty years, this trend was reversed sharply in 1973 and 1974, when farm prices rose at an astonishing rate. Due to poor harvests in other countries and the devaluation of the dollar, as well as trade with the Communist world, there was a marked upward shift to the right of the demand curve for American farm products. As would be predicted by our theory, farm prices rose rapidly in response to this shift in the demand curve. For example, the price of wheat rose from under $2 to over $5 per bushel. Anyone who witnessed the proceedings would have been quick to agree that farm prices behaved in accord with our model.

Government Subsidy Programs

Another important fact about American agriculture that must be added to this picture is government intervention and aid. Both Figures 8.13 and 8.14 are based on the supposition that agricultural markets are free. For about half of all farm products, the government has established price support programs of one sort or another. These programs vary in many respects, but the general idea

---

Thus

$$\frac{dP}{P} \div \frac{d\alpha_0}{\alpha_0} = \frac{1}{\beta_0 + \beta_1}$$

$$\frac{dP}{P} \div \frac{d\alpha_1}{\alpha_1} = \frac{-1}{\beta_0 + \beta_1}.$$

Consequently, as stated in the text, the relative change in price resulting from a small relative change in α_0 or α_1 is bigger if β_0 and β_1 are small than if β_0 or β_1 is large.

behind them is that the federal government has tried to increase farm prices in various ways. For products where such programs exist, the perfectly competitive model is clearly an inappropriate device to predict price and output. But, as we shall see in this section, the basic elements of the theory remain useful in analyzing the effects of these programs.

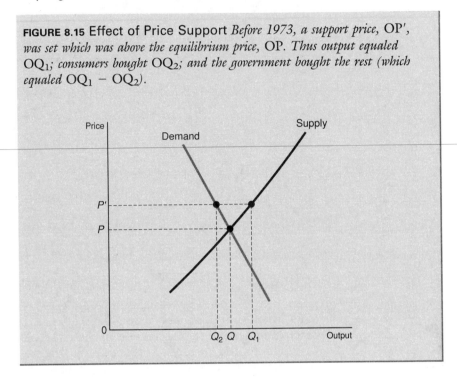

FIGURE 8.15 Effect of Price Support *Before 1973, a support price, OP', was set which was above the equilibrium price, OP. Thus output equaled OQ_1; consumers bought OQ_2; and the government bought the rest (which equaled $OQ_1 - OQ_2$).*

More specifically, the programs in operation until 1973 can be described in terms of Figure 8.15. A support price, OP', was set which was above the equilibrium price, OP, with the consequence that output equaled OQ_1, consumers bought OQ_2, and the rest (which equaled $OQ_1 - OQ_2$) had to be purchased by the government. The imposition of the support price meant, of course, that farmers received more for their crop than they otherwise would have, and the difference in their receipts was $OP' \times OQ_1 - OP \times OQ$.

To cut down on the amount that the government had to purchase (and store or dispose of), production controls were imposed as well. These controls often took the form of quotas on the acreage used to grow the product. With such controls, the situation is shown in Figure 8.16, where OQ_3 is the total quota—in terms of output—for all farms. Because of the imposition of the production control, the government's expenditures were reduced from $OP' \times (OQ_1 - OQ_2)$ in Figure 8.15 to $OP' (OQ_3 - OQ_2)$ in Figure 8.16.

In 1973, an alternative plan, proposed earlier by President Harry Truman's Secretary of Agriculture, Charles Brannan, and President Dwight Eisenhower's Secretary, Ezra Taft Benson, was adopted. According to this plan, which is illustrated in Figure 8.17, farmers are still guaranteed a "target" price of OP', but rather than allow the amount the government buys (which equals $OQ_3 - $

FIGURE 8.16 Effect of Price Support and Production Control *If* OQ₃ *is the total production quota, and* OP′ *is the support price, the government has to purchase an amount of the commodity equaling* (OQ₃ − OQ₂).

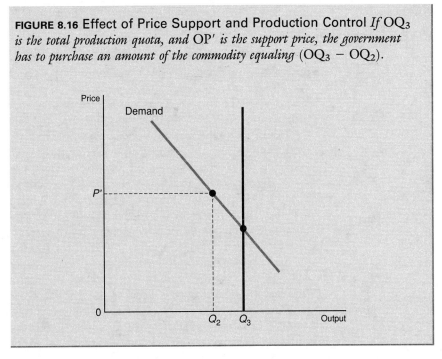

OQ_2) to waste in storage, they sell this amount at whatever consumers will pay for it. Or, what amounts to the same thing, the government lets the competitive market alone, with the result that an output of OQ_3 is produced and sold at a

FIGURE 8.17 Effect of the Brannan Plan *According to the Brannan Plan, farmers sell their output at price* OP₂, *and receive subsidy checks to cover the difference between the price they receive and the target price,* OP′.

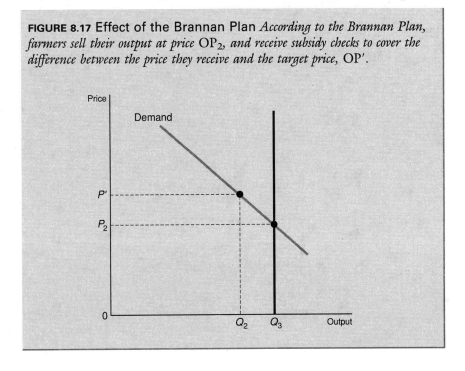

price of OP_2, then the government issues subsidy checks to farmers to cover the difference between the price they received and the target price, OP'.

Clearly, the cost to the government under the Brannan plan is $(OP' - OP_2) \times OQ_3$. An important question is: Will the cost to the Treasury be greater than under the support plan shown in Figure 8.16? The answer depends on the elasticity of demand. If demand is inelastic, it will be greater; if demand is elastic, it will be smaller. To prove this, recall that the cost under the Brannan plan would be $(OP' - OP_2)OQ_3$, and the cost in Figure 8.16 would be $OP'(OQ_3 - OQ_2)$. Thus the former cost would be less than the latter if $OP_2 \times OQ_3 > OP' \times OQ_2$. But since $OP_2 \times OQ_3$ is the revenue at price OP_2 and $OP' \times OQ_2$ is the revenue at price OP', the former will be more than the latter only if the price elasticity of demand exceeds 1. (Recall the discussion on p. 24.)

Since the demand for agricultural products is generally inelastic, this means that the Brannan plan will cost the Treasury more than the support plan in Figure 8.16, if the market price is less than the target price. But this is not a necessarily overwhelming argument against the Brannan plant. For one thing, the market price may be above the target price, in which case the Brannan plan will cost the Treasury nothing. For another, the Brannan plan has the advantage that the market price is closer to the true social cost of producing agricultural products. More will be said about the economic advantages and disadvantages of various types of agricultural price support programs in Chapter 15, when we continue this discussion of agricultural subsidies.

Summary

1. Perfect competition is defined by four conditions: No participant in the market can influence price; output must be homogeneous; resources must be mobile; and there must be perfect knowledge.

2. In the short run, the firm maximizes profit or minimizes losses by producing the output at which marginal cost equals price. However, if market price is less than the firm's average variable costs at all levels of output, the firm will minimize losses by discontinuing production. The firm's short-run supply curve is the same as its marginal cost curve, as long as price exceeds average variable cost.

3. The short-run price of a product is determined by the interaction between the demand and supply sides of the market. As a rough approximation, the industry's short-run supply curve can be regarded as the horizontal summation of the short-run supply curves of the individual firms. However, this is not the case if the supply of inputs to the industry is not perfectly elastic.

4. The short-run equilibrium price level is the price at which the quantity demanded and the quantity supplied in the short run are equal. At the equilibrium price, price will equal marginal cost for all firms that choose to produce, rather than shut down their plants.

5. In the long run, firms can change their plant size and leave or enter the industry. The long-run equilibrium position of the firm is at the point at which its long-run average costs equal price. Moreover, firms must be operating at the minimum point on their long-run average cost curves.

6. Industries can be divided into three types: constant cost, increasing cost, and decreasing cost. Constant-cost industries have horizontal long-run supply curves; increasing-cost industries have positively sloped long-run supply curves; and decreasing-cost industries have negatively sloped long-run supply curves.

Increasing-cost industries are generally regarded as being the most numerous of the three types.

7. Having presented this basic theory, we described the way in which resources are allocated in a perfectly competitive economy. In particular, we considered a case where, because of a shift in consumer demand from potatoes to corn, resources had to be shifted out of potato production and into corn production.

8. Finally, we used the theory to explain some of the characteristics of American agriculture and to analyze government subsidy programs.

**Questions/
Problems**

1. Because New York City imposes ceilings on rents, there is a shortage of apartments. (Recall our discussion in Chapter 2.) According to econometric studies, the price elasticity of demand for rental housing in American cities is 1.0 and the price elasticity of supply of rental housing is 0.5 in the long run. If these elasticities are valid in New York City, and if its government pushes the level of rent down to a point that is 1 percent below its equilibrium value, how big will be the difference between the quantity demanded and the quantity supplied, as a percentage of the equilibrium quantity of rental housing?

2. As pointed out in the previous question, studies indicate that the price elasticity of demand for rental housing in American cities is 1.0 and that the price elasticity of supply of rental housing is 0.5 in the long run. (a) Suppose that a particular city's government decides that the level of rent should be pushed up in order to bring about a 2-percent increase in the supply of rental housing. How big an increase in the rent is required? (b) What will be the effect on the total amount of rental housing that is demanded?

3. In the period between the first and second world wars, the cotton textile industry was sometimes described as being closer to perfect competition than any other manufacturing industry in the United States. Considerable excess capacity existed in the cotton textile industry from about 1924 to 1936. Evidence of this overcapacity is presented in the table below, which shows that the profit rate in cotton textiles was considerably below that in other manufacturing. For example, during 1924–28 and 1933–36, textile profits averaged less than 4 percent of the firms' capitalization, whereas profits as a percentage of capitalization in all manufacturing averaged 8 percent. Also, profit rates in cotton textiles were higher in the South than in the North, due to the fact that the prices of many inputs—like labor and raw cotton—were lower in the South.

	Profits as a percentage of capitalization	
Period	Cotton textiles	All manufacturing
1919–23	15.3	11.0
1924–28	4.7	11.0
1933–36	2.4	4.3

(a) Was the industry in long-run equilibrium? (b) What sorts of changes were required to make the industry approach long-run equilibrium? (c) In fact, did these changes occur—as our theory would predict?

4. "In long-run equilibrium, every firm in a competitive industry earns zero profit. Thus, if the price falls, all of these firms will be unable to stay in business." Evaluate this statement.

5. Richard Webster is a Nebraska farmer who produces corn on 1,000 acres of land, 500 of which are rented and 500 of which are owned. In an interview reported in the *New York Times*, he estimated that his costs per acre for corn produced on his rented land were as

shown on the following list:

Fertilizer	$ 41.84
Herbicides	2.76
Insecticides	5.50
Fuel	18.00
Seed	16.50
Electricity	15.00
Cost of services of plant and equipment	85.46
Labor	15.00
Insurance	10.00
Land rent	110.00
Total	$320.06

(a) Does this mean that the average cost of producing corn is $320.06? Why or why not? (b) On each acre of land that he owns, Mr. Webster does not have to pay a rent of $110, included above. Does this mean that the cost of using his own land is less than that of using rented land? (c) If each acre of land yields 120 bushels of corn, and if the price of a bushel of corn were expected to be 80 cents, should Mr. Webster produce any corn? (d) If the price were expected to be $1.50, should he produce any corn?

6. According to some firms in the paper industry, price controls during the early 1970s resulted in price being below average variable cost. What do you think that these firms did? If you had been a consultant to these firms, what advice would you have given them?

7. According to a 1978 study by Neil Ericsson and Peter Morgan, the supply curve for shale oil was as shown below.

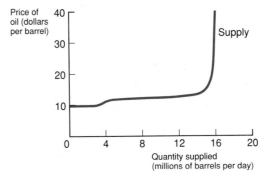

Two problems in producing shale oil is that the producer must dispose of the spent shale and that air pollution may occur. This supply curve assumes that the disposal of spent shale costs $5 per ton, and that federal air pollution standards are applied. (a) If the disposal of spent shale costs $10 per ton, would you expect the quantity supplied to be more or less than 16 million barrels per day if the price of oil is $40 per barrel? (b) Colorado air pollution standards are stricter than federal standards. If the Colorado standards are applied, would you expect the quantity supplied to be more or less than 16 million barrels per day if the price of oil is $40 per barrel? (c) Since no commercial-scale shale oil plants had been built, the above supply curve was based on engineering estimates. Do you think that this supply curve is very accurate? Why or why not? (d) A shale oil plant is estimated to cost over $1 billion. Would an investment in such a plant be risky? Why or why not? Would this influence the position and shape of the supply curve?

8. Explain how it is possible for an industry to be a constant-cost industry even though each firm in the industry has increasing marginal costs.

9. A perfectly competitive firm has the following total cost function:

Total output (dollars)	Total cost (dollars)
0	20
1	30
2	42
3	55
4	69
5	84
6	100
7	117

How much will the firm produce if the price is (a) $13, (b) $14, (c) $15, (d) $16, or (e) $17?

10. If the textile industry is a constant-cost industry, and the demand curve for textiles shifts upward, what are the steps by which a competitive market insures an increased amount of textiles? What happens if the government will not allow textile prices to rise?

11. An economist estimates that, in the short run, the quantity of men's socks supplied at each price is as follows:

Price (dollars per pair)	Quantity supplied per year (millions of pairs)
1	5
2	6
3	7
4	8

Calculate the arc elasticity of supply when the price is between $3 and $4 per pair. (Review Chapter 2 if you do not recall the definition of the arc elacticity of supply.)

12. Suppose that there are 100 firms producing the good in Question 9, and that each firm has the total cost function shown there. If input prices remain constant (regardless of industry output), draw the industry supply curve.

13. According to D. Suits and S. Koizumi, the supply function for onions in the United States is $\log q = 0.134 + .0123\,t + 0.324 \log P - 0.512 \log C$, where q is the quantity supplied in a particular year, t is the year (less 1924), P is the price last season, and C is the cost index last season. Suppose that price is estimated by one forecaster to be 10 cents this season, whereas another says that it will be 11 cents. Holding other factors constant, how much difference will this make in forecasting the quantity supplied next season?

THE MULTIPRODUCT FIRM: THE CHOICE OF OUTPUT COMBINATIONS

In this chapter we assumed that the firm produced only one product. Clearly this is not the case for all firms. Some companies like General Motors or General Electric are engaged in the production of many, many products. To keep things simple, suppose that we are concerned with a firm that produces only two products, windshield wipers and hearing aids. (From the point of view of sheer glamour, the firm's product line is, of course, an advertising account executive's dream.) Suppose that this firm cannot affect the price of either product, that it takes each price as given, and that it can sell as much as it wants of each product at these prices. If it maximizes profits, how much of each product will the firm choose to produce?

For simplicity, we shall assume that the firm has some given quantity of resources: plant, equipment, and so forth. Using this fixed total quantity of resources, the firm can produce various combinations of windshield wipers and hearing aids. For example, the possible combinations of quantities of these two products, given this amount of resources, might be given by T_1 in Figure 8.18. This curve depends, of course, on the amount of resources used by the firm. For example, T_2 is a curve that pertains to a higher level of resources.

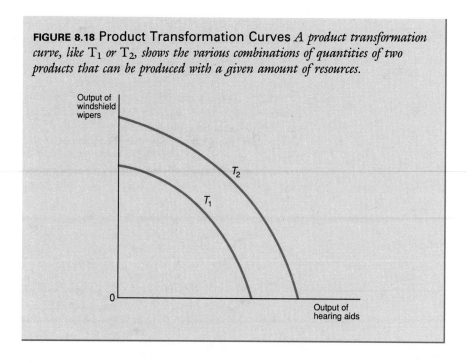

FIGURE 8.18 Product Transformation Curves *A product transformation curve, like* T_1 *or* T_2, *shows the various combinations of quantities of two products that can be produced with a given amount of resources.*

Curves like T_1 and T_2 are called *product transformation curves*. A product transformation curve shows the maximum amount of one product that can be produced, given the output of the other product. A product transformation curve must have a negative slope, since an increase in the output of one product must result in a decrease in the output of the other product.[10] The negative of the slope of the product transformation curve is called the *marginal rate of product transformation* between the two products. It is generally assumed that the marginal rate of product transformation increases as we move to the right along a product transformation curve and decreases as we move to the left. In other words, product transformation curves are generally expected to be concave. For each additional unit of the one product that is given up, the increase in the output of the other product becomes smaller and smaller.

However, two special cases exist where this is not the case. Panel A of Figure 8.19 shows the case in which there is no substitutability at all between the two outputs. This might occur if the products in question (product 1 and product 2) are joint products that occur in fixed proportions. Panel B of Figure 8.19 shows the case in which there is complete substitutability between the two products. This might occur if the two products (again called product 1 and product 2 in Figure 8.19) are two versions of the same commodity. In the rest

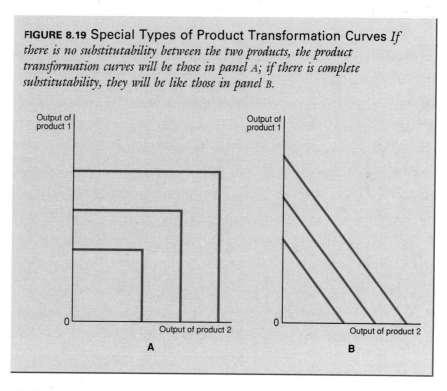

FIGURE 8.19 Special Types of Product Transformation Curves *If there is no substitutability between the two products, the product transformation curves will be those in panel A; if there is complete substitutability, they will be like those in panel B.*

10. Suppose that $g(Z_1, Z_2) = k$ is the product transformation curve, where Z_1 is the output of one good and Z_2 is the output of the other good. The total differential is

$$dk = \frac{\partial g}{\partial Z_1}dZ_1 + \frac{\partial g}{\partial Z_2}dZ_2$$

Since k is a constant, $dk = 0$, and the slope of the product transformation curve, dZ_2/dZ_1, is $-\partial g/\partial Z_1 \div \partial g/\partial Z_2$.

of this section we assume that some substitutability is possible but that it is less than complete.

Since the firm's costs are fixed (because it is using a fixed set of resources), it will maximize profit by maximizing the total revenue from the two products. If π_1 is the price of windshield wipers and π_2 is the price of hearing aids, the total revenue is

$$V = X_1\pi_1 + X_2\pi_2$$

where X_1 is the amount of windshield wipers produced and X_2 is the amount of hearing aids produced. Thus, if the firm takes the prices as given, we can draw

Isorevenue line an *isorevenue line*,

$$X_1 = \frac{V}{\pi_1} - \frac{\pi_2}{\pi_1}X_2,$$

which shows all combinations of outputs of the two commodities that result in a total revenue of V. There is a different isorevenue line for each value of V, but the slope of all such lines is the same and equal to the negative of π_2/π_1. The higher the value of V, the higher the isorevenue line.

By superimposing isorevenue lines on the graph showing the product transformation curve, we can obtain a graphical solution to the firm's problem. Figure 8.20 shows that the optimal combination of outputs is OQ_1 of windshield wipers and OQ_2 of hearing aids. This is the point on the product transformation curve that lies on the highest isorevenue line. If the firm were to produce elsewhere on the product transformation curve, it would be on a lower isorevenue line. Clearly, the isorevenue line is tangent to the product transformation curve at the optimum point. Therefore, π_2/π_1 (the negative of the slope

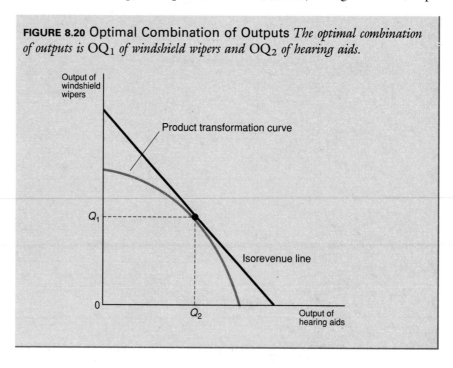

FIGURE 8.20 Optimal Combination of Outputs *The optimal combination of outputs is OQ_1 of windshield wipers and OQ_2 of hearing aids.*

of the isorevenue line) must equal the marginal rate of product transformation (the negative of the slope of the product transformation curve) at the optimum point.

Decision-Making in Municipal Government: An Application

The sort of analysis described in the previous section has a wide range of applications and is useful for many problems confronting public agencies as well as private firms. Consider, for example, a major snowstorm that produced a snow emergency in New York City. As many parts of the city continued to be paralyzed for many days after the storm, politicians, labor leaders, business executives, and even a high United Nations official complained of the slowness with which the snow was cleared. There was an atmosphere of intense dissatisfaction. Eight days after the storm, the mayor of New York directed that a study be made to determine how the city's snow-fighting operations could be improved.

The analysts who carried out the study began by determining how much snow-fighting capability the city had and how this capability was distributed among various parts of the city. To simplify matters, let's divide New York City into two parts: (1) Manhattan and (2) boroughs other than Manhattan. Then let's view New York's snow-fighting capability as a productive unit that can produce two goods: (1) snow removal in Manhattan and (2) snow removal in boroughs other than Manhattan. Clearly, the more of one good that the city's snow-fighting capability produces, the less of the other good it can produce. Given the city's total capability, the various combinations of these two outputs

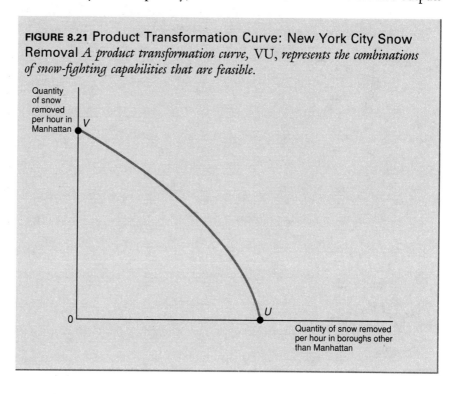

FIGURE 8.21 Product Transformation Curve: New York City Snow Removal *A product transformation curve, VU, represents the combinations of snow-fighting capabilities that are feasible.*

that can be produced are shown in Figure 8.21. This, of course, is a product transformation curve, pure and simple. The points on this curve, like any product transformation curve, are efficient points in the sense that, holding constant the quantity of one output, they show the maximum amount that can be produced of the other output.

Which of the infinity of points on the product transformation curve should the City of New York choose? At one extreme, point U provides no snow removal at all for Manhattan; at the other extreme, point V provides no snow removal at all for the boroughs other than Manhattan. Clearly, the answer lies somewhere in between, but where? In principle, the solution is simple: Choose that point which maximizes the welfare of the city as a whole. Suppose that each curve, like A, B, and C, in Figure 8.22 represents a set of combinations of the two outputs with equal "municipal worth." These curves are analogous to the isorevenue lines of the previous sections. (They are curved, not straight, because the relative worth of the two outputs is assumed constant in the previous section, but not here.) Thus the optimal combination is W, the point at which the product transformation curve touches the highest isorevenue line.

In fact, the analysts' investigations of the extent and distribution of the city's snow-fighting capability showed that the city was allocating its snow plows in such a way that snow was removed much more quickly in Manhattan than in other boroughs of the city. In other words, the municipal government was operating at point X on the product transformation curve. This was not due to a conscious decision, but because most of the plows were fitted on refuse-

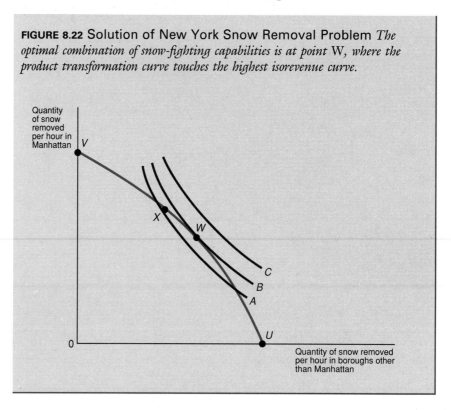

FIGURE 8.22 Solution of New York Snow Removal Problem *The optimal combination of snow-fighting capabilities is at point W, where the product transformation curve touches the highest isorevenue curve.*

collection trucks. Since densely populated Manhattan generated more refuse per mile of street than the other boroughs, it had more refuse-collection trucks per mile of street—and also more plows! Once this was recognized, the mayor reallocated the city's snow-fighting capability so as to move from point X toward point W. In other words, he moved plows and other equipment from Manhattan to the other boroughs. Once this was done, the available evidence indicated that it was very unlikely that the city would be paralyzed in this way again.

This was an interesting and apparently effective application of microeconomic (and engineering) analysis. Before leaving it, note that because the measurement of municipal worth presents difficult problems, it is often hard to draw curves like A, B, and C with confidence. Nonetheless, based on the available evidence (and the intuition of the decision-maker), it may be possible to approximate these curves accurately enough to support a useful analysis. For example, in the case of New York City's snow disposal problem, this did not seem to pose an insurmountable problem. Of course, in the case of business firms, the measurement of the isorevenue lines is much more straightforward. Finally, note too that this same kind of analysis can be used if the decision-maker is viewed as maximizing his or her political fortunes, not the welfare of the city. Under these circumstances, curves like A, B, or C represent combinations of outputs with equal political worth to the decision-maker, not equal municipal worth.[11]

11. Needless to say, this brief discussion can only provide part of the results of the New York study. For a fuller account, see E. S. Savas, "The Political Properties of Crystalline H_2O: Planning for Snow Emergencies in New York," reprinted in E. Mansfield, *Managerial Economics and Operations Research*, 5th ed. The New York analysts did not couch their procedure or their results in the terms used here, but these terms and concepts seem to capture the spirit of their analysis in a sufficiently accurate way to be useful for present purposes. In reality, all that we have done here is to indicate one way in which the New York study can be interpreted in terms of the model discussed in the previous section. There may, of course, be other interpretations.

9

PRICE AND OUTPUT
UNDER MONOPOLY

MONOPOLY

Monopoly

On rainy afternoons, children in the United States often play a game called Monopoly in which they try hard to become the sole owners of related pieces of property. (According to the rules of the game, the amount that a player can get from the other players is greater if he or she is the sole owner of related pieces of property.) Whether or not you have ever played this game, the concept of a *monopoly* is probably familiar: A monopoly is a situation where there is a single source of supply. And whether you live in the United States or Canada or Australia or the United Kingdom, you have probably encountered some firms that are monopolies, or close to it. Electric companies, telephone companies, and water companies often are examples.

In microeconomics monopoly, like perfect competition, is a useful model. The conditions defining monopoly are easy to state: There must exist one, and only one, seller in a market. Monopoly, like perfect competition, does not correspond more than approximately to conditions in real industries. But, as we have noted several times before, a model must be judged by its predictive ability, not the "realism" of its assumptions. The theory of monopoly has proved to be a very useful analytical device. Monopoly and perfect competition are opposites in the following sense: The firm in a perfectly competitive market has so many rivals that competition becomes impersonal in the extreme; the firm under monopoly has no rivals at all. Under monopoly, one firm is the sole supplier. There is no competition.

Having said this, it is important to add that the policies adopted by a monopolist are affected by certain indirect and potential forms of competition.

Clearly, the monopolist is not completely insulated from the effects of actions taken in the rest of the economy. All commodities are rivals for the consumer's favor, as we saw in Chapter 3. Clearly this rivalry occurs among different products, as well as among the producers of a given commodity. For example, meat competes in this sense with butter, eggs, and even men's suits. Of course, the extent of the competition from other products depends on the extent to which other products are substitutes for the monopolist's product. For example, even if a firm somehow could obtain a monopoly on the supply of steel in a particular market, it would still face considerable competition from producers of aluminum, plastics, and other materials that are reasonably good substitutes for steel.

In addition, the threat of potential competition may act as a brake on the policies of the monopolist. The monopolist may be able to maintain its monopoly position only if it does not extract as much short-run profit as possible. If it sets prices above a certain point, other firms may enter its market and try to break its monopoly. If entry can occur, the monopolist must take this possibility into account. Failure to do so may make it an ex-monopolist.

Reasons for Monopoly

Why do monopolies arise? There are many reasons, but four seem particularly important. First, a single firm may control the entire supply of a basic input that is required to manufacture a given product. The example that is cited repeatedly to illustrate this situation is the pre-World War II aluminum industry. Bauxite is an input used to produce aluminum; and for some time, practically every source of bauxite in the United States was controlled by the Aluminum Company of America (Alcoa). For this reason (and others), Alcoa was, for a long time, the sole producer of aluminum in the United States.

Natural monopoly

Second, a firm may become a monopolist because the average cost of producing the product reaches a minimum at an output rate that is big enough to satisfy the entire market at a price that is profitable. In a situation of this sort, if there is more than one firm producing the product, each must be producing at a higher-than-minimum level of average cost. Each may be inclined to cut the price to increase its output rate and reduce its average costs. The result is likely to be economic warfare—and the survival of a single victor, the monopolist. Cases in which costs behave in this fashion are called *natural monopolies*. When an industry is a natural monopoly, the public often insists that its behavior be regulated by the government.

Patents

Third, a firm may acquire a monopoly over the production of a good by having patents on the product or on certain basic processes that are used in its production. The patent laws of the United States permit an inventor to get the exclusive right to make a certain product or to use a particular process. (The patent is in force for seventeen years.) Patents can be very important in keeping competitors out. For example, Alcoa held important patents on basic production processes used to make aluminum. However, it is often possible to "invent around" another company's patents. That is, although a firm cannot use a product or process on which another firm has a patent (without the latter's permission), it may be able to develop a closely related product or process and obtain a patent on it.

Fourth, a firm may become a monopolist because it is awarded a market franchise by a government agency. The firm is granted the exclusive privilege to produce a given good or service in a particular area. In exchange for this right, the firm agrees to allow the government to regulate certain aspects of its behavior and operations. For example, as we shall see in a later section, the government may set limits on the firm's price. Regardless of the form of regulation, the important point is that the monopoly has been created by the government.

The Monopolist's Demand Curve

Since the monopolist is the only firm producing a product, it is obvious that the monopolist's demand curve is precisely the same as the market demand curve for the product. Consequently, the factors determining the shape of the monopolist's demand curve are the same factors that determine the shape of the demand curve for the product. As we saw in Chapter 5 these factors are the prices of other related products (substitutes and complements), incomes, and tastes. However, it should be noted that the monopolist sometimes can affect the prices of related products, as well as consumer tastes. To influence consumer tastes, monopolists often make considerable expenditures on advertising, the purpose being, of course, to shift the demand curve to the right.

Since the monopolist's demand curve is negatively sloped (because the demand curve for a product is negatively sloped, save for a few cases of little significance), average and marginal revenue are not the same. This is quite different from the case of perfect competition where average and marginal revenue were equal. To illustrate the situation faced by a monopolist, consider the hypothetical case in Table 9.1. The price at which each quantity (shown in column 1) can be sold is shown in column 2. The total revenue, the product of the first two columns, is shown in column 3. Obviously, the average revenue corresponding to each output is the price corresponding to that output.

Marginal revenue is of great importance to the profit-maximizing firm. How

TABLE 9.1 Demand and Revenue of Monopolist

Quantity sold	Price (dollars)	Total revenue (dollars)	Marginal revenue* (dollars)
3	100.00	300.00	—
8	80.00	640.00	$68.00 (= \frac{340}{5})$
15	74.00	1,110.00	$67.14 (= \frac{470}{7})$
21	70.00	1,470.00	$60.00 (= \frac{360}{6})$
26	67.50	1,755.00	$57.00 (= \frac{285}{5})$
30	65.50	1,965.00	$52.50 (= \frac{210}{4})$
33	62.00	2,046.00	$27.00 (= \frac{81}{3})$
35	60.00	2,100.00	$27.00 (= \frac{54}{2})$

*These figures pertain to the interval between the indicated quantity of output and one unit less than the indicated quantity of output.

can we estimate marginal revenue from the figures in Table 9.1? Marginal revenue between q and $(q - 1)$ units of output is defined as $R(q) - R(q - 1)$, where $R(q)$ is the total revenue when the output equals q. The problem in Table 9.1 is that the data are not provided for each level of output; we only have data for $q = 3, 8, 15$, and so on. To cope with this problem, we assume that $R(q)$ is approximately a linear function of q between 3 and 8, 8 and 15, 15 and 21, and so on. If this is the case, the marginal revenue is ($640 - $300) ÷ 5 at an output of between 7 and 8, ($1,110 - $640) ÷ 7 at an output of between 14 and 15, and so forth. The results are shown in the last column of Table 9.1.

The Monopolist's Costs

Although a firm is a monopolist in the product market, it may be a perfect competitor in the market for inputs, in which case it buys so small a proportion of the total supply of each input that it cannot affect input prices. If this is the case, there is no need to dwell further on the monopolist's costs, since the theory in Chapter 7 will apply without modification.

In many cases, however, the monopolist is not a perfect competitor in the input markets, because it buys a large proportion of certain specialized resources that have little use other than to produce the commodity in question. In a case of this sort, the price that the firm has to pay for this input depends on how much it buys. The more the firm wants of this resource, the more it will generally have to pay. Cases of this sort are discussed at some length in Chapter 13. In the present chapter we assume that the firm is a perfect competitor in the market for inputs.

Table 9.2 shows the costs of our hypothetical monopolist. Column 1 shows various output rates, column 2 shows the total variable cost at each output rate, and column 3 shows the firm's fixed costs. Finally, column 4 shows the firm's total cost at each output rate, and column 5 shows the firm's marginal costs.

TABLE 9.2 Costs of Monopolist

Output	Total variable cost (dollars)	Fixed cost (dollars)	Total cost (dollars)	Marginal cost* (dollars)
0	0	500	500	—
3	110	500	610	$36.67 (= \frac{110}{3})$
8	240	500	740	$26.00 (= \frac{130}{5})$
15	390	500	890	$21.43 (= \frac{150}{7})$
21	560	500	1,060	$28.33 (= \frac{170}{6})$
26	750	500	1,250	$38.00 (= \frac{190}{5})$
30	960	500	1,460	$52.50 (= \frac{210}{4})$
33	1,190	500	1,690	$76.67 (= \frac{230}{3})$
35	1,440	500	1,940	$125.00 (= \frac{250}{2})$

*These figures pertain to the interval between the indicated quantity of output and one unit less than the indicated quantity of output.

The monopolist, if unregulated and free to maximize profits, will, of course, choose the price and output at which the difference between total revenue and total cost is largest. For example, combining the data from Tables 9.1 and 9.2 into Table 9.3, we find that our hypothetical monopolist will choose an output rate of either 26 or 30 units per time period and a price of $65.50 or $67.50. Figure 9.1 shows the situation graphically.

TABLE 9.3 Cost, Revenue, and Profit of Monopolist

Output	Total revenue (dollars)	Total cost (dollars)	Total profit (dollars)
3	300	610	−310
8	640	740	−100
15	1,110	890	220
21	1,470	1,060	410
26	1,755	1,250	505
30	1,965	1,460	505
33	2,046	1,690	356
35	2,100	1,940	160

Note that either of these optimal output rates is less than the output rate where price equals marginal cost. Under perfect competition, the profit-maximizing output was the one at which price equals marginal cost; indeed, this fact was used to derive the firm's supply curve. It is obvious from Tables 9.1 and 9.2 that this result is not true for monopoly.

Under monopoly, the firm will maximize profit if it sets its output rate at the point at which marginal cost equals marginal revenue. Table 9.4 and Figure 9.2 show that this is true in this example. It is easy to prove that this is generally a *Marginal cost =* necessary condition for profit maximization. At any output rate at which mar-*marginal revenue* ginal revenue exceeds marginal cost, profit can be increased by increasing output, since the extra revenue will exceed the extra cost. Thus profit will not be a maximum when marginal revenue exceeds marginal cost. At any output rate at which marginal cost exceeds marginal revenue, profit can be increased by reducing output, since the decrease in cost will exceed the decrease in revenue. Thus profit will not be a maximum when marginal cost exceeds marginal revenue. Since profit is not a maximum when marginal revenue exceeds marginal cost or when marginal cost exceeds marginal revenue, it must be a maximum only when marginal revenue equals marginal cost.[1]

1. Suppose that the monopolist's demand function is $P = D(q)$, where P is price and q is output. Let $C(q)$ be the monopolist's total cost function. Then the monopolist's profit is

$$\pi = qD(q) - C(q)$$

and

$$\frac{d\pi}{dq} = D(q) + qD'(q) - C'(q).$$

(cont'd.)

FIGURE 9.1 Total Revenue, Total Cost, and Total Profit of
Monopolist *To maximize profit, the monopolist will choose an output rate
of 26 or 30 units per period and a price of $65.50 or $67.50.*

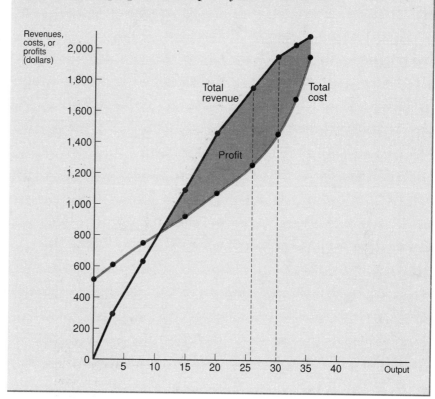

TABLE 9.4 Marginal Cost and Marginal Revenue of Monopolist

Output	Marginal cost* (dollars)	Marginal revenue* (dollars)	Total profit (dollars)
3	36.7	—	−310
8	26.0	68.0	−100
15	21.4	67.1	220
21	28.3	60.0	310
26	38.0	57.0	505
30	52.5	52.5	505
33	76.7	27.0	356
35	125.0	27.0	160

*These figures pertain to the interval between the indicated quantity of output and one unit less
than the indicated quantity of output.

FIGURE 9.2 Marginal Cost and Marginal Revenue of Monopolist *At the monopolist's profit-maximizing output (26 or 30 units), marginal cost equals marginal revenue.*

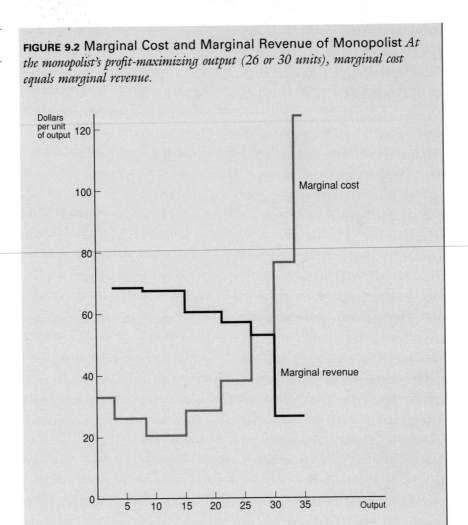

Using this result, it is also simple to represent graphically the short-run equilibrium of the monopolist. Figure 9.3 shows the demand curve, the marginal revenue curve, the marginal cost curve, and the average total cost curve faced by the firm. Short-run equilibrium will occur at the output, OQ, where the marginal cost curve intersects the marginal revenue curve. If the monopolist produces OQ units, the demand curve shows that it must set a price of OP. Moreover, since the average cost curve shows that average costs are OC at an

---

Setting $d\pi/dq = 0$ to obtain the conditions under which profit is a maximum, we find that

$$D(q) + qD'(q) = C'(q).$$

Thus marginal revenue must equal marginal cost when profits are maximized, since the expression on the left-hand side is marginal revenue and the expression on the right-hand side is marginal cost. Of course, this is only the first-order condition for a local maximum. The second-order conditions must also be met, and the maximum may be only a local maximum.

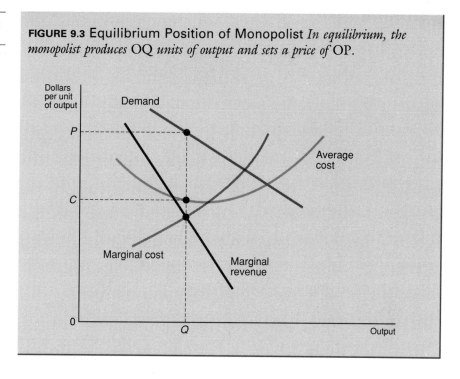

FIGURE 9.3 Equilibrium Position of Monopolist *In equilibrium, the monopolist produces* OQ *units of output and sets a price of* OP.

output of OQ units, the profit per unit of output is $(OP - OC)$, and the firm's total profit is $OQ[OP - OC]$.

In this case, the monopolist earns a profit, but this need not always be the case. It does not follow that a firm that holds a monopoly over the production of a particular product must make a profit. The demand curve for the product may be such that, even when the firm produces at the point at which marginal revenue equals marginal cost, average cost exceeds price. For example, even if one could somehow obtain a monopoly on the sale of cigar-store Indians, it might not be a profitable business to enter. Indeed, in the short run, a monopolist may not be able to cover its variable costs, in which case it will discontinue production.

Relationship between Price and Output

In perfect competition, one can define a unique relationship between the price of the product and the amount supplied. This is the industry's supply curve, which we discussed on pp. 226–28 of Chapter 8. In monopoly, there is no such unique relationship between the product's price and the amount supplied. At first, this is likely to strike the reader as being extremely strange; indeed, one can be pardoned for questioning whether it really is so. The rest of this section is aimed at convincing the reader that it is true.

Figure 9.4 shows the marginal cost curve of the monopolist. It is assumed that the demand curve shifts from D_0 to D_1. When the demand curve is D_0, the firm produces OQ_0 units (since the marginal cost curve intersects the marginal revenue curve, R_0, at OQ_0) and the price must be OP. When the demand curve

**FIGURE 9.4 More Than One Output Level Corresponding to a
Given Price** *A price of* OP *can result in an output of* OQ_0 *or* OQ_1,
depending on whether the demand curve is D_0 *or* D_1.

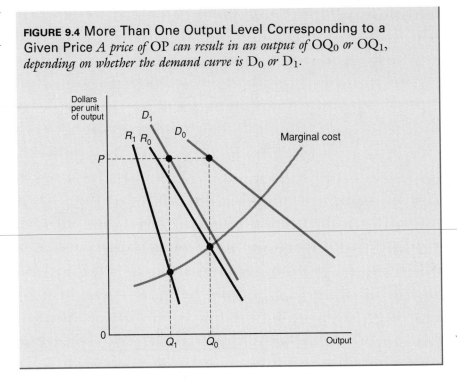

is D_1, the firm produces OQ_1 units (since the marginal cost curve intersects the
new marginal revenue curve, R_1, at OQ_1) and the price must be OP. This result
shows that there is no unique relationship between price and quantity. A price
of OP can result in an output of OQ_0 or OQ_1. Thus a particular price can result
in a wide variety of output levels, depending on the shape and level of the
demand curve.

LONG-RUN EQUILIBRIUM PRICE AND OUTPUT

In contrast to perfect competition, the long-run equilibrium of a monopolistic
industry is not marked by the absence of economic profits or losses. If a monopolist earns a short-run economic profit, it will not be confronted in the long run
with competitors, unless the industry is no longer a monopoly. (The entrance
of additional firms into the industry is, of course, not compatible with the
existence of monopoly.) Thus the long-run equilibrium of an industry under
monopoly may be characterized by economic profits.

On the other hand, if the monopolist incurs a short-run economic loss, it will
be forced to look for other, more profitable uses for its resources. One possibility is that its existing plant is not optimal and that it can earn economic
profits if it alters the scale and characteristics of its plant appropriately. If this is
the case, it will make these alterations in the long run and remain in the indus-

FIGURE 9.5 Long-Run Equilibrium for Monopolist *In the long run, the monopolist will produce the output,* OQ_1, *at which long-run marginal cost equals long-run marginal revenue.*

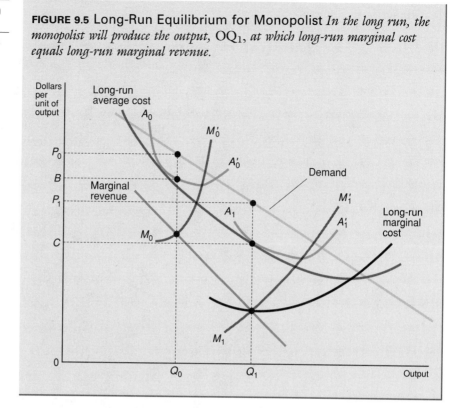

try. However, if there is no scale of plant that will enable the monopolist to avoid economic losses, it will leave the industry in the long run.

Returning to the case in which the monopolist earns short-run profits, it must decide in the long run whether it can make even larger profits by altering its plant. For example, assume that the monopolist's demand curve, marginal revenue curve, long-run average cost curve, and long-run marginal cost curve are as shown in Figure 9.5. Suppose that the firm currently has a plant corresponding to short-run average cost curve, A_0A_0', and short-run marginal cost curve, M_0M_0'. In the short run, it will produce OQ_0 units and set a price of OP_0. Since short-run average cost is OB, the firm's short-run profits will be $OQ_0[OP_0 - OB]$.

However, the firm can adjust its plant in the long run so as to make bigger profits than $OQ_0[OP_0 - OB]$. It is easy to show that the monopolist will maximize profit in the long run when it produces the output at which long-run marginal cost equals long-run marginal revenue. The reasoning behind this rule is precisely the same as that given in the section before last. Thus the firm will produce OQ_1 units in the long run, since this is the point at which the long-run marginal cost curve intersects the marginal revenue curve. The long-run average cost will be OC, the price will be OP_1, and total profit will be $OQ_1[OP_1 - OC]$. The resulting plant will have short-run average and marginal cost curves of A_1A_1' and M_1M_1', respectively.

EXAMPLE 9.1

PREDATORY PRICING AND THE AREEDA-TURNER RULE

The 1970s and 1980s saw a notable increase in the interest among economists in predatory behavior. Although definitions vary somewhat, a firm generally is said to engage in predatory pricing if it sets its price at a low level in an attempt to drive a rival firm out of business. For example, suppose that a monopolist is confronted with a competitor. The monopolist's average and marginal cost curves are shown below. (To avoid cumbersome language, we refer to the firm as "the monopolist," although it clearly is an ex-monopolist once the rival firm enters its market.)

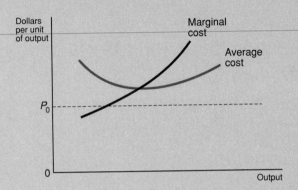

The monopolist sets a price of OP_0, which is below its average costs. Because this price is also below its rival's average cost, its rival experiences losses.

(a) Since both the monopolist and its rival will lose money if price equals OP_0, is it clear that the monopolist is well advised to set this price? (b) If the monopolist succeeds in driving its rival out of business, can it be sure that other entrants will not appear on the scene? (c) A large number of major lawsuits have alleged predatory behavior. For example, the government alleged that IBM's 360 line of computers was priced in a predatory fashion. To help solve the difficult problem of determining when predatory pricing takes place, Phillip Areeda and Donald Turner of Harvard University proposed that it be illegal for a dominant firm to set its price below both its average and marginal costs. What problems can you see in this rule?

SOLUTION

(a) Whether the monopolist is well advised to set this price depends on the likelihood that the rival will be driven out of business. Given the monopolist's larger output, it will lose more money than the rival. However, the monopolist may have larger financial resources and may be in a better position to withstand such losses. (b) No. However, if it manages to impose heavy losses on its rival, this may teach other potential entrants the lesson that it does not pay to challenge the monopolist. (c) Perhaps the most fundamental criticism of the Areeda-Turner test is that the comparison of price with marginal (and average) cost may not be related to predatory pricing. The price set by the monopolist can be viewed as a signal to the entrant. The monopolist may be able to use this signal to convince the entrant that it should withdraw from the industry (to avoid losses), even if its price exceeds marginal (and average) cost. For reasons of this sort, the Areeda-Turner rule has received considerable criticism. Nonetheless, this rule has been used (or at least considered) by many courts.*

*For further discussion, see P. Areeda and D. Turner, "Predatory Pricing and Related Practices Under Section 2 of the Sherman Act," *Harvard Law Review,* 1975; and J. Tirole, *The Theory of Industrial Organization* (Cambridge: MIT Press, 1988).

MULTIPLANT MONOPOLY

In previous sections we have assumed that the monopolist operated only one plant. This, of course, is an unrealistic assumption in many industries. Even readers with the most superficial knowledge of the structure of various industries will recognize that many firms operate more than one plant and that cost conditions may vary among these plants. This section extends the analysis in previous sections to cover the case where the monopolist operates more than one plant.

An illustrative case is shown in Table 9.5, which assumes that the monopolist operates two plants with marginal cost curves shown in columns 2 and 3, output being shown in column 1. Judging from the figures in these columns, if the firm decides to produce only 1 unit of output, it should use plant A, since the marginal cost between zero and 1 unit is lower in plant A than plant B. Thus, for the firm as a whole, the marginal cost between zero and 1 unit of output is $5 (the marginal cost between zero and 1 unit for plant A). Similarly, if the firm decides to produce 2 units of output, both should be produced in

TABLE 9.5 Costs of Multiplant Monopoly

Output	Marginal cost*		Marginal cost for firm* (dollars)	Price (dollars)	Marginal revenue* (dollars)
	Plant A (dollars)	Plant B (dollars)			
1	5	7	5	20.00	—
2	6	9	6	15.00	10
3	7	11	7	13.00	9
4	10	13	7	11.50	7
5	12	15	9	8.00	−6

*These figures pertain to the interval between the indicated output and one unit less than the indicated output.

plant A, and the marginal cost between the first and second unit of output for the firm as a whole is $6 (the marginal cost between the first and second unit in plant A). If the firm decides to produce 3 units of output, two should be produced in plant A and one in plant B, and the marginal cost between the second and third unit of output for the firm as a whole is $7 (the marginal cost between zero and 1 unit of output for plant B). Alternatively, all three could be produced at plant A.

Continuing in this fashion, we can derive the marginal cost curve for the firm as a whole, shown in column 4 of Table 9.5. To maximize profits, the firm should find that output at which marginal revenue equals the marginal cost of the firm as a whole. This is the optimum output. In this case, it is 3 or 4 units: Suppose that the firm picks 4 units.[2] To find out what price to charge, the firm must see what price corresponds to this output on the demand curve. In this case, the answer is $11.50.

This solves most of the monopolist's problems, but not quite all. Given that it will produce 4 units of output per year, how should it divide this production between the two plants? The answer is that it should set the marginal cost in plant A equal to the marginal cost in plant B. Table 9.5 shows that this means that plant A will produce 3 units per year and plant B will produce 1 unit per year. It should also be noted that the common value of the marginal costs of the two plants is also the marginal cost of the firm as a whole. Consequently, this common value must also be set equal to marginal revenue if the firm is maximizing profits.

In the long run the firm can vary the number and size of its plants. The monopolist can construct each plant of optimal size. In other words, in Figure 9.6, the short-run average cost, AA', will equal the long-run average cost, and it will be at the minimum point on the long-run average cost curve. The firm will build plants, each of which produces Oq units of output at an average cost of Ou dollars per unit. Thus, once it has reached Oq units of output, further expansion of output will be accommodated by building more plants of optimal size. Consequently the long-run marginal cost curve is a horizontal line at Ou. Since long-run marginal cost must equal marginal revenue, the firm's total output in the long run will be Oz; it will operate $Oz \div Oq$ plants; and it will charge a price of OP.[3]

COMPARISON OF MONOPOLY WITH PERFECT COMPETITION

It is important to note the differences between the long-run equilibrium of a monopoly and a perfectly competitive industry. Suppose that we could perform an experiment in which an industry was first operated under conditions of

2. If the firm maximizes profit, it is a matter of indifference to the firm whether it produces 3 or 4 units since the profit is the same. Suppose that the firm flips a coin to determine which output it will choose and that 4 units is the winner.

3. Of course, we ignore here the problem that Oz/Oq may not be an integer. For simplicity we assume that it is an integer. Also, Oz will generally be bigger than Oq, the scale in panel A of Figure 9.6 being different from that in panel B.

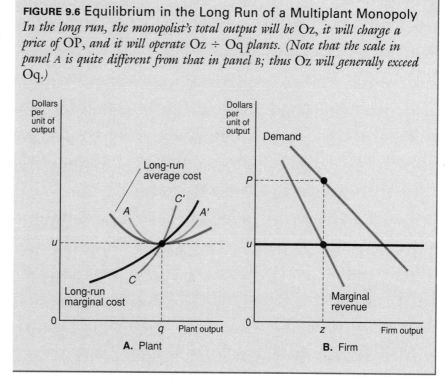

FIGURE 9.6 Equilibrium in the Long Run of a Multiplant Monopoly
In the long run, the monopolist's total output will be Oz, it will charge a price of OP, and it will operate Oz ÷ Oq plants. (Note that the scale in panel A is quite different from that in panel B; thus Oz will generally exceed Oq.)

perfect competition and then under conditions of monopoly. Assuming that the demand curve for the industry's product and the industry's cost curves would be the same in either case,[4] what would be the difference in the long-run equilibrium?

Comparison of costs

First, under perfect competition, each firm operates at the point at which both long-run and short-run average costs are a minimum. However, under monopoly, although the plant that is used will produce the monopolist's long-run equilibrium output at minimum average cost, it is not the plant that will produce the product at the lowest possible average cost. In general, if the monopolist expanded its long-run equilibrium output, it could utilize a plant with lower average costs. This is clearly shown by Figure 9.7, which compares the long-run equilibrium of a firm under perfect competition and monopoly. The monopolist produces OQ_M units of output, which is less than the output corresponding to the minimum point on the long-run average cost curve. Consequently, society's resources tend to be used more effectively in perfectly competitive industries than in monopolized industries.[5] More will be said about this in Chapter 15.

Second, the output of a perfectly competitive industry tends to be greater and price tends to be lower than under monopoly. The perfectly competitive

4. However, the cost and demand curves need not be the same, as we noted above.

5. In multiplant monopoly the monopolist operates fewer plants than would a competitive industry.

FIGURE 9.7 Comparison of Long-Run Equilibria *In contrast to perfect competition, the long-run equilibrium output under monopoly* (OQ_M) *is less than the output corresponding to the minimum point on the long-run average cost curve.*

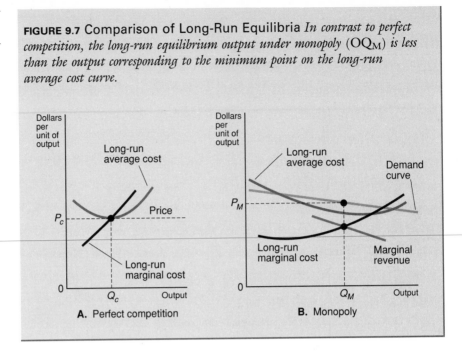

A. Perfect competition

B. Monopoly

Comparison of outputs

firm operates at the point at which price equals marginal cost, whereas the monopolist operates at a point at which price exceeds marginal cost. Under various circumstances, as we shall see in Chapter 15, price is a good indicator of the marginal social value of the good. Consequently, under these conditions, a monopoly produces at a point at which the marginal social value of the good exceeds the good's marginal social cost. In a static sense, society would be better off if more resources were devoted to the production of the good, and if the marginal social value of the product were set equal to the marginal social cost of the product—as it is in perfect competition. Again, more will be said on this score in Chapter 15.

Assuming that the demand curve for the product is linear and that the marginal cost is constant, we compare the equilibrium price and output in monopoly and perfect competition in Figure 9.8. The monopoly price is OP_1 and the competitive price is OM; the monopoly output is OQ_1 and the competitive output is OQ_0. It is assumed, of course, that the marginal cost curve is the long-run supply curve in perfect competition. Under these very special assumptions, the monopoly output will be exactly one-half the competitive output, the reason being that the marginal revenue curve cuts in half any horizontal line from the vertical axis to the demand curve.[6] In general, of course, the ratio of

6. For a proof that this is the case, recall from footnote 9 of Chapter 5 that, if the demand curve is $P = a - bQ$, the marginal revenue curve is $MR = a - 2bQ$. Thus, if a horizontal line is drawn at a height of P from the vertical axis to the demand curve, it will intersect the demand curve at a distance of $(a - P)/b$ from the vertical axis, and it will intersect the marginal revenue curve at a distance of $(a - P)/2b$ from the vertical axis. Consequently, the marginal revenue curve cuts in half the horizontal line from the vertical axis to the demand curve.

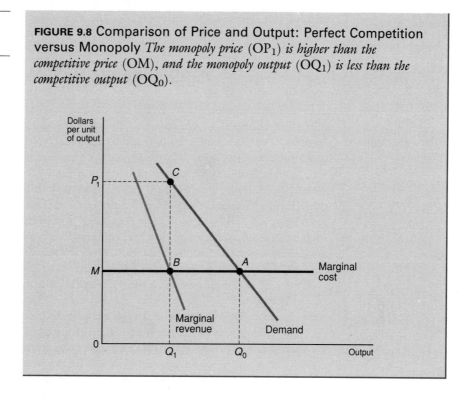

FIGURE 9.8 Comparison of Price and Output: Perfect Competition versus Monopoly *The monopoly price (OP_1) is higher than the competitive price (OM), and the monopoly output (OQ_1) is less than the competitive output (OQ_0).*

the monopoly to the competitive output could be more or less than one-half, depending on the shape of the demand and cost curves.

Using the concept of consumer's surplus described in Chapter 4, some economists believe that the welfare loss to society due to monopoly, rather than perfect competition, can be measured by the so-called welfare triangle, *ABC*, in Figure 9.8. Basically, the idea is that the value to society of the extra output resulting from perfect competition is equal to Q_1CAQ_0, whereas the cost to society of the extra output is equal to Q_1BAQ_0. Thus the net loss due to the smaller output under monopoly is equal to *ABC*. One important limitation of this kind of measure is that it assumes that one can simply add up the gains and losses of various members of society. No attention is paid to the effects of monopoly on the distribution of income.

Welfare triangle

About forty years ago, Arnold Harberger of the University of Chicago estimated the area of the welfare triangle in each manufacturing industry, based on the assumption that marginal cost is constant (as in Figure 9.8) and that the price elasticity of demand is about 1. The results suggested that the misallocation of resources due to monopoly was quite small. Specifically, he found that the elimination of this resource misallocation would result in an increase in consumer welfare of about .1 percent. These conclusions have been challenged on several counts. For example, as Harvey Leibenstein and others have pointed out, Harberger's results do not recognize that monopolies may be less inclined to minimize costs than competitive firms. Further, as Gordon Tullock has pointed out, Harberger's results ignore the social waste which arises because firms use scarce resources in their attempts to obtain monopoly power.[7]

PRICE DISCRIMINATION

Price discrimination

Price discrimination occurs when the same commodity is sold at more than one price. For example, an operation to cure a particular form of cancer may be "sold" to a rich person for $5,000 and to a poor person for $1,000. Even if the commodities are not precisely the same, price discrimination is said to occur if very similar products are sold at prices that are in different ratios to marginal costs. For example, if a firm sells ballpoint pens with a label (cost of label: 1 cent) saying "Super Deluxe" in rich neighborhoods for $2 and sells the same ballpoint pens without this label in poor neighborhoods for $1, this is discrimination. Note that the mere fact that differences in price exist among similar goods is not evidence of discrimination. Only if these differences do not reflect cost differences is there evidence of this sort.

Under what conditions will a monopolist be able and willing to engage in price discrimination? The necessary conditions are that buyers fall into classes with considerable differences in the price elasticity of demand for the product, and that these classes can be identified and segregated at moderate cost. Also, it is important that buyers be unable to transfer the commodity easily from one class to another, since otherwise it would be possible for persons to make money by buying the commodity from the low-price classes and selling it to the high-price classes, thus making it difficult to maintain the price differentials between classes. The differences between classes of buyers in the price elasticity of demand may be due to differences between classes in income level, differences between classes in tastes, or differences between classes in the availability of substitutes. For example, the price elasticity of demand for a certain good may be lower for the rich than for the poor.

If a monopolist practices discrimination of this sort, it must decide two questions: How much output should it allocate to each class of buyer, and what price should it charge each class of buyer? To avoid unnecessary complications, let us assume that there are only two classes of buyers. Also, for the moment, assume that the monopolist has already decided on its total output, and consequently that the only real question is how it should be allocated between the two classes. In each class, there is a demand curve showing how many units of output would be bought by buyers in this class at various prices. In each class, there is also a marginal revenue curve that can be derived from the demand curve.

Setting marginal revenues equal

Given these marginal revenue curves, the monopolist will maximize its profits by allocating the total output between the two classes in such a way that marginal revenue in one class is equal to marginal revenue in the other class.

7. See A. Harberger, "Monopoly and Resource Allocation," and H. Leibenstein, "Allocative Efficiency vs. X-Efficiency," both reprinted in E. Mansfield, *Microeconomics: Selected Readings*, 5th ed.; and G. Tullock, "The Welfare Costs of Monopoly and Theft," *Western Economic Journal*, June 1967. Also, see K. Cowling and D. Mueller, "The Social Costs of Monopoly Power," *Economic Journal*, December 1978, and F. Fisher, "The Social Costs of Monopoly and Regulation: Posner Reconsidered," *Journal of Political Economy*, April 1985.

The reason for this is clear. For example, if marginal revenue in the first class is $5 and marginal revenue in the second class is $3, the allocation is not optimal, since profits can be increased by allocating one less unit of output to the second class and one more unit of output to the first class. Only if the two marginal revenues are equal is the allocation optimal. And if the marginal revenues in the two classes are equal, the ratio of the price in the first class to the price in the second class will equal

$$\left(1 - \frac{1}{n_2}\right) \div \left(1 - \frac{1}{n_1}\right)$$

where n_1 is the elasticity of demand in the first class and n_2 is the elasticity of demand in the second class. Thus it will not pay to discriminate if the two elasticities are equal. Moreover, if discrimination does pay, the price will be lower in the class in which demand is more elastic.

Optimal output

Next consider the more realistic case where the monopolist must also decide on its total output. In this case, the monopolist must look at its costs, as well as demand, in the two classes. It can be shown that it will choose the output where the marginal cost of the monopolist's entire output is equal to the common value of the marginal revenue in the two classes. To see this, consider Figure 9.9, which shows D_1, the demand curve in class 1; D_2, the demand curve in class 2; R_1, the marginal revenue curve in class 1; R_2, the marginal revenue curve in class 2; and the firm's marginal cost curve. The monopolist begins to determine its total output by summing horizontally over the two marginal revenue curves, R_1 and R_2. The curve representing the horizontal summation of the two marginal revenue curves is Z. This curve shows, for each level of mar-

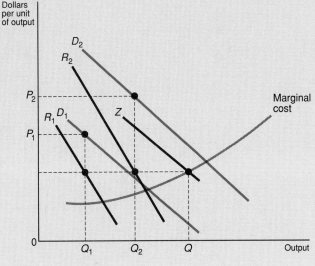

FIGURE 9.9 Price Discrimination: Third Degree *To maximize profit, the firm will produce a total output of* OQ *units, and set a price of* OP_1 *in the class 1 market and a price of* OP_2 *in the class 2 market.*

EXAMPLE 9.2

WHY SHOULD THE PRICE OF BANANAS BE SO MUCH HIGHER IN DENMARK THAN IN IRELAND?

In the 1970s, the United Brands Company marketed its bananas in a variety of countries in Europe. The bananas were sold to wholesalers for distribution in individual national markets. They were all of the same type and entered Europe either through Bremerhaven or Rotterdam. Although the cost of unloading them was essentially the same at these two ports, the prices that United Brands charged distributors differed considerably from country to country. The average difference in price per 20-kilogram box was about 11–18 percent, but some differences were much greater. For example, the price to Denmark was about 2.4 times the price to Ireland.*

Suppose that you are an adviser to the United Brands Company and that the company's president asks you whether its pricing policy resulted in maximum profit. After conversations with the company's marketing personnel, suppose you find that their studies indicate that the price elasticity of demand for the firm's bananas was about 2 in Denmark, about 2.5 in Germany, and about 4 in Ireland. Other company executives state that the marginal cost of shipping bananas to each of these countries (and marketing them) did not differ from country to country. What's the answer?

SOLUTION

To maximize profit, the price to Denmark divided by the price to Ireland should equal

$$\left(1 - \frac{1}{n_i}\right) \div \left(1 - \frac{1}{n_d}\right),$$

where n_i is the price elasticity of demand in Ireland and n_d is the price elasticity of demand in Denmark. (Recall page 275.) Thus, since $n_i = 4$ and $n_d = 2$, the price to Denmark divided by the price to Ireland should have equaled $(1 - \frac{1}{4}) \div (1 - \frac{1}{2}) = 1.5$, which is less than its actual value (2.4) in the 1970s. Based on the information you obtained, your conclusion should be that the firm's profits in the 1970s would have been greater if the price to Denmark had been lower relative to the price to Ireland.**

*S. Martin, *Industrial Economics* (New York: Macmillan, 1988).

**Of course, your conclusions depend on the price elasticities of demand that you are supposed to have obtained. If you somehow misinterpreted the results of the firm's marketing studies and if these elasticities are incorrect, your conclusions may be incorrect as well. Careful empirical research can be very important in cases of this sort.

ginal revenue, the total output that is needed if marginal revenue in each class is to be maintained at this level. The optimal output is shown by the point where the Z curve intersects the marginal cost curve, since marginal cost must be equal to the common value of marginal revenue in each class. If this were not the case, profits could be increased by expanding output (if marginal cost were less than marginal revenue) or by contracting output (if marginal cost were greater than marginal revenue). Thus the firm will produce an output of OQ units and sell OQ_1 units in the class 1 market and OQ_2 units in the class 2 market. Price will be OP_1 in the class 1 market and OP_2 in the class 2 market.[8]

Other Types of Price Discrimination

Price discrimination can take a number of forms. The type discussed in the previous section is often called *third-degree price discrimination*. (This expression was coined by A. C. Pigou, the English economist.)[9] Besides third-degree price discrimination, there are also first-degree and second-degree price discrimination. In *discrimination of the first degree*, the monopolist is aware of the maximum amount that each and every consumer will pay for each amount of the commodity. Since it is assumed that the product cannot be resold, the monop-

First-degree price discrimination

---

8. Let p_1 be the price in the first class, p_2 the price in the second class, q_1 the quantity sold in the first class, and q_2 the quantity sold in the second class. If $C(q)$ is the monopolist's total cost, with q being equal to the sum of q_1 and q_2,

$$\pi = p_1 q_1 + p_2 q_2 - C(q)$$

where π is the monopolist's profits. Then

$$\frac{\partial \pi}{\partial q_1} = \frac{\partial (p_1 q_1)}{\partial q_1} - \frac{\partial C(q)}{\partial q_1} = \frac{d(p_1 q_1)}{dq_1} - \frac{dC(q)}{dq}\frac{\partial q}{\partial q_1}$$

$$= \frac{d(p_1 q_1)}{dq_1} - \frac{dC(q)}{dq} = 0$$

$$\frac{\partial \pi}{\partial q_2} = \frac{\partial (p_2 q_2)}{\partial q_2} - \frac{\partial C(q)}{\partial q_2} = \frac{d(p_2 q_2)}{dq_2} - \frac{dC(q)}{dq}\frac{\partial q}{\partial q_2}$$

$$= \frac{d(p_2 q_2)}{dq_2} - \frac{dC(q)}{dq} = 0.$$

Thus, if π is to be a maximum,

$$\frac{d(p_1 q_1)}{dq_1} = \frac{d(p_2 q_2)}{dq_2} = \frac{dC(q)}{dq}.$$

In other words, $MR_1 = MR_2 = MC$, where MR_1 is marginal revenue in the first class, MR_2 is marginal revenue in the second class, and MC is marginal cost.
  Since

$$MR_1 = P_1\left(1 - \frac{1}{n_1}\right) \text{ and } MR_2 = P_2\left(1 - \frac{1}{n_2}\right),$$

as pointed out in Chapter 5, it follows that, if $MR_1 = MR_2$,

$$P_1\left(1 - \frac{1}{n_1}\right) = P_2\left(1 - \frac{1}{n_2}\right)$$

$$\frac{P_1}{P_2} = \frac{[1 - (1/n_2)]}{[1 - (1/n_1)]}.$$

9. A. C. Pigou, *The Economics of Welfare*, 4th ed. (London: Macmillan, 1950).

olist can charge each consumer a different price. And since the monopolist is assumed to be a profit-maximizer, prices will be established so as to extract from each consumer the full value of his or her consumer's surplus.

To illustrate this case, suppose that each consumer buys only 1 unit of the commodity. In this very simple case, the monopolist will establish a price for each consumer that is so high that the consumer is on the verge of refusing to buy the commodity. In the more realistic case, where each consumer can buy more than 1 unit of the commodity, it is assumed that the monopolist knows each consumer's demand curve for the commodity and that it adjusts its offer accordingly. For example, suppose that the maximum amount that a particular consumer would pay for 20 units of the commodity is $50 and that 20 units is the profit-maximizing amount for the monopolist to sell to this consumer. Then the monopolist will make an all-or-nothing offer of 20 units of the commodity for $50.

First-degree price discrimination is a limiting case that could occur only in the few cases when a monopolist has a small number of buyers and when it is
Second-degree price discrimination able to guess the maximum prices they are willing to accept. *Second-degree price discrimination* is an intermediate case. In second-degree price discrimination, the monopolist takes part, but not all, of the buyers' consumers' surpluses. For example, consider the case of a gas company. Suppose that each of its consumers has the demand curve shown in Figure 9.10. The company charges a high price, OP_0, if the consumer purchases less than OX units of gas per month. For any amount beyond OX units per month, the company charges a medium price, OP_1. For purchases beyond OY, the company charges an even lower price,

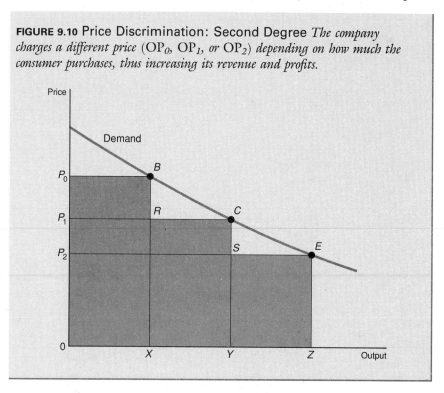

FIGURE 9.10 Price Discrimination: Second Degree *The company charges a different price* (OP$_0$, OP$_1$, *or* OP$_2$) *depending on how much the consumer purchases, thus increasing its revenue and profits.*

OP_2. Consequently, the company's total revenues from each consumer are equal to the shaded area in Figure 9.10, since the consumer will purchase OX units at a price of OP_0, $(OY - OX)$ units at a price of OP_1, and $(OZ - OY)$ units at a price of OP_2.[10]

It is obvious that the gas company, by charging different prices for various amounts of the commodity, is able to increase its revenue and profits considerably. After all, if it were permitted to charge only one price and if it wanted to sell OZ units, it would have to charge a price of OP_2. Thus the firm's total revenue would equal only the rectangle, OP_2EZ, which is considerably less than the shaded area in Figure 9.10. By charging different prices, the monopolist is able to take part of the consumers' surplus. According to some authorities, the schedules of rates charged by many public utilities—gas, water, electricity, and others—can be viewed as a type of second-degree price discrimination.[11]

Discrimination and the Existence of the Industry

Under some circumstances, a good or service cannot be produced without discrimination. For example, consider the case in Figure 9.11, where there are two types of consumers, their demand curves being D_0D_0' and D_1D_1'. Adding the two demand curves, we find that the total demand for the commodity is D_0UV. As shown in Figure 9.11, no output exists at which price is greater than

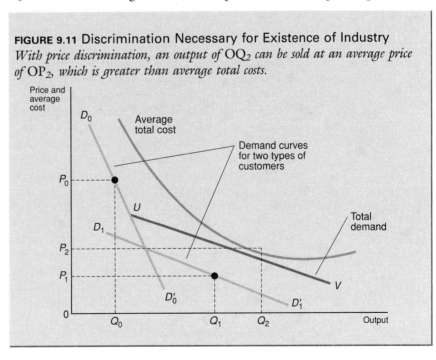

FIGURE 9.11 Discrimination Necessary for Existence of Industry
With price discrimination, an output of OQ_2 can be sold at an average price of OP_2, which is greater than average total costs.

10. Of course, this assumes for simplicity that each consumer purchases OZ units. Also, other simplifying assumptions (which need not concern us here) are made as well in this and the next paragraph.

11. Ralph Davidson, *Price Determination in Selling Gas and Electricity* (Baltimore: Johns Hopkins University Press, 1975); and C. Cicchetti and J. Jurewitz, *Studies in Electric Utility Regulation* (Cambridge, Mass.: Ballinger, 1975).

or equal to average total cost if price discrimination is not practiced. However, with price discrimination, an output of OQ_0 can be sold at a price of OP_0 to one type of consumer; an output of OQ_1 can be sold at a price of OP_1 to the second type of consumer; and the total output (which equals OQ_2) brings an average price of OP_2, which is greater than average total costs.[12]

TWO-PART TARIFFS AND TYING

Two-part tariff

Another pricing technique used by monopolists is the *two-part tariff*, which requires the consumer to pay an initial fee for the right to buy the product as well as a usage fee for each unit of the product that he or she buys. There are many cases where this pricing technique is used. For example, telephone companies charge you a basic monthly fee for telephone service plus an amount for message units, and private golf clubs charge you an annual membership fee plus an amount for each round of golf.

A monopolist that uses this pricing technique must determine how high the initial fee must be, as well as the size of the usage fee. Clearly, the lower the initial fee, the greater the number of consumers that will purchase the right to buy the product. Thus lower initial fees are likely to result in greater profits from the sales of the product. But this may not be best for the firm, since it also receives profits from the initial fees it charges—and if it lowers the initial fee, these profits will fall. Consequently, the monopolist would be expected to choose the initial fee and usage fee so that its total profit—from both the sales of the product and from initial fees—is a maximum. Example 9.3, about the use of a two-part tariff at Disneyland, illustrates the relevant considerations.

Tying

If a monopolist produces a product that will function properly only if it is used in conjunction with another product, it may require its customers to buy the other product from it, rather than from alternative suppliers. This pricing technique, called *tying*, has been used in the office equipment and computer industries, among others. Several decades ago, the Xerox Corporation insisted that firms or individuals that leased its copiers had to buy the copy paper from Xerox, and the IBM Corporation insisted that those who leased its computers had to use paper computer cards that it made. One reason why firms adopt this pricing technique is that it allows them to charge higher prices to customers that use their products intensively than to those that make little use of them. (Price discrimination of this sort often is difficult to carry out otherwise, since a firm often does not know how intensively each customer uses its product.) Thus, by setting the price of its cards above their marginal cost, IBM could obtain a higher total price (from the computer and cards combined) from those that used its computers intensively than from those that used them infrequently. As we know from previous sections, price discrimination of this sort can (under the proper conditions) increase the firm's profits.[13]

12. This section assumes that there are no government subsidies for the product in question. If such subsidies exist, it may be profitable to produce the product in Figure 9.11 even without price discrimination.

13. Firms often argue that tying insures that their products will be used with the proper kind of complementary products so that good performance will result. See B. Klein and L. Salt, "The Law and Economics of Tying Contracts," *Journal of Law and Economics*, May 1985.

EXAMPLE 9.3

A Two-Part Tariff at Disneyland

Monopolists, as we have seen, sometimes charge a two-part tariff, which consists of (1) a fee for the right to buy the product, and (2) an additional fee for each unit of the product the consumer wants to consume. For example, Disneyland, the California amusement park, has charged each person a fee to enter the park and an additional amount for each ride he or she takes. An important problem facing the firm is: how big should the entrance fee be, and how big should the price per ride be?

(a) Suppose that each customer at Disneyland has the demand curve for rides shown below. If the price per ride is $3, how much will be the revenue per customer from the per-ride fees? (b) What is the maximum amount that each consumer would be willing to pay for the number of rides he or she will go on (if the price per ride is $3)? (c) To maximize Disneyland's profits, what entrance fee should be set (if the price per ride is $3)? (d) In the early 1980s, Disneyland eliminated the fee for individual rides and raised the entrance fee. In the graph below, suppose that there is no fee for individual rides. What is the maximum entrance fee that can be charged? (e) In this case, is it more profitable to eliminate the $3 price for individual rides, and raise the entrance fee? (For simplicity, assume that the marginal cost to Disneyland of providing a ride to any person is zero; that is, all costs are fixed costs.) (f) Is it always true that a firm will maximize its profit by relying entirely on a fee for the right to buy the product and by eliminating the fee for each unit of the product the consumer wants to consume?

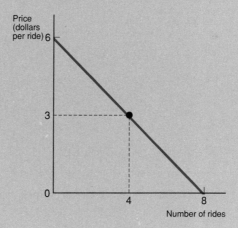

SOLUTION

(a) If the price per ride is $3, each customer will go on 4 rides. Thus the revenue per customer will be $4 \times \$3 = \$12$. (b) The area under the demand curve from zero to 4 rides equals the maximum amount that a customer would pay for the 4 rides. (Recall pp. 90–95.) This area equals $18. (c) Since the maximum total amount that the customer will pay is $18, and since the amount he or she will pay for per-ride fees is $12, the maximum amount he or she will pay for an entrance fee is $18 − $12 = $6. (d) The area under the demand curve from zero to 8 rides equals the maximum amount that a customer would pay for the 8 rides he or she would take if the price per ride were zero. This area equals $24. It is the maximum entrance fee that can be charged if the per-ride fee is zero. (e) Yes. Disneyland receives $24 per customer if the price per ride is zero (and the maximum entrance fee of $24 is charged), whereas it receives $18 per customer if the price per ride is $3 (and the maximum entrance fee of $6 is charged). (f) No. This is sometimes, but not always, true.*

*For further discussion, see W. Oi, "A Disneyland Dilemma: Two-Part Tariffs for a Mickey-Mouse Monopoly," *Quarterly Journal of Economics*, February 1971.

BUNDLING: ANOTHER PRICING TECHNIQUE

Still another pricing technique that is sometimes used by monopolists is *bundling*, which occurs if a firm requires customers that buy one of its products to buy another of its products as well. This procedure can increase the firm's profits if customers have quite different tastes (and if the firm cannot engage in price discrimination). To see why bundling can be profitable, consider a movie company that leases two movies, A and B. For simplicity, suppose that there are only two theaters, the Bijou and the Rialto, and that the maximum amount that each theater is willing to pay to lease each movie is as shown in Table 9.6.

TABLE 9.6 Maximum Price That Each Theater Would Pay for Two Movies, Leased Separately or as a Bundle (Case Where Bundling Is Profitable)

	Theater	
Movie	Bijou	Rialto
A	$11,000	$ 8,000
B	7,000	9,000
Bundle (A and B combined)	$18,000	$17,000

If the movies are leased separately, the most that can be charged for movie A is $8,000, and the most that can be charged for movie B is $7,000. Why? Because if the movie company is foolish enough to set prices above these levels, it will not be able to lease its films to both theaters. Thus the most it can get for both films is $8,000 + $7,000 = $15,000. But what if the movie company insists that a theater must lease both movies? In this case, as shown in Table 9.6, the most that the Bijou is willing to pay for them both is $18,000, and the most that the Rialto is willing to pay is $17,000. Thus the movie company can charge $17,000 for both movies combined, which is more than the amount ($15,000) that it could obtain if it leased them separately.

FIGURE 9.12 Alternative Relationships between the Maximum
Amount a Theater Would Pay for Movie A and the Maximum
Amount It Would Pay for Movie B *In Panel A, bundling is profitable;
in Panel B, it is not profitable.*

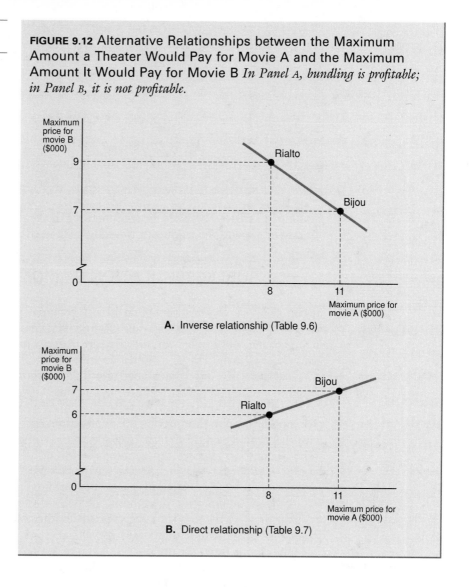

A. Inverse relationship (Table 9.6)

B. Direct relationship (Table 9.7)

The movie company will find it more profitable to lease them as a bundle
than to lease them separately so long as there is an inverse relationship between
the amount that a theater is willing to pay for one movie and the amount that it
is willing to pay for the other movie. (Panel A of Figure 9.12 shows that the
relationship in Table 9.6 is in fact inverse.) But if this relationship is direct,
there will be no advantage to the movie conpany in bundling them. For example, if the maximum prices the theaters would pay are shown in Table 9.7, the
most that can be gotten for movie A (leased separately) is $8,000, and the most
that can be gotten for movie B (leased separately) is $6,000. Thus, if they are
leased separately, the most that can be gotten from them both is $8,000 +
$6,000 = $14,000, which is the same as the amount that can be gotten if they
are bundled. (Panel B of Figure 9.12 shows that there is in fact a direct rela-

TABLE 9.7 Maximum Price That Each Theater Would Pay for Two
Movies, Leased Separately or as a Bundle (Case Where
Bundling Is Not Profitable)

	Theater	
Movie	Bijou	Rialto
A	$11,000	$ 8,000
B	7,000	6,000
Bundle (A and B combined)	$18,000	$14,000

tionship in Table 9.7 between the amount that a theater would be willing to pay
for one movie and the amount it would be willing to pay for the other.)[14]

PUBLIC REGULATION OF MONOPOLY

State regulatory commissions often have substantial power over the prices
charged by public utilities like gas and electric companies. As pointed out earlier
in this chapter, these public utilities often are natural monopolies. Consider the
firm whose demand curve, marginal revenue curve, average cost curve, and
marginal cost curve are shown in Figure 9.13. Without regulation, the firm
would charge a price of OP_0 and it would produce OQ_0 units of the commodity. By setting a maximum price of OP_1, the commission can make the monopolist increase output, thus making price and output correspond more closely to
what they would be if the industry were organized competitively. For instance,
if the commission imposes a maximum price of OP_1, the firm's demand curve
becomes P_1BD', its marginal revenue curve becomes P_1BCR', its optimum
output becomes OQ_1, and it will charge the maximum price of OP_1. By establishing the maximum price, the commission helps consumers who pay a lower
price for more of the good. By the same token, the commission deprives the
monopolist of some of its monopoly power.

Fair rate of return Commissions often set the price—or the maximum price—at the level at
which it equals average total cost, including a "fair" rate of return on the company's investment. For example, in Figure 9.14, the price would be established
by the commission at OP_2, where the demand curve intersects the average total
cost curve. The latter curve includes what the commission regards as a fair profit
per unit of output. Needless to say, there has been considerable controversy
over what constitutes a fair rate of return. There has also been a good deal of
controversy over what should be included in the company's investment on
which the fair rate of return is to be earned.

The regulatory commissions also govern the extent to which price discrimination is used by the public utilities. Intricate systems of price discrimination
exist in the rate structures of the electric and gas companies, the telephone

14. For further discussion, see W. Adams and J. Yellen, "Commodity Bundling and the Burden of
Monopoly," *Quarterly Journal of Economics,* August 1976; and R. Schmalensee, "Commodity
Bundling by Single-Product Monopolies," *Journal of Law and Economics,* April 1982.

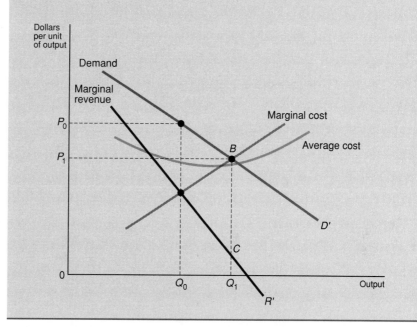

FIGURE 9.13 Regulation of Monopoly: Maximum Price *By setting a maximum price of* OP_1, *a regulatory commission can make the monopolist increase output to* OQ_1.

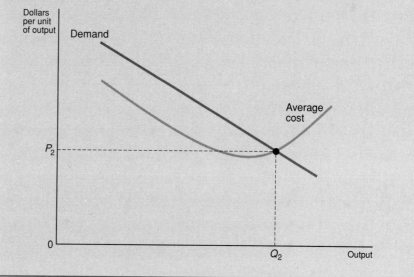

FIGURE 9.14 Regulation of Monopoly: Fair Rate of Return *The regulated price is* OP_2, *where the demand curve intersects the average total cost curve which includes what the commission regards as a fair profit per unit of output.*

EXAMPLE 9.4

THE REJECTION OF THE SANTA FE/SOUTHERN PACIFIC MERGER

In 1983, the Santa Fe and Southern Pacific railroads announced a plan to merge. The two railroads run parallel to one another; they provide the only rail service between southern California and Texas (and the Gulf of Mexico ports). Legislation passed by Congress in 1980 reduced the amount of regulation in this industry. Nonetheless, the Interstate Commerce Commission, which has regulated the railroad industry since 1887, had to approve the merger application, and in 1986 it refused to do so on a 4-to-1 vote of the commissioners.

(a) According to analysts at the U.S. Department of Justice, the merger would have resulted in a substantial price increase by the railroads. In the graph below, the price would have increased from OP to OP'. (For the two firms combined, their demand curve and their marginal cost curve are shown in the graph. For simplicity, marginal cost is assumed to be constant.) These analysts estimated that the area of rectangle C equaled about $404 million. Is this the loss to shippers due to having to pay a price of OP' rather than OP for the OQ' units of railroad services they would buy after the merger? (b) With regard to rectangle C, do the railroads gain what the shippers lose? (c) These analysts estimated that the area of rectangle B equaled about $57 million. Is this the loss to the railroads from the reduction in their output (from OQ to OQ') that was earning more than marginal cost? (d) These analysts estimated that the area of triangle A was about $22 million. Is this the loss to shippers of the consumer's surplus from the railroad services they bought when the price was OP but would not buy when it is OP'? (e) On balance, are shippers hurt by the merger, according to these estimates? Do the railroads benefit? (f) If the merger reduces the firms' costs considerably, should the savings be deducted from the social costs of the merger?

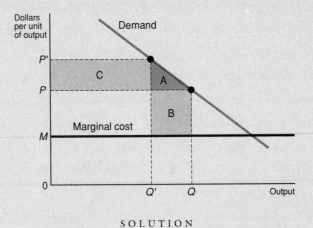

SOLUTION

(a) Yes. The area of rectangle C is $OQ'\,(OP' - OP)$, which equals the amount of railroad services that would be bought after the merger (OQ') times the increase in price ($OP' - OP$). (b) Yes. The extra amount paid by the shippers

goes to the railroads. Thus this is a transfer of income from one group (shippers) to another (railroads). (c) Yes. After the merger, the railroads would sell $(OQ - OQ')$ fewer units of output. On each of these units of output, they earned a profit of $(OP - OM)$. Thus the merger meant a loss to them of $(OQ - OQ') \times (OP - OM)$, which is the area of rectangle B. (d) Yes. The maximum amount that the shippers would pay for these extra $(OQ - OQ')$ units of output is the area under the demand curve from OQ' to OQ. The amount that they would have had to pay for them is $(OQ - OQ')\, OP$, so the consumer's surplus equals the area of triangle A. (Recall pages 90–95.) (e) Yes. Shippers lose \$404 million + \$22 million = \$426 million, while the railroads gain \$404 million − \$57 million = \$347 million. (f) Yes.*

*For further discussion, see R. Pittman, "Railroads and Competition: Why the Santa Fe/ Southern Pacific Merger Had to Die," U.S. Department of Justice, August 1988. It should be recognized that cases of this sort are very complex and that a brief discussion of this sort is bound to be oversimplified. Some experts argue that this merger might have been socially desirable, and that shippers might have gained from the existence of railroad capacity that otherwise might disappear in the long run. All that we present here is a brief summary of the analysis (cited above) by analysts at the Justice Department.

companies, and so forth. Although some types of discrimination are prohibited, other types can be practiced if they are "reasonable." For example, a company may be permitted to charge a lower rate for a service where it must meet stiff competition. It should be noted that rate discrimination raises important questions of equity and of redistribution of income, as well as questions regarding economic efficiency. Particularly in transportation, some of the most nettlesome problems of rate regulation are concerned with questions of discrimination.

CASE STUDIES

De Beers: An Unregulated Monopoly

According to the *New York Times*, the Central Selling Organization, controlled by De Beers Consolidated Mines Ltd., is "probably the world's most successful monopoly."[15] De Beers, founded in 1880 by Cecil Rhodes in South Africa, controlled over 99 percent of world diamond production until about 1900. At

15. *New York Times*, September 7, 1986, p. 4F.

present the firm mines only about 15 percent of the world's diamonds, but it still controls the sales of over 80 percent of the gem-quality diamonds through its Central Selling Organization, which markets the output of other major producing countries like Zaire, the Soviet Union, Botswana, Namibia, and Australia, as well as its own production. In the first half of 1989, its sales were over $2 billion.

No one doubts that De Beers controls the price of diamonds. Buyers are offered small boxes of assorted diamonds at a price set by De Beers on a "take it all or leave it" basis. Those that choose not to buy may have to wait some time before getting another opportunity. If the demand for diamonds falls, as it did during the early 1980s (when inflation slowed and diamonds as an investment lost much of their sparkle), De Beers stands ready to buy diamonds to support the price. Between 1979 and 1984, its stockpile of diamonds increased from about $360 million to about $2 billion.

Besides limiting the quantity supplied, De Beers also works hard and cleverly to push the demand curve for diamonds to the right. An important part of its sales campaign has been to link diamonds and romance. (According to its fifty-year-old slogan, "A Diamond Is Forever.") Of course, this has also been helpful in keeping diamonds, once sold, off the market. A good that is drenched with lasting sentiment is less likely to be sold when times get tough. De Beers's policies have paid off in very substantial profits, but the consumer has paid higher prices than if the diamond market were competitive.

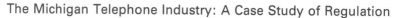

The Michigan Telephone Industry: A Case Study of Regulation

The previous section described a case of unregulated monopoly. To illustrate the case of regulated monopoly, we turn to the telephone industry in Michigan. The two groups that have played a key role in the regulation of the telephone industry in Michigan are one firm, Michigan Bell (a subsidiary of Ameritech[16]), and one commission, the Public Service Commission in Michigan.[17] Although Michigan Bell is not the only telephone company in the state, it is the dominant firm, and there is no direct competition in the industry between firms. The commission, which is composed of three members appointed by the governor , has had authority over the telephone industry for about fifty years.

A general-rate case has been the common sort of regulatory "contest" in the Michigan telephone industry. Such cases have been initiated by the firms and have been based on company claims that earnings are deficient and a higher price level is required. It is generally assumed, though not proved, that demand is inelastic and that higher prices will mean greater revenues. The industry

16. Ameritech (American Information Technologies Corporation) is one of seven regional holding companies resulting from the breakup of the American Telephone and Telegraph Company (AT&T). In 1982, a district court ordered AT&T to divest itself of the exchange telecommunications, exchange access, and Yellow Pages of its 22 wholly-owned Bell operating telephone companies, one of which was Michigan Bell. This decision arose out of an antitrust case brought by the U.S. Department of Justice against AT&T.

17. See C. E. Troxel, "Telephone Regulation in Michigan," in W. G. Shepherd and T. Gies, *Utility Regulation* (New York: Random House, 1966). Also, see M. Irwin, "The Telephone Industry," in W. Adams, *The Structure of American Industry*, 5th ed. (New York: Macmillan, 1977).

usually has received less than it asked for. Moreover, commission decisions have lagged behind the industry's revenue requests. However, it should be recognized that the fact that the commission has not approved all Bell requests does not mean that the company has been constrained much by the commission. The company may ask for more than it thinks it will get.

Nothing in public utility controls is more conventional, more securely established in regulatory methods, than the idea of a "reasonable return on the value of a firm's existing plant."[18] This is what the commission has been interested in establishing. Yet there are a host of questions, some obvious to the most naïve schoolchild, others difficult for a trained engineer or accountant to understand, concerning what is a "reasonable return" and what is "the value of a firm's existing plant." The original cost or historical cost of the plant is the measure on which most commissions base their estimates of the value of the plant; but some allow firms to use replacement-cost valuations instead. In the early 1980s, regulated firms often sought a rate of return of about 10 to 15 percent; commissions in recent years have approved rates of return of about 6 to 10 percent.[19] There are lots of detailed and difficult questions in each case of this sort that provide employment for a great many lawyers, accountants, engineers, and economists.

The Airlines: A Case Study of Deregulation

Considerable controversy has centered on the regulatory process, with many observers feeling that the commissions are lax and that they tend to be captured by the industries they are supposed to regulate. Also, in some cases, regulation, although effective, seems to have had unfortunate consequences. For example, the Civil Aeronautics Board, which was established in 1938, and which regulated the prices charged by the interstate scheduled airlines as well as entry into the industry, was criticized severely during the 1970s for preventing price competition among airlines and for permitting little new entry. After some experimentation with more active price competition in the late 1970s, Congress passed legislation that phased out the CAB's powers. The power to regulate routes terminated at the end of 1981, and the power to regulate rates terminated at the end of 1982.

In subsequent years, deregulation of the airlines became controversial, for at least two reasons. First, because deregulation brought reduced air fares, it also brought an increase in airline passenger traffic, which in turn helped to produce more congestion in airports and more delayed flights. Second, although deregulation initially stimulated an increase in the number of airlines, the airline industry subsequently became much more concentrated, as a number of firms merged. For example, Texas Air took over Eastern (and People Express) in 1986; and Northwest acquired Republic. In 1989, eight airlines controlled more than 90 percent of the domestic market. Some observers felt that this

18. Ibid., p. 162.

19. See W. Shepherd and C. Wilcox, *Public Policies Toward Business*, 6th ed. (Homewood, Ill.: Irwin, 1979); and W. Shepherd, *Public Policies Toward Business: Readings and Cases* (Homewood, Ill.: Irwin, 1979).

increase in concentration was excessive and they blamed the increase in part on deregulation.

Despite these concerns, there is no indication that the clock will be turned back. On the contrary, advocates of deregulation point out that it has increased the industry's efficiency by raising the number of passengers per plane, encouraging the carriers to get more productivity out of their employees, and improving the match between types of equipment and types of market. Further, it has offered the consumer a much greater variety of combinations of price and service quality. As predicted by microeconomic theory, deregulation has resulted in many economic advantages, although not all of its effects have been beneficial.[20]

Summary

1. Monopoly exists when there is one, and only one, seller in a market. Monopolies arise because a single firm controls the entire supply of a basic input, because a firm has a patent on the product or on certain basic processes, because the average cost of producing the product reaches a minimum at an output rate that is big enough to satisfy the entire market at a price that is profitable, because the firm is awarded a franchise, or for other reasons.

2. The demand curve facing the monopolist is the demand for the product. The cost conditions facing a monopolist may be no different from those facing a perfectly competitive firm, if the monopolist is a perfect competitor in the input markets.

3. Under monopoly, the firm will maximize profit if it sets its output rate at the point where marginal cost equals marginal revenue. It does not follow that a firm that holds a monopoly over the production of a particular product must make a profit. If the monopolist cannot cover its variable costs, it will shut down, even in the short run.

4. Under monopoly, there is no unique relationship between the product's price and the amount supplied. The long-run equilibrium of the industry is not necessarily marked by the absence of economic profits. If the monopolist has more than one plant, it should allocate production among its plants so that marginal costs are the same in each plant, and it should set its overall output rate so that this common marginal cost equals marginal revenue.

5. There are a number of important differences between the long-run equilibrium of a monopoly and of a perfectly competitive industry. Under perfect competition, each firm operates at the point where both long-run and short-run average costs are at a minimum; under monopoly, if the monopolist expanded its long-run equilibrium output, it could utilize a plant with lower average costs. The output of a perfectly competitive industry tends to be greater and price tends to be lower than under monopoly. The perfectly competitive firm operates at the point where price equals marginal cost, whereas the monopolist operates at a point where price exceeds marginal cost. Some economists measure the loss in economic welfare due to monopoly by the welfare triangle.

6. Price discrimination occurs when the same commodity is sold at more than one

20. For an appraisal of the airlines' performance, and suggestions for improvement, see S. Morrison and C. Winston, "Enhancing the Performance of the Deregulated Air Transportation System," in M. Baily and C. Winston (eds.), *Brookings Papers on Economic Activity*, 1989.

price, or when similar products are sold at prices that are in different ratios to marginal costs. A monopolist will be able and willing to practice price discrimination if various classes of buyers with different elasticities of demand can be identified and segregated, and if the commodity cannot be transferred easily from one class to another.

7. Another pricing technique used by monopolists is the two-part tariff, which requires the consumer to pay an initial fee for the right to buy the product, as well as a usage fee for each unit of the product that he or she buys. Also, if a monopolist produces a product that will function properly only if it is used in conjunction with another product, it may require its customers to buy the other product from it, rather than from alternative suppliers. This practice is called tying. Still another pricing technique is bundling.

8. Regulatory commissions frequently have the power to set the prices charged by public utilities like gas or electric companies. They often set the price—or the maximum price—at the level at which it equals average total cost, including a "fair" rate of return on the company's investment. There has been considerable controversy over what constitutes a fair rate of return, and over what should be included in the company's investment.

1. Postal service, which since 1845 has been largely a government monopoly in the United States, has been the object of continual controversy. Suppose that the short-run demand and cost curves of the Philadelphia post office are as follows:

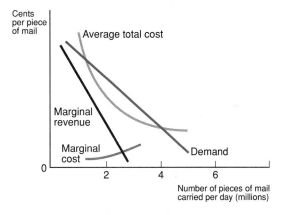

(a) Does the post office appear to be a natural monopoly, as some claim? (b) If the post office is a natural monopoly, must it be operated under government ownership? (c) If the Philadelphia post office wants to carry as many pieces of mail as it can without incurring a short-run deficit, how many should it carry per day? (d) The available evidence indicates that average revenue (per piece of mail) has exceeded average total cost and marginal cost for first-class mail, but not for third-class mail. Which type of mail is likely to attract private competitors? (e) What advantages might accrue if the post office were to face increased private competition?

2. A monopolist has two plants, with the following marginal cost functions:

$$MC_1 = 20 + 2Q_1$$
$$MC_2 = 10 + 5Q_2$$

where MC_1 is marginal cost in the first plant, MC_2 is marginal cost in the second plant, Q_1 is output in the first plant, and Q_2 is output in the second plant. If the monopolist is minimizing its costs, and if it is producing 5 units of output at the first plant, how many units is it producing at the second plant?

3. One of the longest and most expensive antitrust cases in history began in 1969, when the government charged that IBM "has attempted to monopolize and has monopolized . . . interstate trade and commerce in general purpose computers in violation of Section 2 of the Sherman Act." According to IBM's economists, its share of revenue from the sale of electronic data processing products and services in the United States was as follows:

1952	90.1%
1961	56.4
1968	54.0
1972	40.7

(a) Based on these figures, was IBM a monopolist? (b) Even if IBM did not have 100 percent of the market, could it have run afoul of the antitrust laws? (c) If a firm has a very large share of the market, does this mean that it should be prosecuted under the antitrust laws? (d) How should one define a market for these purposes? (e) Whereas IBM argued for a broad definition of the computer industry (including special purpose process control, message switching, and military computers and computer leasing and service activities), the government argued for a narrow definition (general purpose electronic digital computer systems). Why? (f) What was the outcome of this case?

4. Prostatix, Inc., a hypothetical pharmaceutical manufacturer, is a monopolist. Its president says that its price at its profit-maximizing output is triple its marginal cost. What is the price elasticity of demand of its product?

5. A monopolist has the following total cost function and demand curve:

Price (dollars)	Output (units)	Total cost (dollars)
8	5	20
7	6	21
6	7	22
5	8	23
4	9	24
3	10	30

What price should it charge?

6. A. C. Harberger, in his study cited in footnote 7, assumed that the price elasticity of demand was unity everywhere. Will a rational monopolist operate at a point where the price elasticity of demand is unity? Can one be sure that monopoly gains are not included in the cost items reported by accountants?

7. Suppose that you are the owner of a metals-producing firm that is an unregulated monopoly. After considerable experimentation and research, you find that your marginal cost curve can be approximated by a straight line, $MC = 60 + 2Q$, where MC is marginal cost (in dollars) and Q is your output. Moreover, suppose that the demand curve for your product is $P = 100 - Q$, where P is the product price and Q is your output. If you want to maximize profit, what output should you choose?

8. Authors customarily receive a royalty that is a fixed percentage of the price of the book. For this reason, economists have pointed out that an author has an interest in a book's price being lower than the price which maximizes the publisher's profits. Prove that this is true.

9. Suppose that you are hired as a consultant to a firm producing ball bearings. This firm is a monopolist which sells in two distinct markets, one of which is completely sealed off from the other. The demand curve for the firm's output in the one market is $P_1 = 160 -$

$8Q_1$, where P_1 is the price of the product and Q_1 is the amount sold in the first market. The demand curve for the firm's output in the second market is $P_2 = 80 - 2Q_2$, where P_2 is the price of the product and Q_2 is the amount sold in the second market. The firm's marginal cost curve is $5 + Q$, where Q is the firm's entire output (destined for either market). The firm asks you to suggest what its pricing policy should be. How many units of output should it sell in the second market? How many units of output should it sell in the first market? What prices should it charge?

10. The Errata Book Company is a monopolist that sells in two markets. The marginal revenue curve in the first market is

$$MR_1 = 20 - 2Q_1$$

where MR_1 is the marginal revenue in the first market and Q_1 is the number of books sold per day in the first market. The marginal revenue curve in the second market is

$$MR_2 = 15 - 3Q_2$$

where MR_2 is the marginal revenue in the second market and Q_2 is the number of books sold per day in the second market. If the marginal cost of a book is $6, how many books should the Errata Book Company sell in each market?

10

MONOPOLISTIC COMPETITION AND OLIGOPOLY

While perfect competition and monopoly are useful models that shed a great deal of light on how markets work, they are polar cases. In this and the next chapter, we take up models that describe more realistically how many industries function. This chapter focuses attention on monopolistic competition and oligopoly. The theory of monopolistic competition is applicable to industries like retail trade, and oligopoly theory pertains to industries like automobiles, electrical equipment, and computers. In the following chapter, we continue our discussion of oligopoly, the primary focus being on game theory and strategic decision-making.

MONOPOLISTIC COMPETITION

Product differentiation

Bergdorf Goodman has a monopoly on the sale of its dresses. However, other firms like Macy's and Bloomingdale's sell roughly similar dresses. Each firm has a monopoly over the sale of its own product, but the various brands are close substitutes. This is a case of *product differentiation*. In other words, there is no single, homogeneous commodity called a dress; instead, each seller differentiates its product from that of the next seller. This, of course, is a prevalent case in the modern economy. Each seller tries to make its product a little different, by altering the physical makeup of the product, the services it offers, and other such variables. Other differences—which may be spurious—are based on brand name, image-making, advertising claims, and so forth. In this way, each seller

Monopolistic competition

has some amount of monopoly power, but it usually is small, because the products of other firms are very similar.

Monopolistic competition is a market structure where product differentiation exists and where there are elements of both monopoly and perfect competition. Under monopolistic competition, there is a large number of firms producing and selling goods that are close substitutes, but that are not completely homogeneous from one seller to another. For example, retail trade is often cited as an industry with many of the characteristics of monopolistic competition. Edward Chamberlin[1] of Harvard University pioneered in the development of the theory of monopolistic competition. While his theory has met with considerable criticism, it was a famous and noteworthy attempt to develop a model to handle the important middle ground between perfect competition and monopoly.[2]

To begin with, let's consider Chamberlin's concept of a product group. In perfect competition, the firms included in an industry are easy to determine, because they all produce the same product. But if there is product differentiation, it is no longer easy to define an industry, since each firm produces a somewhat different product. Nevertheless, Chamberlin believes that it is useful to group together firms producing similar products and call them a *product group*. For example, we can formulate a product group called dresses. Of course, the process by which we combine firms into product groups is bound to be somewhat arbitrary, since there is no way to decide how close a pair of substitutes must be in order to be included in the same product group. However, Chamberlin asserts that meaningful product groups can be formulated.

Product group

The assumptions underlying Chamberlin's theory are as follows: First, he assumes that the product, which is differentiated, is produced by a large number of firms, with each firm's product being a fairly close substitute for the products of the other firms in the product group. Second, he assumes that the number of firms in the product group is sufficiently large so that each firm expects its actions to go unheeded by its rivals and to be unimpeded by any retaliatory measures on their part. Third, he assumes that both demand and cost curves are the same for all of the firms in the group. This, of course, is a very restrictive assumption since, if the products are dissimilar, one would ordinarily expect their demand and cost curves to be dissimilar, too.

EQUILIBRIUM PRICE AND OUTPUT IN THE SHORT AND LONG RUNS

Because each firm's product is somewhat different from that of its rivals, the demand curve for its product is downward sloping, as shown in Figure 10.1. This demand curve is for one firm's product, but its position depends on other

1. E. Chamberlin, *The Theory of Monopolistic Competition* (Cambridge, Mass.: Harvard University Press, 1933). Another very important work of the same period was J. Robinson, *The Economics of Imperfect Competition* (New York: Macmillan, 1933).

2. Perfect competition and monopoly are two polar extremes. There is an extremely large number of firms in a perfectly competitive industry, but only one firm in a monopoly. Obviously, many industries in the real world fall between these two extremes.

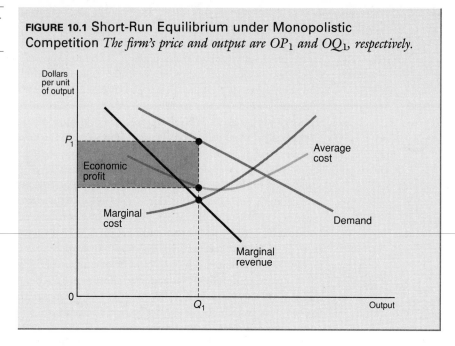

FIGURE 10.1 Short-Run Equilibrium under Monopolistic
Competition *The firm's price and output are OP_1 and OQ_1, respectively.*

Short run

firms' prices. (An increase in other firms' prices would cause this demand curve
to shift to the right, while a decrease would cause it to shift to the left.) In the
short run, an equilibrium will be reached when the situation is like that in
Figure 10.1. The short-run equilibrium price and output of each firm are OP_1
and OQ_1, respectively. It can easily be verified that the firm has no incentive to
change its price from OP_1. Since marginal revenue equals marginal cost at an
output of OQ_1, the firm believes that it is maximizing profits by maintaining its
price at OP_1.

In the case shown in Figure 10.1, the firm earns a short-run profit equal to
the shaded area; but this need not always be the case in short-run equilibrium.
On the contrary, in some cases, firms may experience losses in short-run equilibrium. However, as long as OP_1 exceeds the firm's average variable costs, the
firm will continue to produce in the short run.

Long run

As in perfect competition, firms in the long run are able to change the scale
of their plant and to leave or enter the industry. The long-run equilibrium price
and output of the representative firm are shown in Figure 10.2; the equilibrium
price is OP_2 and the equilibrium output is OQ_2. Since there is free entry and
exit in a monopolistically competitive industry, the long-run equilibrium is a
situation in which all firms in the industry, although they are maximizing profits, have zero economic profits. This is similar to the long-run equilibrium in a
perfectly competitive industry. Note that the cost curves in Figure 10.2 are
long-run cost curves, not the short-run cost curves shown in Figure 10.1. The
long-run equilibrium position is at the output where the long-run average cost
curve is tangent to the demand curve and where the marginal cost curve intersects the marginal revenue curve. Because marginal revenue equals marginal

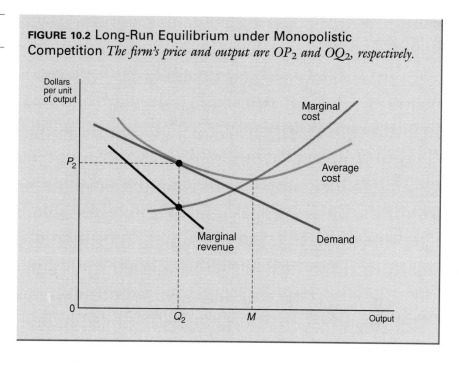

FIGURE 10.2 Long-Run Equilibrium under Monopolistic
Competition *The firm's price and output are OP_2 and OQ_2, respectively.*

cost, the firm is maximizing profit. Because average cost equals price, economic
profits equal zero.

How is this long-run equilibrium position reached? The adjustments that
take place can be described in terms of changes in the position of the demand
curve facing the representative firm. The demand curve shifts in response to the
entry of new firms and the exit of old firms. Increases in the number of firms in
the industry shift the demand curve facing the representative firm to the left,
because the market (which is relatively fixed) must be divided among more
firms. Reductions in the number of firms shift the demand curve facing the
representative firm to the right, because the market must be divided among
fewer firms. As a result of entry and exit, the demand curve is pushed toward
the equilibrium position, where it is tangent to the long-run average cost
curve.

Consider Figure 10.1, which shows the short-run situation. This firm (and
the others in the group) is making an economic profit since the current price is
OP_1. The existence of profit encourages new firms to enter the group, and the
demand curve facing the representative firm shifts to the left. As entry continues, this demand curve may shift further to the left. Only when at last the
situation in Figure 10.2 is reached will a long-run equilibrium be established.
In this situation, the demand curve is tangent to the long-run average cost
curve, with the result that there is no incentive for entry or exit, since economic
profits are nonexistent. Moreover, in this situation, the demand curve is always
below the long-run average cost curve, except at the point where the firm is
operating. Thus the firm has no incentive to change its price or output, since
any such change appears to be unprofitable.

EXCESS CAPACITY AND PRODUCT DIVERSITY

A famous and controversial conclusion of the theory of monopolistic competition is that a firm under this form of market organization will tend to operate with excess capacity. In other words, it is alleged that the firm will construct a plant smaller than the minimum-cost size of plant and operate it at less than the minimum-cost rate of output. Why? Because, as shown in Figure 10.2, the demand curve must be tangent in long-run equilibrium to the long-run average cost curve. Thus, since the demand curve is downward sloping, the long-run average cost curve must also be downward sloping at the long-run equilibrium output rate. Consequently, the firm's output must be less than $OM,$ the output rate at which long-run average cost is minimized, since the long-run average cost curve slopes downward only at outputs less than $OM.$ Moreover, since each firm builds a smaller than minimum-cost plant and produces a smaller than minimum-cost output, more firms can exist under these circumstances than if there were no excess capacity. Thus it has been argued that there will be some "overcrowding" of monopolistically competitive industries.

Product diversity   More recent research suggests that this argument may be somewhat myopic because, as pointed out by Avinash Dixit, Michael Spence, Joseph Stiglitz, and others, an important benefit to society of monopolistic competition is *product diversity.* Like most consumers, you probably value the ability to choose among a wide variety of clothes, restaurant meals, and other styles and types of products and services. The social benefits from product diversity can be substantial, and they may exceed the social costs cited in the previous paragraph.[3]

MARKUP PRICING

Empirical studies suggest that markup (or cost-plus) pricing is used by many monopolistically competitive (and other) firms. For example, many retail stores use markup pricing. There are two basic steps in this approach to pricing. First, the firm estimates the cost per unit of output of the product. Since this cost will generally vary with output, the firm must base this computation on some assumed output level. Usually, firms seem to use for this purpose some percentage, generally between two-thirds and three-quarters, of capacity. Second, *Markup pricing*   the firm adds a *markup* (generally put in the form of a percentage) to the estimated average cost. This markup is meant to include certain costs that cannot be allocated to any specific product and to provide a return on the firm's investment. The size of the markup depends on the rate of profit that the firm believes it can earn. Some firms have set up a *target return* figure that they hope to earn, which determines the markup. For example, a firm may establish a target rate of return of 20 percent.

3. See A. Dixit and J. Stiglitz, "Monopolistic Competition and Optimum Product Diversity," *American Economic Review,* June 1977; M. Spence, "Product Selection, Fixed Costs, and Monopolistic Competition," *Review of Economic Studies,* June 1976; K. Lancaster, "Socially Optimal Product Differentiation," *American Economic Review,* September 1975; and H. Leland, "Quality Choices and Competition," *American Economic Review,* March 1977.

There has been considerable controversy over the extent to which markup pricing is compatible with profit maximization. At first glance, it seems extremely unlikely that this form of pricing can result in the maximization of profits. Indeed, this pricing technique seems naïve, since it takes no account, explicitly at least, of the extent or elasticity of demand or of the size of marginal, rather than average, costs. Nevertheless, if marginal cost (not average cost) is really what is being marked up, and if the price elasticity of demand is used to determine the size of the markup, markup pricing can readily be used to maximize profit.

To see this, recall from Equation 5.3 that

$$MR = P\left[1 - \frac{1}{\eta}\right]$$

where MR is the firm's marginal revenue, P is its price, and η is the price elasticity of demand of the firm's product. Solving this equation for P, and recognizing that marginal revenue will be equal to marginal cost if the firm is maximizing profit, we get

$$P = MC\left[\frac{1}{1 - \frac{1}{\eta}}\right] = MC\left[1 + \frac{\frac{1}{\eta}}{1 - \frac{1}{\eta}}\right]. \qquad [10.1]$$

Thus, if marginal cost (rather than average cost) is what is being marked up, and if the markup (in absolute terms) equals $MC[1/\eta \div (1 - 1/\eta)]$, the firm can obtain the profit-maximizing price in this way.

From the point of view of a firm's managers, Equation 10.1 is a very useful result. Surprising as it may seem, this equation shows that, to determine the price that maximizes profit, all that a firm's managers need to know is their product's marginal cost and its price elasticity of demand, which can be inserted into Equation 10.1 to obtain the optimal price. As we saw in Chapters 5 and 7, even though very precise estimates of a product's marginal cost and its price elasticity of demand may be hard to come by, rough estimates generally can be obtained. These estimates often are good enough to be helpful in guiding firms' pricing policies. For example, if marginal cost equals $10 and the price elasticity of demand is about 2, price should be established at about $10 $\left[\frac{1}{1 - \frac{1}{2}}\right]$,

or $20, if the firm wants to maximize profit. (It is also worth noting that Equation 10.1 can be useful for monopolists and other firms, as well as under monopolistic competition.)

COMPARISONS WITH PERFECT COMPETITION AND MONOPOLY

Frequently, attempts are made to compare the long-run equilibria that result from various market organizations. If we suppose that an industry were monopolistically competitive, rather than purely competitive or purely monopolistic, what difference would it make in the long-run behavior of the industry? It is difficult to interpret this question in a meaningful way, let alone answer it, since the output of the industry would be heterogeneous in one case and homogeneous in the other, and since the cost curves of the industry would probably vary with its organization. Nevertheless, many economists seem to believe that differences of the following kinds can be expected.

First, the firm under monopolistic competition is likely to produce less, and set a higher price, than under perfect competition. The demand curve confronting the monopolistic competitor is not perfectly elastic, as it is in perfect competition. Since marginal revenue is less than price in monopolistic competition, the firm will produce less than the amount at which price equals marginal cost, the consequence being that it will produce less than under perfect competition. However, the difference may not be very great, since the demand curve facing the firm under monopolistic competition may be close to perfectly elastic.

Second, relative to monopoly, monopolistically competitive firms are likely to have lower profits, greater output, and lower prices. The firms in a product group might obtain economic profits if they were to collude and behave as a monopolist. Of course, the increase in profit resulting from the monopoly would make the producers better off, but consumers would be worse off because of higher prices and a smaller output of goods.

Third, as noted in the section before last, firms in monopolistic competition are sometimes accused of being (somewhat) inefficient because they produce an output that is less than that which would minimize long-run average cost. However, if the differences among their products are real and are understood by consumers, the greater variety of alternatives available under monopolistic competition may be worth a great deal to consumers. Indeed, the social benefits from product diversity may outweigh these apparent inefficiencies.[4]

ADVERTISING EXPENDITURES: A SIMPLE MODEL

Industries with the characteristics of monopolistic competition spend very large amounts on advertising. Newspapers, which account for about 30 percent of total advertising expenditure in the United States, are full of advertisements by food stores, clothing stores, and other retailers. How much should a profit-maximizing firm spend on advertising? This is a very important question, and one that has occupied the attention of many economists in the sixty years since

---

4. Many criticisms have been made of Chamberlin's theory. For example, Chicago's George Stigler and others have argued that the definition of the group of firms included in the product group is extremely ambiguous. It may contain only one firm or all of the firms in the economy. Moreover, in Stigler's view, the concept of the group is not salvaged by the assumption that each firm neglects the effects of its decisions on other firms in the group, and that each firm has essentially the same demand and cost curves. Indeed, according to Stigler, the firms in the group must be selling homogeneous commodities if the assumption of similar demand and cost curves for all firms in the group is to be at all realistic. But if the commodities are homogeneous, there is no reason why firms should have downward-sloping demand curves.

Chamberlin's work. In this section, we derive a simple rule that helps to answer this question.

For a particular firm, suppose that the quantity that it sells of its product is a function of the product's price and the level of the firm's advertising expenditure for the product. In particular, assume that there are diminishing marginal returns to advertising expenditures, which means that beyond some point successive increments of advertising outlays will yield smaller and smaller increases in additional sales. (Table 10.1 shows an illustrative case where successive increments of $100,000 in advertising outlays result in smaller and smaller increases in quantity sold. For example, the quantity sold increases by 2.0 million units when advertising expenditures rise from $800,000 to $900,000, but by only 1.5 million units when they rise from $900,000 to $1 million.)

TABLE 10.1 Relationship between Advertising Expenditures and the Quantity Sold of the Firm's Product

Advertising expenditures (millions of dollars)	Quantity sold of product (millions of units)
0.8	5.0
0.9	7.0
1.0	8.5
1.1	9.5
1.2	10.0

We assume too that neither price nor the marginal cost of producing an extra unit of the product will be altered by small changes in advertising expenditures. Letting P be the price of a unit of the product and MC be the marginal cost of production, the firm receives a gross profit of $(P - MC)$ from each additional unit of the product that it makes and sells. Why is this the *gross* profit of making and selling an additional unit of output? Because it takes no account of whatever additional advertising expenditures were required to sell this extra unit of output. To obtain the *net* profit, the firm must deduct these additional advertising outlays from the gross profit.

To maximize its total net profits, a firm must set its advertising expenditures at the level where an extra dollar of advertising results in extra gross profit equal to the extra dollar of advertising cost. Unless this is the case, the firm's total net profits can be increased by changing its advertising outlays. If an extra dollar of advertising results in more than a dollar increase in gross profit, the extra dollar should be spent on advertising (since this will raise total net profits). If an extra dollar (as well as the last dollar) of advertising results in less than a dollar increase in gross profit, advertising outlays should be cut.[5] Thus, if ΔQ is the number of extra units of output sold due to an extra dollar of advertising, the

---

5. For simplicity, we assume here that the gross profit due to an extra dollar spent on advertising is essentially equal to the gross profit due to the last dollar spent. This is an innocuous assumption.

firm should set its advertising expenditures so that

$$\Delta Q(P - MC) = 1, \qquad [10.2]$$

because the right-hand side of this equation equals the extra dollar of advertising cost and the left-hand side equals the extra gross profit due to this advertising dollar.

Multiplying both sides of Equation 10.2 by $P \div (P - MC)$, we obtain

$$P\Delta Q = \frac{P}{P - MC}. \qquad [10.3]$$

Since the firm is maximizing profit, it is producing an output where marginal cost (MC) equals marginal revenue (MR). Thus we can substitute MR for MC in Equation 10.3, the result being

$$P\Delta Q = \frac{P}{P - MR}. \qquad [10.4]$$

Marginal revenue from an extra dollar of advertising

Using Equation 5.3, it can be shown that the right-hand side of Equation 10.4 equals η, the price elasticity of demand for the firm's product.[6] The left-hand side of Equation 10.4 is the *marginal revenue from an extra dollar of advertising* (since it equals the price times the extra number of units sold due to an extra dollar of advertising). Consequently, to maximize profit, the firm should set its advertising expenditure so that

$$\text{Marginal revenue from an extra dollar of advertising} = \eta. \qquad [10.5]$$

This rule, derived by Harvard's Robert Dorfman and Michigan's Peter Steiner,[7] is interesting and useful. To illustrate its use, consider the Terratech Corporation, which knows that the price elasticity of demand for its product equals 1.5. If this firm maximizes profit, the rule in Equation 10.5 says that it must set the marginal revenue from an extra dollar of advertising equal to 1.5. Suppose that Terratech's managers believe that an extra $100,000 of advertising would increase the firm's sales by $180,000, which implies that the marginal revenue from an extra dollar of advertising is about $180,000 ÷ $100,000, or 1.8, rather than 1.5. Because the marginal revenue exceeds the price elasticity, Terratech will increase its profit if it does more advertising.[8] To maximize profit, it should increase its advertising up to the point where the marginal revenue from an extra dollar of advertising falls to 1.5, the value of the

---

6. According to Equation 5.3, $MR = P\left[1 - \frac{1}{\eta}\right]$. Thus $1 - \frac{1}{\eta} = MR/P$, and $\frac{1}{\eta} = 1 - MR/P$, which means that

$$\eta = \frac{1}{1 - MR/P} = \frac{P}{P - MR},$$

which is the right-hand side of Equation 10.4.

7. R. Dorfman and P. Steiner, "Optimal Advertising and Optimal Quality," *American Economic Review*, December 1954.

8. Had Terratech's managers believed that the marginal revenue from an extra dollar of advertising was *less* than the price elasticity of demand, a *reduction* in the firm's advertising expenditures would increase profit.

price elasticity of demand. (Since diminishing returns are assumed, marginal revenue falls as advertising increases.)[9]

OPTIMAL ADVERTISING EXPENDITURES: A GRAPHICAL ANALYSIS

Going a step further, we can use a simple graphical technique to see how much a firm, if it maximizes profit, will spend on advertising. Take the case of the Miller Electronics Company. Suppose that curve F in Figure 10.3 shows the relationship between the price elasticity of demand of this firm's product and the amount it spends on advertising. With little or no advertising, this firm's product would be regarded by consumers as similar to a host of other products; hence, its price elasticity of demand would be very high. However, because appropriate advertising can induce consumers to attach importance to this product's distinguishing features, increases in advertising expenditure reduce its price elasticity considerably.[10] At each level of advertising expenditure, the G curve shows the marginal revenue from an extra dollar of advertising. Since the F curve intersects the G curve when Miller's advertising expenditure is OV

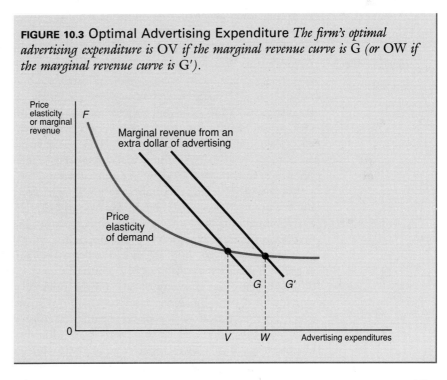

FIGURE 10.3 Optimal Advertising Expenditure *The firm's optimal advertising expenditure is* OV *if the marginal revenue curve is* G *(or* OW *if the marginal revenue curve is* G'*).*

9. Of course, this analysis is highly simplified, and the rule in Equation 10.5 is by no means a full or adequate answer to the complex question of how much a firm should spend on advertising. Nonetheless, it is of interest. For a discussion of the game theoretic considerations involved, see pp. 343–44.

10. In some cases, the price elasticity of demand is directly, not inversely, related to the amount spent on advertising. More is said later on this score.

dollars, this, based on Equation 10.5, is Miller's optimal level of advertising expenditure.

Clearly, a firm's optimal advertising expenditure depends on the position and shape of its G curve and its F curve. For example, suppose Miller's G curve shifts rightward to G', as shown in Figure 10.3. Such a shift might occur if the firm or its advertising agency found ways to increase the effectiveness of its advertisements. The result would be an increase in the optimal level of the firm's advertising expenditures (to OW dollars in Figure 10.3).

THE SOCIAL VALUE OF ADVERTISING

Thus far, we have considered advertising from the point of view of the firm, rather than of society as a whole. From society's point of view, there are obvious disadvantages stemming from certain kinds of advertising. To begin with, although private groups like the National Advertising Review Board and government agencies like the Federal Trade Commission try to stamp out blatantly deceptive advertising, some advertising misleads, rather than informs, consumers. Many consumers are properly skeptical about advertising claims, but the rest may be duped into making purchasing decisions that are far from optimal from their own point of view (but fine from the advertiser's perspective).

Negative effects

In addition, advertising may tend to augment the advertiser's monopoly power and may permit the advertiser more latitude to raise its price and profits. According to William Comanor and Thomas Wilson, the higher the ratio of advertising expenditures to sales in an industry, the higher the industry's profit rates.[11] If advertising makes customers recognize certain brands and if it encourages them to be loyal to these brands, sellers may have more power to raise prices without losing sales to competitors. In many retail establishments, advertised brands are priced higher than lesser-known brands. Advertising encourages customers to think that advertised brands are better than other brands, even though they may be essentially the same.

Positive effects

On the other hand, there also are advantages of advertising from a consumer's point of view. As Nobel laureate George Stigler[12] and Phillip Nelson[13] have pointed out, the consumer frequently does not know the minimum price that he or she must pay for a commodity, and it is costly and time-consuming for the consumer to shop around in order to obtain this information. For example, it may cost a consumer $12 worth of time and travel expense to locate the store that offers a saving of $10 on the price of an item. If so, it is not worthwhile for the consumer to try to locate this store. On the other hand, if advertising (of various stores' prices) enables all consumers to identify and get to the lowest-price seller of this item at an additional cost of only $2, the identification of this lowest-price store is worthwhile—and the consumer will be better off as a result of this advertising.

11. W. Comanor and T. Wilson, *Advertising and Monopoly Power* (Cambridge, Mass.: Harvard University Press, 1974).

12. G. Stigler, "The Economics of Information," *Journal of Political Economy,* June 1961.

13. P. Nelson, "The Economic Consequences of Advertising," *Journal of Business,* April 1975.

EXAMPLE 10.1

ADVERTISING, SPECTACLES, AND THE FTC

The theory of monopolistic competition emphasizes the significance of selling expenses, including advertising. The market for eyeglasses in large cities has many of the characteristics of monopolistic competition, there being a large number of sellers of eyeglasses, each one's product being slightly different from the others. Some states have banned advertising of prices by sellers of eyeglasses. The following table shows the average price of eyeglasses in these states, as well as in states with no advertising restrictions:

	Average price	
Nature of state law	Eyeglasses	Eyeglasses and eye examinations
Ban on advertising	$33.04	$40.96
No ban on advertising	26.34	37.10

(a) Since advertising is a selling expense which requires the use of resources, is it reasonable to expect that a firm's costs would be lower if it didn't have to advertise? (b) If advertising increases costs, why did the price of eyeglasses tend to be lower in states with no ban on advertising? (c) In 1978, the Federal Trade Commission (FTC) declared restrictions on eyeglass advertising to be illegal. Why did the FTC take this action?

SOLUTION

(a) Yes. Since advertising must be paid for, it increases a firm's costs. (b) In the markets studied, it appears that advertising improved the consumer's knowledge of the prices and services being offered by various sellers of eyeglasses. Without advertising, the cost to consumers of obtaining such knowledge is relatively high. Armed with such information, consumers were in a better position to seek out relatively low prices, and sellers were more likely to offer them. (Also, see p. 306.) (c) Because the FTC felt that such restrictions impaired the effectiveness of the competitive process. In particular, as shown in the above table, consumers seem to pay higher prices when such restrictions exist. In fact, there tended to be a drop in eyeglass prices after this FTC ruling.*

*For further discussion, see L. Benham, "The Effect of Advertising on the Price of Eyeglasses," *The Journal of Law and Economics,* October 1972.

Also, if advertising is successful in enlarging the market for a firm's product, and if this product's average cost falls as more of it is produced, then the saving in production costs may more than offset the advertising cost. A case in point is the retailing of eyeglasses. (See Example 10.1.) Apparently, significant economies of scale can be realized by achieving a relatively large sales volume in an eyeglass retailing firm, but it is difficult to achieve that volume if sellers are constrained by bans on advertising and other restrictive provisions sometimes found in optometrists' codes of ethics.

In contrast to the view that advertising promotes monopoly power, both Stigler and Nelson conclude that advertising tends to increase the price elasticity of demand for products. According to their findings, the demand for goods that are not widely advertised tends to be price inelastic. The greater the advertising effort, the more price elastic the demand for a good becomes. And the more elastic the demand for a good, the more competitive is the market for that good—and frequently the lower is the price.

Based on the foregoing discussion, it is clear that advertising has a variety of social effects, some positive, some negative. To the extent that it provides trustworthy information to consumers about product quality and other matters, its effects may be positive, but if it is grossly misleading, they may be negative. To the extent that it enables consumers to shop around for lower prices more efficiently and at lower cost, its effects tend to be positive, but if it is used to increase the advertiser's monopoly power, they may be negative.

Because advertising is of so many kinds, it really is impossible to generalize about whether or not it is socially beneficial. The answer depends on the nature of the advertising and the circumstances under which it takes place.[14] Advertising by retail stores, which informs consumers of the price and availability of goods, is more likely to be socially beneficial than radio commercials consisting of mindless ditties. Advertising aimed at professional purchasers of equipment is more likely to be socially beneficial than television commercials that feature lots of movie stars and sports heroes but few facts.

OLIGOPOLY

Having sketched out the theory of monopolistic competition, and having discussed the firm's decision regarding advertising expenditures, we turn now to

14. For some recent studies concerning advertising and its effects, see the papers by T. Bresnahan, R. Higgins and F. McChesney, Y. Kotowitz and F. Mathewson, and K. Leffler and R. Sauer in P. Ippolito and D. Scheffman (eds.), *Empirical Approaches to Consumer Protection Economics* (Washington, D.C.: Federal Trade Commission, 1986). Also, see G. Becker and K. Murphy, "A Simple Theory of Advertising as a Good," University of Chicago, 1990.

oligopoly. *Oligopoly* is a market structure characterized by a small number of firms and a great deal of interdependence, actual and perceived, among them. Unlike the case of monopolistic competition, oligopolies contain so few firms that each oligopolist formulates its policies with an eye to their effect on its rivals. Since an oligopoly contains a small number of firms, any change in the firm's price or output influences the sales and profits of competitors. Moreover, each firm must recognize that changes in its own policies are likely to elicit changes in the policies of its competitors as well.

Because of this interdependence, oligopolists face a situation where the optimal decision of one firm depends on what other firms decide to do, and where there is opportunity for both conflict and cooperation. A good example is the American beer industry, in which a handful of firms, led by Anheuser-Busch, account for the bulk of the industry's sales. Each of the major beer producers must take account of the reaction of the others when it formulates its price and output policy, since its optimal strategy is likely to depend in part on how they are likely to respond. Thus, in 1989, when Miller and Coors cut the price of their beers by as much as 25 percent, they had to anticipate what the reactions of other firms, like Anheuser-Busch, would be. In fact, Anheuser-Busch met their price reductions.

Oligopoly Oligopoly is a common market structure in the United States. The automobile industry is dominated by three domestic firms—General Motors, Ford, and Chrysler—and a handful of foreign producers. Many parts of the electrical equipment industry are dominated by General Electric and Westinghouse. The aerospace industry is dominated by Boeing, General Dynamics, Lockheed, McDonnell Douglas, United Technologies, and a few others. And these are only some highly visible examples. Not all oligopolists are large firms. If two grocery stores exist in an isolated community, they are oligopolists, too; the fact that they are small firms does not change this situation.

There are many reasons for oligopoly, one being economies of scale. In some industries, low costs cannot be achieved unless a firm is producing an output equal to a substantial percentage of the total available market, with the consequence that the number of firms will tend to be rather small. In addition, there may be economies of scale in sales promotion as well as in production, and this too may promote oligopoly. Further, there may be barriers that make it very difficult to enter the industry. (A variety of such barriers are discussed later in this chapter.) Finally, of course, the number of firms in an industry may decrease in response to the desire to weaken competitive pressures.

COLLUSION AND CARTELS

Conditions in oligopolistic industries tend to promote collusion, since the number of firms is small and the firms recognize their interdependence. The advantages to the firms of collusion seem obvious: increased profits, decreased uncertainty, and a better opportunity to prevent entry. However, collusive arrangements are often hard to maintain, since once a collusive agreement is made, any of the firms can increase its profits by cheating on the agreement. Moreover, collusive arrangements generally are illegal, at least in the United States.

When a collusive arrangement is made openly and formally, it is called a *cartel*. In many countries in Europe, cartels have been common and legally acceptable. In the United States, most collusive agreements, whether secret or open cartels, were declared illegal by the Sherman Antitrust Act, which dates back to 1890. However, this does not mean that such agreements do not exist. For example, there was widespread collusion among American electrical equipment manufacturers during the 1950s.[15] Moreover, trade associations and professional organizations may sometimes perform functions somewhat similar to a cartel. In addition, some types of cartels have the official sanction of the United States government.[16]

Cartel Suppose that a cartel is established to set a uniform price for a particular (homogeneous) product. What price will it charge? To begin with, the cartel must estimate the marginal cost curve for the cartel as a whole. If input prices do not increase as the cartel expands, this marginal cost curve is the horizontal sum of the marginal cost curves of the individual firms. Suppose that the resulting marginal cost curve for the cartel is as shown in Figure 10.4. If the demand curve for the industry's product and the relevant marginal revenue curve are as shown there, the output that maximizes the total profit of the cartel members is OQ_0. Thus, if it maximizes cartel profits, the cartel will choose a price of OP_0. This, of course, is the monopoly price.

Another important task of a cartel is to distribute the industry's total sales among the firms belonging to the cartel. If the aim of the cartel is to maximize cartel profits, it will allocate sales to firms in such a way that the marginal cost of all firms is equal. Otherwise the cartel could make more money by reallocating output among firms so as to reduce the cost of producing the cartel's total output. For example, if the marginal cost at firm I was higher than at firm II, the cartel could increase its total profits by transferring some production from firm I to firm II.

Negotiation However, this allocation of output—sometimes called the ideal allocation by economists—is unlikely to occur, since the allocation of output usually determines the allocation of cartel profits. For this reason, allocation decisions are the result of negotiation between firms with varying interests and varying capabilities. This is a political process in which various firms have different amounts of influence. Those with the most influence and the shrewdest negotiators are likely to receive the largest sales quotas, even though this increases total cartel costs. Moreover, high-cost firms are likely to receive larger sales quotas than

15. In early 1960 the Department of Justice charged that a large number of companies and individuals in the electrical equipment industry were guilty of fixing prices and dividing up the market for circuit breakers, switchgears, and other important products. Most of the defendants were found guilty; the companies, including General Electric and Westinghouse, received fines; and some of the guilty executives were sent to prison. The price-fixing agreements were reached in various ways. Many of the meetings occurred at conventions of the National Electric Manufacturers Association and other trade groups. Some agreements were made through telephone calls and written memoranda transmitted from one sales executive to another. Efforts were made to keep the meetings and agreements secret. For example, codes were used, and the participants at meetings sometimes disguised their records and did not use their companies' names when registering at hotels. The executives recognized that these agreements were illegal.

16. For example, airlines flying transatlantic routes have been members of the International Air Transport Association, which can agree on uniform prices for transatlantic flights.

FIGURE 10.4 Price and Output Determination by a Cartel *The cartel chooses a price of* OP_0 *and an output of* OQ_0.

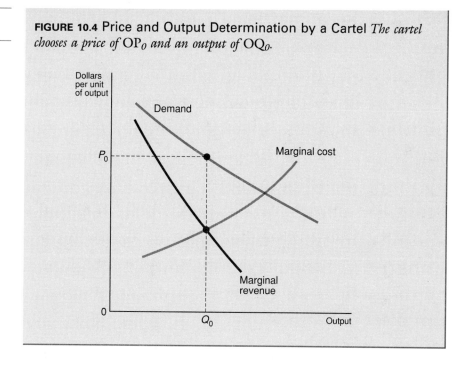

THE INSTABILITY OF CARTELS

We have already noted that collusive agreements tend to break down. Of course, the difficulty in keeping a cartel from breaking down increases with the number of firms in the cartel. To see why firms are tempted to leave the cartel, consider the case of the firm in Figure 10.5. If this firm were to leave the cartel, it would be faced with a demand curve of DD' as long as the other firms in the cartel maintain a price of OP_0. This demand curve is very elastic; the firm is able to expand its sales considerably by small reductions in price. Even if the firm were not to leave the cartel, but if it were to grant secret price concessions, the same sort of demand curve would be present.

Cheating   Under these circumstances the firm's maximum profit if it leaves the cartel or secretly lowers price will be attained if it sells an output of OQ_1, at a price of OP_1, since this is the output at which marginal cost equals marginal revenue. (RR' is the firm's marginal revenue curve.) This price would result in a profit of $OQ_1 \times BP_1$, which is higher than if the firm conforms to the price and sales quota dictated by the cartel. A firm that breaks away from a cartel—or secretly

cost minimization would dictate, since they would be unwilling to accept the small quotas dictated by cost minimization. In practice, there is some evidence that sales are often distributed in accord with a firm's level of sales in the past, or the extent of its productive capacity. Also, a cartel sometimes divides a market geographically, with some firms being given certain regions or countries and other firms being given other regions or countries.

FIGURE 10.5 The Instability of Cartels *If it leaves the cartel, the firm's profit equals $OQ_1 \times BP_1$, which is higher than if it adheres to the price and sales quota established by the cartel.*

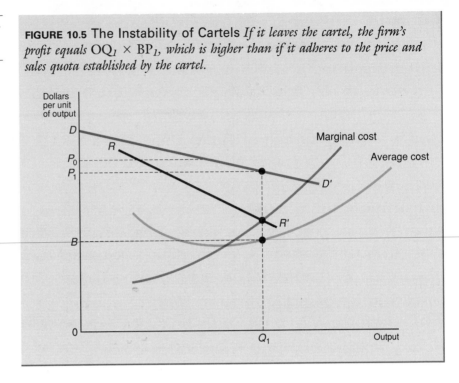

cheats—can increase its profits as long as other firms do not do the same thing and as long as the cartel does not punish it in some way. But if all firms do this, the cartel breaks down.

Consequently, as long as a cartel is not maintained by legal provisions, there is a constant threat to its existence. Its members have an incentive to cheat, and once a few do so, others may follow. Price concessions made secretly by a few "chiselers" or openly by a few malcontents cut into the sales of cooperative members of the cartel who are induced to match them. Thus the ranks of the unfaithful are expanded; and ultimately the cartel may break down completely.

THE OPEC OIL CARTEL: AN APPLICATION

To illustrate the nature and behavior of a cartel, consider the Organization of Petroleum Exporting Countries (OPEC) cartel. This cartel first hit the headlines in late 1973 when its Arab members precipitated a crisis in the United States by announcing a cutback in oil exports to us. Then it attracted further attention by taking a series of actions resulting in very large increases in the price of crude oil. For example, the price of Saudi Arabian crude oil (delivered to the U.S. East Coast) jumped from $4 in 1973 to over $10 in early 1974. Again in 1979, in the wake of the Iranian revolution, OPEC raised the price enormously, to over $30 a barrel.

What is OPEC, and how has it functioned? OPEC consists of thirteen major oil-producing countries, including Saudi Arabia, Iran, Venezuela, Libya, and

Nigeria. The OPEC countries imposed an excise tax of so many cents per barrel on each barrel of oil produced in their countries. These taxes were well publicized and, like any excise tax, they were treated as a cost of production by any of the international oil companies operating in these countries. Thus, by increasing these taxes, the OPEC countries raised the price of crude oil, since no company can afford to sell oil for less than its production costs plus the tax. According to the model discussed on pp. 307–9, one would expect the OPEC cartel to have pushed the crude oil price up toward the monopoly level, since this would have increased their tax revenues. In fact, this seems to have been exactly what occurred. Experts estimate that hundreds of billions of dollars were transferred by this means from oil consumers to OPEC.

However, OPEC's economic power seemed to wane in the 1980s, as evidenced by the fact that the price of oil fell until it was below $15 per barrel. To a considerable extent, the downward pressure on price was due to a continuing shift away from the use of oil. For example, while national output in the United States increased at a 5 percent annual rate in the first three quarters of 1983, oil consumption dropped nearly 2.5 percent. Because of conservation of oil and competition from other fuels (due partly to the great increases in the oil price in earlier years), there was a reduction in the quantity of oil demanded. In addition, non-OPEC oil production (in Mexico and the North Sea, for example) has soared, thus putting additional pressure on OPEC. In 1990, Iraq invaded Kuwait and took over its oil fields. Both Iraq and Kuwait were members of OPEC. The situation was fraught with danger, both economic and military. Fearing an attack by Iraq on Saudi Arabia, the United States moved large amounts of military personnel and equipment into that country.[17]

EXAMPLE 10.2

A CARTEL IN THE ORANGE GROVES

Cartels can occur in competitive, as well as oligopolistic, industries if the government creates the cartel. Since the 1930s, federal marketing orders have empowered producers in the California-Arizona orange industry (which supplies about two-thirds of the fresh oranges in the United States) to get together to determine how much of each year's crop will be sold for consumption in fresh form; the rest is sold in the processed market (where it is made into orange juice, among other things).[*] The price received by producers is much higher in the fresh market than in the processed market. Yet, according to the following estimates based on recent economic studies, the percentage of the orange crop that the cartel chooses to sell in the fresh market is much lower than would be the case if the cartel were disbanded:

| | Percent sold in the fresh market | |
	Valencia oranges	*Navel oranges*
Cartel	42	55
Without cartel	58	80

---

17. For further discussion of OPEC, see J. Griffin and H. Steele, *Energy Economics and Policy*, 2d ed. (New York: Academic Press, 1985).

(a) The California-Arizona orange industry contains more than 4,000 growers and 100 packers. Is it an oligopoly? Why or why not? (b) Does the cartel have control over entry into the industry? (c) The price elasticity of demand for oranges in the fresh market is about 0.8 for Navel oranges and about 1.2 for Valencia oranges. In the processed market, the price elasticity for both types of oranges is more than 2.0. Does this help to explain why the cartel's price is higher in the fresh market than in the processed market? (d) Why does the cartel sell a smaller proportion of oranges in the fresh market than would be the case if the cartel were disbanded?

SOLUTION

(a) No. There are far more producers in the market than in an oligopoly. (b) No. (c) Yes. According to economists that have studied the situation, the cartel is engaging in price discrimination. To increase producers' profits, it is selling oranges at a higher price in the less price-elastic market (the fresh market) than in the more price-elastic market (the processed market). In accord with the discussion in Chapter 9, this is the way to maximize the profit from a given quantity of oranges supplied. (d) In effect, the cartel must divert some oranges from the fresh to the processed market in order to maintain the price in the fresh market at a substantially higher level than in the processed market. If the cartel did not exist, this diversion would not occur.**

*Congress has provided that these decisions operate with the force of law, and that the antitrust laws do not apply in this area.

**For further discussion, see L. Shepard, "Cartelization of the California-Arizona Orange Industry, 1934–1981," *Journal of Law and Economics*, April 1986.

PRICE LEADERSHIP

Faced with the difficulties of forming an effective cartel, oligopolists may attempt to collude implicitly. In other words, they may attempt to cooperate without actually making explicit agreements with one another. A useful model of oligopolistic behavior is based on the supposition that one of the firms in the industry is the *price leader*. This form of behavior seems to be quite common in oligopolistic industries, where one or a few firms apparently set the price and the rest follow their lead. Examples of industries that have been characterized by price leadership, according to various studies, are steel, nonferrous alloys, and agricultural implements.

Let's assume that there is a single large dominant firm in the industry and a number of small firms (the "competitive fringe"). We assume too that the dominant firm sets the price for the industry, but that it lets the small firms sell all they want at that price. Whatever amount the small firms do not supply at that price is supplied by the dominant firm. If this model holds, it is easy to derive the price that the dominant firm will set if it maximizes profits. Since each small firm takes the price as given, it produces the output at which price equals marginal cost. Thus a supply curve for all small firms combined can be drawn by summing horizontally the marginal cost curves of the small firms. This supply curve is labeled S in Figure 10.6. The demand curve for the dominant firm can be derived by subtracting the amount supplied by the small firms at each price from the total amount demanded at that price. Consequently, if D is the demand curve for the industry's product, the demand curve for the output of the dominant firm, d, can be determined by finding the horizontal difference at each price between the D curve and the S curve.

To illustrate the derivation of d, suppose that the dominant firm sets a price of OP_0. The S curve shows that the small firms will supply OR_0, and the D curve shows that the total amount demanded will be OV_0 Thus the amount to be supplied by the dominant firm is $OV_0 - OR_0$, which is the quantity on the d

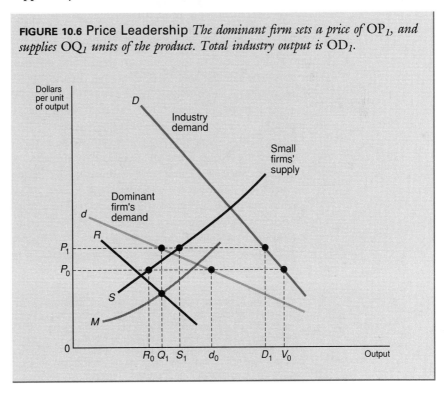

FIGURE 10.6 Price Leadership *The dominant firm sets a price of* OP_1, *and supplies* OQ_1 *units of the product. Total industry output is* OD_1.

curve at price OP_0. In other words, Od_0 is set equal to $OV_0 - OR_0$. The process by which the other points on the d curve are determined is exactly the same; this procedure is repeated at various price levels.

Given the demand curve for the output of the dominant firm, d, and the dominant firm's marginal cost curve, M, it is a simple matter to determine the price and output that will maximize the profits of the dominant firm. The dominant firm's marginal revenue curve, R, can be derived from the dominant firm's demand curve, d, in the usual way. The optimal output for the dominant firm is the output, OQ_1, where its marginal cost equals its marginal revenue. This output will be achieved if the dominant firm sets a price of OP_1. The total industry output will be OD_1, and the small firms will supply OS_1 ($= OD_1 - OQ_1$).[18]

THE LONG RUN AND BARRIERS TO ENTRY

So far we have been concerned primarily with oligopolistic behavior in the short run. In the long run it may be possible for entry or exit of firms to occur. We are already familiar, of course, with the in-migration and out-migration of firms from our discussions of other market structures in this and the previous two chapters. However, the importance of entry of new firms—and the exit of old firms—in modifying the structure of an industry should be noted once more. In particular, an oligopolistic industry may not be oligopolistic for long if every Tom, Dick, and Harry can enter.

Whether or not the industry remains oligopolistic in the face of relatively easy entry depends on the size of the market for the product relative to the optimum size of firm. Above-average profits will attract new firms. If the market is small relative to the optimum size of firm in this industry, the number of firms will remain sufficiently small so that the industry will still be an oligopoly. If the market is large relative to the optimum size of the firm, the number of firms will grow sufficiently large so that the industry will no longer be an oligopoly.

Ease of entry also tends to erode collusive agreements. We have seen in this chapter that existing firms are tempted continually to "cheat" on a collusive agreement, since they can attract business from their rivals by lowering prices. The situation is similar for entrants. They, too, are faced by a relatively elastic demand curve as long as existing firms adhere to collusive agreements to maintain price at its existing level. As long as profits exist in the industry, firms will be tempted to enter and take business away from the collusive group by lowering the price a bit. Once entry of this sort occurs, it becomes more and more difficult to keep a cartel together.

18. If (as is often the case) a cartel controls only part, not all, of an industry's output, this model can be used to describe the behavior of such a cartel. Thus, in the case of OPEC (discussed on pages 310–11), this model has sometimes been applied, with OPEC playing the role of the "dominant firm." Obviously, the extent to which the cartel can push up the price depends on how price elastic the d curve in Figure 10.6 is. If it is very price elastic, perhaps because the output supplied by firms outside the cartel (which play the role of the "small firms") is highly price elastic, the cartel cannot push up the price very much.

Since it may not be possible to maintain an oligopoly for long if firms can enter the industry, it is important that we discuss the various kinds of barriers to entry. The first barrier to entry, already noted, is smallness of the market relative to the optimum size of firm. For example, suppose that the industry demand curve is D in Figure 10.7. If the industry is composed of two identical duopolists (producing a homogeneous product) which split the market equally, each firm faces a demand curve of E, which is half of D at each price. On the other hand, if the industry is composed of three identical oligopolists (producing a homogeneous product) which split the market equally, each firm faces a demand curve of F, which is one-third of D at each price. If the average cost curve of a firm in this industry is as shown in Figure 10.7, only two firms can exist for long in this industry; once there are two firms, there is a barrier to entry. Although each of the existing firms may be displaced by a newcomer, there is room for only two firms in this industry.

Large scale required

Another barrier to entry is the requirement in some industries that a firm build and maintain a large, complicated, and expensive plant. It is difficult to obtain the funds required to build a modern automobile or steel plant, which may cost hundreds of millions of dollars. Also, skilled personnel must be acquired, distribution channels must be established, and various types of production and repair facilities must be set up. Of course, it is not impossible for newcomers to obtain the necessary capital, even if it is very large, but the scale of the undertaking is likely to discourage some potential entrants.

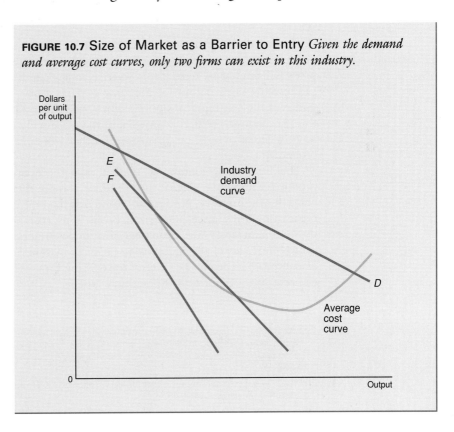

FIGURE 10.7 Size of Market as a Barrier to Entry *Given the demand and average cost curves, only two firms can exist in this industry.*

Dollars per unit of output

E

F

Industry demand curve

D

Average cost curve

0

Output

Still another barrier to entry is the unavailability of natural resources. This factor is often cited in the case of nickel, sulfur, diamonds, and bauxite. A further barrier to entry is the existence of important patents. The holder of these patents, which may relate to the product itself or key processes by which the product is made, may license only a few firms to produce the product. Moreover, the firms in an industry may allow one another to use their patents but refuse to permit any outsider to use them. Finally, the government is sometimes responsible for other important barriers to entry. For example, taxicabs and buses must obtain franchises, and local licensing laws may be used to limit the number of plumbers, barbers, and so on.

CONTESTABLE MARKETS

Although entry into some oligopolistic industries may be very difficult, this is not always the case. A *contestable market* is one in which "entry is absolutely free, and exit is absolutely costless."[19] In other words, firms can enter and leave the market readily. For example, if the government permits, the owner of a commercial jet aircraft can use it to fly passengers on a particular route, then devote it to other uses. The essence of contestable markets is that they are vulnerable to hit-and-run entry. "Even a very transient profit opportunity need not be neglected by a potential entrant, for he can go in, and before prices change, collect his gains and then depart without cost, should the climate grow hostile."[20]

Contestable market

Despite the fact that a contestable market contains only a few firms (or perhaps only one), it will perform much like a competitive market. Economic profit will tend to be zero. If it is positive, a new entrant can enter the market, produce the same output (at the same cost) as a firm already in the market, undercut the existing firm's price slightly, and make a profit. Entrants will do this if economic profit is positive, and the price will be pushed down to the point where economic profit is zero. In other words, if they like, entrants can hit and run.

The firms in a contestable market, like those under competition, will produce at minimum cost. If they produce at more than minimum cost, firms will enter the industry, produce at lower costs than the existing firms, undercut the existing firms' price, and make a profit. Thus costs will be pushed down to the minimum level. Also, in an oligopoly, price cannot exceed marginal cost. If existing firms are charging a price in excess of marginal cost, it is profitable for an entrant to undercut the price of the existing firms. Thus, for an equilibrium to occur, price cannot exceed marginal cost.

19. W. Baumol, "Contestable Markets: An Uprising in the Theory of Industry Structure," *American Economic Review*, March 1982, p. 3. Also see W. Baumol, J. Panzar, and R. Willig, *Contestable Markets and the Theory of Industry Structure* (San Diego: Harcourt Brace Jovanovich, 1982).

20. Ibid., p. 4. For criticism of this theory, see W. Shepard, "Competition versus Contestability," *American Economic Review*, 1984.

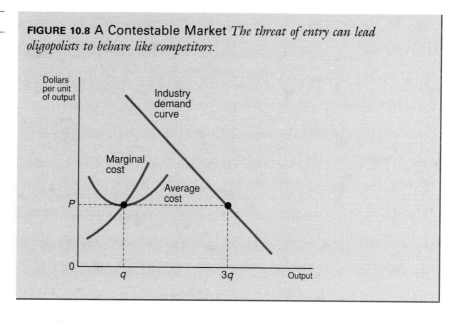

FIGURE 10.8 A Contestable Market *The threat of entry can lead oligopolists to behave like competitors.*

To illustrate the workings of a contestable market, suppose that an industry contains three firms, each with the marginal and average cost curves shown in Figure 10.8. If each firm produces Oq units of output, and charges a price of OP, total output will be 3 times Oq, and all three firms will earn zero economic profit. Although they could attempt to collude and push up the price, they do not do so because they know that new firms would enter the market very quickly and undercut their price. Given that entrants could sell the product at a price of OP, each firm maximizes its profit by producing Oq units of output and selling it at that price.

The theory of contestable markets, which is only about ten years old, has provoked considerable controversy. Its critics charge that it is based on extremely unrealistic assumptions concerning entry and exit. (In reality, of course, entry is not free and exit is not costless.) However, as stressed in Chapter 1, models based on simplified assumptions can be very useful. At this point, it is too early to tell how important this relatively new theory will turn out to be, but without question it has had a noteworthy impact on many economists' views concerning oligopoly.

Summary

1. Under monopolistic competition, there is a large number of firms producing and selling goods that are close substitutes, but that are not completely homogeneous from one seller to another. Each seller tries to make its product a little different, by altering the physical makeup of the product, the services it offers, and other such variables.

2. The firm under monopolistic competition is likely to produce less, and set a higher price, than under perfect competition. It is likely to operate with excess capacity, but the greater variety of alternatives available under monopolistic competition may be worth a great deal to consumers.

3. To maximize profit, a firm should set its advertising expenditures at the level where the marginal revenue from an extra dollar of advertising equals the price elasticity of demand for its product. If the marginal revenue is greater than the price elasticity, the firm should increase its advertising expenditures; if the marginal revenue is less than the price elasticity, it should decrease its advertising expenditures.

4. Whether or not advertising is socially beneficial depends on the nature of the advertising and the circumstances under which it takes place. From society's point of view, there are obvious disadvantages in advertising that misleads, rather than informs, consumers, and in advertising that augments the advertiser's monopoly power. On the other hand, advertising that enables sellers to take advantage of economies of scale in production, as well as advertising that allows consumers to shop around for lower prices more efficiently, can be socially beneficial.

5. Oligopoly is characterized by a small number of firms and a great deal of interdependence, actual and perceived, among them. A good example of an oligopoly is the American beer industry, where a small number of firms accounts for the bulk of the industry's capacity.

6. Conditions in oligopolistic industries tend to promote collusion, since the number of firms is small and firms recognize their interdependence. The advantages to be derived by the firms from collusion seem obvious: increased profits, decreased uncertainty, and a better opportunity to control the entry of new firms. However, collusive arrangements are often hard to maintain, since once a collusive agreement is made, any of the firms can increase its profits by "cheating" on the agreement. Also, such arrangements are illegal in the United States. An interesting example of collusion is the OPEC cartel, which has played so important a role in the oil markets.

7. Faced with the difficulties of forming an effective cartel, oligopolists may attempt to cooperate without making explicit agreements with one another. One useful model of oligopolistic behavior is based on the supposition that one of the firms in the industry is a price leader.

8. In the 1980s, an interesting development was the theory of contestable markets, which assumed that entry is absolutely free and exit is absolutely costless. According to this theory, oligopolists will behave much like perfectly competitive firms, because of the threat of entry into their market. However, this theory remains controversial.

Questions/Problems

1. In 1989, the top four firms—Anheuser-Busch, Miller, Coors, and Stroh's—accounted for over three-quarters of all beer produced in the United States. Anheuser-Busch alone had 42 percent of the market. (a) Do you think that the market for beer is a contestable market? (b) In the 1960s, the long-run average cost of producing beer was at a minimum when a firm produced about 2 million barrels per year. In the late 1970s, it was at a minimum when a firm's output was about 18 million barrels per year. Can you guess why this change occurred? (c) Do you think that this change in the long-run average cost curve helped to cause the decrease shown on p. 319 in the number of firms in the brewing industry?

Year	Number of firms	Year	Number of firms
1963	171	1972	108
1967	125	1976	49

2. Explain in detail why you believe that each of the following industries can or cannot be represented by the theory of monopolistic competition: (a) copper, (b) outboard motors, (c) airlines, (d) cement. To answer this question, what characteristics of each industry should you look at? Why?

3. Suppose that you are on the board of directors of a firm which is the price leader in the industry. That is, it lets all of the other firms, which are much smaller, sell all they want at the existing price. In other words, the smaller firms act as perfect competitors. Your firm, on the other hand, sets the price, which the other firms accept. The demand curve for your industry's product is $P = 300 - Q$, where P is the product's price (in dollars per unit) and Q is the total quantity demanded. The total amount supplied by the other firms is equal to Q_r, where $Q_r = 49\,P$. If your firm's marginal cost curve is $2.96\,Q_b$, where Q_b is the output of your firm, at what output level should you operate to maximize profit? What price should you charge? How much will the industry as a whole produce at this price? (Q, Q_b and Q_r are expressed in millions of units.)

4. In the United States agreements to fix prices and restrict output are illegal. Section 1 of the Sherman Antitrust Act says, "Every contract, combination . . . , or conspiracy in restraint of trade or commerce among the several states, or with foreign nations, is hereby declared to be illegal." (a) Does this mean that oligopoly is illegal? (b) Is any formal agreement among firms necessary to constitute an unlawful conspiracy? (c) For decades, the Big Three of the cigarette industry—American Tobacco, Liggett and Meyers, and Reynolds—followed a pattern of setting the same price. Even at the pit of the Great Depression, the other two firms matched a price increase by Reynolds. Also, they behaved in such a way as to make it likely that each would pay much the same price for tobacco. Can such parallel action be used in court as convincing circumstantial evidence of illegal collusion? (d) Is mere recognition of mutual interdependence and parallel behavior by a group of firms sufficient to make conspiracy charges against them stick?

5. There has been considerable criticism of the historically high price of milk in New York City. In 1986, Farmland Dairies, a New Jersey milk producer, began selling milk on Staten Island, one of New York City's five boroughs. Its low price drove down the retail price of milk by 40 cents per gallon. New York state law dictated that each milk producer like Farmland must get a license to sell milk, borough by borough. Existing dairies in New York City argued that the entry of Farmland into other parts of the city would not benefit consumers because it costs a great deal to distribute milk there. Further, they said that New York jobs should not go to New Jersey. In January 1987, a Federal judge ruled in favor of Farmland, saying that a state decision barring its expansion of sales in New York was unconstitutional. Evaluate in detail the above arguments of the existing New York dairies.

6. Suppose that two firms are producers of spring water, which can be obtained at zero cost. The marginal revenue curve for their combined output is

$$MR = 10 - 2Q$$

where MR is marginal revenue and Q is the number of gallons per hour of spring water sold by both together. If the two producers collude to maximize their total profits, how much will be their combined output? Why?

7. Suppose that a cartel is formed by three firms. Their total cost functions are as shown on the following page:

| | Total cost | | |
Units of output	Firm 1	Firm 2	Firm 3
0	20	25	15
1	25	35	22
2	35	50	32
3	50	80	47
4	80	120	77
5	120	160	117

If the cartel decides to produce 11 units of output, how should the output be distributed among the three firms, if they want to minimize cost?

8. The Sonora Software Company estimates that the price elasticity of demand for its product is 2 and that an extra $100,000 in advertising expenditure would increase its sales by $150,000. Is this firm maximizing profit? Why or why not? If not, should it increase or reduce its advertising expenditures? Why?

9. Describe in detail the social advantages and disadvantages of advertising. If a particular advertising campaign is profitable to the advertisers, does this mean that it is socially desirable? Why or why not?

10. Under what circumstances are increases in advertising likely to reduce a product's price elasticity of demand? Under what circumstances are they likely to increase it?

*11. Suppose that a computer manufacturer's perceived demand curve is DVD', its marginal revenue curve is RAR', and its marginal cost curve is MM' in panel A below.**

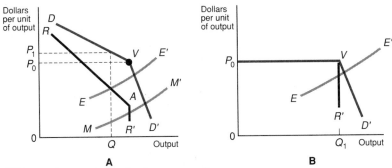

A

B

*This question pertains to the chapter appendix.

**In both panels of the graph, only parts of the marginal revenue are shown, but these parts are sufficient for present purposes.

Suppose further that, because of a jump in materials prices, the firm's costs increase sharply, with the result that the marginal cost curve rises from MM' to EE'. (a) An economist says that, because the firm's demand curve is kinked, this will not increase its price. Is he correct? (b) Fearful that the cost increase will result in a price hike, the government specifies that the firm's price must not exceed OP_0. What effect does this have on the firm's demand curve? Marginal revenue curve? Output?

12. According to the Senate Subcommittee on Antitrust and Monopoly, there has been a long history of international cartels that have controlled the price and output of quinine. What do you think the effects of the cartels have been? Do you think that such cartels should be broken up? If so, how can individual governments go about doing this?

13. A firm estimates its average total cost to be $10 per unit of output when it produces 10,000 units, which it regards as 80 percent capacity. Its goal is to earn 20 percent on its total investment, which is $250,000. If it were sure that it could sell 10,000 units, what price should it set to achieve this goal? Can it be sure of selling 10,000 units if it sets this price?

APPENDIX

THE KINKED DEMAND CURVE

An early oligopoly model was due to Paul Sweezy, who in 1939 advanced a theory to explain the rigidity of prices in oligopolistic markets.[21] At that time, there was a widespread feeling that prices in such markets tended to be rigid. A classic example occurred in the steel industry. From 1901 to 1916, the price of steel rails remained at $28 a ton, and from 1922 to 1933, it remained at $43 a ton. Of course, this was an extreme example, but it illustrates the basic point, which was that prices in oligopolistic industries sometimes remain unchanged for fairly long periods.[22] To explain this price rigidity, Sweezy asserted that, if an oligopolist cuts its price, it can be pretty sure that its rivals will meet the reduction. On the other hand, if an oligopolist increases its price, it is likely to find that its rivals will not change their prices. In such a case, the demand curve

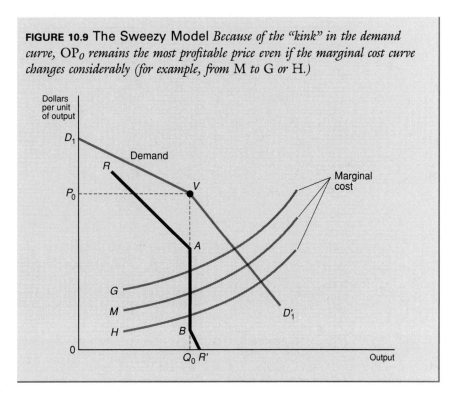

FIGURE 10.9 The Sweezy Model *Because of the "kink" in the demand curve, OP_0 remains the most profitable price even if the marginal cost curve changes considerably (for example, from M to G or H.)*

21. P. Sweezy, "Demand under Conditions of Oligopoly," *Journal of Political Economy*, August 1939.

22. For some relevant recent discussion, see Dennis Carlton, "The Rigidity of Prices," *American Economic Review,* September 1986.

for the oligopolist's product would be much more elastic for price increases than for price decreases.

Figure 10.9 shows the situation, the oligopolist's demand curve being represented by D_1VD_1' and the current price being OP_0. Because of the "kink" in the demand curve, the marginal revenue curve is not continuous: It consists of two segments RA and BR'. Given that the firm's marginal cost curve is M, marginal revenue does not equal marginal cost at any level of output. But it can be shown that OQ_0 is the most profitable output of the firm.[23] Moreover, OQ_0 remains the most profitable output—and OP_0 the most profitable price—even if the marginal cost curve changes considerably. For example, it remains the most profitable output if the marginal cost curve shifts to G or H. Also, OQ_0 remains the most profitable output—and OP_0 the most profitable price—for some changes in demand, as long as the kink remains at the same price level. Hence, under these circumstances, one might expect price to be quite rigid.

Soon after Sweezy's theory first appeared, it was regarded by some economists as a general theory of oligopoly. However, subsequent research has cast doubt on its general usefulness. For example, George Stigler found that in seven oligopolistic industries there was little indication that an increase in price by one firm would not be matched, in general, by other firms.[24] Thus, in these industries at least, there seemed to be little evidence for the existence of a kink in the demand curve. Moreover, although this theory may be useful under some circumstances in explaining why price tends to remain at a certain level (OP_0 in Figure 10.9), it is of no use in explaining why this level, rather than another, currently prevails. For example, it simply takes as given that the current price is OP_0 in Figure 10.9; it does not explain why the current price is OP_0. Thus this theory is an incomplete model of oligopolistic pricing.[25]

23. To see that OQ_0 is the most profitable output, note that, if output is pushed above OQ_0, the increase in revenues (given by the marginal revenue curve) is less than the increase in cost (given by the marginal cost curve). On the other hand, if output falls below OQ_0, the loss in revenue (given by the marginal revenue curve) is greater than the reduction in cost (given by the marginal cost curve). Since profit decreases when output is pushed above, or falls below, OQ_0, it must be maximized when output equals OQ_0.

24. G. Stigler, "The Kinky Oligopoly Demand Curve and Rigid Prices," *Journal of Political Economy*, 1947. Also see W. Primeaux, Jr., and W. Smith, "Pricing Patterns and the Kinky Demand Curve," *Journal of Law and Economics*, April 1976; and J. Simon, "A Further Test of the Kinky Oligopoly Demand Curve," *American Economic Review*, December 1969.

25. Research also suggests that oligopolists tend to change price more often than monopolists. Since monopolists do not face a kinked demand curve (because they are the only firm in their industry), the rigidity of their prices must be explained on other grounds.

11

GAME THEORY AND STRATEGIC BEHAVIOR

INTRODUCTION

Since oligopolies abound in the modern economy, and since some of the most fundamental theories of oligopoly behavior have yet to be presented, we continue our treatment of oligopoly in this chapter. As we already know, a basic feature of oligopoly is that each firm must take account of its rivals' reactions to its own actions. For example, General Electric cannot tell what effect an increase in its output will have on the price of dishwashers and on its profits unless it understands how its rivals will respond to its output increase. Thus it seems clear that oligopolistic behavior has some of the characteristics of a game.

One of the most interesting developments in the theory of oligopoly in recent decades has been the appearance and elaboration of the theory of games, which has enriched oligopoly theory enormously.[1] In this chapter, we present a basic description of the objectives and concepts of game theory, including the important concept of a Nash equilibrium. Then we show how game theory sheds new light on some of the topics of the previous chapter, such as the firm's decision to cheat (or not cheat) on a cartel agreement and ways that a firm can deter entrants from invading its market, as well as on a variety of new topics. Finally, we discuss the effects of an oligopolistic market structure on price, output, and profits.

1. A seminal work on game theory was J. von Neumann and O. Morgenstern, *Theory of Games and Economic Behavior* (Princeton, N.J.: Princeton University Press, 1944). For more recent descriptions of game theory, see J. Tirole, "Noncooperative Game Theory: A User's Manual," in *The Theory of Industrial Organization* (Cambridge: MIT Press, 1988); and J. Eatwell, W. Milgate, and P. Newman (eds.), *Game Theory* (New York: W. W. Norton, 1989).

Game theory

Game theory attempts to study decision-making in situations where there is a mixture of conflict and cooperation, as in oligopoly. A *game* is a competitive situation where two or more players pursue their own interests and no player can dictate the outcome. For example, poker is a game, and so is a situation in which two firms are engaged in competitive advertising campaigns. A game is described in terms of the players, the rules of the game, the payoffs of the game, and the information conditions that exist during the game. These elements, common to all conflict situations, are the fundamental characteristics of a game.

More specifically, a player, which may be a single person or an organization, is a decision-making unit. Each player has a certain amount of resources; the *rules of the game* describe how these resources can be used. For example, the rules of poker indicate how bets can be made and which hands are better than other hands. A *strategy* is a complete specification of what actions a player will take under each contingency in the playing of the game. For example, a corporation president might tell his subordinates how he wants an advertising campaign to start, and what should be done at subsequent points in time in response to various actions of competing firms.

Strategy

The game's outcome clearly depends on the strategies used by each player. A player's *payoff* varies from game to game: It is win, lose, or draw in checkers, and various sums of money in poker. For simplicity this section deals only with *two-person games,* games with only two players. The relevant features of a two-person game can be shown by constructing a *payoff matrix.* To illustrate, suppose that two firms are about to stage rival advertising campaigns and that each firm has a choice of strategies. Firm I can choose strategy *A* or *B*, and firm II can choose strategy 1 or 2. The payoff, expressed in terms of profits for each firm, is shown in Table 11.1 for each combination of strategies. For example, if firm I adopts strategy *A* and firm II adopts strategy 2, firm I makes a profit of $1 million, and firm II makes a profit of $2 million.

Payoff matrix

This is an example of a game where the players move simultaneously. Each player selects a strategy before observing any action or strategy chosen by the other player. Not all games are of this type. As we shall see, in some games one of the players goes first, after which the other player responds.

Dominant strategy

In this game, there is a *dominant strategy* for each player. Regardless of whether firm II adopts strategy 1 or 2, firm I will make more profit if it chooses

TABLE 11.1 Payoff Matrix: Advertising Campaigns

Possible strategies for firm I	Possible strategies for firm II	
	1	2
A	Firm I's profit: $2 million Firm II's profit: $3 million	Firm I's profit: $1 million Firm II's profit: $2 million
B	Firm I's profit: $3 million Firm II's profit: $2 million	Firm I's profit: $2 million Firm II's profit: $1 million

strategy B rather than A. Thus strategy B is firm I's dominant strategy. Similarly, regardless of whether firm I adopts strategy A or B, firm II will make more profit if it chooses strategy 1 rather than 2. Thus strategy 1 is firm II's dominant strategy. The solution to this game is quite simple. Firm I chooses strategy B, and firm II chooses strategy 1. Firm I's profit equals $3 million, and firm II's profit equals $2 million. This is the best that either player—that is, either firm—can do.

One additional point should be noted regarding this game: The best strategies are the same regardless of whether the players choose their strategies simultaneously or whether one or the other player goes first. Thus firm I will choose strategy B regardless of whether it moves before, after, or at the same time as firm II. As we shall see, this is not always true. In some games, a player's best strategy depends on the timing of the player's move.

NASH EQUILIBRIUM

Not all games have a dominant strategy for every player. For example, suppose that the payoff matrix for firms I and II is that shown in Table 11.2. (This is the same as the payoff matrix in Table 11.1 except that firm II's profit is $3 million, not $1 million, if it adopts strategy 2 and firm I adopts strategy B.) Under these circumstances, firm I still has a dominant strategy: strategy B. Regardless of which strategy firm II adopts, strategy B is firm I's best strategy. But firm II no longer has a dominant strategy, since its optimal strategy depends on what firm I decides to do. If firm I adopts strategy A, firm II will make more profit if it chooses strategy 1 rather than 2. If firm I adopts strategy B, firm II will make more profit if it chooses strategy 2 rather than 1.

TABLE 11.2 Payoff Matrix: No Dominant Strategy for Firm II

Possible strategies for firm I	Possible strategies for firm II	
	1	2
A	Firm I's profit: $2 million Firm II's profit: $3 million	Firm I's profit: $1 million Firm II's profit: $2 million
B	Firm I's profit: $3 million Firm II's profit: $2 million	Firm I's profit: $2 million Firm II's profit: $3 million

To figure out what to do, firm II must try to determine what action firm I is likely to take. In other words, firm II must put itself in firm I's place, and see whether strategy A or strategy B is best for firm I. As pointed out in the previous paragraph, firm I's dominant strategy is strategy B. Since firm II knows all of the numbers in the payoff matrix, it can readily determine that this is the case. Thus it will conclude that firm I will choose strategy B, and that it should therefore pick strategy 2 (because strategy 2 is more profitable than strategy 1 if firm I adopts strategy B).

Consequently, firm I would be expected to adopt strategy B, and firm II would be expected to adopt strategy 2. This is the *Nash equilibrium* (named after John F. Nash, a Princeton mathematician) for this game. A Nash equilibrium occurs if each player's strategy is optimal, given the strategies chosen by the other player(s). Put differently, *a Nash equilibrium is a set of strategies (in this case, strategy B for firm I and strategy 2 for firm II) such that each player believes (accurately) that it is doing the best it can given the strategy of the other player(s).* Taking the other firm's decision as given, both firm I and firm II are pursuing their own best interests by adopting strategy *B* and strategy 2, respectively. Neither regrets its own decision, or has any incentive to change it.

It is important to recognize the difference between a Nash equilibrium and an equilibrium where each player has a dominant strategy (as in Table 11.1). If each player has a dominant strategy, this strategy is its best choice *regardless of what other players do.* In a Nash equilibrium, each player adopts a strategy that is its best choice *given what the other players do.* It is also important to recognize that some games do not have a Nash equilibrium, and that some games have more than one Nash equilibrium. Table 11.3 contains the payoff matrix for a game with two Nash equilibria. If firm I adopts strategy *A* and firm II adopts strategy 1, each is doing the best it can, given the other's choice of strategy. Also, if firm I adopts strategy *B* and firm II adopts strategy 2, each is doing the best it can, given the other's choice of strategy. Hence, there are two Nash equilibria in this game.

TABLE 11.3 Payoff Matrix: Two Nash Equilibria

Possible strategies for firm I	Possible strategies for firm II	
	1	2
A	Firm I's profit: $3 million Firm II's profit: $3 million	Firm I's profit: zero Firm II's profit: zero
B	Firm I's profit: zero Firm II's profit: zero	Firm I's profit: $3 million Firm II's profit: $3 million

AN EXAMPLE OF NASH EQUILIBRIUM: THE COURNOT MODEL

As a further illustration of the concept of a Nash equilibrium, we consider a theory put forth by Augustin Cournot[2] about a hundred and fifty years ago. Although this theory is too simple to capture much of the richness of the oligopolistic situation, it has attracted considerable attention and is still cited. Cournot considers the case in which there are two sellers, that is, the case of *Duopoly* *duopoly;* but his model can easily be generalized to include the case of three or more sellers. To describe his model, it is convenient to assume that the two firms, firm I and firm II, produce the same product, have the same cost func-

2. A. Cournot, *Recherches sur les Principes Mathématiques de la Théorie des Riches,* translated by Nathaniel Bacon (New York: Macmillan, 1897). He first published his model in 1838.

tions, and are perfectly aware of the demand curve for their product, which is supposed to be linear.

Turning to behavioral assumptions, both firms are supposed to maximize profits. Each assumes that, regardless of what output it produces, the other will hold its output constant at the existing level. Taking the other firm's output level as given, each firm chooses its own output level to maximize profit. Of course, the level of output that it chooses will depend on how much it thinks its rival will produce. For example, consider the situation in Figure 11.1, which shows the demand curve for firm I's product, based on three alternative assumptions by firm I concerning firm II's output:

1. *Firm I thinks that firm II will produce and sell nothing.* If this is what firm I thinks, the demand curve for firm I's product is believed to be the market demand curve, since firm I is expected to be the sole producer. Panel A of Figure 11.1 shows this demand curve and the corresponding marginal revenue curve. To maximize profit, firm I will choose the output where marginal revenue equals marginal cost, this output being 150 units per month. (For simplicity, we assume that marginal cost is constant in Figure 11.1.)

2. *Firm I thinks that firm II will produce and sell 100 units per month.* If this is what firm I thinks, the demand curve for firm I's product is believed to be the market demand curve *shifted to the left by 100 units.* Why? Because at each possible level of price firm I expects to sell the total amount demanded less the 100 units that firm II is expected to produce and sell. Panel B of Figure 11.1 shows this demand curve, and the corresponding marginal revenue curve. To maximize profit, firm I will choose the output where marginal revenue equals marginal cost, this output being 100 units per month in this case. (See Panel B of Figure 11.1.)

3. *Firm I thinks that firm II will produce and sell 200 units per month.* If this is what firm I thinks, the demand curve for firm I's product is believed to be the market demand curve *shifted to the left by 200 units,* since at each possible level of price, firm I expects to sell the total amount demanded less the 200 units that firm II is expected to produce and sell. Panel C of Figure 11.1 shows this demand curve, and the corresponding marginal revenue curve. To maximize profit, firm I will choose the output where marginal revenue equals marginal cost, this output being 50 units per month in this case (as shown in Panel C of Figure 11.1).

Using these results, it is a simple matter to draw a curve showing how firm I's output depends on how much it thinks that firm II will produce and sell. In the previous three paragraphs, we derived three points on this curve. These three points are plotted in Figure 11.2. Other points on this curve could be *Reaction curve* derived in the same way. This curve is called firm I's *reaction curve* because it shows how firm I will react, as a function of how much it thinks firm II will produce and sell. Firm II also has a reaction curve which is shown in Figure 11.2. Firm II's reaction curve shows how much firm II will produce, as a function of how much it thinks that firm I will produce and sell. It can be derived in precisely the same way that we derived firm I's reaction curve.

According to the Cournot model, an equilibrium will occur at the point where the firms' reaction curves intersect. Thus, in Figure 11.2, an equilibrium will occur if both firm I and firm II are producing and selling 100 units per

FIGURE 11.1 Optimal Output of Firm I if Firm II Produces 0, 100, or 200 Units of Output per Month *Firm I will produce and sell 150, 100, or 50 units, depending on whether it believes that firm II will produce and sell 0, 100, or 200 units.*

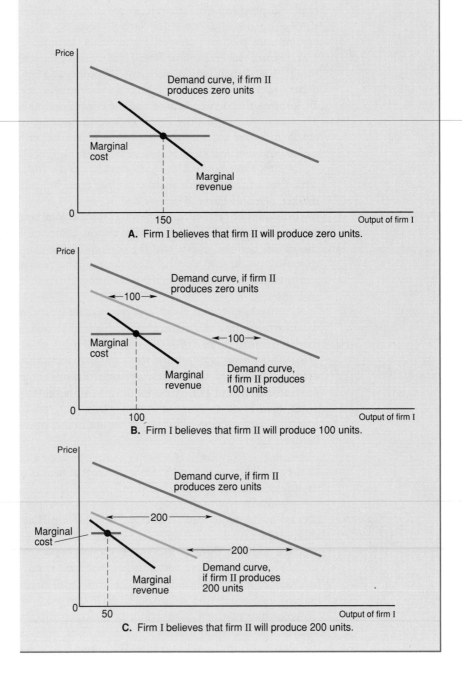

A. Firm I believes that firm II will produce zero units.

B. Firm I believes that firm II will produce 100 units.

C. Firm I believes that firm II will produce 200 units.

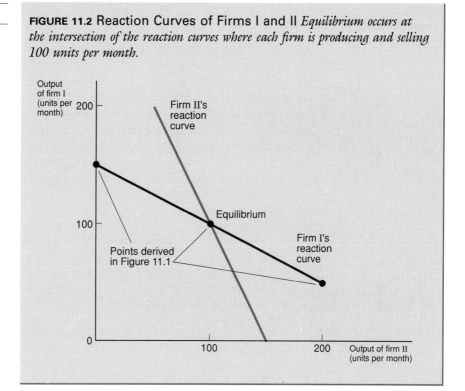

FIGURE 11.2 Reaction Curves of Firms I and II *Equilibrium occurs at the intersection of the reaction curves where each firm is producing and selling 100 units per month.*

month. Why is this a Nash equilibrium? Because each firm's expectation concerning the other's output is correct, and because each firm is maximizing its profit (given that its rival's output is what it is). To see that each firm's expectations concerning the other's output is correct at this intersection point, note that at this point firm I expects firm II to produce 100 units per month—and this in fact is what firm II produces. Similarly, at this point firm II expects firm I to produce 100 units per month—and this in fact is what firm I produces. Thus there are no surprises, and equally important, there are no incentives for either firm to alter its behavior. Each firm is maximizing its profit, if (as is the case) the other produces 100 units per month.

Although the Cournot model is useful in illustrating the concept of a Nash equilibrium, its limitations should be noted. For one thing, it provides no satisfactory description or explanation of the way in which firms move toward this equilibrium. Cournot's own explanation is naïve in many respects, and is rejected by most economists today. The lack of any explanation of the dynamic adjustment process is regarded as a serious problem by many economists. In later sections, we will take up models that pay more attention to dynamic considerations, and are far richer and more interesting.[3]

3. Another way to describe the Cournot model is as follows: There is a demand curve for the industry's product, $p = f(q_1 + q_2)$, where q_1 is the output of firm I, q_2 is the output of firm II, and p is the price of the product. The total cost function of firm I is $C_1(q_1)$ and the total cost function of firm II is $C_2(q_2)$. Thus the profit of firm I is

$$\pi_1 = q_1 f(q_1 + q_2) - C_1(q_1),$$ *(cont.'d)*

EXAMPLE 11.1

SHOULD AMHERST BUY ALL ITS STEEL FROM DUQUESNE?

The Amherst Company must decide whether to buy all or part of its steel from the Duquesne Corporation. If Duquesne provides prompt delivery of the steel it sells Amherst, Amherst will make $2 million if it buys all its steel from Duquesne and $1 million if it buys only part from Duquesne. But if Duquesne does not provide prompt delivery, Amherst will lose $50 million if it buys all its steel from Duquesne and $1 million if it buys only part from Duquesne. If it receives an order for all of Amherst's steel requirements, Duquesne will make $3 million if it provides prompt delivery and $2 million if it does not do so. If it receives an order for part of Amherst's steel requirements, Duquesne will make $2 million if it provides prompt delivery and $1 million if it does not do so.

(a) Amherst must decide whether to buy all or part of its steel from Duquesne, and Duquesne must decide whether or not to provide prompt delivery. What is the payoff matrix for this game? (b) Does each player have a dominant strategy? If so, what is it? (c) Does this game have a Nash equilibrium? If so, what is it? (d) Suppose that Duquesne's managers are known to be inefficient and not much interested in how much money their firm makes. Do you think that Amherst will act in accord with the Nash equilibrium? Why or why not?

SOLUTION

(a) The payoff matrix is as follows:

Possible strategies for Amherst	Possible strategies for Duquesne	
	Provide prompt delivery	Do not provide prompt delivery
Buy all steel from Duquesne	Amherst's profit: $2 million Duquesne's profit: $3 million	Amherst's profit: −$50 million Duquesne's profit: $2 million
Buy part of steel from Duquesne	Amherst's profit: $1 million Duquesne's profit: $2 million	Amherst's profit: −$1 million Duquesne's profit: $1 million

(b) Duquesne has a dominant strategy, which is to provide prompt delivery. Regardless of which strategy is chosen by Amherst, Duquesne makes more

and the profit of firm II is

$$\pi_2 = q_2 f(q_1 + q_2) - C_2(q_2).$$

If each firm takes the other firm's output as given and maximizes profit,

$$\frac{\partial \pi_1}{\partial q_1} = f(q_1 + q_2) + q_1 \frac{\partial f(q_1 + q_2)}{\partial q_1} - \frac{\partial C_1}{\partial q_1} = 0$$

$$\frac{\partial \pi_2}{\partial q_2} = f(q_1 + q_2) + q_2 \frac{\partial f(q_1 + q_2)}{\partial q_2} - \frac{\partial C_2}{\partial q_2} = 0.$$

Solving these two equations simultaneously, we obtain the equilibrium values of q_1 and q_2, which in turn tell us what the equilibrium value of p will be.

money if it provides prompt delivery than if it does not do so. Amherst does not have a dominant strategy, since its optimal strategy depends on whether or not Duquesne provides prompt delivery. (c) Yes. The Nash equilibrium is for Amherst to buy all its steel from Duquesne and for Duquesne to provide prompt delivery. Each firm is doing the best it can, given the other firm's strategy. (d) Probably not. A Nash equilibrium assumes that all players are "rational" in the sense that they will adopt whatever strategy results in maximum profit. If Duquesne is not "rational" in this sense, it might not provide prompt delivery even though its failure to do so would reduce its profit, the result being that Amherst would lose $50 million if it bought all its steel from Duquesne. If Amherst has strong enough doubts about Duquesne's "rationality" (or is uncertain about what Duquesne's true payoffs are), it may buy only part of its steel from Duquesne, thus cutting its potential loss (if Duquesne does not provide prompt delivery) from $50 million to $1 million. In this way, it minimizes its maximum potential loss.*

*For further relevant discussion, see J. Tirole, *The Theory of Industrial Organization, op. cit.*

THE PRISONERS' DILEMMA

Prisoners' dilemma

Having described the basic features of a Nash equilibrium, we turn our attention to an important type of game, known as the *prisoners' dilemma,* which has proved of use in oligopoly theory, as well as in many other areas of economics and behavioral (and political) science. Consider a situation where two persons, John Dillinger and Dutch Schultz, are arrested after committing a crime. The police lock each person in a separate room and offer each one the following deal: "If you confess, while your partner does not confess, you will get a 2-year jail term, while he will get 12 years." Each person knows that if they both confess, each will get 10 years (not 12 years because they cooperated with the police). If neither confesses, each will get only 3 years because the evidence against them is weak.

Both Dillinger and Schultz have two possible strategies: to confess or not to confess. The four possible outcomes, depending on which strategy each person chooses, are shown in the payoff matrix in Table 11.4. What strategy will Schultz choose? If Dillinger does not confess, the better strategy for Schultz is to confess, since Schultz will serve less time (2 years) than if he does not confess

TABLE 11.4 Payoff Matrix: Dillinger and Schultz

Possible strategies for John Dillinger	Possible strategies for Dutch Schultz	
	Confess	Do not confess
Confess	Both get 10-year jail terms.	Dillinger gets 2 years; Schultz gets 12 years.
Do not confess	Dillinger gets 12 years; Schultz gets 2 years.	Both get 3-year jail terms.

(3 years). If Dillinger confesses, the better strategy for Schultz is to confess, since Schultz will serve less time (10 years) than if he does not confess (12 years). Thus Schultz will confess, since regardless of which strategy Dillinger adopts, Schultz is better off to confess than not to confess.

Similarly, Dillinger too will confess since, regardless of which strategy Schultz adopts, Dillinger is better off to confess than not to confess. To see this, note that, if Schultz does not confess, the better strategy for Dillinger is to confess, since Dillinger will serve less time (2 years) than if he does not confess (3 years). Also, if Schultz confesses, the better strategy for Dillinger is to confess, since Dillinger will serve less time (10 years) than if he does not confess (12 years).

Thus, in this situation, it appears that both Dillinger and Schultz will confess. This is the dominant strategy for each player. But it is important to recognize that each is doing worse than if neither of them confessed. If they could trust each other not to confess, or if they were able to communicate with one another (and thus if each could assure himself that the other would not confess), each could serve 3 years rather than 10 years. However, because there is no way for them to coordinate their decisions (and to trust each other), they serve the longer prison term.

CHEATING ON A CARTEL AGREEMENT

The type of game discussed in the previous section—the so-called prisoners' dilemma—is useful in analyzing oligopoly behavior. For example, it can help to indicate the circumstances under which firms will tend to cheat (that is, secretly cut price) on a cartel agreement. As we stressed in the previous chapter, there frequently is a temptation for cartel members to cheat in this way.

Suppose that the only two producers of lasers—Ambler, Inc., and the Elysian Company—form a cartel. Each firm has two possible strategies: to stick by the cartel agreement or to cheat. There are four possible outcomes, depending on which strategy each firm pursues. They are shown in Table 11.5.

What should Ambler do? If Elysian sticks by the agreement, it appears that the better strategy for Ambler is to cheat, since Ambler's profits will be greater than if it sticks by the agreement. If Elysian cheats, the better strategy for Ambler seems to be to cheat as well, since Ambler's profits will be higher than if

TABLE 11.5 Payoff Matrix: Ambler and Elysian

Possible strategies for Ambler	Possible strategies for Elysian	
	Stick by agreement	Cheat
Stick by agreement	Ambler's profit: $4 million Elysian's profit: $4 million	Ambler's profit: $1 million Elysian's profit: $5 million
Cheat	Ambler's profit: $5 million Elysian's profit: $1 million	Ambler's profit: $3 million Elysian's profit: $3 million

it sticks by the agreement. Thus it appears that *Ambler will choose the strategy of cheating since regardless of which strategy Elysian adopts, Ambler seems better off by cheating than by sticking by the agreement.*

What should Elysian do? If Ambler sticks by the agreement, the better strategy for Elysian appears to be to cheat, since Elysian's profits will be greater than if it sticks by the agreement. If Ambler cheats, the better strategy for Elysian appears to be to cheat as well, since Elysian's profits will be higher than if it sticks by the agreement. Thus it seems that *Elysian will choose the strategy of cheating, since regardless of which strategy Ambler adopts, Elysian is better off by cheating than by sticking by the agreement.*

Consequently, in this situation it appears that both firms will cheat. Like the game in Table 11.4 involving John Dillinger and Dutch Schultz, this is an example of the prisoners' dilemma. Recall that, because neither Dillinger nor Schultz could trust the other not to confess, both wound up serving more time in jail (10 years versus 3 years) than if they had trusted each other. Similarly, Ambler and Elysian, because they do not trust each other to stick by their agreement, wind up with lower profits than if they both were to stick by the agreement ($3 million versus $4 million).

REPEATED PRISONERS' DILEMMA AND "TIT FOR TAT"

Repeated prisoners' dilemma

At this point, it is essential to recognize that there is an important difference between the situation facing Ambler and Elysian and that facing Dillinger and Schultz. In the case of Dillinger and Schultz, if this was the only crime they performed together and if they did not intend to work together again, it may have been reasonable for each of them to assume that they would play this game only once. But for Ambler and Elysian, such an assumption would not be reasonable. At every point in time, each of these firms must decide whether it will cheat or not. Since they are continually dealing with customers, they must continually decide whether or not to secretly cut price.

Because Ambler and Elysian play this game repeatedly, the analysis in the previous section may not be correct. To see this, suppose that Ambler refuses to cheat the first time it must make a decision and that it continues to stick by the agreement so long as Elysian does so. But if Elysian fails even once to cooperate, Ambler will revert forever to the safe policy of cheating. If Elysian adopts the same sort of policy, then each can reap profits of $4 million. If either one cheats, it will raise its profit to $5 million for a brief period of time, but subsequently its profit will fall permanently to $3 million. Thus it will not be in the interest of either firm to cheat.[4]

It is important to recognize that Ambler and Elysian can achieve this outcome even if they do not collude or make any binding agreements. If each presumes that the other will have the intelligence to maintain the monopoly price, their presumptions will tend to be correct. As David Hume, the eighteenth-century British economist, put it over 200 years ago,

> I learn to do a service to another, without bearing him any real kindness; because I foresee that he will return my service, in expectation of another of the same kind, and in order to maintain the same correspondence of good offices with me or with others. And accordingly, after I have served him, and he is in possession of the advantage arising from my action, he is induced to perform his part, as foreseeing the consequences of his refusal.[5]

Tit for tat According to Robert Axelrod of the University of Michigan, a good strategy for each player is *"tit for tat,"* which means that each player should do on this round whatever the other player did on the previous round. If Ambler pursues a "tit-for-tat" strategy, it should abide by the agreement on the first round. If Elysian also abides by it, Ambler should continue to do so, but once Elysian cheats, Ambler should retaliate by cheating as well. Robert Axelrod's experimental results, based on a computer analysis of the results of various strategies, suggest that this is a very effective approach.[6]

In accord with Axelrod's findings, some cartels seem to have adopted tit-for-tat strategies in the past. For example, the cartel that set the price of railroad freight in the United States in the 1880s (prior to the Sherman Antitrust Act) retaliated against member firms that cut price to increase their market shares. When such cheating occurred, the other members of the cartel would cut their own price as well, thus inflicting economic damage on the price cutters.[7]

---

4. This assumes that the game is repeated indefinitely. If it is repeated only a finite number of times, there may, of course, be a tendency to cheat in the final periods. Indeed, in an effort to be the first to start cheating, players may cause the situation to unravel, and cheating may begin immediately. However, if firms have doubts about the rationality (in the narrow sense of the word used here) of their rivals, they may not cheat even if the game is played only a finite number of times. See D. Kreps, P. Milgrom, J. Roberts, and R. Wilson, "Rational Cooperation in the Finitely Repeated Prisoners' Dilemma," *Journal of Economic Theory,* 1982.

5. J. Friedman, *Game Theory with Applications to Economics* (New York: Oxford University Press, 1986), p. 70. Of course, this assumes that each firm can quickly detect whether the other firm is cheating. In fact, this may not be so easy. In some cases, trade associations have been authorized to collect detailed information concerning each firm's transactions. In this way, an attempt has been made to detect cheating quickly. Of course, the quicker cheating is detected, the less profitable it tends to be.

6. R. Axelrod, *The Evolution of Cooperation* (New York: Basic Books, 1984).

7. R. Porter, "A Study of Cartel Stability," *Bell Journal of Economics,* Autumn 1983.

STRATEGIC MOVES

In previous sections of this chapter, we have emphasized that oligopolists must recognize that their own profits depend on the decisions and behavior of their rivals, as well as on their own decisions and behavior. Given that this is the case, each oligopolist must decide on which strategic moves to make. According to Harvard's Thomas Schelling, who has made important contributions to the theory of strategic decision-making, "A strategic move is one that influences the other person's choice in a manner favorable to one's self, by affecting the other person's expectations on how one's self will behave."[8] For example, if DuPont reacts to a rival's price cut by reducing its own price to a level that imposes losses on its rival, this is a strategic move. It influences how other firms can expect DuPont to behave.

Nonthreatening moves

Firms can engage in a variety of types of strategic moves. Some moves are not in any sense threatening to a firm's rivals. Thus Hewlett Packard may raise its price, hoping that its rivals will go along with the price increase. The problem with such a move is that other firms may not cooperate. For example, Hewlett Packard's rivals may not go along with the price increase. If such a move can be rescinded quickly and cheaply, this problem may not be very important, but if this is not the case, such a move can be very risky.

Threatening moves

Other moves are threatening to a firm's rivals. For example, the American Hospital Supply Corporation developed a new container for intravenous solutions, which it began to market. This move threatened Baxter Travenol Laboratories, which already sold products of this type. In weighing the pros and cons of making such a move, a firm must try to estimate how likely it is that there will be retaliation, and how quick and effective this retaliation will be. In the case of the American Hospital Supply Corporation, it met substantial retaliation from Baxter, which cut its prices considerably and tried hard to wrest business away from American Hospital Supply Corporation.[9]

To prevent its rivals from carrying out threatening moves, a firm often behaves in such a way as to lead its rivals to believe that they can expect rapid and effective retaliation if they carry out such a move. For example, firms often engage in vicious price cutting to drive out a firm that enters their market, the idea being that this will teach other potential entrants that it does not pay to threaten or challenge them.

An important element of a firm's strategic planning is *commitment*. If a firm can convince its rivals that it is unequivocally committed to a particular move that it is making, they may back down without retaliating, since they may be convinced that they would lose more than they would gain from a protracted struggle. If a firm can convince its rivals that it is unequivocally committed to retaliate if a rival makes particular moves, no rival may make such a move. And if a firm can convince its rivals that it is unequivocally committed to take no

---

8. T. Schelling, *The Strategy of Conflict* (New York: Oxford University Press, 1960). Another important book in this area is M. Porter, *Competitive Strategy* (New York: Free Press, 1980). Many of the concepts and results discussed in this chapter are treated in more detail in these two books.

9. M. Porter, ibid.

(threatening) actions of a particular type, they may eventually begin to trust this firm not to do so.

A commitment tends to be more persuasive if it seems binding and irreversible. For example, suppose that a firm commits itself to enter a particular market. If this firm buys a plant rather than leases it, or if it signs a long-term, rather than a short-term, contract for raw materials, this is an indication that this firm is irreversibly committed to entering the market in question. Or suppose that a firm commits itself to meet price reductions by its rivals. If this firm makes written or verbal agreements with customers to meet price cuts, these agreements can make such a commitment irreversible—and hence more persuasive. On the other hand, if a firm's rivals feel that it can easily renounce or ignore a particular commitment that it makes (much as politicians frequently do), they are not likely to pay as much attention to this commitment.

To be credible, a firm's commitments must be backed up with the assets and expertise required to carry out the commitment. Thus, if a firm commits itself to invade another firm's market if the latter firm invades its market, it must have the financial and technological power and skills needed to carry out this commitment. Also, a firm's commitments are more credible if it has a long history of adherence to past commitments. Here, as in other aspects of life, a firm's (and its managers') reputation counts. If a firm has a well-deserved reputation for honoring its past commitments, its rivals are likely to pay careful attention to whatever new commitments it makes.

THREATS: EMPTY AND CREDIBLE

Firms frequently send signals to one another indicating their intentions, motives, and objectives. Some signals are threats. For example, suppose that the Smith Company learns that the Jones Corporation, its principal rival, intends to lower its price. Smith may announce its intention of lowering its own price significantly, thus signaling to Jones that it is willing to engage in a price war if Jones goes ahead with its price reduction. Indeed, some of Smith's executives may see to it that this message gets transmitted indirectly to some of Jones's executives.

But not all threats are credible. If, for example, the payoff matrix is as shown in Table 11.6, Smith's threat is not very credible. To see why, let's compare

TABLE 11.6 Payoff Matrix: Smith and Jones

Possible strategies for Smith	Possible strategies for Jones	
	Low price	High price
Low price	Smith's profit: $1 million Jones's profit: $2 million	Smith's profit: $2 million Jones's profit: −$1 million
High price	Smith's profit: $6 million Jones's profit: $10 million	Smith's profit: $10 million Jones's profit: $7 million

Smith's profits if it sets a low price with its profits if it sets a high price. (For simplicity, we assume that price can be set at only these two levels.) If Jones sets a high price, Smith makes $10 million if it sets a high price and $2 million if it sets a low price. If Jones sets a low price, Smith makes $6 million if it sets a high price and $1 million if it sets a low price. Thus, regardless of whether Jones sets a high or low price, Smith will do better if it sets a high price than a low price.

Given that this is the case, it certainly seems unlikely that Smith will carry out its threat to cut its price to the low level. After all, as we've just seen, if Jones does cut its price to the low level, Smith will earn higher profits by keeping its price at the high level. Consequently, if Jones can be sure that Smith will take the course of action that maximizes Smith's profit, it can dismiss Smith's threat as no more than an empty gesture.

However, if Smith can convince Jones that it is *not* going to take the course of action that maximizes its profit, it can make its threat credible. Specifically, if it can convince Jones that, if Jones sets the low price, it will match it, *even though this lowers Smith's own profits,* Jones may decide not to set the low price. After all, Jones's profits are higher ($7 million versus $2 million) if it maintains a high price (and Smith does the same) than if Jones sets a low price (and Smith does the same).

How can Smith convince Jones that it will lower its price, even though this seems to be irrational? One way is for Smith's managers to develop a reputation for doing what they say, "regardless of the costs." They may have a well-publicized taste for facing down opponents and for refusing to back down, regardless of how crazy they may seem. Faced with the "irrational" Smith Company, the Jones Corporation may decide not to cut price. But if Smith cannot convince Jones of its "irrationality," Jones will rightly regard Smith's threat to lower price as not being credible.

THE DETERRENCE OF ENTRY

Firms, like nations and politicians, try to discourage entrants from invading their turf. As we saw in the previous chapter, the entry of new firms tends to reduce the profits of existing firms. To illustrate the situation, consider the Martin Company, which faces the threat of entry by the Newton Company. Table 11.7 shows the profits of each firm, depending on whether or not Newton enters the market and on whether or not Martin resists Newton's entry (for example, by cutting price and increasing output).[10]

In this game, the first move is up to Newton, which must decide whether or not to enter. If it enters, Martin must decide whether or not to resist. Based on the payoff matrix in Table 11.7, Martin, if it is "rational," will not resist because its profits will be $1 million less (that is, $2 million rather than $3 million) if it resists than if it does not resist. Knowing this, Newton will enter because its profits will be $3 million higher (that is, $11 million rather than $8 million) if it

---

10. If Newton does not enter the market, there is no difference between Martin's resisting and not resisting, so the profit figures are the same, regardless of which strategy Martin is assumed to adopt.

TABLE 11.7 Payoff Matrix, Before Martin Makes Credible Its Threat to Resist

Possible strategies for Martin Company	Possible strategies for Newton Company	
	Enter	Do not enter*
Resist entry	Martin's profit: $2 million Newton's profit: $5 million	Martin's profit: $12 million Newton's profit: $8 million
Do not resist entry	Martin's profit: $3 million Newton's profit: $11 million	Martin's profit: $12 million Newton's profit: $8 million

*See footnote 10.

enters than if it does not enter. Of course, Martin may well threaten to resist, but given the nature of the payoff matrix in Table 11.7, this threat is not credible (if Martin is "rational") because resistance by Martin would lower its profits.

Making resistance credible

What can Martin do to deter Newton's entry into the market? It can alter the payoff matrix. For example, suppose that it builds excess production capacity—capacity that is unnecessary if Newton does not enter, but that will be used to increase output (and lower price) if Newton enters. Because it costs money to keep excess capacity on hand, Martin's profits are reduced by $2 million if it does not resist entry or if Newton does not enter;[11] the new payoff matrix is as shown in Table 11.8. Martin's profits are now greater ($2 million versus $1 million) if it resists Newton's entry than if it does not resist. Thus Martin's threat to resist becomes credible, and Newton will not enter because its profits will be $3 million lower (that is, $5 million rather than $8 million) if it enters than if it does not enter.

Paradoxical as it may seem, Martin has succeeded in convincing Newton not to enter *by reducing its own profits if it does not resist entry.* This is an irrevocable

TABLE 11.8 Payoff Matrix, After Martin Makes Credible Its Threat to Resist

Possible strategies for Martin Company	Possible strategies for Newton Company	
	Enter	Do not enter
Resist entry	Martin's profit: $2 million Newton's profit: $5 million	Martin's profit: $10 million Newton's profit: $8 million
Do not resist entry	Martin's profit: $1 million Newton's profit: $11 million	Martin's profit: $10 million Newton's profit: $8 million

11. For simplicity, we assume that these are the only changes in the payoff matrix due to Martin's construction of excess production capacity. In fact, there may be other changes, but from a pedagogical point of view, it is convenient to assume that they do not exist.

commitment by Martin to fight. If Newton enters, Martin is ready to fight (by increasing output and driving price down), and has an incentive to fight (since its profits are higher than if it does not fight). It has gained an advantage by committing itself in this way to resist entry.

But harking back to the section before last, this is not the only way for Martin to convince Newton not to enter. If Martin has imposed huge losses on every firm that has tried to enter in the past, and has a reputation for "irrational" resistance to entry, Newton may decide that Martin is too tough an opponent to challenge. Thus it may be in Martin's interests to foster such a reputation by declaring total war on every entrant that appears, since the short-term losses from these wars may be more than offset by the longer-term gains from the prevention of entry.

LIMIT PRICING

A *limit price* is a price that discourages or prevents entry. Economists often have asserted that a firm can deter entry by keeping its price relatively low. In recent years, Stanford's Paul Milgrom and John Roberts have provided an interesting explanation, based on game theory, of why this may be true.[12] Suppose that the Moran Manufacturing Company is a very low-cost producer of hardware. If potential entrants knew how low its costs really are, they would not be foolish enough to enter the industry (because they would recognize that they have no chance to survive). But they have no reliable way of telling what Moran's costs are, since hardware is only one of its products, and its accounting statements are useless for this purpose.

Price as a signal

To signal potential entrants that it is a very low-cost producer, Moran may find it worthwhile and effective to set a relatively low price. Of course, this will lower Moran's profits in the short run, but it may result in bigger profits over the long run because of the reduced likelihood that Moran will have to compete with entrants. Why can't Moran simply announce that its costs are very low? Because potential entrants are smart (and suspicious) enough to recognize that such announcements may be lies aimed at discouraging entry. However, under the proper circumstances, a relatively low price may be reasonably convincing evidence that Moran really is a very low-cost producer—and that entry would be unwise.

FIRST-MOVER ADVANTAGES

In many situations, the firm that makes the first move has a substantial advantage. For example, suppose that two firms, A and B, are about to introduce a new product, and that each must choose whether to tailor its product for the civilian or military market. Table 11.9 shows the relevant payoff matrix. If both firms tailor their products for the same market (civilian or military), both will lose $10 million because these markets are too small to support two (profitable)

---

12. Paul Milgrom and John Roberts, "Limit Pricing and Entry under Incomplete Information: An Equilibrium Analysis," *Econometrica*, March 1982.

TABLE 11.9 Payoff Matrix: Firms A and B

Possible strategies for firm A	Possible strategies for firm B	
	Tailor product for civilian market	Tailor product for military market
Tailor product for civilian market	Firm A's profit: −$10 million Firm B's profit: −$10 million	Firm A's profit: $30 million Firm B's profit: $15 million
Tailor product for military market	Firm A's profit: $15 million Firm B's profit: $30 million	Firm A's profit: −$10 million Firm B's profit: −$10 million

producers. If one firm tailors its product for the civilian market while the other firm focuses on the military market, it will make $30 million, and its rival will make $15 million, since the civilian market for this product is more profitable than the military market.

If each firm must make this choice independently and without any information concerning what the other firm will do, it is likely that both will tailor their products to the civilian market. After all, this is the more profitable market. But the result (as Table 11.9 shows) will be that both will lose $10 million.

First-mover advantages

On the other hand, if one of these firms—say firm A—can introduce its product before the other firm does so, it enjoys a great advantage. It can tailor its product to the civilian market, since this market is more profitable than the military market. Of course, if the other firm—firm B—enters the civilian market too, both will lose money. But given that firm A has already entered the civilian market, firm B is unlikely to enter it too. Why? Because this would result in a substantial loss for firm B, whereas if firm B enters the military market, it will earn a tidy profit—not as big a profit as if it had made the first move (and thus could have been the sole producer in the civilian market), but a tidy profit nonetheless. Hence, it seems likely that, if one of these firms has the first move, it will tailor its product to the civilian market, and that the other firm will tailor its product to the military market.

Frequently, firms try to commit themselves first to a particular move, even if they cannot be first to actually carry out this move. For example, suppose that neither of the above firms can introduce its product before the introduction of the other firm's product. Firm A may announce that it is about to introduce a new product tailored for the civilian market. It may engage in an expensive advertising campaign, and begin to order the sorts of materials needed to produce a civilian version of the new product. It may even go so far as to begin seeking orders from civilian customers. In this way, firm A tries to persuade firm B that it is committed to entering the civilian market and that there is nothing that firm B can do to prevent it. Firm A's intention is to convince firm B to settle for the military market, thus offering no resistance to firm A's entry into the civilian market.

EXAMPLE 11.1

HOW GOVERNMENTS CAN TILT THE OUTCOME OF OLIGOPOLY

In recent years, some economists like MIT's Paul Krugman have argued that governments, by supporting their firms in international competition, may be able to raise national welfare at another country's expense. Suppose that America and France are the only two countries capable of producing a 150-seat passenger aircraft, and that only one firm in each country, Boeing and Airbus, has this production capability. Each firm has the choice of producing or not producing the aircraft, but Boeing has a headstart that permits it to commit itself to produce before Airbus's decision. In the absence of government intervention, the payoff matrix is as shown below:

Possible strategies for Boeing	Possible strategies for Airbus	
	Produce the aircraft	Do not produce it
Produce the aircraft	Boeing's profit: −$25 million Airbus's profit: −$25 million	Boeing's profit: $300 million Airbus's profit: zero
Do not produce it	Boeing's profit: zero Airbus's profit: $300 million	Boeing's profit: zero Airbus's profit: zero

(a) Without government intervention, will each firm produce this aircraft? Why or why not? (b) If France's government commits itself in advance to pay a subsidy of $50 million to Airbus if it produces the plane, will this alter the payoff matrix? If so, how? (c) Will this French subsidy alter the behavior of Boeing and Airbus? If so, how? (d) Will the profits of Airbus increase by more than the amount of the subsidy? (e) If France adopts a strategic trade policy of this sort, is this likely to provoke retaliation from the United States?

SOLUTION

(a) Boeing will produce the aircraft, since it will earn profits of $300 million if Airbus does not produce it. This is more than what Boeing would earn (zero) if it did not produce it. Airbus will not produce it, since it would lose $25 million if it did so, once Boeing is committed to do so. This is less than what Airbus would earn (zero) if it did not produce it. (b) Because of this subsidy, Airbus will earn profits of $-25 + 50 = 25$ million dollars if it produces this aircraft, once Boeing is committed to do so. Thus the payoff matrix now is as follows:

Possible strategies for Boeing	Possible strategies for Airbus	
	Produce the aircraft	Do not produce it
Produce the aircraft	Boeing's profit: −$25 million Airbus's profit: $25 million	Boeing's profit: $300 million Airbus's profit: zero
Do not produce it	Boeing's profit: zero Airbus's profit: $350 million	Boeing's profit: zero Airbus's profit: zero

(c) If Boeing commits itself to produce this aircraft, this will no longer deter Airbus from doing so, since Airbus will make $25 million if it does so and nothing if it does not do so. Recognizing this fact, Boeing will not produce it, because if it did so, it would lose $25 million. Thus Airbus will produce it, and Boeing will not. (d) Yes. Airbus's profits increase by $300 million; the subsidy is only $50 million. (e) If any country adopts policies of this sort and carries them out aggressively, the country that is hurt by them may feel that it is worthwhile to retaliate, sooner or later.*

*For further discussion, see Paul Krugman, "Is Free Trade Passé?" *The Journal of Economic Perspectives*, Fall 1987, and J. Brander and B. Spencer, "International R and D Rivalry and Industrial Strategy," *Review of Economic Studies*, 1983.

CAPACITY EXPANSION AND PREEMPTION

Preemptive strategy

The decision of whether—and if so, how much—to expand production capacity is one of the most important strategic decisions made by a firm. Some firms adopt a preemptive strategy; that is, they try to expand before their rivals do, thus discouraging their rivals from building extra capacity of their own. If the future growth of demand for a particular product is known with reasonable precision, such a strategy can be effective.

Suppose that two firms, Monroe Company and the Madison Corporation, are the only producers and sellers of a particular kind of machine tool. Since the demand for this type of machine tool is growing substantially, each firm is considering the construction of an additional plant. The payoff matrix is shown in Table 11.10. If only one of the firms builds an additional plant, it will make $10 million, but if both firms build an additional plant, both will lose $5 million, since there will be too much capacity. If neither firm builds an additional plant, both will earn zero profits.

In this game, there are two Nash equilibria—one where Madison alone builds an additional plant, and one where Monroe alone builds an additional plant. Which equilibrium takes place is dependent on which firm moves first. If Madison moves first, it will choose to build an additional plant, since the rational response of Monroe is not to build an additional plant too (because if it did

TABLE 11.10 Payoff Matrix: Monroe and Madison

Possible strategies for Monroe	Possible strategies for Madison	
	Build additional plant	Do not build additional plant
Build additional plant	Monroe's profit: −$5 million Madison's profit: −$5 million	Monroe's profit: $10 million Madison's profit: zero
Do not build additional plant	Monroe's profit: zero Madison's profit: $10 million	Monroe's profit: zero Madison's profit: zero

so, it would lose $5 million). Similarly, if Monroe moves first, it will choose to build an additional plant, since Madison's rational response is not to build an additional plant too.

However, such a preemptive strategy can be risky. For example, if the demand for the product grows more slowly than expected (or not at all), a firm that pursues this strategy may be stuck with a plant that is an unprofitable white elephant. Also, if a firm pursues this strategy, it must be careful to insure (as best it can) that its rival will respond "rationally." If its rival refuses to yield to this preemptive strategy, and builds its own additional plant, the industry is plunged into a war that may do serious harm to both firms. A firm that adopts a preemptive strategy of this sort could regret it.

NONPRICE COMPETITION

In many oligopolistic industries, firms tend to use nonprice competition, like advertising and variation in product characteristics, more than price, as strategic weapons. They seem to view price-cutting as a dangerous tactic, since it can start a price war that may have grave consequences. On the other hand, advertising and product variation are viewed as less risky ways of wooing customers away from competitors.

When a firm advertises, it attempts to shift the demand curve for its product to the right. An effective advertising campaign will make it possible for a firm to sell more at the same price. (Recall page 301.) Firms use advertising to differentiate their product from those of their competitors. In this way customers may be induced to stick with a particular brand name, even though the products of all firms in the industry are much the same. For example, various brands of cigarettes are quite similar, although not identical. The cigarette industry has spent over $200 million a year on advertising to impress their brand names, and whatever differences exist among brands, on the consumer.[13]

Sometimes advertising expenditures only have the effect of raising the costs of the entire industry, since one firm's advertising campaign causes other firms

13. Other industries that spend very heavily on advertising are department stores, retail food stores, drugs and medicines, and beer. See L. Telser, "Advertising and Cigarettes," *Journal of Business,* 1963; and W. Comanor and T. Wilson, *Advertising and Market Power* (Cambridge, Mass.: Harvard University Press, 1974) for historical material and analysis.

to increase their advertising. The total market for the industry's product may not increase in response to the increased advertising, and the effects on the sales of individual firms may be small, since the effects of the advertising may cancel out. However, once every firm has increased its advertising expenditures, no single firm can reduce them to their former size without losing sales. Thus the cost curves—including both production and selling costs—of the firms in the industry are pushed upward.

Prisoners' dilemma revisited

To see why an individual firm may spend a large amount on advertising even though its profits might have been higher with a smaller advertising budget, recall the prisoners' dilemma. If each firm believes that its profits will fall if its rival spends more on advertising, it may feel that a large advertising budget is in its own interest, although its profits, as well as those of its rival, would be greater if both it and its rival agreed to spend less on advertising. Consider the situation in Table 11.11. Both firms X and Y may adopt large advertising budgets (since this is the dominant strategy for each firm), even though both would enjoy higher profits ($4 million rather than $1 million) if they both adopted small advertising budgets.

Frequently a firm varies the characteristics of its product as well as advertises in order to differentiate its product from those of its competitors. Like advertising, one purpose of varying the firm's product is to manipulate the firm's demand curve. Of course, changes in product, like other competitive tactics, often result in retaliatory moves by competitors. Successful changes in product design or product quality tend to be imitated by competitors, although with a lag of varying length. The costs of competition through style and quality of product can be very great. For example, the automobile industry has been engaged for many years in intense competition of this sort; the annual cost of model changes has sometimes been $5 billion or more.[14]

TABLE 11.11 Payoff Matrix: Firms X and Y

Possible strategies for firm Y	Possible strategies for firm X	
	Large advertising budget	Small advertising budget
Large advertising budget	Firm Y's profit: $1 million Firm X's profit: $1 million	Firm Y's profit: $5 million Firm X's profit: zero
Small advertising budget	Firm Y's profit: zero Firm X's profit: $5 million	Firm Y's profit: $4 million Firm X's profit: $4 million

EFFECTS OF OLIGOPOLY

Finally, having completed our discussion of game theory, let's return to the general topic of oligopoly. In this and the previous chapter, we have taken up

14. See L. White, *The Automobile Industry Since 1945* (Cambridge, Mass.: Harvard University Press, 1971); and F. Fisher, Z. Griliches, and C. Kaysen, "The Cost of Automobile Model Changes since 1949," *Journal of Political Economy,* October 1962, for historical data.

some of the oligopoly models that economists have constructed. Since there is no agreement that any of these models is an adequate general representation of oligopolistic behavior, it is difficult to estimate the effects of an oligopolistic market structure on price, output, and profits. Nevertheless, a few things can be said.

First, the models we have discussed usually indicate that price will be higher than under perfect competition. The difference between the oligopoly price and the perfectly competitive price will depend, of course, on the number of firms in the industry and the ease of entry. The larger the number of firms and the easier it is to enter the industry, the closer the oligopoly price will be to the perfectly competitive level.

Second, if the demand curve is the same under oligopoly as under perfect competition, it also follows that output will be less under oligopoly than under perfect competition. However, it is not always reasonable to assume that the demand curve is the same under oligopoly as under perfect competition, since the large expenditures for advertising and product variation that are incurred by some oligopolies may tend to shift the demand curve to the right. Consequently, in some cases both price and output may tend to be higher under oligopoly than under perfect competition.

Third, oligopolistic industries tend to spend large amounts on advertising and product differentiation. The use of some resources for these purposes is certainly worthwhile, since advertising provides buyers with information, and product differentiation allows greater freedom of choice. Whether or not oligopolies spend too much for these purposes is by no means obvious, although it is sometimes claimed that in some oligopolistic industries such expenditures have been expanded beyond the levels that are socially optimal.[15]

Fourth, one would expect on the basis of most oligopoly models that the profits earned by oligopolists should be higher, on the average, than the profits earned by perfectly competitive firms. About forty years ago, a seminal study by Berkeley's Joe Bain found that firms in industries in which the few largest firms had a high proportion of total sales tended to have higher rates of return than firms in industries in which the few largest firms had a small proportion of total sales. However, there has been considerable disagreement over the interpretation of such evidence. According to some economists, these results are due in considerable part to the largest firms' superior efficiency in oligopolistic industries.[16]

15. Note that we are not talking here about expenditures on relatively fundamental research and development, when we talk about product differentiation. A great deal of existing product differentiation is based on relatively superficial differences among products. For some discussion of research and development, see Chapter 17.

16. See J. Bain, "Relation of Profit Rate to Industry Concentration: American Manufacturing 1936–1940," *Quarterly Journal of Economics,* August 1951; H. Demsetz, "Industry Structure, Market Rivalry, and Public Policy," *Journal of Law and Economics,* April 1973; L. Weiss, "The Concentration-Profits Relationship and Antitrust," in H. Goldschmid, H. M. Mann, and J. F. Weston, *Industrial Concentration: The New Learning* (Boston: Little, Brown, 1974); and J. Kwoka, "The Effect of Market Share Distribution on Industry Performance," *Review of Economics and Statistics,* Feburary 1979.

1. A game is a competitive situation where two or more players pursue their own interests and no player can dictate the outcome. The relevant features of a two-person game can be shown by constructing a payoff matrix. In some games, each player has a dominant strategy—a strategy that is best regardless of what strategy the other player chooses.

2. A Nash equilibrium is a situation where each player's strategy is optimal, given the strategy of the other players. To illustrate the concept of a Nash equilibrium, we considered the Cournot model, an early theory based on the supposition that each firm believes that the other firm will hold its output constant at the existing level. The solution of this model (the point where the firms' reaction curves intersect) is a Nash equilibrium.

3. The prisoners' dilemma is a type of game that has proved very useful in analyzing oligopoly behavior. In particular, it helps to explain why firms have a tendency to cheat on cartel agreements. However, if this game is played repeatedly, firms may not cheat; for example, they may adopt a "tit-for-tat" strategy.

4. A firm can engage in a variety of types of strategic moves. Some are threatening to its rivals; others are not. An important element of a firm's strategic planning is commitment. For example, if a firm can convince its rivals that it is unequivocally committed to a particular move that it is making, they may back down without retaliating, since they may be convinced that they would lose more than they would gain from a protracted struggle.

5. Although firms frequently threaten their rivals, not all threats are credible. One way for a firm to make its threats credible is to develop a reputation for doing what it says, "regardless of the costs." Also, the firm can alter the payoff matrix to make its threat credible. For example, this can be effective in deterring entry.

6. The firm that makes the first move often has an advantage. For instance, with regard to capacity expansion, some firms adopt a preemptive strategy; that is, they try to expand before their rivals do.

7. The effects of oligopoly are difficult to predict, but most models suggest that price and profits will tend to be higher than under perfect competition. Also, oligopolists frequently engage in nonprice competition; advertising and product differentiation can be very important.

Questions/ Problems

1. Two firms, A and B, exist in a particular market. Each has two strategies, the payoff matrix being as follows:

Possible strategies for firm B	Possible strategies for firm A	
	1	2
I	Firm A's profit: −$6 million Firm B's profit: −$5 million	Firm A's profit: $10 million Firm B's profit: $5 million
II	Firm A's profit: $5 million Firm B's profit: $10 million	Firm A's profit: −$5 million Firm B's profit: −$6 million

(a) If firm A has the first move, what strategy is it likely to choose? What strategy is firm B likely to choose?

(b) If firm B has the first move, what strategy is it likely to choose? What strategy is firm A likely to choose?

2. The industrial robot is one of the most important technological innovations of this century. In 1985, about 50 American firms produced robots, with the following six firms accounting for about 70 percent of total sales:

	Sales (millions of dollars)		Sales (millions of dollars)
GMF Robotics	180	ASEA	39
Cincinnati Milacron	59	GCA	35
Westinghouse	45	DeVilbiss	33

(a) Robotics firms devoted about 17 percent of their sales to research and development in 1983. Is nonprice competition important in this industry? (b) During 1979–82, the robotics industry experienced substantial losses, although its sales increased at a relatively rapid rate. Why did firms stay in this industry in the face of these losses? (c) Does the fact that they stayed in the industry mean that they were "irrational"?

3. Two firms, C and D, exist in a particular market. Each has two strategies, the payoff matrix being as follows:

Possible strategies for firm D	Possible strategies for firm C	
	1	2
I	Firm C's profit: $8 million Firm D's profit: $5 million	Firm C's profit: $4 million Firm D's profit: $7 million
II	Firm C's profit: $6 million Firm D's profit: $9 million	Firm C's profit: $3 million Firm D's profit: $8 million

(a) Does firm C have a dominant strategy? If so, what is it? (b) Does firm D have a dominant strategy? If so, what is it? (c) What is the solution to this game?

4. The Brooks Company's managers begin to sense that the Harris Corporation may attempt to enter their market. (a) What steps might they take to dissuade Harris from doing so? (b) What factors are likely to determine whether they will succeed? (c) What actions that they have taken (or not taken) in the past may play an important role in influencing whether or not Harris tries to enter?

5. Firms A and B are the only producers of a homogeneous good. Firm A's marginal revenue (in dollars) equals $100 - 8(Q_A + Q_B)$, where Q_A is firm A's monthly output and Q_B is firm B's monthly output. (Both Q_A and Q_B are expressed in units of output per month.) If firm A's marginal cost equals $4 per unit of output, obtain the equation for firm A's reaction curve.

6. Suppose the payoff matrix is as given below. What strategy will firm I choose? What strategy will firm II choose?

Possible strategies for firm I	Possible strategies for firm II		
	1	2	3
	(Profits for firm I, or losses for firm II, in millions of dollars)		
A	10	9	11
B	8	7	10

7. In the previous question, the game is a zero-sum game; that is, the amount that one player wins is exactly equal to the amount that the other player loses. Is this realistic in the case of duopoly? Why or why not?

8. The Miller Company must decide whether to advertise its product or not. If its rival, the Morgan Corporation, decides to advertise its product, Miller will make $4 million if it advertises and $2 million if it does not advertise. If Morgan does not advertise, Miller will make $5 million if it advertises and $3 million if it does not. (a) Is it possible to determine the payoff matrix? Why or why not? (b) Can you tell whether Miller has a dominant strategy? If so, what is it?

9. The Morgan Company, introduced in the previous question, must decide whether or not to advertise its product. If its rival, the Miller Company, decides to advertise, Morgan will make $2.5 million if it advertises and $2 million if it does not advertise. If Miller does not advertise, Morgan will make $2 million if it advertises and $2.5 million if it does not advertise. (a) Based on the data in this and the previous question, is it possible to determine the payoff matrix? If so, what is it? (b) Do both firms have dominant strategies? If so, what are they? (c) Is there a Nash equilibrium? If so, what is it?

10. (a) Is the game in Question 1 an example of the prisoners' dilemma? Why or why not? (b) Is the game in Question 3 an example of the prisoners' dilemma? Why or why not? (c) Is the game in Question 6 an example of the prisoners' dilemma? Why or why not?

THE ECONOMICS OF 1992

Europe, which for centuries has been divided into a number of relatively small national markets, has come much closer to being a single market. During the 1960s, the European Economic Community—or Common Market—was established. The members of the Common Market (first Belgium, France, West Germany, Holland, Italy, and Luxembourg, then Britain, Denmark, and others) agreed to reduce tariffs on one another's goods. A tariff is a tax imposed by a government on imports. Thus this was a step toward converting Europe into a single market.

However, there still are significant barriers to free trade among European countries. For example, there are technical regulations that thwart free trade. Take the humble (but tasty) case of pasta. In Italy, the law states that the name "pasta" can only be used for products consisting exclusively of durum wheat, even though experts believe that pasta made with a combination of durum and common wheat is quite acceptable. Thus non-Italian products made with a combination of durum and common wheat—which are 10–15 percent less expensive than pasta made exclusively of durum wheat—are kept out of the Italian market.

In addition, each government favors firms from its own country when it awards contracts for construction, defense, highway, and other projects. Only about 2 percent of public construction projects have been awarded to foreign firms. Also, there are restrictions on a firm's freedom to engage in particular service transactions, or to enter particular service industries, in another European country. For example, it can be difficult for a bank or airline in one European country to establish itself in a neighboring country.

*EEC Headquarters
in Brussels*

In 1985, the member states of the European Community undertook to remove the remaining barriers to free trade by 1992. Economists have tended to favor this step, because it seems likely to promote competition, thus bringing prices in monopolistic or oligopolistic markets down toward perfectly competitive levels. For example, suppose that a French machinery producer is a monopolist in the French market; that is, it is the only seller of the kind of machinery it produces. If its marginal revenue and marginal cost curves are as shown in Figure 1, its price will be *OP*. But if its customers are allowed to import machinery of the relevant kind from producers in Germany, Italy, and

FIGURE 1 Effect of Imports on Monopoly Price *If imports become available at a price of* OP$_1$, *the monopolist must lower its price from* OP *to* OP$_1$.

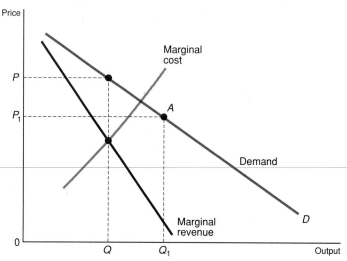

other countries, the French firm may have to cut its price. For example, if imported machinery is available in France for a price of OP_1, the French producer will have to lower its price from OP to OP_1. For reasons discussed in Chapter 9, this movement of price from the monopoly level toward the perfectly competitive level is likely to result in an increase in social welfare.

Also, the increase in competition may force firms to be more efficient. According to a report of the European Community,

> The basic idea is that, in the absence of sufficient competitive pressures, there would be, for a given level of inputs, a poor exploitation of production facilities, an inefficient internal allocation of human, physical, or financial resources, an under-employment of certain factors and duplications and redundancies that reflect excess "organizational fat." Such phenomena are particularly important in the area of managerial and executive duties. These excessive overhead costs are generally brought to light by internal or external audits. Consultants thus frequently succeed in identifying ways of reducing overhead costs by between 10 and 25% through internal reorganization alone.[1]

Still another way that the removal of barriers to free trade in Europe will result in economic benefits is through the exploitation of economies of scale. As we have seen in previous chapters, it sometimes is necessary for a plant to be quite large if the average cost of its product is to be close to the minimum

---

1. M. Emerson, M. Aujean, M. Catinet, P. Goybet, and A. Jacquemin, *The Economics of 1992* (Oxford: Oxford University Press, 1988), p. 156.

FIGURE 2 Minimum Efficient Size of Plant *If the long-run average cost curve is as shown here, the minimum efficient size of plant is* OQ.

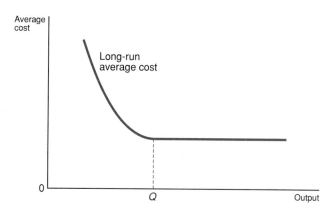

attainable level. Let's define the *minimum efficient size of plant* as the smallest output at which long-run average cost is a minimum. Thus, if the long-run average cost curve in a particular industry is as shown in Figure 2, the minimum efficient size of plant is *OQ*. Why? Because average cost for this size of plant is much lower than for an appreciably smaller size of plant, but no different from that for bigger plants.

Due to limitations on the size of their markets, some European firms have plants that are too small to produce at relatively low cost. By making Europe into a single market, the removal of trade barriers can enable firms to expand so as to reach the minimum efficient size. Table 1 shows the average estimated effect on cost of the removal of trade barriers in 1992, according to a sample of business executives in six European countries. In practically all countries, it was estimated that costs would be reduced by about 2 percent.

The European Community, with 323 million inhabitants in 1987, has more inhabitants than either the United States (244 million) or Japan (122 million). In terms of total output, it is about on a par with the United States and well ahead of Japan. According to estimates made by European economists, the 1992 reforms are likely to increase the European Community's output by 2.5 to 6.5 percent, a very considerable achievement.

Although the removal of barriers to free trade within Europe is likely to benefit the Europeans, some American firms fear that a Fortress Europe may be created. While the easier movement of goods within Europe will encourage more intra-European trade, it may put non-European sellers at a disadvantage. The United States hopes, of course, that the European Community will remain open to products from the rest of the world.

The Ford Motor Company is an American firm that has very large European operations. About 20 percent of its profits in 1988 stemmed from its European business. To be ready for the 1992 reforms, Ford plans to spend $7.5 billion from 1989 to 1994 to modernize its European plant and equipment and to redesign its European product line. General Electric, which has been much less

TABLE 1 Estimated Percentage Cost Reduction Due to Removal of Barriers to Free Trade in European Community

Industry	Percentage cost reduction	Industry	Percentage cost reduction
Food and tobacco	2.3	Artificial fibers	3.3
Textiles	1.3	Fabricated metal	
Footware and clothing	1.4	products	1.6
Timber and furniture	1.5	Mechanical engineering	2.0
Paper and publishing	1.5	Office machinery	0.4
Leather	1.3	Electrical engineering	2.1
Plastics	1.6	Motor vehicles	2.2
Oil refining	0.6	Other transportation	
Metals	3.5	equipment	1.3
Mineral products	1.4	Rubber	0.5
Chemicals	1.3	Precision engineering	1.9

Source: M. Emerson, M. Aujean, M. Catinet, P. Goybet, and A. Jacquemin, *op. cit.,* p. 225. The titles of some industries have been simplified.

involved in Europe than Ford, has reacted to the 1992 reforms by carrying out mergers and joint ventures. For example, it has formed a $580 million joint venture with Britain's General Electric Company, bought Borg Warner's European chemical business for over $2 billion, and invested nearly $2 billion to produce plastics in Spain.

No one can be sure that the reforms scheduled to occur in 1992 will actually take place then. Some, such as Britain's Prime Minister Margaret Thatcher, are opposed to at least some of the proposed changes. (Also, the dramatic political developments in Eastern Europe may tend to delay these scheduled reforms.) But if these changes occur, many business and political leaders feel that it will be a very major step. For example, according to the president of Phillips, Europe's largest consumer electronics company, "What Europe is doing is gigantic. The drive for economic unity is the most important thing that will happen here in the next fifty years."

Analytical Questions

1. One stated reason for removing barriers to free trade in the European Community is that prices in monopolistic or oligopolistic markets will be driven down toward competitive levels. Why is this regarded as a good thing?

2. If imports become available at a price of OP_1, does this change the monopolist's demand curve in Figure 1? If so, how is the demand curve altered?

3. If imports become available at a price of OP_1, will the monopolist in Figure 1 change its output level? If so, what will be its new output level?

4. In February 1990, two European auto makers, France's Renault and Sweden's Volvo, established an alliance under which each would own large shares of the other.[2] Observers suggested that Renault and Volvo wanted to share the very large cost of developing new cars. Do you think that there are economies of scale in the development of new cars?

2. "Alliance Established by Renault and Volvo," *New York Times,* February 24, 1990.

5. According to the report of the European Community (cited in note 1), more competition may force European firms to be more efficient. Doesn't this contradict the economist's assumption that firms maximize profit?
6. What political difficulties stand in the way of one country's awarding government contracts to another country's firms? Do you think that the United States is likely to buy its key military hardware from Sweden or France?

PART FIVE

MARKETS FOR INPUTS

12

PRICE AND
EMPLOYMENT OF
INPUTS

INCOMES: DISTRIBUTION AND INEQUALITY

No one needs to be convinced that income is an interesting topic. Both a struggling member of the working class and a dowager whose labor is confined to endorsing dividend checks recognize the significance of income. Moreover, no one has to be intimately acquainted with government statistics to know that there are enormous differences in the amounts of money that people make. For example, a stroll through midtown Manhattan will provide plenty of evidence of abject poverty and great affluence existing almost side by side.

Why do these differences in income exist? Why is it that one person receives so much more income than another? As we pointed out in Chapter 1, a person's income depends partly on the quantity of resources owned. Some people own lots of land; others own none. Some people have unusual skills and talents; others do not. Some people own equipment and factories; others own little beyond their clothes (and even their clothes may not be completely paid for).

But the quantity of resources a person owns is by no means the only determinant of income. The other important determinant is the price received for the services of each type of resource. For example, if a man is a landowner with 100 acres of land, he will receive $10,000 per year if the price he obtains from the farmers who work his land is $100 per acre (annually); however, if the price goes down to $50 per acre, he will receive only $5,000 per year. Similarly, a laborer's income will obviously depend on the price received for the services performed.

Thus, to understand why differences in income exist, we must understand why the prices of the services of each type of resource are what they are. We must ask questions like: Why is the wage rate for physicians frequently in the neighborhood of $100 an hour while the wage rate for secretaries is often about $10 an hour? Why is the wage rate for mathematicians so much higher than it was several decades ago? Why is it that land of one kind yields a higher financial return than land of another kind?

Input prices

In other words, we must try to understand the determinants of input prices. In a free-enterprise economy, input prices are important determinants of the incomes of consumers. In the typical household, the breadwinner sells his or her services to a firm; the wage that the worker receives is an input price from the viewpoint of the firm. Wages are a cost to the firm but to the worker they are an important determinant of income, which (as we saw in Chapter 3) helps to determine the worker's choice of consumers' goods. The distribution of income among individuals in the economy is determined to a considerable extent by the configuration of input prices.

DETERMINANTS OF INPUT PRICES

The previous four chapters were concerned with the analysis of the pricing and output of consumers' goods. We turn now to the determinants of the price and employment of inputs, which will be the topic of the present chapter as well as Chapter 13. Throughout most of this chapter we assume that there is perfect competition in both commodity and input markets, and that firms have perfect information concerning the productivity of all inputs, including workers. Then we take up cases where information of this sort is imperfect.

At the outset, two points should be noted. First, a good deal of the theory presented in the previous four chapters is applicable to inputs as well as commodities; for example, the price of inputs as well as commodities is determined by the interaction of supply and demand. However, the demand for inputs differs in important respects from the demand for commodities, and the supply of inputs differs in important respects from the supply of commodities. These differences stem largely from the fact that inputs are demanded by firms, not consumers; and that some important inputs, like labor, are supplied by consumers, not firms.

Second, in the nineteenth century it was customary for economists to classify inputs into three categories: land, labor, and capital. The theory of input pricing was therefore a theory of the distribution of income among landowners, wage earners, and capitalists, three important economic and social classes. (The incomes of these classes were rent, wages, and profits, respectively.) A disadvantage of this simple classification of inputs is that each category contains such an enormous amount of variation. For example, labor includes the services of a Nobel Prize–winning biochemist and the services of a secretary whose typing is strictly hunt-and-peck. In this chapter we shall seldom use this tripartite classification;[1] instead we ordinarily present our results in general terms so that the user of the model can classify inputs to fit any particular problem.

---

1. Toward the end of the nineteenth century, a fourth "factor of production"—or type of input— was recognized: entrepreneurship. Then profits were viewed as the return to the entrepreneur, and interest was viewed as the return to the owner of capital.

Fortunately, we do not have to start from scratch in constructing a model of input pricing and utilization under perfect competition. We learned a great deal that is relevant and useful in Chapters 7 and 8 when we analyzed the firm's decisions concerning input combinations and output level. A moment's reflection should convince you that, when we determined how much the firm would produce and the input combination it would use to produce this output, we in effect determined how much of each input the firm would demand under various sets of circumstances. This, of course, is an important beginning.

To make sure that the implications of our findings in Chapter 7 are clear, we shall review a few of these findings. In particular, recall the way in which a firm combines inputs in order to minimize costs. We showed that the firm will pick a combination of inputs where the ratio of each input's marginal product to its price is equal. That is, it will set

$$\frac{MP_x}{P_x} = \frac{MP_y}{P_y} = \cdots = \frac{MP_z}{P_z} \qquad [12.1]$$

where MP_x is the marginal product of input x, P_x is the price of input x, MP_y is the marginal product of input y, P_y is the price of input y, and so on. If Equation 12.1 does not hold, the firm can always reduce costs by changing the utilization of certain inputs. For example, if the marginal product of a unit of input x is 2 units of output, the price of a unit of input x is $1, the marginal product of a unit of input y is 6 units of output, and the price of a unit of input y is $2, the firm can reduce its costs by using 1 unit less of input x—which reduces output by 2 units and cost by $1—and by using $\frac{1}{3}$ unit more of input y—which increases output by 2 units and cost by $0.67. This substitution of input y for input x has no effect on output but reduces the cost by $0.33.

Going a step further, it can be shown that, if a firm minimizes cost, each of the ratios in Equation 12.1 equals the reciprocal of the firm's marginal cost. In other words,

$$\frac{P_x}{MP_x} = \frac{P_y}{MP_y} = \cdots = \frac{P_z}{MP_z} = MC \qquad [12.2]$$

where MC is its marginal cost. To prove this, consider input x. What is the cost of producing an extra unit of output if this extra unit of output is achieved by increasing the utilization of input x, while holding constant the utilization of other inputs? Since an extra unit of input x results in MP_x extra units of output, $(1/MP_x)$ units of input x will result in 1 unit of extra output. Since $(1/MP_x)$ units of input x will cost $(1/MP_x)P_x$, $P_x \div MP_x$ equals marginal cost. This same type of reasoning can be used for any input, not just input x, with the consequence that Equation 12.2 holds.[2]

2. Let $Q = f(X_1, \cdots, X_n)$, where Q is the firm's output, X_1 is the amount of the first input used by the firm, X_2 is the amount of the second input used by the firm, and so on. To minimize cost subject to the constraint that output equals Q^*, we form the Lagrangian function:

$$L = \sum_{i=1}^{n} P_i X_i - \lambda[f(X_1, \cdots, X_n) - Q^*]$$

(cont'd.)

As an illustration, suppose that there are only two inputs, input x and input y. Suppose that the marginal product of a unit of input x is 2 units of output, the price of a unit of input x is \$1, the marginal product of a unit of input y is 4 units of output, and the price of a unit of input y is \$2. The extra cost of producing an extra unit of output, if the extra production occurs by increasing the use of input x, is \$0.50, since an extra $\frac{1}{2}$ unit of input x—at \$1 a unit—will result in an extra unit of output. Similarly, the extra cost of producing an extra unit of output, if the extra production comes about by increasing the use of input y, is \$0.50, since an extra $\frac{1}{4}$ unit of input y—at \$2 a unit—will result in an extra unit of output. Thus the ratio of the price of each input to its marginal product equals marginal cost, which is \$0.50.

Going another step, the firm, if it maximizes profit, must be operating at a point at which marginal cost equals marginal revenue. Thus it follows that

$$\frac{P_x}{MP_x} = \frac{P_y}{MP_y} = \cdots = \frac{P_z}{MP_z} = MR \qquad [12.3]$$

where MR is the firm's marginal revenue. Rearranging terms,

$$MP_x \cdot MR = P_x \qquad [12.4a]$$

$$MP_y \cdot MR = P_y \qquad [12.4b]$$

$$\vdots$$

$$MP_z \cdot MR = P_z. \qquad [12.4c]$$

Thus we conclude that the profit-maximizing firm employs each input in an amount such that the input's marginal product multiplied by the firm's marginal revenue equals the input's price. This result, as we shall see in the following section, provides the basis for the firm's demand curve for an input.

---

where P_i is the price of the ith input and λ is a Lagrangian multiplier. Setting $\partial L/\partial X_i = 0$, we have

$$P_i - \frac{\lambda \partial f}{\partial X_i} = 0 \qquad \text{where } i = 1, \cdots, n.$$

Thus,

$$P_i \div \frac{\partial f}{\partial X_i} = \lambda \qquad \text{where } i = 1, \cdots, n.$$

The point in the text is that λ equals marginal cost. To prove this, note that

$$dC = \sum_{i=1}^{n} P_i dX_i$$

$$dQ = \sum_{i=1}^{n} \frac{\partial f}{\partial X_i} dX_i$$

where dC is a small change in cost, dQ is a small change in output, and dX_i is a small change in X_i. Since marginal cost equals $dC \div dQ$, it follows that marginal cost equals

$$\frac{\sum_{i=1}^{n} P_i dX_i}{\sum_{i=1}^{n} (\partial f/\partial X_i) dX_i} = \sum_{i=1}^{n} \lambda \frac{(\partial f/\partial X_i) dX_i}{\sum_{i=1}^{n} (\partial f/\partial X_i) dX_i} = \lambda.$$

This proves the point in the text.

THE FIRM'S DEMAND CURVE: THE CASE OF ONE VARIABLE INPUT

Our first step in analyzing the demand for an input is to consider the demand curve of an individual firm for an input, assuming that this input is the only variable input in the firm's production process. In other words, the quantities of all other inputs are fixed. This assumption is relaxed in the next section. The demand curve of a firm for this input—call it input x—shows the quantity of input x that the firm will demand at each possible price of input x. Assuming that the firm maximizes its profits, it will demand that amount of input x at which the value of the extra output produced by an extra unit of input x is equal to the price of input x. This is the meaning of Equation 12.4a.

To make this more concrete, suppose that we know the firm's production function, from which we deduce that the marginal product of input x (at each level of utilization of input x) is as shown in Table 12.1. Suppose that the price of the product is \$3. Since the product market is perfectly competitive, the marginal revenue is also \$3. The value to the firm of the extra output resulting from its increasing its utilization of input x by 1 unit is shown in the last column of Table 12.1. This is called the *value of the marginal product* of input x, and equals $MP_x \cdot P$, where P is the price of the product. Since $P = MR$ in perfect competition, the value of the marginal product is the left-hand side of Equation 12.4a.

Value of the marginal product

TABLE 12.1 Value of Marginal Product of Input x

Quantity of x	Marginal product*	Value of marginal product* (dollars)
3	8	24
4	7	21
5	6	18
6	5	15
7	4	12
8	3	9
9	2	6

*The figures pertain to the interval between the indicated quantity of input x and one unit less than the indicated quantity of input x.

How many units of input x should the firm use if input x costs \$10 a unit? A 1-unit increase in the utilization of input x adds to the firm's revenues the amount shown in the last column of Table 12.1, and it adds \$10 to the firm's costs. (Since the input markets are perfectly competitive, the firm cannot influence the price of any input.) Thus the firm should increase its utilization of input x as long as the increase in revenue exceeds the increase in costs; in other words, as long as the figure in the last column of Table 12.1 exceeds \$10. For example, if the firm is using 5 units of input x, the use of an extra unit will

increase revenues by $15 and increase costs by $10; consequently, the extra unit
should be used. What about adding still another unit? If the firm is using 6 units
of input x, the use of an extra unit will increase revenue by $12 and increase
costs by $10; thus it too should be added. Increases in the utilization of input x
are profitable up to 7 units; beyond this point, an extra unit of input x increases
costs more than revenues. Thus the firm should use 7 units of input x.

The optimal number of units of input x is the number at which the value of
the marginal product of input x equals the price of input x. This, of course, is
just another way of stating the result in Equation 12.4a, since under these
circumstances the value of the marginal product of input x is equal to the
left-hand side of the equation and the price of input x is the right-hand side of
the equation.[3]

Firm's demand curve If the firm demands the optimal amount of input x at each price of input x,
its demand schedule for input x must be the value-of-marginal-product schedule in the last column of Table 12.1. For example, if the price of input x is
between $6 and $9, the firm will demand 8 units of input x; if the price of input
x is between $9 and $12, the firm will demand 7 units of input x. Thus the
firm's demand curve for input x is the value-of-marginal-product curve, which
shows the value of input x's marginal product at each quantity of input x used.
This curve will slope downward and to the right, because it is proportional to
the curve showing the input's marginal productivity.

THE FIRM'S DEMAND CURVE: THE CASE OF SEVERAL VARIABLE INPUTS

Suppose now that the firm uses a number of inputs that can be varied in quantity and input x is only one of them. Under these circumstances, the firm's
demand curve for input x is no longer the value-of-marginal-product curve.
This is because a change in the price of input x will result in a change in the
quantities of the other variable inputs used, and these changes in the quantities
of the other variable inputs will affect the quantity of input x used.

As an example, suppose that the price of input x is initially $10 and the
quantity of input x used is 100 units. Holding constant the use of other inputs,
suppose that the value-of-marginal-product curve is V_1 in Figure 12.1. If none
of the other inputs were variable, this would be the demand curve for input x.
In fact, however, a number of other inputs are variable. Suppose that the price
of input x falls to $6. What will happen to the quantity of input x demanded by
the firm? Since the value of its marginal product exceeds its new price, the firm
will tend to expand its use. But the increase in its use will shift the value-
of-marginal-product curves of other inputs. For example, if another variable
input is complementary to input x, its value-of-marginal-product curve will
shift to the right. These shifts in the value-of-marginal-product curves of other
variable inputs will result in changes in the amounts used of them. And the

3. This assumes that the quantity of the input can be varied continuously, which is often the case.
However, it is not the case in Table 12.1. Since only integer values can be used, according to
Table 12.1, this rule must be changed somewhat here. In this case, the optimal number of units
of input x is the largest integer at which the value of the marginal product of input x is greater
than or equal to the price of input x.

FIGURE 12.1 Demand Curve of the Firm for Input *x* Points A *and* B
are on the firm's demand curve for input x. (V*₁ and* V*₂ are*
value-of-marginal-product curves.)

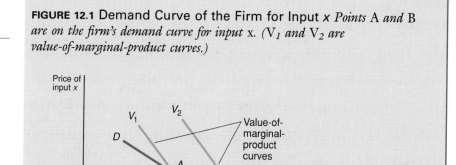

changes in the amounts used of other inputs will in turn shift the value-of-marginal-product curve of input *x*.

When all of these effects have occurred, the firm will be on another value-of-marginal-product curve for input *x*, say V_2 in Figure 12.1. And the amount demanded of input *x* will be such that the value of its marginal product will be equal to its new price. Thus the firm will demand 200 units of input *x*. Points *A* and *B* are both on the firm's demand curve for input *x*. Other points can be determined in a similar fashion; the complete demand curve is *D*. It can be shown that all demand curves of this type slope down and to the right, as would be expected.[4]

4. In passing, we should note that economists of the past were bothered by the question of whether or not, if each input was paid the value of its marginal product, the total amount paid by firms for inputs would be equal to the firm's revenues. Much of the discussion of this question was beside the point, and need not concern us here (see P. Samuelson, *Foundations of Economic Analysis* [Cambridge, Mass.: Harvard University Press, 1947], pp. 81–87). However, it may be worth noting that, if the production function exhibits constant returns to scale, Euler's theorem states that the total physical output of a firm will be identically equal to the sum of the amount of each input used multiplied by the input's marginal product:

$$Q = X_1 MP_1 + X_2 MP_2 + \cdots + X_n MP_n \qquad [12.5]$$

where Q is the firm's output level, X_1 is the amount of the first input used by the firm, X_2 is the amount of the second input used by the firm, X_n is the amount of the *n*th input used by the firm, MP_1 is the marginal product of the first input, MP_2 is the marginal product of the second input, MP_n is the marginal product of the *n*th input, and *n* is the number of inputs used by the firm. Thus, multiplying both sides of Equation 12.5 by *P*, the price of the product, we have

$$PQ = X_1 P(MP_1) + X_2 P(MP_2) + \cdots + X_n P(MP_n). \qquad [12.6]$$

(cont.'d)

EXAMPLE 12.1

THE VALUE OF THE MARGINAL PRODUCT OF IRRIGATION WATER

Under the auspices of the U.S. Department of Agriculture, controlled experiments have been carried out to determine the production functions for a variety of crops. One such experiment estimated the effects of various amounts of irrigation water on the output of cotton in medium-textured soil in Arizona. Based on this experiment, the value of the marginal product of irrigation water in the production of Arizona cotton (if the cotton price is 76 cents or 51 cents per pound of lint) is as follows:

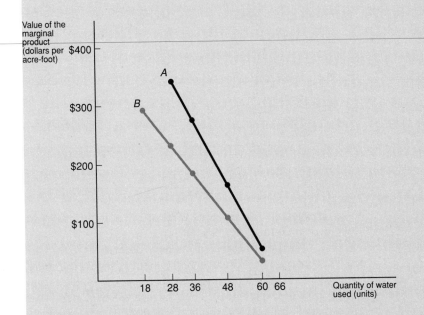

(a) Which of these curves is based on the cotton price of 76 cents? Which is based on the cotton price of 51 cents? (b) If the price of water is $50 per acre-foot, about how much water will be demanded for irrigation purposes, if the price of cotton is 76 cents? (c) Most studies indicate that the demand for irrigation water is price inelastic. Is this in accord with the above curves, if the price of water is $50 per acre-foot? (d) If substantial increases occur in the price of irrigation water, farmers can respond by installing a completely dif-

---

If each input is paid the value of its marginal product, it follows that

$$PQ = X_1P_1 + X_2P_2 + \cdots + X_nP_n \qquad [12.7]$$

where P_1 is the price of the first input, P_2 is the price of the second input, and P_n is the price of the nth input. The left-hand side of Equation 12.7 is the firm's receipts. The right-hand side of Equation 12.7 is the total amount paid by the firm to inputs. Thus, if there are constant returns to scale, the firm's total receipts will be identically equal to the amount necessary to pay all inputs the value of their marginal products. Finally, note that Equation 12.7 is an identity under these circumstances. In general, Equation 12.7 holds as a condition of long-run competitive equilibrium (see Samuelson, ibid.).

ferent type of irrigation apparatus which conserves water. If this were to occur, would the above curves still show the demand curve for water? Why or why not?

SOLUTION

(a) The higher curve, *A,* is based on the higher price; the lower curve, *B,* is based on the lower price. The value of the marginal product at any quantity of water equals the marginal product of water times the price of cotton. Thus the higher the price of cotton, the higher the value of the marginal product. (b) About 60 units of water. (c) Yes. For example, if the price of water increases from $50 to $100, the quantity of water demanded is reduced from about 60 to about 55 units of water, based on curve A in the graph on p. 362. Thus the arc elasticity of demand is about

$$\frac{-(55 - 60)}{57.5} \div \left(\frac{100 - 50}{75}\right) = .13.$$

(d) No. The value-of-marginal-product curve is the demand curve for water only if the amount used of all other inputs remains constant. If a different apparatus were used, the quantity (and perhaps the type) of other inputs used would change.*

*For further discussion, see D. Gibbons, *The Economic Value of Water,* Washington, D.C.: Resources for the Future, 1986.

THE MARKET DEMAND CURVE

When we derived a market demand curve for a commodity in Chapter 5, we summed horizontally over the demand curves of individual consumers of the commodity. At first glance it may seem that we can derive the market demand curve for an input by simply summing horizontally over the demand curves of individual firms for the input. Although this would provide a first approximation, it would not yield the correct result because it neglects the effect of changes in the input price on the product price.

Each firm's demand curve for the input is based on the supposition that the firm's decisions cannot affect the price of its output. For example, in Table 12.1, the firm assumes that the price of its product will be $3, regardless of how it alters its utilization of input x in response to changes in the price of input x. This is a perfectly reasonable assumption for the firm to make, because it is only a very small portion of the industry. But this is not the situation underlying the market demand curve. The market demand curve shows the total amount of the input demanded at various possible prices of the input. Thus it shows the effect of changes in input price on the utilization of the input *when all firms in the industry respond at the same time.*

Suppose that the price of input x decreases substantially. This will result in increased utilization of input x by all firms in the industry and in increased output by all members of the industry. Although the increased output by any single firm cannot affect the price of the industry's product, the combined expansion of output by all firms results in a decrease in the price of the product. This decrease in the price of the product shifts each firm's value-of-marginal-product curve, and consequently it shifts each firm's demand curve for input x.

Market demand curve To derive the market demand curve for input x, suppose that its initial price is $8 and that each firm in the market is in equilibrium, with its demand curve for input x being d in Figure 12.2. Each firm uses Oq units of input x. Multiplying Oq by the number of firms in the market we get OQ, the total amount taken off the market at a price of $8. Thus A is a point on the market demand curve.

Suppose that the price of input x falls to $6. Each firm will increase its use of input x and increase output, with the consequence that the price of the product

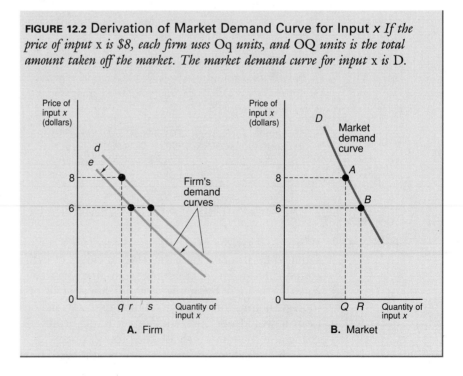

FIGURE 12.2 Derivation of Market Demand Curve for Input x *If the price of input* x *is $8, each firm uses* Oq *units, and* OQ *units is the total amount taken off the market. The market demand curve for input* x *is* D.

will fall and the individual firm demand curves for input x will shift toward e. When all adjustments have been made, each firm will be using Or units of input x. This is less than the Os units that each would have used if it had remained on the demand curve, d. Multiplying Or by the number of firms in the market, we get OR, the total amount taken off the market at a price of \$6. Thus B is another point on the market demand curve. Other points on the market demand curve can be obtained in similar fashion; the complete market demand curve for input x is D.

DETERMINANTS OF THE PRICE ELASTICITY OF DEMAND FOR AN INPUT

In Chapter 5 we pointed out that, in the case of commodities, the price elasticity of market demand varies enormously, the quantity demanded of some commodities being very sensitive to price changes, and the quantity demanded of other commodities being quite insensitive to price changes. This is true of inputs as well. The quantity demanded of some inputs is very sensitive to price changes, whereas the quantity demanded of other inputs is not at all sensitive to price changes. Why is this the case? What determines whether the price elasticity of demand for a particular input will be high or low? Several rules are important.

1. The more easily other inputs can be substituted for a certain input, say input x, the more price elastic is the demand for input x. This certainly makes sense. If the technologies of the firms using input x allow these firms to substitute other inputs readily for input x, a small increase in the price of input x may result in a substantial decrease in its use. But if these firms cannot substitute other inputs readily for input x, a large increase in the price of input x may result in only a small decrease in its use.

2. The larger the price elasticity of demand for the product that input x helps to produce, the larger the price elasticity of demand for input x. This, too, seems clear enough. The demand for an input is prompted by the demand for the product it produces; in other words, the demand for an input is a *derived demand*. The greater the price elasticity of demand of the product, the more sensitive is the output of the product to changes in its price that occur in response to changes in the price of input x.

Derived demand

3. The greater the price elasticity of supply of other inputs, the greater is the price elasticity of demand for input x. The supply curve for an input is the relationship between the amount of the input that is supplied and the input's price. The price elasticity of supply of an input is the percentage increase in the quantity supplied of the input resulting from a 1 percent increase in the price of the input.[5] Thus, if small increases in price bring forth large increases in the quantity of other inputs supplied, this will mean that the demand for input x will be more price elastic than if large increases in price are required to bring forth small increases in the quantity supplied of other inputs.

---

5. More accurately, the price elasticity of supply is $dQ/dP \div Q/P$, where Q is the quantity supplied of the input and P is its price.

4. The price elasticity of demand for an input is likely to be greater in the long run than in the short run. The reasoning here is like that underlying the similar proposition in Chapter 5 concerning the demand for commodities. Basically, the point is that it takes time to adjust fully to a price change. For example, if the price of skilled labor increases, it may not be possible for many plants to reduce very greatly the quantity of skilled labor demanded in the short run, since their plants are built to use fairly rigidly defined amounts of this input. But in the long run, firms can build new plants to reduce their utilization of skilled labor.[6]

THE MARKET SUPPLY CURVE

Market supply curve

Under perfect competition, the supply of an input to an individual firm is infinitely elastic. In other words, the firm can buy all it wants without influencing the price of the input. When we consider the market supply curve, which is the relationship between the price of the input and the total amount of the input supplied in the entire market, it is often untrue that the supply is infinitely elastic. In many cases, the total amount of the input supplied in the entire market will increase only if the price of the input is increased. Indeed, in some cases it is alleged that the market supply curve is perfectly inelastic, that is, the total amount of the input supplied in the entire market is fixed and unresponsive to the price of the input.

There is, of course, no contradiction between the assertion that the supply of an input *to an individual firm* is perfectly elastic under perfect competition and the assertion that the *market* supply curve may not be perfectly elastic under perfect competition. For example, arable land might be available to any one farmer in as great an amount as he could possibly use at a given price; yet the aggregate amount of arable land available to all farmers may increase little with increases in the price per acre. The situation is similar to the sale of commodities: We saw in Chapter 8 that any firm under perfect competition believes that it can sell all it wants at the existing price; yet the total amount of a commodity sold in a given market can usually be increased only by reducing price.

There is sometimes a tendency to underestimate the extent to which the market supply of an input will be increased in response to an increase in the price of the input. For example, it is sometimes argued that the nation is provided with a certain amount of land and mineral resources, and that there is no way to change these amounts. For this reason, it is assumed that their market supply is perfectly inelastic, the available supply being completely unresponsive to price. But this can be quite wrong. For present purposes, what is important is the amount of land and mineral resources that is used, not the amount in existence. A large increase in price generally will increase the amount of these resources in use. This will occur because a higher price will result in more exploration for resources, in the reopening of high-cost mines and farms, and in the irrigation and upgrading of poorer land.

6. For durable inputs, this proposition may not hold. See footnote 2 on page 111.
   Another proposition that is frequently advanced is that the demand for an input will be less elastic if the payments to this input are a small, rather than a large, proportion of the total cost of the product. There may be a good deal of truth in this proposition, but it does not always hold.

Most inputs are *intermediate goods,* goods that are bought from other business firms. For example, an important input in the electric power industry is coal, which is bought from the coal industry. The supply curve for inputs of this kind is already familiar, and there is no need to discuss once again the determinants of the nature and shape of the market supply curve in these cases.

However, not all inputs are supplied by business firms. One of the most significant inputs—labor—is provided by individuals. (In addition, individuals provide other inputs like savings.) When individuals supply an input like labor, they are supplying something that they themselves can use, since the time that they do not work can be used for leisure activities. Thus sellers of these inputs want to keep some of them for themselves. And the amount of these inputs that is supplied to firms depends on the quantities of these inputs that are produced and the quantities that the suppliers want to keep for themselves.

In Chapter 8, we saw that the market supply curve for inputs supplied by business firms will generally slope upward and to the right. In other words higher prices generally are required to bring forth an increased supply. An interesting feature of the market supply function for inputs supplied by individuals is that it, unlike the supply function for inputs supplied by business firms, may be *backward-bending*. That is, increases in price may result in smaller amounts of the input being supplied. An example of a backward-bending supply curve is *SS'* in Figure 12.3.

Backward-bending supply curve

To see how such a case can occur, consider the labor time supplied by a single worker, Bill Jones. Jones has twenty-four hours a day to allocate between work and leisure. To him leisure time is a commodity he desires, and its price is the hourly wage rate—the amount of money he gives up to enjoy an hour of leisure time. What will be the effect of an increase in the wage rate on the

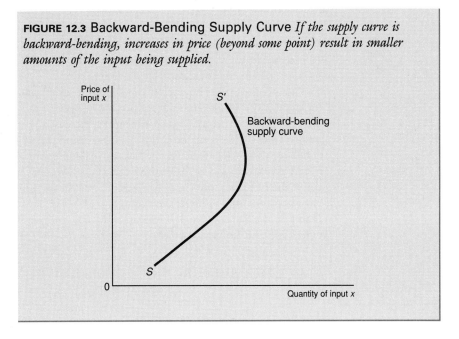

FIGURE 12.3 Backward-Bending Supply Curve *If the supply curve is backward-bending, increases in price (beyond some point) result in smaller amounts of the input being supplied.*

amount of leisure time that Jones will demand? Clearly, this is a problem of consumer choice, since the question can be restated: What is the effect of an increase in the price of leisure time on the quantity of leisure time that Jones demands? The theoretical tools discussed in Chapter 4 can help us to answer this question.

Substitution effect

As we learned in Chapter 4, we can divide the effect of the price increase into two parts: the substitution effect and the income effect. The substitution effect is the effect of the increase in the cost of leisure relative to other commodities. Since other consumer goods will become relatively less expensive, the substitution effect will result in his reducing his leisure time and increasing his purchase of other consumer goods. Thus the substitution effect will result in his increasing the amount of labor time he puts forth.

Income effect

In addition, there is an income effect, which is quite different from the income effect in the case of the purchase of most consumer products. In the first place, the income effect here works in the opposite direction from the income effect in the case of the purchase of the typical consumer product. As we saw in Chapter 4, the income effect of a price increase of a good is generally to reduce the consumption of the good, since the price increase reduces the consumer's real purchasing power. But this is not the case here. An increase in the price of his leisure time due to an increase in his wage makes Jones more affluent and better able to afford the things he wants, including leisure. Thus the income effect of an increase in the price of leisure is likely to be an increase in the demand for leisure.

The income effect in this case differs from the income effect for most consumer products in another important respect: It is likely to be much stronger than for most consumer products. In general, the consumer spends only a small percentage of his budget on the product in question, with the result that an increase in its price has only a small impact on his real income. However, in the case of leisure, an increase in its price will almost certainly have a great effect on his real income, since most of his income is likely to stem from the sale of his labor. (Remember that the price of leisure time is equal to the wage rate.) Thus an increase in the price of leisure time is likely to have a great effect on Jones's income and on his consumption pattern.

The income effect may offset the substitution effect, with the result that an increase in the wage rate may reduce the supply of labor. In other words, an increase in the price of leisure time may increase the quantity demanded of leisure time. Of course, institutional constraints often prevent workers from choosing their own working hours; for example, the 40-hour week is commonly worked in industry. But the typical, or average, work week responds to the shape of the supply curve for labor. Thus, in the United States, as workers have become more affluent the average work week has tended to decrease. For example, the average work week in 1850 was almost 70 hours, as contrasted with about 40 hours at present.

EQUILIBRIUM PRICE AND EMPLOYMENT OF AN INPUT

The market demand and supply curves for an input determine the input's equilibrium price. The price of the input will tend in equilibrium to the level at

FIGURE 12.4 Determination of Equilibrium Price and Quantity *The equilibrium price is OP_0, and the equilibrium quantity is OQ_0.*

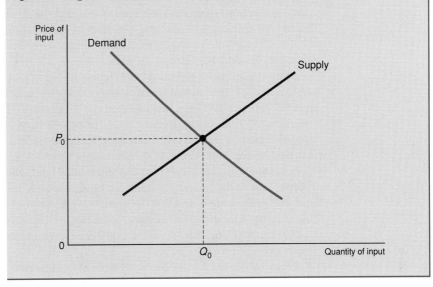

Equilibrium price

which the quantity of the input demanded equals the quantity of the input supplied. Thus, in Figure 12.4, the equilibrium price of the input is OP_0. If the price were higher than OP_0, the quantity supplied would exceed the quantity demanded, and there would be downward pressure on the price. If the price were lower than OP_0, the quantity supplied would fall short of the quantity demanded, and there would be upward pressure on the price.

Equilibrium employment

The equilibrium amount of the input that is employed is also given by the intersection of the market demand and supply curves. For example, in Figure 12.4, OQ_0 units of the input will be employed in equilibrium. In equilibrium the value of the marginal product of an input will be equal in each and every place where the input is used. In all uses the value of the marginal product of an input will equal the price of the input—and the price of the input will, of course, be the same to all firms under perfect competition.

The Market for Engineers: An Application

At this point, it is advisable to pause for a moment and illustrate how the theory we have been discussing has been put to use. During much of the period since World War II, top government policy-makers have been concerned with the adequacy of the national supply of engineers. During the late 1960s and early 1970s, there was a feeling that too many engineers were being turned out by the nation's colleges and universities. The situation turned around in the late 1980s, when the National Science Board worried that a 23 percent decline in the college-age population between 1980 and 1995 "may impose restraints on the supply of newly trained scientists and engineers."[7] Both during the period

7. National Science Board, *Science and Engineering Indicators—1987* (Washington, D.C.: Government Printing Office, 1988), p. 69.

of apparent surplus and that of apparent shortage, questions were repeatedly raised by knowledgeable people concerning the workings of the market for engineers. In particular, it was asked whether the sort of model described in previous sections of this chapter really explained the quantity of engineers graduated in a particular period and the level of their salaries.

To help answer this question, Richard Freeman of Harvard University gathered detailed data concerning the annual number of freshmen enrolling in engineering, the annual number of engineers graduating and seeking work, and the annual level of starting salaries of engineers (with a bachelor's degree). Based on careful statistical analysis, he estimated the supply and demand curves for engineers during this period. In the case of the supply curve, he divided the analysis into two parts. First, he estimated the effect of the level of engineering starting salaries on the number of freshmen enrolling in engineering. Holding other factors (like the total number of freshmen in all fields and the previous levels of salaries and enrollments) constant, he found that the relationship between the number of freshmen enrolling in engineering and the level of engineering starting salaries was as shown in panel A of Figure 12.5. Specifically, a 1 percent increase in starting salaries results in a 2.9 percent increase in freshman enrollment in engineering.

Next, taking the freshman enrollment in engineering as given, he estimated the effect of the level of engineering starting salaries on the number of engineers graduating four years later and seeking work. Holding the freshman enrollment (and other factors) constant, he found that the relationship between the number of engineers graduating (and seeking work) and the level of starting salaries[8] was as shown in panel B of Figure 12.5. Specifically, a 1 percent increase in starting salaries results in about a 1 percent increase in the number of graduate engineers. In other words, more students switched to engineering or stayed in

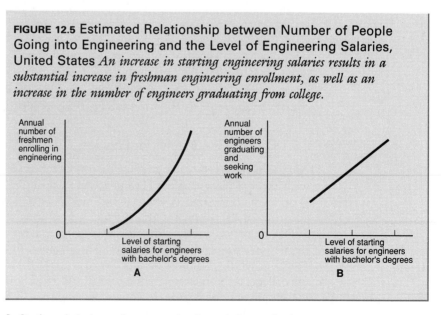

FIGURE 12.5 Estimated Relationship between Number of People Going into Engineering and the Level of Engineering Salaries, United States *An increase in starting engineering salaries results in a substantial increase in freshman engineering enrollment, as well as an increase in the number of engineers graduating from college.*

8. Starting salaries here refer to a couple of years before graduation.

engineering when engineering salaries were relatively high than when they were relatively low. But as one would expect, the quantitative impact of salaries was smaller here than on freshman enrollment in engineering.

Together, the two panels of Figure 12.5 provide some interesting insights concerning the supply curve for engineers in the United States. To government policy-makers, information of this sort is of great importance. For example, if national goals seem to require a certain number of engineers, the information such as that in Figure 12.5 can be used to indicate the level of starting salaries that, in the absence of other measures, would be required to call them forth.

EXAMPLE 12.2

HOW MUCH EFFECT WOULD A WAGE INCREASE HAVE ON THE NURSING SHORTAGE?

Recent years have seen widespread complaints of a shortage of nurses. In 1986, a survey of the American Hospital Association indicated that about 1 out of 7 nursing positions was unfilled. Enrollment in nursing schools dropped substantially between 1983 and 1986, due in part (according to many observers) to the feeling among young people that the nursing profession does not get the public esteem and status that it deserves. At the same time, rises in the elderly population and a variety of other factors have increased the demand for nurses.

Nurses' wages have risen substantially. For example, in 1987 the Westchester County Medical Center raised starting salaries from $22,350 to $26,500. Yet in 1989 a federal nursing commission concluded that wages should be increased further. Suppose that you are an adviser to a U.S. senator who asks you to estimate how much of an effect a 1-percent increase in the wage for nurses would have on the size of the shortage. He claims that the quantity of nurses demanded currently exceeds the quantity supplied by 14 percent, that the price elasticity of demand for nurses is 0.3, and that the price elasticity of supply for nurses is 0.1. If these estimates are correct, what is the answer?

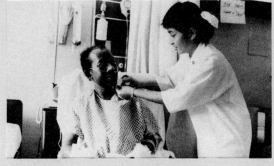

SOLUTION

If it is true that the quantity of nurses demanded currently exceeds the quantity supplied by 14 percent, the current shortage equals

$$H = Q_D - Q_S = 1.14Q_S - Q_S = .14Q_S,$$

where Q_D is the quantity of nurses demanded and Q_S is the quantity supplied. Letting ΔH be the change in the size of the shortage due to the wage increase, it follows that

$$\Delta H = \Delta Q_D - \Delta Q_S,$$

where ΔQ_D is the change in the quantity of nurses demanded and ΔQ_S is the change in the quantity supplied. Based on the elasticities provided by the senator, a 1-percent increase in the wage for nurses would result in a 0.3 percent reduction in the quantity demanded and a 0.1 percent increase in the quantity supplied, which means that $\Delta Q_D = -.003Q_D$ and $\Delta Q_S = .001Q_S$. Thus

$$\Delta H = -.003Q_D - .001Q_S.$$

Recalling that $Q_D = 1.14Q_S$,

$$\Delta H = -.003(1.14Q_S) - .001Q_S$$
$$= -.00442Q_S.$$

Since the shortage currently equals $.14Q_S$, this means that the percentage change in the size of the shortage would be

$$\frac{\Delta H}{H} = \frac{-.00442Q_S}{.14Q_S} = -3.2 \text{ percent.}$$

In other words, based on the senator's estimates, the answer is that a 1-percent increase in the wage for nurses would reduce the shortage by about 3.2 percent. However, before putting any confidence in this result, you would do well to check the senator's estimates against the results of studies carried out by economists and others.*

*It should be recognized that the shortage of nurses is a very complex topic and that this discussion is only an elementary introduction to it. While we assume here that the market for nurses is competitive, it may have monopsonistic characteristics. (Monopsony is discussed in Chapter 13.) Also, the government has intervened in this market in a variety of ways. See, for example, D. Yett, *An Economic Analysis of the Nursing Shortage* (Lexington: D.C. Heath, 1975). Further, the estimates attributed to the senator are meant only to be illustrative.

Further, Freeman's results shed valuable light on the extent to which the theory presented in previous sections can explain the workings of the market for engineers. He concludes that "traditional market forces—shifts in supply and demand—explain changes in engineering starting salaries, though with a lag due to sluggish adjustment to unexpected supply conditions."[9]

THE CONCEPT OF RENT

Earlier in this chapter we stated that there is sometimes a tendency to underestimate the extent to which the market supply of an input will be increased in

9. In panel B of Figure 12.5, the annual numbers of engineers graduating and seeking work is estimated holding constant the number of freshmen enrolled in engineering four years earlier.

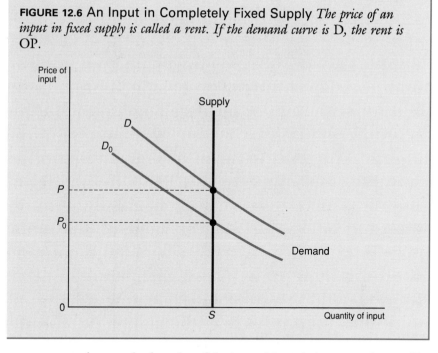

FIGURE 12.6 An Input in Completely Fixed Supply *The price of an input in fixed supply is called a rent. If the demand curve is* D, *the rent is* OP.

response to an increase in the price of the input. Nevertheless, some inputs, like certain types of land, may be in relatively fixed supply. Suppose that the supply of an input is completely fixed: Increases in its price will not increase its supply and decreases in its price will not decrease its supply. Following the terminology of the classical economists of the nineteenth century, the price of such an input is rent. This use of the word *rent* is quite different from everyday usage, according to which *rent* is the price of using an apartment or a car or some other object owned by someone else.

Rent

If the supply of an input is fixed, its supply curve is a vertical line, as shown in Figure 12.6. Thus the price of this input, that is, its rent, is determined entirely by the demand curve for the input. For example, if the demand curve is D, the rent is OP; if the demand curve is D_0, the rent is OP_0. Since the supply of the input is fixed, the price of the input can be lowered without influencing the amount of the input that is supplied. Thus a rent is a payment above the minimum necessary to attract this amount of the input.[10]

In recent years, there has been a tendency among economists to extend the use of the word *rent* to encompass all payments to inputs that are above the minimum required to make these inputs available to the industry or to the economy. To a great extent these payments are costs to individual firms, since these firms must make such payments in order to attract and keep these inputs, which are useful to other firms in the industry. But, if the inputs have no use in

10. Note that whether rent is or is not price-determined depends on whether we are looking at the matter from the point of view of a firm, a small industry, a large industry, or the whole economy. Although a payment to an input that is in fixed supply to the whole society or a large industry may be a rent from the point of view of the society or the industry, it may appear to be a price-determining cost to an individual small firm or a small industry.

EXAMPLE 12.3

DOES IMMIGRATION BENEFIT THE UNITED STATES?

In the 1980s, the United States accepted about 600,000 immigrants per year, many from Asia, Mexico, and Europe. In addition, despite the Immigration Reform and Control Act of 1986, illegal immigration continues. Suppose that the economy is competitive (with constant returns to scale) and that the value-of-marginal-product curve for labor is shown below.

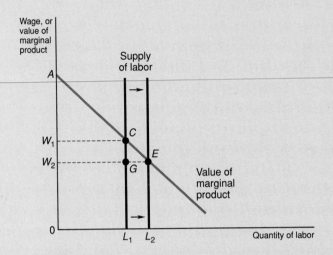

(a) If immigration results in an increase from OL_1 to OL_2 in the supply of labor, what is the effect on the equilibrium wage? (b) What is the effect on the total amount of wages received by nonimmigrant U.S. labor? (c) What is the effect on the total income of U.S. owners of capital (and other nonlabor resources)? Assume that all capital (and other nonlabor resources) is owned by Americans other than the immigrants. (d) Taking account of the effects of the immigration on both the wages received by nonimmigrant U.S. labor and the income of owners of capital (and other nonlabor resources), is there a net benefit to Americans other than the immigrants? If so, how big is it?

SOLUTION

(a) The equilibrium wage will drop from OW_1 to OW_2. Before the immigration, the intersection of the demand and supply curves for labor was at point C; after the shift in the supply curve for labor, it is at point E. (b) The quantity of nonimmigrant U.S. labor is OL_1. Since the wage rate was OW_1 before the immigration, nonimmigrant U.S. labor received total wages amounting to OW_1 times OL_1, which equals area OW_1CL_1. After the immigration, nonimmigrant U.S. labor received total wages amounting to OW_2 times OL_1, which equals area OW_2GL_1. Thus the immigration reduced the total wages of nonimmigrant U.S. labor by an amount equal to area W_2W_1CG. (c) The value of the total output produced by n workers is the sum of the values of the marginal products of the first, second, . . . , and n^{th} workers.* Thus, since OL_1 workers were hired before the immigration, the value of the total output at that time equaled the sum of the values of the marginal products of the OL_1 workers—which amounts to area $OACL_1$. Since wages equaled area OW_1CL_1, owners of capital (and other nonlabor resources) received an amount equal to W_1AC (the difference between area $OACL_1$ and area OW_1CL_1). After the immigration, the value of the total output produced by the OL_2 workers is the sum of the values of their marginal products, which equals $OAEL_2$. Subtracting total wages, owners of capital (and other nonlabor resources) received an amount equal to area W_2AE (the difference between area $OAEL_2$ and area OW_2EL_2). Thus owners of capital (and other nonlabor resources) received an increase in income amounting to the area W_2W_1CE (the difference between area W_2AE and area W_1AC). (d) The increase in the total income of U.S. owners of capital and other nonlabor resources (area W_2W_1CE) exceeds the loss to nonimmigrant U.S. labor (area W_2W_1CG), the difference equaling triangle CGE.**

*To see this, let the value of total output be $V(n)$ when n workers are hired. Since the value of the marginal product of the first worker is $V(1) - V(0)$, the value of the marginal product of the second worker is $V(2) - V(1), \ldots$, and the value of the marginal product of the nth worker is $V(n) - V(n - 1)$, it follows that the sum of the values of the marginal products of the n workers equals

$$[V(1) - V(0)] + [V(2) - V(1)] + \ldots + [V(n) - V(n - 1)].$$

Since $V(1), V(2), \ldots V(n - 1)$ appear with both positive and negative signs, they cancel out; and since $V(0) = 0$, this sum must equal $V(n)$.

**For further discussion, see B. Chiswick, "Illegal Immigration and Immigration Control," and Clark Reynolds and Robert McCleery, "The Political Economy of Immigration Law: Impact of Simpson-Rodeno on the United States and Mexico," *The Journal of Economic Perspectives,* Summer 1988. J. Simon has written extensively on this topic.

other industries, these payments are not costs to the industry as a whole (or to the economy as a whole) because the inputs would be available to the industry whether or not these payments are made.

Why is it important to know whether or not a certain payment for inputs is a rent? Because a reduction of the payment will not influence the availability and use of the inputs if the payment is a rent; whereas, if it is not a rent, a reduction of the payment is likely to change the allocation of resources. For example, if the government imposes a tax on rents, there will be no effect on the supply of resources to the economy.

Quasi-Rents

The payment to any input in temporarily fixed supply is called a quasi-rent. In previous chapters, we have seen that many inputs are in fixed supply to a firm in the short run. For example, a firm's plant cannot be changed appreciably. In the short run, fixed inputs cannot be withdrawn from their current use and transferred to a use where the returns are higher. Also, fixed inputs cannot be supplemented with other similar inputs in the short run. Thus the payments to the fixed inputs are determined differently from the payments to the variable inputs. Whereas inputs that are variable in quantity are free to move where the returns are highest, fixed inputs are stuck where they are, at least in the short run. Consequently, firms must pay the variable inputs as much as they can earn in alternative uses, and the fixed inputs receive whatever is left over.

Quasi-rent

The return to the fixed inputs is a *quasi-rent*. It is a residual. To understand its nature, it is useful to consider the diagram in Figure 12.7, which shows a firm's short-run cost curves. Suppose that the price is OP_0, with the result that the firm will produce OQ_0 units and its total variable costs will be $OGBQ_0$ (since OG equals its average variable cost). This area, $OGBQ_0$, represents the amount that the firm must pay in order to attract and keep the amount of variable inputs corresponding to an output of OQ_0. It cannot pay less and expect to keep them. The fixed inputs get the residual, which is GP_0CB. This is the quasi-rent.

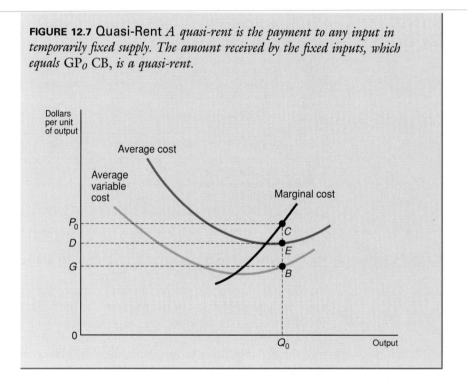

FIGURE 12.7 Quasi-Rent *A quasi-rent is the payment to any input in temporarily fixed supply. The amount received by the fixed inputs, which equals* GP_0 CB, *is a quasi-rent.*

The short-run average total cost curve includes both the average variable costs and the average fixed costs. To determine the average fixed costs, we see what the returns on the firm's fixed assets would be if the rate of return were equal to that available elsewhere in the economy. Thus, since the firm's average total cost curve is as shown in Figure 12.7, the total fixed costs of the firm are equal to $GDEB$. Consequently, this amount of the quasi-rent is not pure economic profit; only DP_0CE is economic profit. Needless to say, quasi-rent need not be greater than total fixed costs. Firms with pure economic losses do not have quasi-rents that are large enough to cover total fixed costs.

EXAMPLE 12.4

THE EFFECTS OF MINIMUM-WAGE LAWS

The minimum wage, which was only 25 cents per hour in 1938, is $4.25 in 1991. Suppose that a minimum wage, OP_m, is instituted in a competitive labor market, with the demand and supply curves for labor as follows:

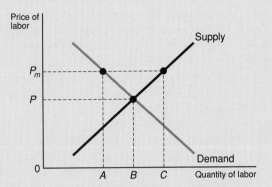

(a) Will the minimum wage affect the level of employment? If so, how big will its effect be? (b) How may employers (and workers) get around the minimum wage? (c) Are certain types of workers affected more than others by the minimum wage? If so, which types are affected most?

SOLUTION

(a) Yes. The minimum wage will cause employment to fall from OB to OA workers, as employers move along their demand curve for labor to the point where labor's price equals the minimum wage. Thus AB workers will be laid off. Note that this is less than the excess supply of workers (the difference between the quantity of workers supplied and the quantity demanded), which now equals AC, since OC workers supply their services but only OA workers are demanded. The excess supply of workers is the total number who would like to work at the minimum wage, but cannot do so. (b) Sometimes employers can provide less in-kind benefits, such as meals, or employees are willing to pay for items that normally would be the responsibility of the employer. In this way, the *net* amount paid by the employer is below the minimum wage, although the wage appears to be above it. (c) Unskilled workers and occupations are affected much more than skilled workers and occupations, because only in unskilled labor markets does the minimum wage exceed the equilibrium wage. There is a strong effect on teenagers, particularly black teenagers. One study indicated that the unemployment rate for black teenagers increases about 1.8 percentage points for each percentage point rise in the ratio of the minimum wage to the average hourly earnings of production workers in private nonagricultural employment.*

*For further discussion, see C. Brown, C. Gilroy, and A. Kohen, "The Effect of the Minimum Wage on Employment and Unemployment," *Journal of Economic Literature,* June 1982; and C. Brown, "Minimum Wage Laws: Are They Overrated?" *Journal of Economic Perspectives,* Summer 1988. A lower training wage now exists for teenagers.

In previous sections, we have assumed that a firm can readily determine the marginal productivity of an input. For business firms in the real world, this may or may not be true. To illustrate the situation where it is not true, consider Melissa Harvey, personnel director of an electronics firm, who is interviewing several applicants for a particular job. Although she can obtain information concerning their previous experience and education, it is very difficult for her to predict how productive each will be, if hired. In contrast to our discussion in previous sections, this is a case of *asymmetric information;* that is, the prospective employer—Ms. Harvey—knows less about the productivity of these workers than do the workers themselves. (For other cases of asymmetric information we have encountered, recall the used car market in Chapter 2 and the limit pricing model in Chapter 11.)

Asymmetric information

One way that the firm can solve this problem is to hire a number of workers, see which ones are most productive, and let the rest go. Although this procedure can be used, it frequently is too expensive to be worthwhile. In many cases, a firm must invest considerable money in on-the-job training for a new worker and wait months (even years) to determine how productive the new worker will be. Moreover, if an employee has been on the job more than a few months, the firm may have to provide severance pay, unless it can give good reasons for the employee's dismissal (which may not be easy). Thus firms are intensely interested in evaluating potential employees before they hire them.

Signal

To make such evaluations, firms frequently use education as an important indicator, or *signal,* of a person's productivity. This is understandable, since more highly educated people tend to be more productive on many jobs because schooling imparts information and skills that help them work more effectively. But this is not the only reason. Even if schooling really had no effect at all on a person's productivity, it still might be a valuable signal.

To see why, consider a model proposed by Stanford's Michael Spence.[11] Suppose that all workers fall into two groups: high-productivity workers and low-productivity workers. The value of the marginal product of a high-productivity worker is greater than that of a low-productivity worker. If firms could determine (before hiring them) which group a particular job applicant falls into, they would offer a higher wage to the high-productivity workers than to the low-productivity workers; but they cannot tell in advance whether a particular applicant falls into one group or the other.

Suppose that firms decide to use education as an indicator of whether a person is high-productivity or low-productivity. Specifically, firms assume that any applicant who has a college degree is high-productivity, and that any applicant without a college degree is low-productivity. The fact that firms are using education as a signal of this sort becomes known to people who are making decisions concerning how much schooling they should get. They realize that if they graduate from college, they will receive a higher wage than if they do not graduate from college. Specifically, let's assume that, if a person graduates from college, he or she will receive $90,000 more in lifetime earnings than if he or she does not go to college or graduate. (See Table 12.2.)

11. Michael Spence, *Market Signaling* (Cambridge: Harvard University Press, 1974).

TABLE 12.2 Increase in Lifetime Earnings Due to College Graduation and Cost of College Education, High-Productivity and Low-Productivity Workers

	Type of worker	
	High-productivity	Low-productivity
Increase in lifetime earnings due to graduation from college	$90,000	$90,000
Cost of a college education	75,000	110,000
Net earnings gain from college graduation	15,000	−20,000

Suppose too that high-productivity workers find it much less costly than low-productivity workers to get a college education. Because they are abler, they can get through college more quickly, and with more financial aid. (Low-productivity people may find it difficult, if not impossible, to meet the standards for graduation.) Specifically, let's assume that the cost of a college education would be $75,000 for a high-productivity worker and $110,000 for a low-productivity worker. Under these circumstances, only high-productivity workers would get a college education, since it would be profitable for them—but not for low-productivity workers—to do so. (As shown in Table 12.2, the $75,000 cost is less than the $90,000 earnings gain for high-productivity workers; whereas for low-productivity workers, the $110,000 cost is greater than the $90,000 earnings gain.)

Education as signal

Thus education turns out to be a very good indicator, or signal, of whether a job applicant is high-productivity or low-productivity. Indeed, in this highly simplified model, it is a perfect indicator, since all college graduates are high-productivity workers and all job applicants without a college degree are low-productivity workers. Consequently, firms will continue to use education as an indicator of this sort—and high-productivity workers will continue to find it profitable to go to college. An equilibrium exists in the sense that firms and workers (both high-productivity and low-productivity) have no reason to change their behavior.

Education and productivity

One important point to note about this model is that the results are the same even if education has no effect at all on a person's productivity. Nowhere in this section have we made any assumptions about the nature or effect of education. Whether a person's college degree is in music, physics, or basket-weaving makes no difference for present purposes, since all that education really provides is a signal. In reality, of course, education does have an effect on productivity. Engineers who graduate from Cornell or Caltech are more productive than they would have been without a college education. But this does not deny that education also serves as a signal. Many employers insist on a college degree or an MBA, even though this specific training is much less important to them than the perseverance, intelligence, and drive of the job applicant. What they recognize is that a college degree or an MBA is a useful (if imperfect) signal of a person's intelligence and willingness to work.

EMPLOYERS AND WORKERS: A PRINCIPAL-AGENT PROBLEM

Agency relationship

Once a worker is hired, the employer still faces difficulties because of asymmetric information since the worker may pursue his or her interests, not those of the employer. This is called a principal-agent problem (recall pp. 140–41), reflecting the fact that an *agency relationship* exists between the employer and the worker. (The worker is an *agent* who works for the employer, who is the *principal.*) The employer's welfare depends on the actions of the worker, but often it is not feasible for the employer to measure at all accurately how hard a particular employee is working and the extent to which this work is in accord with the employer's goals (as distinct from the worker's goals, which may be quite different).

Consider the case of John Wheeler, a salesman for a computer manufacturer. If he works hard, he generates $50,000 per month in profit for his employer if he is lucky, but only $30,000 if he is unlucky. If he does not work hard, he generates $30,000 per month in profit if he is lucky, but only $20,000 if he is unlucky. (Wheeler's salary has not been subtracted from these profit figures; to obtain the net profit to his employer, it must be subtracted.) Thus, if Mr. Wheeler generates a $30,000 profit in a particular month, there is no way that his employer can tell whether he worked hard and was unlucky, or whether he did not work hard and was lucky. Even if his employer took the trouble to monitor his behavior (which could be prohibitively expensive), there may be no accurate method of gauging how much effort he is really putting forth.

Mr. Wheeler's employer would like to induce him to work hard because this will increase the firm's profit. It is instructive to compare how effective two alternative payment schemes are in this regard. According to the first payment scheme, Wheeler receives a *fixed monthly wage* (say $4,000), regardless of how much profit he generates for his employer. Clearly, this payment scheme will not induce him to work hard, since he will receive no more pay if he works hard than if he doesn't work hard. Thus, unless he likes work for its own sake, he will not work hard. If there is a 50-50 chance that he will be lucky in any month (and a 50-50 chance that he will be unlucky), his employer can expect that he will generate, on the average, 0.5 ($20,000) + 0.5 ($30,000) = $25,000 in profit per month. Deducting his wage of $4,000 from this gross profit figure, his employer receives an average net profit of $21,000 per month. (See Table 12.3.)

Bonus

According to the second payment scheme, Wheeler receives a *bonus* if he generates high levels of profit. Specifically, he gets a *low* wage (say $2,000) if he generates a $20,000 or $30,000 profit in a particular month, but a *much higher wage* (say $10,000) if he generates a $50,000 profit in that month. Since there is a 50-50 chance that he will be lucky in any month (and a 50-50 chance that he will be unlucky), he can expect, on the average, to receive 0.5 ($2,000) + 0.5 ($10,000) = $6,000 per month if he works hard. (Why? Because he will receive $2,000 during those months when he is unlucky and $10,000 during those months when he is lucky.) On the other hand, if he does not work hard, he is certain to receive $2,000 per month. (Why? Because regardless of whether he is lucky or unlucky, he will generate only a $20,000 or $30,000 profit, which means he will receive $2,000 per month.)

Fixed monthly wage

TABLE 12.3 John Wheeler's Expected Monthly Income and His Employer's Expected Monthly Profit, Two Alternative Payment Schemes

Payment scheme	Wheeler's expected income		Wheeler's maximum expected income*	Employer's expected profit
	If he works hard	If he does not work hard		
Fixed monthly wage of $4,000	$4,000	$4,000	$4,000	$25,000 – $4,000 = $21,000
$10,000 wage if he generates $50,000 profit; $2,000 wage otherwise	$6,000	$2,000	$6,000	$40,000 – $6,000 = $34,000

*This is his expected income if he works hard or his expected income if he does not work hard, whichever is higher (if they differ).

In contrast with the first payment scheme, Mr. Wheeler now has an incentive to work hard, since his monthly wage is much higher if he works hard than if he doesn't. His employer can expect that Wheeler will generate, on the average, 0.5 ($30,000) + 0.5 ($50,000) = $40,000 in profit per month. Subtracting his average wage of $6,000 per month from this gross profit figure, his employer receives an average net profit of $34,000 per month, which is greater than under the first payment scheme. (See Table 12.3.) Clearly, both Wheeler and his employer are better off under the second payment scheme than under the first.

This example illustrates an important point: *A bonus payment system can be used by firms to help induce workers to further the aims of the firm when there is no way to measure directly the amount of effort that a worker puts out.* Other incentive systems can be used as well. For example, Mr. Wheeler's employer could have instituted a profit-sharing system whereby Wheeler would have earned a basic wage plus a certain percentage of the profits in excess of a particular amount. If properly designed, this type of system would also provide an incentive for Wheeler to work hard—and to increase the firm's profit.

EFFICIENCY WAGE THEORY

Another recent development in the analysis of input pricing is *efficiency wage theory*. One interesting feature of this theory is that it helps to explain the fact that substantial unemployment exists in many labor markets. Based on the simple competitive model presented on pages 356–72, such unemployment would not be expected if unemployed persons were willing to work for a lower wage than employed persons, because firms would find it profitable to lower

FIGURE 12.8 The Efficiency Wage *The efficiency wage is* OW_1. *At this wage, there will be* $(OQ_0 - OQ_1)$ *units of labor unemployed.*

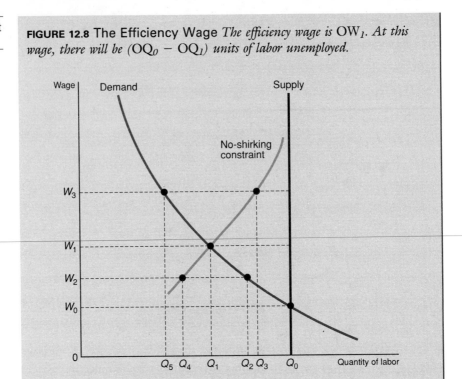

wage rates and increase employment. In this way, unemployment would tend to disappear.

However, the efficiency wage theory makes a quite different assumption than the simple model presented above; it assumes that a worker's productivity—that is, his or her output per hour of labor—depends on the level of the wage rate. As pointed out in the previous section, it can be difficult for firms to measure how much effort a worker is really making. Under such circumstances, if a firm pays the wage where the quantity of labor demanded equals the quantity of labor supplied (OW_0 in Figure 12.8),[12] its workers may have an incen-

Shirking tive to *shirk*. Why? Because the firm's managers may not be able to detect the shirking, and even if they do detect it and fire the workers who are involved, these workers can readily obtain employment elsewhere at the wage they formerly earned. Thus there is little incentive for workers to work hard.

To get workers not to shirk, a firm must pay workers a higher wage than OW_0 in Figure 12.8. They will not shirk under these circumstances, because if they are fired for shirking (or for any other reason), they will have to take a substantial pay cut if they go to work for some other firm at the perfectly competitive wage, OW_0. Because they do not want to give up the relatively high pay that they are earning, they are induced to work hard. The wage rate

Efficiency wage where no shirking takes place is called the *efficiency wage*; it is higher than the perfectly competitive wage.

12. For simplicity, we assume in Figure 12.8 that the supply curve for labor is vertical.

Since all firms in the labor market are in the same situation, they all pay the efficiency wage rather than the perfectly competitive wage. This does not mean, however, that workers are less motivated to work hard. Since the efficiency wage is higher than the perfectly competitive wage, less labor is demanded than supplied, and there is unemployment. Consequently, if a worker is fired for shirking, he or she is likely to occupy a place among the unemployed before finding another job at some other firm. This prospect induces workers to work hard.

What factors determine the level of the efficiency wage? According to Berkeley's Janet Yellen, Stanford's Joseph Stiglitz, and others,[13] the minimum wage rate that workers have to earn in order not to shirk is inversely related to the level of unemployment. For example, if the wage rate is OW_2 in Figure 12.8, $(OQ_0 - OQ_4)$ units of labor must be unemployed in order to induce workers not to shirk. On the other hand, if the wage rate is OW_3, $(OQ_0 - OQ_3)$ units of labor must be unemployed to keep workers from shirking. The curve showing the amount of unemployment (measured horizontally from OQ_0 to the left) required at each wage rate to prevent shirking is the so-called *no-shirking-constraint* curve. The efficiency wage will tend to be at the point where this curve intersects the market demand curve for labor—OW_1 in Figure 12.8.

Why is OW_1 the equilibrium value of the efficiency wage? Because at this wage unemployment (the horizontal distance between the supply and demand curves) is at the level required to prevent shirking. (Recall that the horizontal difference between the supply and no-shirking-constraint curves is this required level). If the efficiency wage is OW_2 (which is lower than OW_1), unemployment—$(OQ_0 - OQ_2)$ units of labor—is less than the $(OQ_0 - OQ_4)$ units of labor required to prevent shirking. Thus the efficiency wage will tend to rise. If the efficiency wage is OW_3 (which is higher than OW_1), unemployment—$(OQ_0 - OQ_5)$ units of labor—is greater than the $(OQ_0 - OQ_3)$ units of labor required to prevent shirking. Thus the efficiency wage will tend to fall.

Although this is a highly simplified model, it has been used to help explain a variety of phenomena, such as Henry Ford's famous decision to pay $5 a day for labor in 1914. On January 12, 1914, Ford reduced the length of the working day from 9 to 8 hours and raised the minimum daily pay from $2.34 to $5.00. This was a decision that received international attention. It is very unusual for a firm to announce that it will double the wage rate it pays. Yet Ford himself said it ". . . was one of the finest cost cutting moves we ever made."[14] Detailed analysis bears out the fact that the average cost of Ford's cars declined (and the average product of labor increased) after this announcement. The higher wage resulted in fewer layoffs, discharges, and resignations; and the workers seemed to exert more intensive and productive effort. The available evidence indicates that what Ford did was to pay an efficiency wage.[15]

13. J. Yellen, "Efficiency Wage Models of Unemployment," *American Economic Review,* May 1984; and J. Stiglitz, "The Causes and Consequences of the Dependence of Quality on Price," *Journal of Economic Literature,* March 1987.

14. H. Ford, *My Life and Work* (Garden City, NY: Doubleday, Page, 1922), p. 147.

15. For a detailed discussion, see D. Raff and L. Summers, "Did Henry Ford Pay Efficiency Wages?" *Journal of Labor Economics,* 1987.

1. In a free-enterprise economy, input prices are an important determinant of any consumer's income. Our first step in analyzing the demand for an input is to consider the demand curve of an individual firm. If there is only one variable input, the firm's demand curve is the same as the value-of-marginal-product schedule. If there is more than one variable input, the situation is somewhat more complicated.

2. The market demand curve for the input can be derived from the demand curves of the individual firms in the market; however, it cannot be derived by simply taking their horizontal sum.

3. Under perfect competition, the supply of an input to an individual firm is infinitely elastic. However, when we consider the market supply curve, which is the relationship between the price of the input and the amount of the input supplied in the entire market, it is often not true that supply is infinitely elastic.

4. Many inputs are supplied by business firms, and the factors influencing their supply have been discussed in previous chapters. But other inputs—notably labor—are supplied by individuals, not business firms. For inputs supplied by individuals, the supply curve may be backward bending; that is, increases in input price may result in a smaller supply of the input, at least over some range of variation of input price.

5. Given the market demand and supply curves for an input, the price of the input will tend in equilibrium to the level at which the quantity of the input demanded equals the quantity of the input supplied. The equilibrium amount of the input that is utilized is also given by the intersection of the market demand and supply curves. To illustrate how these concepts can be used to help solve important problems of public policy, we described how economists have used these concepts to analyze the market for engineers.

6. The payment to an input that is completely fixed in supply is called a rent; and the payment to an input in temporarily fixed supply is a quasi-rent.

7. There frequently is asymmetric information in the labor market. Firms know less about the productivity of workers and about how much effort a worker is exerting than do the workers themselves. To evaluate workers before they hire them, firms frequently use education as an important indicator, or signal, of a person's productivity.

8. A principal-agent problem often exists because the worker's goals may be quite different from the firm's goals. To help induce workers to further the aims of the firm (when there is no way to measure directly the amount of effort that a worker puts forth), bonus payment systems are often used. Also, to get workers not to shirk, firms may have to pay workers a higher wage than the one that equates the quantity of labor demanded and the quantity of labor supplied: this is called the efficiency wage.

1. Martin Feldstein estimated that physicians have a backward-bending supply curve for labor. He found that the price elasticity of supply of physicians' services was about -0.91. (a) Draw a graph where hours per week devoted to leisure are plotted along the horizontal axis, and income derived from working is plotted along the vertical axis. Letting leisure be one good and income derived from working be the other, construct an individual physician's budget line and indifference curves. (b) Using the graph constructed in (a), show how the physician's desired amount of leisure is influenced by a decrease in his or her wage rate, if his or her supply curve for labor is backward-bending. (c) The American Medical Association has argued that any legislation that reduces the fees that physicians can charge

will cut the supply of physicians' services. Based on Feldstein's results, does this appear to be true?[16]

2. Using the concepts presented in this chapter, describe the effect on the market for unskilled labor if the existing minimum wage is abolished.

3. Suppose that a negative income tax is enacted. If a family's income level is as shown in the first column of the table below, the amount that it will receive from the government is given in the second column, and the family's total income (including the cash payment from the government) is given in the third column. Thus, if a family's income is $2,000, it will receive $3,500 from the government (this being its *negative* tax payment), and its total income (including the cash payment from the government) is $5,500. (a) In the absence of a negative income tax, suppose that the relationship between a worker's after-

Family income	Government's cash payment to family	Family's total income (including payment by government)
$ 0	$4,500	$4,500
1,000	4,000	5,000
2,000	3,500	5,500
3,000	3,000	6,000
4,000	2,500	6,500
5,000	2,000	7,000
6,000	1,500	7,500
7,000	1,000	8,000
8,000	500	8,500
9,000	0	9,000

tax income and his number of hours of leisure would be the straight line *EF* in the graph on p. 386. If he devoted no time at all to leisure, he would earn an income of *OE*. If he devoted no time at all to work (and 8,760 hours[17] to leisure), he would earn a zero income. The slope of line *EF* equals − 1 times the worker's (after-tax) hourly wage rate, because every extra hour devoted to leisure reduces the amount of income received from working by an amount equal to the after-tax hourly wage rate. What point on the line *EF* will the worker choose? How many hours of work per year will he do? (b) How many hours of work will he do if the government establishes a minimum annual income of $4,500 per year? (c) If the negative income tax in the table above is adopted, how many hours per year will he work? (d) Will all workers devote more time to work under the negative income tax than under the guaranteed annual income?

4. According to 1981 Nobel laureate James Tobin, "When there are only a few people left in the population whose capacities are confined to garbage-collecting, it will be a high-paid calling. The same is true of domestic service and all kinds of menial work." Do you agree? Using the concepts presented in this chapter, explain why you agree or disagree.

5. A biotechnology firm uses labor and capital. The price of a unit of labor is $5 and the price of a unit of capital is $6. The marginal product of a unit of labor is the same as the marginal product of a unit of capital. Is this firm (which is a perfect competitor) maximizing its profit? Explain.

6. Rome Stifler, a Harley-Davidson employee, is reported to have suggested a new cutting-tool design that reduced the tool's cost by 60 percent. What sorts of incentive systems can be adopted by a firm to encourage such performance? Is there a principal-agency problem with regard to inventive activity of this sort? If so, what is it?

16. Note that Martin Feldstein's study, while very influential, is not the only one bearing on this topic, and that results vary from study to study.

17. The number of hours in a year equals 365 times 24, or 8,760.

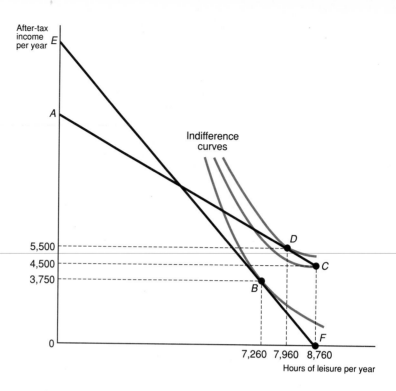

7. A perfectly competitive firm can hire labor at $30 per day. The firm's production function is as follows:

Number of days of labor	Number of units of output
0	0
1	8
2	15
3	21
4	26
5	30

If each unit of output sells for $5, how many days of labor should the firm hire?

8. A firm sells its product for $10 per unit. It produces 100 units per month, and its average variable cost is $5. What is its quasi-rent? If its average fixed cost is $4, does its quasi-rent equal its economic profit?

9. (Advanced) Suppose that a chemical firm's production function is $Q = L^{.8}K^{.2}$, where Q is output, L is the amount of labor used, and K is the amount of capital used. If the firm takes the product price and the input prices as given, show that total wages paid by the firm will equal 80 percent of its revenues.

10. Using the conventional supply and demand apparatus, show why nonwhite labor receives lower wages than white labor, if racial discrimination exists in a society. What would happen to nonwhite wages, white wages, and total output if discrimination were to cease?

13

PRICE AND EMPLOYMENT OF INPUTS UNDER IMPERFECT COMPETITION

INTRODUCTION

In some parts of the economy, perfect competition is clearly not the best model. In this chapter, we continue our discussion of the determinants of the price and employment of inputs, but we relax the assumption that there is perfect competition. (As in most of Chapter 12, we assume that firms and individuals have perfect information.) More specifically, this chapter is divided into three parts. In the first part, we consider the case in which there is perfect competition in the market for the input, but imperfect competition (that is, monopoly, oligopoly, or monopolistic competition) in the relevant product markets. In other words, we allow some of the firms that are potential buyers of the input to have some monopoly power in the sale of their products. In the second part, we take up the case in which there is only a single buyer of an input. In the third part, we discuss an important and highly visible form of market imperfection in the market for labor—the labor union.[1]

PROFIT MAXIMIZATION AND INPUT EMPLOYMENT: IMPERFECT COMPETITION IN THE PRODUCT MARKET

In the previous chapter we showed that a firm, if it maximizes profit, will employ inputs in such a way that each input's marginal product multiplied by

---

1. Of course, this is only a brief introduction to the economics of collective bargaining; the material presented here is chosen and viewed from the vantage point of microeconomic theory. Readers with a particular interest in this field should take a specialized course in labor economics.

the firm's marginal revenue will equal the price of the input. Put in symbols, this condition for profit maximization is

$$MP_x \cdot MR = P_x \qquad [13.1a]$$

$$MP_y \cdot MR = P_y \qquad [13.1b]$$

$$\vdots$$

$$MP_z \cdot MR = P_z \qquad [13.1c]$$

where MP_x is the marginal product of input x, MP_y is the marginal product of input y, MP_z is the marginal product of input z, P_x is the price of input x, P_y is the price of input y, P_z is the price of input z, and MR is the marginal revenue of the firm's output.

Suppose that the firm is a monopolist or an oligopolist or a monopolistic competitor, rather than a perfect competitor as assumed in the previous chapter. Will the firm still employ inputs in the way described by Equations 13.1a, 13.1b, . . . , 13.1c if it maximizes profit? The answer is yes. As long as the market for the input is perfectly competitive and the firm cannot influence the price of the input by its purchases, it must conform to Equations 13.1a, 13.1b, . . . , 13.1c if it maximizes profit. It is a simple matter to prove to yourself that this is the case: Merely turn back to pp. 357–58 of Chapter 12 and work through the derivation of the conditions in Equations 12.4a, 12.4b, . . . , 12.4c. Nowhere in that derivation is it assumed that the firm's product is sold in a perfectly competitive market. Thus the results hold whether the firm is a perfect competitor or an imperfect competitor in the product market.

The Firm's Demand Curve: The Case of One Variable Input

Equations 13.1a, 13.1b, . . . , 13.1c are the basis for the theory of input demand under imperfect competition in the product market (just as they are under perfect competition in the product market). As in the previous chapter our first step in analyzing the demand for an input is to consider the demand of an individual firm for an input, assuming that this input is the only variable input in the firm's production process. In other words, the quantities of all other inputs are fixed. This assumption is relaxed in the next section. In the section after next, we discuss the market demand for the input and the determination of input price and employment.

Suppose that the only variable input is input x. The demand curve of a firm for this input shows the quantity of input x that the firm will take at various possible prices of input x. Assuming that the firm maximizes its profits, it will take that amount of input x at which the value of the extra output produced by an extra unit of input x is equal to the price of a unit of input x. This is the meaning of Equation 13.1a.

To be more specific, suppose that the marginal product of input x at various levels of utilization of input x is that shown in Table 13.1; the total amount of output that can be derived from each number of units of input x is shown in the third column of Table 13.1. Because the firm is an imperfect competitor, the price of its product will vary with the amount it sells; the fourth column of

TABLE 13.1 Marginal Revenue Product of Input x

Quantity of x	Marginal product of x*	Total output	Price of good (dollars)	Total revenue (dollars)	Marginal revenue product of x* (dollars)
3	10	33	20.00	660.00	—
4	9	42	19.50	819.00	159.00
5	8	50	19.00	950.00	131.00
6	7	57	18.50	1,054.50	104.50
7	6	63	18.00	1,134.00	79.50
8	5	68	17.50	1,190.00	56.00
9	4	72	17.00	1,224.00	34.00

*These figures pertain to the interval between the indicated amount of input x and one unit less than the indicated amount of input x.

Table 13.1 provides the price that corresponds to each output in the third column. Multiplying the output in the third column by the price in the fourth column, we get the total revenue corresponding to each number of units of input x used; this is shown in column 5.

Finally, in column 6 of Table 13.1 we show the increase in total revenue that stems from the use of each additional unit of input x. For example, the fifth unit of input x (that is, going from 4 units to 5 units of input x) increases the firm's total revenue by $131. Similarly, the seventh unit of input x (that is, going from 6 units to 7 units of input x) increases the firm's total revenue by $79.50. The increase in total revenue due to the use of an additional unit of input x is called the *marginal revenue product* of input x, which explains the heading of column 6. The marginal revenue product of input x is equal to the marginal physical product of input x times the firm's marginal revenue.[2] Thus it is equal to the left-hand side of Equation 13.1a.

Marginal revenue product

If the firm maximizes profit it sets the marginal revenue product of input x equal to the price of input x. This is the meaning of Equation 13.1a. Thus the firm's demand schedule for input x must be the marginal-revenue-product schedule in column 6 of Table 13.1. For example, suppose the the price of input x is $56. Then according to Equation 13.1a the firm will set the marginal revenue product of input x equal to $56, which means that it will demand 8

2. It is easy to prove that the marginal revenue product (*MRP*) is the product of the marginal product (*MP*) and marginal revenue (*MR*). By definition,

$$MRP = \frac{\Delta R}{\Delta I}$$

where ΔR is the change in total revenue and ΔI is the change in the quantity of the input. Since $MR = \Delta R \div \Delta Q$, where ΔQ is the change in output, it follows that

$$MRP = \frac{MR\Delta Q}{\Delta I}.$$

But since $MP = \Delta Q \div \Delta I$, it also follows that $MRP = MR \times MP$, as we set out to prove.

units of input x. Or suppose that the price of input x is \$34. Then the firm will set the marginal revenue product of input x equal to \$34, which means that it will demand 9 units of input x. Thus the number of units of input x that the firm will demand at any price is given by the marginal-revenue-product curve, which shows the marginal revenue product of input x at various quantities of input x used. This curve is shown in Figure 13.1.

Two points should be noted concerning the marginal-revenue-product curve. First, it will slope downward and to the right (as a demand curve should for an input) for two reasons: the input's marginal product will decrease as more of it is used, and the firm's marginal revenue will decrease as its output increases. Since the marginal revenue product is the product of the input's marginal product and the firm's marginal revenue, it will decrease for both reasons as more of the input is used. Second, the value-of-marginal-product schedule in the previous chapter can be regarded as a special case of the marginal-revenue-product schedule. If marginal revenue is equal to price (as it is in perfect competition), the marginal-revenue-product schedule becomes precisely the same as the value-of-marginal-product schedule.

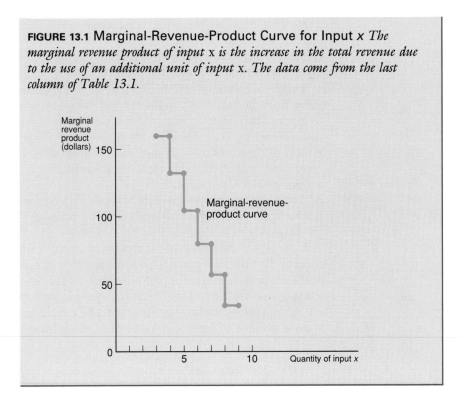

FIGURE 13.1 Marginal-Revenue-Product Curve for Input x *The marginal revenue product of input* x *is the increase in the total revenue due to the use of an additional unit of input* x. *The data come from the last column of Table 13.1.*

The Firm's Demand Curve: The Case of Several Variable Inputs

Suppose that the firm uses a number of inputs that can be varied in quantity, with input x being only one of them. As in the case of perfect competition, the firm's demand curve for input x is no longer its marginal-revenue-product curve. This is because a change in the price of input x will result in changes in

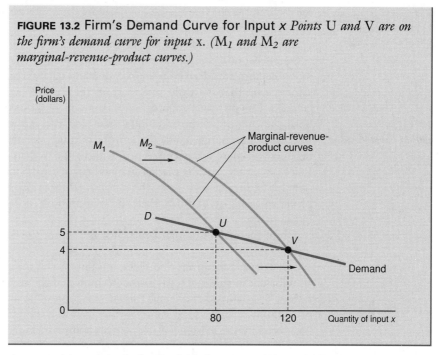

FIGURE 13.2 Firm's Demand Curve for Input x *Points* U *and* V *are on the firm's demand curve for input* x. (M$_1$ *and* M$_2$ *are marginal-revenue-product curves.)*

Firm's demand curve

the quantities used of other variable inputs, and these changes in the quantities used of other inputs will affect the quantity used of input x.

For example, suppose that the price of input x is initially $5 and that 80 units of input x are used at this price. Holding constant the use of other inputs, the marginal-revenue-product curve is assumed to be M_1 in Figure 13.2. This would be the demand curve for input x if the other inputs were not variable. Suppose that the price of input x falls to $4. Since the marginal revenue product of input x exceeds its new price, the firm will tend to increase its use of input x. But this will shift the marginal-revenue-product curves of other variable inputs, which in turn will change the amount used of them, which in turn will shift the marginal-revenue-product curve of input x.

When all of these effects have taken place, the firm will be on another marginal-revenue-product curve for input x, say M_2 in Figure 13.2. Since the amount demanded of input x will be such that the marginal revenue product of input x will equal its new price, the firm will demand 120 units. Points U and V are both on the firm's demand curve for input x. Other points can be determined in similar fashion; the complete demand curve is D.

The Market Demand Curve and Input Price

The previous sections derived the demand curve of an individual firm for an input. The next step is to combine the demand curves of the individual firms in the market (for the input) into a single market demand curve for the input. This step can be accomplished in different ways, depending on whether the firms are all monopolists or whether some are oligopolists or monopolistic competitors. If all firms are monopolists in their product markets, the market demand curve for the input would simply be the horizontal summation of the demand curves of the individual firms.

On the other hand, if some of the firms are oligopolists or monopolistic competitors, one cannot simply sum (horizontally) the demand curves of the individual firms to derive the market demand curve. This will not work for the same reason that it would not work in the case of perfect competition (discussed in the previous chapter): A change in the price of the input will affect both the output of the individual firm and the outputs of its competitors. Because of the change in its competitors' outputs, the demand curve for its own product will change, and this in turn will change its demand curve for the input. In a case of this sort, the market demand curve for the input can be determined only by finding at each price the amount of the input that will maximize the profits of each firm in the market, and by summing these amounts over all firms in the market.

Market demand curve

Given the market demand curve for the input, the equilibrium price of the input will be the price at which this demand curve intersects the input's market supply curve. Moreover, the total amount of the input that will be used in equilibrium in this market is also determined in the usual way by the intersection of this demand curve and this supply curve. The nature and determinants of an input's market supply curve, discussed in the previous chapter, need not be altered by the existence of imperfect competition in the product market.

MONOPSONY

Monopsony

Up to this point we have assumed that there is perfect competition in the input market. Now we change this assumption. We begin by considering the case of monopsony. *Monopsony* is a situation in which there is a single buyer. For example, a group of small firms may be set up to provide tooling, supplies, or materials for a single large manufacturing firm, and because this large firm is the only one of its type in the area and its requirements are highly specialized, this large firm may be the only buyer for the product of the small firms. This is a case of monopsony.

Note the difference between monopsony and monopoly: Monopsony is a case of a single buyer; monopoly is a case of a single seller. Other market situations that could also be studied are oligopsony (where there are a few buyers) and monopsonistic competition (where there are many buyers but the inputs are not homogeneous and some buyers prefer some sellers' inputs to other sellers' inputs). However, it is sufficient for present purposes to limit our attention to monopsony.

Monopsony can occur for various reasons. In some cases, a particular type of input is much more productive in one kind of use than in others. For example, some land that is rich in iron ore may be much more profitably devoted to iron mining than to any other use. Or a person with certain specialized skills may be much more profitably employed using these skills than working at other jobs. If there is only one firm that rents such land or hires such labor, the result is a monopsonistic situation.

The classic case of monopsony is the company town in which a single firm is the sole buyer of labor services. Many "mill towns" and "mining towns" have been dominated by a single firm. As long as workers are unable or unwilling to move elsewhere to work, this firm is a monopsonist. If the mobility of labor can be increased, the monopsony can be broken, at least partially. However, the difficulties in increasing the mobility of labor should not be underestimated: Workers become emotionally attached to a particular area and to their friends and family located there; they often are ignorant of opportunities elsewhere; and they sometimes lack the money and skills that are required to move.

Input Supply Curves and Marginal Expenditure Curves

The supply curve of the input facing the monopsonist is the market supply curve: This is the key feature of monopsony. The reason why the monopsonist faces the market supply curve of the input is that the monopsonist is the entire market for the input: It is the sole buyer. Since the market supply curve of an input is generally upward sloping, as we saw in the previous chapter, this means that the supply curve for the input that the monopsonist faces is upward sloping. In other words, the monopsonist is forced to increase the price of the input if it wishes to use more of it, and it can reduce the input's price if it chooses to use less of it.

The contrast between this situation and the situation under perfect competition in the input market should be noted. In the case of perfect competition in the input market, each firm buys only a very small proportion of the total supply of any input, the consequence being that each firm faces a perfectly elastic supply curve for the input. In other words, each firm can buy all it wants of an input without affecting the input's price.

The situation under monopsony is illustrated by the case in Table 13.2. Suppose that a firm is a monopsonist with respect to input x. Suppose that the market supply schedule for input x is that shown in columns 1 and 2. For example, 8 units of input x will be supplied if the price of input x is $10.00; 9 units of input x will be supplied if the price of input x is $10.50; and so forth. Column 3 shows the total cost to the firm of buying the quantities of input x in column 1. For example, the total cost of 8 units of input x is $80.00; and the

---

TABLE 13.2 Marginal Expenditure for Input x

Quantity of x	Price of x (dollars)	Total cost of x (dollars)	Marginal expenditure for x* (dollars)
8	10.00	80.00	—
9	10.50	94.50	14.50
10	11.00	110.00	15.50
11	11.50	126.50	16.50
12	12.00	144.00	17.50
13	12.50	162.50	18.50
14	13.00	182.00	19.50

*Each figure pertains to the interval between the indicated amount of input x and one unit less than the indicated amount of input x.

total cost of 9 units of input x is $94.50. Of course, column 3 is simply the product of the figures in column 1 and column 2.

Column 4 shows the additional cost to the firm of increasing its utilization of input x by one unit. This is called the *marginal expenditure* for input x. For example, the marginal expenditure for the ninth unit of input x is $14.50; and the marginal expenditure for the tenth unit of input x is $15.50. When the market supply curve for the input is upward sloping, the marginal expenditure for the input will be greater than the input price. The reason for this is simple. Suppose, for example, that the firm in Table 13.2 increases its use of input x from 8 units to 9 units. If it did not have to increase the price of input x in order to expand the supply of the input, it would have to pay only the price, $10, of another unit. But because the supply curve *is* upward sloping, the firm *will* have to increase the price of input x in order to increase the supply. *Moreover, this will mean paying all 9 units the higher price, not just paying more for the ninth unit.* Consequently, the marginal expenditure will exceed the input's price.

Figure 13.3 shows input x's supply curve, SS'. If the input is bought by a single buyer, the monopsonist's marginal expenditure curve, which shows the marginal expenditure for the input at various quantities used of the input, is EE'. Since the supply curve is upward sloping, the marginal expenditure curve lies above it.

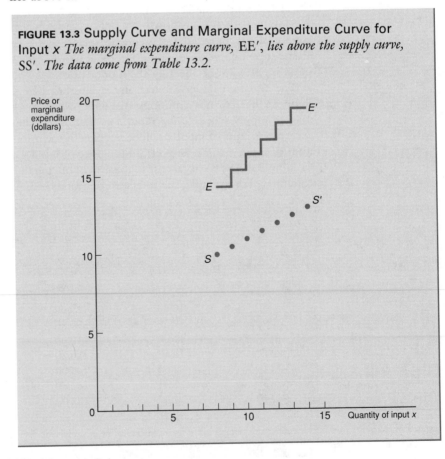

FIGURE 13.3 Supply Curve and Marginal Expenditure Curve for Input x *The marginal expenditure curve, EE', lies above the supply curve, SS'. The data come from Table 13.2.*

Suppose that there is only one variable input. If the monopsonist maximizes profit, it will purchase larger amounts of the input as long as the extra revenues derived from the additional quantity of input are at least as large as the extra cost of the additional quantity of input. When this is no longer the case, the monopsonist will no longer increase its employment of the input. Indeed, if the extra revenues derived from an additional quantity of input are less than the extra cost of the additional quantity of input, the monopsonist will cut back its employment of the input.

More specifically, consider the case in Table 13.3. Column 3 shows the marginal revenue product of the input, that is, the additional revenue derived from an additional unit of the input. For example, the addition of the sixth unit of the input results in $38 of additional revenue. Column 4 shows the marginal expenditure for the input, that is, the additional cost of an additional unit of the input. For example, the addition of the sixth unit of the input results in $15 of additional costs.

TABLE 13.3 Optimal Employment of Input x: Monopsony

Quantity of input x used by monopsonist	Price of x (dollars)	Marginal revenue product of $x*$ (dollars)	Marginal expenditure for input $x*$ (dollars)
5	9	40	—
6	10	38	15
7	11	35	17
8	12	30	19
9	13	24	21
10	14	18	23
11	15	10	25
12	16	2	27

*These figures pertain to the interval between the indicated amount of input x and one unit less than the indicated amount of input x.

Clearly, the monopsonist, if it maximizes profit, will employ additional units of the input as long as the marginal revenue product of the input exceeds the marginal expenditure. When the marginal revenue product no longer exceeds the marginal expenditure, it will stop adding further units of the input. Thus, in Table 13.3, the monopsonist will employ 9 units of the input. Also, in Figure 13.4, if the marginal-revenue-product curve is DD' and the marginal expenditure curve is EE', the firm will hire OQ units of the input.

Note the difference between the condition for profit maximization under monopsony and the condition for profit maximization when there is perfect competition in the input market. Under perfect competition in the input markets, we saw in the previous chapter and in Equation 13.1a of this chapter that the firm must set

$$MP_x \cdot MR = P_x. \qquad [13.2]$$

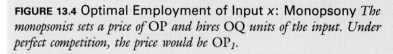

FIGURE 13.4 Optimal Employment of Input *x*: Monopsony *The monopsonist sets a price of* OP *and hires* OQ *units of the input. Under perfect competition, the price would be* OP₁.

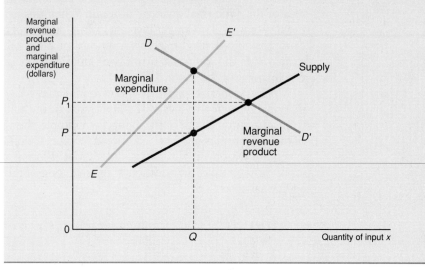

However, if the firm is a monopsonist, it must set

$$MP_x \cdot MR = ME_x \qquad\qquad [13.3]$$

where ME_x is the marginal expenditure for input *x*.

The difference between Equation 13.2 and 13.3 lies in the quantities on the right-hand side: P_x in one case and ME_x in the other. Since ME_x is greater than P_x if the input's supply curve is upward sloping (see p. 394) and since the marginal revenue product of input *x* (which equals $MP_x \cdot MR$) decreases as more of input *x* is used, it follows that less of input *x* is used if Equation 13.3 is met than if Equation 13.2 is met. Thus the monopsonist will employ less of the input than would be used if the input market were perfectly competitive.

Monopsony price   The monopsonist sets the input's price at the level at which the quantity it demands—the quantity at which marginal revenue product equals marginal expenditure—will be supplied. Thus, in Table 13.3, it sets a price of $13. And in Figure 13.4 it sets a price of *OP,* if the supply curve for input *x* is as shown there. Note that the price set by the monopsonist is lower than would be set in a competitive market for the input. For example, in Figure 13.4, if *DD'* were the demand curve for the input in a competitive market, the equilibrium price of the input would be *OP₁* rather than *OP*.

Price and Employment: Several Variable Inputs

The previous section dealt with the case where the monopsonist uses only one variable input. It is easy to generalize our results to the case in which it uses more than one variable input. For example, suppose that there are a number of variable inputs: input *x*, input *y*, . . . , input *z*. For each of these inputs, it will pay the monopsonist to increase its use of the input only as long as the extra

EXAMPLE 13.1

EFFECTS OF MINIMUM-WAGE LAWS UNDER MONOPSONY

In Example 12.4, we examined the effects of a minimum wage when a labor market is perfectly competitive. Now let's test its effects when a labor market is monopsonistic. In the absence of a minimum wage, suppose that the supply curve for labor, the marginal-revenue-product curve for labor, and the marginal expenditure curve for labor are as shown below.

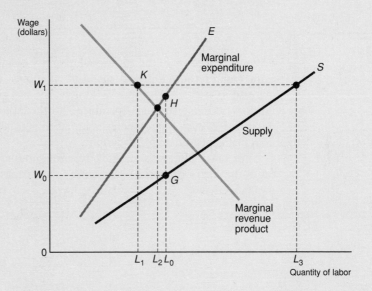

(a) If the minimum wage is set at OW_0, how much labor will the monopsonist hire? Will there be unemployment? If so, how much? (b) If the minimum wage is set at OW_1, how much labor will the monopsonist hire? Will there be unemployment? If so, how much? (c) Under monopsony, does a minimum wage reduce employment? (d) Do you think that most low-wage labor markets are monopsonistic?

SOLUTION

(a) If the minimum wage is set at OW_0, the effective supply curve of labor to the monopsonist is W_0GS. Thus the marginal expenditure curve is W_0GHE. The monopsonist will hire OL_0 units of labor, since this is the point where the marginal expenditure curve (W_0GHE) intersects the marginal-revenue-product curve. There is no unemployment perceived. (b) If the minimum wage is set at OW_1, the effective supply curve of labor to the monopsonist is W_1K. Since this effective supply curve is horizontal, it is also the marginal expenditure curve, which means that the monopsonist will hire OL_1 units of labor. Since OL_3 units of labor will be supplied at this wage, there will be ($OL_3 - OL_1$) units of labor trying to find jobs but not succeeding. (c) A minimum wage of OW_0 will increase, not decrease, employment. Without the minimum wage, employment would be OL_2; with it, employment is OL_0. However, if the minimum wage is high enough (OW_1, for example), it will reduce employment. A minimum wage of OW_1, would result in employment of OL_1, which is less than OL_2, the level of employment without a minimum wage. (d) No. One study of 1,774 labor markets found that the four largest employers employed at least half of the unskilled and semi-skilled workers in less than 4 percent of the labor markets.*

*See C. Brown, C. Gilroy, and A. Kohen, "The Effect of the Minimum Wage on Employ- ment and Unemployment," *Journal of Economic Literature*, June 1982; and F. Welch, *Mini- mum Wages: Issues and Evidence* (Washington, D.C.: American Enterprise Institute, 1978).

revenue derived from the additional quantity of input is at least as large as the extra cost of the additional quantity of input. Thus the monopsonist will increase its use of each input as long as the marginal revenue product of the input exceeds its marginal expenditure for the input. The firm will stop increasing its use of each input when the input's marginal revenue product equals the marginal expenditure for the input.

Thus, since an input's marginal revenue product equals its marginal product times the firm's marginal revenue, it follows that the monopsonist will hire inputs so that

$$MP_x \cdot MR = ME_x \qquad [13.4a]$$

$$MP_y \cdot MR = ME_y \qquad [13.4b]$$

$$\vdots$$

$$MP_z \cdot MR = ME_z \qquad [13.4c]$$

where ME_x is the marginal expenditure for input x, ME_y is the marginal expenditure for input y, and ME_z is the marginal expenditure for input z.

These equations are the basic conditions for profit maximization under monopsony. Note that Equations 13.1a $\cdots$ 13.1c can be regarded as a special case of Equations 13.4a $\cdots$ 13.4c. If the markets for the inputs are perfectly competitive, the marginal expenditure for each input is simply equal to the price of each input, since a firm can buy all it wants of each input without affecting its price. Thus Equations 13.1a $\cdots$ 13.1c are special cases of Equations 13.4a $\cdots$ 13.4c that hold under perfect competition in the input markets.

It is often stated that a monopsonist will hire inputs so that

$$\frac{MP_x}{ME_x} = \frac{MP_y}{ME_y} = \cdots = \frac{MP_z}{ME_z}. \qquad [13.5]$$

To see that Equation 13.5 follows from Equations 13.4a, 13.4b, $\cdots$, 13.4c, note that Equations 13.4a, 13.4b, $\cdots$, 13.4c imply

$$MP_x \div ME_x = \frac{1}{MR}$$

$$MP_y \div ME_y = \frac{1}{MR}$$

$$MP_z \div ME_z = \frac{1}{MR}.$$

Thus Equations 13.4a, 13.4b, . . ., 13.4c imply that Equation 13.5 is true. Note also that Equation 13.5 is equivalent to the standard condition for cost minimization under perfect competition,

$$\frac{MP_x}{P_x} = \frac{MP_y}{P_y} = \cdots = \frac{MP_z}{P_z}$$

if there is perfect competition in the input markets. This follows from the fact, noted previously, that the marginal expenditure for an input equals its price under perfect competition.

Baseball: A Case Study

Before leaving the subject of monopsony, sports fans (and others) may be interested to note that the labor market in professional baseball has had many monopsonistic characteristics. There has been a tight set of rules governing contractual arrangements between players and teams. Until the mid-1970s, once a player signed his first contract, the club could renew his contract for the following year at a price that the club could set (as long as it was not less than about 75 percent of his current salary). Another stipulation was that the team had exclusive rights to the use of the player's services. He could not play baseball for anyone else without the team's consent.

Consequently, once a player had signed his first contract in organized baseball, he was no longer able to sell his services in any way he chose. He could not move freely from one team to another. He could, of course, drop out of organized baseball and take up some other occupation. But if he stayed in organized baseball, he had to do what the team with his contract said. If the team assigned his contract to another team, the player had to work for the assignee team. No other team in organized baseball could hire him.

Given these rules, one would expect, on the basis of the analysis in the previous four sections, that baseball players would receive less than they would if the labor market for baseball players were perfectly competitive. It may seem hard to believe that baseball stars making very large salaries were being exploited—in the sense that their salaries were less than they would have received in a free labor market. But leading labor economists like Simon Rottenberg of the University of Massachusetts reached this conclusion after careful study of the market for baseball players.

According to some observers, the situation could be represented (in simplified form) by Figure 13.5, which shows the club owners' demand curve for baseball players and the supply curve for baseball players. Assuming that the club owners did not compete among themselves for players, but acted as a monopsonist, they would hire players up to the point where the marginal expenditure curve (EE') intersected the demand curve. That is, they would hire OU players and pay a wage of OX thousands of dollars per year. On the other hand, if the market for players was competitive, the club owners would hire OV

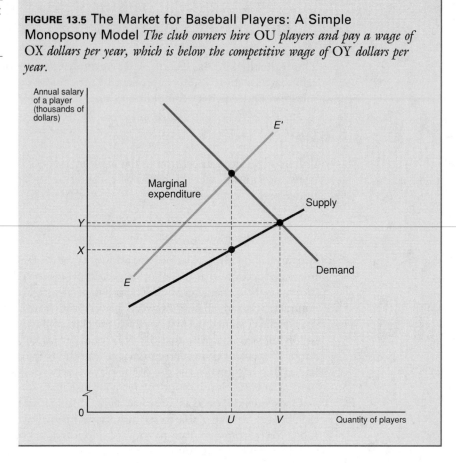

FIGURE 13.5 The Market for Baseball Players: A Simple Monopsony Model *The club owners hire* OU *players and pay a wage of* OX *dollars per year, which is below the competitive wage of* OY *dollars per year.*

players and pay a wage of *OY* thousands of dollars per year. In this highly simplified situation, it is clear that the wage was lower in the former case than in the latter.[3]

A number of reasons were given for the restrictive rules built into contracts for professional athletes. For example, it was frequently asserted that they were necessary to maintain a relatively equal distribution of playing talent among the various teams. Without these rules, it was claimed that the wealthier clubs would buy up most of the best players, with the result that games would be uneven and attendance would drop. This argument was challenged by many observers. According to Rottenberg and others, a free market for players would

3. For an early, influential study, see S. Rottenberg, "The Baseball Players' Labor Market," *Journal of Political Economy*, June 1956. Note that Figure 13.5 is highly simplified. For one thing, it assumes that the players do not band together to try to counteract the monopsony power of the club owners. In fact, the players have formed an association and have carried out strikes on occasion. For further discussion, see R. Noll and B. Okner, *The Economics of Professional Baseball* (Washington, D.C.: Brookings Institution, 1973); J. Quirk and M. El Hodiri, "Model of a Professional Sports League," *Journal of Political Economy*, December 1971; and G. Scully, "Pay and Performance in Major League Baseball," *American Economic Review*, December 1974. I am indebted to Edward D. Mansfield for sharing his extensive knowledge of this subject with me, and for doing his best to keep me from error.

produce better results: "It appears that free markets would give as good aggregate results as any other kind of market for industries, like the baseball industry, in which all firms must be nearly equal if each is to prosper. On welfare criteria, . . . the free market is superior to the others, for in such a market each worker receives the full value of his services and exploitation does not occur."[4]

In the mid-1970s, after protracted legal battles, the rules governing the hiring of baseball players were changed. Players were allowed to declare themselves free agents, and other teams were allowed to bid for their services. These and other such changes (some of which were factors in the baseball strike of 1981) meant a reduction in the monopsonistic power of the baseball clubs.[5]

LABOR UNIONS

One of the most important inputs is, of course, labor, and an important feature of the labor market is the existence of unions. About one in six nonfarm workers in the United States belongs to a union. The four largest unions are the Teamsters, the National Education Association, the Food and Commercial Workers, and the State, County, and Municipal Employees. Until the 1930s, there was strong opposition to unions, but since the passage of the Wagner Act in 1935, many manufacturing industries have become unionized. In the remainder of this chapter, we discuss briefly the ways in which unions can try to increase wages, the nature of union objectives, and the economic effects of unions.

How unions increase wages

For the moment, let us suppose that a union wants to increase the wage rate paid its members. How might it go about accomplishing this objective? First, the union might try to shift the supply curve of labor to the left. For example, it might shift the supply curve from S to S_0 in Figure 13.6, with the result that the price of labor will rise from OP to OP_0. To cause this shift in the supply curve, the union might restrict entry into the union, or it might not let nonunion workers obtain jobs, or it might restrict the labor supply in other ways.

Second, the union might try to get the employers to pay a higher wage, while allowing some of the supply of labor forthcoming at this higher wage to find no opportunity for work. For example, in Figure 13.7, the union might exert pressure on the employers to get them to raise the price of labor from OP to OP_0. At OP_0, not all of the available supply of labor can find jobs, because the quantity of labor supplied is OQ_1, while the amount of labor demanded is OQ_0. The effect is the same as in Figure 13.6, but in this case the union does not limit the supply directly: It lets the higher wage reduce the opportunity for work.

Third, the union might try to shift the demand for labor upward and to the right. For example, in Figure 13.8 it might shift the demand curve from D to

4. S. Rottenberg, ibid.

5. However, in 1989, an arbitrator awarded about $10 million to players he said were financially damaged during the 1986 season due to the owner's collusion. According to the arbitrator, "In the place of competition among the clubs the owners substituted a common understanding that no club would bid on the services of a free agent until and unless his former club no longer desired to sign that free agent." See "Collusion Award Exceeds $10 Million," *New York Times,* September 1, 1989.

FIGURE 13.6 Shift in Supply Curve for Labor *If the union shifts the supply curve from S to S₀, the price of labor will rise from OP to OP₀.*

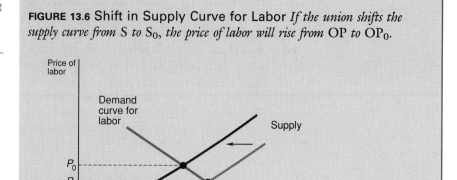

FIGURE 13.7 Increase in Price of Labor *If the union gets employers to raise the price of labor from OP to OP₀, not all of the available supply of labor will find jobs. While the quantity of labor supplied will be OQ₁, the quantity demanded will be OQ₀.*

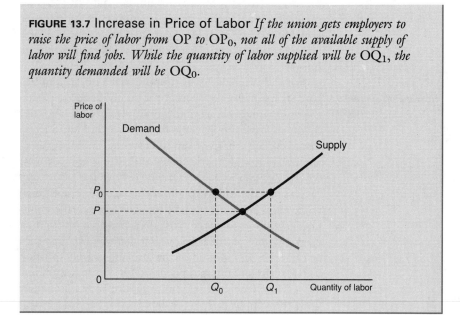

D_1, with the result that the price of labor will increase from OP to OP_1. To cause this shift in the demand curve for labor, the union might help the employers advertise their products; it might help them to be more efficient and better able to compete against other industries; or it might try to get Congress to pass legislation to protect the employers from foreign competition. Also, it might try to force employers to hire more workers than are needed for particular jobs.

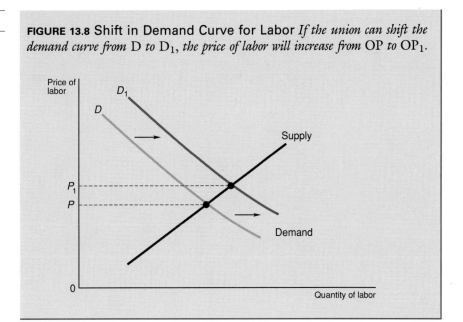

FIGURE 13.8 Shift in Demand Curve for Labor *If the union can shift the demand curve from* D *to* D_1, *the price of labor will increase from* OP *to* OP_1.

The Nature of Union Objectives

Possible union objectives

What are the objectives of unions? This is a difficult matter to settle, since unions, like firms, have diverse goals that are not easy to encapsulate and measure. Indeed, the problem is even more difficult for unions than for firms, because there is less agreement that any relatively simple objective like profits is a reasonable first approximation. Nevertheless, it is worthwhile discussing the implications of some simple hypotheses concerning union motivation that have been put forth. Three possible union objectives that are often considered are: (1) The union wants to keep its members fully employed; (2) the union wants to maximize the aggregate income of its members; and (3) the union wants to maximize the wage rate subject to the condition that a certain minimum number of its members be employed. All three hypotheses concerning union motivation have a certain amount of plausibility. It is easy to show, however, that they lead to quite different conclusions regarding union behavior.

Suppose that the demand curve for labor that faces the union is as shown in Figure 13.9. If the union has objective 1 and if it contains OM_1 members, it will have to accept a wage of OP_1, since this is the highest wage that will enable all of its members to find work.

But suppose that it has objective 2. Then it will choose OP_2, since this is the wage that maximizes the total wage bill of the union. To prove this, note that the wage bill is the union's total revenue from its product, labor; and that consequently the wage bill is maximized when the union's marginal revenue is zero. Since the union's marginal revenue curve is RR^1, and since this marginal revenue curve intersects the horizontal axis at OM_2, the union's wage bill is maximized when OM_2 workers are employed, which means that the wage must

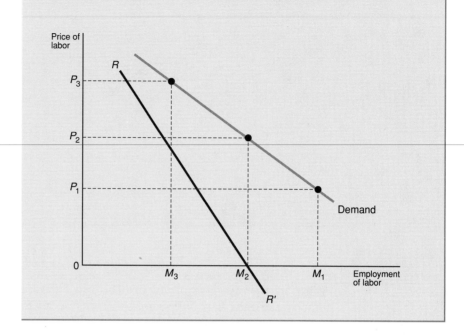

FIGURE 13.9 Three Types of Union Behavior *If the union wants to keep its members fully employed, it will have to accept a wage of* OP_1. *If it wants to maximize the aggregate income of its members, it will choose* OP_2. *If it wants the employment level to equal* OM_3, *it will choose* OP_3.

be OP_2. Note that, if the union has objective 2, it must be prepared to see a great many of its members out of work.[6]

On the other hand, suppose that the union has objective 3. Specifically, suppose that it wants to maximize the wage rate subject to the condition that OM_3 of its members are employed, these members being perhaps those with considerable seniority. If this is its objective, it will choose a wage of OP_3, since this is the highest wage at which the employment level is at least OM_3.

It is clear that the wage desired by the union—and the supply of labor—will vary considerably, depending on which of these objectives is pursued. After all, OP_1, OP_2, and OP_3 are quite different wage levels, and OM_1, OM_2, and OM_3 are quite different labor supplies. Moreover, it is also perfectly clear that the three objectives stated above are only three possibilities out of a very large number. For example, the union leadership obviously has as one objective the maintenance of its own position in the union.

6. And there is the difficult question of which members should be unemployed and which members should work.

EXAMPLE 13.2

ECONOMIC EFFECTS OF UNIONS

Suppose that the economy can be divided into a unionized sector and a nonunion sector. The demand curve for labor in the union sector is D_u, the demand curve for labor in the nonunion sector is D_n, and the demand curve for labor in both sectors combined is D_c. The supply curve for labor in the economy as a whole is shown below.

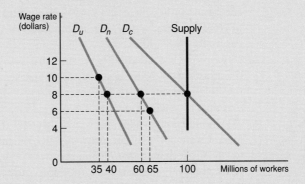

(a) Before the entry of the union, what will be the wage rate? (b) If the union raises the wage rate to $10 in the unionized sector, how many workers will the union sector lay off? (c) If all of these workers get jobs in the nonunion sector, what will be the effect on the wage rate in the nonunion sector? (d) Unions sometimes engage in featherbedding, which requires employers to hire more workers than they would otherwise. For example, railroads often have been required to hire more operating employees per train than they deemed necessary (or profitable). In the short run, such practices often increase the employment of union members. Does this effect persist in the long run as well?

SOLUTION

(a) $8, since this is where the combined curve, D_c, intersects the supply curve. (b) Its employment will fall from 40 million to 35 million, so 5 million will be laid off. (c) The wage rate in the nonunion sector will have to fall to $6 if an additional 5 million workers are to be hired there. (d) In the long run, the effect is unpredictable since the increase in the labor costs may accelerate types of substitution that the union cannot block. For example, new technologies utilizing fewer or other types of labor may be developed more quickly, or the product (made more expensive by featherbedding) may lose some of its markets to competing products or to imports.*

*For further discussion, see A. Rees, *The Economics of Work and Pay,* 2d ed. (New York: Harper & Row, 1979).

Summary

1. If there is imperfect competition in product markets but perfect competition in the market for an input, a firm will use an input in such a way that the marginal revenue product of the input equals the price of the input. Thus, if there is only one variable input, the firm's demand curve for the input is the same as the marginal-revenue-product curve. If there are several variable inputs, the firm's demand curve for an input is no longer the same as the marginal-revenue-product curve, since a change in the price of one input will result in changes in the quantity used of other inputs.

2. The market demand curve for an input can be derived by finding at each price the amount of the input that will maximize the profits of each firm in the market, and by summing these amounts over all firms in the market. The equilibrium price of the input is given by the intersection of the market demand and supply curves for the input.

3. Monopsony is a situation in which there is a single buyer. The supply curve of the input facing the monopsonist is the market supply curve. If the monopsonist maximizes profit, it sets the marginal expenditure for the input equal to the marginal revenue product of the input.

4. The monopsonist will employ less of the input than would be used if the input market were perfectly competitive. Also, the monopsonist will set a lower price for the input than if the input market were perfectly competitive. The market for baseball players has had some monopsonistic aspects.

5. An important feature of the market for labor is the existence of labor unions. To some extent, unions can be viewed as labor monopolies. However, it is difficult to know what the objectives of the union are. Under certain circumstances the union might want to keep its members fully employed. Under other circumstances, a union might want to maximize the aggregate income of its members. And these two objectives are only two possibilities out of a very large number.

Questions/Problems

1. Studies by John Landon and Robert Baird indicate that, when other factors are held equal, the level of teachers' salaries in a school district depends on the number of other school districts in the county containing the district in question. (a) If there are a relatively large number of other districts in the county containing a particular school district, would you expect the salary level of teachers in this district to be relatively high or relatively low? Why? (b) Suppose that teachers could move costlessly to school districts outside the county. Would this influence your answer to question (a)? (c) In recent years, there has been a tendency for large metropolitan school districts to decentralize into a number of autonomous districts, each of which makes its own hiring and firing decisions. What effect, if any, do you think that such decentralization will have on teachers' salaries? (d) What are some of the arguments put forth by those who favor such decentralization?

2. An input is said to be "exploited" when it receives less than the value of its marginal product. Is labor exploited under (a) perfect competition, (b) unions, (c) monopsony?

3. A firm's demand curve for its product is given in the table on the next page:

Output	Price of good (dollars)
23	5.00
32	4.00
40	3.50
47	3.00
53	2.00

Also, suppose that the marginal product and total product of labor (the only variable input) is

Amount of labor	Marginal product of labor	Total output
2	10	23
3	9	32
4	8	40
5	7	47
6	6	53

(Note that the figures regarding marginal product pertain to the interval between the indicated amount of labor and one unit less than the indicated amount of labor.) Given these data, how much labor should the firm employ if labor costs $12 a unit?

4. According to Albert Rees, there is evidence that agreements sometimes exist "among employers not to raise wages individually or not to hire away each other's employees . . . . Except in the unusual case of professional sports, however, these agreements must be very difficult to enforce." Using the concepts presented in this chapter, analyze the effects on wages and employment of such agreements. Also, indicate some of the reasons why they may be difficult to enforce.

5. Suppose that the market supply schedule for input Y is as follows:

Quantity of Y	Price of Y (dollars)
10	1
11	2
12	3

Plot the marginal expenditure curve for Y in the relevant range. (Assume that input Y must be used in integer amounts.)

6. If the market supply curve for an input is a horizontal line, will the marginal expenditure curve for this input differ from the market supply curve? Explain.

7. A craft union is formed, which forces employers to hire only union members. The union membership is restricted by high initiation fees and a variety of other devices. What are the effects on the demand curve, supply curve, and price of labor?

8. What would be the effect of a union on a monopsonistic labor market? Would it necessarily lead to unemployment?

9. According to Allan Carter and F. Ray Marshall, former President Carter's Secretary of Labor, the impact of unionism on wage levels of organized workers is most noticeable during periods of recession. Why?

10. Several hundred colleges and universities belong to the National Collegiate Athletic Association (NCAA), which investigates and enforces the rules pertaining to over twenty sports. The NCAA rules prohibit bidding for college athletes in an open manner, and the NCAA regulates the number of student athletes, as well as the prices, wages, and conditions under which colleges can hire them. Is the NCAA a monopsonist? Why or why not? Do colleges tend to cheat on the NCAA rules? If so, how?

11. The Davis-Bacon Act, passed by Congress during the Great Depression of the 1930s, has required that an area's "prevailing wage" be paid to workers on construction projects receiving some federal funding. The original purpose of this law was to make sure that northern contractors could not import relatively cheap southern workers unless they were willing to pay them the relatively high wage received by northerners. More recently, the Department of Labor has had the task of specifying what the "prevailing wage" is in a particular area. According to many studies, the department often specifies that it is the union wage, even in areas where the bulk of the workers do not belong to unions. Many observers have criticized this law; indeed, the U.S. General Accounting Office recommended its repeal. Suppose that you are an adviser to a U.S. senator who asks you to indicate the economic effects of this law and why it has been criticized. What answer would you give?

SEX DISCRIMINATION AND COMPARABLE WORTH

Most adult American women (two-thirds of those between the ages of 25 and 54) work outside the home. One reason why more women enter the labor force today than in the early twentieth century (when only about 20 percent of adult American women worked outside the home) is that household management requires less time than it did then. Technological advances have resulted in a variety of labor-saving devices in the home. In addition, the decline in the birth rate has provided women with more time for work, while the demand for women's services has increased as physical strength has become less important in many jobs and the service sectors of the economy have grown. Also, prevailing attitudes toward the proper role of women have changed.

Despite the tremendous growth in the participation of women in the labor force, women's earnings tend to be considerably lower than men's. Among workers between the ages of 20 and 24, the percentage gap in earnings averages about 15 percent; among workers between 45 and 54, it averages about 40 percent. This pay differential can be attributed to many factors. For example, as pointed out by the Council of Economic Advisers, the "average employed man has more work experience, fewer interruptions in that work experience, and longer tenure with his current employer than does his female counterpart of a comparable age."[1] Econometric evidence suggests that these factors explain some but not all of the earnings gap. It is not always clear which way the causality runs, either; to some extent, low earnings may encourage interrupted work lives, since the opportunity cost of leaving the work force is low.

Although Congress has passed laws, such as the Equal Pay Act of 1964, that prohibit discrimination against women, many observers believe that this pay differential is due partly to discrimination. If there were only one employer of a particular type of labor, it is easy to see how discrimination of this sort might occur. Even if men and women are equally productive, this monopsonist can increase its profits if it separates the labor supply into two groups—men and women—and if it pays different wages to each group. To see this, recall from

---

1. *Economic Report of the President* (Washington, D.C.: U.S. Government Printing Office, 1987), p. 220.

Equation 13.4 that a monopsonist will maximize profit by setting each input's marginal revenue product equal to the marginal expenditure on the input. Suppose that, as shown in Figure 1, the supply curve for labor is less elastic for women than for men because women have fewer opportunities other than this type of work. Thus the marginal expenditure curves are E_M for men and E_W for women. If the marginal revenue product of both men and women equals OX, the wage will be OP_M for men and OP_W for women. Clearly, men are paid more than women even though their marginal revenue product is the same.

But this model assumes that labor markets are monopsonies, which, as pointed out in Example 13.1, is seldom the case. If labor markets are competitive and if men and women are hired for the same jobs, there are limitations on the extent to which firms can discriminate. Suppose, for example, that male lawyers earn $70,000 and (equally talented and productive) female lawyers earn $60,000. Under these circumstances, an employer can make $10,000 (that is, $70,000 − $60,000) by hiring a female lawyer rather than a male. As more and more employers respond in this way to the profit motive, the wage of female lawyers will be bid up and the wage of male lawyers will decline until the wage differential between them tends to disappear.

However, it is important to recognize that discrimination of this sort can be due to the preferences of consumers, not employers. For example, the clients of some law firms may not trust female lawyers as much as males. Also, other employees of law firms (including male lawyers) may prefer not to work with female lawyers. If prejudice and discriminatory attitudes are sufficiently widespread, and if people are willing to absorb significant costs rather than change

FIGURE 1 Sex Discrimination under Monopsony *The monopsonist pays women a lower wage (OP_W) than men (OP_M).*

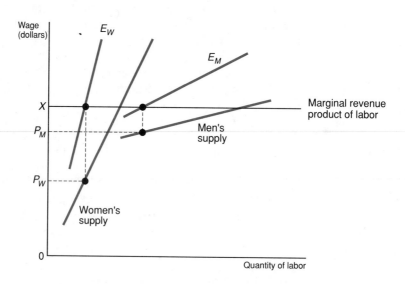

their attitudes, women will be paid less than men, even for equivalent performance.

A striking fact about female employment is that women tend to be found in a relatively small cluster of occupations. In recent years, women have constituted about 94 percent of registered nurses, 98 percent of secretaries, and 85 percent of waiters and waitresses in the United States. Some believe that these jobs are underpaid because they tend to be filled by women, and to eliminate what they regard as a major inequity, they argue for "equal pay for work of comparable worth." The idea is to compare the worth of one occupation with that of another occupation, and to press for equal wage rates for them if they are judged to be of equal worth. Thus, if a nurse does work that is of equal worth to that of a stevedore, nurses should get the same wage as stevedores.

How do the proponents of "comparable worth" propose to measure the worth of an occupation? A common answer is to use a job evaluation point system. In 1983, a federal court found the state of Washington guilty of discrimination because it paid male-dominated occupations more than "comparable" female-dominated occupations. To determine what occupations were comparable, every state job was evaluated in terms of "accountability," "knowledge and skills," "mental demands," and "working conditions." A committee decided how many points to give each occupation on each of these criteria, and two occupations were regarded of comparable worth if they got the same total number of points.

This decision by the federal court, which said that Washington should raise women's wages and grant restitution for past injuries to them (cost to the state: $800 million), has caused a great deal of controversy. So has the law enacted in Ontario, Canada, in 1989 which says that employers with more than 10 workers must assess jobs in which at least 60 percent of the employees are women and use such a job evaluation system to determine how much women should be paid. In the York (Ontario) Region Board of Education, this has meant that the wage rate for switchboard receptionists has had to be raised to equal that of grasscutters, since these jobs have been determined to be comparable. (See Table 1.)

TABLE 1 Three Pairs of Jobs Determined to Be of Comparable Worth, York Region Board of Education, Ontario, Canada, 1989

Pairs of jobs of comparable worth	Hourly wage rates (prior to Ontario Pay Equity Act)
Switchboard receptionist (generally female)	$ 9.26
Grasscutter (generally male)	10.84
Health assistant (generally female)	11.66
Maintenance person (generally male)	12.66
Head secretary (generally female)	11.33
Maintenance foreman (generally male)	15.11

Many economists have criticized the idea that an occupation's wage rate should be determined in this way by "comparable worth." For example, Rutgers' Mark Killingsworth is reported to have said that "The solution is worse than the disease."[2] Nonetheless, this idea has not gone away. Although higher courts reversed the Washington decision described above, a considerable number of states have implemented policies based on "comparable worth," and leading politicians have espoused the idea. Whether or not this concept should be employed more widely in the public and private sectors of the economy is a lively issue.

Analytical Questions

1. How can one determine how many points to give a particular occupation with regard to "mental demands"? Are the four criteria given above the only ones that could be used? How can one determine the proper weights to apply to various criteria? Is a point system of this sort largely arbitrary?

2. According to the point system described above, the value of each occupation can be determined from its characteristics alone. But the marginal revenue product of workers in a particular occupation decreases as more and more of them are hired. Can one legitimately determine the value of an occupation to society without specifying how many people are in this occupation?

3. Suppose that the doctrine of "comparable worth" is accepted by Boston's municipal government and that a study concludes that the value of a typist's job is comparable to that of an electrician, the result being that the wage of typists is raised from $8 to $12 an hour. Will this result in more and better applicants for the city's typing jobs?

4. If skilled typists not working for Boston's municipal government can displace the typists currently working there, is such a displacement likely to occur (under the conditions described in Question 3)? Will the increase in the wage rate be of benefit to the typists currently working there in the short run? In the long run?

5. The doctrine of comparable worth has received more serious attention and has been put into effect more often in government agencies than in business firms. (A majority of state governments have studied the idea, and some have begun to apply it.) Why would such a scheme be more likely to encounter resistance among firms than government agencies?

6. Is adoption of the idea of "comparable worth" the only way that women can improve their access to high-paid jobs? If not, what are some other important ways? According to Chicago's Gary Becker, "Changes in the earnings and occupations of women in this country are much more closely related to changes in their productivity than to government action."[3] Do you agree?

2. "Wage Gap Between Sexes Is Cut in Test, but at a Price," *New York Times*, May 31, 1990.

3. *Business Week*, April 27, 1987, p. 18.

PART SIX

GENERAL EQUILIBRIUM, ECONOMIC EFFICIENCY, EXTERNALITIES, AND PUBLIC GOODS

14

GENERAL EQUILIBRIUM ANALYSIS AND RESOURCE ALLOCATION

INTRODUCTION

At the beginning of this book we said that microeconomics is concerned with the economic behavior of individual decision-making units like consumers, resource owners, and firms. At first glance one might interpret this statement to mean that microeconomics views the behavior of such individual units and the workings of individual markets in isolation, with each unit or market being considered separately. Such an interpretation would be quite wrong. Microeconomics is also concerned in an important way with how these units and these markets fit together. Indeed, some of the intellectually most exciting, and practically most significant, aspects of microeconomics deal with the interrelations among individual units and among various markets.

In previous chapters we looked in detail at the behavior of individual decision-making units and the workings of individual markets. Our approach has been like that of a movie-maker who, sitting with a camera in a helicopter, depicts a battle by zooming in to get a close-up picture of what the infantry is doing, then by zooming in to get a picture of what the artillery is doing, then by zooming in to get a picture of what the commanding generals are doing, and so on. After taking these pictures, the movie-maker has the problem, of course, of showing how the pieces fit together.

At this point, we face the same kind of problem. We, like the movie-maker, have zoomed in to study the behavior of people acting as consumers; then we have zoomed in to study the behavior of people acting as managers and as workers. And we have zoomed in to look at the workings of various kinds of markets, each considered separately. Now we must show how economists have attempted to form an integrated model of the economy as a whole. This clearly is an important task: Every schoolchild knows that it is important not to get so engrossed in the trees that one loses sight of the forest.

In this chapter, we provide a brief introduction to general equilibrium analysis, the branch of microeconomics that deals with the interrelations among various decision-making units and various markets. After defining general equilibrium analysis, we see whether we can be reasonably sure that a state of general equilibrium can exist in a perfectly competitive economy. Then we build a simple general equilibrium model and take up some questions concerning the efficient allocation of resources.

PARTIAL EQUILIBRIUM ANALYSIS VERSUS GENERAL EQUILIBRIUM ANALYSIS

As stressed in the last section, our analysis in previous chapters has focused on a single market, viewed in isolation. According to the models we have used, the price and quantity in each such market are determined by supply and demand curves, and these supply and demand curves are drawn on the assumption that other prices are given. Each market is regarded as independent and self-contained for all practical purposes. In particular, it is assumed that changes in price in this market do not have significant repercussions on the prices existing in other markets.

But this assumption in reality may be seriously wrong. No market can adjust to a change in conditions without there being a change in other markets, and in some cases the change in other markets may be substantial. For example, suppose that a shift to the left occurs in the demand for pork. In previous chapters, it was assumed that when the price and output of pork changed in response to this change in conditions, the prices of other products would remain fixed. However, the market for pork is not sealed off from the markets for lamb, beef, and other meats.[1] (For that matter, it is not completely sealed off from the markets for other food products or from the markets for other less similar products, like washing machines and autos.) Thus the market for pork cannot adjust without disturbing the equilibrium of other markets *and without having these disturbances feed back on itself.*

Partial equilibrium analysis

General equilibrium analysis

An analysis that assumes that changes in price can occur without causing significant changes in price in other markets is called a *partial equilibrium analysis.* This is the kind of analysis we carried out in previous chapters. An analysis that takes account of the interrelationships among prices is called a *general equilibrium analysis.* Both kinds of analysis are very useful, each being valuable in its own way. Partial equilibrium analysis is perfectly adequate in cases in

1. Quantitative evidence on this point was presented in Table 5.4, where the cross elasticity of demand for beef with respect to the price of pork was given.

which the effect of a change in market conditions in one market has *little* reper-
cussion on prices in other markets. For example, in studying the effects of a
proposed excise tax on the production of a certain commodity, the assumption
that prices of other commodities are fixed may be a good approximation to the
truth. However, if the effects of a change in market conditions in one market
result in *important* repercussions on other prices, a general equilibrium analysis
may be required.

THE NATURE AND EXISTENCE OF GENERAL EQUILIBRIUM

General equilibrium analysis, like partial equilibrium analysis, can be used to
solve problems of many kinds. One of the most fundamental problems that
general equilibrium analysis has been used to help solve is as follows: If we
could somehow establish a perfectly competitive economy, would it be possible
for equilibrium to occur simultaneously in all markets? That is, does a set of
prices exist such that all of the markets would be in equilibrium simultaneously?

General equilibrium   Approaching this problem somewhat differently, let us define a state of *general equilibrium* as a state of the economy in which the following conditions
hold: (1) Every consumer chooses his or her preferred market basket subject to
his or her budget line, which is determined by the prices of inputs and the prices
of products; (2) every consumer supplies whatever amount of inputs he or she
chooses, given the input and product prices that prevail; (3) every firm maximizes its profits subject to the constraints imposed by the available technology,
the demand for its product, and the supply of inputs; but in the long run profits
are zero; and (4) the quantity demanded equals the quantity supplied at the
prevailing prices in all product and input markets.

Given this definition of a state of general equilibrium, the problem is: Can
we be sure that a state of general equilibrium can be achieved? It is evident from
the definition of general equilibrium that a great many conditions must be
satisfied simultaneously if a state of general equilibrium is to be achieved. Can
we be sure that all of these conditions can always be satisfied at the same time?
Or can they all be satisfied only under certain conditions? And if so, what are
these conditions? This is an important question that has received considerable
attention from economic theorists.

The Conditions for the Existence of General Equilibrium

Work by Nobel laureates Kenneth Arrow and Gerard Debreu, as well as Lionel
McKenzie and others, has established that in a perfectly competitive economy a
general equilibrium can be achieved under a fairly wide set of conditions. As
Robert Kuenne has put it,

> Judged . . . against the characteristics of our abstract economic models [of
> consumption and production], the pragmatic assertion of a faith that our
> data would need to be constrained in wholly acceptable ways to guarantee

No unique equilibrium

a solution under all allowable conditions of their initial values seems to be well justified on the whole.[2]

But are the prices and outputs that make up a general equilibrium unique? That is, is there only one set of prices and outputs at which supply equals demand in all markets? Clearly the answer is no. Only relative prices affect the decisions of consumers, firms, and resource owners. Thus, if all markets are in equilibrium at one set of prices, they will also be in equilibrium if all prices are increased or decreased in the same proportion. Whether there is more than one set of *relative* prices that can result in equilibrium is a more difficult question that is taken up in advanced texts but is beyond the scope of this book.

It is important to know that general equilibrium can be achieved under a wide set of conditions in a perfectly competitive economy. As we shall see in the next chapter, economists have concluded that, under certain circumstances, a perfectly competitive economy has a variety of desirable characteristics; for this reason, a perfectly competitive economy is sometimes held up as an ideal. For those who put forth this view, it would be embarrassing to find that this kind of economy is based on behavioral assumptions and market mechanisms that are incompatible in the sense that general equilibrium cannot be achieved. Fortunately, no such embarrassment is necessary.

A SIMPLE MODEL OF GENERAL EQUILIBRIUM

In the next three sections, we present in somewhat more detail a simple general-equilibrium model of the economy. This model shows more completely the nature of general equilibrium in a perfectly competitive economy. The nature of the analysis being such that it is necessary for the reader to be familiar with the idea of, and notation for, a set of equations, readers who do not have this familiarity can skip to p. 422 without losing the thread of the argument.

For simplicity, we assume in this model that the economy is composed of two sectors, a business sector and a consumer sector. A diagram describing the flows of income, payments, products, and services in such an economy is shown in Figure 14.1. Note that there is no government sector or foreign sector. Although they could be added, the essential features of general equilibrium can be described without them. We assume that all production is done by firms (not consumers) and that all inputs come from consumers (not firms). This means that there are no intermediate goods—goods made by one firm to be used by another firm.

2. R. Kuenne, *The Theory of General Economic Equilibrium* (Princeton, N.J.: Princeton University Press, 1963), p. 566. Also see K. Arrow and G. Debreu, "Existence of an Equilibrium for a Competitive Economy," *Econometrica*, July 1954; G. Debreu, *Theory of Value* (New York: Wiley, 1959); L. McKenzie, "On the Existence of General Equilibrium for a Competitive Market," *Econometrica*, January 1959; J. Quirk and R. Saposnik, *Introduction to General Equilibrium Theory and Welfare Economics* (New York: McGraw-Hill, 1968); and K. Arrow and F. Hahn, *General Competitive Analysis* (San Francisco: Holden-Day, 1971).

To be more specific, Arrow and Debreu show that a general equilibrium exists if increasing returns to scale exist for no firm, at least one primary input must be used to produce each commodity, the quantity of a primary input supplied by a consumer must not be greater than his or her initial stock of the input, each consumer can supply all primary inputs, each consumer's ordinal utility function is continuous, his or her wants cannot be satiated, and his or her indifference curves are convex. Of course, these conditions are sufficient but not necessary.

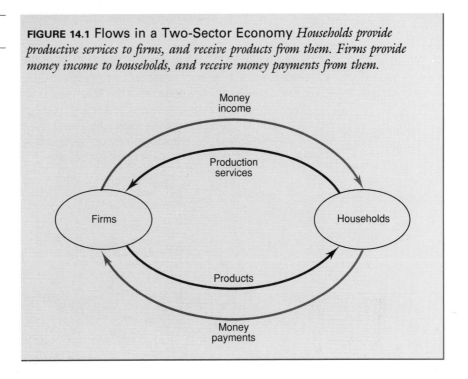

FIGURE 14.1 Flows in a Two-Sector Economy *Households provide productive services to firms, and receive products from them. Firms provide money income to households, and receive money payments from them.*

In addition, we assume that consumers obtain their incomes only from the sale of inputs to firms, and that this income is spent entirely on the products of these firms. Moreover, we assume that the amount of inputs supplied by each consumer is fixed and independent of the level of input prices. This assumption is made because it simplifies the analysis, not because of necessity or realism; it can easily be relaxed in more advanced treatments of this topic. Finally, we also assume that there are fixed coefficients of production. This assumption too can easily be relaxed.

When this simple two-sector model is in equilibrium, the total flow of money income from firms to households is equal to the flow of payments from households to firms. We shall be concerned here with the characteristics of this simple economy in equilibrium, not with the path by which it moves from one equilibrium to another. Let the economy consist of A consumers, C consumer products, and D types of inputs. Thus, if there are 2 million consumers, 500 consumer products, and 1,000 types of inputs, A equals 2 million, C equals 500, and D equals 1,000. We assume that all markets are perfectly competitive.

Equations of the Model

There are three kinds of equations in this simple model of general equilibrium. First, there are equations representing the demand by consumers for commodities. Let r_{ca} be the amount of the cth commodity demanded by the ath consumer. We know from Chapter 5 that r_{ca} will depend on the prices of all commodities and on the tastes of the ath consumer. Also, r_{ca} will depend on the

EXAMPLE 14.1

THE DEREGULATION OF RAILROADS AND TRUCKS

During the 1980s, steps were taken toward the deregulation of both the railroad and trucking industries. In 1981, Ann Friedlander and Richard Spady of Massachusetts Institute of Technology published a study attempting to forecast the effects of the deregulation of both industries. Before deregulation, they found that the demand curve for rail services for bulk commodities in the South and West was as shown below.

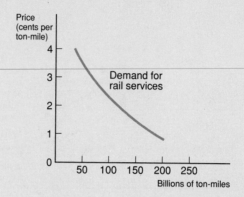

(a) If deregulation would result in a cut in the price of rail service from 2 cents to 1 cent per ton-mile, what would be the effect on the number of ton-miles carried by the railroads in the South and West, based on the above graph? (b) Could the market for rail service adjust to deregulation without disturbing the equilibrium in the market for trucking service? (c) Would the disturbances in the market for trucking service (due to railroad deregulation of this sort) have an impact on the market for rail services? (d) In trying to estimate the effects on each industry of the simultaneous deregulation of them both, what were the advantages of general equilibrium analysis over partial equilibrium analysis? (e) Friedlander and Spady estimated that, when all the reverberations of deregulation from one market to the other (and vice versa) had worked themselves out, the prices of some (but by no means all) types of rail service were likely to rise. Did this mean that deregulation would not be a success?

SOLUTION

(a) The number of ton-miles carried by the railroads would increase from about 120 billion to about 180 billion. (b) No. The lower price of railroad services would push the demand curve for trucking services to the left since railroad and trucking services were substitutes. Consequently, the price of trucking services was likely to fall. (c) Yes. The fall in the price of trucking services described in the answer to part (b) was likely to shift the demand curve for railroad services to the left, thus causing a change in the price and quantity of rail service. (d) Since the demand for rail service depended on the

price of truck service, a change in the price of truck service due to deregulation would have an effect on the demand curve for rail service. Similarly, the demand for truck service depended on the price of rail service. Further, each industry's costs depended on the way in which traffic was divided between them. When both the prices of rail service and of truck service changed due to deregulation, it was very hazardous to carry out a partial equilibrium analysis of either the market for rail service or the market for truck service, since such an analysis would disregard many of the interdependencies between the two markets. In fact, Friedlander and Spady carried out a general equilibrium analysis. (e) No. In these cases, the price before deregulation was below marginal cost, which meant that railroads were losing money on these services. The test of the success of deregulation was whether economic efficiency and equity were promoted, not the direction in which particular prices moved.*

*See A. Friedlander and R. Spady, *Freight Transport Regulation* (Cambridge, Mass.: MIT Press, 1981).

prices of all of the inputs, since they (together with the amount of each input supplied by the consumer) determine the consumer's income. Thus there are AC equations of the form

$$r_{ca} = r_{ca}(p_1, \cdots, p_C, W_1, \cdots, W_D) \qquad \begin{array}{l} (c = 1 \cdots C) \\ (a = 1 \cdots A) \end{array} \qquad [14.1]$$

where p_c is the price of the cth commodity, and W_d is the price of the dth input. The consumer's tastes (and his or her supply of inputs) determine the functional form of each of these equations.

Letting R_c be the total quantity demanded by consumers of the cth commodity, it is obvious that

$$R_c = r_{c1} + r_{c2} + \cdots + r_{cA} \qquad (c = 1 \cdots C). \qquad [14.2]$$

Consequently, it follows from the equations in (14.1) that

$$R_c = R_c(p_1, \cdots, p_C, W_1, \cdots, W_D) \qquad (c = 1 \cdots C). \qquad [14.3]$$

In other words, the total quantity demanded of each commodity depends on all commodity and input prices, with the form of the relationship differing from commodity to commodity.

Second, there are equations that insure that the total amount of each input employed by firms is equal to the total amount of the input supplied by consumers. That is, firms cannot use more inputs than are supplied, and there is no unemployment of inputs. If u_{cd} is the amount of the dth type of input used to produce one unit of the cth consumer good, this means that

$$X_d = u_{1d}R_1 + u_{2d}R_2 + \cdots + u_{Cd}R_C \qquad (d = 1 \cdots D) \qquad [14.4]$$

where X_d is the total amount of the dth type of input supplied by consumers.

Third, there are equations that insure that the long-run conditions of perfect competition are met, with neither profit nor loss in the production of each commodity. In other words, price must equal average cost for each commodity. And since there are fixed coefficients of production, the average cost of producing the cth commodity is

$$A_c = u_{c1}W_1 + u_{c2}W_2 + \cdots + u_{cD}W_D \qquad (c = 1 \cdots C) \qquad [14.5]$$

where W_1 is the price of the first input, W_2 is the price of the second input, and so on. Consequently, if the price of the cth commodity equals its average cost,

$$p_c = u_{c1}W_1 + u_{c2}W_2 + \cdots + u_{cD}W_D \qquad (c = 1 \cdots C). \qquad [14.6]$$

Existence of a Solution

We have constructed a simple general equilibrium model composed of equations in 14.3, 14.4, and 14.6.[3] However, the fact that we have written down these equations does not insure that a solution exists. In other words, it does not insure that at least one consistent and feasible set of numbers can be assigned to all the variables so that all these equations are satisfied. One step in telling whether a solution exists is to compare the number of equations in the model with the number of variables to be determined. Table 14.1 shows the number of equations in the model and the number of variables to be determined. Note that the number of equations in 14.4 is given as $(D - 1)$, rather than D. This is because one of the equations in 14.4 is not independent. If all

TABLE 14.1 Number of Equations versus Number of Variables

Equations		Variables	
Equation	Number	Variable	Number
14.3	C	R_c	C
14.4	$D - 1$	W_d	D
14.6	C	p_c	C

3. This is an extremely simple model. For more complete accounts of general equilibrium analysis, see R. G. D. Allen, *Mathematical Economics;* and J. Quirk and R. Saposnik, *Introduction to General Equilibrium Theory and Welfare Economics;* as well as R. Kuenne, *The Theory of General Economic Equilibrium.*

the other equations in the model hold, it can be shown that this equation must hold too. Thus there are only $(D - 1)$ independent equations in 14.4.[4]

Table 14.1 shows that the number of equations is one less than the number of variables. This means that the model cannot determine values for each of the variables to be determined. The situation is similar to having one equation and two variables to be determined: Although only certain pairs of numbers can be solutions, there is no single solution. However, we can obtain a solution if we take the price of one commodity or input as being given: If we arbitrarily select one commodity or input as the *numeraire* and assign this commodity or input a price of 1, we have an exactly determined system. This is just like setting one variable equal to 1 and solving for the other variable in a case where there are two variables and one equation. In effect, the prices of all commodities and inputs are expressed in terms of the price of the numeraire. For example, if $p_3 = 3$, this means that the price of the third commodity is 3 times the price of the numeraire.

Numeraire

We stated above that one step in telling whether a solution exists is to compare the number of equations in the model with the number of variables to be determined. However, for reasons that are too technical to concern us here, the equality of the number of variables and the number of equations does not always guarantee that a solution exists. Whether or not it does depends on the functional form of the equations; and whether the solution is economically meaningful depends on the solution's satisfying various nonnegativity constraints.[5] But as we saw earlier in this chapter, it can be shown that a meaningful state of general equilibrium exists under a fairly wide set of conditions.

---

4. Suppose that each of the equations in 14.6 holds and that all but one of the equations in 14.4 hold. That is, assume that

$$p_c = \sum_d u_{cd} W_d \qquad \text{where } c = 1 \cdots C$$

$$X_d = \sum_c u_{cd} R_c \qquad \text{where } d = 1 \cdots (D - 1).$$

It is easy to show that the remaining equation in 14.4 must hold too. Since the total amount spent by consumers must equal their total income,

$$\sum_c R_c p_c = \sum_d X_d W_d.$$

And since $p_c = \sum_d u_{cd} W_d$, it follows that

$$\sum_d X_d W_d = \sum_c R_c \sum_d u_{cd} W_d.$$

Moreover, since $\sum_{d=1}^{D-1} X_d W_d = \sum_{d=1}^{D-1} \sum_c u_{cd} R_c W_d$,

$$X_D W_D = \sum_c R_c \sum_d u_{cd} W_d - \sum_{d=1}^{D-1} \sum_c u_{cd} R_c W_d$$

$$= \sum_c R_c \sum_d u_{cd} W_d - \sum_c R_c \sum_{d=1}^{D-1} u_{cd} W_d$$

$$= \sum_c R_c u_{cD} W_D.$$

Therefore, since $W_D > 0$, $X_D = \sum_c u_{cD} R_c$, which is what we set out to prove.

5. These nonnegativity constraints are like those discussed in the Appendix to this book; it makes no sense for some variables, like the production of corn, to be negative.

We now turn our attention to a somewhat different, but related, topic. In previous chapters, we have stated repeatedly that microeconomics is concerned with the way in which resources should be allocated. Once we consider more than a single market, it becomes possible to consider many interesting questions concerning the efficient allocation of resources. The rest of this chapter is devoted to a discussion of some of these questions.

Edgeworth box diagram

In the simple models that we shall take up, the Edgeworth box diagram finds extensive use. The Edgeworth box diagram shows the interaction between two economic activities when the total amount of commodities consumed or inputs used by these activities is fixed in quantity. To see how the Edgeworth box diagram is constructed, and how it should be interpreted, see Figure 14.2. We assume that there are two goods, food and medicine, and two consumers, Tom and Harry. The total amount of food that they have is *OF* and the total amount of medicine that they have is *OM*.

The amount of food that Tom has is measured horizontally from the origin at *O*. The amount of medicine that Tom has is measured vertically from *O*. Thus any point in the box diagram indicates a certain amount of food and a certain amount of medicine consumed by Tom. For example, the point *P* indicates that Tom consumes *OR* of food and *OS* of medicine. The amount of food that Harry consumes is measured by the horizontal distance to the left of the

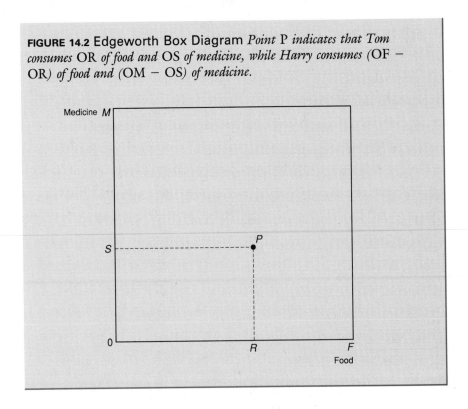

FIGURE 14.2 Edgeworth Box Diagram *Point* P *indicates that Tom consumes* OR *of food and* OS *of medicine, while Harry consumes (*OF − OR*) of food and (*OM − OS*) of medicine.*

upper right-hand corner of the box diagram. And the amount of medicine that Harry consumes is measured by the vertical distance downward from the upper right-hand corner of the box diagram. Thus every point in the diagram indicates an amount of food and medicine consumed by Harry. For example, the point P indicates that Harry consumes $(OF - OR)$ of food and $(OM - OS)$ of medicine.

The important points to remember about the Edgeworth box diagram are that its length and width represent the total amounts of the two commodities that both consumers together have, and that each point in the box represents an allocation of the total supplies of the two goods between the two consumers.

The Edgeworth box diagram can be used for production problems, as well as consumption problems. For example, suppose that there are two industries, industry A and industry B, and that there are two inputs, labor and capital. Suppose that the total amount of labor available to the two industries is OL and the total amount of capital available to the two industries is OK. Figure 14.3 shows the relevant Edgeworth box diagram, the height of which equals the total amount of labor, OL, and the width of which equals the total amount of capital, OK.

Any point in the box represents an allocation of this total supply of labor and total supply of capital between the two industries. The amount of labor allocated to industry A is represented by the vertical distance upward from the origin, and the amount of capital allocated to industry A is represented by the horizontal distance to the right of the origin. For example, point Q indicates that industry A has OU of labor and OV of capital. The amount of labor allo-

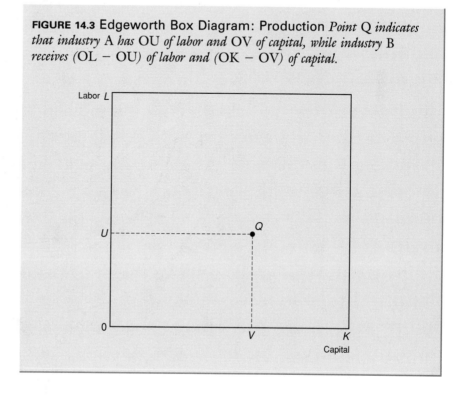

FIGURE 14.3 Edgeworth Box Diagram: Production *Point* Q *indicates that industry* A *has* OU *of labor and* OV *of capital, while industry* B *receives* (OL − OU) *of labor and* (OK − OV) *of capital.*

cated to industry B is represented by the distance downward from the upper right-hand corner of the box diagram, and the amount of capital allocated to industry B is represented by the distance leftward from the upper right-hand corner of the box diagram. Thus point Q indicates that industry B receives $(OL - OU)$ of labor and $(OK - OV)$ of capital.

EXCHANGE

Let's return now from production to consumption, and discuss the process of exchange. To begin with, consider an economy of the simplest sort. There are only two consumers, Tom and Harry, and only two commodities, food and medicine. There is no production; the only economic problem is the allocation of a given amount of food and medicine between the two consumers. If it helps, you may regard Tom and Harry as two shipwrecked sailors marooned on a desert island with a certain amount of food and medicine that they rescued from their ship.

The amount of food and medicine brought by Tom to the island is indicated in the Edgeworth box diagram in Figure 14.4: He arrives with OH units of food and OI units of medicine. The amount of food and medicine brought by Harry to the island is also indicated in Figure 14.4: He arrives with $(OF - OH)$ units of food and $(OM - OI)$ units of medicine. The total amount of food brought to the island by both men is OF, and the total amount of medicine brought to the island by both men is OM.

FIGURE 14.4 Exchange *Points* P_0, P_1, *and* P_2 *are on the contract curve, which includes all points where the marginal rates of substitution are the same for both consumers.*

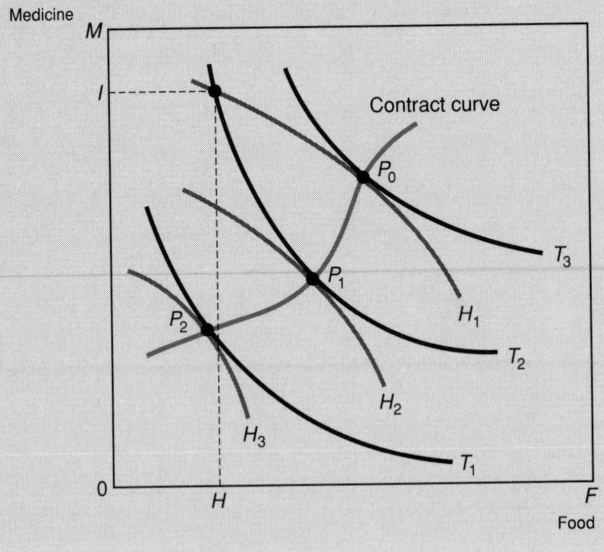

If the two men are free to trade with one another, what sort of trading will take place? What can be said about the efficient allocation of the commodities between the two men? To find out, we must insert the indifference curves of Tom and Harry into the Edgeworth box diagram in Figure 14.4. Three of Tom's indifference curves are T_1, T_2, and T_3. The highest indifference curve is T_3; the lowest is T_1. Three of Harry's indifference curves are H_1, H_2, and H_3. The highest indifference curve is H_3; the lowest is H_1. In general, Tom's satisfaction is increased as we move from points close to the origin to points close to the upper right-hand corner of the box. Conversely, Harry's satisfaction is increased as we move from points close to the upper right-hand corner of the box to points close to the origin.

Given the initial allocation of food and medicine, we find that Tom is on indifference curve T_2 and Harry is on indifference curve H_1. At this point, Tom's marginal rate of substitution of food for medicine is much higher than Harry's, as shown by a comparison of the slope of T_2 with the slope of H_1 at this point. Thus, if both men are free to trade, Tom will trade some medicine to Harry in exchange for some food. The exact point to which they will move cannot be predicted, however. If Tom is the more astute bargainer, he may get Harry to accept the allocation at point P_0, where Harry is no better off than before (since he is still on indifference curve H_1) but Tom is better off (since he has moved to indifference curve T_3). On the other hand, if Harry is the better negotiator, he may be able to get Tom to accept the allocation at point P_1, where Tom is no better off than before (since he is still on indifference curve T_2) but Harry is better off (since he has moved to indifference curve H_2). The ultimate point of equilibrium is very likely to be between P_0 and P_1.

One thing is certain. If the object is to make the men as well off as possible, the efficient allocation of the commodities is one in which the marginal rate of substitution of food for medicine will be the same for both men. Otherwise one man can be made better off without making the other worse off. In other words, the efficient allocation is a point at which Tom's indifference curve is tangent to Harry's. The locus of points at which such a tangency occurs is called the *contract curve*. This curve, shown in Figure 14.4, includes all points, like P_0, P_1, and P_2, where the marginal rates of substitution are equal for both consumers. The contract curve is an efficient (or optimal) set of points in the sense that, if the consumers are at a point *off* the contract curve, it is always preferable for them to move to a point *on* the contract curve, since one or both can gain from the move while neither incurs a loss.

Contract curve: exchange

PRODUCTION[6]

In the previous section we discussed the case in which consumers exchange quantities of commodities, when there is no production. In this section and the next, we take up a simple case in which there is production but no consumption. Then, in the section after next, we combine the results and consider a case in which there is both consumption and production.

6. The following sections are based to some extent on the work of F. Bator, among others.

FIGURE 14.5 Production *Points* U *and* V *are on the contract curve, which includes all points where the marginal rates of technical substitution between the inputs are the same for both industries.*

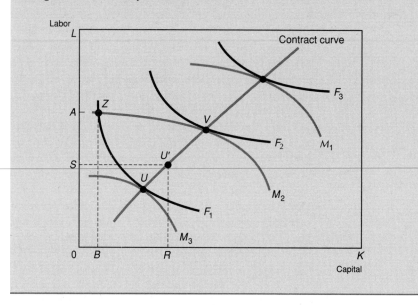

Consider a simple economy in which only two goods are being produced, the production sector of the economy being composed of a food industry and a medicine industry. Suppose that there are two inputs, labor and capital, and that the total amount of labor to be allocated between the two industries is OL and the total amount of capital to be allocated between the two industries is OK. Suppose that the initial allocation of labor and capital is that represented by point Z in the Edgeworth box diagram in Figure 14.5. That is, the food industry has OA units of labor and OB units of capital, and the medicine industry has $(OL - OA)$ units of labor and $(OK - OB)$ units of capital.

On the basis of the production functions for food and medicine one can insert isoquants for both food production and medicine production in Figure 14.5. Three isoquants for food production are F_1, F_2, and F_3. The isoquant pertaining to the highest output level is F_3; the isoquant pertaining to the lowest output is F_1. Three isoquants for medicine production are M_1, M_2, and M_3. The isoquant pertaining to the highest output level is M_3; the isoquant pertaining to the lowest output level is M_1.

Efficient allocation of inputs

What will be the efficient allocation of inputs between the two industries? At the original allocation at point Z, the marginal rate of technical substitution of capital for labor in producing food is higher than in producing medicine. This is indicated by the fact that the slope of F_1 is steeper than the slope of M_2 at point Z. The fact that the marginal rates of technical substitution are unequal means that the inputs are not being allocated efficiently. For example, suppose that at point Z the food industry can substitute 2 units of labor for 1 unit of capital without changing its output level, while the medicine industry must substitute 1 unit of labor for 2 units of capital to maintain its output level. In this case if the medicine industry uses more labor and less capital and if the food industry uses less labor and more capital, it will be possible for one industry to expand its output without any reduction in the other industry's output. Specifically, it is possible to move to point U, where the output of food is the same as at Z but the output of medicine is at the level corresponding to M_3. It is also possible to move to point V, where the output of medicine is the same as at Z but the output of food is at the level corresponding to F_2. Or it is possible to move to a point between U and V.

Regardless of which point is chosen, production should occur at a point at which the marginal rate of technical substitution between inputs is the same for all producers, if the allocation of inputs is to be efficient in the sense that an increase in the output of one commodity can be achieved only by reducing the output of the other commodity. Thus the efficient allocation of inputs will lie somewhere along the locus of points where the marginal rates of technical substitution are equal—and consequently where a food isoquant is tangent to a medicine isoquant. This locus of points, like the analogous set in the previous

Contract curve: production

section, is called the *contract curve*,[7] and is shown in Figure 14.5. This curve is an efficient (or optimal) set of points in the sense that, if producers are at a point *off* the contract curve and if society is interested in producing as much as possible of each good, it is always socially desirable for them to move to a point *on* the contract curve, since output in one industry or the other can be increased without a reduction in the other's output.

Note that this analysis of production is entirely analogous to the analysis of exchange in the previous section. The total amounts of the two inputs determine the dimensions of the Edgeworth box in this section; the analogous quantities in the previous section are the total amounts of the two commodities. The isoquant maps play an analogous role to the indifference maps in the previous section.

THE PRODUCT TRANSFORMATION CURVE

The contract curve in Figure 14.5 shows the various allocations of inputs that are efficient. Corresponding to each point on this contract curve is a level of output of food and a level of output of medicine. For example, consider U. If the level of output of food corresponding to isoquant F_1 is 100 and if the level of output of medicine corresponding to isoquant M_3 is 200, then an output of 100 units of food and 200 units of medicine corresponds to the point U. Similarly, if the level of output of food corresponding to isoquant F_2 is 200 and if the level of output of medicine corresponding to isoquant M_2 is 100, then an output of 200 units of food and 100 units of medicine corresponds to the point V.

Proceeding in this way, we can find the pair of outputs corresponding to each point on the contract curve. Then we can plot each such pair of points in a graph like Figure 14.6, where the amount of food produced is shown on the horizontal axis and the amount of medicine produced is shown on the vertical axis. For example, the pair of outputs corresponding to point U on the contract

7. Other terms could be used as well, but this is the term that is often applied.

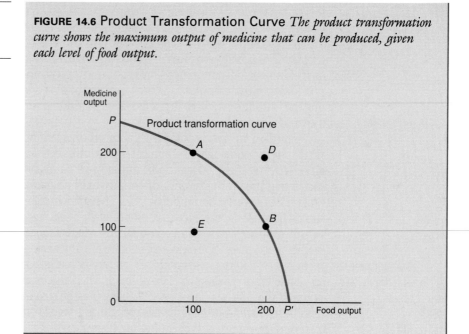

FIGURE 14.6 Product Transformation Curve *The product transformation curve shows the maximum output of medicine that can be produced, given each level of food output.*

curve are plotted as point *A* in Figure 14.6, and the pair of outputs corresponding to point *V* on the contract curve are plotted as point *B* in Figure 14.6. The curve, *PP′*, which results when all of these points are plotted in Figure 14.6, is called the product transformation curve.

Product transformation curve

The product transformation curve shows the various combinations of food output and medicine output that can be derived from the economy's input base (which is *OL* units of labor and *OK* units of capital). More specifically, it shows the maximum output of one good that can be produced, holding fixed the output of the other good. Given the economy's input base, it is impossible, given existing technology, to attain a point (like *D*) that is outside the product transformation curve. It is possible to attain a point like *E* that is inside the product transformation curve, but it would be inefficient to do so. As long as production is efficient, production occurs at some point along the product transformation curve.

PRODUCTION AND EXCHANGE

In this section, we take up a simple model that includes both production and exchange. Our simple economy contains two consumers, Tom and Harry, and two commodities, food and medicine, and two inputs, labor and capital. As in the previous two sections, this economy can use a total of *OL* units of labor and *OK* units of capital. If the input base, the indifference maps of the consumers, and the production functions in the two industries are given, how should these inputs be allocated between industries, and how should the output of goods be allocated between the consumers?

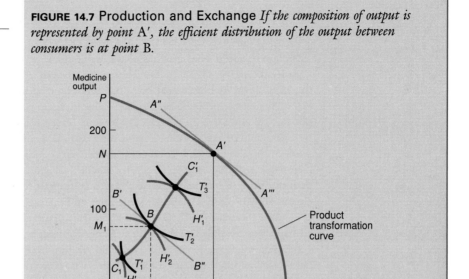

FIGURE 14.7 Production and Exchange *If the composition of output is represented by point A', the efficient distribution of the output between consumers is at point B.*

If the isoquant map in each industry is that shown in Figure 14.5, we know from the previous section that the various combinations of food output and medicine output that can be derived from this input base are given by the product transformation curve, PP', in Figure 14.6. This curve, PP', is reproduced in Figure 14.7. Suppose that we know the composition of output in the economy, that is, the amount of food and medicine that will be produced. Then we can insert an Edgeworth box diagram similar to Figure 14.4 in Figure 14.7, the upper right-hand corner of the box being the point on the product transformation curve corresponding to the composition of output.

More specifically, suppose that we know that the composition of output in the economy will be represented by point A', where the quantity of food produced is OQ and the quantity of medicine produced is ON. Then we can draw a box diagram with OQ as its width and ON as its height. Since OQ is the total amount of food to be distributed to Tom and Harry, and ON is the total amount of medicine to be distributed to them, this box diagram can be used to see how much of the total output of each good will go to each consumer. Figure 14.7 shows the indifference curves of each consumer (T'_1, T'_2, and T'_3 for Tom and H'_1, H'_2, and H'_3 for Harry) within the box, $OQ\,A'N$. It also shows the contract curve, $C_1C'_1$, the locus of points where Tom's indifference curves are tangent to Harry's.

We know from pp. 424–25 that the distribution of output between the two consumers should be such that they will be on the contract curve, $C_1C'_1$. But at what point on the contract curve should they be? We show in the following

*Marginal rate of
transformation*

section that, if the economy's output is allocated so that consumer satisfaction is maximized, the marginal rate of product transformation—the negative of the slope of the product transformation curve—must equal the marginal rate of

EXAMPLE 14.2

THE ALLOCATION OF FISSIONABLE MATERIAL

Although the 1990s have witnessed a notable thaw in the cold war, it is still important that our military establishment be efficient. A classic illustration of the application of Edgeworth box diagrams occurred in the 1950s, when a key U.S. defense problem was how to allocate fissionable material between our tactical and strategic forces. There were a fixed total number of aircraft (OA) and a fixed supply of fissionable materials (OM) in the short run. Every point in the Edgeworth box diagram shown below indicates an allocation of fissionable material and airplanes to the tactical and strategic forces. For example, point P represents a case where our strategic forces get OU units of aircraft and OV units of fissionable material, and our tactical forces get ($OA - OU$) units of aircraft and ($OM - OV$) units of fissionable material. Within limits, it was possible to substitute airplanes for fissionable material and vice versa. For example, fewer aircraft would be required to destroy a certain number of targets if atomic weapons, rather that conventional weapons, were used. Curve T_1 contains combinations of aircraft and fissionable material that result in equal effectiveness of the tactical forces. Curve T_0 also contains combinations that result in equal effectiveness of the tactical forces—but at a lower level than curve T_1. Curve S_2 contains combinations of aircraft and fissionable material that result in equal effectiveness of the strategic forces. Curve S_3 also contains combinations that result in equal effectiveness of the strategic forces—but at a higher level than curve S_2. The allocation at that time was represented by point W. Was this an efficient choice?

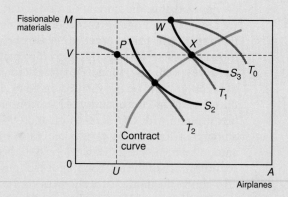

SOLUTION

No, because point W is not on the contract curve. The Defense Department could increase the effectiveness of either the tactical or strategic forces without reducing the effectiveness of the other by moving to a point on the contract curve. For example, point X results in the same effectiveness of our strategic forces as point W, since both points are on curve S_3. But point X results in more effectiveness of our tactical forces than point W. In fact, this simple kind of economic analysis was used to help solve this important policy problem.*

*For further discussion, see S. Enke, "Using Costs to Select Weapons." *American Economic
Review,* May 1965; and "Some Economic Aspects of Fissionable Materials," *Quarterly Journal of Economics,* May 1964.

substitution. Thus, if the economy's output is allocated to maximize consumer satisfaction, the consumers should be at the point on the contract curve at which the common slope of their indifference curves equals the slope of the product transformation curve at A'.

At what point on the contract curve does the common slope of their indifference curves equal the slope of the product transformation curve at A'? An examination of Figure 14.7 shows that this condition is fulfilled at point B on the contract curve, where Tom gets OF_1 units of food and OM_1 units of medicine and Harry gets $(OQ - OF_1)$ units of food and $(ON - OM_1)$ units of medicine. The slope of the indifference curves at point B equals the slope of the product transformation curve at point A', as demonstrated by the fact that the tangents, $B'B''$ and $A''A'''$ are parallel. Thus, given the amount to be produced of each commodity, we can find in this way the amount of each commodity that should be allocated to Tom and Harry.

In addition, we can find the amount of labor and capital that should be allocated to the production of each commodity by consulting the Edgeworth box diagram in Figure 14.5 that underlies the product transformation curve. Recall from the previous section that each point on the product transformation curve corresponds to a point on the contract curve in Figure 14.5, and that each point on the contract curve in Figure 14.5 corresponds to a particular allocation of labor and capital between the production of the two commodities. For example, point A' on the product transformation curve corresponds to point U' on the contract curve in Figure 14.5. Thus, given that the composition of output in the economy will be given by point A', we know that OS units of labor will be devoted to the production of food, $(OL - OS)$ units of labor will be devoted to the production of medicine, OR units of capital will be devoted to the production of food, and $(OK - OR)$ units of capital will be devoted to the production of medicine.

To sum up, we have answered the two questions set forth at the beginning of this section. Given the amount of each commodity to be produced, we have shown how this output should be distributed between consumers and how the available inputs should be distributed between industries if production is to be efficient and if consumer satisfaction is to be maximized. However, it is important to note that our model is incomplete even for this simple two-commodity, two-consumer, two-input economy, since we take as given the amount of each commodity to be produced. In the next chapter, we shall discuss some of the problems involved in trying to complete this model.

The Marginal Rate of Product Transformation, the Marginal Rate of Substitution, and Consumer Satisfaction

In the previous section, it was asserted that consumer satisfaction will not be maximized unless the marginal rate of product transformation between two goods is equal to the marginal rate of substitution between the two goods. The purpose of this section is to demonstrate that this is the case. For simplicity, suppose that firm A produces both food and medicine and that it supplies all of these commodities consumed by Tom. Suppose, too, that Tom initially consumes M_T units of medicine and F_T units of food, and that his marginal rate of substitution of medicine for food is X. Finally, suppose that firm A produces M units of medicine and F units of food and that the marginal rate of product transformation between food and medicine is Y.

The first thing we shall show is that consumer satisfaction is not being maximized if X is less than Y. If X is less than Y, suppose that we decrease the amount of medicine produced by firm A and the amount of medicine consumed by Tom by 1 unit. For Tom to maintain the same level of satisfaction, he can be given X additional units of food to offset the loss of the 1 unit of medicine. (This follows from the definition of the marginal rate of substitution, given in Chapter 3.)

Suppose that firm A gives him the extra X units of food. By decreasing its production of medicine by 1 unit, firm A can make an additional Y units of food. (This follows from the definition of the marginal rate of product transformation, given in the appendix to Chapter 8. As indicated there, the marginal rate of product transformation equals the extra number of units of one good that can be produced if one less unit of another good is produced.) After decreasing its output of medicine, firm A supplies Harry just as much medicine as before, since both its total output of medicine and Tom's consumption of medicine are reduced by 1 unit. But it can supply Harry with an extra $(Y - X)$ units of food (the extra Y units it can produce less the X units it has given Tom). Consequently, Harry can be made better off without hurting Tom, if X is less than Y. Thus consumer satisfaction is not being maximized if X is less than Y.[8]

The next thing we shall show is that consumer satisfaction is not being maximized if X is greater than Y. If X is greater than Y, suppose that we increase the amount of medicine produced by firm A and the amount of medicine consumed by Tom by 1 unit. For Tom to maintain the same level of satisfaction, he must give up X units of food. Suppose that he gives them to firm A. By increasing its output of medicine by 1 unit, firm A can make Y fewer units of food. Firm A can supply Harry with as much medicine as before but it can supply him with an extra $(X - Y)$ units of food (the X units Tom has given up minus the Y units by which its output of food has fallen). Consequently Harry can be made better off without hurting Tom if X is greater than Y. Thus consumer satisfaction is not being maximized if X is greater than Y.[9]

8. A numerical example may help make this easier. If Tom's marginal rate of substitution of medicine for food is 1 and if the marginal rate of product transformation between food and medicine is 2, firm A can reduce its output of medicine by 1 unit and provide Tom with 1 less unit of medicine. Firm A can also increase its production of food by 2 units and give Tom 1 extra unit of food to compensate for his loss of medicine. There is 1 unit of food left over, which can make Harry better off without hurting Tom.

9. A numerical example may help make this easier. If Tom's marginal rate of substitution of medicine for food is 2 and if the marginal rate of product transformation between food and medicine is 1, firm A can increase its output of medicine by 1 unit and provide Tom with 1 extra unit of medicine. Firm A can also obtain 2 units of food from Tom to compensate for the extra unit of medicine, but to produce the extra unit of medicine, firm A had to produce 1 less unit of food. Thus firm A has 1 unit of food left over, which can make Harry better off without hurting Tom.

If consumer satisfaction is not being maximized if X is less than Y, and if it is not being maximized if X is greater than Y, it follows that consumer satisfaction can be maximized only if X is equal to Y. This, of course, is what we set out to prove.

Summary

1. Previous chapters have been concerned with partial equilibrium analysis, which assumes that changes in price can occur in whatever market is being studied without causing significant changes in price in other markets, which in turn affect the market being studied. An analysis that takes account of the interrelationships among prices in various markets is called a general equilibrium analysis.

2. One of the most fundamental problems that general equilibrium analysis has been used to help solve is whether or not it is possible for equilibrium to occur simultaneously in all markets in a perfectly competitive economy. Modern work has established that in a perfectly competitive economy a state of general equilibrium can be achieved under a fairly wide set of conditions.

3. General equilibrium analysis provides a framework of price and output relations for both commodities and inputs for the economy as a whole. Its purpose is to show what the equilibrium configuration of prices, outputs, and inputs will be in various markets, given a certain set of consumer preferences, production functions, and input supply functions.

4. In the simple model presented on pp. 416–21, there are three kinds of equations. This model is extremely simple, since it assumes that the supply of inputs is given (and independent of prices) and that production coefficients are fixed. However, it illustrates the nature of general equilibrium models.

5. Once we consider more than a single market, it becomes possible to consider many interesting questions concerning the efficient allocation of resources. Using the Edgeworth box diagram, we showed that the efficient allocation of commodities between consumers lies on the contract curve.

6. Turning to production, the efficient allocation of inputs between industries also lies on a contract curve. From this contract curve we can construct the production transformation curve.

7. We also studied a simple model that included both production and exchange. It was shown that consumer satisfaction will not be maximized unless the marginal rate of product transformation between two goods is equal to the marginal rate of substitution between them.

Questions/Problems

1. Gasohol is a blend of 10 percent ethanol and 90 percent regular gasoline. Ethanol can be made from corn. In late 1979, the cost of a gallon of ethanol made from corn was estimated at $1.20. The refinery price of regular gasoline was 85 cents per gallon. To encourage the production of gasohol, the federal government exempted gasohol from the federal gasoline tax, worth 40 cents on the 10 percent ethanol content of gasohol. And many states exempted it from their motor fuel taxes, worth another 40 cents to $1 per gallon of ethanol. (a) Does each gallon of ethanol used in gasohol result in a one-gallon reduction in the amount of regular gasoline (or other fuels) used in the United States? (b) Given the above tax incentives, was it profitable to produce gasohol? If so, was it likely that gasohol would displace regular gasoline completely? (c) What are the effects of these tax exemptions on corn prices? On the value of corn-producing land? Can a partial equilibrium analysis answer these questions?

2. According to Bertrand de Jouvenel, "In an economic policy-making committee I recently happened to suggest that the Parthenon was an addition to the wealth of Athe-

nians, and its enjoyment an element of their standard of life. This statement was regarded as whimsical." Do you agree with de Jouvenel's statement? Why or why not?

3. John takes a date, Joan, to a Chinese restaurant, and they order a portion of lemon chicken and a portion of sweet and sour pork. When the food arrives, they divide each portion between them. Indicate how the Edgeworth box diagram might be used to analyze the way in which they should divide the food. Is it reasonable to assume that John's satisfaction depends only on the amount of food he consumes and not on the amount Joan consumes too?

4. Based on partial equilibrium analysis, how would you go about predicting the effect on the output of butter of a tax on butter of $1 per pound? Recognizing that margarine is a substitute for butter, what are the advantages, if any, of using a general equilibrium analysis to answer this question?

5. Suppose that you have 6 bottles of beer (and no potato chips) and your roommate has 4 bags of potato chips (and no beer). It is late at night, and the stores are closed. You decide to swap some of your beer for some of her potato chips. The Edgeworth box diagram is the following:

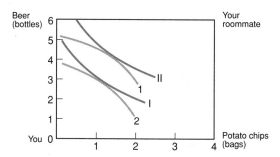

Your indifference curves are labeled I and II; hers are labeled 1 and 2. Label the point on the diagram which represents your pretrade situation.

6. In the previous question, suppose that you decide to swap 3 bottles of your beer for 1 bag of your roommate's potato chips. Is this a rational offer? That is, will it make you better off? Explain.

7. In Question 5, suppose that you offer to swap 2 bottles of your beer for 1½ bags of your roommate's potato chips. Will your roommate agree to this? Is this a rational offer for you to make? (That is, will it make you better off?)

8. Suppose that the simple economy in Figure 14.5 is endowed with more labor (perhaps due to immigration). What will be the effect on Figure 14.5? What will be the effect on the product transformation curve in Figure 14.6?

9. Suppose that the government orders a 4 percent reduction in the price of a particular good. (a) Based on a partial equilibrium analysis, would the output of this good be expected to fall? Would a shortage of this good be expected? (b) Besides ordering a 4 percent reduction in the price of this good, the government orders a reduction in the price of many other goods, including substitutes for this good. Based on a general equilibrium analysis, would you come to the same conclusions as in part (a)? Why or why not?

10. Martin Cantine leaves an estate consisting of 200 acres of land and 50 paintings. In his will, he states that his estate should be divided equally between his two children, Mary and John. (That is, each child should receive half of the land and half of the paintings.) (a) Construct an Edgeworth box diagram showing the various ways in which the estate might be divided. (b) Show the point in this diagram that represents the division of the estate according to the will. (c) Can we be sure that this point is on the contract curve?

15

THE PROMOTION OF ECONOMIC EFFICIENCY

INTRODUCTION

At the beginning of this book, we made the claim that microeconomics is of use in clarifying public-policy issues. Having made this claim, we hastened to add that microeconomics alone is seldom able to provide a clear-cut solution to such issues, but that, in combination with other relevant disciplines, it frequently can provide useful ways of structuring and analyzing these issues. The purpose of this chapter is to describe and discuss the nature of the policy recommendations that economists can make to promote economic efficiency.

More specifically, microeconomics is concerned with policy issues concerning the allocation of resources. In other words, it deals mainly with questions concerning how inputs should be allocated among industries and how goods should be allocated among consumers. These are general equilibrium problems, since the efficient usage of any input cannot be determined by looking at the market for this input alone, and the efficient output of any commodity cannot be determined by looking at the market for this commodity alone. On the contrary, the efficient allocation of resources between two products depends on the relative strength of the demands for the products and their relative production costs.

We have already begun the study of efficient resource allocation. The latter part of the previous chapter was concerned with this topic in the very simple case of a two-commodity, two-consumer, two-input economy. This chapter provides a further introduction to the fundamental principles of economic efficiency. We begin by taking up the conditions that must be satisfied by an efficient allocation of resources. Then we deal with the role of perfect competition, in promoting an efficient allocation of resources. Finally, we discuss the effects of external economies and diseconomies, increasing returns, and incomplete information.

THE DEFINITION OF ECONOMIC EFFICIENCY

To understand the definition of economic efficiency, it is important to recognize an important limitation of microeconomics: *There is no scientifically meaningful way to compare the utility levels of various individuals.* The reader will recall that in our previous discussion of utility and demand theory in Chapters 3 and 4 we were not required to make any such interpersonal comparisons.[1] This was fortunate, and intentional. There is no way that one can state scientifically that a piece of Aunt Mary's apple pie will bring you more satisfaction than it will me, or that your headache is worse than mine. This is because there is no scale on which we can measure pleasure or pain in such a way that interpersonal comparisons can be made validly.

Distribution of income

Because we cannot make interpersonal comparisons of utility, we cannot tell whether one distribution of income is better than another. For example, suppose you receive twice as much income as I do. Economics cannot tell us whether this is a better distribution of income than if I receive twice as much income as you do. This is a value judgment, pure and simple. However, most problems of public policy involve changes in the distribution of income. For example, even a decision to increase the production of numerically controlled machine tools and to reduce the production of conventional machine tools may mean that certain stockholders and workers will gain, while others will lose (since some machine tool firms specialize more heavily than others in the production of numerically controlled tools). Because it is so difficult to evaluate the effects of such a decision on the distribution of income, it is correspondingly difficult to come to any conclusion as to whether or not such a decision is good or bad.

Faced with this problem, economists have adopted a number of approaches, all of which have important difficulties. Some economists simply have paid no attention to the effects of proposed policies on the income distribution. Others have taken the existing income distribution as optimal, while still others have asserted that income distributions exhibiting less inequality of income are preferable to those exhibiting more inequality of income. Purists have argued that we really cannot be sure a change is for the better unless it hurts no member of society. Others have suggested that we must accept the judgment of Congress (or the public as a whole) as to what is an optimal distribution of income.[2]

1. However, there were two exceptions. In the treatment of government restrictions on sugar imports in Chapter 4, we simply added the reductions in consumer's surplus of various consumers to get an aggregate measure of the loss to consumers due to the restrictions. We noted that this treatment, although sometimes adopted in applied work, suffers from difficulties. In this chapter, these difficulties are explained at length. Also, in Chapter 9, when we computed the welfare loss due to monopoly, we simply added up the areas under the demand curves of various persons. We indicated that this entailed problems which are discussed here in detail.
2. One contribution to this literature that has received considerable attention is J. Rawls, *A Theory of Justice* (Cambridge, Mass.: Harvard University Press, 1971). Rawls argues that "all social values . . . are to be distributed equally unless an unequal distribution . . . is to everyone's advantage." Needless to say, this proposition has aroused much controversy. (See Example 15.1.)

For present purposes, the important thing to note is that practically all economists accept the proposition that a change that harms no one and improves the lot of some people (in their own eyes) is an improvement. This criterion, put forth by Vilfredo Pareto at about the turn of the century and often called the *Pareto criterion*,[3] evades the question of income distribution. If a change benefits one group of people and harms another group, this criterion is not applicable. Nonetheless, this criterion is by no means useless, as we shall see below, and most economists would agree that all changes that satisfy this criterion should be carried out. That is, they believe that society should make any change that harms no one and that improves the lot of some people. *If all such changes are carried out—and thus no opportunity to make such changes remains—the situation is termed economically efficient.* In the next two sections, we will describe and discuss the marginal conditions for an economically efficient allocation of resources.

MARGINAL CONDITIONS FOR ECONOMIC EFFICIENCY

Fundamentally, there are three necessary conditions for economic efficiency. The first pertains to the allocation of commodities among consumers. It states

that *the marginal rate of substitution between any two commodities must be the same for any two consumers.* The proof that this condition is necessary to maximize consumer satisfaction is quite simple. All that needs to be noted is that, if the marginal rates of substitution were unequal, both consumers could benefit by trading. For example, suppose that the first consumer regards an additional unit of product *A* as having the same utility as 2 extra units of product *B*, whereas the second consumer regards an additional unit of product *A* as having the same utility as 3 extra units of product *B*. Then, if the first consumer trades 1 unit of product *A* for 2.5 units of product *B* from the second consumer, both consumers are better off.

This condition implies that commodities should be distributed in such a way that consumers are on their contract curve, since the contract curve is composed of points where the marginal rates of substitution are equal for the consumers. In the case of only two commodities and two consumers, we showed in the previous chapter (pp. 424–25) that this condition must be met if consumer satisfaction is to be maximized. We are now stating the more general proposition that this condition must also be met in the more realistic case in which there are more than two commodities and two consumers.

The second condition pertains to the allocation of inputs among producers. It states that *the marginal rate of technical substitution between any two inputs must be the same for any pair of producers.* If this condition does not hold, it is possible to increase total production merely by reallocating inputs among producers. For example, suppose that, for the first producer, the marginal product of input 1 is twice that of input 2, whereas for the second producer the marginal product of input 1 is 3 times that of input 2. Then, if the first producer gives 1 unit of

3. V. Pareto, *Manuel d'Economie Politique* (1909).

input 1 to the second producer in exchange for 2.5 units of input 2, both firms can expand their output.

To see this, suppose that the marginal product of input 1 is M_1 for the first producer and M_2 for the second producer. Then the output of the first producer is reduced by M_1 units because of its loss of the unit of input 1, but it is increased by $2.5 \times M_1/2$ units because of its gain of the 2.5 units of input 2, with the consequence that, on balance, its output increases by $M_1/4$ units because of the trade. Similarly, the output of the second producer is increased by M_2 units because of its gain of the 1 unit of input 1, but it is decreased by $2.5 \times M_2/3$ units because of its loss of the 2.5 units of input 2, with the consequence that, on balance, its output increases by $M_2/6$ units because of the trade.

This condition implies that inputs should be allocated so that producers are on their contract curve, since the contract curve is made up of points at which the marginal rates of technical substitution are equal for producers. In the case of only two inputs and two producers, we showed in the previous chapter (pp. 425–27) that this condition must be met if the output of each producer is maximized, holding constant the output of the other producer. We are now stating the more general proposition that this condition must also be met in the more realistic case in which there are more than two inputs and two producers.

Condition #3 The third condition pertains to both the allocation of inputs among industries and the allocation of commodities among consumers. It states that *the marginal rate of substitution between any two commodities must be the same as the marginal rate of product transformation between these two commodities for any producer.* Suppose that PP' in Figure 15.1 is the product transformation curve, the curve that shows the maximum amount of good X that can be produced, given various output levels for good Y. The marginal rate of product transformation is the negative of the slope of the product transformation curve; it shows the number of units of good Y that society must give up in order to get an additional unit of good X.

Suppose that curves A and B in Figure 15.1 represent the indifference curves of a consumer who, for simplicity, is assumed to be the only consumer in the economy. To maximize the consumer's satisfaction, production must take place at point T, where the output of good X is OX and the output of good Y is OY. Clearly, T is the point on the product transformation curve that is on the consumer's highest indifference curve. Since the product transformation curve is tangent to the indifference curve at point T, it follows that the marginal rate of product transformation equals the marginal rate of substitution at point T. Thus the marginal rate of product transformation equals the marginal rate of substitution if consumer satisfaction is maximized. This result will hold for any number of consumers, not just for one.

In the case of two products and two consumers, we showed in the previous chapter (pp. 431–33) that this condition must hold if the satisfaction of one consumer is maximized, holding constant the other consumer's satisfaction. We are now stating the more general proposition that this condition must also be met in the more realistic case in which there are more than two commodities and two consumers.

FIGURE 15.1 Product Transformation Curve and Indifference
Curves *To maximize consumer satisfaction, production must take place at
point* T.

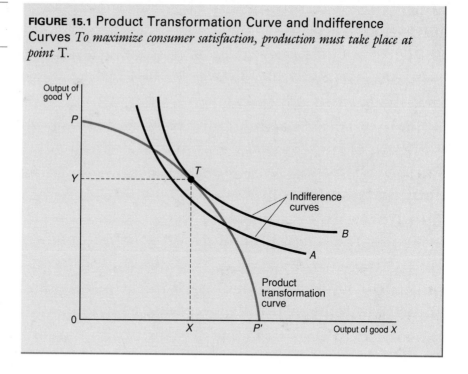

Agricultural Price Supports: An Application

We can use these three conditions for economic efficiency to analyze many
interesting questions, such as the choice among alternative agricultural price
support schemes. From Chapter 8 it will be recalled that in the past such
schemes have commonly specified that each farm can produce a certain quota,
represented by OX in panel A of Figure 15.2. The total quota for the entire
industry is OY in panel B of Figure 15.2. Also, a support price has frequently
been set by the government, which is OP in this case. Since the demand curve
for the product is as shown in panel B of Figure 15.2, consumers will purchase
OQ_1 units of product, and the government will buy $(OY - OQ_1)$ units of the
product. This is in contrast to the situation that would prevail if there were no
quotas and price supports; under these circumstances, price would be OP_1 and
the total output of the product would be OQ_2. The purpose of the quotas and
price supports is to increase the income of farmers.

Unfortunately, this type of support scheme leads to inefficiencies of various
kinds in the use of resources. First, because the marginal cost at OX will certainly vary from farm to farm, the industry's total output will be produced

 inefficiently. That is, the total cost of producing the total output could be
decreased by reducing the output of farms with high marginal costs at OX and
increasing the output of farms with low marginal cost at OX. Since the industry's total output is being produced inefficiently, it is clear that the second
condition in the previous section is being violated. Second, part of the industry's output is unnecessary, and is taken off the market by the government.

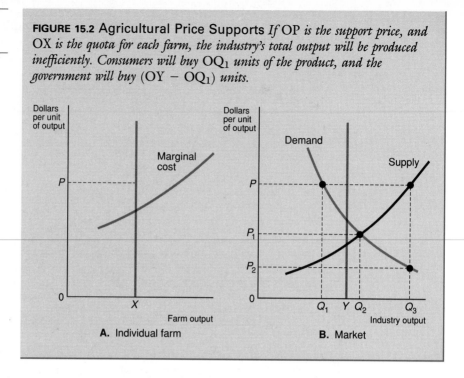

FIGURE 15.2 Agricultural Price Supports *If* OP *is the support price, and* OX *is the quota for each farm, the industry's total output will be produced inefficiently. Consumers will buy* OQ₁ *units of the product, and the government will buy* (OY − OQ₁) *units.*

Third, since price is above marginal cost for this product (see panel A of Figure 15.2), the third condition in the previous section is also violated, if the prices of other goods equal marginal cost (as they would in a perfectly competitive economy). The reasoning underlying this statement is explained in some detail in the section after next. For the moment, it is sufficient to accept it on faith.

On the other hand, suppose that the government adopts a different sort of scheme, one closer to that adopted in 1973. Suppose that the government guarantees each farmer a price of *OP,* with the result that the industry produces *OQ₃* units of the product. But then suppose that it lets the free market alone, with the result that the *OQ₃* units of the agricultural product command a price of only *OP₂* in the market and the government pays each farmer (*OP − OP₂*) per unit. The first type of inefficiency would be eliminated because each farmer would set marginal cost equal to *OP,* with the result that the marginal cost for each farm would be the same. The second type of inefficiency would be eliminated because the government no longer would take part of the industry's output off the market. The third type of inefficiency remains, since the price to consumers would be less than marginal cost.[4]

However, this does not mean that this scheme is necessarily an improvement. For instance (as noted earlier in this chapter), any choice among policies must take into account their effects on the income distribution. This kind of plan would result in a different distribution of benefits and costs among consumers and farmers. For example, the abandonment of the quota system would

4. See G. Stigler, *The Theory of Price* (New York: Macmillan, 1966), pp. 187–90.

hurt farmers who possess quotas. These aspects of the choice may outweigh all others in many people's minds. (Congressmen in particular may be sensitive to the question of whose ox is gored). More will be said on this score in the next two sections.

THE UTILITY-POSSIBILITY CURVE[5]

Earlier in this chapter, we stated that the three necessary conditions for economic efficiency (described on pp. 437–38) are incomplete guides to an optimal allocation of resources, since they say nothing concerning the question of income distribution. In this and the following section we show more explicitly how these conditions are incomplete. To do this, it is convenient to return to the two-commodity, two-consumer, two-input case discussed at the end of the previous chapter. There are two consumers, Tom and Harry; two commodities, food and medicine; and two inputs, labor and capital. There are a total of OL units of labor and OK units of capital.

Given that the production functions are as shown in Figure 14.5 (p. 426), the previous chapter shows that the product transformation curve is that shown in Figure 14.6 (p. 428). This curve, PP', is reproduced in Figure 15.3. At any point on this curve, inputs are allocated so that the second condition for economic efficiency (described on p. 437) is met (see pp. 425–28 of Chapter 14).

FIGURE 15.3 Production and Exchange *If the total quantity of food produced is* OF *and the total quantity of medicine produced is* OM, *the commodities should be distributed between the consumers so that they are at point* G. *Only at point* G *does the slope of each indifference curve equal the slope of the product transformation curve at point* N.

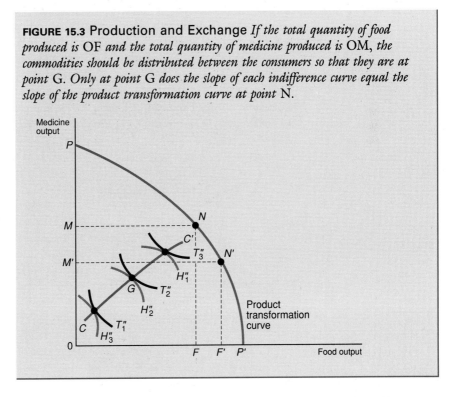

5. This section is based to a considerable extent on an expository approach advanced by F. Bator.

If we know the amount of food and the amount of medicine that will be produced, we can construct an Edgeworth box diagram for the two consumers. For example, if the total quantity of food produced is OF and the total amount of medicine produced is OM, the Edgeworth box diagram has OF as its width and OM as its height. Figure 15.3 also shows the indifference curves of Tom and Harry (T''_1, T''_2, and T''_3 for Tom; and H''_1, H''_2, and H''_3 for Harry) and the contract curve, CC'. At any point on this contract curve, commodities are allocated so that the first condition for economic efficiency (described on p. 437) is met (see pp. 424–25 of Chapter 14).

If the total quantity of food produced is OF and the total quantity of medicine produced is OM, the third condition for economic efficiency (described on p. 438) dictates that the commodities be distributed between the consumers so that they are at point G. Only at point G does the common slope of their indifference curves (the negative of the marginal rate of substitution) equal the slope of the product transformation curve at point N (the negative of the marginal rate of product transformation). The distribution of commodities at point G between Tom and Harry means that Tom achieves a certain level of utility and Harry achieves a certain level of utility. Suppose that this pair of utility levels corresponds to point R in Figure 15.4.

Now suppose that we take another point on the product transformation curve in Figure 15.3, say N'. On the basis of this amount of food output and this amount of medicine output, a new Edgeworth box diagram can be drawn; its width is OF' and its height is OM'. Drawing Tom's and Harry's indifference curves in this new Edgeworth box diagram, we can find the contract curve for this new box diagram, and we can find the point on this contract curve at which the common slope of the indifference curves (the negative of the marginal rate

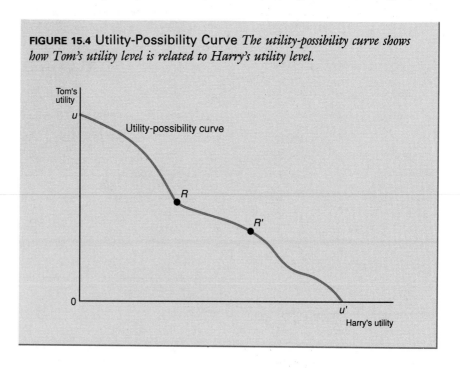

FIGURE 15.4 Utility-Possibility Curve *The utility-possibility curve shows how Tom's utility level is related to Harry's utility level.*

of substitution) equals the slope of the product transformation curve at point N' (the negative of the marginal rate of product transformation). Then we can see what levels of Tom's utility and Harry's utility correspond to this point and we can plot these utility levels in Figure 15.4, the result being point R'.

Utility-possibility curve

If we repeat this process for all points on the product transformation curve, we shall obtain a locus of points, UU', that shows the various possible pairs of utility levels of Tom and Harry if the three conditions for economic efficiency are met. This locus of points is called the *utility-possibility curve*. As would be expected, UU' is negatively sloped: If these conditions are met, the greater satisfaction obtained by Tom, the less satisfaction obtained by Harry. Some point on UU' must be chosen. Basically, the choice of a point on the utility-possibility curve is the choice of an income distribution. If this choice is made, the problem of finding an optimal allocation of resources in this case is solved.

EQUITY CONSIDERATIONS

The choice of a point on the utility-possibility curve involves questions of equity. If point R' in Figure 15.4 is chosen, Tom's utility level is lower, and Harry's utility level is higher, than if point R is chosen. Obviously, Harry prefers point R' to point R, whereas Tom prefers point R to point R'. But which point is fairer? Unfortunately, there is no simple way to answer this question, since people's views concerning fairness differ considerably.

Distribution of income

According to some people, the most equitable allocation of goods and services is completely egalitarian. That is, each person should receive the same amount of goods and services (that is, the same income). According to other people, the most equitable allocation is that which results from the workings of competitive markets because, in their view, this rewards the ablest and most diligent persons. According to still other people like Harvard philosopher John Rawls, income inequality is justified only to the extent that it benefits the least advantaged. (See Example 15.1.)

Given the diversity of opinion concerning the meaning of fairness, it is difficult, if not impossible, to say with authority that any particular point on the utility-possibility curve is best, or most equitable. Of course, this does not mean that you or I should not have strong views concerning what is or is not fair, but we must be careful not to regard our views as scientific propositions which should be accepted by all. Because there is no way to tell whether one distribution of income is better than another, the problem of finding an optimal allocation of resources cannot be solved completely.[6]

---

6. Note that this and the previous section as well as pp. 422–33 of Chapter 14 specify nothing about the institutional context. All that we have done is to figure out how resources should be allocated in this situation. We have not said anything about the sorts of institutional arrangements that will result in such an allocation of resources. The next few sections deal with the latter subject.

EXAMPLE 15.1

JOHN RAWLS ON SOCIAL JUSTICE

In most democratic societies, an equitable distribution of income is a major political objective. There are, of course, many arguments for and against more equality of income. John Rawls has put forth a theory of social justice in which he asserts that inequality is justified only to the extent that it benefits the least advantaged. Suppose that society consists of two people, Tom and Mary, and that any combination of their incomes on curve *ABCDE* below is attainable.

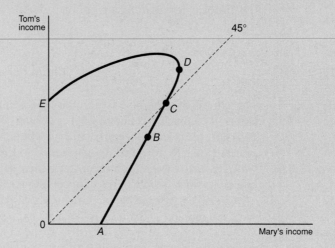

(a) If society moves from point *B* to *C*, does this reduce income inequality? Is this an improvement, according to Rawls? (b) If society moves from point *C* to *D*, does this reduce income inequality? Is this an improvement, according to him? (c) Is it really possible to define what is a "just" distribution of income without considering how various people act (how much and what sort of work each does, what other contributions they make, and so on) and the process by which the distribution of income is determined?

SOLUTION

(a) Yes. At point *B*, Mary's income exceeds Tom's income (since point *B* lies below and to the right of the 45° line).* At point *C*, Mary's income equals Tom's income (since point *C* lies on the 45° line). This is an improvement, according to Rawls. (b) Whereas Mary's income equals Tom's income at point *C*, her income is less than Tom's income at point *D* (since point *D* lies above and to the left of the 45° line). Thus the movement from point *C* to point *D* does not reduce income inequality. However, this is an improvement, according to Rawls, because even the poorer person (Mary) is benefited by the change, since her income at point *D* exceeds that at point *C*. (c) Many economists would argue that justice occurs when a person's rewards (or lack of them) are related properly to his or her actions. One criticism of Rawl's theory is that it is concerned with the distribution of benefits without much regard for the actions of Mary and Tom.**

*The 45° line is the locus of points where the value measured along the horizontal axis (Mary's income) equals the value measured along the vertical axis (Tom's income). At points below and to the right of the 45° line, the former value exceeds the latter value; at points above and to the left of the 45° line, the reverse is true.

**For further discussion, see J. Rawls, *A Theory of Justice* (Cambridge, Mass.: Harvard University Press, 1971).

PERFECT COMPETITION AND ECONOMIC EFFICIENCY

One of the most important, and most fundamental, findings of microeconomics is that a perfectly competitive economy satisfies the three conditions for economic efficiency set forth on pp. 437–38. The argument for competition can be made in various ways. For example, some people favor competition simply because it prevents the undue concentration of power and the exploitation of consumers. But to the economic theorist, the basic argument for a perfectly competitive economy is the fact that such an economy satisfies the three conditions on pp. 437–38. In this section we prove that this is indeed a fact. In the next two sections, we discuss how prices can be used in planned economies and by regulated industries to achieve the same kinds of results.

The first condition for economic efficiency is that the marginal rate of substitution between any pair of commodities must be the same for all consumers. To see that this condition is met under perfect competition, we must recall from Chapter 4 that under perfect competition consumers choose their purchases so that the marginal rate of substitution between any pair of commodities is equal to the ratio of the prices of the pair of commodities. Since prices, and thus price ratios, are the same for all buyers under perfect competition, it follows that the marginal rate of substitution between any pair of commodities must be the same for all consumers. For example, if every consumer can buy bread at 50 cents a loaf and butter at $1 a pound, each one will arrange his or her purchases so that the marginal rate of substitution of butter for bread is 2. Thus the marginal rate of substitution will be the same for all consumers: 2 for everyone.

The second condition for economic efficiency is that the marginal rate of technical substitution between any pair of inputs must be the same for all producers. To see that this condition is met under perfect competition, we must recall from Chapter 7 that, under perfect competition, producers will choose the quantity of each input so that the marginal rate of technical substitution between any pair of inputs is equal to the ratio of the prices of the pair of inputs. Since input prices, and thus price ratios, are the same for all producers under perfect competition, it follows that the marginal rate of technical substitution must be the same for all producers. For example, if every producer can buy labor services at $8 an hour and machine tool services at $16 an hour, each one will arrange the quantity of its inputs so that the marginal rate of technical substitution of machine tool services for labor is 2. Thus the marginal rate of technical substitution will be the same for all producers: 2 for each of them.

The third condition for economic efficiency is that the marginal rate of product transformation must equal the marginal rate of substitution for each pair of goods. The proof that this condition is met under perfect competition is somewhat lengthier than in the case of the other conditions. To begin with, we must note that the marginal rate of product transformation is the number of units of good A that must be given up to produce an additional unit of good B. The additional cost of producing the extra unit of good B is, of course, the marginal cost of good B. To see how many units of good A must be given up to get this extra unit of good B, we must divide the marginal cost of good B by the marginal cost of good A. This will tell us how many extra units of good A cost as much as one extra unit of good B. Thus the marginal rate of product transformation under perfect competition equals the ratio of the marginal cost of good B to the marginal cost of good A.

From Chapter 8 it will be recalled that price equals marginal cost under perfect competition. Consequently, the ratio of the marginal cost of good B to the marginal cost of good A equals the ratio of the price of good B to the price of good A under perfect competition. Coupled with the result of the previous paragraph, this means that the marginal rate of product transformation is equal to the ratio of the price of good B to the price of good A under perfect competition. But, as we noted in connection with our discussion of the first condition, the marginal rate of substitution is equal to the ratio of the price of good B to the price of good A under perfect competition. Consequently, it follows that the marginal rate of product transformation equals the marginal rate of substitution for any pair of products under perfect competition.

Referring back to our earlier discussion of agricultural price supports in this chapter, it is obvious now why these price supports violate the third condition for economic efficiency. Since the price of the agricultural good does not equal marginal cost (see Figure 15.2), the third condition must be violated if the prices of other goods equal marginal cost. For example, take some other good with marginal cost, MC_x, and price, P_x. The marginal rate of product transformation between this good and the agricultural product is $MC_A \div MC_x$, where MC_A is the marginal cost of the agricultural good. Moreover, if consumers maximize satisfaction, the marginal rate of substitution between the two goods is $P_A \div P_x$, where P_A is the price of the agricultural product. However, since $P_x = MC_x$ and $MC_A \neq P_A$, it follows that the marginal rate of substitution does not equal the marginal rate of product transformation.

*Case for perfect
competition*

Returning to the original topic of this section, we find that all three conditions for economic efficiency are satisfied under perfect competition. This is one of the principal reasons why economists are so enamored of perfect competition and so wary of monopoly. If a formerly competitive economy is restructured so that some industries become monopolies, these conditions for economic efficiency are no longer met. As we know from Chapter 9, each monopolist produces less than the perfectly competitive industry that it replaces would have produced. Thus too few resources are devoted to the industries that are monopolized, and too many resources are devoted to the industries that remain perfectly competitive. This is one of the economist's chief charges against monopoly. It wastes resources because its actions result in an overallocation of resources to competitive industries and an underallocation of resources to monopolistic industries. Society is then less well off.[7]

ECONOMIC PLANNING AND MARGINAL COST PRICING

The previous section showed that the three conditions for economic efficiency are satisfied under perfect competition. Economists interested in the functioning of planned, or socialist, economies have argued that a price system could be used in a similar way to increase social welfare in such economies.[8] In their view, rational economic organization could be achieved in a socialist economy that is decentralized, as well as under perfect competition. For example, the government might try to solve the system of equations that is solved automatically in a perfectly competitive economy, and obtain the prices that would prevail under perfect competition. Then the government might publish this price list, together with instructions for consumers to maximize their satisfaction and for producers to maximize profit. (Of course, the wording of the instructions to consumers might be a bit less heavy-handed than "Maximize your satisfaction!")

An important advantage claimed for planning and control of this sort is that the government does not have to become involved in the intricate and detailed business of setting production targets for each plant. It need only compute the proper set of prices. As long as plant managers maximize "profits," the proper production levels will be chosen by them. Thus decentralized decision-making, rather than detailed centralized direction, could be used, with the result that administrative costs and bureaucratic disadvantages might be reduced.

Marginal cost pricing

The prices that the government would publish, like those prevailing in a perfectly competitive economy, would equal marginal cost. Many economists have recommended that government-owned enterprises in basically capitalist economies also adopt *marginal cost pricing,* that is, that they set price equal to marginal cost. For example, Harold Hotelling argued that this should be the case.[9] Taking the case of a bridge where the marginal cost (the extra cost involved in allowing an additional vehicle to cross) is zero, he argued that the socially optimal price for crossing the bridge is zero, and that its cost should be defrayed by general taxation. If a toll is charged, the conditions for economic efficiency are violated.

7. In evaluating this result and judging its practical relevance, it is important to note that it stems from a very simple model that ignores such things as technological change and other dynamic considerations, risk and uncertainty, and externalities. Some of these factors are taken up in subsequent sections of this chapter and in Chapters 16–18. The reader should be very careful to note the qualifications and assumptions that must be made. Sometimes the argument for perfect competition is made without full recognition of these qualifications.

8. A. Lerner, *The Economics of Control* (New York: Macmillan, 1944). In 1990, a fascinating economic debate took place in the Soviet Union and Eastern Europe. Many influential economists argued that a decentralized, market-oriented economic system would be more efficient than the existing system of economic planning.

9. See H. Hotelling, "The General Welfare in Relation to Problems of Taxation and of Railway and Utility Rates," *Econometrica,* July 1938.

Marginal cost pricing has fascinated economists during the more than fifty years that have elapsed since Hotelling's article.[10] But there are a number of important problems in the actual application of this idea. One of the most important is that, if (as is frequently the case in public utilities) the firm's average costs decrease with increases in its scale of output, it follows from the discussion in Chapter 7 that marginal cost must be less than average cost, with the consequence that the firm will not cover its costs if price is set equal to marginal cost. This means that marginal cost pricing must be accompanied by some form of subsidy if the firm is to stay in operation. However, the collection of the funds required for the payment of the subsidy may also violate the conditions for economic efficiency. Moreover, this subsidy means that there is a change in the income distribution favoring users of the firm's output and penalizing nonusers of its output. Whether or not marginal cost pricing results in improved economic welfare depends on how one views this change in the income distribution.

Marginal Cost Pricing: A Case Study

During the mid-fifties, Électricité de France, the French nationalized electricity industry, introduced marginal cost pricing for its high-tension service. The ultimate goal of the new pricing scheme was that the price paid for a kilowatt-hour of electricity at a given time of day in a given season of the year in a given region was to approximate the cost of an additional kilowatt-hour at this time in this season in this region.

Of course, a great many simplifications had to be made in computing the new price schedule. First, consider price differences at various times of day. In the winter, the day is divided into three periods: the peak daytime hour, the other daytime hours, and the night. In the summer, it is divided into two periods: day and night. A consumer in a given region must pay a different price for kilowatt-hours in each period, with the differences reflecting differences in marginal costs. Next, consider price differences among regions. To estimate the marginal costs in each region, a pattern of movements of electricity from generating stations to consumption areas is derived that meets estimated demands at minimum total cost given present capacity. The marginal costs corresponding to this pattern are used to determine prices in various regions.

Finally, consider price differences among seasons. Differences among seasons in demand curves, as well as differences in hydroelectric reservoir levels and river flows, are responsible for these differences in price. The seasonal differences in demand are assumed by the industry to be like those observed in the past. Average snow and rainfall levels in each season can be used in the calculations. Since water tends to be less abundant in the winter, peak demands for electricity have to be satisfied by using less efficient thermal plants than have to be used in the summer. Also, demand for electricity tended to be higher in the winter. Both of these factors clearly influence the level of the marginal cost of electricity.

10. For example, see the papers by M. Boiteux and others in J. Nelson (ed.), *Marginal Cost Pricing in Practice* (Englewood Cliffs, N.J.: Prentice-Hall, 1964); W. Vickrey, "Some Implications of Marginal Cost Pricing for Public Utilities," reprinted in Mansfield, *Microeconomics: Selected Readings*, 5th ed.: and A. Kahn, *The Economics of Regulation* (New York: Wiley, 1970).

What has the new pricing scheme achieved? According to Berkeley's Thomas Marschak, who made a careful study of the French experience, Électricité de France's marginal cost pricing had a number of important beneficial results. In his view, a

> clear improvement over the [old] pricing scheme is very plausibly claimed. Preliminary observation suggests that a leveling of consumption between the daytime and the nighttime periods may be expected. One immediate result is a reduction by 5 percent in the capacity required to meet peak demands. . . . Another is a substantial saving of imported (American) coal in winter, since the flattening of peaks eliminates the need for some of the inefficient thermal output previously required.[11]

EXTERNAL ECONOMIES AND DISECONOMIES

Up to this point, we have generally assumed implicitly that there is no difference between private and social benefits, or between private and social costs. For example, costs to producers have been assumed to be costs to society, and costs to society have been assumed to be costs to producers; benefits to producers have been assumed to be benefits to society, and benefits to society have been assumed to be benefits to producers. In fact, however, there are many instances in which these assumptions do not hold. Instead, producers sometimes confer benefits on other members of the economy but are unable to obtain payment for these benefits, and they sometimes act in such a way as to harm others without having to pay the full costs. In these cases, the pursuit of private gain will not promote the social welfare. The purpose of this section is to describe how differences between private and social returns are likely to arise and the ways in which these differences influence our results. The following sections show how this theory can illuminate public policies toward basic research and toward multinational firms.

It is convenient, and customary, to classify these divergences into four types. First, there are *external economies of production*. An external economy occurs when an action taken by an economic unit results in uncompensated benefits to others; when such benefits are due to an increase in a firm's production, they are called external economies of production. The firm may benefit others directly. For example, it may train workers that eventually go to work for other firms that do not have to pay the training costs. Or the firm may benefit other firms indirectly because its increased output may make it more economical for firms outside the industry to provide services to other firms in the industry. For example, a great expansion in an aircraft firm may make it possible for aluminum producers to take advantage of economies of scale, with the result that other metal fabricating firms can also get cheaper aluminum. In either case, there is a difference between private and social returns; the gains to society are greater than the gains to the firm.

External economies of production

11. T. Marschak, "Capital Budgeting and Pricing in the French Nationalized Industries," *Journal of Business,* January 1960, p. 151.

EXAMPLE 15.2

TIME-OF-DAY ELECTRICITY RATES

Time-of-day pricing of electricity calls for higher electricity rates during the times of day when the use of electricity is relatively great than during the times of day when it is relatively small. For example, in England, Indonesia, and Kenya, the charge at various times of day is as follows:

	England	Indonesia	Kenya
	(cents per kilowatt-hour)		
Period of peak demand (7 a.m. to midnight)*	5.91	4.64	3.75
Period of off-peak demand (midnight to 7 a.m.)**	2.78	3.20	2.25

*This is the peak period in England. In Indonesia it is 6 p.m. to 10 p.m. In Kenya it is 8 a.m. to 10 p.m.

**This is the off-peak period in England. In Indonesia it is 10 p.m. to 6 p.m. In Kenya it is 10 p.m. to 8 a.m.

(a) Can time-of-day pricing be viewed as a form of marginal cost pricing? (b) What effect does time-of-day pricing have on the way in which electricity use is distributed among hours of the day? (c) Are the benefits from applying time-of-day pricing to large industrial firms and office buildings frequently greater than those resulting from its application to residential consumers? If so, why? (d) Until the mid-1970s, was time-of-day pricing customarily used in the United States? If not, has it become more widely used?

SOLUTION

(a) If the prices in the peak and off-peak periods are set in such a way that they approximate the marginal costs in these respective periods, the results will be a form of marginal cost pricing. As shown in the table, the peak-period price is set higher than the off-peak-period price in each of these countries. This difference is reasonable because marginal cost tends to be higher in peak than off-peak periods. (b) Buyers are discouraged from using electricity at the peak hours, when it is relatively expensive to produce, and they are encouraged to use it at the off-peak hours, when it is cheaper to produce. Thus there may be more use of electricity in off-peak hours and less use in peak hours. (c) Yes.

There are hundreds of thousands of residences in a major urban area, and many of these customers use relatively small amounts of electricity and have limited flexibility with regard to the time of day when they demand electricity. The cost of installing the meters required to determine how much electricity each customer used at each time of day may exceed the benefits. For example, in Los Angeles, Jan Acton and Bridger Mitchell found that "if time-of-day rates were applied to all residential customers, the additional costs of metering would greatly exceed the benefits of more efficient energy use."* (d) Time-of-day pricing, while well established in the electricity industries of Europe, was seldom used in the United States until the mid-1970s. Because of public concern over environmental issues and our energy problems, state regulatory commissions began to hold hearings in the early 1970s to examine electricity rate structures. These hearings led to the adoption of time-of-day rates for very big electricity consumers (generally large industrial firms and office buildings). In 1978, the Public Utility Regulatory Policy Act required public utilities to implement time-of-day pricing or to "show cause" why such pricing should not be implemented in their service areas.**

* J. Acton and B. Mitchell, "Evaluating Time-of-Day Electricity Rates for Residential Customers," in B. Mitchell and P. Kleindorfer, *Regulated Industries and Public Enterprise* (Lexington, Mass.: Lexington Books, 1980), p. 248.

** For further discussion, see J. Acton and B. Mitchell, ibid.; M. Munasinghe and J. Warford, *Electricity Pricing: Theory and Case Studies* (Baltimore: Johns Hopkins Press, 1982); and D. Hill, D. Ott, L. Taylor, and J. Walker, "Incentive Payments in Time-of-Day Electricity Pricing Experiments: The Arizona Experience," *Review of Economics and Statistics*, February 1983.

External economies of consumption

Second, there are *external economies of consumption,* which occur when an action taken by a consumer, rather than a producer, results in an uncompensated benefit to others. For example, if I maintain my house and lawn, this benefits my neighbors as well as myself. If I educate my children and make them more responsible citizens, this too benefits my neighbors as well as myself. The list of external economies from consumption could easily be extended, but the idea should be clear at this point.

External diseconomies of production

Third, there are *external diseconomies of production.* An external diseconomy occurs when an action taken by an economic unit results in uncompensated costs to others; when such costs are due to increases in a firm's production, they are called external diseconomies of production. For example, a firm may pollute a stream by pumping out waste materials, or it may pollute the air with smoke or materials. Such actions result in costs to others; for instance, Chesapeake Bay's oyster beds and Long Island's clam beds continually are being threatened by water pollution. However, the private costs do not reflect the full social costs, since the firms and cities responsible for the pollution are not charged for their contribution to poorer quality water and their harm to industries dependent on good water. There are many cases of external diseconomies of production, such as traffic congestion and defacing of scenery.

External diseconomies of consumption

Fourth, there are *external diseconomies of consumption,* which occur when an action taken by a consumer results in an uncompensated cost to others. Some external diseconomies of consumption can be fairly subtle. For example, Mrs.

White may be trying hard to keep up with the social leader in town, Mrs. Brown. If Mrs. Brown obtains a new mink coat, this may make Mrs. White worse off, since she may become dissatisfied with her old mink coat. Similarly, a family that feels that a three-year-old Chevrolet is perfectly adequate may become dissatisfied with it after moving to a community where everyone drives a new Cadillac.

The foregoing are some of the most important cases where social and private costs and benefits differ. At first glance, these cases may not seem very important. But when all of these types of external economies and diseconomies are considered, their aggregate significance can be substantial. For example, the fact that environmental pollution of various kinds resulting from industrial output is important has been stressed repeatedly in the United States in recent years. The importance of various types of external economies of production is undeniable, and the fact that consumer tastes and well-being are determined by the tastes and well-being of other members of society is obvious as well.

How do these external economies and diseconomies alter the efficiency of the allocation of resources under perfect competition? If a person takes an action that contributes to society's welfare but receives no payment for it, he or she is likely to take this action less frequently than would be socially desirable. The same holds true for firms. Thus, if the production of a certain good, say beryllium, is responsible for external economies, less than the socially efficient amount of beryllium is likely to be produced under perfect competition, since the producers are unlikely to increase output simply because it reduces the costs of other companies. By the same token if a person takes an action that results in costs borne by others, he or she is likely to take this action more frequently than is socially desirable. The same holds true for firms. Thus, if the production of a certain good is responsible for external diseconomies, more of this good is likely to be produced under perfect competition than is socially efficient. Much more will be said about these and other effects of externalities in Chapter 16.[12]

Public Policy Toward Basic Research: An Application

To illustrate how the theory of external economies and diseconomies, together with the other principles discussed in this chapter, can be used to throw light on problems of public policy, consider the nature of social policy toward basic research. One of the most fundamental questions in this area is: Why should the government support basic research? Why not rely on private enterprise to support sufficient basic research?

To answer this question, it is important to recognize that basic scientific research is likely to generate substantial external economies. Important additions to fundamental knowledge often have an impact on a great many fields. If a firm produces an important scientific breakthrough, it generally cannot hope to capture the full value of the new knowledge it creates. It cannot go into the full range of activities in which the knowledge has use, and it is seldom able to capture through patent rights the full social value of the new knowledge.

---

12. See W. Baumol, *Economic Theory and Operations Analysis,* 3d ed. (Englewood Cliffs, N.J.: Prentice-Hall, 1972), pp. 392–95 and 399–404.

Indeed, fundamental discoveries, such as natural laws, cannot be patented at all.

Because of these external economies, there is likely to be a divergence between the private and social benefits from basic research, with the result that a perfectly competitive economy would be expected to devote fewer resources to basic research than is socially optimal. Consequently, there seems to be a good case on purely economic grounds for the government (or some other agency not motivated by profit) to support basic research. As pointed out in the 1987 report of the Council of Economic Advisers, "the Federal Government has an important role in funding basic scientific research. Such research can contribute to technological advance in the longer term. However, its benefits are often too diffuse and difficult to profit from for it to be undertaken by private business."[13]

Based on similar considerations, there is a strong argument for government support of fundamental research to extend the technological underpinnings of broad industrial areas. For example, the National Advisory Committee on Aeronautics carried out research and development concerning wind tunnels, aircraft fuels, aircraft design, and other fundamental matters regarding aviation. No individual firm had much incentive to do such work because it could appropriate only a small share of the benefits. But because the benefits to the economy as a whole were substantial, the government intervened to finance work of this sort. The simple principles of microeconomics help to indicate why such a policy was justified.[14]

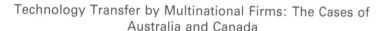

Technology Transfer by Multinational Firms: The Cases of Australia and Canada

A remarkable economic development of the last forty years has been the growth of multinational firms, firms which operate in a very significant way in many countries. The reasons why firms have become multinational are varied. In some cases, firms have established overseas branches to control foreign sources of raw materials. In other cases, firms have invested overseas for defensive reasons. But in a great many cases, firms have established foreign branches to exploit a technological lead. After exporting a new product (or a modified version of an existing product) to foreign markets, firms have decided to establish plants overseas to supply these markets. Once the foreign market was big enough to accomodate a plant of minimum efficient size, this decision did not conflict with scale economies. Moreover, freight costs and tariffs often hastened such a decision. Also, in some cases, the only way that a firm could introduce its innovation into a foreign market was through the establishment of overseas production facilities.

Multinational firms, by carrying their technology overseas, have played a

---

13. Economic Report of the President (Washington, D.C.: U.S. Government Printing Office, 1987), p. 49.
14. J. Hirshleifer has pointed out that, if new information provides an individual or firm with a competitive edge, there may be a tendency to overinvest in it. The kinds of information discussed in this section can seldom be translated into an important competitive advantage, for reasons discussed above. See J. Hirshleifer, "The Private and Social Value of Information and the Reward to Inventive Activity," *American Economic Review,* September 1971.

very significant role in the international diffusion of innovations. Moreover, they have often been responsible for important external economies, since the new technology that they introduced into other countries often spread quickly to other firms in these countries. Thus the transfer of technology benefited other firms as well as the multinational firm that transferred the technology. For example, in the case of Australia, Donald Brash concludes that the technologies of multinational firms "tend to become disseminated throughout the economy in a variety of ways. Executives with experience in [multinational] companies often move to Australian-owned companies . . . . Often the mere example of [multinational] firms is sufficient to induce a change in the operating methods of Australian firms."[15]

Canada is another important example of this sort. In a recent study of 283 major Canadian innovations, it was found that 96 of them were based wholly or in part on externally controlled technology. In over half of these 96 cases, the technology came from another part of a multinational firm of which the innovator was a member. Usually the source of the technology was the United States.[16]

Of course, the fact that multinational firms result in such external economies does not mean that the activities of these firms always benefit the host country. As Canada's Watkins Committee has suggested, there may be considerable costs to the host country associated with its receipt of technology via the multinational firm. To the host countries, multinational firms are sometimes viewed as instruments of their parent country's policies. Also, the host country sometimes fears that the multinational firm, in pursuit of its own profits, may engage in activities that are contrary to the host country's interests and policies. A basic consideration here is the locus of control: Host countries do not feel comfortable about foreign control of much of their resources and capability.[17]

INCREASING RETURNS, PUBLIC GOODS, AND IMPERFECT INFORMATION

Increasing returns

If there are external economies or diseconomies, the simple conditions for economic efficiency described above (on pp. 437–38) are not valid. Other cases in which these conditions are not valid occur when some industries operate under increasing returns or when a good is a public good. First, consider the case of a good that is produced under increasing returns. In such a case the product transformation curve may look like that in panel A of Figure 15.5, rather than like that in panel B of Figure 15.5. Let curves 1 and 2 be the indifference curves of the sole consumer in our simple society. Then, if the marginal rate of product

15. Donald Brash, *American Investment in Australian Industry* (Cambridge, Mass.: Harvard University Press, 1966), pp. 178–79. Also see E. Mansfield and A. Romeo, "Technology Transfer by U.S.-Based Firms to Overseas Subsidiaries," *Quarterly Journal of Economics,* December 1980.

16. For a discussion of studies in this area, see E. Mansfield, "Technological Change and the International Diffusion of Technology," in D. G. McFetridge (ed.), *Technological Change in Canadian Industry* (Toronto: University of Toronto Press, 1985).

17. See R. Caves, *Multinational Enterprise and Economic Analysis* (Cambridge, Eng.: Cambridge University Press, 1982).

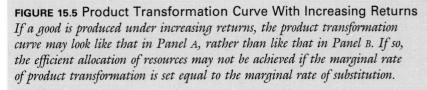

FIGURE 15.5 Product Transformation Curve With Increasing Returns

*If a good is produced under increasing returns, the product transformation
curve may look like that in Panel A, rather than like that in Panel B. If so,
the efficient allocation of resources may not be achieved if the marginal rate
of product transformation is set equal to the marginal rate of substitution.*

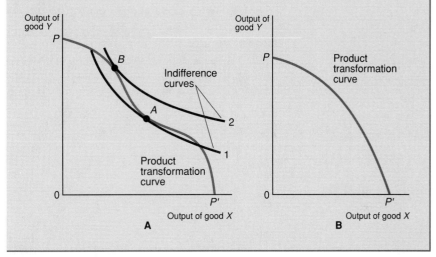

transformation is set equal to the marginal rate of substitution, in accord with
the third condition for economic efficiency (on p. 438), the efficient allocation
of resources may not be achieved, since this condition is fulfilled at point *A*,
which is not the efficient point, as well as at point *B*, which is the efficient point.
In cases like this, the price system, as well as the conditions described on pp.
437–38, can give faulty signals to producers and consumers.

Turning to public goods, it is important to recognize that one person can
enjoy some goods without reducing the enjoyment they give others. The market mechanism does not work properly for such goods because excluding those
who do not pay reduces their satisfaction and does not increase the satisfaction
of others. Also, the consumer cannot be made to pay a price for these commodities, because a person cannot be barred from using them whether or not he
Public goods or she pays. Examples of such goods, called *public* or *collective goods,* are major
items like national defense. Perfect competition will not result in an efficient
allocation of resources to such goods. Instead, the government or private char-
ities generally provide goods of this type. Much more will be said about public
goods in Chapter 16.

Another reason why the market mechanism may not work properly is that
consumers (and others) may have imperfect information about market prices
Imperfect information and product quality. Because consumers have imperfect information, producers
may produce too much of some goods and services and too little of others. To
illustrate the effects of imperfect information, take the case of the used car
market. If consumers are unable to evaluate the quality of a used car until after
they buy it, the price of a used car may be so low that relatively few good used
cars are put on the market. Many consumers would be glad to pay a higher price

EXAMPLE 15.3

EXTERNAL DISECONOMIES ON THE HIGHWAYS

Each morning, thousands of motorists travel the route from Philadelphia's western suburbs to the central business district where they work or shop. Suppose that the full cost of this auto trip—including both the money costs (of fuel, oil, tire wear, and so on) and *the value of the driver's (and passengers') time*—is measured along the vertical axis of the graph below, and that the number of vehicles attempting this trip between 7 a.m. and 8 a.m. on a particular day is measured along the horizontal axis. The relationship between the full cost of this trip to a motorist and the number of vehicles attempting this trip is CC'. The demand curve shows at each price of this trip (including both money and time costs) the number of vehicles that will set out on this route.

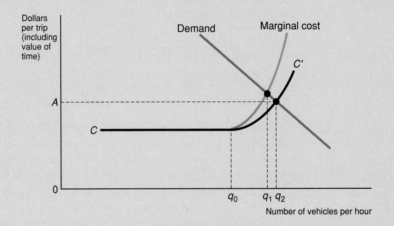

(a) If more than Oq_0 vehicles attempt this trip, the cost of the trip increases as more and more vehicles per hour set out on this route. Why? Is this due to external diseconomies? (b) How many autos per hour will travel along this route? (c) Is this the economically efficient number? (d) What measures might be taken to push the actual number closer to the efficient number?

SOLUTION

(a) If more than Oq_0 vehicles per hour travel this route, the highway becomes congested. Traffic becomes tied up, it takes longer to make the trip, and the full cost (including time) increases. As more and more vehicles travel this route, the congestion gets worse. Each extra vehicle, by delaying other vehicles taking this route, is responsible for external diseconomies. (b) Oq_2 vehicles per hour. If less than Oq_2 vehicles per hour travel this route, the full cost of the trip (indicated by the CC' curve) is less than the value of the trip to the motorist (indicated by the demand curve), and more vehicles will make the trip. If more than Oq_2 vehicles per hour travel this route, the full cost of the trip exceeds the value of the trip to the motorist, and less vehicles will make the trip. (c) No. The economically efficient number is Oq_1 vehicles per hour. If more than Oq_0 vehicles per hour travel this route, the marginal cost to society of an extra vehicle's traveling this route (shown by the colored line in the graph) exceeds the cost to the motorist driving this extra vehicle because the extra vehicle delays other motorists. Up to Oq_1 vehicles per hour, the marginal cost to society of an extra vehicle (shown by the colored line) is less than the marginal benefit (shown by the demand curve), and society gains if more vehicles per hour take this route. But above Oq_1 vehicles per hour, this is no longer true. (d) Some economists have suggested that a tax be imposed on motorists that travel congested highways.* In this way, the private costs would be brought closer to the true social costs. Also, tolls can be used, at least under some circumstances.

*See A. Walters, "The Theory and Measurement of Private and Social Cost of Highway Congestion," *Econometrica*, October 1961.

if they could be sure they were getting a good used car, but because they find it so difficult to obtain reliable information on this score, the market for used cars may not function effectively, as we saw in Chapter 2.

Summary

1. Microeconomics is concerned with the nature of the policy recommendations that economists can make. An important limitation of microeconomics is that there is no scientifically meaningful way to compare the utility levels of different individuals, with the result that we cannot tell whether one distribution of income is better than another.

2. Putting aside the question of income distribution, there are three conditions for an efficient allocation of resources: (1) The marginal rate of substitution between any two commodities must be the same for any two consumers; (2) the marginal rate of technical substitution between any two inputs must be the same for any pair of producers; and (3) the marginal rate of substitution between any two commodities must be the same as the marginal rate of product transformation between these two commodities for any producer.

3. One of the most fundamental findings of microeconomics is that a perfectly competitive economy satisfies these three sets of conditions for economic efficiency. To the economic theorist, this is one of the basic arguments for a perfectly competitive economy.

4. Economists interested in the functioning of planned, or socialist, economies have argued that a price system could be used in a similar way to increase social welfare in such economies. The prices that would be set would equal marginal cost.

5. There have been recommendations that government-owned enterprises in basically capitalist economies also adopt marginal cost pricing. The French electric industry is a case study along these lines.

6. If the production of a certain good is responsible for external economies, less than the socially efficient amount of this good is likely to be produced under perfect competition. If the production of a certain good is responsible for external diseconomies, more of this good is likely to be produced under perfect

competition than is socially efficient. Basic research is an example of a good that
is likely to be underproduced in a perfectly competitive economy.

7. Perfect competition is unlikely to result in economic efficiency in the presence of
increasing returns or when a good is a public good. Also, if consumers (and
others) have imperfect information concerning market prices and product quality, this too can interfere with the workings of competitive markets.

Questions/ Problems

1. The paper industry has been a notable source of water pollution. Suppose that every ton
of paper which is produced imposes costs on others (for example, to people using local
rivers for recreation and fishing) of $5. The supply and demand curves for paper are
given below.

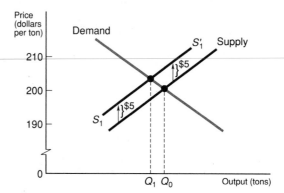

What will be the output of the paper industry? What is the efficient output of the paper
industry?

2. According to Milton Friedman, significant external economies are gained from the education of children: "The gain from the education of a child accrues not only to the child
or its parents but also to other members of the society." Moreover, "It is not feasible to
identify the particular individuals (or families) benefited and so to charge for the services
rendered." What kind of government action is justified by these considerations?

3. In some cities (for example, Los Angeles), the price of water is lower for some water
uses—irrigation, for example—than for others. Will this result in a malallocation of
resources? If so, how? What may be a preferable water pricing system?

4. In 1986, Congress passed a bill making business entertainment expenses partly, but not
wholly, tax deductible. (Previously they had been completely deductible.) What segments of the population did this hurt? What segments did it help? Is there any way to tell
whether, on balance, it was good or bad for society?

5. Suppose that two consumers, after swapping goods back and forth, have arrived at a
point on the contract curve. In other words, neither can be made better off without
making the other worse off. Does this mean that neither of them can find a point *off* the
contract curve which is preferable to the point at which they have arrived? If it does not
mean this, why do economists claim that points on the contract curve are to be preferred?

6. Microeconomics is concerned with the determination of ways to satisfy human wants as
best we can. But is this really a sensible goal? For example, suppose that people want the
wrong things. Is it still sensible to try to satisfy these wants as completely as possible?
Shouldn't microeconomics be concerned, too, with how wants are created?

7. A small private jet lands at Kennedy Airport in New York at the busiest time of day. It
pays a nominal landing fee. What divergences may exist between the private and social

costs of this plane's landing there at that time? What policies might help to eliminate such divergencies?

8. In judging various social mechanisms and policies, microeconomics tends to emphasize the outcomes of these mechanisms and policies, as measured by the extent to which various human wants are satisfied. But shouldn't microeconomics be concerned with *means* as well as *ends*? For example, suppose that a particular policy resulted in an ideal allocation of resources, but that it was achieved by trickery or coercion. Doesn't this matter?

9. According to Nicholas Kaldor, a change is an improvement if the people who gain from the change evaluate their gains at a higher dollar figure than the dollar figure that the losers attach to their losses. For example, if a proposed change benefits Tom and harms Harry, and if Tom would be willing to pay up to $100 to see the change occur, while Harry would pay up to $50 to avoid the change, the change, according to Kaldor, is an improvement (even though no money is paid by Tom to Harry). Can you see any problems with this view? If so, what are they?

10. Suppose that the market for videocassette recorders is in disequilibrium; that is, the actual price does not equal the equilibrium price. If all industries in the economy are perfectly competitive (including videocassette recorders), will the necessary conditions for economic efficiency be met?

16

PUBLIC GOODS, EXTERNALITIES, AND THE ROLE OF GOVERNMENT

INTRODUCTION

A perfectly competitive economy, despite its attractive features, is unlikely to allocate resources efficiently in the production of public goods and of goods that are responsible for important external diseconomies and economies. This was one of the lessons of the previous chapter. Thus the government is charged with the responsibility for providing (but not necessarily producing) public goods and for trying to offset the distortions caused by externalities. In this chapter, we provide a more complete discussion of the nature of public goods, and of the amount of a public good that should be provided to promote economic efficiency. Also, using environmental pollution as a case study, we describe in more detail the effects of externalities on resource allocation and what the government can do to offset them. Further, we discuss Coase's theorem, which indicates circumstances under which a perfectly competitive economy will allocate resources efficiently, even in the face of seemingly important external costs or benefits.

In addition, although a full discussion of the microeconomic analysis of government activities would take us too far afield, it is worthwhile considering two aspects of this subject. First, we discuss and illustrate the use of benefit-cost analysis, a technique frequently used by government agencies to help improve their decision-making. Second, we discuss some of the limitations of government agencies as allocators of resources. To obtain a balanced picture, it is essential to recognize that both competitive markets and government agencies can be quite imperfect in this respect.

CHARACTERISTICS OF A PUBLIC GOOD

In Chapter 15, we learned that under the specified conditions (and with the proper qualifications), a perfectly competitive economy results in an efficient allocation of resources. However, it was assumed that the goods being produced were not public goods. A public good has two characteristics: it is non-*Nonrival* rival and nonexclusive. By *nonrival* we mean that the marginal cost of providing the good to an additional consumer is zero. Thus a public good can be enjoyed by an extra person without reducing the enjoyment it gives others. Consider the case of national defense. If a baby is born in the United States at this moment, he or she can enjoy the protection of our military establishment without reducing the protection it affords the rest of us. Thus national defense is a nonrival good.

Nonexclusive By *nonexclusive,* we mean that people cannot be excluded from consuming the good. Ordinarily, whether or not a person consumes a good depends on whether or not he or she pays the price. Those who pay for the good can consume it, while those who do not pay cannot consume it. But this is not always the case, as illustrated again by national defense. Once a country has created a military establishment, all citizens enjoy its protection. Since there is no practical way of excluding citizens from its protection, national defense is a nonexclusive good.

A public good is defined here as a good that is *both* nonrival and nonexclusive. Not all nonrival goods are nonexclusive goods (and not all nonexclusive goods are nonrival goods). Consider an uncrowded bridge. If Mr. Smith crosses the bridge, this does not interfere with Mr. Jones's crossing it, which indicates that the use of this bridge is a nonrival good. But it is not a nonexclusive good, as shown by the fact that it is perfectly feasible to charge a fee for crossing the bridge, and to prevent people who do not pay from crossing it.

Public goods will not be provided in the right amounts by the market mechanism, which operates on the principle that those who do not pay for a good cannot consume it. As we have just seen, it is impossible to prevent people from consuming a public good whether or not they pay for it. For example, there is no way to prevent someone from benefiting from national defense, regardless of whether or not he or she helps pay for it. Thus, in many cases, the market mechanism simply is not applicable.

THE EFFICIENT OUTPUT OF A PUBLIC GOOD

If resources are to be allocated efficiently, how much should be produced of a public good? In this section, we analyze this question from the point of view of partial equilibrium analysis. Suppose for simplicity that there are only two consumers, the Adams family and the Brown family. Suppose that D_A is the Adams family's demand curve for a good, D_B is the Brown family's demand curve for the same good, and the supply curve for the good is as shown in Figure 16.1.

FIGURE 16.1 Determination of Efficient Output: Private Good and Public Good *For a private good, the efficient output is* OQ *in panel* A. *For a public good, the efficient output is* OR *in panel* B.

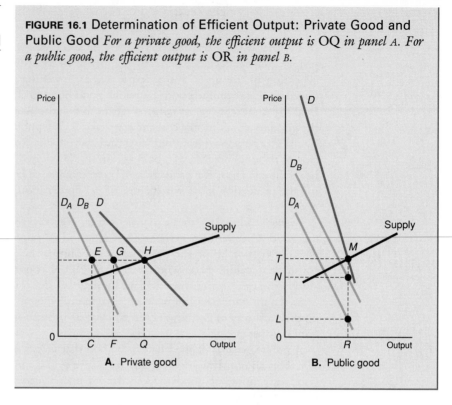

A. Private good

B. Public good

The left-hand panel of Figure 16.1 shows the efficient output of this good, assuming that it is a *private* good produced under perfect competition. Summing horizontally the demand curves of the two consumers, we obtain the market demand curve for the good, *D*. The efficient output is *OQ*, where this market demand curve intersects the market supply curve. Why is this efficient? Because at this output, the marginal benefit each consumer would obtain from an extra unit of the good equals its marginal cost. Assuming that the marginal benefit can be measured by the maximum amount that each family will pay for the extra unit, the marginal benefit for the Adams family would be *CE*, and the marginal benefit for the Brown family would be *FG*. The marginal cost of the extra unit is *QH* at an output of *OQ*. (Recall from Chapter 8 that the supply curve shows the marginal cost at each level of output.) Since *CE = FG = QH*, it follows that the marginal benefit to each consumer equals the marginal cost.

If, on the other hand, the good is a *public* good, the efficient output is shown in the right-hand panel of Figure 16.1. In this case, the market demand curve is obtained by summing the individual demand curves[1] *vertically*, not horizontally. This fundamental difference stems from the fact that both consumers consume the *total* amount of the good, and that the combined price paid by the two consumers is the sum of the prices paid by each one. The efficient output of

Efficient output of private good

Efficient output of public good

---

1. These demand curves are sometimes called pseudo-demand curves or willingness-to-pay curves. See R. and N. Dorfman, *Economics of the Environment*, 2d ed. (New York: Norton, 1977).

the good is now *OR,* and the total price (the sum of the prices paid by each consumer) is *OT.*

To see why *OR* is the efficient output, recall (from pp. 271–72 of Chapter 9) that the efficient output is the one where marginal social benefit equals marginal social cost. Next, note that the marginal social benefit from an extra unit of output of a public good is obtained by adding vertically the distances under every consumer's demand curve. This is because all consumers share entirely in the consumption of whatever quantity of the good is available, and because the marginal social benefit is the sum of the marginal benefits to each consumer. (Also, if an extra unit of the good is worth to an individual the maximum amount that he or she is willing to pay for it, the marginal benefit to each consumer is the distance under his or her demand curve.) Thus, if output is *OR,* the marginal social benefit from an extra unit of output is the vertical sum of *OL* and *ON,* which equals *OT.* Since the marginal social cost of an extra unit of output is *RM* (as in the case of a private good), and since the optimal output is where marginal social benefit equals marginal social cost, it follows that *OR* must be the efficient output, since marginal social benefit (*OT*) and marginal social cost (*RM*) are equal at this output.

This analysis is illuminating. For example, Figure 16.1 shows the important fact that, whereas economic efficiency requires that each consumer's marginal benefit equal marginal cost for a private good, it requires that the *sum* of the marginal benefits of all consumers equals marginal cost for a public good. But despite its good points, this kind of analysis can take us only so far. For one thing, the demand curves in Figure 16.1 will not be revealed voluntarily if citizens believe that the amount they pay will be related to the preferences they reveal. Consumers will find it worthwhile to be *free riders.* In other words, when consumers feel that the total output of the good will not be affected significantly by the action of any single person, they are likely to make no contribution to supporting the good, although they will use whatever output of the good is forthcoming.[2]

Free riders

THE PROVISION OF PUBLIC GOODS

If the number of people in a society is quite small, it may be worthwhile for people acting individually to provide some quantity of public goods. For example, consider a case where there are two families on an island that is infested with poisonous snakes. The reduction of the number of such snakes is a public good, if there is no way of preventing the snakes from moving from one family's land to the other's, and if providing enhanced protection against the snakes for one family automatically provides it for the other family at no additional cost. Under these conditions, one of the families may well deem it worthwhile to engage in some activities to kill the snakes, even though this benefits the other family as well. Thus, when numbers are small, it is a mistake to say that no public goods will be produced unless the government does so. However, this

2. In addition, a partial equilibrium analysis of this problem has obvious limitations. For a general equilibrium analysis, see P. Samuelson, "Diagrammatic Exposition of a Theory of Public Expenditure," reprinted in E. Mansfield, *Microeconomics: Selected Readings,* 5th ed.

does not mean that the proper amount of public goods will be produced, which brings us to the next point.

Even if there are few people in the society, there is a tendency for the provision of a public good to be too small, if its provision is left entirely up to the people acting individually in their own self-interest. To see why, suppose that a family lives alone for some time on the island cited above, and then is joined by a family that formerly lived alone on another island. Once the second family arrives, the first family will reduce its efforts to kill poisonous snakes because it will count on the other family to do some such work. Similarly, the other family will do less work of this sort than when it lived alone on the other island, for the same reasons. Both will cut back too much on their efforts because, whereas each family pays the full cost of devoting its time to this activity, it receives only part of the benefits, some of which accrue to the other family. Thus less will be produced of this public good than is socially efficient.

If there are few people in the society, there is a tendency for those who have the biggest interest in the outcome, or the biggest share of the resources, to provide a disproportionately large share of the amount of a public good that is supplied. For example, suppose that the first family in the previous paragraph owns 90 percent of the land (and other resources) on the island, and the second family owns 10 percent. Then the first family will recognize that whatever attempts are made to control the snake nuisance will rest largely on its shoulders, and it will act almost as if it were by itself on the island. On the other hand, the second family, recognizing that the first family has an incentive to do an effective job of this sort, is likely to reduce its efforts to a minimal level. Consequently, the first family is likely to do more than 90 percent of the snake-control work, and the second family is likely to do less than 10 percent.

The larger the number of people in the society, the farther it will fall short of producing an efficient amount of a public good. Thus, in large societies like the United States, the government intervenes in an attempt to insure the proper amount of public goods. There is general agreement that the government must provide public goods like national defense, and the provision of such goods unquestionably accounts for a significant portion of the government's expenditure. In democratic societies, the ballot box is used to determine the amount spent on various public goods. Each person votes for candidates that represent (often imperfectly) the set of public expenditures and taxes that is closest to his or her own preferences.[3]

EXTERNALITIES: THE CASE OF ENVIRONMENTAL POLLUTION

Besides providing public goods, the government sometimes intervenes in an attempt to offset distortions caused by external diseconomies and economies. In the previous chapter, we discussed briefly how considerations of this sort influence public policy. Now we look in more detail at a case of fundamental

3. To a considerable extent, this section is based on M. Olson, *The Logic of Collective Choice*, rev. ed. (New York: Shocken, 1971). Also, see M. Olson and R. Zeckhauser, "An Economic Theory of Alliances," *The Review of Economics and Statistics,* August 1966.

EXAMPLE 16.1

ECONOMICS OF A LIGHTHOUSE

A lighthouse warns fishing boats away from a treacherous rock. Different
levels of service can be provided by the lighthouse, resulting in different probabilities that a boat will be warned of its nearness to the rock. For example, the
more powerful the beacon or signal emitted by the lighthouse, the higher the
probability that a boat will receive the warning. The marginal cost of attaining
various probabilities that a boat will be warned is as shown in the graph
below. There are three boats in the area, owned by Captains Amos, Barnaby,
and Columbus. The price that each captain is willing to pay for each level of
service (that is, each probability that a boat will be warned) is shown by the
individual demand curves in the graph below.

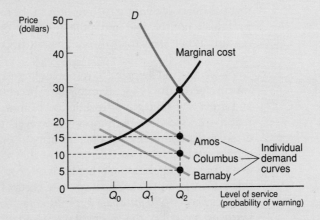

(a) Is the service provided by the lighthouse a nonrival good? (b) Is it a
nonexclusive good? (c) What is the efficient level of service (if it is a public
good)? That is, what should be the probability that a boat will be warned? (d)
Is it impossible for a lighthouse to be privately owned and operated?

SOLUTION

(a) It is a nonrival good because, if the service is provided for any fishing boat,
it is available to all other boats at no extra cost. (b) It is a nonexclusive good
because the light can be used by all boats that see it. (c) To obtain the market
demand curve for the service, we must sum the three individual demand
curves vertically, the result being D. The efficient level of service is at the point
where the marginal cost curve intersects the D curve; that is, the efficient level
of service is OQ_2. (d) No. In England lighthouses were private for many
years. They assessed the shipowners at the docks. Ordinarily only one ship
was in sight of the lighthouse at a particular point in time. The light would
not be shown if the ship (which was identified by its flag) had not paid.*

*For further discussion, see N. Singer, *Public Microeconomics* (Little, Brown, 1976); and R.
Coase, "The Lighthouse in Economics," *Journal of Law and Economics,* October 1974.

importance—the problem of environmental pollution—and discuss in what ways and to what extent the government should intervene. The pollution problem affects vital aspects of our environment. Many of our streams and lakes receive chemical wastes generated by industrial plants and mines, as well as pesticides, fertilizers, and detergents used by farms and homes. Automobiles are the prime source of many air pollutants. Also, factories generate particles of various kinds, often through the combustion of fossil fuels, that pollute the air.

Why does our economy tolerate such pollution of the environment? The answer lies largely in the concept of external diseconomies, discussed in Chapter 15. An external diseconomy, as you recall, occurs when one person's (or firm's) use of a resource damages other people who cannot obtain proper compensation. When this occurs, a competitive economy is unlikely to function properly. For market prices to produce an efficient allocation of resources, it is necessary that the full cost of using each resource is borne by the person or firm that uses it. If this is not the case, and if the user bears only part of the full costs, then the resource is not likely to be directed by the price system into the socially optimal use.

As we saw in Chapter 15, resources are used in their socially most valuable way in a perfectly competitive economy because they are allocated to the people and firms that find it worthwhile to bid most for them, assuming that prices reflect true social costs. Suppose, however, that because of the presence of external diseconomies, people and firms do not pay the true social costs for certain resources. In particular, suppose that some firms or people can use water or air for nothing, but that other firms or people incur costs as a consequence of this prior use. In this case, the private costs of using air and water differ from the social costs: *The price paid by the user of water and air is less than the true cost to society.* In a case like this, users of water and air are guided in their decisions by the private cost of water and air—by the prices they pay. Since they pay less than the true social costs, water and air are artificially cheap to them, so that they will use too much of these resources, from society's point of view.

Note that the divergence between private and social cost occurs if and only if the use of water or air by one firm or person imposes costs on other firms or persons. Thus, if a paper mill uses water and then treats it to restore its quality, there is no divergence between private and social cost. But when the same mill dumps untreated wastes into streams and rivers—and causes firms and towns downstream that use the water to incur costs to restore its quality—there is a divergence between private and social cost. The same is true of air pollution. When an electric power plant uses the atmosphere as a cheap and convenient place to dispose of wastes, but people living and working nearby incur costs (including poorer health) as a result, there is a divergence between private and social cost.

Efficient Pollution Control

In general, an industry can vary, at each level of output, the amount of pollution it generates. For example, it may install pollution-control devices like scrubbers or electrostatic precipitators to reduce the amount of pollution it generates at each level of output. Holding the industry's output fixed, what is the econom-

FIGURE 16.2 Cost of Pollution *The cost of pollution increases as larger
quantities of pollutants are emitted.*

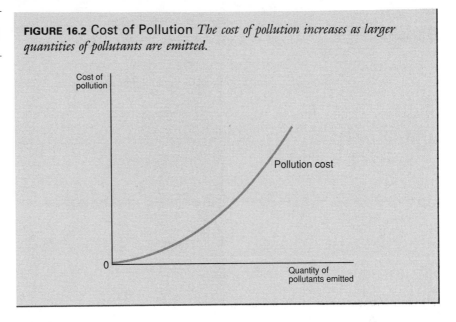

Cost of pollution

*Cost of pollution
control*

Sum of costs

ically efficient level of pollution control? At first blush, it may appear that this is
a foolish question. Isn't it obvious that zero pollution is the best level? Strange
as it may seem, the answer is no. Instead, the best solution for society is generally to tolerate a certain amount of pollution. This statement may not warm
the hearts of some environmentalists, but it is true nonetheless, as we shall
see.

Figure 16.2 shows the total social cost of each level of discharge of an industry's wastes, holding constant the industry's output. Clearly, the more untreated
waste the industry dumps into the environment, the greater the total costs.
Figure 16.3 shows the costs of pollution control at each level of discharge of the
industry's wastes. Clearly, the more the industry cuts down on the amount of
wastes it discharges, the higher are its costs of pollution control. Figure 16.4
shows the sum of these two costs—the cost of pollution and the cost of pollution control—at each level of discharge of the industry's wastes.

From the point of view of society as a whole, the industry should reduce its
discharge of pollution to the point where the sum of these two costs—the cost
of pollution and the cost of pollution control—is a minimum. Specifically, the
efficient level of pollution in the industry is *OR* in Figure 16.4. Why is this the
efficient level? Because if the industry discharges *less* than this amount of pollution, a one-unit increase in pollution will reduce the cost of pollution control
by more than it will increase the cost of pollution, whereas if the industry
discharges *more* than this amount of pollution, a one-unit reduction in pollution will reduce the cost of pollution by more than it will increase the cost of
pollution control.

To make this more evident, Figure 16.5 shows the marginal cost of an extra
unit of discharge of waste at each level of discharge of the industry's wastes:
This is designated by *AA'*. Figure 16.5 also shows the marginal cost of reducing
the industry's discharge of waste by one unit: This is designated by *BB'*. The

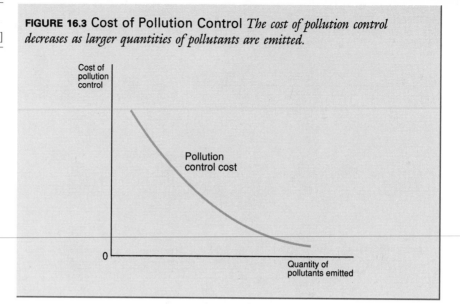

FIGURE 16.3 Cost of Pollution Control *The cost of pollution control decreases as larger quantities of pollutants are emitted.*

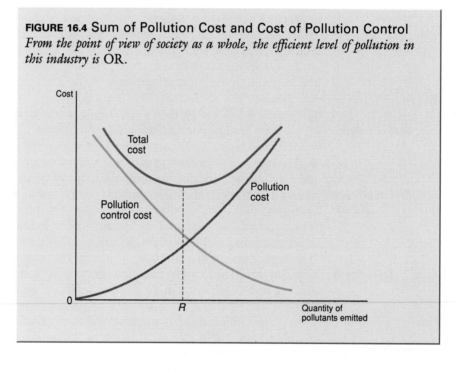

FIGURE 16.4 Sum of Pollution Cost and Cost of Pollution Control *From the point of view of society as a whole, the efficient level of pollution in this industry is* OR.

economically efficient level of pollution for the industry is at the point where the two curves intersect. At this point, the cost of an extra unit of pollution is just equal to the cost of reducing pollution by an extra unit. Regardless of whether we look at Figure 16.4 or 16.5, the answer is the same: *OR* is the economically efficient level of pollution.

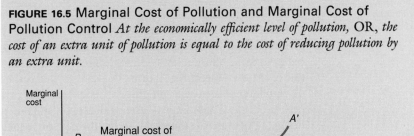

FIGURE 16.5 Marginal Cost of Pollution and Marginal Cost of
Pollution Control *At the economically efficient level of pollution,* OR, *the
cost of an extra unit of pollution is equal to the cost of reducing pollution by
an extra unit.*

Finally, let's return to our statement that the efficient level of pollution is
generally not zero. Based on our discussion in previous paragraphs, it should be
clear that this is true. Why? Because beyond some point, the cost of reducing
pollution exceeds the benefits. In Figures 16.4 and 16.5, this point is reached at
a pollution level of *OR*.[4]

Direct Regulation, Effluent Fees, and Transferable
Emission Permits

Left to its own devices, the industry in Figure 16.5 will not reduce its pollution
level to *OR*, because it does not pay all of the social costs of its pollution. This,
as we saw in the section before last, is the heart of the problem. How can the
government establish incentives that will lead to the efficient amount of pollu-
Direct regulation   tion control? One way is by direct regulation. For example, the government
may decree that this industry is to limit its pollution to *OR* units. Direct regulation of this sort is relied on in many sectors of the American economy.

Another way for the government to influence the amount of pollution is to
Effluent fee   impose an *effluent fee,* which is a fee that a polluter must pay to the government
for discharging waste. The idea behind the imposition of effluent fees is that
they can bring the private cost of waste disposal closer to the true social costs.
For example, in Figure 16.5, an effluent fee of *OE* per unit of pollution discharge might be charged. If so, the marginal cost of an additional unit of
pollution discharge to the industry is *OE*, with the result that it will cut back its
pollution to the efficient level, *OR* units. Why? Because it will be profitable to
cut back pollution so long as the marginal cost of reducing pollution by a unit is
less than *OE*—and, as you can see from Figure 16.5, this is the case so long as

4. For further discussion, see A. Freeman, R. Haveman, and A. Kneese, *The Economics of Environmental Policy* (New York: Wiley, 1973).

the pollution discharge exceeds *OR*. Thus, to maximize their profits, the firms in the industry will reduce pollution to *OR* units.

Effluent fees often have at least two advantages over direct regulation. First, it obviously is socially desirable to use the cheapest way to achieve any given reduction in pollution. A system of effluent fees is more likely to accomplish this result than direct regulation. To see why this is the case, consider a particular polluter. Faced with an effluent fee—that is, a price it must pay for each unit of waste it discharges—the polluter will find it profitable to reduce its discharge of waste to the point where the cost of reducing waste discharges by one unit equals the effluent fee. (Recall our discussion in the previous paragraph.)

It follows that, since the effluent fee is the same for all polluters, the cost of reducing waste discharges by one extra unit is then the same for all polluters. But if this is so, the total cost of achieving the resulting decrease in pollution must be a minimum. To see this, suppose that the cost of reducing waste discharges by an additional unit is not the same for all polluters. Then there is a cheaper way to reduce pollution to its existing level—by getting polluters whose cost of reducing waste discharges by an additional unit is low to reduce their waste disposal by an additional unit, and by allowing polluters whose cost of reducing waste discharges by an additional unit is high to increase their pollution commensurately.

Second, effluent fees have the advantage that they require far less information in the hands of the relevant government agencies than does direct regulation. After all, when effluent fees are used, all the government has to do is meter the amount of pollution a firm or household produces (which admittedly is sometimes not easy) and charge accordingly. It is left to the firms and households to figure out the most ingenious and effective ways to cut down on their pollution and save on effluent fees.

Transferable emissions permits

Still another way that the government can curb the amount of pollution is to issue *transferable emissions permits,* which are permits to generate a certain amount of pollution. These permits, which are limited in total number so that the aggregate amount of pollution equals (approximately) the economically efficient amount, are allocated among firms. They can be bought and sold. Firms that find it very expensive to reduce pollution are likely to buy these permits; firms that find it cheap to do so are likely to sell them.

To illustrate how market mechanisms can be used to curb pollution, consider President Bush's 1989 proposal to reduce the pollutants that cause acid rain. His plan called for a reduction of 10 million tons of sulfur dioxide and 2 million tons of oxides of nitrogen emitted over the next ten years. If one plant reduced its pollutants more than required, it could sell its surplus to another plant that could deduct that amount of pollutants from the reduction it otherwise would have to make.[5]

---

5. "Bush's Acid Test," *New York Times,* October 31, 1989. Still another way for the government to intervene is to establish tax credits for firms that introduce pollution-control equipment. Such subsidies may not be very effective, since it still may be cheaper for the firms to continue polluting. Also, they may not be very efficient, since pollution-control equipment may not be the most economical means of reducing some kinds of pollution. Further, they are frequently attacked on the grounds that they are not equitable.

PROPERTY RIGHTS AND COASE'S THEOREM

Under certain circumstances, a perfectly competitive economy will allocate resources efficiently, even in the face of seemingly important external benefits or costs. For example, consider a firm that pollutes a stream by pumping out waste materials. Suppose that the downstream water users have well-defined property rights to water of a specified quality level, which means that they can sue the firm for damages if it passes water on to them that is below this quality level. In such a case, the firm can be required to pay for the pollution costs it imposes on others. Or consider a firm that upgrades the water in a stream, thus benefiting downstream water users. If this firm raises the water quality above the legally required level, it can seek compensation from the water users if property rights of this sort are well defined.

If the costs of negotiating are not too large, the parties responsible for an external benefit or cost can negotiate with the parties affected by this externality. For example, if downstream water users are entitled to water of a particular quality, a firm may purchase from them the right to pollute the stream to a certain extent. Or the downstream users may purchase from the firm the right to water of better quality than they would otherwise be entitled to. In this way, the externality is brought into the calculations of the interested parties. Thus there is no divergence between social and private costs because a firm or individual that harms others must pay for this right, and a firm or individual that benefits others receives compensation.

Coase's theorem   According to Ronald Coase of the University of Chicago, a competitive economy will allocate resources efficiently, even in the face of seemingly important external effects, if it is possible to carry out such negotiations at little or no cost. In the course of these negotiations, the relevant parties will be led to take proper account of the effects of their actions on others. For example, if downstream water users are endowed with a property right to obtain water of a particular quality, a firm that wants to pollute a stream will be led to offer compensation to them, and, pursuing its own interest, it will not find it worthwhile to pollute beyond the economically efficient point. Moreover, Coase has shown that, *regardless of which party is endowed with the relevant property rights,* the outcome will be the same. That is, regardless of whether the downstream users are endowed with the right to obtain water of a particular quality or the firm is endowed with the right to emit a certain amount of pollutants into the stream, the parties will be led to buy or sell these rights so that the economically efficient amount of pollution results.[6]

This theorem, often referred to as Coase's theorem, is of considerable interest and importance. However, it is important to recognize that it assumes that the costs of negotiating and contracting by the interested parties are relatively small. For example, it assumes that the downstream water users can get together with the polluting firm and that they can negotiate effectively without prohibitive expense. In fact, however, when there are more than a relatively small number of interested parties, the costs of such negotiations may be so

6. R. Coase, "The Problem of Social Cost," reprinted in E. Mansfield, *Microeconomics: Selected Readings,* 5th ed.

high that they are not feasible. Indeed, even if the costs are moderate, negoti-ations of this sort may not be practical. If the number of interested parties is large, it may not be possible to get the unanimity required to make the nego-tiations effective. And if the number of interested parties is small, the fact that mutually advantageous deals are possible does not mean that they will neces-sarily be consummated.

Nonetheless, Coase's theorem suggests that the assignment of well-defined property rights might help to promote economic efficiency. For example, to get around the difficulties caused by external diseconomies arising from waste dis-posal, society might find it useful to try to establish more unambiguous prop-erty rights for individuals and firms with respect to environmental quality. Then, assuming that the relevant negotiations are feasible, the interested parties in a particular area might try to negotiate to determine how much pollution will occur. Note that if these negotiations are to be effective, property rights must be exchangeable, as well as unambiguous. It must be possible for a person (or firm) to buy or sell his or her property rights of this sort.

GOVERNMENT INTERVENTION AND BENEFIT-COST ANALYSIS

The government intervenes in the economy in a wide variety of ways, ranging from the provision of public goods to the redistribution of income, and from the regulation of monopoly to the regulation of pollution. Government offi-cials (and more fundamentally, the general public) must continually decide whether it is worthwhile for the government to carry out particular projects. Frequently, it is extremely difficult to make such decisions because it is so hard to measure the benefits and costs to society of the projects in question. But in some cases, these benefits and costs can be measured well enough so that benefit-cost analysis can be used to help guide these decisions. Although benefit-cost analysis is by no means a panacea, it has frequently proved useful in this context.

Benefit-cost analysis

To understand how benefit-cost analysis operates, it is convenient to begin by assuming that a government agency has a fixed budget that limits the amount that it can spend and that it can carry out a number of alternative projects, each of which is relatively indivisible or lumpy. For example, suppose that the Department of Transportation has a fixed amount to spend on roads and that it is considering the construction of each of the roads in Table 16.1. Its problem is to decide which ones to build. As shown in Table 16.1, certain benefits accrue to the people from each of these projects, and each project entails costs.

The government agency tries to maximize the difference between total ben-efits and total costs. Since we are assuming (for the moment) that its total costs are fixed, it follows that it will maximize this difference if it maximizes the total benefits obtained from this fixed expenditure. But how can it determine which projects will maximize the total benefits? For example, in Table 16.1, if the Department of Transportation has $1 billion to spend on roads, which roads will maximize the total benefits? The answer is simple. It should calculate the

TABLE 16.1 Benefit-Cost Analysis, Fixed Budget

Possible roads	Benefits	Costs	Benefit-cost ratio
		(billions of dollars)	
A to B	.30	.20	1.50
A to D	.30	.24	1.25
B to C	.10	.08	1.25
C to D	.18	.20	0.90
D to E	.70	.40	1.75
F to H	.40	.30	1.33
G to R	.40	.20	2.00
H to S	.36	.30	1.20
S to T	.35	.20	1.75

ratio of benefits to costs for each project, and accept those projects with the highest values of this ratio. Thus, in Table 16.1, the roads from A to B, D to E, G to R, and S to T should be built. These projects have the highest benefit-cost ratios (and together their costs sum to $1 billion).[7]

Up to this point, we have assumed that the government agency's budget is fixed. But in reality, of course, the budget of most government agencies is variable, not fixed. If its budget is variable, which projects should it carry out? For example, if the Department of Transportation can spend as much as it likes on the roads in Table 16.1, which ones should it build? The answer is that all projects with a benefit-cost ratio exceeding 1 should be carried out. Why? Because all projects where benefits exceed costs (that is, where the benefit-cost ratio exceeds 1) are assumed to be carried out in the private sector. Under perfect competition, this will be true, since spending in the private sector will be carried to the point where the marginal benefit of an extra dollar of spending will equal one dollar. Thus, so long as a public project has a benefit-cost ratio exceeding 1, a transfer of resources from private to public use will result in a social gain.[8]

7. It is easy to see that this procedure will maximize the sum of the benefits received. Looking at the benefits and costs columns of Table 16.1, it is clear that if only $.2 billion could be spent, the optimal choice would be the road from G to R; if $.4 billion could be spent, the optimal choice would be the road from G to R and the road from S to T; and if $.8 billion could be spent, the optimal choice would be the road from G to R, the road from S to T, and the road from D to E. In each case, these same results can be gotten by picking the projects with the highest benefit-cost ratios. (If you aren't convinced, try it in each case, and see.) Note, too, that we are assuming that the costs and benefits of each project do not depend on whether any of the other projects is carried out. Sometimes this assumption holds; but sometimes it doesn't, and more advanced techniques may be required.

8. If projects are divisible, the government agency should allocate funds among projects so that the marginal benefit from an extra dollar of expenditure on each project (carried out) is equal—and the same as the marginal benefit from an extra dollar of expenditure in the private sector of the economy.

From our discussion so far, one could get the impression that benefit-cost analysis involves little more than a straightforward calculation of the benefit-cost ratio for each project and a simple comparison of these ratios.[9] Unfortunately, things are not so simple. The application of this analysis is often marked by great difficulties in measuring the benefits and costs of each project. Although it would be inappropriate for us to dwell at length on the ways in which benefits and costs should be measured, two important principles should be borne in mind. First, it is important to distinguish between *real* benefits (and costs) and *pecuniary* benefits (and costs). Real benefits augment society's welfare; consequently, they should be weighed against the real costs of a project. Pecuniary benefits and costs, on the other hand, arise because of changes in relative prices that come about as the economy adjusts to the project. Pecuniary benefits and costs change the income distribution since some people gain from them, while others lose. But since the pecuniary gains of one individual are offset by the pecuniary losses of another, they are not benefits or costs to society as a whole.

Real vs. pecuniary costs and benefits

To illustrate the distinction between real and pecuniary benefits (and costs), consider a dam that is built by the government. The construction of the dam may result in an increase in wage rates for construction workers in the locality. Although this is a benefit to them, it is offset by a reduction in relative wage rates somewhere else in the economy, due to reduced demand because of higher taxes. Thus this is a pecuniary, not a real, benefit. Or the dam may result in a higher price for food in restaurants near the dam site. Since such gains to the restaurant owners are offset by the losses to the restaurant patrons who pay the higher prices, they too are pecuniary, not real, benefits.

Second, in carrying out a benefit-cost analysis, one should try to estimate *all* of the benefits and costs of each public project. This is much easier said than done. One problem is that some benefits may accrue indirectly. For example, the dam may have indirect effects on consumers, laborers, investors, and firms in many parts of the nation. Another problem is that many benefits and costs are intangible. For example, one of the costs of the dam may be that it will mar the scenery, an intangible effect that cannot be valued in the marketplace. The situation has been described very well by Roland McKean:

> Needless to say, in reaching decisions, one should attempt to take into account all gains and all costs. Some people feel that there are two types of gain or cost, economic and noneconomic, and that economic analysis has nothing to do with the latter. This distinction is neither very sound nor very useful. People pay for—that is, they value—music as well as food, beauty or quiet as well as aluminum pans, a lower probability of death as well as garbage disposal. The significant categories are not economic and noneconomic items but (1) gains and costs that can be measured in mon-

9. Although the basics are easy to master, the theory is not so straightforward once one gets beyond fundamentals. There are a number of theoretical problems that we have not taken up, since they would take us too far afield. In particular, a great deal of attention has been devoted in the literature to the question of what is the proper discount rate. For some relevant discussion, see J. Stiglitz, *Economics of the Public Sector,* 2d ed (New York: Norton, 1988).

EXAMPLE 16.2

THE EFFECT OF VOTING RULES

Voting rules differ from situation to situation. Although there is a simple majority rule in many elections, in other situations (such as the passage of school bonds), two-thirds of the vote may be required, and in the case of juries a unanimous vote is required to find a defendant guilty of a criminal offense. Economists like 1986 Novel laureate James Buchanan have studied the effects of various voting rules. Suppose that a (small) society is composed of the following five individuals, who must vote on whether or not a particular change in public policy should be carried out. For simplicity, suppose that the benefit and cost of this change to each individual are as shown below.

	John	Jane	Martin	Mary	Tom
Cost	$50	$60	$80	$500	$70
Benefit	$60	$80	$90	$ 10	$80

(a) Do the people who gain from the change gain more than the loser loses? (b) If there is majority rule, will the change be made? (c) Under a unanimous voting rule, will the change be made? (d) Will any change that does not satisfy the Pareto criterion be approved under a unanimous voting rule? (e) Suppose that four commissioners must decide which of four projects, (A, B, C, or D) will be carried out. Each commissioner is asked to rank the projects. A project receives 4 points if it is a commissioner's first choice, 3 points if it is his or her second choice, 2 points if it is his or her third choice, and 1 point if it is his or her fourth choice. The project with the most points will be carried out. Commissioner Mary Flynn, who is strongly committed to project A, believes that the vote will be very close, A and B being the favorites to win. Even if project B is in fact her second choice, is it reasonable for her to declare that it is her fourth choice? Why or why not?

SOLUTION

(a) No. Jane's net gain is $80 − $60 = $20, and John, Martin, and Tom each
have net gains of $10; thus the total net gain is $20 + $10 + $10 + 10 =
$50. On the other hand, Mary's net loss is $500 − $10 = $490. (b) Yes. Since
Jane, John, Martin, and Tom gain from the change, they will vote for it.
However, this assumes that Mary does not attempt (or is not able) to bribe at
least two of the others to vote against it. (c) No. Mary will vote against it. (d)
No. If a change does not satisfy the Pareto criterion, at least one person must
be hurt by it, and he or she will vote against it. Under a unanimous voting
rule, this one negative vote will be sufficient to prevent the change from
taking place. (e) Yes. In this way, she will try to reduce the total number of
points received by project B, and increase project A's chance of winning.*

*For further discussion, see J. Buchanan and G. Tullock, *The Calculus of Consent* (Ann
Arbor: University of Michigan, 1962); A. Downs, *An Economic Theory of Democracy* (New
York: Harper & Row, 1957); and H. Sonnenschein, *The Economics of Incentives: An Intro-
ductory Account* (Evanston, Ill.: Northwestern University Press, 1983).

etary units (for example, the use of items like typewriters that have market
prices reflecting the marginal evaluations of all users); (2) other commen-
surable effects (impacts of higher teacher salaries, on the one hand, and of
teaching machines, on the other hand, on students' test scores);
(3) incommensurable effects that can be quantified but not in terms
of a common denominator (capability of improving science test scores
and capability of reducing the incidence of ulcers among students); and
(4) nonquantifiable effects. Examples of the last category are impacts of
alternative policies on the morale and happiness of students, on the probability of racial conflicts, and on the probability of protecting individual
rights. In taking a position on an issue, each of us implicitly quantifies
such considerations. But there is no way to make quantifications that
would necessarily be valid for other persons. This sort of distinction
between types of effects does serve a useful purpose, especially in warning
us of the limitations of cost-benefit analysis.[10]

ANEMIA REDUCTION IN INDONESIA, KENYA, AND MEXICO: AN APPLICATION

Let us examine how benefit-cost analysis has been used in connection with
proposed measures to reduce anemia in less developed countries. Anemia is a
condition in which the concentration of hemoglobin in the blood is relatively
low. In many less developed countries, between one-third and two-thirds of the
population are affected by anemia, which is typically caused by not consuming
enough absorbable iron. Anemic people tend to be weak and listless, and their
work capacity is limited. To reduce anemia, it has been proposed that govern-

10. R. McKean, "The Nature of Cost-Benefit Analysis," reprinted in E. Mansfield, *Microeconomics:
Selected Readings,* 5th ed.

ment or international agencies provide nutrients to be added to the population's food, which would supply extra iron. For example, iron can be added to sugar.

One of the major benefits of such a program is that people are able to work harder and more effectively. Studies indicate that a 10 percent increase in the amount of hemoglobin in the blood is associated with an increase of between 10 to 20 percent in the amount of output produced by a worker. Also, there is some evidence that anemia affects a person's learning ability. Thus extra iron provided to children should help them to learn more rapidly. Henry Levin has made rough estimates of the value of the extra output that would result if the amount of hemoglobin were increased by 10 percent through the provision of extra iron in Indonesia, Kenya, and Mexico.[11] As shown in Table 16.2, he found that the per capita annual benefit would be about $7 in Indonesia, $43 in Kenya, and $71 in Mexico.

TABLE 16.2 Annual Per Capita Benefits and Costs of Nutritional Programs to Reduce Anemia in Indonesia, Kenya, and Mexico

	Indonesia	Kenya	Mexico
Benefit	$7.32	$42.64	$71.10
Cost			
Iron	.20	.20	.20
Additional energy intake	.82	.82	.82
Total	1.02	1.02	1.02
Benefit-cost ratio	7	42	70

Source: H. Levin, *op. cit.* These figures pertain to iron fortification programs.

The costs of such a program are basically of two types. First, there is the cost of the iron supplements, which is only about 20 cents per person annually. Second, there is the cost of the extra food that a worker must consume if he or she is to be able to produce the extra output permitted by his or her having a greater amount of hemoglobin in the blood. According to Levin, this amounts to about 82 cents per year. Thus the benefit-cost ratio of such a program in each of these countries seems to be high—about 7 in Indonesia, 42 in Kenya, and 70 in Mexico. Although Levin points out that there are many limitations of his study, he concludes that programs to reduce anemia are highly productive investments in many less developed countries.[12]

11. H. Levin, "A Benefit-Cost Analysis of Nutritional Programs for Anemia Reduction," *World Bank Research Observer*, July 1986.

12. Of course, an important question is: Why should the investment in these programs be made by governments, rather than consumers and firms in these countries? As an exercise, suppose that you had to make recommendations as to whether or not this is a proper activity of government. What factors would you consider? Why? (Hint: Consider the discussion in the previous chapter as well as in this chapter.)

Pressure groups

Before concluding this brief discussion of selected aspects of government activity, we should point out that government intervention need not always be beneficial. Although we cannot do more than scratch the surface of this topic in the available space, certain salient points should be recognized. For one thing, the political process is characterized by the existence of various pressure groups, which are groups of citizens who band together to advocate certain policies to the people's representatives. These groups usually contain only a small proportion of the population, but they may be successful in getting enough representatives on their side to push through measures that benefit them at the expense of the general public. For example, industry groups lobby for and get special tax breaks and tariffs or subsidies. Because these groups have a great deal to gain from such measures, they have the incentive to spend large amounts to influence legislation. Also, because they contain relatively few members, the free-rider problem is not as great for them as if they had a larger number of members. (Recall pp. 463–64.) Further the general public, which frequently loses more than the pressure group gains through such measures, is often unaware of its losses because the amount each individual loses is small and hard for the individual to identify, let alone measure. For these and other reasons, pressure groups are sometimes successful in persuading the people's representatives to adopt the policies they support, even though these policies may be detrimental to the welfare of the public at large.

Bureaucracy

Our understanding of the determinants of the behavior of civil servants is limited, but, according to some economists, two of their principal goals are tenure of office and agency growth. Certainly, it is not surprising they they should be interested in tenure of office. Without the sorts of civil-service regulations that currently exist, it would be relatively easy for an incoming administration to replace hordes of civil servants with deserving cronies (and their deserving relatives and loved ones). Without these regulations, it would also be very difficult for civil servants to withstand any serious pressure from elected officials or pressure groups. As for the goal of agency growth, it has been pointed out repeatedly that there are many reasons why civil servants may want their agencies to expand, not contract. For one thing, the prestige (as well as pay and perquisites) of a bureau chief is related to the size of the bureau. Also, a bureaucrat's power tends to increase with the size and rate of growth of the bureau he or she heads. For example, if the bureau has lots of building funds, the chief has some latitude in choosing which congressional districts will receive new facilities, a fact which few members of Congress are likely to ignore. Also, if the bureau has lots of jobs to keep filled, the chief has some latitude in choosing who will fill them, a fact which few jobseekers and ambitious junior bureaucrats are likely to ignore.

It is also alleged that civil servants have too little incentive to do away with activities and personnel that are not worth their costs. For instance, the Department of Defense has repeatedly been charged with "gold-plating"—that is, with the development of increments of technical performance and other features of weapons systems that are not worth their cost. Since there are strong incentives for agency growth and weak ones for reduced scope and expenditure,

EXAMPLE 16.3

SHOULD REFUSE COLLECTION BE PRIVATIZED?

The word *privatize,* which entered the dictionary in the 1980s, means "to change from public to private control or ownership." During the 1980s there was considerable pressure for privatization, both in the United States and in other countries like Great Britain, due in part to evidence that private firms have been more efficient at particular activities than government agencies. The most thoroughly-studied case is refuse collection. The following data compare the inputs used to collect refuse (and the productivity of these inputs) in two cities of the same size in the New York metropolitan area, one of which used private firms to collect refuse, the other of which relied on the municipal government to perform this service.

	City with private refuse collection	City with municipal refuse collection
Truck shifts per week	39	63
Persons per truck	2	4
Person-days of labor per week	78	237
Tons collected per person-day of labor	9.67	3.40

(a) Do private firms seem to be more efficient at the performance of this service? (b) In 1975, about 21 percent of American cities hired private firms to collect refuse; in 1982, about 35 percent did so. Is this growth in accord with the above figures? (c) According to many observers, the basic reason for the greater efficiency of private firms is competition. Why is competition important? (d) Some cities have fostered competition between municipal agencies and private firms and have allowed both to collect refuse. What are the advantages of this arrangement? (e) Does the fact that private firms often are more efficient than municipal agencies at refuse collection mean that the provision of most government services should be turned over to private firms?

SOLUTION

(a) Yes. The number of tons of refuse collected per person-day of labor is almost three times as high in the city with private refuse collection as in the city with municipal refuse collection. (Also, the number of tons per truck shift is higher in the former than in the latter city.*) (b) Yes. With evidence of this sort accumulating, one would expect more and more cities to turn from municipal to private refuse collection. (c) Municipal agencies responsible for refuse collection often face little or no competition. Thus they can allow their efficiency to fall without having to worry about the work going elsewhere. (d) This subjects the municipal agencies to competition from private firms. For example, in Minneapolis, city officials, citing superior practices by private crews, have gotten the municipal crews to adopt similar practices and to match the private performance. (e) By no means all the studies comparing public and private organizations find that public ones are less efficient.

Whether private firms are more efficient than government agencies at providing a particular service depends on the nature of the service. One cannot
generalize from the above table.**

*The number of tons of refuse collected per week in the former city is 9.67 (the number of
tons collected per person-day) times 78 (the number of person-days per week), or 754.26.
Thus the number of tons of refuse collected per truck shift equals 754.26 divided by 39 (the
number of truck shifts per week), or 19.34. Making similar calculations for the latter city,
one finds that the number of tons of refuse collected per truck shift equals 12.79.

**For further discussion, see E. S. Savas, *Privatization,* (Chatham, N.J.: Chatham House,
1987); J. Pack, "Privatization of Public Sector Services in Theory and Practice," *Journal of
Policy Analysis and Management,* Summer 1987; F. Sloan, "Property Rights in the Hospital
Industry," in H. E. Frech III (ed.), *Health Care in America* (San Francisco: Pacific Research
Institute, 1988); and W. Stanbury and F. Thompson (eds.), *Managing Public Enterprises*
(New York: Praeger, 1982).

some observers believe that there is a built-in tendency for government agencies
to grow regardless of whether their responsibilities and work load expand at all.
For example, C. Northcote Parkinson claims that in public administration,
"there need be little or no relationship between the work to be done and the size
of the staff to which it may be assigned."[13] (For a sampling of Parkinson's
reasoning and wit, see his "Parkinson's Law.")[14]

Although these allegations should be taken seriously, it is difficult to know
how much truth they contain, because of the lack of reasonably reliable measures of how efficient (or inefficient) various agencies are and of how much
each of the various services is worth. Perhaps the most important lesson to be
derived from this section is that *one cannot justify government intervention in a
particular area of the economy merely by showing that market forces work imperfectly
there.* Why? Because it is necessary to show (or to have substantial reason to

13. C. N. Parkinson, "Parkinson's Law," reprinted in E. Mansfield, *Managerial Economics and
Operations Research,* 5th ed. (New York: Norton, 1987), p. 20. Apparently international orga-
nizations are not free of these problems either. According to the *New York Times's* United
Nations bureau chief, Parkinson's observations apply remarkably well to the U.N., as reflected
in the old saw, "How many people work at the United Nations?" Answer: "About half." See
"Parkinson's Law at the U.N.," *New York Times Magazine,* November 23, 1980.

14. "Picture a civil servant called A who finds himself overworked. . . . For this real or imagined
overwork there are, broadly speaking, three possible remedies: (1) He may resign. (2) He may
ask to halve the work with a colleague called B. (3) He may demand the assistance of two
subordinates to be called C and D. There is probably no instance in civil service history of A
choosing any but the third alternative. By resignation he would merely bring in a rival for
promotion to W's vacancy when W (at long last) retires. So A would rather have C and D,
junior men, below him. They will add to his consequence; and, by dividing the work into two
categories, as between C and D, he will have the merit of being the only man who compre-
hends them both.

"It is essential to realize, at this point, that C and D are, as it were, inseparable. To appoint
C alone would have been impossible. Why? Because C, if by himself, would divide the work
with A and so assume almost the equal status which has been refused in the first instance to B; a
status the more emphasized if C is A's only possible successor. Subordinates must thus number
two or more, each being kept in order by fear of the other's promotion. When C complains in
turn of being overworked (as he certainly will) A will, with the concurrence of C, advise the
appointment of two assistants to help C. But he can then avert internal friction only by
advising the appointment of two more assistants to help D, whose position is much the same.
With this recruitment of E, F, G and H, the promotion of A is now practically certain. Seven
officials are now doing what one did before. . . . These seven make so much work for each other
that all are fully occupied and A is actually working harder than ever" (ibid., pp. 64–65).

expect) that government intervention will do more good than harm. Just as the private sector cannot be trusted to work in all instances for the public good (because of monopoly, external diseconomies, and other factors discussed above), so government agencies cannot be trusted always to do so either (because politicians may not represent the people's preferences and interests properly, civil servants may build empires and pursue their own interests, and so on). Further economic analysis of the behavior of government agencies is badly needed to indicate more clearly the circumstances under which government intervention of various sorts will be effective and worthwhile. Fortunately, economists in increasing numbers seem to be turning their attention to this topic.[15]

Summary

1. A public good has two characteristics: it is nonrival and nonexclusive. By nonrival, we mean that the marginal cost of providing the good to an additional consumer is zero. By nonexclusive, we mean that people cannot be excluded from consuming the good (whether or not they pay for it).
2. Whereas economic efficiency requires that each consumer's marginal benefit equal marginal cost for a private good, it requires that the sum of the marginal benefits of all consumers equal marginal cost for a public good. An important problem is to get people to reveal their true preferences since, if they can avoid paying, they can get the benefits from public goods anyway.
3. If the number of people in a society is quite small, it may be worthwhile for people acting individually to provide some quantity of public goods. However, there is a tendency for the provision of a public good to be too small; the larger the number of people in the society, the farther it will fall short of providing an efficient amount of a public good. Thus the government tends to intervene in an attempt to insure the proper amount of such goods.
4. Besides providing public goods, the government sometimes intervenes in an attempt to offset distortions caused by external diseconomies and economies. An important example is the problem of environmental pollution. To a large extent, undesirably high levels of pollution are due to external diseconomies in waste disposal.
5. The efficient level of pollution (holding output constant) is at the point where the marginal cost of pollution equals the marginal cost of pollution control. In general, this will be at a point where a nonzero amount of pollution occurs. To establish incentives that will lead to a more nearly efficient level of pollution, the government can establish effluent fees, enact direct regulations, and issue transferable emissions permits, among other things.
6. If the costs of negotiating are not too large, the parties responsible for an external benefit or cost can negotiate with the parties affected by this externality. Under these circumstances, a perfectly competitive economy can allocate resources efficiently, even in the face of seemingly important externalities. Moreover, regardless of which party is endowed with the relevant property rights, the

15. For some work by economists concerning political processes, see A. Downs, *An Economic Theory of Democracy* (New York: Harper and Brothers, 1956); A. Hirschman, *Exit, Voice, and Loyalty* (Cambridge, Mass.: Harvard University Press, 1970); M. Olson, *The Logic of Collective Choice;* and G. Tullock, *Towards a Mathematics of Politics* (Ann Arbor: University of Michigan Press, 1967).

outcome is the same. However, it is important to recognize that the costs of negotiating and contracting by the interested parties may not be small and that negotiations of this sort may not be feasible in many situations.

7. Benefit-cost analysis is aimed at helping government agencies come to rational decisions concerning how much should be spent on various projects. If a government agency has a fixed amount to spend on projects of a certain kind (and the projects are indivisible), it should choose those projects with the highest benefit-cost ratios, if it wants to maximize social benefits. If its total budget is variable, it should accept all projects where the benefit-cost ratio exceeds 1, if it wants to maximize net social benefits. Although the basic theory underlying benefit-cost analysis is relatively simple, the application of this theory is often by no means straightforward, because of the difficulties in measuring the benefits and costs of each project.

8. Government intervention in a particular area of the economy cannot be justified merely by showing that market forces work imperfectly there. It is necessary to show (or have substantial reason to expect) that government intervention will do more good than harm. Just as the private sector cannot be trusted to work in all instances for the public good (because of such factors as monopoly and externalities), so government agencies cannot be trusted to do so either (because politicians may not represent the people's preferences and interests properly, civil servants may build empires and pursue their own interests, and so on).

Questions/ Problems

1. The Department of the Interior made a benefit-cost study of four alternative dam sites on the Middle Snake River in Idaho, the results being shown below:

	Alternative sites			
	Appaloosa and Low Mountain Sheep	High Mountain Sheep and China Gardens	High Mountain Sheep only	Pleasant Valley and Low Mountain Sheep
	(millions of dollars)			
Benefits				
Power	49.3	60.7	35.9	44.2
Fish and wildlife	6.6	None	None	None
Recreation	.4	.3	.3	.3
Flood control	.2	.2	.2	.1
Total*	56.5	61.3	36.5	44.5
Costs				
Total	20.8	24.3	13.6	19.0
Benefit-cost ratio	2.72	2.53	2.69	2.35

*Individual figures may not sum to total because of rounding errors.

(a) Does it appear that a dam should be built at one of these sites? (b) Critics pointed out that this analysis took no account of fish and wildlife destruction. When these and other costs were included, the staff of the Federal Energy Regulatory Commission estimated that the benefit-cost ratio for none of these sites exceeds 1. Does it appear that a dam should be built at one of these sites?

2. Suppose that the Department of Transportation has a budget of $5 billion to spend on roads, and that the costs and benefits from all roads under consideration are as follows:

Road	Benefits	Costs
	(billions of dollars)	
A	10	1
B	12	4
C	20	5

Which roads should the department finance, and why? If you were an adviser to the department, what questions would you ask concerning the derivation of these figures?

3. A. R. Prest and Ralph Turvey point out that the benefit-cost ratio for a cross-Florida barge canal was estimated to be 1.20 by the Corps of Engineers, but only 0.13 by some consultants retained by the railroads. What factors might account for the difference in these results?

4. Education and health services can be provided by private enterprise on a fee basis. What is the rationale for government intervention in these areas? To what extent are education and health services public goods? In what ways can microeconomics help to shed light on proper public policy in these areas?

5. Suppose that there are only three citizens of a (very small) nation and that the amount of national defense each would demand (at various prices) is as follows:

Price of a unit of national defense (dollars)	Citizen A	Citizen B	Citizen C
	(number of units demanded)		
1	10	8	12
2	9	7	9
3	8	6	7
4	7	5	5

If the marginal cost of a unit of national defense is $9, what is the efficient amount of national defense for this nation?

6. In the previous question, suppose that the members of this small nation agree that if any citizen refuses to pay for national defense, his or her property and person will not be protected by the nation's defense forces. Under these circumstances, could a nongovernmental organization sell some of the services normally provided by the nation's defense forces? If so, will ordinary market forces result in the efficient amount of national defense being provided?

7. "All public goods must be provided by the government." Comment and evaluate.

8. In an oil field, each owner of a well is motivated to pump out the oil relatively fast, because this makes it more likely that the well owner can capture some oil under others' land and prevent others from capturing oil under his or her land. Are there externalities present in this situation? Do you think that they lead to inefficiencies? If so, what sorts of inefficiencies result?

9. C. N. Parkinson presents the following data concerning the British Admiralty in 1914 and 1928:

	1914	1928
Capital ships in commission	62	20
Officers and men in Royal Navy	146,000	100,000
Dockyard workers	57,000	62,439
Dockyard officials and clerks	3,249	4,558
Admiralty officials	2,000	3,569

Did the number of civil servants in the Admiralty vary in proportion to the size of the Royal Navy? What factors might have accounted for these results?

10. A paint plant is upstream from plant A. Plant A's costs reflect the fact that it has to clean up the water that the paint plant pollutes. The firm that owns the paint plant decides to buy plant A because it believes that the price of the product made by plant A will increase dramatically. Is it likely that the paint plant will emit the same amount of pollutants as before the purchase of plant A? What factors influence how much the paint plant will change the amount of pollutants it emits?

11. The Times Mirror Company wanted to complete the $120 million expansion of a paper-making plant near Portland, Oregon. State and federal officials were concerned about the effects on air quality. Eventually, the firm bought the right to emit about 150 tons of extra hydrocarbons into the air per year from a wood-coating plant that had gone out of business, the price being $50,000. If the firm had not bought this right, it would not have been able to get permission from the state and federal regulators to make this expansion, according to the firm's manager of environmental and energy services.

One way that government agencies can reduce pollution is to issue transferable emissions permits, as we saw on page 470. These permits can be bought and sold, much as the Times Mirror Company did. Suppose that you are an adviser to the Environmental Protection Agency, and that you are asked to tell the agency's officials what determines the price of a permit. What's the answer? (For simplicity, assume that there are many buyers and sellers of such permits, so the market for them is competitive, and that each permit allows its owner to emit one ton of pollutants.)

EFFECTS OF QUOTAS ON STEEL IMPORTS INTO THE UNITED STATES

In July 1989, President Bush extended steel import quotas until March 31, 1992, but said that they would end then. To understand the nature and origins of steel import quotas in the United States, you must recognize that during the 1980s, the system of free trade that helped to bring about the economic prosperity of the 1960s and 1970s came under increasing attack. The recession of 1981–82 resulted in serious unemployment in many nations of the world. With over 20 million people out of work in 1983 in the United States and Western Europe alone, a growing number of industrialists, labor leaders, and politicians raised their voices to demand protectionist barriers against foreign competition. Nowhere was there more concern over foreign competition than in the American steel industry, which rolled up an impressive record of losses in the early 1980s. (For example, Bethlehem Steel Corporation lost about $1.5 billion in 1982.) Faced with great difficulties in competing with Japanese and other foreign steelmakers, American steel firms pleaded with the government to set quotas limiting the quantity of steel that could be imported into the United States, and their petitions were heard. In 1984, quotas were established. By 1989, steel imports were limited to about 20 percent of the U.S. market.

An enormous amount of controversy resulted among economists and others. Traditionally, most economists have argued against quotas of this sort on the grounds that they reduce trade, raise prices, protect domestic industry at the expense of consumers, and reduce the standard of living of the nation as a whole. To estimate the effects of such a quota, the staff of the Federal Trade Commission (FTC) carried out a detailed economic study,[1] which is useful in demonstrating how microeconomic theory can contribute to the analysis of major public policies. To begin with, the FTC economists estimated the demand curve for steel in the United States and the supply curve for U.S.-produced steel, both shown in Figure 1. The supply curve for foreign-produced

1. Federal Trade Commission, *Staff Report on the United States Steel Industry and Its International Rivals,* November 1977.

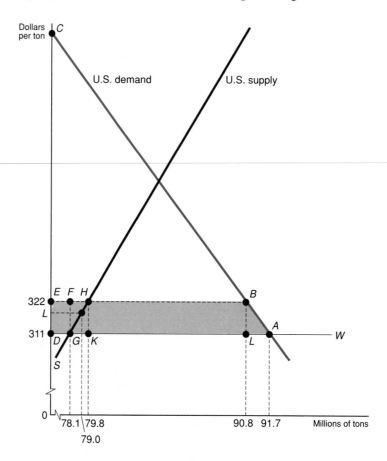

FIGURE 1 Effects of a Steel Import Quota *U.S. steel producers gain $868.5 million per year from the quota, while U.S. consumers lose $1,003.75 million per year. Thus consumers lose more than producers gain.*

steel was a horizontal line at $311. Thus, adding horizontally the supply curve for U.S. steel and the supply curve for foreign steel, we get the supply curve of all steel in the United States, which is *SGW*. Since this supply curve intersects the demand curve at point *A*, the equilibrium price is $311 per ton and the equilibrium quantity is 91.7 million tons of steel. The U.S. steel industry supplies 78.1 million tons, and foreigners supply 13.6 million tons.

What is the effect if the U.S. government imposes a quota which limits imports to 11 million tons? In other words, what would happen if American steel imports could not exceed 11 million tons? The demand and supply curves show that, if the price is $322, American demand will exceed American supply by 11 million tons. Thus, once the quota is imposed, the price will rise to $322, since this is the price that will reduce our imports to the amount of the quota. Consequently, the equilibrium will be at point *B*, where price is $322 per ton and the equilibrium quantity is 90.8 million tons of steel. The U.S. steel industry supplies 79.8 million tons, and foreigners supply 11 million tons.

Who gains and who loses from this quota? American consumers lose an amount equal to the shaded area in Figure 1. Before the imposition of the quota, consumer's surplus in the United States equals the area under the demand curve above the price of $311 (that is, it equals the area of triangle *DCA*). After the imposition of the quota, consumer's surplus in the United States equals the area under the demand curve above the price of $322 (that is, it equals the area of triangle *ECB*). The reduction in consumer's surplus due to the imposition of the quota is area *DCA* minus *ECB*, or area *DEBA* (which is shaded). This area equals ½(322 − 311) (90.8 + 91.7) = 1,003.75 millions of dollars. Thus consumers stand to lose about $1 billion per year from the quota.

American steel producers gain from the quota, their gain being of two types. First, they are able to sell the 78.1 million tons that they would have sold without the quota at a higher price ($322 rather than $311). The extra profit equals the area of rectangle *DEFG*, or (322 − 311) (78.1) = 859.1 millions of dollars. Second, they are able to sell 79.8, rather than 78.1 million tons. Their profit from the extra 1.7 million tons equals the area of triangle *GFH*, or ½(322 − 311) (79.8 − 78.1) = 9.4 millions of dollars. (Why is this their profit? Because the supply curve shows the industry's marginal cost at each level of output. For example, the marginal cost of the 79-millionth ton of U.S.-produced steel equals *OL*. Thus, the profit earned from the 79-millionth ton equals its price minus *OL*, or $322 − *OL*. If we add up the difference between price and marginal cost for all of the extra 1.7 million tons, we get the area of triangle *GFH*.) Adding the two types of gain, American steel producers increase their profits by 859.1 + 9.4 = 868.5 millions of dollars per year.

Part of the U.S. consumers' losses find their way into the pockets of foreign steelmakers. After the imposition of the quota, U.S. consumers buy 11 million tons of foreign steel products, which cost 322 − 311 = 11 dollars per ton more than before the imposition of the quota. Thus 11 × 11 = 121 millions of dollars per year (the area of rectangle *KHBL*) of U.S. consumers' losses are transferred to foreign steelmakers.[2]

In addition, part of U.S. consumers' losses is due to their consuming 90.8 rather than 91.7 million tons of steel products. The loss in consumer's surplus arising from their forgoing the consumption of these 0.9 million tons equals the area of triangle *LBA*, or ½(322 − 311) (91.7 − 90.8) = 5.0 millions of dollars. As we know from Chapter 4, the area of this triangle equals the consumer's surplus from the consumption of these 0.9 million tons.

Finally, part of U.S. consumers' losses is due to the fact that more costly U.S. steel is being substituted for less costly foreign steel. After the quota is introduced, U.S. steel firms produce 79.8 million tons, in contrast to 78.1 million tons before the imposition of the quota. The extra 79.8 − 78.1 = 1.7 million tons could be obtained more cheaply from foreign producers. The total extra amount that U.S. consumers pay for this 1.7 million tons equals the area of

2. This assumes that foreign exporters would be called upon to monitor exports to comply with the quota. Alternatively, with restrictive licensing of domestic importers, the importers extract this profit. According to the FTC economists, the former assumption is more likely.

triangle *GHK*, or ½(322 − 311) (79.8 − 78.1) = 9.4 millions of dollars. (Why is this the correct measure? Because the extra amount paid for each ton is the difference between the marginal cost of producing it in the United States and the cost of obtaining it from abroad. For example, for the 79-millionth ton produced in the United States this difference equals *OL* − $311, since its marginal cost equals *OL* and the cost of obtaining it from abroad is $311. Thus, if we sum up the differences for all 1.7 million extra tons, the total extra amount that consumers pay for this reason equals the area of triangle *GHK*.)

To sum up, this analysis indicates that U.S. steel producers gain $868.5 million per year from the quota, while U.S. consumers lose $1,003.75 million per year. Thus consumers lose more than producers gain. Part of the difference goes to foreign producers; the rest is due to lower consumption of steel products and the substitution of high-cost U.S. steel for cheaper foreign steel. Other studies have been made of the effects of the quota. They too indicate that consumers lose more than producers gain.[3]

Analytical Questions

1. This analysis looks at how all U.S. consumers and all U.S. steel producers are affected by the import quotas. In what ways are the results clouded by the fact that we cannot make interpersonal comparisons of utility?

2. According to the Congressional Budget Office, if imports of steel are limited to 15 percent of the U.S. market, the cost to consumers would be about $178,000 for each American steel job created (or saved). Relative to the quotas, under what circumstances would both consumers and steelworkers be better off if the former paid the latter not to work?

3. Can the transfer of income from consumers to steelworkers due to the import quotas be defended on the grounds that it helps the poor? (Hint: In 1984, the average wage of steelworkers was about 65 percent higher than that of all American workers in manufacturing.)

4. Proponents of quotas often argue that quotas provide the protected industry with the time and resources to modernize, thus enabling it to become competitive internationally. According to the *New York Times*, "American steel is, in fact, competitive now in the domestic market and gaining abroad. Forced to retrench by the severe 1981–82 recession, the industry has invested heavily in technology and slashed its high-cost work force."[4] How can you tell whether the industry is competitive?

5. What pressure groups have favored steel import quotas? Why have government officials adopted these quotas?

3. For further discussion, see W. Cline, "U.S. Trade and Industrial Policy: The Experience of Textiles, Steel, and Automobiles," in P. Krugman (ed.), *Strategic Trade Policy and the New International Economics* (Cambridge, Mass.: MIT Press, 1986); National Academy of Engineering, *The Competitive Status of the U.S. Steel Industry*, (Washington, D.C.: National Academic Press, 1985); and D. Tarr, *A General Equilibrium Analysis of the Welfare and Employment Effects of U.S. Quotas in Textiles, Autos, and Steel* (Washington, D.C.: Federal Trade Commission, 1989).

4. "Uncoddle Steel," *New York Times*, July 15, 1989.

PART SEVEN

INTERTEMPORAL CHOICE AND DECISION-MAKING INVOLVING RISK

17

INTERTEMPORAL CHOICE AND TECHNOLOGICAL CHANGE

INTRODUCTION

Many problems that are central to economics involve a choice between doing something now and doing it later. For example, consumers must decide whether they will consume all of their income now or save some for the future, and producers must decide whether they will devote some of their present resources to investment projects that will increase their future profits. These problems of intertemporal choice are of great practical importance. In this chapter, we describe some of the models that economists have devised to deal with them. These models are dynamic, in the sense that they focus attention on more than one time period. They enable (indeed, force) us to take up such major concepts as saving, investment, the interest rate, and present value.

Once we focus attention on dynamic considerations, we must reckon too with a very important force in the economy—technological change. Our discussion in previous chapters of the efficient allocation of resources was concerned largely with static conditions. We took as given the production functions in various industries and the indifference maps of consumers, and attempted to determine the allocation of resources that, given these production functions and indifference maps, would be efficient. Although an analysis of this kind is interesting, it is incomplete in important aspects, since one of the most significant ways that economic welfare is increased is through the alteration of production functions due to technological change. In the latter part of this chapter, we discuss the microeconomics of technological change. First we take up the definition and measurement of the rate of technological change. Then we discuss the limitations of static efficiency and the effects of market structure on the rate of technological change and the rate of productivity increase.

Consumers try to maintain a desired balance between consumption in the present and consumption in the future. For example, if Frank Olcott receives a lump-sum payment of $50,000 upon retirement, he is likely to save much of it to tide him over in subsequent years. In this section, we take up the consumer's intertemporal choice with regard to consumption. To simplify matters, we assume that there is only a single commodity. Consumers must choose how much of this commodity they will consume at various points in time. In making this decision, they recognize that they can borrow or lend this commodity. To begin with, we consider only two periods: this year and next year. This assumption will be relaxed later on in this chapter.

The consumer's choice between the amount consumed this year and the amount consumed next year can be analyzed by the simple model of consumer behavior presented in Chapter 3. The consumer has preferences between consumption this year and consumption next year, just as he or she has preferences between meat and potatoes in a particular time period. (Recall Figure 3.1.) These preferences are represented by an indifference map like that shown in Figure 17.1. In addition, the consumer is confronted by a budget line, also shown in Figure 17.1, which indicates the combinations of present and future consumption that he or she can attain. The optimal choice for the consumer is represented by the point on the budget line that is on the highest indifference

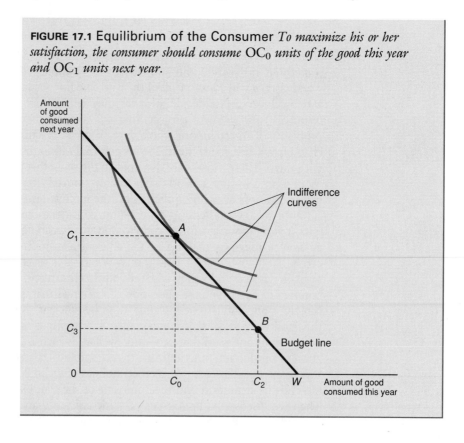

FIGURE 17.1 Equilibrium of the Consumer *To maximize his or her satisfaction, the consumer should consume* OC_0 *units of the good this year and* OC_1 *units next year.*

curve. In Figure 17.1, this optimal point is A, where OC_0 units are consumed this year and OC_1 units are consumed next year.

Endowment position

The position of the consumer's budget line is determined by his or her endowment position, which is represented by point B in Figure 17.1. The consumer's *endowment position* is the number of units of the good that the consumer will receive in each year. In Figure 17.1, the consumer knows that he or she will *receive* OC_2 units of the good this year and OC_3 units next year. Thus, in this case, this is the consumer's endowment position. Note that the consumer does not have to consume this amount each year, because the consumer can borrow or lend. By borrowing or lending, the consumer can move to other points on the budget line. If the consumer moves upward from B along the budget line, this represents *lending* (because less is consumed this year, and more is consumed next year). If the consumer moves downward from B along the budget line, this represents *borrowing* (because more is consumed this year, and less is consumed next year). In Figure 17.1, the consumer's optimal choice is to lend $(OC_2 - OC_0)$ units of the good this year. Whereas OC_2 units of the good are received this year by the consumer, only OC_0 units are consumed, and the rest are lent out.

Lending and borrowing

The slope of the budget line indicates the terms on which the consumer can borrow or lend. Recall from Chapter 3 that the slope of the budget line equals -1 times the extra number of units of the good on the vertical axis that can be consumed if the consumer gives up one unit of the good on the horizontal axis. Thus the slope of the budget line in Figure 17.1 must equal -1 times the extra number of units of the good that can be consumed next year if the consumer gives up (and lends) one unit of the good this year. The *rate of interest* is the premium received by the consumer one year hence if he or she lends a dollar for a year. In other words, if the consumer lends a dollar, and if the interest rate equals r, he or she receives $(1 + r)$ dollars a year hence. (Similarly, if the consumer borrows a dollar, he or she pays $(1 + r)$ dollars a year hence.) *The interest rate can be viewed as a price,* since $(1 + r)$ is the price of a dollar today in terms of dollars a year hence. For example, if the interest rate equals 0.10, a dollar today is worth \$1.10 a year hence. If the price of the good is the same next year as this year, it follows that the slope of the budget line in Figure 17.1 must equal $-(1 + r)$, since the number of units of the good that can be consumed next year if the consumer gives up (and lends) one unit of the good this year equals $(1 + r)$.

Rate of interest

Endowed wealth

The intercept of the budget line on the horizontal axis in Figure 17.1 is called the consumer's *endowed wealth*. As noted above, the consumer's endowment position is at point B, which indicates that he or she will receive OC_2 units of the good this year and OC_3 units of the good next year. The consumer's endowed wealth will *not*, in general, be the same as his or her endowment position. The consumer's endowed wealth shows how much the consumer could consume this year if he or she borrowed against all of next year's receipts of the good. Clearly, the consumer's endowed wealth equals

$$W = OC_2 + \frac{OC_3}{1 + r}, \qquad [17.1]$$

because, besides the OC_2 units of the good that the consumer receives this year, he or she can consume an additional $OC_3/(1 + r)$ units of the good this year.

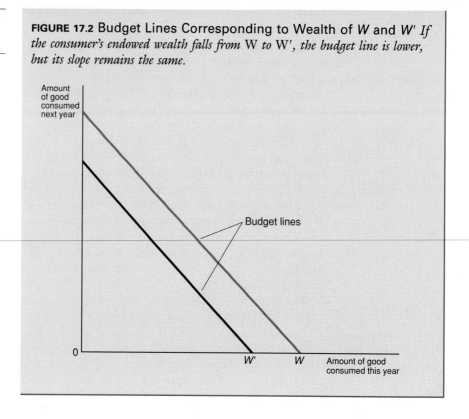

FIGURE 17.2 Budget Lines Corresponding to Wealth of *W* and *W'* *If the consumer's endowed wealth falls from* W *to* W', *the budget line is lower, but its slope remains the same.*

Why? Because the consumer can borrow $OC_3/(1 + r)$ units of the good. This is the most that the consumer can borrow because, if he or she borrows this much, the amount (including interest) that must be paid next year is $OC_3/(1 + r)$ times $(1 + r)$, or OC_3, which is all the consumer will receive then.

Note that, if the interest rate is held constant, how much a person can consume is determined by his or her wealth. For example, Figure 17.2 shows that, if the consumer's wealth is reduced to W', the budget line is lower. (But its slope remains the same, since it equals $- [1 + r]$.) Just as the consumer's money income determined how high or low his or her budget line would be in the single-period model of consumer behavior in Chapter 3, so the consumer's wealth determines how high or low it will be in the present intertemporal model.

INTERTEMPORAL CHOICE: PRODUCTION

Producers, like consumers, must make choices involving more than one time period. To make things as simple as possible, suppose that Mary McGann lives on an island and that she both produces and consumes the single good that exists. She is endowed with a certain amount of the good this year and next; this endowment is represented by point *G* in Figure 17.3. Specifically, she knows that she will produce OC_4 units of the good this year and OC_5 units of the good

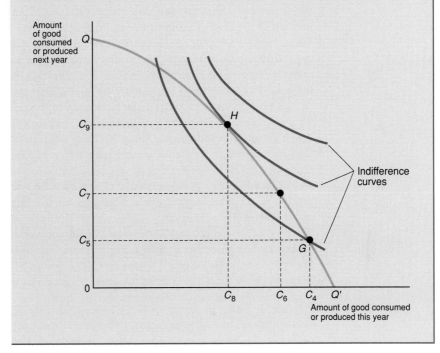

FIGURE 17.3 Equilibrium of the Producer-Consumer *The consumer will choose point* H, *the point on curve* QQ' *that lies on the highest indifference curve. She saves and invests* $(OC_4 - OC_8)$ *units of the good.*

Saving and investment

next year. Curve QQ' shows how much she can produce (and consume) next year if she saves some of the present year's output and invests it to increase next year's output.[1] By *saving*, we mean refraining from consumption. By *investment*, we mean the formation of new capital assets.

To illustrate the meaning of curve QQ', suppose that she consumes only OC_6 units of the good this year. Curve QQ' shows that, under these circumstances, she will produce OC_7 units of the good next year. That is, if she saves and invests $(OC_4 - OC_6)$ units of the good this year, she will receive $(OC_7 - OC_5)$ additional units next year. The reason for the extra output next year is that the investment pays off then. For example, if a farmer uses some corn for seed for next year's crop, rather than consuming it this year, this investment will add to next year's output.

To determine what is the optimal choice for this producer-consumer, we must consider her indifference curves, shown in Figure 17.3. Since all attainable combinations of present and future consumption are points on curve QQ', she will choose point H, the point on curve QQ' that lies on the highest indifference curve. Let's look at exactly what point H signifies. Clearly, this is the

---

1. QQ' also indicates that she can dissave; that is, she can consume somewhat more than she produces this year, at the expense of next year's output. She does this if she chooses points along QQ' between G and Q'.

point where she consumes OC_8 units of the good this year and consumes OC_9 units of the good next year. But more can be said than this. Since she knows that she will produce OC_4 units of the good this year, and yet she chooses to consume only OC_8 units of it, she is *saving* $(OC_4 - OC_8)$ units of the good. At the same time, she is also *investing* these $(OC_4 - OC_8)$ units of the good. That is, the $(OC_4 - OC_8)$ units of the good that she saves will be put to work to expand next year's output. Moreover, the amount by which this investment will expand next year's output can be determined from Figure 17.3. If she had invested nothing, her output next year would be OC_5 units, so this investment must increase next year's output by $(OC_9 - OC_5)$ units.

Since single life on an island can be dull, even for economists, it is time that we move on to somewhat more interesting (and realistic) circumstances. Suppose that another individual, James McBride, can both produce the good and lend or borrow it. His endowment, like Mary McGann's, is represented by point G. That is, he knows that he will produce OC_4 units of the good this year and OC_5 units of the good next year. Once again, QQ' shows how much he can produce (and consume) next year if he saves some of the present year's output and invests it to increase next year's output. But now, after he chooses a point on the QQ' curve, he can lend some (or all) of his current year's output to others, or he can borrow against some (or all) of his next year's output. For example, if he chooses point K on the QQ' curve in Figure 17.4, he can then borrow $(OC_{12} - OC_{10})$ units of the good from others, thus moving to point L.

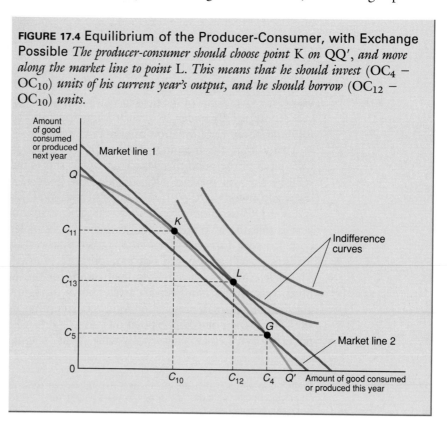

FIGURE 17.4 Equilibrium of the Producer-Consumer, with Exchange Possible *The producer-consumer should choose point K on QQ', and move along the market line to point L. This means that he should invest* $(OC_4 - OC_{10})$ *units of his current year's output, and he should borrow* $(OC_{12} - OC_{10})$ *units.*

Clearly, his options are much richer than in Figure 17.3. What decision will he make?

As a first step toward answering this question, it is necessary to recognize that, corresponding to each choice of a point on QQ', there exists a *market line* which shows the various amounts of the good that he can consume in each period, if he lends or borrows various amounts. For example, if the producer-consumer chooses point K, he is then confronted with market line 1 when he subsequently decides how much to borrow or lend. This market line (like the budget lines in Figures 17.1 and 17.2) has a slope equal to $-(1 + r)$. It goes through the point that he chooses on QQ' because this point indicates how much of the good he will have in the present and next year. Since one of his options is to borrow (and lend) nothing, the market line must go through this point. The market line corresponding to his choosing point G on QQ' is market line 2 in Figure 17.4.

Each market line is associated with a particular level of *attained wealth,* which is equal to the market line's intercept on the horizontal axis. The producer-consumer's first step toward an optimal decision is to *choose the point on* QQ' *that is on the highest market line.* In other words, he should choose the point on QQ' that is associated with the maximum possible attained wealth. In Figure 17.4, this point is K. Next, *he should move along the market line corresponding to this point until he reaches the highest possible indifference curve.* In Figure 17.4, this point is L. In this way, he reaches the optimal decision. The opportunity to borrow or lend will usually result in the producer-consumer's being on a higher indifference curve than if he could not borrow or lend. For example, in Figure 17.4, he achieves a higher indifference curve at point L (which he can reach only by borrowing) than at point K (where he neither borrows nor lends).

In sum, the producer-consumer in Figure 17.4 should choose point K on QQ'. That is, he should invest $(OC_4 - OC_{10})$ units of his current year's output. This amount should be added to his capital assets. But he should not save this entire amount. Instead, he should borrow $(OC_{12} - OC_{10})$ units of this amount, thus moving along the market line to point L. This is his optimal decision. Of course, some other member of society must save enough to lend him the $(OC_{12} - OC_{10})$ units of the good. In the aggregate, the total amount that people desire to save must equal the total amount that people desire to invest, if equilibrium occurs. More will be said on this score in the next section.

THE INTEREST RATE: EFFECTS AND DETERMINANTS

The choices made by individuals and firms are influenced by the rate of interest. To see that this is the case, suppose that the consumer in Figure 17.1 is confronted with a higher rate of interest. As shown in Figure 17.5, the increase in the interest rate will shift the budget line. Specifically, the budget line will be steeper after the increase in the interest rate, since the slope of the budget line equals $-(1 + r)$, as we know from p. 491. Thus, with the higher interest rate, the consumer will choose a different amount to consume each year than with

FIGURE 17.5 Effect of Increase in the Interest Rate on the Equilibrium of the Consumer *With the higher interest rate, the consumer saves* $(OC_2 - OC_{14})$ *units. With the lower interest rate, the consumer saves* $(OC_2 - OC_0)$ *units.*

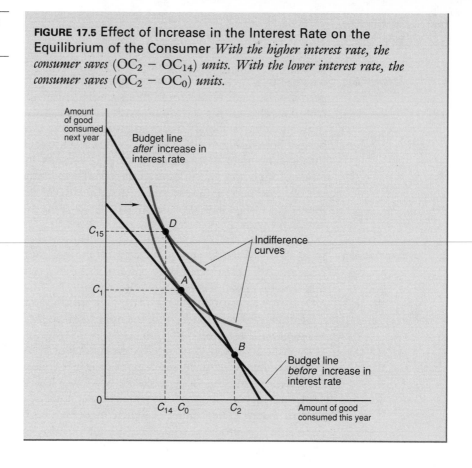

the lower interest rate. Specifically, with the higher interest rate, the consumer will consume OC_{14} units of the good this year and OC_{15} units next year. With the lower interest rate, the consumer will consume OC_0 units this year and OC_1 units next year.

The increase in the interest rate also affects the amount the consumer saves this year. With the higher interest rate, the consumer saves $(OC_2 - OC_{14})$ units. (Recall from p. 491 that the consumer receives OC_2 units this year. Since he or she decides to consume only OC_{14} units this year, it follows that $(OC_2 - OC_{14})$ units must be saved.) With the lower interest rate the consumer saves $(OC_2 - OC_0)$ units. (Since he or she consumes OC_0 units this year, it follows that $(OC_2 - OC_0)$ units are saved.)

Producers, like consumers, are also influenced by the rate of interest. For example, suppose that the producer-consumer in Figure 17.4 is confronted with a higher rate of interest. As shown in Figure 17.6, the increase in the interest rate will shift the market lines. Specifically, the market line in panel B of Figure 17.6 (which shows the situation when the interest rate is *higher*) is steeper than the market line in panel A of Figure 17.6 (which shows the situation when the interest rate is *lower*). This is true because the slope of a market line equals $-(1 + r)$, as we know from the previous section. As we also know

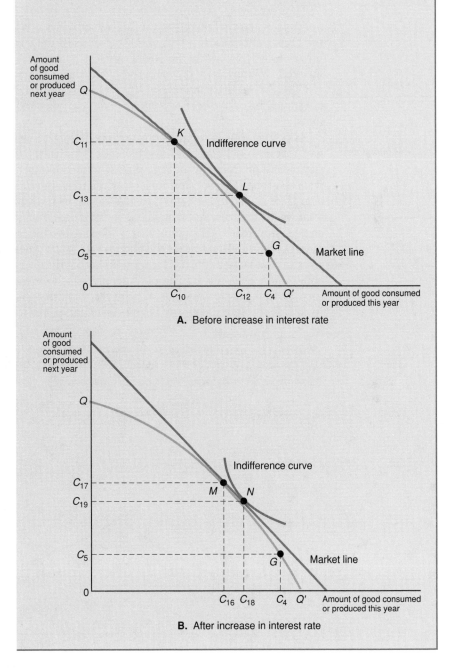

FIGURE 17.6 Effect of Increase in the Interest Rate on the Equilibrium of the Producer-Consumer *Before the increase in the interest rate, $(OC_4 - OC_{10})$ units are invested and $(OC_{12} - OC_{10})$ units are borrowed. After the increase in the interest rate, $(OC_4 - OC_{16})$ units are invested, and $(OC_{18} - OC_{16})$ units are borrowed.*

A. Before increase in interest rate

B. After increase in interest rate

from the previous section, the producer-consumer's first step toward an optimal decision is to choose the point on QQ' that is on the highest market line. In panel A of Figure 17.6, this point is K, whereas in panel B, it is M. Next, the producer-consumer should move along the market line corresponding to this point until he or she reaches the highest possible indifference curve. In panel A of Figure 17.6, this point is L; in panel B, it is N.

Thus the producer-consumer is led to make different investment and saving decisions when the interest rate is high than when it is low. Specifically, with the higher interest rate, $(OC_4 - OC_{16})$ units of the current year's output are invested, whereas with the lower interest rate, $(OC_4 - OC_{10})$ units are invested. With the higher interest rate, the producer-consumer borrows $(OC_{18} - OC_{16})$ units and saves $(OC_4 - OC_{18})$ units, whereas with the lower interest rate, he or she borrows $(OC_{12} - OC_{10})$ units and saves $(OC_4 - OC_{12})$ units.

Saving = investment

As pointed out in the previous section, aggregate saving must equal aggregate investment if equilibrium is to occur. That is, the total amount that consumers and producers want to save must equal the total amount that producers want to invest. The equilibrium level of the rate of interest is the level at which aggregate saving equals aggregate investment, as shown in Figure 17.7. Curve S shows the total amount that will be saved at each level of the interest rate, and curve I shows the total amount that will be invested at each level of the interest rate. The equilibrium level of the interest rate is OR, the level at which the total amount saved equals the total amount invested. If the interest rate is above this equilibrium level, the total amount people want to invest will be less than the total amount people want to save, with the result that the interest rate will tend to fall. If the interest rate is below this equilibrium level, the total amount

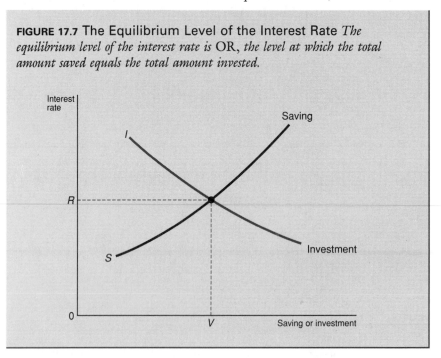

FIGURE 17.7 The Equilibrium Level of the Interest Rate *The equilibrium level of the interest rate is* OR, *the level at which the total amount saved equals the total amount invested.*

people want to invest will exceed the total amount people want to save, wit|
result that the interest rate will tend to rise. Thus, assuming perfect com|
tion, the interest rate, like any other price, is determined through the int|
tion of individuals and firms in the market.

THE PRESENT-VALUE RULE FOR INVESTMENT DECISIONS

The models of intertemporal choice presented in previous sections are hig|
simplified, and you may wonder whether they are of any practical significan|
The fact is that they are the basis for some extremely valuable decision ru|
used by business firms and government agencies to determine which inve|
ment projects they should carry out. The typical firm or agency is confront|
with a great many proposals for investment projects, far more than it can |
should carry out. The economic health (perhaps even the survival) of the fir|
or agency depends on whether it accepts the right ones.

How do the models presented in previous sections provide a useful guide f|
investment decisions of this sort? As a first step toward answering this question
let's return to the case of the producer-consumer in Figure 17.4. It is clear fron
Figure 17.4 that *the optimal point on* QQ' *is unaffected by the producer-consumer*
preferences. That is, regardless of the shape or location of his indifference curves
the decision-maker should choose that point on QQ' that is on the highes|
market line—or, putting it differently, *he should choose that point that is associatea*
with the maximum possible attained wealth. The fact that this is the optimal
decision, regardless of the decision-maker's preferences, is important, because it
means that, to establish a rule to guide decisions of this sort, one does not have
to worry about differences among decision-makers in preferences. Regardless
of such differences, the same rule applies: *Maximize attained wealth.*[2]

To see how this rule can be applied, consider a particular investment project
Any such project can be characterized by an amount that the decision-make
Present value of an
investment:
two periods
gives up this year and an amount that he or she receives next year. In the case o
this investment project, suppose that the decision-maker, if he or she gives up y
units of output this year, will gain y_1 units of output next year. The *present valı*
of this investment is defined to be

$$V = -y_0 + \frac{y_1}{1 + r}.$$

[17.

Comparing this definition of present value with the definition of wealth
p. 491, it is clear that *the present value of this investment project is the change in*
decision-maker's wealth resulting from carrying out the project. To see this, supp|
that the decision-maker, if he or she does not carry out the project, receives
units of output this year and X_1 units of output next year, which means that
or her wealth equals $X_0 + \dfrac{X_1}{1 + r}$. If the project is carried out, he or

2. The implicit assumption is made here that there are perfect and costless markets where boi
ing and lending occur. If this is not (approximately) true, the analysis must be altered, as s|
in more specialized texts concerning investment and capital budgeting.

receives $X_0 - y_0$ units this year and $X_1 + y_1$ units next year, which means that his or her wealth equals $X_0 - y_0 + \dfrac{X_1 + y_1}{1 + r}$, or $\left(X_0 + \dfrac{X_1}{1 + r}\right) + V$. The difference between his or her wealth if the project is carried out and his or her wealth if it is not carried out equals V, the present value of the project.

Since the decision-maker should maximize his or her wealth, and since the present value of an investment project is the change it effects in the decision-maker's wealth, it follows that *the decision-maker should carry out any investment project with a positive present value*. For example, suppose that, if a decision-maker gives up 1 unit of output this year, he or she will receive 1.2 units of output next year. If the interest rate is .10, should he or she carry out this project? Since $y_0 = 1$, $y_1 = 1.2$, and $r = .10$,

$$V = -1 + \frac{1.2}{1 + .10} = .09.$$

Since its present value is positive, this project should be carried out. Why? Because the decision-maker's wealth will be .09 units higher if the project is accepted than if it is rejected.

To see why the expression in Equation 17.2 is called the present value of the investment, note that *each unit of output received next year is worth only $1/(1 + r)$ units of output this year*. This is because, if one has $1/(1 + r)$ units of output this year, they can be lent out for a year; and because the rate of interest is r, they will return $(1 + r)$ times $1/(1 + r)$, or 1 unit next year. Since the value this year—that is, the *present* value—of each unit of output received next year is $1/(1 + r)$ units, the value this year—that is, the *present* value—of y_1 units received next year is $y_1[1/(1 + r)]$ units. Subtracting the y_0 units that are given up this year from $y_1 [1/(1 + r)]$, we obtain the net value this year—that is, the *present* value—of the investment.

THE PRESENT-VALUE RULE: THE MULTIPERIOD CASE

Present value of an investment: more than two periods

Since most investment projects extend over more than two periods, we must generalize the rule given in the previous section. To begin with, let's define the *present value* of a project as

$$V = z_0 + \frac{z_1}{1 + r} + \frac{z_2}{(1 + r)^2} + \cdots + \frac{z_n}{(1 + r)^n} \qquad [17.3]$$

where z_0 is the change (positive or negative) in the decision-maker's output this year, z_1 is the change in his or her output next year, z_2 is the change in his or her output two years hence, . . . , and z_n is the change in his or her output n years hence. Of course, Equation 17.2 is a special case of this equation, where $n = 1$, $z_0 = -y_0$, and $z_1 = y_1$. Equation 17.3 generalizes the earlier definition of present value (contained in Equation 17.2) to cases where more than two periods are relevant.

To see whether an investment project should be carried out, a decision-maker should determine whether the present value of the project is positive. If so, he or she should accept it. This is the rule to follow, regardless of the

number of periods that must be included in the analysis. For example, suppose that a decision-maker is presented with the following investment opportunity: If he or she gives up 1 unit of output this year, he or she will receive 1 unit of output next year and $\frac{1}{2}$ unit of output in the following year. If the interest rate is .10, should he or she carry out this project? Since $z_0 = -1$, $z_1 = 1$, $z_2 = .50$, and $r = .10$,

$$V = -1 + \frac{1}{1 + .10} + \frac{.50}{(1 + .10)^2} = .32.$$

Thus, since the present value of the project is positive, the project should be carried out.

The reason why the decision-maker should accept a project if its present value is positive is the same as in the two-period case discussed in the previous section. Regardless of the number of periods that must be included in the analysis, the decision-maker's wealth will increase if he or she carries out a project whose present value is positive (and the decision-maker's wealth will decrease if he or she carries out a project whose present value is negative). In effect, the present value puts the outflows and inflows of output resulting from the investment in comparable form. Specifically, it converts these inflows and outflows (which occur in various periods) into their equivalent amounts in the *present* period. For example, the present value of the investment in the previous paragraph is .32, because the receipt of 1 unit next year is the equivalent of receiving $1 \div (1 + .10)$, or .91 units this year, and the receipt of $\frac{1}{2}$ unit two years hence is the equivalent of receiving $\frac{1}{2} \div (1 + .10)^2$, or .41 units this year. Thus, since the investment entails giving up 1 unit this year, its present value is $-1 + .91 + .41$, or .32 units.

Why is the receipt of 1 unit next year the equivalent of receiving $1 \div (1 + .10)$ units this year? Because, as pointed out in the previous section, each unit of output received next year is worth only $1/(1 + r)$ units this year. Why is the receipt of $\frac{1}{2}$ unit two years hence the equivalent of receiving $\frac{1}{2} \div (1 + .10)^2$ units this year? Because, if one has $\frac{1}{2} \div (1 + .10)^2$ units of output this year, they can be lent out for two years. Since the rate of interest is .10, they will return $(1 + .10)^2$ times $\frac{1}{2} \div (1 + .10)^2)$, or $\frac{1}{2}$ unit in two years. (At this point, it should be obvious that the receipt of 1 unit of output n years hence is the equivalent of receiving $1/(1 + r)^n$ units this year. Why? Because, if one has $1/(1 + r)^n$ units this year, they can be lent out for n years, and at that time they will be worth $(1 + r)^n$ times $1/(1 + r)^n$, or 1 unit, because of the accumulated interest.)

Present value of
indefinite stream of
income

Finally, suppose that an investment yields a constant stream of output indefinitely into the future. Specifically, suppose that it yields z units of output next year, the following year, and every future year. What is the present value of this stream of output? Applying the principles described above, it is

$$\frac{z}{1 + r} + \frac{z}{(1 + r)^2} + \frac{z}{(1 + r)^3} + \cdots = z\left[\frac{1}{1 + r} + \frac{1}{(1 + r)^2} + \frac{1}{(1 + r)^3} \cdots\right],$$

which can be shown to equal z/r. (See footnote 3.) Thus, if the present value of

3. If x is any number less than 1,

$$1 + x + x^2 + x^3 + \cdots = 1/(1 - x).$$

(cont'd.)

this investment is to be positive, the decision-maker must give up less than z/r units of output this year to get this stream of future output. For example, if an investment yields 1 unit of output next year, the following year, and so on, what is the most that a decision-maker should be willing to give up this year in order to obtain this stream of future output, if the interest rate is .05? The answer is $1 \div .05$, or 20 units of output, since $z = 1$ and $r = .05$.

THE INVESTMENT DECISION: AN EXAMPLE

The present-value rule, described in the previous two sections, has found wide-spread application throughout business and government. To illustrate its use, consider a firm that had to decide whether or not to purchase a machine which would reduce the firm's labor requirements. The machine had a price of $25,000 and an anticipated life of five years with no salvage value at the end of that time. If the firm bought the machine, it would incur savings of labor costs in subsequent years, as shown in Table 17.1. If the interest rate was .10, should the firm have bought the machine? According to the present-value rule, the answer depends on whether the present value of the investment is positive. Using Equation 17.3, the present value of this investment was

TABLE 17.1 Effects of Machine on Firm's Stream of Cash Inflows

Number of years hence	Effect on cash inflow* (dollars)
0	−25,000
1	2,000
2	6,000
3	8,000
4	14,000
5	12,000

*Positive numbers indicate cash savings; negative numbers indicate cash outflows.

Thus, since $\dfrac{1}{1 + r}$ is less than 1,

$$\frac{1}{1 + r} + \left(\frac{1}{1 + r}\right)^2 + \left(\frac{1}{1 + r}\right)^3 + \cdots =$$
$$1/\left(1 - \frac{1}{1 + r}\right) - 1 = \frac{1 + r}{r} - 1 = \frac{1}{r}.$$

Consequently,

$$z\left[\frac{1}{(1 + r)} + \left(\frac{1}{1 + r}\right)^2 + \left(\frac{1}{1 + r}\right)^3 + \cdots\right] = \frac{z}{r}.$$

$$V = -25{,}000 + \frac{2{,}000}{1 + .10} + \frac{6{,}000}{(1 + .10)^2} + \frac{8{,}000}{(1 + .10)^3}$$

$$+ \frac{14{,}000}{(1 + .10)^4} + \frac{12{,}000}{(1 + .10)^5} = 4{,}800,$$

because $z_0 = -25{,}000$, $z_1 = 2{,}000$, $z_2 = 6{,}000$, $z_3 = 8{,}000$, $z_4 = 14{,}000$, $z_5 = 12{,}000$, and $r = .10$. Since the present value of the investment was positive, the firm should have bought the machine.

In this case, the amount that the decision-maker gains or loses each year is expressed in terms of money, not output.[4] This is because we no longer are making the assumption that only one good is present in the economy. The firm must estimate the effect of the investment—in this case, the new machine—on its cash inflow and outflow each year. The net change in its cash inflow (positive or negative) during each year is the value of z for this year. Thus, in this illustration, z_0 equals $-25{,}000$, since the machine reduces the firm's net cash inflow by $25,000 in the year when the machine is purchased (because the firm must spend this amount on the machine). And z_1 equals 2,000, since the machine increases the firm's net cash inflow by $2,000 during the first year after the machine is purchased (because the firm spends $2,000 less on labor than if it did not buy the machine).

Although the present-value rule is useful in guiding investment decisions, it sometimes cannot be applied in the straightforward way described here because of a variety of complications. For one thing, investment projects may be interdependent; that is, the stream of cash inflow or outflow from one project may depend on whether another project is undertaken. For another thing, there may be limitations on how many projects a firm can accept, perhaps because of limits on how much it is willing to borrow.[5] For still another thing, it is impossible to predict with certainty the stream of cash inflow or outflow from any investment project. One of the most difficult tasks facing any firm or agency is forecasting. In the present discussion, we have bypassed this problem and assumed that the firm's forecasts are correct. Techniques that help to deal with all of these complications are available in more advanced texts.[6]

INTERNAL RATES OF RETURN AND BOND YIELDS

The present value of an investment project is not the only commonly used indicator of the project's profitability. Another indicator is the *internal rate of*

4. We assume that the money figures are corrected for inflation and that r is the *real* interest rate (that is, the nominal interest rate minus the rate of inflation). If the money figures are not corrected for inflation, the *nominal* interest rate (that is, the interest rate unadjusted for inflation) should be used instead.

5. In Chapter 16, we pointed out that a government agency's budget often is variable, but this is only within certain limits. Thus government agencies, too, must operate within limitations of this sort.

6. For example, see I. Fisher, *The Theory of Interest* (New York: Macmillan, 1930); J. Lorie and L. Savage, "Three Problems in Rationing Capital," reprinted in E. Mansfield, *Microeconomics: Selected Readings*, 5th ed.; E. Solomon, "The Arithmetic of Capital Budgeting Decisions," *Journal of Business*, 1956; and F. Lutz and V. Lutz, *The Theory of Investment of the Firm* (Princeton, N.J.: Princeton University Press, 1951). These are classic studies in this area.

return, which is defined as the interest rate that equates the present value of the net cash inflows from the project to the project's investment outlay. In other words, it is the interest rate that the investor is really earning from his or her investment in the project. Holding constant the riskiness of a project, investors

---

EXAMPLE 17.1

SHOULD THE CARBORUNDUM CORPORATION EXPAND ITS CAPACITY?

The Carborundum Corporation had to decide whether to expand its production capacity for Ceramax, a high-porosity ceramic material it manufactured. Sales for this material had been growing rapidly, and its only maufacturing plant had reached capacity. The firm could expand its existing plant at Lockport, New York, or build a new plant in Birmingham, Alabama. Carborundum's staff calculated the present value of each of these investments, the results being as follows:

	Present value (millions of dollars)
Expand Lockport plant	−.163
Build new plant	−.153

(a) Based on these results, does it appear that Carborundum should expand the Lockport plant? (b) Does it appear that it should build a new plant? (c) In calculating the present value of the investment in the new plant, Carborundum's staff considered only the first five years after its construction. Does that seem to be the relevant period? (d) In calculating the above present values, Carborundum's staff used an interest rate of 15 percent, although the firm's return on equity capital during the previous decade had averaged less than 10 percent. Does this figure of 15 percent seem too high? (e) If the interest rate that is used is too high, will this bias the present values upward or downward? Why?

SOLUTION

(a) No, since the present value of such an investment is negative. (b) No, since the present value of this investment is negative too. (c) If the new plant is expected to operate for as long as many plants do, a five-year period seems rather short because the new plant's effects on profits are likely to extend for much longer than five years. (d) If the firm can only obtain 10 percent or less on alternative investment possibilities, the figure of 15 percent is too high (assuming that the investment in the new plant is no riskier than the alternative investment possibilities). The interest rate that is used should be the interest rate the firm can obtain if it does not invest in this project. (e) It will tend to bias the present values downward because net costs occur early and net benefits occur late in the life of such investment projects.*

*For further discussion, see R. Hayes, S. Wheelwright, and K. Clark, *Dynamic Manufacturing* (New York: Free Press, 1988).

generally prefer projects with high rates of return over those with low rates of return.

Suppose that you invest $47,550 in a project that yields cash inflows of $15,000 per year for each of the next four years. To determine the internal rate of return for this project, you must find the value of r^* that satisfies the following equation:

$$\$47,550 = \frac{\$15,000}{1 + r^*} + \frac{\$15,000}{(1 + r^*)^2} + \frac{\$15,000}{(1 + r^*)^3} + \frac{\$15,000}{(1 + r^*)^4}.$$

Why is r^* the interest rate that is earned on this investment? Because it is the interest rate that makes the present value of the net cash inflows from the project—which is shown on the right-hand side of this equation—equal to the investment outlay of $47,550. Using available computer programs (or trial-and-error techniques), we can solve this equation for r^*, the result being .10. Thus the internal rate of return for this investment is 10 percent.[7]

This same technique can be used to determine the interest rate earned on a bond. (This interest rate is often called the bond's *yield*.) Bonds are, of course, a very important type of security. A bond is a certificate bearing the issuer's promise to pay a stipulated amount of interest each year until the bond's maturity date, at which time the issuer promises to pay the bondholder the principal as well. Banks, brokers, and others must calculate the yields on a huge number of bonds each day. To see how such a yield is calculated, suppose that you pay $1,066 today for a bond that will mature in four years, at which time you will receive the face value of the bond (the principal), which is $1,000. In addition, since the bond pays annual interest of 10 percent (of the principal), you will receive interest of $100 per year, this amount being paid one, two, three, and four years from today.

To find the yield on this bond, you must find the interest rate that makes the present value of the cash inflows from the bond equal the amount paid for the bond. That is, you must find the value of r^* that satisfies the following equation:

$$\$1,066 = \frac{100}{1 + r^*} + \frac{\$100}{(1 + r^*)^2} + \frac{100}{(1 + r^*)^3} + \frac{\$100}{(1 + r^*)^4} + \frac{\$1,000}{(1 + r^*)^4}.$$

Because the present value of the cash inflow from the bond is given by the right-hand side of this equation, r^* is the interest rate that makes the present value of this cash inflow equal the amount paid for the bond ($1,066). In other words, r^* is the interest rate earned on this bond. Like the previous equation, this one can be solved for r^* using available computer programs (or trial-and-error techniques), the result being that $r^* = .08$. Thus the yield on this bond is 8 percent.

---

7. Hand calculators that compute rates of return are constructed to solve equations of this sort. For a description of trial-and-error methods, as well as a discussion of the relationship between the present-value rule and the internal rate of return, see E. Mansfield, *Managerial Economics* (New York: Norton, 1990). One disadvantage of the internal rate of return is that it is not always unique. That is, more than one value of r^* will sometimes make the present value of the cash flows equal to the investment outlay.

EXAMPLE 17.2

DID PROPOSITION 13 RESULT IN LOWER HOUSING PRICES?

In 1978, California's voters supported Proposition 13 by an overwhelming margin. During the 1970s, their property taxes had increased considerably. One Los Angeles family bought a house for $64,000 in 1968 and its property tax then was $1,800. By 1976, it had increased to $3,500, and without Proposition 13, it soon would have gone to $7,000. Angry at such increases in their property taxes, Californians voted for Proposition 13, which called for a more than 50 percent reduction in the property tax.

One argument frequently advanced by the supporters of Proposition 13 was that property taxes had gotten so high that many families were unable to scrape up the funds required to buy a house. According to this argument, a reduction in the property tax would lower housing prices and make it easier for families to purchase houses. Suppose that you are an adviser to the governor of California, and that you are asked whether this argument really holds water. What's the answer?

SOLUTION

A reduction in the property tax means that owners of houses have to pay less each year to the government. Because of Proposition 13, the owner of a particular house in Palo Alto may have had to pay $1,000 less in property taxes in 1979, 1980, and in all subsequent years. Assuming for simplicity that these savings continue indefinitely, the present value of this stream of annual savings was

$$PV = \frac{1,000}{r}, \qquad [17.4]$$

where r is the interest rate. (Recall page 501.) Given this stream of annual savings, a house was worth more than before the property tax cut. Specifically, its value increased by an amount equal to the present value of the annual savings, given in Equation 17.4.

At the time, the rate of interest was in the neighborhood of 15 percent, so the present value of a $1,000 annual reduction in property taxes was approximately

$$PV = \frac{1000}{.15} = \$6,667.$$

(To get this result, we substitute .15 for r in Equation 17.4.) Thus we would expect that a $1,000 annual reduction in property taxes would increase a house's value by about $6,667. In fact, Kenneth Rosen, based on a careful study, has shown this to be the case. According to his findings a $1,000 reduction in property taxes triggered an increase of about $7,000 in property values.*

*K. Rosen, "The Impact of Proposition 13 on House Prices in Northern California," *Journal of Political Economy*, February 1982.

TECHNOLOGICAL CHANGE[8]

In the previous sections of this chapter, we have presented models pertaining to intertemporal choice by consumers and producers. Now we turn to another essentially dynamic phenomenon—technological change. Technology is society's pool of knowledge regarding the industrial and agricultural arts. The technology existing at a given point in time sets limits on how much can be produced with a given amount of inputs. Given the level of technology, there is generally a wide range of possible methods of producing a given good or service. Some require little capital and much labor, some require much capital and little labor; some are old, some are new. Given a certain amount of various inputs, it is possible to determine which method results in the maximum output and what the maximum output is. We know from Chapter 6 that the production function shows, for a given level of technology, the maximum output rate that can be achieved from a given amount of inputs.

Technological change

Technological change is the advance of technology; such advance often takes the form of new methods of producing existing products and new techniques of organization, marketing, and management. Technological change results in a change in the production function. If the production function were readily observable, a comparison of the production function at two points in time would provide the economist with a simple measure of the effect of technological change during the intervening period. For example, if there were only two inputs, labor and capital, and if there were constant returns to scale, the characteristics of the production function at a given date could be captured fully by a single isoquant.[9] Under these circumstances, one could simple look at the changing position of this isoquant to see the effects of technological change.

For example, if this isoquant shifted from position 1 to position 2 in Figure 17.8 during a certain period of time, technological change had less impact during this period than if the curve shifted to position 3. As we shall see in subsequent sections, it is sometimes possible to estimate the average rate of movement of the production function by a single number, and economists often use this number to measure the rate of technological change. Of course, it is only an indirect measure, but there is no way to measure the rate of technological change directly.

Technological change also results in the availability of new products. In many cases, the availability of new products can be regarded as a change in the production function, since they are merely more efficient ways of meeting old wants if these wants are defined with proper breadth. This is particularly true in the case of new intermediate goods, which may result in little or no change in the final product. In other cases, however, the availability of new products

---

8. For a much more extensive and detailed discussion of technological change, see E. Mansfield, *The Economics of Technological Change* (New York: Norton, 1968); and E. Mansfield, A. Romeo, M. Schwartz, D. Teece, S. Wagner, and P. Brach, *Technology Transfer, Productivity, and Economic Policy* (New York: Norton, 1982).

9. Recall from Chapter 6 that, if there are constant returns to scale, an x percent increase in all inputs results in an x percent increase in output. Thus, if there are constant returns to scale, there is at a given point in time a unique relationship between capital input per unit of output and labor input per unit of output. This relationship holds for any output and completely summarizes the efficient input combinations.

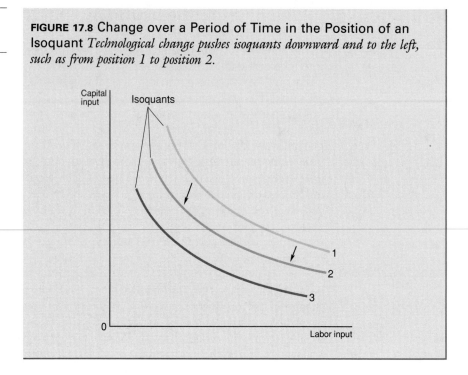

FIGURE 17.8 Change over a Period of Time in the Position of an Isoquant *Technological change pushes isoquants downward and to the left, such as from position 1 to position 2.*

cannot realistically be viewed as a change in the production function, since they entail an important difference in kind.[10]

PRODUCTIVITY GROWTH AND THE MEASUREMENT OF TECHNOLOGICAL CHANGE

Labor productivity

Economists have long been interested in productivity—the ratio of output to input. In recent decades, American economists have shown a particular interest in this topic because there has been a well-publicized fall in the U.S. rate of productivity increase. The oldest and most commonly studied measure of productivity is *labor productivity,* output per hour of labor. One determinant of the rate of growth of labor productivity is the rate of technological change; a high rate of technological change is likely to result, all other things equal, in a high rate of growth of labor productivity. However, the rate of technological change is not the only determinant of the rate of growth of labor productivity, with the consequence that the latter is a very incomplete, though frequently used, measure of the rate of technological change.

10. It is sometimes asserted that it is unrealistic to emphasize cost-reducing technological change, since firms report that only about 13 percent of their expenditures on research and development go for pure process improvement. But this is wrong because much of the research and development concerning new products and product improvements is devoted to new and improved intermediate goods and capital goods. In civilian industry, perhaps 80 percent of the reported research and development goes for new processes, new intermediate goods, and new capital goods. See E. Mansfield, J. Rapoport, J. Schnee, S. Wagner, and M. Hamburger, *Research and Innovation in the Modern Corporation* (New York: Norton, 1971).

A more adequate measure of the rate of technological change is the *total productivity index,* which relates changes in output to changes in both labor and capital inputs, not changes in labor inputs alone. Suppose that the production function is of the simple form

$$Q = \alpha(bL + cK) \qquad [17.5]$$

where Q is the quantity of output, L is the quantity of labor, K is the quantity of capital, b and c are constants, and α is a number that varies over time in response to technological change. Suppose that $Q_0, L_0, K_0,$ and α_0 are the values of $Q, L, K,$ and α in an early period and that $Q_1, L_1, K_1,$ and α_1 are the values of $Q, L, K,$ and α in a later period. To determine $\alpha_1 \div \alpha_0$, which is a measure of the rate of technological change, one can compute

$$\frac{Q_1}{Q_0} \div \left(U\frac{L_1}{L_0} + V\frac{K_1}{K_0} \right) \qquad [17.6]$$

where $U = bL_0/(bL_0 + cK_0)$ and $V = cK_0/(bL_0 + cK_0)$. This is the total productivity index. It is equal to the relative increase in output divided by a weighted average of the relative increase in labor input and the relative increase in capital input.[11]

Of course, the production function in Equation 17.5 is a very special case. Economists have tried to devise better measures of the rate of movement of the production function than the total productivity index. These measures rest on somewhat different assumptions about the shape of the production function, with the Cobb-Douglas production function sometimes, but not always, being used. One of the pioneering studies of this type was carried out in 1957 by Nobel laureate Robert Solow of the Massachusetts Institute of Technology.[12] The resulting estimates have proved useful in many contexts, but their limitations should be noted. In particular, since they equate the effects of technological change with whatever increase in output is unexplained by other inputs, they may not isolate the effects of technological change alone. In addition, they may contain the effects of whatever inputs may have been excluded from the analysis because of convenience, lack of data, ignorance, or some other reason.

THE LEARNING CURVE

In many industries like aircraft, electronics, and machine tools, technological change is due in considerable part to learning and on-the-job experience that occurs as a firm produces more and more of a given item. Thus, holding the firm's output rate constant, its average cost declines with increases in its *cumulative* total output (that is, the total number of items of this sort that it has

---

11. For historical data concerning labor productivity and total productivity in the United States, see J. Kendrick, *Productivity Trends in the United States* (New York: National Bureau of Economic Research, 1961), and his more recent publications, as well as D. Jorgenson, F. Gollop, and B. Fraumeni, *Productivity and U.S. Economic Growth* (Cambridge: Harvard University Press, 1987).

12. R. Solow, "Technical Change and the Aggregate Production Function," *Review of Economics and Statistics,* August 1957.

EXAMPLE 17.3

THE GROWTH OF LABOR PRODUCTIVITY AT GENERAL MOTORS AND TOYOTA

Labor productivity at General Motors and Toyota, the biggest American and Japanese auto producers, are shown below for 1950 to 1985.

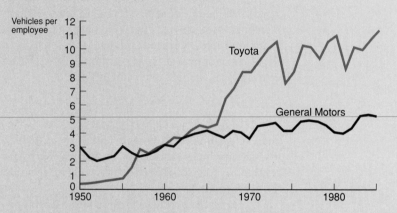

(a) Did labor productivity increase as rapidly during 1950–85 at General Motors as at Toyota? (b) From 1960 to 1985, the amount of capital per worker approximately doubled at both General Motors and Toyota. Can the higher rate of increase of labor productivity at Toyota than at General Motors be attributed to more substitution of capital for labor at Toyota than at General Motors? (c) According to many observers, the internal organization of Japanese firms often differs from that of American firms. Workers' jobs are seldom specified in detail, and employees are often rotated among a variety of jobs. Relative to American firms, there is less emphasis on job specialization and hierarchical control. Can organizational factors of this sort affect the rate of increase of labor productivity? (d) General Motors and Toyota have a joint venture in California. Using Japanese managerial and organizational techniques, the managers in California raised labor productivity considerably over the levels achieved when the plant was operated under purely American management. Were these managerial and organizational changes a form of technological change?

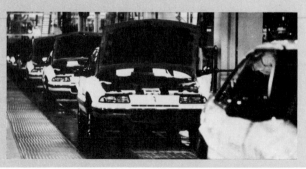

SOLUTION

(a) No. (b) Apparently not, since capital per worker increased as much at General Motors as at Toyota. (c) Yes. Studies indicate that the Japanese approach is particularly effective in industries where process improvements depend on interdepartmental coordination and many small modifications on the factory floor that are not easily recognized at higher levels of the managerial hierarchy. (d) Yes. To the economist, technological change includes alterations in organization and management.*

*For further discussion, see M. Lieberman, "Learning, Productivity, and Industrial Competitiveness," in K. Ferdows (ed.), *Managing International Manufacturing* (Amsterdam: North-Holland, 1988).

produced in the past). For example, production of the first thousand C-46 transport planes required about 75 percent more hours of labor than production of the second thousand aircraft of this type, even though the number of aircraft produced per month remained about the same. Thus the average cost of this airplane fell substantially as cumulative total output grew.

Learning   It is important to distinguish between cost reductions due to *learning* and cost reductions due to *economies of scale*. Holding constant the number of C-46 transport planes produced by this firm in the past, if the average cost of producing such a plane during the current period declines as more of them are produced, the decline is due to economies of scale. Holding constant the number of such planes produced per period of time, if the average cost falls (as in the previous paragraph) when the firm's cumulative total output of this plane increases, this is due to learning.

Economists often use the *learning curve* to represent the extent to which the average cost of producing an item falls in response to increases in its cumulative total output. Figure 17.9 shows the learning curves for two products, a machine tool and a semiconductor chip. (A semiconductor chip is a key component employed to store information in computers and other electronic products.) As you can see, learning results in bigger reductions in average cost for the semiconductor chip than for the machine tool. Of course, these cost reductions are not automatic: They occur only if workers and managers strive for increased efficiency. But for many products of this sort, a doubling of cumulative output tends to produce about a 20 or 30 percent reduction in average cost. As would be expected, this implies that learning results in more dramatic cost reductions (in absolute terms) when cumulative total output is small than when it is large.

The learning curve has played an important role in decision-making in both government and industry. As an illustration, consider the case of Texas Instruments, a major producer of semiconductor chips and other electronic products. When the semiconductor industry was relatively young, Texas Instruments priced its product at less than its then-current average costs in order to increase its output rate and its cumulative total output. Believing that the learning curve was relatively steep, it hoped that this would reduce its average costs to such an extent that it would be profitable to produce and sell at this low price. This

FIGURE 17.9 Learning Curve for Semiconductor Chip and Machine Tool* *For both products, average cost falls as cumulative total output increases.*

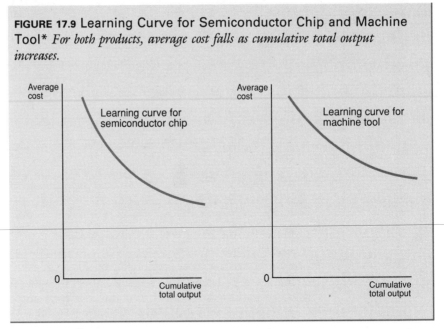

*The horizontal and vertical scales are different in the left-hand figure than in the right-hand figure, but it is clear that a doubling of cumulative output results in a greater percentage reduction in average cost in the left-hand figure than the right-hand figure.

strategy was extremely successful. As Texas Instruments continued to cut price, its rivals began to withdraw from the market, its output continued to increase, its costs fell further, and its profits increased.[13]

STATIC EFFICIENCY AND ECONOMIC PROGRESS

In Chapter 15, we presented several conditions for economic efficiency: The marginal rate of substitution between any pair of commodities must be the same for all consumers, the marginal rate of technical substitution between any pair of inputs must be the same for all producers, and the marginal rate of product transformation must equal the marginal rate of substitution for each pair of goods. Given a fixed level of technology these conditions must be fulfilled (with certain qualifications discussed in Chapter 15) if economic efficiency is to be achieved.

Static efficiency   It is important to note that these conditions result only in efficiency in a static sense. That is, they show how inputs and commodities must be allocated

13. For a classic paper concerning learning curves, see K. Arrow, "The Economic Implications of Learning by Doing," *Review of Economic Studies,* June 1962. The Boston Consulting Group was a leading advocate of their application to corporate planning. Also see A. Michael Spence, "Competition, Entry, and Antitrust Policy," in E. Mansfield, *Microeconomics: Selected Readings,* 5th ed.; and L. Argote and D. Epple, "Learning Curves in Manufacturing," *Science,* February 23, 1990.

if economic performance is to be maximized, *given a fixed level of technology*. It is possible that an allocation of inputs and commodities that violates these conditions might lead to a higher level of performance than any allocation that meets these conditions, because it might result in a faster rate of technological change and productivity increase.

Economists like Joseph Schumpeter and John Kenneth Galbraith of Harvard University[14] have argued that this is the case, and have gone on to suggest that a perfectly competitive economy is likely to be inferior in a dynamic sense to an economy including many imperfectly competitive industries (that is, monopolies, oligopolies, etc.). In their view, although (as we showed in Chapter 15) a perfectly competitive economy will satisfy the conditions for static economic efficiency, it will not result in as high a rate of technological change and productivity increase as an imperfectly competitive economy.

To illustrate what they have in mind, suppose that we compare the performance of two economies, one perfectly competitive, the other imperfectly competitive. Suppose that they start off with comparable technology in 1991, but that the rate of technological change is higher in the imperfectly competitive economy than in the perfectly competitive economy, with the result that the annual rate of productivity change is 3 percent in the imperfectly competitive economy and 2 percent in the perfectly competitive economy. Assuming that the quantity of inputs is the same in each economy and constant over time, it follows that

$$Q(t) = Q_0(1.02)^t \qquad\qquad [17.7]$$

$$Q'(t) = Q'_0(1.03)^t \qquad\qquad [17.8]$$

where $Q(t)$ is the output in year t in the perfectly competitive economy, $Q'(t)$ is the output in year t in the imperfectly competitive economy, and t is measured in years from 1991.

Suppose too that, because of the static inefficiencies due to its violation of the conditions in Chapter 15, the imperfectly competitive economy produces 98 percent as much as the perfectly competitive economy when their technology levels are the same. Thus $Q'_0 = .98Q_0$, and

$$Q(t) = Q_0(1.02)^t \qquad\qquad [17.9]$$

$$Q'(t) = .98Q_0(1.03)^t. \qquad\qquad [17.10]$$

Thus it follows that

$$Q'(t) \div Q(t) = .98(1.03 \div 1.02)^t, \qquad\qquad [17.11]$$

which implies that $Q'(t) \div Q(t)$ will be greater than one when t is greater than about 2. Consequently, despite its being relatively inefficient in a static sense, the imperfectly competitive economy out-produces the perfectly competitive economy from about 1993 on, because it has the higher rate of technological change and productivity increase.

14. J. Schumpeter, *Capitalism, Socialism, and Democracy* (New York: Harper & Row, 1947); and J. K. Galbraith, *American Capitalism* (Boston: Houghton Mifflin, 1952).

EXAMPLE 17.4

ROBOTS AND THEIR ECONOMIC EFFECTS

Robots are becoming increasingly important in many industries. In the United States, about 49 percent of all robots have been used for welding and painting, and 21 percent for machine tool loading and assembly operations. Suppose that the metal cabinet industry devises a new way to use robots to reduce its costs, and that the market demand curve for metal cabinets in 1992 is as shown below. Because of this new method, the cost of producing a metal cabinet is OP_1, whereas it would have been OP_0 without the new method. Suppose that the market supply curve for metal cabinets in 1992 is S_1; without this method, it would have been S_0.

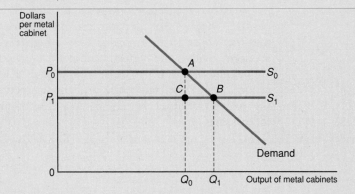

(a) During the period covered by the graph above, what is the social value of the extra output of metal cabinets due to this new method? (b) What is the social value of the saving in resources due to this new method? (c) Prove that the social value of the extra output, which you found in question (a), plus the social value of the resource savings, which you found in question (b), equals the area P_1P_0AB. (d) If the resources saved consist in part of labor that cannot find alternative work, are your answers to questions (a) and (b) correct?

SOLUTION

(a) Output is OQ_1 with the new method, whereas it would have been OQ_0 without it. The social value of the extra output is the area under the demand curve from Q_0 to Q_1—that is, the area Q_0ABQ_1. (Recall p. 273.) (b) With the new method, OQ_1 metal cabinets are produced, and each one costs OP_1, so the total value of resources used is OQ_1 times OP_1, which equals the area OP_1BQ_1. Without the new method, OQ_0 metal cabinets would have been produced, and each one would have cost OP_0, so that the total value of resources used would have been OQ_0 times OP_0, which equals the area OP_0AQ_0. Thus the saving equals the area OP_0AQ_0 minus the area OP_1BQ_1. Since these areas have in common the area OP_1CQ_0, it follows that this saving equals the area P_1P_0AC minus the area Q_0CBQ_1. (c) From above, we know that the social value of the extra output equals the area Q_0ABQ_1, and that the social value of the savings equals the area P_1P_0AC minus the area Q_0CBQ_1. Thus the sum of these social values must equal the area Q_0ABQ_1 plus the area P_1P_0AC minus the area Q_0CBQ_1. Since the area Q_0ABQ_1 minus the area Q_0CBQ_1 equals the area CAB, it follows that the sum of these social values must equal P_1P_0AC plus the area CAB, or the area P_1P_0AB. (d) No. The answers to questions (a) and (b) assume that labor and other resources no longer required in producing metal cabinets find employment elsewhere. If not, the social benefits must be scaled down.*

*For further discussion of this topic, see E. Mansfield, J. Rapoport, A. Romeo, S. Wagner, and G. Beardsley, "Social and Private Rates of Return from Industrial Innovations," *Quarterly Journal of Economics,* May 1977. This article shows how the benefits from an innovation can be related to the costs of developing it to determine the rate of return from the investment in the innovation. Also, it extends the results of this example to more complicated cases.

Imperfect Competition and Technological Change

This example shows that the static inefficiencies of an imperfectly competitive economy *can* be offset by its having a higher rate of technological change and productivity increase, but it does not tell us why we should expect the rate of technological change and productivity increase to be higher in an imperfectly competitive economy. This is a question that has been debated at great length. On the one hand, some economists, like Schumpeter and Galbraith, believe that there are a number of good reasons why the rate of technological change and productivity increase will be higher in an imperfectly competitive economy. On the other hand, other economists stick with the view of John Stuart Mill and J. B. Clark that this is not the case.[15]

Members of the Schumpeter-Galbraith group argue that firms under perfect competition have less resources to devote to research and experimentation than do firms under imperfect competition. Because profits are at a relatively low level, it is difficult for firms under perfect competition to support large expenditures on research and development. Moreover, it is argued that, unless a firm has sufficient control over the market to reap the rewards of an innovation, the introduction of the innovation may not be worthwhile. If competitors can imitate the innovation very quickly, the innovator may be unable to make any money from the innovation.

Defenders of perfect competition retort that there is likely to be less pressure for firms in imperfect markets to introduce new techniques and products, since such firms have fewer competitors. Moreover, such firms are better able to drive out entrants who, uncommitted to present techniques, are likely to be relatively quick to adopt new ones. (Entrants, unlike established producers, have no vested interest in maintaining the demand for existing products and the profitability of existing equipment.) Also, there are advantages in having a large

15. J. S. Mill, *Principles of Political Economy* (London, 1852), Book IV, Ch. VII, p. 351; and J. B. Clark, *Essentials of Economic Theory* (New York, 1907), p. 374.

number of independent decision-making units, since there is less chance that an important technological advance will be blocked by the faulty judgment of a few people.

It is difficult to obtain evidence to help settle this question, if it is posed in this way, since perfect competition is, of course, a hypothetical construct that does not exist in the real world. However, it does seem unlikely that a perfectly competitive industry (if such an industry could be constructed) would be able in many areas of the economy to carry out the research and development required to promote a high rate of technological change.[16] Moreover, if entry is free and rapid, firms in a perfectly competitive industry will have little motivation to innovate. Although the evidence is not at all clear-cut, this much certainly seems reasonable.[17]

But it is one thing to grant that a certain amount of market imperfection may promote the rate of technological change, and another thing to say, as does Galbraith, that the "modern industry of a few large firms [is] an almost perfect instrument for inducing technical change."[18] If true, this is an extremely important point. But is it true? Does the evidence indicate that an industry dominated by a few giant firms is generally more progressive than one composed of a large number of smaller firms?

Advantages in diversity

Contrary to the allegations of Galbraith, there is little evidence that industrial giants are needed in all or even most industries to insure rapid technological change and rapid utilization of new techniques. Of course, this does not mean that industries composed only of small firms would necessarily be optimal for the promotion and diffusion of new techniques either. On the contrary, there seem to be considerable advantages in a diversity of firm sizes; no single firm size is optimal in this respect. Moreover, the optimal average size is likely to be directly related to the costliness and the scope of the inventions that arise. However, in general, these factors do not make giantism necessary. To repeat, there is little evidence that industrial giants are needed in all or even most industries to promote rapid technological change and rapid utilization of new techniques.[19]

Summary

1. The consumer has preferences between consumption this year and consumption next year, and these preferences can be represented by a set of indifference curves. The consumer is confronted by a budget line which indicates the combinations of present and future consumption that he or she can attain. The intercept of the budget line on the horizontal axis is called the consumer's endowed wealth. The slope of the budget line is $-(1 + r)$, where r is the interest rate. The optimal choice between the amount consumed this year and the

---

16. Even if supplier firms emerge that specialize in research and development, the members of the competitive industry must still carry out some technical work to be able to accept new technology rapidly. Moreover, there may have to be imperfect competition in the supplying industry if it is to be viable.

17. Also, technological change may result in a certain amount of market imperfection, although the extent of the market imperfection is likely to vary greatly from case to case.

18. J. K. Galbraith, *American Capitalism,* p. 91.

19. See E. Mansfield, A. Romeo, M. Schwartz, D. Teece, S. Wagner, and P. Brach, *Technology Transfer, Productivity, and Economic Policy* (New York: W. W. Norton, 1982.)

amount consumed next year is represented by the point on the budget line that is on the highest indifference curve.

2. Suppose that a producer-consumer can both produce the good and lend or borrow it. He or she is confronted by a curve, QQ', showing how much he or she can produce (and consume) next year if he or she saves various amounts of the present year's output and invests it to increase next year's output. Corresponding to each point on this curve is a market line which shows the various amounts of the good that he or she can consume in each period, if he or she borrows or lends various amounts. A market line's intercept on the horizontal axis equals the level of attained wealth associated with this market line.

3. To maximize his or her utility, the producer-consumer should choose the point on QQ' that corresponds to the market line with the highest level of attained wealth. Then he or she should move along this market line until he or she reaches the point that is on the highest possible indifference curve. For an equilibrium to occur in the economy as a whole, aggregate saving must equal aggregate investment. The equilibrium level of the interest rate is the level where aggregate saving equals aggregate investment.

4. The present value of an investment project is the change in the decision-maker's wealth resulting from carrying out the project. Clearly, the decision-maker should carry out any investment project with a positive present value. In calculating the present value of an investment, it is important to note that the receipt of a dollar n years hence is the equivalent of receiving $1/(1 + r)^n$ dollars now, since, if one has $1/(1 + r)^n$ dollars now, they can be lent out for n years, and at that time they will be worth $(1 + r)^n$ times $1/(1 + r)^n$, or \$1, because of the accumulated interest. The present-value rule—accept investment projects that have a positive present value—has found widespread application in business and government. Several examples of its uses were presented.

5. To measure the profitability of an investment, firms sometimes calculate the internal rate of return, which is the interest rate that equates the present value of the net cash inflows from the investment to the cost of the investment. Holding constant the riskiness of an investment, firms and individuals generally prefer investments with high rates of return over those with low rates of return.

6. Technology is society's pool of knowledge concerning the industrial and agricultural arts. Technological change is the advance of technology, and such advance often results in a change in the production function for an existing product or in a new product.

7. The rate of technological change is often measured by changes in labor productivity. A more adequate measure is the total productivity index, which relates changes in output to changes in both labor and capital inputs, not changes in labor inputs alone.

8. Schumpeter, Galbraith, and others have argued that, although a perfectly competitive economy will satisfy the conditions for static economic efficiency, it will not result in as high a rate of technological change and productivity increase as an imperfectly competitive economy. Although a certain amount of market imperfection may help to increase the rate of technological change and productivity increase, there is little evidence that giant firms are needed in all or even most industries to insure rapid technological change and rapid utilization of new techniques.

1. Government agencies, as well as business firms, use the present-value rule to determine whether investments should be carried out. In 1977, there was a famous controversy at the highest levels of government over water projects (such as dams). President Jimmy Carter objected to eighteen water projects that had been approved when interest rates were lower. He said, "A more realistic interest rate must be used in calculating the costs and benefits of projects." (a) Suppose that a project costs $1.5 billion in 1991 and $3 billion in 1992 and that it results in the following benefits (in billions of dollars) in subsequent years:

1993	1	1995	1	1997	1
1994	1	1996	1	1998	1

If the interest rate is .10, what is the present value of the costs and benefits? Should the project be carried out? (b) If the interest rate really is .05 rather than .10, should the project be carried out? (c) Why do reductions in the interest rate tend to increase a project's chances of being accepted? (d) What value of the interest rate should government agencies use for this purpose?

2. In 1982, American semiconductor manufacturers explored the possibility of filing complaints with the U.S. government against their Japanese rivals, the charge being that the Japanese were involved in predatory pricing of semiconductor chips. (Predatory pricing is aimed at driving a rival firm out of business.) The Japanese denied this allegation. The Semiconductor Industry Association decided not to file charges (at that time) due in part to the difficulty of proving the allegation.

(a) Given the fact that the average cost of producing a chip tends to fall considerably because of the learning curve (see Figure 17.9), is the marginal cost of a chip equal to the cost in the current period of producing an extra chip, as we stated in Chapter 7? Why or why not? (b) Might a profit-maximizing producer of chips set its price below its current average cost? Why or why not? (c) Based on your answers to (a) and (b), explain why it might have been hard for the Semiconductor Industry Association to prove its allegation.

3. A major oil company evaluated a proposed investment in improvements in visbreakers, a particular type of petroleum-refining equipment. According to the company's analysts, such improvements would require an investment of $15 million and would result in a saving of $2 million per year for the following nine years. Thus, if the investment were made in 1992, the effect on the firm's cash flow would be as follows:

Year	Effect on cash flow (millions of dollars)	Year	Effect on cash flow (millions of dollars)
1992	−15	1997	2
1993	2	1998	2
1994	2	1999	2
1995	2	2000	2
1996	2	2001	2

(a) If the interest rate was 10 percent, what was the present value of this investment? (b) If cost overruns resulted in the investment being $20 million rather than $15 million, what would be the present value of the investment? (c) In fact, the oil company decided not to carry out this investment project. Was this a wise decision? Why or why not?

4. (a) If there is a learning curve in a particular industry, it can be an important barrier to entry. Why? (b) According to A. Michael Spence, "Entry barriers are greatest when the learning curve is neither very steep (rapid learning) nor very flat (slow learning), but rather somewhere in the middle. It is the moderately rapid learning that creates the largest cost differentials among firms—and hence the greatest entry barriers." Explain.

5. A firm developed and introduced a new product used in connection with the drilling of wells. The product results in lower drilling costs because the drilling goes faster. This is an actual (not hypothetical) case. The effect of the investment in this new product on the firm's cash flow is shown below. (These figures, which were provided by the firm, have been updated and rounded to make the computations simpler.)

Year	Effect on cash flow (dollars)	Year	Effect on cash flow (dollars)
1980	−100,000	1990	15,000
1981	−100,000	1991	200,000
1982	−100,000	1992	700,000
1983	−100,000	1993	700,000
1984	−100,000	1994	700,000
1985	−100,000	1995	700,000
1986	−100,000	1996	700,000
1987	15,000	1997	700,000
1988	15,000	1998	700,000
1989	15,000	1999	700,000

(a) Was the firm wise to make this investment if the interest rate was 10 percent? (b) If the effect of this investment on the firm's cash flow is zero in 1987–91, (but the figures for the other years in the above table are correct), would the firm have been wise to make this investment?

6. An investment will have the following effect on a firm's annual cash inflow:

1992	−$5,000
1993	+$2,000
1994	+$2,000
1995	+$1,000
1996	+$1,000

If the interest rate is .10, should this firm carry out this investment?

7. Suppose that Mary Brown's situation is as follows, where *AB* is her budget line:

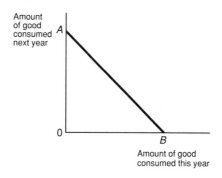

If *OA* = 10 units of the good, and the interest rate equals .08, what does *OB* equal? What is Mary Brown's endowed wealth?

8. John Brown is notified that his aunt has died and that she has willed him $5,000, which will be paid when her estate is settled in two years. If the interest rate is .10, what is the present value of his inheritance?

9. A government bond pays $10 per year, and has no due date. That is, the interest payment of $10 per year goes on forever. If the interest rate is .05, how much would you be willing to pay for the bond?

10. In Question 9, how much would you be willing to pay for the bond described there if the interest rate is .10?

11. Historical data provided by the Bureau of Labor Statistics show that output per hour of labor in blast furnaces using the most up-to-date techniques has sometimes been about twice as large as the industry average. How can such large differences exist at a given point in time? Why don't all firms adopt the most up-to-date techniques at every point in time? Do you think that differences of this sort exist today?

12. Suppose that you were given the job of forecasting the rate of growth of sales of a new product to be introduced by Du Pont. What factors would you expect to determine the rate of growth of sales? How would you go about measuring these factors?

18

DECISION-MAKING AND CHOICE INVOLVING RISK

INTRODUCTION

As we have seen, consumers, firms, and government agencies are constantly involved in decision-making. In previous chapters, we generally have made the simplifying assumption that certainty prevailed in the decision-making process. For example, consumers were assumed to know with certainty what present and future prices would be, and firms were assumed to know what their present and future demand curves and cost functions would be. Although this assumption seldom is entirely correct, it is good enough for many purposes. But in other cases, it is inadequate because risk is an important factor which should not be ignored.

Risk

Risk refers to a situation where the outcome is not certain, but where the probability of each possible outcome is known or can be estimated. Under such circumstances, one can apply the theory of decision-making and choice involving risk, which is the subject of this chapter. To understand the theory, it is essential to begin by defining what we mean by a probability, after which we take up expected monetary value, decision trees, the expected value of perfect information, and Neumann-Morgenstern utility functions. Then we consider moral hazard, diversification, and the capital asset pricing model, which has been used extensively by Wall Street analysts.

DEFINITIONS OF PROBABILITY

Suppose that a situation exists where one of a number of possible outcomes can take place. For example, if a gambler throws a single die, the number that comes up may be 1, 2, 3, 4, 5, or 6. A *probability* is a number that is attached to each outcome. It is the proportion of times that this outcome occurs over the long run if the situation exists over and over again. Thus the probability that a particular die will come up a 1 is the proportion of times this will occur if the die is thrown many, many times and the probability that the same die will come up a 2 is the proportion of times this will occur if the die is thrown many, many times; and so on.

Similarly, the probability that a forty-five-year-old American male will die before his forty-sixth birthday is the proportion of times that this outcome occurs. Detailed statistics are available concerning the proportion of people in a particular age group that die each year. Based on such statistics, one can calculate the proportion of forty-five-year-old American males that die before their forty-sixth birthdays. This proportion equals the probability in question.

In general, if a situation exists a very large number of times M, and if outcome U occurs m times, the probability of U is

$$P(U) = \frac{m}{M}. \qquad [18.1]$$

Thus, if a die is "true" (meaning that each of its sides is equally likely to come up when the die is rolled), the probability of its coming up a 1 is $\frac{1}{6}$, or 0.167, because if it is rolled many, many times, this will occur $\frac{1}{6}$ of the time. Moreover, even if the die is not true, this definition can be applied. Suppose, for instance, that a local mobster injects some loaded dice into a crap game, and that one of the players (who is suspicious) asks to examine one of them. If he rolls the die, what is the probability that it will come up a 1? To answer this question, we must imagine the die in question being rolled again and again. After many thousands of rolls, if the proportion of times that it has come up a 1 is 0.195, then this is the probability of its coming up a 1.

Based on our definition of a probability in Equation 18.1, the following three fundamental propositions must be true: First, the probability of an impossible outcome must be zero. If an outcome is impossible, the number of times the outcome occurs (that is, m) must equal zero. Second, the probability of an outcome that is certain must equal 1. If an outcome is certain, the number of times the outcome occurs (m) must equal the number of times the situation takes place (that is, M). Third, the probability of any outcome must be no less than zero and no greater than 1. Since the number of times any outcome occurs (m) cannot be negative, its probability cannot be less than zero. Since the number of times any outcome occurs cannot exceed the number of times the situation takes place (M), its probability cannot exceed 1.

The foregoing is the so-called *frequency definition of probability*. In some situations, this concept of probability may be difficult to apply because these situations cannot be repeated over and over. When Digital Equipment Corporation launched its new type of computer (the VAX 9000 series) in October 1989, this was an "experiment" that could not be repeated over and over again under essentially the same set of circumstances. Market and other conditions vary from month to month. If Digital's computer had not been introduced that month, the state of consumer expectations, the prices and capabilities of other firms' computers, the advertising campaigns of other firms, and a host of other relevant factors would probably have been different.

In dealing with cases of this sort, economists and statisticians sometimes use a *subjective* or *personal definition of probability*. According to this definition, the probability of an event is the degree of confidence or belief on the part of the decision-maker that the event will occur. For example, if the decision-maker believes that outcome *A* is more likely to occur than outcome *B*, the probability of *A* is higher than the probability of *B*. If the decision-maker believes that it is equally likely that a particular outcome will or will not occur, the probability attached to the occurrence of this outcome equals 0.50. The important factor in this concept of probability is what the decision-maker believes.

EXPECTED MONETARY VALUE

Expected monetary value

Firms and individuals frequently are in situations where a variety of outcomes can occur, each of which results in a certain amount of money being gained or lost. If the probability of each outcome is known, it is possible to compute the *expected monetary value* in this situation, which is the sum of the amount of money gained (or lost) if each outcome occurs times the probability of occurrence of the outcome. For example, suppose that the Wilson Corporation, a producer of automobile tires, is thinking of raising the price of its product by $1 per tire. Based on the firm's estimates, such a price increase will result in an $800,000 increase in profit if its current advertising campaign is successful and a $500,000 decrease in profit if its current advertising campaign is not successful. The firm believes that there is a 0.5 probability that its current advertising campaign will be successful and a 0.5 probability that it will not be successful.

In this situation, the expected monetary value to the firm if it raises its price equals

$$(\$800,000) (0.5) + (-\$500,000) (0.5) = \$150,000.$$

As indicated above, the expected monetary value is the sum of the amount of money gained (or lost) if each outcome occurs times the probability of occurrence of the outcome. In this case, there are two possible outcomes: (1) the firm's current advertising campaign is successful, or (2) it is not successful. If we multiply the amount of money gained (or lost) if the first outcome occurs times its probability of occurrence, the result is ($800,000) (0.5). If we multiply the amount of money gained (or lost) if the second outcome occurs times its probability of occurrence, the result is (−$500,000) (0.5). Summing these two results, the result is $150,000, which is the expected value if the firm raises its price.

The expected monetary value is important because it is the mean amount that a decision-maker would gain (or lose) if he or she were to accept a gamble over and over again. For example, if the Wilson Corporation were to raise its price (under the above circumstances) repeatedly, sometimes the advertising campaign would be successful, and sometimes it would not. Over the long run, it would be successful in half of the cases and not successful in half of them. Thus the mean amount that the firm would make (per price increase) would be $150,000.

What would be the expected monetary value if the Wilson Corporation did *not* increase its price? If it were certain that there would be no effect on its profit if it did not increase its price, the expected monetary value under these circumstances would be zero. (Since it would be certain that the effect would be no effect on profit, the expected monetary value would equal the amount of money gained if this outcome occurs [zero] times its probability of occurrence [one].) That is, the mean amount that the firm would make (per decision not to increase price) would be zero.

Under some circumstances, it is rational to choose the action or gamble that has the largest expected monetary value; under other circumstances, it is not. In the next three sections we shall make the simplifying assumption that the decision-maker wants to maximize expected monetary value. Under such circumstances, the Wilson Corporation will increase its price, because the expected monetary value if it increases its price equals $150,000, whereas the expected monetary value if it does not increase its price equals zero. Later on in this chapter we shall discuss at length the circumstances under which it is rational to maximize expected monetary value—and how to proceed if it is not rational to do so.

DECISION TREES

Any problem of decision-making under conditions of risk has the following characteristics. First, the decision-maker must make a choice, or perhaps a series of choices, among alternative courses of action. Second, this choice leads to some consequence, but the decision-maker cannot tell in advance the exact nature of this consequence because it depends on some unpredictable event, or series of events, as well as on the choice itself. For example, consider the case of the Wilson Corporation, which must decide whether or not to increase its price. In this case, the choice is between two alternatives: increase price or do not do so. And the consequence of increasing it is uncertain since the firm cannot be sure of whether or not its current advertising campaign will be a success.

Decision tree

To represent any such problem, a decision tree is useful. A *decision tree* is a diagram that helps one visualize the relevant choices. It represents a decision problem as a series of choices, each of which is depicted by a fork (sometimes called a juncture or branching point). A *decision fork* is a juncture representing a choice where the decision-maker is in control of the outcome; a *chance fork* is a juncture where "chance" controls the outcome. To differentiate between a decision fork and a chance fork, we shall place a small square at the former juncture but not at the latter.

Figure 18.1 shows the decision tree for the problem facing the Wilson Corporation, which must decide whether or not to increase its price. Beginning at the left-hand side of the diagram, the first choice is up to the firm, which can either follow the branch representing a price increase or the branch representing no such increase. Since this fork is a decision fork, it is represented by a square. If the branch representing no price increase is followed, the consequence is certain: The firm will have no extra profits or losses. Thus zero extra profit is shown at the end of this branch. If the branch representing a price increase is followed, we come to a chance fork since it is uncertain whether the

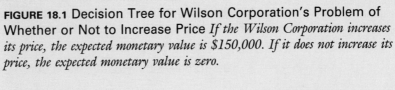

FIGURE 18.1 Decision Tree for Wilson Corporation's Problem of Whether or Not to Increase Price *If the Wilson Corporation increases its price, the expected monetary value is $150,000. If it does not increase its price, the expected monetary value is zero.*

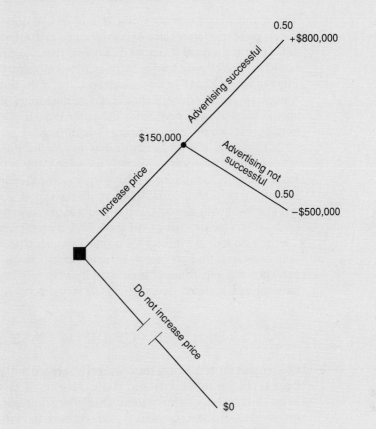

firm's current advertising campaign is successful. The upper branch following this chance fork represents the consequence that it is successful, in which case the extra profit to the firm is $800,000, shown at the end of this branch. The lower branch following this chance fork represents the consequence that it is not successful, in which case the outcome is −$500,000 (a loss), shown at the end of this branch. The probability that "chance" will choose each of these branches is shown above the end of each branch.

Given such a decision tree, it is easy to determine which branch the firm should choose in order to maximize the expected monetary value. The processs by which we solve this problem, known as *backward induction*, requires that we begin at the right-hand side of the decision tree, where the monetary payoff figures are located. The first step is to calculate the expected monetary value of being situated at the chance fork immediately to the left of these payoff figures. In other words, this is the expected monetary value to the firm given that "chance" will choose which subsequent branch will be followed. Since there is a

Backward induction

0.50 probability that the branch culminating in a profit increase of $800,000 will be followed, and a 0.50 probability that the branch culminating in a profit decrease of $500,000 will be followed, the expected monetary value of being situated at this chance fork is

$$0.50(\$800,000) + 0.50(-\$500,000) = \$150,000.$$

This number is written above the chance fork in question to show that this is the expected monetary value of being located at that fork. Moving further to the left along the decision tree, it is evident that the firm has a choice of two branches, one of which leads to an expected monetary value of $150,000, the other of which leads to a zero monetary value. If the firm wants to maximize the expected monetary value, it should choose the former branch. In other words, it should increase its price. Since the latter branch (Do not increase price) is nonoptimal, we place two vertical lines through it.

At this point, it is worth noting that this graphic procedure for analyzing the firm's problem amounts to precisely the same thing as the calculations we made in the previous section. Recall that we compared the expected monetary value if the price was increased ($150,000) with the expected monetary value if it was not increased ($0) and followed the course of action that resulted in the larger of the two. Our procedure in Figure 18.1 is exactly the same. Note, too, that the decision tree in Figure 18.1 is much simpler than those required to represent many practical problems. In many cases, decision trees have dozens of branches. But regardless of how complex they may be, decision trees are constructed and analyzed essentially in the way described in this section.

DRILLING FOR OIL: A CASE STUDY

One important area where the concepts presented in the previous sections have been applied is oil exploration. Huge amounts of money have been, and are being, invested in oil exploration. Due in large measure to the efforts of economists like C. Jackson Grayson,[1] many oil firms have used these analytical tools as an aid to decision-making. Of course, this does not mean that these tools are the only ones that are used, or that they are used by all firms. But they do seem to have played a role in this area, which is so important to both the oil firms and the nation as a whole.

To illustrate how these concepts can be applied to oil exploration, consider the case of the Beard Oil Company.[2] Suppose that this firm must decide whether or not to drill a well in a particular location. The firm has information concerning the cost of drilling and the price of oil, as well as geologists' reports concerning the likelihood of striking oil. Based on the geologists' reports, the firm believes that, if the well is drilled, there is a 0.60 probability that no oil will be found, a 0.10 probability that 50,000 barrels will be found, a 0.15 probability that 100,000 barrels will be found, a 0.10 probability that 500,000 bar-

1. C. Jackson Grayson, *Decisions Under Uncertainty: Drilling Decisions by Oil and Gas Operators* (Boston: Harvard University Press, 1960). This was an early (and classic) study.

2. The Beard Oil Company is an actual firm included in Grayson's study (ibid.). The situation described below is taken from Grayson.

rels will be found, and a 0.05 probability that 1 million barrels will be found.

Based on these probabilities alone, the firm cannot decide whether or not to drill the well. In addition, information is needed concerning the profit (or loss) that will accrue to the firm if each of these outcomes occurs. Suppose that the firm believes that, if it drills the well, it will incur a $50,000 loss if it finds no oil, a $20,000 loss if it finds 50,000 barrels of oil, a $30,000 profit if it finds 100,000 barrels, a $430,000 profit if it finds 500,000 barrels, and a $930,000 profit if it finds 1 million barrels. Based on this information, should the firm drill the well?

If the firm wants to maximize the expected monetary value, it can answer this question by constructing the decision tree shown in Figure 18.2. Beginning at the left-hand side of the diagram, the first choice is up to the firm, which can

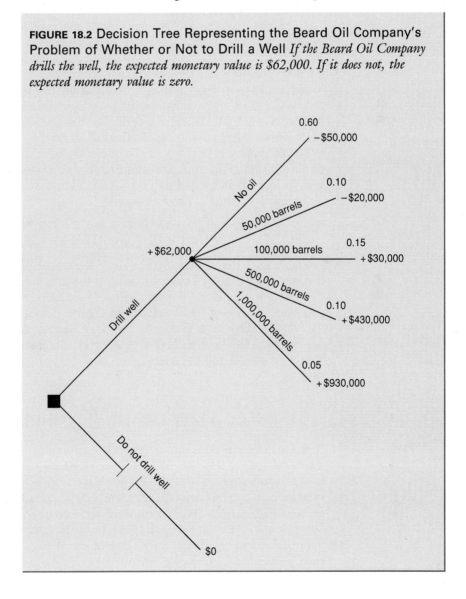

FIGURE 18.2 Decision Tree Representing the Beard Oil Company's Problem of Whether or Not to Drill a Well *If the Beard Oil Company drills the well, the expected monetary value is $62,000. If it does not, the expected monetary value is zero.*

follow the branch representing the drilling of the well or the branch representing not drilling. If the branch representing not drilling is followed, the expected monetary value is zero, which is shown at the end of this branch. If the branch representing the drilling of the well is followed, we come to a chance fork since it is uncertain whether the firm will strike oil and if so, how much oil it will find. The highest branch following this chance fork represents the consequence that no oil is found, in which case the firm loses $50,000, shown at the end of this branch. The second highest branch following this chance fork represents the consequence that 50,000 barrels are found, in which case the firm loses $20,000, shown at the end of this branch. Similarly, the middle, second lowest, and lowest branches following this chance fork represent respectively the consequences that 100,000, 500,000, and 1 million barrels are found; the number at the end of each of these branches is the corresponding profit to the firm.

Once this decision tree is constructed, the next step is to calculate the expected monetary value to the firm if it is situated at the chance fork immediately to the left of the profit (or loss) figures. If the firm is at this fork, there is a 0.60 probability that the branch culminating in a $50,000 loss will be followed, a 0.10 probability that the branch culminating in a $20,000 loss will be followed, a 0.15 probability that the branch culminating in a $30,000 profit will be followed, a 0.10 probability that the branch culminating in a $430,000 profit will be followed, and a 0.05 probability that the branch culminating in a $930,000 profit will be followed. To obtain the expected monetary value if the firm is situated at this fork, we must multiply each possible value of profit (or loss) by its probability, and sum the results. Thus the expected monetary value if the firm is situated at this fork equals

$$0.60(-\$50,000) + 0.10(-\$20,000) + 0.15(+\$30,000) +$$
$$0.10(+\$430,000) + 0.05(+\$930,000) = +\$62,000.$$

In Figure 18.2, this result is written above the chance fork in question to show that this is the expected monetary value if the firm is located at that fork.

Moving further along the decision tree to the left, the firm has a choice of two branches, one of which leads to an expected monetary value of $62,000, the other of which leads to a zero expected monetary value. If the firm wants to maximize the expected monetary value, it should choose the former branch. That is, it should drill the well.

THE EXPECTED VALUE OF PERFECT INFORMATION

In many cases, the decision-maker can obtain information that will dispel (at least some of) the relevant risk. If the decision-maker can get perfect information, how much is it worth? To answer this question, we define the expected value of perfect information as the increase in expected monetary value if the decision-maker could obtain completely accurate information concerning the outcome of the relevant situation (but if he or she does not yet know what this information will be). Thus, in the case of the Wilson Corporation (the firm cited above that must decide whether or not to increase its tire price), this expected value is the increase in expected monetary value if the firm could obtain perfectly accurate information indicating whether or not its current advertising campaign will be successful.

To see how one can compute the expected value of perfect information, let's return to this case. To determine the expected value of perfect information, we carry out two steps. First, we evaluate the expected monetary value to the Wilson Corporation if it can obtain access to perfectly accurate information of this sort. Then we calculate the extent to which this expected monetary value exceeds the expected monetary value based on the information actually available to the firm.

Step 1: If the Wilson Corporation obtains perfect information, it will be able to make the correct decision, regardless of whether or not its current advertising campaign is successful. If it is successful, the firm will be aware of this fact, and will increase the price. If it is not successful, the firm will be aware of this fact also, and will not increase the price. Thus, given that the firm has access to perfect information, the expected monetary value is

$$0.5(\$800,000) + 0.5(0) = \$400,000.$$

To see why this is the expected monetary value if the Wilson Corporation has access to perfect information, it is important to recognize that although it is assumed that the firm has access to perfect information, *it does not yet know what this information will be.* There is a .5 probability that this information will show that its advertising campaign is successful, in which case the Wilson Corporation will increase its price and the gain will be $800,000. There is also a .5 probability that the information will show that it is not successful, in which case the Wilson Corporation will not increase its price and the gain will be zero. Thus, as shown above, the expected monetary value if the firm has access to perfect information (that is not yet revealed to the firm) is $400,000.

Step 2: The expected monetary value if the firm bases its decision on exist-

*Expected value of
perfect information*

ing information is $150,000 (as we saw on pp. 523–24), not $400,000. The difference between these two figures—$400,000 minus $150,000 or $250,000—is the expected value of perfect information. It is a measure of the value of perfect information. *It shows the amount by which the expected monetary value increases as a consequence of the firm's having access to perfect information.* Put differently, *it is the maximum amount that the firm should pay to obtain perfect information.*

In many situations, it is very important that the decision-maker knows how much perfect information would be worth. Whether the decision-maker is a business executive, government official, or consumer, he or she is continually being offered information by testing services, research organizations, news bureaus, and a variety of other organizations. Unless the decision-maker knows how much particular types of information are worth, he or she will not be able to tell whether their worth exceeds their cost. Thus it will be difficult to decide rationally whether various types of information should or should not be bought. The sort of analysis presented in this section is useful to guide such decisions.[3]

3. In this section, we have dealt only with the relatively simple case where information is perfect. If the only available information is less than perfect (that is, if it contains errors), can we determine whether its expected worth exceeds its cost? Under many circumstances, the answer is yes. To see how, consult the sections on preposterior analysis in any modern statistics text.

IS IT RATIONAL TO MAXIMIZE THE EXPECTED MONETARY VALUE?

In discussing both the Wilson Corporation's pricing decision and the Beard Oil Company's drilling decision, we have assumed that the decision-maker wants to maximize the expected monetary value. In this and the following sections we will discuss how a more realistic criterion can be formulated. To understand why a decision-maker may not want to maximize the expected monetary value, consider a situation where you are given a choice between (1) receiving $1,000,000 for certain and (2) a gamble in which a fair coin is tossed, and you will receive $2,100,000 if it comes up heads or you will lose $50,000 if it comes up tails. The expected monetary value for the gamble is

$$0.50(\$2,100,000) + 0.50(-\$50,000) = \$1,025,000,$$

so you should choose the gamble over the certainty of $1,000,000 if you want to maximize the expected monetary value. However, it seems likely that many persons would prefer the certainty of $1,000,000 since the gamble entails a 50 percent chance that you will lose $50,000, a very substantial sum. Moreover, many people may feel that they can do almost as much with $1,000,000 as with $2,100,000, and therefore the extra amount is not worth the risk of losing $50,000.

Clearly, whether or not you will want to maximize the expected monetary value in this situation depends on your attitude toward risk. If you are a widow of modest means, you will probably be overwhelmed at the thought of taking a 50 percent chance of losing $50,000. On the other hand, if you are the president of a big corporation, the prospect of a $50,000 loss may not be the least bit unsettling, and you may prefer the gamble to the certainty of a mere $1,000,000 profit. And if you are the sort of person who enjoys danger and risk, you may prefer the gamble even though a $50,000 loss may wipe you out completely.

Fortunately, there is no need to assume that the decision-maker wants to maximize the expected monetary value. Instead, we can construct a so-called *Utility function* *Neumann-Morgenstern utility function*[4] for the decision-maker which is based on his or her attitudes toward risk. From this, we can then go on to find the alternative that is best for the decision-maker, given his or her attitudes toward risk. The Neumann-Morgenstern utility function was named after John von Neumann and Oskar Morgenstern,[5] who developed this kind of utility function in their famous work on the theory of games (Chapter 11). A utility function of this sort should not be confused with the utility functions discussed in Chapter 3. As we shall see, it is quite a different sort of concept.

4. John von Neumann and Oskar Morgenstern, *Theory of Games and Economic Behavior* (Princeton, N.J.: Princeton University Press, 1944). For alternative approaches, see M. Machina, "Dynamic Consistency and Non-Expected Utility Models of Choice Under Uncertainty," *Journal of Economic Literature,* December 1989.

5. Von Neumann was a famous mathematician at the Institute for Advanced Study; Morgenstern was an economist at Princeton University.

CONSTRUCTING A NEUMANN-MORGENSTERN UTILITY FUNCTION

According to the theory put forth by von Neumann and Morgenstern, *a rational decision-maker will maximize expected utility.* In other words, the decision-maker should choose the course of action with the highest expected utility. But what (in this context) is a *utility?* It is a number that is attached to a possible outcome of the decision. Each outcome has a utility. The decision-maker's Neumann-Morgenstern utility function shows the utility that he or she attaches to each possible outcome. The utility function, as we shall see, shows the decision-maker's preferences with respect to risk. What is *expected utility?* It is the sum of the utility if each outcome occurs times the probability of occurrence of the outcome. For example, if a situation has two possible outcomes, S and T, if the utility of outcome S is 5 and the utility of outcome T is 10, and if the probability of each outcome is 0.5, the expected utility equals

Expected utility

$$0.5(5) + 0.5(10) = 7.5.$$

To take a more complicated and realistic case, what is the expected utility if the Beard Oil Company drills the well under the circumstances described on pp. 526–27? It equals

$$0.60\ U(-50) + 0.10\ U(-20) + 0.15\ U(30) + 0.10\ U(430) + 0.05\ U(930),$$

where $U(-50)$ is the utility that the decision-maker attaches to a monetary loss of $50,000, $U(-20)$ is the utility attached to a loss of $20,000, $U(30)$ is the utility attached to a gain of $30,000, and so on. Since there is a 0.60 probability of a $50,000 loss, a 0.10 probability of a $20,000 loss, a 0.15 probability of a $30,000 gain, a 0.10 probability of a $430,000 gain, and a 0.05 probability of a $930,000 gain, this is the expected utility. What is the expected utility if the firm does not drill the well? It equals $U(0)$, since under these circumstances it is certain that the gain will be zero.

To determine the utility that the decision-maker attaches to each possible outcome, he or she must respond to a series of questions which indicate his or her preferences with regard to risk. The required utilities can be found in two steps. The first step is simple: *We set the utility attached to two monetary values arbitrarily.* The utility of the better consequence is set higher than the utility of the worse one. In the case of the decision-maker in the oil-drilling problem, we might set $U(-50)$ equal to zero and $U(930)$ equal to 50. It turns out that the ultimate results of the analysis do not depend on which two numbers we choose, as long as the utility of the better consequence is set higher than the utility of the worse one. Thus we could set $U(-50)$ equal to 1 and $U(930)$ equal to 10. It would make no difference to the ultimate outcome of the analysis.[6]

6. It is important to note that the utility function that we construct is not unique. Since we set two utilities arbitrarily, the results will vary, depending on the values of the utilities that are chosen. If $X_1, X_2, \ldots, X_n$ are the utilities attached to n possible monetary values, $(\alpha + \beta X_1)$, $(\alpha + \beta X_2)$, $\ldots$, $(\alpha + \beta X_n)$ can also be utilities attached to them (where α and β are constants, and $\beta > 0$).

The second step is somewhat more complicated: *In this step we present the decision-maker with a choice between the certainty of one of the other monetary values and a gamble where the possible outcomes are the two monetary values whose utilities we set arbitrarily.* For example, in the oil-drilling problem, suppose that we want to find $U(-20)$. To do so, we ask the decision-maker whether he or she would prefer the certainty of a $20,000 loss to a gamble where there is a probability of P that the gain is $930,000 and a probability of $(1 - P)$ that the loss is $50,000. We then try various values of P until we find the one where the decision-maker is indifferent between the certainty of a $20,000 loss and this gamble. Suppose that this value of P is 0.10.

If the decision-maker is indifferent between the certain loss of $20,000 and this gamble, it must be that the expected utility of the certain loss of $20,000 equals the expected utility of the gamble. (Why? Because the decision-maker maximizes expected utility.) Thus

$$U(-20) = 0.10\ U(930) + 0.90\ U(-50).$$

And since we set $U(930)$ equal to 50 and $U(-50)$ equal to zero, it follows that

$$U(-20) = 0.10(50) + 0.90(0) = 5.$$

In other words, the utility attached to a loss of $20,000 is 5.

Similarly, we can find $U(30)$, $U(430)$, and $U(0)$, the other utilities required to calculate the expected utility if the oil company drills the well and the expected utility if it does not drill it. For example, to obtain $U(30)$, we ask the decision-maker whether he or she would prefer the certainty of a $30,000 gain to a gamble where there is a probability of P that the gain is $930,000 and a probability of $(1 - P)$ that the loss is $50,000. Then we try various values of P until we find the one where the decision-maker is indifferent between the certainty of a $30,000 gain and this gamble. Suppose that this value of P is 0.20. Then the expected utility of a certain gain of $30,000 must equal the expected utility of this gamble, which means that

$$U(30) = 0.20\ U(930) + 0.80\ U(-50).$$

And since $U(930)$ equals 50 and $U(-50)$ equals zero, it follows that $U(30)$ equals 10.

The decision-maker's utility function is the relationship between his or her utility and the amount of his or her monetary gain (or loss). Based on our evaluation of $U(-50)$, $U(-20)$, $U(30)$, and $U(930)$ in previous paragraphs, we can identify four points on the decision-maker's utility function, as shown in Figure 18.3. Through the repeated use of the procedure described above, we can obtain as many such points as we like—or as the decision-maker's patience permits.

Should the Decision-Maker Accept or Reject Particular Gambles?

Once a decision-maker's Neumann-Morgenstern utility function has been constructed, it can be used to indicate whether he or she should accept or reject

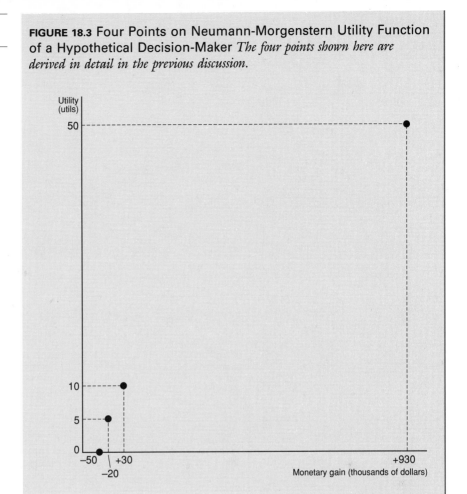

FIGURE 18.3 Four Points on Neumann-Morgenstern Utility Function of a Hypothetical Decision-Maker *The four points shown here are derived in detail in the previous discussion.*

particular gambles. To illustrate, consider the actual case of William Beard, one of the owners of the Beard Oil Company. Using the above procedures, C. Jackson Grayson constructed Mr. Beard's utility function, the result being shown in Figure 18.4.[7] Of course, Mr. Beard's actual utility function differs from that shown in Figure 18.3, since the latter was based on hypothetical data, not on Mr. Beard's responses.[8]

Suppose that Mr. Beard must decide whether or not to drill the well described on p. 526. According to the theory put forth by von Neumann and Morgenstern, he should maximize expected utility. Thus he should drill the well if his expected utility if the well is drilled exceeds his expected utility if it is not drilled. As pointed out in the previous section, his expected utility if the

---

7. C. Jackson Grayson, *Decisions Under Uncertainty.* This utility function was read from Grayson's graph on p. 304 and is only approximate, but it is sufficiently accurate for present purposes.

8. Note that, unlike the hypothetical case in the previous section, Grayson did not set $U(930)$ equal to 50 and $U(-50)$ equal to zero. See Figure 18.4.

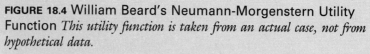

FIGURE 18.4 William Beard's Neumann-Morgenstern Utility Function *This utility function is taken from an actual case, not from hypothetical data.*

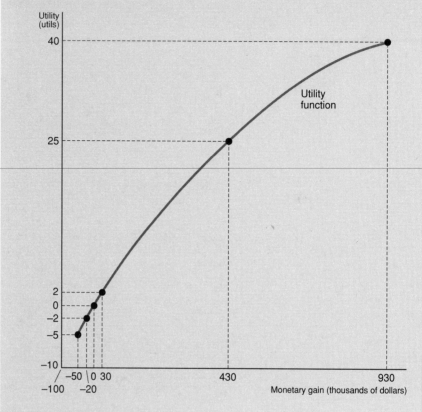

well is drilled equals

$$0.60 \, U(-50) + 0.10 \, U(-20) + 0.15 \, U(30) + 0.10 \, U(430) + 0.05 \, U(930).$$

Now that Mr. Beard's utility function has been constructed, this expression can be evaluated. For Mr. Beard, $U(-50)$ equals -5, $U(-20)$ equals -2, $U(30)$ equals 2, $U(430)$ equals 25, and $U(930)$ equals 40, according to Figure 18.4. Thus, if the well is drilled, his expected utility is

$$0.60(-5) + 0.10(-2) + 0.15(2) + 0.10(25) + 0.05(40) = -0.2.$$

As pointed out in the previous section, if the well is not drilled, Mr. Beard's expected utility equals $U(0)$, which is zero, according to Figure 18.4. Thus he should not drill the well. Why? Because if he does not drill it, his expected utility is zero, whereas if he drills it, his expected utility is -0.2. Since he should maximize expected utility, he should choose the action with the higher expected utility, which is not to drill. Note that this is not the decision that maximizes the expected monetary value. As we saw on p. 528, if Mr. Beard wants to maximize the expected monetary value, he should drill the well. But because of Mr.

Beard's preferences with respect to risk, as shown by his utility function, this is not the best decision for him.

Besides being useful in indicating the sorts of decisions that individuals and firms should make, utility functions can also be useful in predicting the decisions that they actually will make. To the extent that they conform to the theory put forth by von Neumann and Morgenstern, decision-makers will choose the course of action that maximizes expected utility. Thus, if we have a decision-maker's utility function, we can predict which course of action he or she will choose by comparing the expected utility of each one. For example, suppose that William Beard is confronted with a choice between (1) the certainty of a $430,000 gain and (2) a gamble where there is a 0.50 probability that he will gain $930,000 and a 0.50 probability that he will gain $30,000. Which will he choose?

Using Mr. Beard's utility function in Figure 18.4, we can readily determine the utility he attaches to $30,000, $430,000, and $930,000. These utilities are 2, 25, and 40, respectively. Thus the expected utility from the certainty of a $430,000 gain equals 25. And the expected utility from the gamble equals

$$0.50(2) + 0.50(40) = 21.$$

Since the expected utility from the certain gain of $430,000 exceeds that from the gamble, we would predict that Mr. Beard will choose the certainty of a $430,000 gain over the gamble.[9]

Attitudes Toward Risk

Not all utility functions look like the one in Figure 18.4. Although one can expect that utility increases with monetary gain, the shape of the utility function can vary greatly, depending on the preferences of the decision-maker. Figure 18.5 shows three general types of utility functions. The one in panel A is like that in Figure 18.4 in the sense that utility increases with monetary value, but *at a decreasing rate*. In other words, an increase in monetary gain of $1 is associated with *smaller and smaller* increases in utility as the monetary gain increases in size. People with utility functions of this sort are *risk averters*. That is, when confronted with gambles with equal expected monetary values, they prefer a gamble with a more certain outcome to one with a less certain outcome.[10]

Risk averter

9. Of course, decision-makers sometimes are inconsistent and, like all of us, they make mistakes. Thus it would be foolish to expect that predictions of this sort would always be correct, even if the theory were basically correct. For an early (and classic) study that attempted to determine the accuracy of such predictions, see F. Mosteller and P. Nogee, "An Experimental Measurement of Utility," *Journal of Political Economy* 59 (October 1951).

10. Consider a gamble where there is a probability of P that the gain is M_1 and a probability of $(1 - P)$ that the loss is M_2. A person is a risk averter if the utility of the gamble's expected monetary value, $U[(P)M_1 + (1 - P)M_2]$, is *greater than* the expected utility of the gamble, $PU(M_1) + (1 - P)U(M_2)$.

Suppose that you are offered the opportunity to play a game in which a coin is tossed until it comes up heads. The game then ends and you receive a sum equal to $(\$2)^n$, where n is the number of times the coin was tossed. The expected value of this sum is $\frac{1}{2}(\$2) + \frac{1}{4}(\$4) + \frac{1}{8}(\$8) + \ldots = 1 + 1 + 1 + \ldots$, which is an infinitely large amount. (To see why this is the expected value of this sum, note that the probability of heads on the first toss is $\frac{1}{2}$, and of tails on the first and heads on the second toss is $\frac{1}{4}$. In general, the probability of $(n - 1)$ tails followed by a heads on the nth toss equals $(\frac{1}{2})^n$.) You are unlikely to be willing to pay an infinite amount for the opportunity to play this game. Thus, with respect to this gamble, you are likely to be a risk averter. This is the so-called *St. Petersburg paradox*.

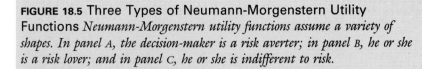

FIGURE 18.5 Three Types of Neumann-Morgenstern Utility
Functions *Neumann-Morgenstern utility functions assume a variety of
shapes. In panel A, the decision-maker is a risk averter; in panel B, he or she
is a risk lover; and in panel C, he or she is indifferent to risk.*

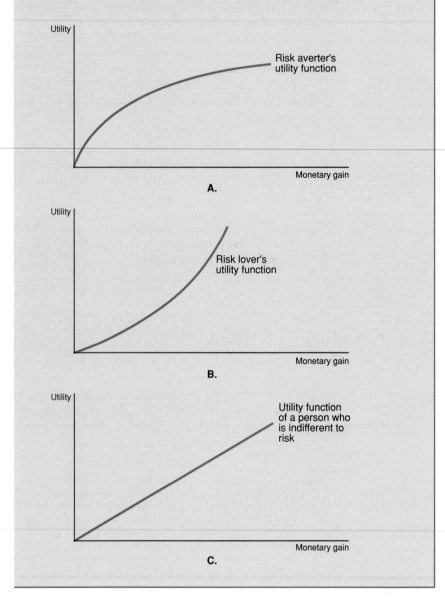

The utility function in panel B of Figure 18.5 is one where utility increases
with monetary value, but *at an increasing rate*. In other words, an increase in
monetary gain of $1 is associated with *larger and larger* increases in utility as the

Risk lover   monetary gain increases in size. People with utility functions of this sort are *risk*
lovers. That is, when confronted with gambles with equal expected monetary

EXAMPLE 18.1

WHO BUYS STATE LOTTERY TICKETS?

Many states, like Connecticut, Massachusetts, Michigan, New Jersey, and Pennsylvania, run lotteries that provide them with revenues. In 1986, the average adult living in a state with lotteries spent about $110 on lottery tickets. According to Charles Clotfelter and Philip Cook, betting is heaviest among males, Hispanics, blacks, the middle-aged, Catholics, laborers, and those with less than a college degree. In an earlier year, the total sales of lottery tickets and the total prize money in six states were as follows (in millions of dollars):

	Ticket sales	Prize money		Ticket sales	Prize money
Connecticut	34.7	15.6	Michigan	135.7	61.1
Maryland	40.1	16.0	New Jersey	112.7	51.8
Massachusetts	70.6	30.5	Pennsylvania	124.4	54.4

(a) Is the expected monetary value of a lottery ticket positive or negative in these states? (b) On the average, about how much do these state lotteries pay out per dollar bet? (c) Will a risk averter buy a lottery ticket in any of these states? (d) Will one of these lottery tickets be bought by a person who is indifferent to risk?

SOLUTION

(a) Negative, because the prize money is much less in each state than the ticket sales. (b) The amount paid out in prizes per dollar bet ranged from 40 cents in Maryland to 46 cents in New Jersey. Thus the expected amount that a buyer of a $1 ticket will win is only 40 to 46 cents, which is considerably less than the price of the ticket. (c) The expected monetary value of *not* buying a lottery ticket is zero, and there is no risk if he or she does not buy the ticket. A risk averter would prefer not buying the ticket to buying it *even if the ticket's expected monetary value were zero* (because the risk would be less if it were not bought than if it was bought, and the expected monetary value would be the same). Consequently, he or she would certainly not buy it if its expected monetary value is *negative,* as it is here. (d) People who are indifferent to risk maximize expected monetary value, regardless of risk. Since the expected monetary value of not buying the ticket (zero) is higher than that of buying the ticket (negative), such people will not buy the ticket.*

*For further discussion, see R. Brinner and C. Clotfelter, "An Economic Appraisal of State Lotteries," *National Tax Journal,* 1975; and C. Clotfelter and P. Cook, "The Demand for Lottery Products," National Bureau of Economic Research, 1989.

values, they prefer a gamble with a less certain outcome to one with a more certain outcome.[11]

Finally, the utility function in panel C is one where utility increases with monetary value and *at a constant rate*. In other words, an increase of $1 in monetary gain is associated with a *constant* increase in utility as the monetary gain grows larger and larger. Stated differently, utility in this case is a linear function of monetary gain:

$$U = a + bM \qquad [18.2]$$

where U is utility, M is monetary gain, and a and b are constants (of course, $b > 0$). People with utility functions of this sort are *indifferent to risk*.[12] That is, they maximize expected monetary value, regardless of risk. It is easy to show that this is true. If Equation 18.2 holds,

$$E(U) = a + bE(M) \qquad [18.3]$$

where $E(U)$ is expected utility and $E(M)$ is expected monetary value.[13] Thus, since expected utility is directly related to expected monetary value, it can only be a maximum when expected monetary value is a maximum.

THE OPTIMAL AMOUNT OF INSURANCE

One important way in which firms and individuals try to cope with risk is through a purchase of insurance. The analytical tools described in previous sections can help to solve the problem of how much insurance a person (or firm) should buy. To see how, let's consider a specific case. Suppose that Richard Abbot, a jeweler, owns a diamond worth $100,000, and that he wants to determine how much insurance he should purchase against the theft of the diamond. He can buy theft insurance at a cost of 20 percent of the face value of the insurance. That is, if he buys $100,000 worth of insurance, he must pay $20,000 for the insurance; and if he buys $50,000 worth of insurance, he must pay $10,000. If we measure Mr. Abbot's Neumann-Morgenstern utility function, we can determine how much insurance he should buy.

To see how the optimal amount of insurance can be determined, we must

---

11. Consider a gamble where there is a probability of P that the gain is M_1 and a probability of $(1 - P)$ that the loss is M_2. A person is a risk lover if the utility of the gamble's expected monetary value, $U[(P)M_1 + (1 - P)M_2]$, is *less than* the expected utility of the gamble, $PU(M_1) + (1 - P) U(M_2)$.

12. It is important to recognize that a person can be a risk averter under some circumstances, a risk lover under other circumstances, and indifferent to risk under still other circumstances. The utility functions in Figure 18.5 are "pure" cases where the person is always only one of these types, at least in the range covered by the graphs. For a "hybrid" case, see Example 18.2.

13. To see that Equation 18.3 is correct, suppose that M can assume two possible values, M_1 and M_2, and that the probability that M_1 occurs is P and the probability that M_2 occurs is $(1 - P)$. Then, if $U = a + bM$,

$$\begin{aligned} E(U) &= P(a + bM_1) + (1 - P)(a + bM_2) \\ &= a + b[(P)M_1 + (1 - P)M_2] \\ &= a + bE(M), \end{aligned}$$

since $E(M)$ equals $(P)M_1 + (1 - P)M_2$.

recognize that Mr. Abbot is in a situation where there are two possible outcomes: (1) the diamond is stolen and (2) it is not stolen. The more insurance he buys, the greater the value of his assets if the diamond is stolen, but the less the value of his assets if it is not stolen. For example, if he buys $50,000 worth of insurance, he will have $40,000 (that is, $50,000 less the insurance cost of $10,000) if it is stolen, and $90,000 (the value of the diamond, which is $100,000, less the insurance cost of $10,000) if it is not stolen. But if he buys $100,000 worth of insurance, he will have $80,000 (that is, $100,000 less the insurance cost of $20,000) if it is stolen, and $80,000 (the value of the diamond, $100,000, less the insurance cost of $20,000) if it is not stolen.

Table 18.1 shows, for various possible amounts of insurance that he can buy, the value of his assets if the diamond is stolen, and their value if it is not stolen. Since the value of his assets if it is stolen is inversely related to their value if it is not stolen, we can plot the former value of his assets against the latter value in Figure 18.6. As you can see, the relationship between these two values is a straight line, AB. To obtain the equation for this line, note that

$$Y_n = \$100{,}000 - 0.2I \qquad [18.4]$$

where Y_n is the value of his assets if the diamond is not stolen, and I is the amount of insurance he buys. The equation says that the value of his assets if the diamond is not stolen is $100,000 (the value of the diamond) less the cost of the insurance (which is $.2I$). Also, note that

$$Y_T = I - 0.2I = 0.8I, \qquad [18.5]$$

where Y_T is the value of his assets if the diamond is stolen. Under these circumstances, he receives the insurance (I) less the cost of the insurance ($0.2I$).

TABLE 18.1 Outcomes for Mr. Abbot if the Diamond Is or Is Not Stolen, Given That He Purchases Various Amounts of Insurance

Amount of insurance (I) (dollars)	Cost of insurance ($0.2I$) (dollars)	Value of Mr. Abbot's assets if:	
		Diamond is stolen (Y_T) (dollars)	Diamond is not stolen (Y_n) (dollars)
0	0	0	100,000
10,000	2,000	8,000	98,000
20,000	4,000	16,000	96,000
30,000	6,000	24,000	94,000
40,000	8,000	32,000	92,000
50,000	10,000	40,000	90,000
60,000	12,000	48,000	88,000
70,000	14,000	56,000	86,000
80,000	16,000	64,000	84,000
90,000	18,000	72,000	82,000
100,000	20,000	80,000	80,000

FIGURE 18.6 Relationship between Value of Mr. Abbot's Assets if
the Diamond Is Stolen and Their Value if It Is Not Stolen *The value
of Mr. Abbot's assets if the diamond is stolen is inversely related to their value
if it is not stolen.*

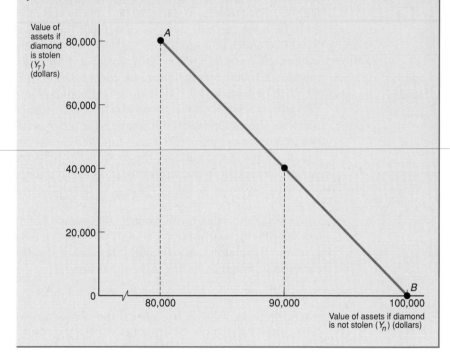

From Equation 18.4, it follows that

$$I = \frac{1}{0.2}(\$100,000 - Y_n) = \$500,000 - 5Y_n. \qquad [18.6]$$

Substituting the right-hand side of Equation 18.6 for I in Equation 18.5, we
have

$$Y_T = 0.8(\$500,000 - 5Y_n) = \$400,000 - 4Y_n, \qquad [18.7]$$

which is the equation for the line in Figure 18.6.[14]

To determine the amount of insurance that Mr. Abbot should buy, it is
obvious that some account should be taken of his preference regarding risk. If P
is the probability that the diamond will be stolen, his expected utility equals

$$P \cdot U(Y_T) + (1 - P) \cdot U(Y_n) \qquad [18.8]$$

where $U(Y_T)$ is the utility he attaches to having assets equal in value to Y_T, and
$U(Y_n)$ is the utility he attaches to having assets equal in value to Y_n. Mr. Abbot

---

14. Since the amount of insurance, I, must be between zero and $100,000, the line in Figure 18.6
only exists for the interval where $\$80,000 \leq Y_n \leq \$100,000$.

EXAMPLE 18.2

THE UTILITY FUNCTION FOR INCOME

In a famous article, Milton Friedman and L. J. Savage hypothesized that a person's Neumann-Morgenstern utility function for income typically has the shape indicated below.

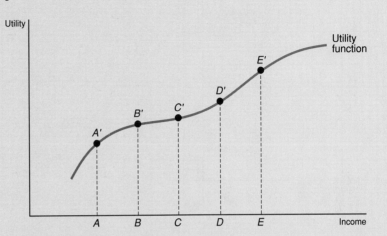

(a) If John Jones has this utility function, will he prefer the certainty of an income of B to a gamble in which there is a 0.5 probability that his income is A and a 0.5 probability that his income is C? (Note that B is the average of A and C.) (b) Will he prefer the certainty of an income of D to a gamble where there is a 0.5 probability that his income is C and a 0.5 probability that his income is E? (Note that D is the average of C and E.)

SOLUTION

(a) Yes. The expected utility attached to the certainty of an income of B equals BB' (the distance from B to B'). To determine the expected utility from the gamble, draw a straight line from A' to C'. The vertical distance from B to this line equals the expected utility of the gamble because it equals 0.5 times AA' plus 0.5 times CC'. (AA' is the utility of an income of A, and CC' is the utility of an income of C.) Since this vertical distance is less than BB', the expected utility of the gamble is less than the expected utility of the certainty of an income of B. (b) No. The expected utility attached to the certainty of an income of D equals DD'. To determine the expected utility from the gamble, draw a straight line from C' to E'. The vertical distance from D to this line equals the expected utility of the gamble because it equals 0.5 times CC' plus 0.5 times EE'. Since this vertical distance is more than DD' the expected utility of the gamble is more than the expected utility of the certainty of an income of D.*

*For further discussion, see Milton Friedman and L. J. Savage, "The Utility Analysis of Choices Involving Risk," *Journal of Political Economy* 56 (August 1948).

FIGURE 18.7 Combinations of Y_T and Y_n with Same Expected Utility for Mr. Abbot *Each curve shows combinations of* Y_T *and* Y_n *that result in the same expected utility for Mr. Abbot.*

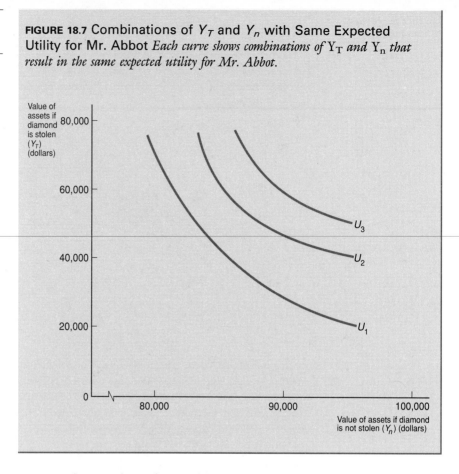

wants to choose values of Y_T and Y_n so that his expected utility is as large as possible.

Each curve in Figure 18.7 shows combinations of Y_T and Y_n that result in the same expected utility for Mr. Abbot. To derive each curve, we set his expected utility equal to some constant, a. Thus

$$P \cdot U(Y_T) + (1 - P) \cdot U(Y_n) = a. \qquad [18.9]$$

Since increases in either Y_T or Y_n result in increases in his expected utility,[15] it follows that if his expected utility is held constant (at a), increases in Y_n must be accompanied by decreases in Y_T. (Why? Because if both Y_T and Y_n increased, or if one increased and the other remained constant, his expected utility would increase, not remain constant.) Thus each of the curves in Figure 18.7 is downward sloping to the right. Higher curves like U_3 represent higher levels of expected utility than lower ones like U_1. And since Mr. Abbot would like to

---

15. Mr. Abbot's utility would be expected to increase with increases in the value of his assets. Thus $U(Y_T)$ increases with increases in Y_T, and $U(Y_n)$ increases with increases in Y_n. And since both P and $(1 - P)$ are positive, increases in either $U(Y_T)$ or $U(Y_n)$ result in increases in expected utility.

FIGURE 18.8 Determination of Optimal Expenditure on Insurance
Mr. Abbot should choose point C, which means that Y_T = $56,000 *and* Y_n = $86,000.

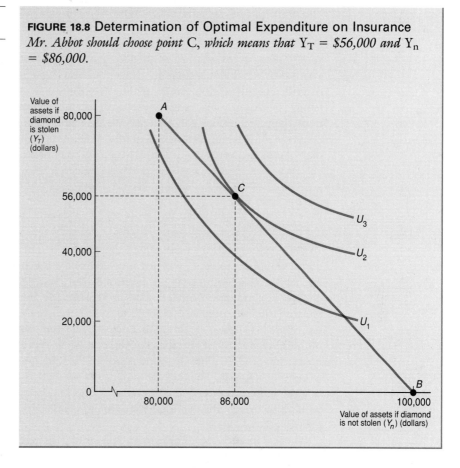

maximize expected utility, points on higher curves like U_3 are preferred over points on lower curves like U_1.

To solve Mr. Abbot's problem, we must add line *AB* (in Figure 18.6) to Figure 18.7, the result being shown in Figure 18.8. As pointed out above, line *AB* contains all the possible combinations of the value of his assets if the diamond is stolen and their value if it is not stolen. In other words, line *AB* shows the combinations of Y_T and Y_n that he can achieve, given the existing insurance rates. Mr. Abbot must choose some point on line *AB*; but which point is best? Clearly, he should choose the point that is on the highest of the attainable curves shown in Figure 18.8, since each of these curves contains combinations of Y_T and Y_n that result in the same value of expected utility. Given that he must choose a point on line *AB*, the highest such curve that is attainable is U_2. He can reach this curve if he chooses point *C*, where Y_T = $56,000 and Y_n = $86,000.

To reach point *C*, he must buy $70,000 worth of insurance. Why? Because, as shown in Table 18.1, if he buys this amount of insurance, the value of his assets if the diamond is stolen is $56,000, and their value if it is not stolen is $86,000. In other words, if he buys this amount of insurance, Y_T = $56,000 and Y_n = $86,000, which means that he attains point *C*. Thus, since point *C* is the optimal point, $70,000 is the optimal amount of insurance for Mr. Abbot to purchase.

This sort of analysis can be used to determine the optimal amount of insurance of many types, not just insurance against theft. For example, suppose that a family owns a house that it wants to insure against fire. The techniques described in this section can be used to determine how much fire insurance this family should buy. (As an exercise, prove to yourself that this is true.) In addition, these techniques can be used to analyze certain aspects of investment behavior. Although this model is quite simple, it can shed considerable light on many kinds of decisions, if used with some imagination.

MORAL HAZARD

In the previous section, we assumed that the probability that Mr. Abbot's diamond would be stolen, P, was not affected by how much insurance he buys. For Mr. Abbot, this assumption may be correct, but for other people it may be quite wrong. For example, Ann Flanders, who (like Mr. Abbot) owns a diamond worth $100,000, purchases $100,000 worth of insurance at a cost of $20,000, the result (as shown in Table 18.1) being that the value of her assets will be $80,000 regardless of whether her diamond is stolen or not. Feeling that she has nothing to lose if her diamond is stolen, she does not take many precautions to prevent its theft. Thus the probability of its theft is greater than if she had bought less insurance. Why? Because if she had bought less insurance, she would lose more if the diamond were stolen—and consequently she would take greater precautions.

Moral hazard

The fact that a person's or firm's behavior may change after buying insurance in such a way as to alter the probability of theft results in the so-called problem of *moral hazard*. This problem exists for various kinds of insurance, not for theft insurance alone. For example, people who buy lots of accident insurance may drive less carefully because they are insured, the result being that they are more likely to have an accident than if they had less insurance. Similarly, people with lots of medical insurance may spend less on preventive health care, and if they get sick, they may make more visits to the physician and incur more expensive treatments than if they had less insurance.

If the problem of moral hazard is severe enough, insurance companies may have to increase their premiums or stop selling insurance of this sort. Otherwise they will lose money because the probability that they will have to pay out to a policy holder will be too high to allow them to break even. One way that insurance companies try to cope with this problem is by insisting that the policy holder bear part of the risk through co-insurance and deductibles. For example, as we saw in Example 3.2, a medical insurance policy may stipulate that the patient must pay the first $200 of medical expenses that he or she incurs per year, and that the insurance company will pay 80 percent (not all) of the patient's medical expenses above $200. These stipulations give the policy holder incentives to behave in ways that reduce the probability of having to make an insurance claim.

Having discussed insurance, let's turn to the stock market, a part of the economy characterized by considerable risk. Assuming that investors are risk averse, they would like to construct portfolios of stocks so as to minimize risk (when the expected return is held constant). One way that this can be achieved is through diversification. Suppose, for example, that one can buy stock in only two firms, a sweater manufacturer and a bathing suit producer. If next year's weather is mild, stock in the bathing suit producer will earn 30 cents per dollar invested, while stock in the sweater manufacturer will earn nothing. If next year's weather is not mild, stock in the sweater manufacturer will earn 30 cents per dollar invested, while stock in the bathing suit producer will earn nothing.

If there is a 0.5 probability that next season's weather will be mild (and a 0.5 probability that it will not be mild), the expected return from a dollar's worth of stock in the bathing suit producer is

$$0.5(30 \text{ cents}) + 0.5(0) = 15 \text{ cents},$$

and the expected return from a dollar's worth of stock in the sweater manufacturer is

$$0.5(0) + 0.5(30 \text{ cents}) = 15 \text{ cents}.$$

Thus, regardless of which stock is purchased, the expected return is 15 cents per dollar invested. However, if the investor buys either one of these stocks, there is a considerable amount of risk. Specifically, there is a 0.5 probability that the actual return will be nothing (and a 0.5 probability that it will be 30 cents per dollar invested).

Diversification

One way to reduce the risk is to *diversify*. Rather than buying only one stock or the other, suppose that the investor puts half of his or her money into each stock. The expected return from this diversified portfolio, denoted by E, is

$$E = P_M R_M + P_N R_N, \qquad [18.10]$$

where P_M is the probability of mild weather, R_M is the return if the weather is mild, P_N is the probability that the weather is not mild, and R_N is the return if the weather is not mild. From the previous paragraph, we know that $P_M = P_N = 0.5$. But what do R_M and R_N equal? If the weather is mild, the return, R_M, is $0.5(30) + 0.5(0) = 15$ cents per dollar invested, because the half of the portfolio devoted to bathing suit stock earns 30 cents per dollar invested, while the half devoted to sweater stock earns nothing. If the weather is not mild, the return, R_N, is $0.5(0) + 0.5(30) = 15$ cents per dollar invested, because the half of the portfolio devoted to sweater stock earns 30 cents per dollar invested, while the half devoted to bathing suit stock earns nothing. Inserting the above values of P_M, P_N, R_M and R_N into Equation 18.10, we find that the expected return from this diversified portfolio is

$$0.5(15) + 0.5(15) = 15.$$

Thus this diversified portfolio has precisely the same expected return as a portfolio consisting of either stock alone—15 cents per dollar invested.

The key point to recognize and understand is that the diversified portfolio has much less risk than a portfolio consisting of either stock alone. To see this, note that, regardless of whether next year's weather is mild or not, the return from the diversified portfolio (R_M or R_N) equals 15 cents per dollar invested. Thus there is *no* risk at all! The investor can be *sure* of getting 15 cents per dollar invested. On the other hand, as pointed out above, there is considerable risk in a portfolio consisting of either stock alone.

The reason why risk is eliminated through diversification is that the stocks of the two firms are affected differently by different weather conditions. Because the one firm's stock always does well when the other firm's stock does poorly, diversification can, as we have seen, do away with risk. However, this is a very unusual situation. In most cases, it is possible to reduce, but not eliminate, risk through diversification. This is because there generally is not a simple, dependable inverse relation (of the sort posited above) between the returns from various firms' stock.

DIVERSIFIABLE AND NONDIVERSIFIABLE RISK

Diversifiable risk

Nondiversifiable risk

Some types of risk can be eliminated by diversification; other types cannot. Risk that can be eliminated in this way is called *diversifiable* (or *nonsystematic*) risk; risk that cannot be eliminated in this way is called *nondiversifiable* (or *systematic*) risk. Nondiversifiable risk is the risk that the general level of the stock market will fall because of a recession or for some other reason. Since the prices of stocks of various companies tend to go up and down together, this sort of risk cannot be eliminated by diversification. If you buy stock in a wide variety of companies (such as IBM, DuPont, General Motors, Sears Roebuck, and Citibank), their prices will tend, on the average, to move up during some periods and down in others—such as October 19, 1987, when the Dow-Jones average of stock prices fell by about 20 percent on a single day. Diversification will not prevent the average price of your stocks from fluctuating.

On the other hand, risk due to factors that are specific to a particular firm can be eliminated through diversification. For example, IBM's stock may be adversely affected by a new product's being introduced by one of its rivals, or General Motors' stock may fall because of a strike. Risk of this sort can be eliminated by diversification, because whereas some firms are hurt by new products or strikes during a particular period, other firms benefit from them. Thus, if one buys a considerable number of stocks representing a variety of industries, it is likely that the effects of such factors will be very small, on the average. They will tend to cancel each other out.

Figure 18.9 illustrates the relationship between diversification and risk. If we choose stocks at random,[16] the total risk of our portfolio of stocks goes down as the number of stocks goes up. This is because the diversifiable risk declines. But the nondiversifiable risk cannot be reduced in this way; no matter how many stocks we buy, it remains equal to *OR* in Figure 18.9.

---

16. In Figure 18.9, we assume that all of the stocks have the same amount of nondiversifiable risk.

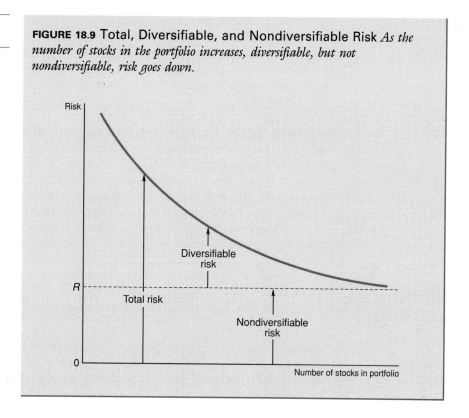

FIGURE 18.9 Total, Diversifiable, and Nondiversifiable Risk *As the number of stocks in the portfolio increases, diversifiable, but not nondiversifiable, risk goes down.*

THE CAPITAL ASSET PRICING MODEL

In recent years, the capital asset pricing model, developed by economists like Stanford's William Sharpe and the late John Lintner of Harvard, has become very important, both to theorists and to Wall Street practitioners. This theory builds on the long-accepted proposition that investors must receive a higher expected return to induce them to accept higher risk. Thus, if stock in firm A is riskier than stock in firm B, the expected return from firm A's stock must exceed that from firm B's stock. Otherwise, risk-averse investors would not purchase firm A's stock.

In contrast to older thinking, this new theory emphasizes that not all of the risk in a particular stock must be taken into account in determining how high this stock's expected return must be to compensate the investor for risk-bearing. Surprising as it may seem, only the nondiversifiable risk is relevant. Why? Because the diversifiable risk can readily be avoided by diversification. Since the diversifiable risk can be eliminated so easily, one cannot obtain a higher expected return by assuming this risk. People won't pay you for bearing unnecessary risks.

The capital asset pricing model says that the expected return[17] from a par-

17. The return from a stock is defined as its price at the end of the period it will be held minus its price at the beginning of this period plus any dividends that are paid, divided by its price at the beginning of this period.

ticular stock should depend on three variables: (1) the return from a riskless
investment (such as U.S. Treasury securities), i; (2) the expected return from all
available stocks (such as the Standard and Poor's 500-stock index), r_m; and
(3) the amount of nondiversifiable risk one assumes by buying this particular
stock. Specifically, this theory concludes that

$$r = i + (r_m - i)\beta, \qquad\qquad [18.11]$$

where r is the expected return from this particular stock and β is this stock's
beta, a measure of nondiversifiable risk for this stock that is defined in the
paragraph after next.[18]

Figure 18.10 shows the relationship between the expected return from a
stock and the extent of its nondiversifiable risk, as measured by its beta. As you
can see, there is a direct, linear relationship between them. Let's define $(r - i)$ as
Risk premium   the *risk premium* for this stock; it is the increase in the expected return over and
above what could be earned on a riskless investment (such as U.S. Treasury
securities). Both Equation 18.11 and Figure 18.10 show that, according to the
capital asset pricing model, the risk premium for a stock is proportional to the
stock's beta.

Beta   But what exactly is a stock's beta? *It is a measure of how sensitive the stock's*

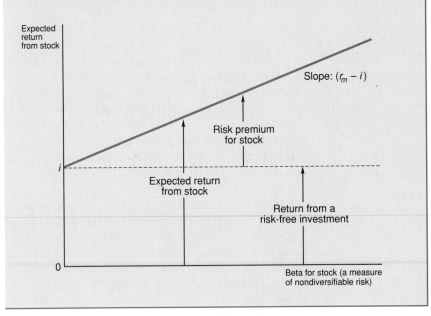

FIGURE 18.10 Relationship between the Expected Return from a
Stock and the Stock's Value of Beta *According to the capital asset
pricing model, expected return is a direct, linear function of beta, a measure
of nondiversifiable risk.*

18. For derivations of Equation 18.11, see W. Sharpe, "Capital Asset Prices: A Theory of Market
Equilibrium under Conditions of Risk," *Journal of Finance*, September 1964; and J. Lintner,
"The Valuation of Risk Assets and the Selection of Risky Investments in Stock Portfolios and
Capital Budgets," *Review of Economics and Statistics*, February 1965.

return is to changes in the return from all available stocks (such as the Standard and Poor's 500-stock index). If an increase of 1 percentage point in the return from all available stocks is associated with an increase, on the average, of 2 percentage points in this stock's return, this stock's beta equals 2. If an increase of 1 percentage point in the return from all available stocks is associated with an increase, on the average, of 0.8 percentage points in this stock's return, this stock's beta equals 0.8. Table 18.2 shows the beta for selected stocks in June 1987. The fact that IBM's beta equals 1.05 means that an increase of 1 percentage point in the return from all available stocks is associated with an increase, on the average, of 1.05 percentage points in this stock's return.

TABLE 18.2 Betas for Selected Stocks, June 1987

Stock	Beta
Bristol Myers	1.00
Control Data Corporation	1.30
Dow Chemical	1.15
Eastman Kodak	0.80
Exxon	0.85
General Electric	1.05
Hewlett-Packard	1.30
IBM	1.05
McDonnell-Douglas	1.00

Source: J. Van Horne, *Financial Management and Policy,* 8th ed. (Englewood Cliffs, N.J.: Prentice Hall, 1989).

To illustrate how this theory is used, suppose that the expected annual rate of return from U.S. Treasury securities is 8 percent, that the expected annual rate of return from the Standard and Poor's 500-stock index is 13 percent, and that the beta for company X's stock is 1.1. Given this information and using Equation 18.11, we find that the expected annual rate of return from company X's stock is

$$r = .08 + (.13 - .08)1.1 = .135.$$

What this means is that, on the average, the stock market expects company X's stock to show a 13.5 percent annual rate of return. This is the rate of return that investors require to hold this stock. Results of this sort are used continually by Wall Street analysts. The capital asset pricing model and other such techniques have had a profound effect on the field of corporate finance.[19] (In 1990, Markowitz, Miller, and Sharpe won the Nobel Prize in Economics.)

19. This, of course, is not the place to delve deeply into this topic. But even in the present brief summary, it is important to recognize that the capital asset pricing model has many limitations. For a more comprehensive treatment, see texts on corporate finance like R. Westerfield, S. Ross, and J. Jaffe, *Corporation Finance,* 2d ed. (Homewood, Ill.: Irwin, 1990); or J. Van Horne, *Financial Management and Policy.*

1. The probability of a particular outcome is the proportion of times that this outcome occurs over the long run if this situation exists over and over again. The expected monetary value of a gamble is the sum of the amount of money gained (or lost) if each outcome occurs times the probability of occurrence of the outcome. The expected monetary value is important because it is the average amount that the decision-maker would gain (or lose) if he or she were to accept this gamble repeatedly.

2. A decision tree represents a decision problem as a series of choices, each of which is depicted by a decision fork or a chance fork. A decision tree can be used to determine the course of action with the highest expected monetary value. As an example, we took up the decision of whether or not to drill an oil well.

3. The expected value of perfect information is the increase in expected monetary value if the decision-maker could obtain completely accurate information concerning the outcome of the relevant situation (but he or she does not yet know what this information will be). This is the maximum amount that the decision-maker should pay to obtain such information. Using methods described in this chapter, one can calculate the expected value of perfect information.

4. Whether a decision-maker wants to maximize expected monetary value depends on his or her attitudes toward risk, which can be measured by his or her Neumann-Morgenstern utility function. To construct such a utility function, we begin by setting the utility attached to two monetary values arbitrarily. Then we present the decision-maker with a choice between the certainty of one of the other monetary values and a gamble where the possible outcomes are the two monetary values whose utilities we set arbitrarily. Repeating this procedure over and over, we can construct the decision-maker's utility function (which should not be confused with a cardinal utility function of the sort described in the Appendix to Chapter 3).

5. The Neumann-Morgenstern utility function is useful in indicating the courses of action that the decision-maker should choose, and in predicting those that he or she will choose. As an illustration, we described the utility function of William Beard, an actual owner of an oil firm.

6. To cope with risk, firms and consumers often buy insurance. For example, a man must decide how much insurance (if any) to buy against the theft of an asset he owns. The more insurance he buys, the more money he will have if the asset is stolen, but the less money he will have if it is not stolen. Under the circumstances described above, the relationship between the amount of money he will have if it is stolen and the amount of money he will have if it is not stolen can be represented by a straight line. To find the optimal amount of insurance, we must find the point on this line where his expected utility is highest. The amount of insurance corresponding to this point is the optimal amount.

7. The problem of moral hazard occurs if a person's or firm's behavior changes after buying insurance in such a way as to increase the probability of a loss. For example, people with lots of medical insurance may spend less on preventive medical care, and if they get sick, they may make more visits to the physician and incur more expensive treatments than if they had less insurance.

8. If investors are risk averse, they would like to construct portfolios of stocks so as to minimize risk (when the expected return is held constant). Diversifiable risk can be eliminated by diversification; nondiversifiable risk cannot. The capital

asset pricing model says that the risk premium for a stock (the difference between its expected return and that of a riskless investment) is proportional to the stock's beta, a measure of the stock's nondiversifiable risk.

1. Professional tennis has become a big business with big prizes. There frequently is a large disparity between the prize for the winner and that for the runner-up; for example, the former may receive $100,000; the latter $32,000. Michael Mewshaw has asserted that finalists often have secret deals before the match to divide the pot; that is, they have agreed that both winner and loser get $\frac{\$100,000 + \$32,000}{2}$, or $66,000. This practice, known as "splitting," has been particularly likely to occur, he said, "in special events and exhibitions, and on the [World Championship Tennis] circuit, all of which [have] tended to have huge prize-money differences."[20]

a) If a player believes that he has a 50-50 chance of winning, will he be willing to "split" if he is a risk lover? (b) Suppose a player has the following utility function:

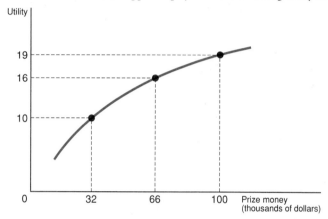

If the first prize is $100,000 and the second prize is $32,000 and if he believes that he has a 50-50 chance of winning, will he be willing to split? (c) Mewshaw quotes some players who doubted that the top-seeded player would "split" with his opponent the next day because he "was on a hot streak and thought he would win." If these players were correct, if the prizes were as indicated in (b) and if the top-seeded player had the utility-function shown above, how large must his probability of winning have been (in his eyes)?

2. According to R. A. Fisher, a famous British statistician, advocates of subjective probability "seem forced to regard mathematical probability not as an objective quantity measured by observed frequencies, but as measuring psychological tendencies, theorems respecting which are useless for scientific purposes." Do you agree? Do you think that subjective probabilities are useless in solving microeconomic problems?

3. The beta for the Hoffman Company's stock equals 1.4. If the expected annual rate of return from U.S. Treasury securities is 9 percent and if the expected annual rate of return from the Standard and Poor's 500-stock index is 12 percent, what is the rate of return that investors require to hold the Hoffman Company's stock?

4. A firm must decide whether or not to go forward with an R and D project to develop a new process. If the project is successful, it will gain $5 million; if it is not successful, it will lose $1 million. It believes that the probability is 0.2 that it will be successful and 0.8

20. M. Mewshaw, "Say It Ain't So, Bjorn," *Harper's*, June 1983.

that it will not be successful. What is the expected value of perfect information concerning whether or not it will be successful?

5. The Tremont Corporation is considering the purchase of a firm that produces tools and dies. Tremont's management feels that there is a 50-50 chance, if Tremont buys the firm, that it can make the firm into an effective producer of auto parts. If the firm can be transformed in this way, Tremont believes that it will make $1 million if it buys the firm; if it cannot be transformed in this way, Tremont believes that it will lose $2 million. What is the expected monetary value to Tremont of buying the firm?

6. Construct a decision tree to represent Tremont's problem (described in the previous question). If Tremont maximizes expected monetary value, should it purchase the firm?

7. In fact, the Tremont Corporation decides to purchase the firm described in Question 5. Does this mean that Tremont's management is (a) indifferent to risk, (b) a risk averter?

8. Suppose that insurance rates go up. Theft insurance now costs 30 percent of the face value of the insurance. Will line AB in Figure 18.6 shift? If so, draw its new position in the graph below.

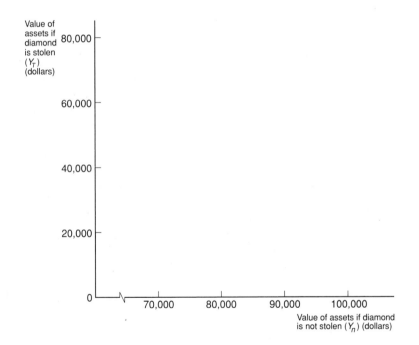

9. Mrs. Cherrytree's Neumann-Morgenstern utility function can be represented by the following equation:

$$U = 10 + 2M$$

where U is utility and M is monetary gain (in thousands of dollars).[21] She has the opportunity to invest $25,000 in Archie Dallas's Bar and Grill. She believes that there is

21. As pointed out in footnote 6, this utility function is not unique. But that does not mean that this utility function cannot be used to solve this problem. Like any other such utility function, it is based on the arbitrary setting of the utilities attached to two monetary values.

a 0.5 probability that she will lose her entire investment and a 0.5 probability that she will gain $32,000. (a) If she makes the investment, what is her expected utility? (b) Should she make the investment?

10. The Dennis Company is the principal supplier of the Johnson Corporation. The fortunes of the two firms are closely intertwined. When one firm's profits go up or down, the other's profits generally behave in the same way. An investor who owns only Johnson stock decides to buy Dennis stock in order to reduce risk through diversification. Comment on this decision.

11. During some periods in the 1960s, Mead Johnson and Company (now part of Bristol-Myers Company) seemed to have a beta that was *negative*. In other words, an increase of 1 percentage point in the return from all available stocks was associated with a *decrease* in the return from Mead Johnson stock. The reason was that Mead Johnson came out with a very profitable new product, Metrecal, in 1962, when the stock market as a whole declined. During the subsequent period when the stock market went up, the returns from Mead Johnson stock went down as Metrecal became less popular.[22]

When using the capital asset pricing model, Wall Street analysts often assume that the historical relationship between the return from a particular stock and the return from all available stocks will continue to prevail in the future. Thus, if the return from Mead Johnson stock happened to be inversely related to the return from all available stocks in the past, it is assumed that the same sort of relationship will be maintained in the future. Suppose that you are an adviser to a stock brokerage firm, and that you are asked to comment on the soundness of this assumption. What would your answer be?

22. B. Malkiel, *A Random Walk Down Wall Street*, 5th ed. (New York: Norton, 1990).

AIRCRAFT DEVELOPMENT AND THE SST

Enormous advances have been made in the commercial aircraft industry in recent decades. In part, this has been due to government policies and programs. As pointed out in Chapter 15, research and development activities often result in external economies. Nowhere is this more obvious than in the aircraft industry, where research supported by the Department of Defense and other government agencies has resulted in important spillovers to the commercial aircraft industry. For example, military-supported research on power plants for the huge C-5A military transport led to the development of the jet engines that now power the wide-body commercial airliners.

Aircraft research and development is an activity that is characterized by great risk, as well as by externalities. Chance plays a crucial role, and a long string of failures often occurs before any kind of success is achieved. A research or development project can be regarded as a process of risk reduction or learning. Suppose, for example, that a firm that is trying to fabricate a part can use one of two alloys and that it is impossible to use standard sources to determine their characteristics. Suppose that strength is of paramount importance and that the firm's estimates of the strengths of the alloys, alloy 1 and alloy 2, are represented by the probability distributions in part A of Table 1. If the firm were forced to make a choice immediately, it would probably choose alloy 2, since it believes that there is better than a 50–50 chance that alloy 2 will turn out to be stronger than alloy 1.

TABLE 1 Subjective Probability Distribution of Strength of Alloys 1 and 2, before and after Test

Extent of strength	A. Before test		B. After test	
	Alloy 1	Alloy 2	Alloy 1	Alloy 2
	(probabilities)			
Exceptionally high	.20	.20	.10	.10
Very high	.40	.50	.20	.80
High	.20	.20	.60	.10
Medium	.10	.05	.10	.00
Low	.10	.05	.00	.00
Total	1.00	1.00	1.00	1.00

However, there is a good chance that this decision might turn out to be wrong, the consequence being that the part would be weaker than if alloy 1 had been used. Thus the firm may decide to perform a test prior to making the selection. On the basis of the test results, the firm will formulate new estimates, represented by the probability distributions in part B of Table 1. These probability distributions show less dispersion than the ones in part A; in other words, the firm believes it is able to pinpoint more closely the strength of each alloy than in part A. Because of the tests, the firm is less uncertain as to which alloy is stronger.

Research and development is more risky than most other economic activities, and many development projects use parallel efforts to help cope with risk. For example, in the development of the atomic bomb, there were several methods of making fissionable materials, and no consensus existed among scientists as to which of these alternatives was most promising. To make sure that the best one was not discarded, all methods were pursued in parallel. The wisdom of this decision was borne out by the fact that the method that was first to produce appreciable quantities of fissionable material was one that had been considered relatively unpromising early in the development program.

Under what conditions is it optimal to run parallel research and development efforts? What factors determine the optimal number of parallel efforts? Suppose that a firm can select x approaches, spend C dollars on each one over a period of m months, choose the one that looks most promising at the end of the period, and carry it to completion, dropping the others. Suppose that the only relevant criterion is the extent of the development costs, the usefulness of the result and the development time being assumed to be the same regardless of which parallel effort is pursued. For further simplification, suppose that all approaches look equally promising. Under these circumstances, the optimal value of x—the number of parallel research and development efforts—is inversely related to C and directly related to the amount learned in the next m months. As the cost of running each effort increases, the optimal number of parallel efforts decreases. As the prospective amount of learning increases, the optimal number of parallel efforts increases.

To illustrate why it is sometimes cheaper to run parallel development efforts, consider a case in which each approach has a 50–50 chance of costing $2 million and a 50–50 chance of costing $1 million. Since we assume that all approaches are equally promising, these probabilities are the same for all approaches. The expected total cost of development is the sum of the total costs of development if each possible outcome occurs times the probability of the occurrence of this outcome. (Recall our discussion of expected monetary value in Chapter 18.) If a single approach is used, the expected total costs of development are

$$.5(\$2 \text{ million}) + .5(\$1 \text{ million}) = \$1.5 \text{ million}, \qquad [1]$$

since there is a .5 probability that total costs with any single approach will be $2 million and a .5 probability that they will be $1 million.

If two approaches are run in parallel and if the true cost of development using each approach can be determined after C dollars are spent on each approach, the expected total costs of development are

$$.25(\$2 \text{ million}) + .75(\$1 \text{ million}) + C = \$1.25 \text{ million} + C \qquad [2]$$

if each approach is carried to the point at which C dollars have been spent on it, and if the cheaper approach is chosen at that point (and the other approach is dropped). Why? Because there is a .25 probability that total costs with the better of the two approaches will be $2 million and a .75 probability that they will be $1 million. In addition, there is the certainty that a cost of C will be incurred for the approach that is dropped. (The reason why there is a .25 chance that total costs with the better of the two approaches is $2 million is that this will occur only when the total cost of both approaches turns out to be $2 million—and the probability that this will occur is .5 times .5 or .25.) Comparing Equation 1 with Equation 2, it is obvious that the expected total cost of development is lower with two parallel approaches than with a single approach if C is less than $250,000.

The results of the previous few paragraphs are important because they put in perspective some of the criticisms of "duplication" and "waste" in research and development. Contrary to popular belief, parallel efforts may produce results more cheaply than attempting in advance to choose the optimal approach and concentrating all one's efforts on pursuing it. The fact that most of the parallel paths are ultimately rejected does not mean that they are a waste. On the contrary, this may be the cheapest way to proceed.

The previous discussion indicates how the theory of decision-making under risk can be of use in understanding aircraft R and D. Another technique that has often been applied in this area is the present-value rule described in Chapter 17. To illustrate, let's turn to a particularly famous case, the SST or supersonic transport plane. This program, begun in the late 1960s, was a response to the fear that American dominance of commercial aircraft sales might be threatened by the Concorde, which was being developed jointly by the British and the French. The federal government set in motion a design competition and proposed to finance the development activities of the winning firm. The prototype development contract was awarded to Boeing. There was a considerable amount of opposition to the development of the SST, both among environmentalists (who objected to its noise and other characteristics) and among economists (who felt that it was a poor use of resources). For example, in the late 1960s, the Institute for Defense Analysis presented estimates to Congress of the present value of the net benefits from developing the SST. The results, shown in Table 2, indicate that, if the interest rate was 5 percent or more, the present value of the project was negative. Thus, based on the criteria discussed in Chapter 17, this was not a promising investment.

Nonetheless, the SST program was not easy to kill. As Senator William Proxmire put it in 1970: "Last year, we had the President's own ad hoc advisory committee on the SST which came down as hard as any group of experts I have ever seen against the SST. . . . In spite of that, we were not able to muster a great deal of opposition to it in Congress. And even more shocking is the fact that the President went ahead over the decision of his own committee."[1] Yet the anal-

1. U.S. Joint Economic Committee, Subcommittee on Economy in Government, *Hearings on Economic Analyses and the Efficiency of Government,* Part 4, *Supersonic Transport Development* (Washington, D.C.: U.S. Government Printing Office, 1970).

TABLE 2 Present Value of Estimated Net Benefits from the Supersonic Transport Program

Interest rate (percent)	Present value (millions of dollars)
5	−344
10	−528
15	−579

Source: U.S. Joint Economic Committee, *Economic Analysis of Public Investment Decisions: Interest Rate Policy and Discounting Analysis* (Washington, D.C.: Government Printing Office, 1968), pp. 20–21.

yses of the economists, environmentalists, and others eventually had a decisive impact, and the SST program ended in 1971. Based on the experience of the British and French, who went ahead with the development of the Concorde, the United States was smart to quit when it did. In 1979, after spending many billions of dollars (according to some accounts, $500 for every man, woman, and child in the two countries), Britain and France stopped producing the Concorde. They had not been able to sell one of the planes commercially. Because its operating costs were several times as high as a Boeing 747 (discussed in Example 7.2), the Concorde's services could not be priced low enough to attract sufficient demand. Thus the economic analyses that helped to kill the SST in the United States seem to have promoted the right decision.

Analytical Questions

1. According to the National Academy of Engineering, an aircraft manufacturer must risk about $3 billion to develop and introduce a new commercial transport plane.[2] If the probability of success is 0.4, how large must the profit be (if the plane is a success) for the expected monetary value of the gamble to be at least zero?

2. Suppose that an aircraft manufacturer must decide whether to run two parallel development efforts, each of which has a 50–50 chance of costing $5 million and a 50–50 chance of costing $10 million. If a single approach is used, what is the expected cost of development? If the two approaches are run in parallel, what is the expected cost of development?

3. If the true cost of development using each approach can be determined after $1 million is spent on each approach, should the aircraft manufacturer (in the previous question) run both efforts in parallel? Why or why not?

4. In Table 2, the present value of the estimated net benefits from the SST program decreases as the interest rate rises. Why?

5. What value of the interest rate should have been used to estimate the present value of the net benefits from the SST program?

6. An aircraft manufacturer can invest in a project that costs $100 million now and that provides the manufacturer with a cash inflow of $25 million annually for each of the next five years. If the interest rate is .10, should the firm accept the project? Why or why not?

2. National Academy of Engineering, *The Competitive Status of the U.S. Civil Aviation Manufacturing Industry* (Washington, D.C.: National Academy Press, 1985).

APPENDIX

LINEAR PROGRAMMING

Linear programming is the most famous of the mathematical programming methods that have come into existence since World War II. It is a technique that allows decision-makers to solve maximization and minimization problems where there are certain constraints that limit what can be done. Some of the principal figures in the development of linear programming were Tjalling Koopmans and Leonid Kantorovich (who received the 1975 Nobel Memorial Prize in Economics for their work), and George Dantzig, an American mathematician at Stanford. First used shortly after World War II to help schedule the procurement activities of the United States Air Force, linear programming has become an extremely important part of microeconomic theory and a very powerful tool for the solution of managerial problems. Its remarkable growth has been helped along by the development of computers which can handle the many computations that are required to solve large linear programming problems.

Although linear programming is an important tool of microeconomists, it is purely a mathematical technique. By itself it can only tell us the implications of the data that the decision-maker or the analyst has gathered (or assumed). If these data (or assumptions) are wrong, the solution will in general be wrong, too. The great advantage of linear programming is that it provides computational advantages, not that it performs magic.

In this Appendix we reexamine the theory of production from the point of view of linear programming. There are at least two reasons for doing so. First, the programming analysis is more fundamental in one respect than the conventional analysis presented in Chapters 6 and 7. The conventional theory is built on the foundation of the production function, which assumes that the technically efficient production processes have been determined and given to the economist before he or she attacks the problem. But in the real world, the economist is usually confronted with a number of feasible production processes, and it is very difficult to tell which ones—or which combinations—are efficient. The choice of the optimal combination of production processes is an extremely important decision, and it can be analyzed by linear programming.

Second, the programming analysis seems to conform more closely to the way that managers tend to view production. The language and concepts of linear programming, though abstract and by no means the same as those of management, seem to be closer to those of management people than the ones used by the conventional theory. Although this is less important than the first reason, it is of some importance, since it makes it easier to apply linear programming than conventional theory. The development of linear programming has enabled the economist to solve many types of production problems for industry and government.

THE FIRM'S PRODUCTION DECISIONS AS A LINEAR PROGRAMMING PROBLEM

Linear programming views the technology available to the firm as being composed of a finite number of processes. A *process* uses inputs and produces one or more outputs. For example, a man using a wheelbarrow to carry bricks is a process. An important assumption in linear programming is that each process uses inputs in fixed proportions. Consequently, each process can be described by a set of technical coefficients, $(a_1, \cdots, a_m)$, that shows the amount of the first input, $\cdots$, mth input that is needed to produce one unit of output. For example, if the first input were hours of labor, the second input were wheelbarrow-hours, and a unit of output were the transportation of 1 ton-mile of bricks, the technical coefficients for the "person-wheelbarrow" process might be $(5, 5)$, which would indicate that it takes 5 hours of labor and 5 hours of use of the wheelbarrow to "produce" 1 ton-mile of transportation of bricks.

Activity level   Each process can be operated at various *activity levels*. The activity level of a process is the number of units of output that is produced with the process. For example, if 2 ton-miles of bricks are "produced" with the "person-wheelbarrow" process described above, its activity level is 2; on the other hand, if 0.5 ton-miles of bricks are transported with this process, its activity level is 0.5. It is assumed that, if the output of any process is varied, the quantity of inputs used by the process varies proportionately with the output of the process. Thus the quantity of any input used by a process is equal to the activity level of the process multiplied by the input's technical coefficient for this process. For example, the amount of labor used by the "person-wheelbarrow" process is $5 \times 5 = 25$ hours, if this process is operated at an activity level of 5. When two or more processes are used simultaneously, it is assumed that they do not interfere with one another or make each other more productive. (In other words, it is assumed that the processes are additive in the inputs.)

Viewed in the context of linear programming, the firm's production problem is as follows: The firm has certain fixed amounts of a number of inputs at its disposal. For example, if the firm is a steel mill, it has a limited amount of land, raw materials, managerial labor, and equipment of various types. (These limi-
Constraints   tations on the amounts of inputs that the firm can use are called *constraints*.) Each unit of output resulting from a particular process yields the firm a certain amount of profit. This amount of profit varies in general from process to process; indeed, the product itself may vary from process to process. Knowing the profit to be made from a unit of output from each process and recognizing the limited amount of inputs at its disposal, the firm must determine the activity level at which each process should be operated to maximize profit.

THE FINISHING OF COTTON CLOTH: AN ILLUSTRATION

The previous section provided a general description of the firm's production decision, as it is pictured from the viewpoint of linear programming. But such a description is of limited use unless it is supplemented by illustrations. Recognizing this fact, the next few sections of this Appendix are devoted to a fairly detailed description of several cases that illustrate how linear programming can be used to solve the production problems of the firm.

To begin with, consider the following situation. Suppose that one of the operations of a textile mill is the finishing of cotton cloth. The output rate of the finishing department is limited by the capacity of its finishing equipment and the amount of labor available to carry out the work. The firm is considering three finishing processes: processes 1, 2, and 3. Suppose that the firm knows that the profit per batch of cotton cloth finished with process 1 is $1.00; similarly, it is $0.90 for process 2, and $1.10 for process 3. Suppose too that process 1 uses 3 machine-hours of finishing capacity per batch of cotton cloth processed, that process 2 uses 2.50 machine-hours, and that process 3 uses 5.25 machine-hours. Also, suppose that process 1 uses 0.4 hours of labor per batch of cotton cloth processed, that process 2 uses 0.50 hours, and that process 3 uses 0.35 hours. These are the technical coefficients.[1] Finally, suppose that 6,000 machine-hours per week is the maximum finishing capacity, and 600 hours per week is the maximum amount of labor that the firm can use.

If Q_1 is the number of batches of cotton cloth processed per week on process 1, Q_2 is the number processed on process 2, and Q_3 is the number processed on process 3, the firm's production problem can be regarded as the following linear programming problem: Maximize

$$\pi = 1.00Q_1 + 0.90Q_2 + 1.10Q_3 \qquad [A.1]$$

subject to the constraints

$$3Q_1 + 2.50Q_2 + 5.25Q_3 \leq 6,000 \qquad [A.2]$$

$$0.40Q_1 + 0.50Q_2 + 0.35Q_3 \leq 600 \qquad [A.3]$$

$$Q_1 \geq 0; Q_2 \geq 0; Q_3 \geq 0. \qquad [A.4]$$

Objective function The *objective function*, sometimes called the criterion function, is the function to be maximized in a linear programming problem. In this case, it is the expression for the firm's profits given in Equation A.1. The *constraints* are given in Inequalities A.2 to A.4. Inequality A.2 states that the total machine-hours per week of finishing capacity must be less than or equal to 6,000. Inequality A.3 states that the total hours of labor per week must be less than or equal to 600. Inequality A.4 contains nonnegativity constraints, which may seem so obvious as to be unnecessary to state. But they are not obvious to a computer, which might otherwise come up with a solution with a negative output. Finally, note that the

---

1. If machine-time is the first input and labor is the second input, the a's, in the terminology of the previous section, are (3, 0.4) for process 1, (2.50, 0.5) for process 2, and (5.25, 0.35) for process 3. A unit of output is a batch of cotton cloth finished.

FIGURE A.1 Feasible Input Combinations *Since a maximum of 600 labor-hours and 6,000 machine-hours are available, the feasible region is the rectangle* OXYZ.

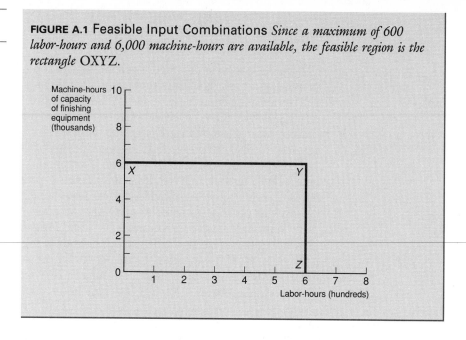

objective function and the constraints are all linear in Q_1, Q_2, and Q_3, the levels at which the processes are operated.

To see how this problem can be solved, we begin by providing a graphical representation of the feasible input combinations and of a process.[2] Figure A.1, which has the total hours per week of labor-time used by all three processes along the horizontal axis and the total machine-hours per week of finishing capacity used by all three processes along the vertical axis, shows the combinations of total labor-hours and total machine-hours that are feasible. The feasible region is the rectangle $OXYZ$, since a maximum of 600 labor-hours and 6,000 machine-hours are available.

Recall that a process is defined to have fixed input proportions. Since all points where input proportions are unchanged lie along a straight line through the origin, we can represent each process by such a line, or *ray*. In Figure A.2, the ray OR_1 represents process 1. Process 1 uses 3 machine-hours of finishing capacity and 0.4 hours of labor per batch processed. That is, it uses 7.5 machine-hours of finishing capacity for every hour of labor. Thus the ray OR_1 includes all points at which finishing capacity is combined with labor in the ratio of 7.5 : 1. Each point on this ray implies a certain output level. For example, point A, where 100 hours of labor and 750 machine-hours of finishing capacity are used, implies an output of 250 batches per week, since process 1 uses 0.4 hours of labor and 3 machine-hours of finishing capacity per batch. Moreover, since all points at which labor and finishing capacity are combined in

2. The ensuing discussion of this problem is similar in many respects (although the problem itself is quite different) to W. Baumol, *Economic Theory and Operations Analysis*, 3d ed. (Englewood Cliffs, N.J.: Prentice-Hall, 1972), pp. 296–310. Baumol's discussion in Chapters 5, 6, and 12 of his book are highly recommended for those readers who are interested in a more detailed treatment of linear programming.

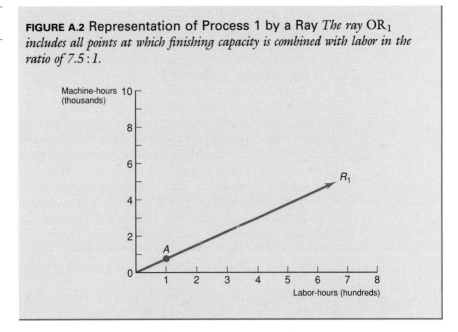

FIGURE A.2 Representation of Process 1 by a Ray *The ray* OR_1 *includes all points at which finishing capacity is combined with labor in the ratio of 7.5:1.*

the ratio of 7.5:1 are included in the ray OR_1, every possible output corresponds to some point on OR_1. It is possible to construct rays representing each of the three processes. Figure A.3 shows all of them, with OR_2 representing process 2, and OR_3 representing process 3. Each ray is constructed in the same

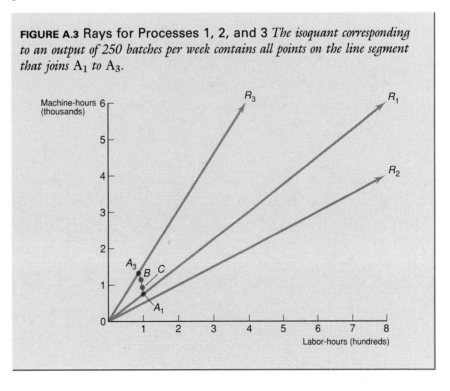

FIGURE A.3 Rays for Processes 1, 2, and 3 *The isoquant corresponding to an output of 250 batches per week contains all points on the line segment that joins* A_1 *to* A_3.

way as OR_1 was constructed for process 1. Using these rays, we can draw isoquants—curves that include all input combinations that can produce a particular amount of output. An isoquant means the same thing here as in Chapter 6; the only difference is that an isoquant here does not exhibit the smoothness of the isoquants in Chapter 6.

To begin with, we focus on processes 1 and 3. In Figure A.3, point A_1 on OR_1 is the point corresponding to an output of 250 batches per week, and point A_3 on OR_3 is the point corresponding to an output of 250 batches per week. Thus A_1 and A_3 are points on the isoquant corresponding to an output of 250 batches per week. Moreover, any point on the line segment that joins A_1 to A_3 is also on this isoquant, because the firm can simultaneously use both process 1 and process 3 to produce 250 batches per week. For example, point B corresponds to the case in which process 1 is used to produce 25 batches and process 3 is used to produce 225 batches, and point C corresponds to the case in which process 1 is used to produce 150 batches and process 3 is used to produce 100 batches. By varying the proportion of total output produced by each process, one can obtain all points on the line segment that joins A_1 to A_3.

In Figure A.4, to complete the isoquant corresponding to an output of 250 batches per week, we join A_1 to A_2, the point on OR_2 that represents an output of 250 batches per week. Thus the entire isoquant is $A_3A_1A_2$. (At first glance, one might wonder why the line segment joining A_3 to A_2 is not part of the isoquant. After all, it does represent various combinations of labor and finishing capacity that can produce 250 batches a week. The reason for its exclu-

FIGURE A.4 Isoquants for Selected Output Levels $A_3A_1A_2$ *is the isoquant corresponding to an output of 250 batches per week;* $B_3B_1B_2$ *is the isoquant corresponding to an output of 500 batches per week; and* $C_3C_1C_2$ *is the isoquant corresponding to an output of 750 batches per week.*

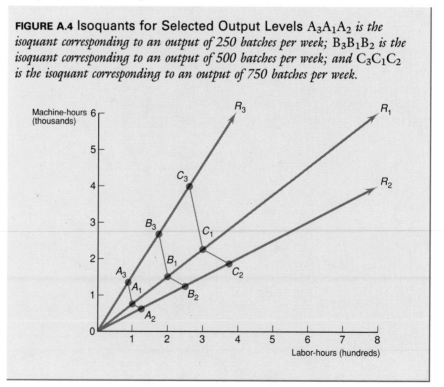

sion is that all points on the line segment joining A_3 to A_2 are inefficient. They use as much of one input and more of the other input than some point on $A_3A_1A_2$. Thus the points on A_3A_2 are clearly not on the isoquant—and they are not part of the solution to the firm's problem.) Other isoquants are also shown in Figure A.4; $B_3B_1B_2$ is the isoquant corresponding to an output of 500 batches per week and $C_3C_1C_2$ is the isoquant corresponding to an output of 750 batches per week.

Several things should be noted about the characteristic shape of isoquants in linear programming problems. First, they consist of a series of connected line segments, not the smooth curves of conventional theory. If the number of possible processes is very large, however, the isoquants may approximate the smooth conventional curves.[3] Second, their slope is negative, or at least non-positive. Third, they are convex, which means that the marginal rate of technical substitution of one input for another decreases as more of the first input is substituted for the other. Disregarding the fact that they do not exhibit the smoothness assumed in conventional theory, the isoquants of linear programming have the same basic shape as the isoquants of conventional theory.

Since the isoquants show a decreasing marginal rate of technical substitution of one input for another, linear programming is quite compatible with the law of diminishing returns, which plays an important role in conventional theory. However, the linearity assumptions in linear programming problems imply that there are neither diminishing nor increasing returns to scale. In other words, the production function is always assumed to be linear and homogeneous, which means that there are constant returns to scale.

ISOPROFIT CURVES AND A GRAPHICAL SOLUTION

Returning to the firm's problem, our next step toward a solution of this linear programming problem is the construction of isoprofit curves. Once this is done, we can obtain a solution by graphical means. Just as each isoquant in Figure A.4 represents the locus of input combinations that can produce a given *Isoprofit curve* output, each *isoprofit curve* is constructed to include all input combinations that can produce a given level of profit.

For example, suppose that we construct the isoprofit curve corresponding to a profit of $200. Since the profit per batch is $1.00 for process 1, the point on OR_1 corresponding to an output of 200 batches per week is on this isoprofit curve. Since each batch produced with process 1 requires 3 machine-hours of finishing capacity and 0.4 hours of labor, the point on OR_1 corresponding to an output of 200 batches per week is A in Figure A.5. Similarly, since the profit per batch is $0.90 for process 2, the point on OR_2 corresponding to an output of 222.2 batches per week is on this isoprofit curve. This is point B. Moreover, since the profit per batch is $1.10 for process 3, the point on OR_3 corresponding to an output of 181.8 batches per week is also on this isoprofit curve. This is

---

3. The basic reason why they are not smooth is that only a finite number of processes is assumed to be available to the firm. As the number of processes grows larger and larger, the isoquants become closer and closer to the smooth isoquants of conventional theory.

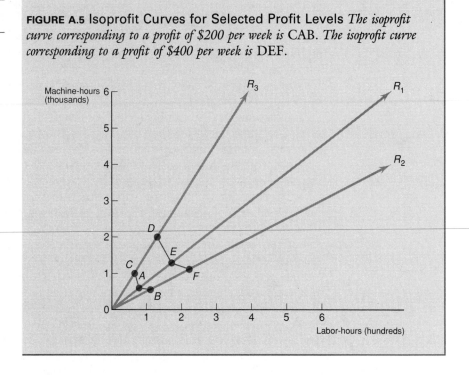

FIGURE A.5 Isoprofit Curves for Selected Profit Levels *The isoprofit curve corresponding to a profit of $200 per week is* CAB. *The isoprofit curve corresponding to a profit of $400 per week is* DEF.

point C. Finally, for the same reason as in the case of the isoquants, we can also include all points on the lines that join these points. Thus the isoprofit curve corresponding to a profit of $200 per week is *CAB* in Figure A.5.

Isoprofit curves corresponding to other levels of profit can be constructed in a similar manner. As in the case of the isoquants in Figure A.4, the isoprofit curves in Figure A.5 are parallel to one another. For example, if we compare *DEF,* the isoprofit curve corresponding to $400, with *CAB,* the isoprofit curve corresponding to $200, we find that they are parallel. That is, the slope of *CA* equals the slope of *DE,* and the slope of *AB* equals the slope of *EF.*

Given the isoprofit curves, we can easily solve the firm's problem. All that we need to do is add the isoprofit curves to the diagram (Figure A.1) showing the feasible input combinations. This is done in Figure A.6. Clearly, the problem is to find the point in the rectangle *OXYZ* of feasible input combinations that lies on the highest isoprofit curve. It is evident from Figure A.6 that this optimal point is Y. If we construct various isoprofit curves, like $U_3U_1U_2, V_3V_1V_2,$ and so forth, the highest isoprofit curve we can construct that includes any points in *OXYZ* is $V_3V_1V_2$. The only point in *OXYZ* that lies on $V_3V_1V_2$ is Y.

Granting that Y is the optimum point, how can we tell what the original values of $Q_1, Q_2,$ and Q_3 are? First, since Y lies on the line segment V_3V_1, it means that it is optimal only to use processes 3 and 1. This illustrates the fact that the optimal solution of a linear programming problem of this sort will generally entail the use of no more processes than there are constraints: two, in this case (excluding the nonnegativity constraints). Second, since Y is the point where a total of 6,000 machine-hours of finishing capacity and 600 hours of

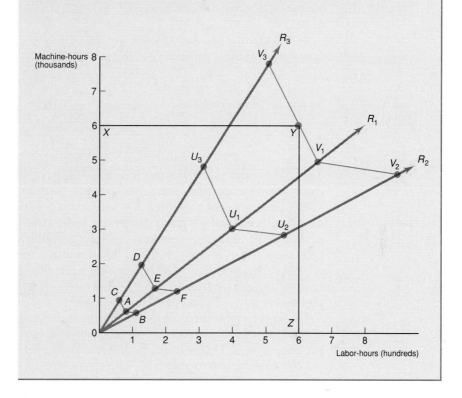

FIGURE A.6 Isoprofit Curves and Feasible Input Combinations *The optimum point is* Y, *where 6,000 machine-hours of finishing capacity and 600 hours of labor are used. It is optimal to use only processes 3 and 1.*

labor are used,

$$3Q_1 + 5.25Q_3 = 6,000 \qquad [A.5]$$

$$0.40Q_1 + 0.35Q_3 = 600. \qquad [A.6]$$

Solving Equations A.5 and A.6 simultaneously, we find that the optimal values are $Q_3 = 571.4$ and $Q_1 = 1,000$. In other words, the firm will maximize its profit if it produces about 571 batches per week on process 3 and 1,000 batches per week on process 1.

MINIMIZATION OF COSTS

As another simple illustration of the use of linear programming in solving production problems, consider a variant of the above example. Suppose that the textile firm is no longer constrained by limits on the amount of labor and finishing capacity it can use. Instead, it can hire all of the labor it wants at $6.00 an hour, and it can rent all of the finishing capacity it wants at $0.80 per machine-hour. Suppose that it can use any of the three processes just described, and that its problem is to choose that combination of processes that will produce 400 batches per week of finished cotton cloth at minimum cost. The price received per batch is the same for all processes. (Note that the figures given on p. A-3 concerning the profit per batch made by each process are no longer valid, since the price received per batch is now the same for all processes.)

In this case the firm's production problem can be regarded as the following linear programming problem: Minimize

$$C = 4.80Q_1 + 5.00Q_2 + 6.30Q_3 \qquad\qquad [A.7]$$

subject to the constraints

$$Q_1 + Q_2 + Q_3 = 400 \qquad\qquad [A.8]$$

$$Q_1 \geq 0;\ Q_2 \geq 0;\ Q_3 \geq 0. \qquad\qquad [A.9]$$

The objective function in this case is cost, C, which is given in Equation A.7. To derive this equation, note that the cost of each batch produced by process 1 is $4.80, since process 1 requires 3 machine-hours of finishing capacity (at $0.80 a machine-hour) and 0.4 hours of labor (at $6.00 an hour). Thus the total cost of the batches produced by process 1 is $4.80Q_1$. Similarly, the total cost of the batches produced by process 2 is $5.00Q_2$, and the total cost of the batches produced by process 3 is $6.30Q_3$. The only constraint, other than the nonnegativity constraints in Inequality A.9, is Equation A.8, which states that the total production from all processes must equal 400.

It is easy to solve this problem. Using the methods described in the section before last, we can construct the isoquant corresponding to an output of 400 batches per week. This isoquant, labeled ABC, is shown in Figure A.7. Next we can construct isocost curves, each of which shows the various combinations of quantities of labor and finishing capacity that can be obtained at a given level of cost. The isocost curves corresponding to costs of $2,000 and $1,800 are labeled KK' and MM' in Figure A.7. Clearly, the problem is to find the point on the isoquant, ABC, that lies on the lowest isocost curve. It is evident that the optimal point is B, which means that all of the output should be produced with process 1.

Two things should be noted at this point. First, a comparison of this problem with the one discussed on p. 171 of Chapter 7 shows that they are one and the same. In both cases, we are determining the input combination and production technique that minimize the cost of producing a given output. Moreover, Figure 7.3 (p. 171), which shows the solution according to conventional theory, is very similar to Figure A.7, which shows the solution in this case. What is the difference between the two cases? It boils down to the fact that in Chapter 7 we assumed that we were somehow given a smooth production function, whereas here we assume that there are three processes that can be used and that their characteristics are as described in this Appendix.

Second, was it really necessary to use linear programming—even the simplified version relying only on graphical techniques that we use here—to solve this problem? The answer clearly is no. All that the problem entails is a choice among three methods of production in a case in which the unit costs of production are constant for each process and there is no constraint on the amount

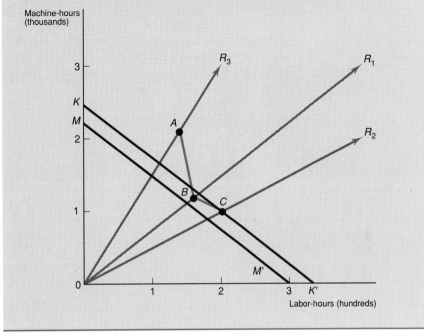

FIGURE A.7 Optimal Solution: Cost-Minimization Problem *Since the isoquant is* ABC *and the isocost curves are* KK' *and* MM', *the optimal point is* B, *which means that all of the output should be made with process 1.*

that can be produced using a particular process. In such a case the answer is obvious: Produce the required volume of output with the process with the lowest unit cost. The moral is clear. Although relatively high-powered analytical devices like linear programming are often required to help solve large and complicated problems, nothing is gained by using them to handle problems that can just as readily be solved by simpler means. Students—and economists long out of school—sometimes become so infatuated with complex tools that they use them even when much simpler methods would do just as well.

EXAMPLE A.1

THE CHOICE OF PRODUCTION PROCESSES

A firm can use three processes, *A, B,* or *C,* to produce a particular good. To make one unit of the good, process *A* requires 2 hours of labor and 1 hour of machine-time, process *B* requires 1.5 hours of labor and 1.5 hours of machine-time, and process *C* requires 1.1 hours of labor and 2.2 hours of machine-time. The firm must pay $3 per hour for labor and $2 per hour for machine-time, but it cannot use more than 120 hours of machine-time, since this is all that is available in the short run. If it has committed itself to produce 100 units of the product, how many units should it produce with process A?

SOLUTION

The following graph contains the isoquant corresponding to an output of 100 units of the product. U_A is the input combination if all 100 units are produced with process A; U_B is the input combination if all 100 units are produced with process B; and U_C is the input combination if all 100 units are produced with process C. The graph also contains isocost curves, which show the combinations of labor-time and machine-time that can be purchased for a certain amount. (Specifically, the isocost curves corresponding to expenditures of $600 and $780 are given.)

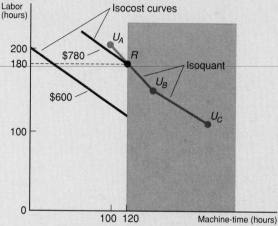

To minimize the cost of producing the 100 units of product, this firm should choose the point on the isoquant that is on the lowest isocost curve. However, the shaded area in the graph is not feasible since it requires more than 120 hours of machine-time. Thus the firm should choose the feasible point on the isoquant that is on the lowest isocost curve. Clearly, this is point R, where 120 hours of machine-time and 180 hours of labor are used. Since this point lies on the line segment between U_A and U_B, the firm should use process A to make some units of the product and process B to make the rest. Let Q_1 be the number of units that should be made with process A and Q_2 be the number that should be made with process B. Because process A uses 2 hours of labor per unit of product, process B uses 1.5 hours per unit of product, and a total of 180 hours should be used, it follows that

$$2Q_1 + 1.5Q_2 = 180.$$

And since $Q_1 + Q_2 = 100$ (since 100 units in all are produced),

$$2Q_1 + 1.5(100 - Q_1) = 180$$

$$.5Q_1 = 30$$

$$Q_1 = 60.$$

Thus the number of units of product produced with process A should be 60, and the number of units produced with process B should be 40 (since $Q_2 = 100 - Q_1$).

THE PRODUCTION OF AUTOMOBILES AND TRUCKS: ANOTHER ILLUSTRATION

Turning now to a more complex case, suppose that a firm produces two kinds of output, automobiles and trucks.[4] It has four kinds of facilities, each of which is fixed in capacity: automobile assembly, truck assembly, engine assembly, and sheet metal stamping. The problem is: How many automobiles and how many trucks should the firm produce? The profit per automobile or the profit per truck depends on the price of an automobile or a truck, the variable costs of producing an automobile or a truck, and the firm's fixed costs. Assume that the price and average variable cost of each product are constant; that is, they do not vary with output in the relevant range. Specifically, assume that the price of an automobile is $12,000, the price of a truck is $20,000, the average variable costs of an automobile are $11,700, and the average variable costs of a truck are $19,750.

The firm wants to maximize profits. Neglecting fixed costs (which will be the same regardless of what the firm does), the firm's profits (per hour) equal

$$\pi = 300Q_a + 250Q_t \qquad [\text{A.}10]$$

where Q_a is the number of automobiles produced by the firm per hour and Q_t is the number of trucks produced by the firm per hour. Since the firm receives $300 (that is, $12,000 − $11,700) above variable cost for each automobile that it produces, and since the firm receives $250 (that is, $20,000 − $19,750) above the variable cost for each truck it produces, the firm's profits (before deducting fixed costs) must equal $300 times the output of automobiles plus $250 times the output of trucks.

The constraints on the firm's decisions are the fixed capacities for automobile assembly, truck assembly, engine assembly, and sheet metal stamping. Table A.1 shows the proportion of each facility's total capacity required to produce one automobile or one truck. From this table, we can represent the constraints on the production of automobiles and trucks by the following inequalities:

$$0.5Q_a \leq 1 \qquad [\text{A.}11]$$

$$.04Q_t \leq 1 \qquad [\text{A.}12]$$

$$.02Q_a + .033Q_t \leq 1 \qquad [\text{A.}13]$$

$$.033Q_a + .025Q_t \leq 1 \qquad [\text{A.}14]$$

$$Q_a \geq 0;\ Q_t \geq 0. \qquad [\text{A.}15]$$

To begin with, Inequalities A.11 and A.12 represent the constraints imposed by existing automobile and truck assembly capacity. Since each automobile that is produced per hour takes up 5 percent of the automobile assembly capacity, it follows that .05 times the output per hour of automobiles must be

---

4. This is an adaptation of the well-known example found in R. Dorfman, "Mathematical or Linear Programming: A Nonmathematical Exposition," reprinted in E. Mansfield, *Microeconomics: Selected Readings*, 5th ed. Different numbers have been used to simplify the results.

TABLE A.1 Percent of Capacity of Each Division of Plant Required to Make a Car or a Truck (per hour)

Capacity	Car	Truck
Auto assembly	5	0
Engine assembly	2	$3\frac{1}{3}$
Sheet metal	$3\frac{1}{3}$	$2\frac{1}{2}$
Truck assembly	0	4

less than or equal to 1. Figure A.8 plots the firm's automobile production against its truck production. The vertical line at 20 automobiles per hour shows the effects of this constraint, since 20 is the maximum automobile output compatible with this constraint. Similarly, since each truck that is produced per hour takes up 4 percent of the truck assembly capacity, it follows that .04 times the output per hour of trucks must be less than or equal to 1. The horizontal line in Figure A.8 at 25 trucks per hour shows the effects of this constraint, since 25 is the maximum truck output compatible with this constraint.

Inequality A.13 states that no more than the existing capacity for engine assembly can be used. Since each automobile produced per hour takes up 2 percent of the existing engine assembly capacity and since each truck produced per hour takes up $3\frac{1}{3}$ percent of the existing engine assembly capacity, it follows that .02 times the output per hour of automobiles plus .033 times the output per hour of trucks, must be less than or equal to 1. Thus the line AB in Figure A.8 separates feasible combinations of automobile and truck outputs from

FIGURE A.8 Feasible Output Combinations *The feasible combinations of output of automobiles and trucks all lie within the area OEFGHI.*

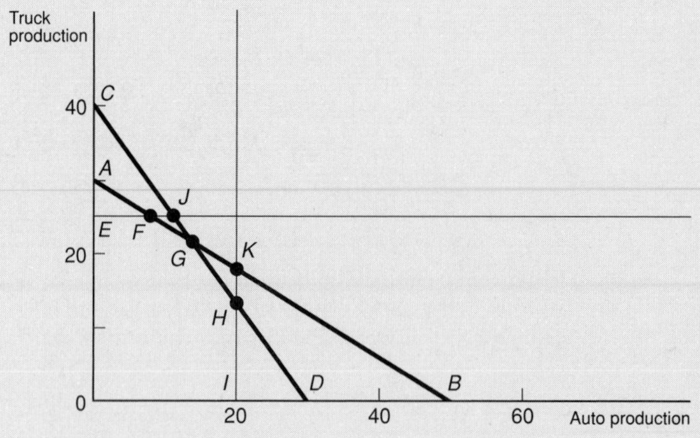

those that are beyond the existing engine assembly capacity. To be feasible, the combination of outputs must be on, or within, the triangle *OAB*.

Inequality A.14 states that no more than the existing sheet metal stamping capacity can be used. Since each automobile produced per hour takes up $3\frac{1}{3}$ percent of the available metal stamping capacity and since each truck produced per hour takes up $2\frac{1}{2}$ percent of the available metal stamping capacity, it follows that .033 times the output per hour of automobiles plus .025 times the output per hour of trucks, must be less than or equal to 1. Thus the line *CD* in Figure A.8 separates feasible combinations of automobile and truck outputs from those that are beyond the existing sheet metal stamping capacity. To be feasible, the combination of outputs must be on, or within, the triangle *OCD*.

Combining these constraints, the combination of output of automobiles and trucks must lie within the area *OEFGHI* in Figure A.8. Any point outside this area violates at least one of the constraints. For example, point *C* uses more engine assembly capacity and truck assembly capacity than is available, and point *K* uses more sheet metal stamping capacity than is available.

This is a linear programming problem. The objective function is given by Equation A.10, and the constraints are given in Inequalities A.11 to A.15. There are two processes, automobile production and truck production, each of which uses the four types of capacities in fixed (but different) proportions. The optimal solution to this problem can be found graphically by adding a family of isoprofit lines to Figure A.8. This is done in Figure A.9. Each black line shows the various combinations of automobile production and truck production that will result in the same total profit (gross of fixed costs). If π is the profit, the

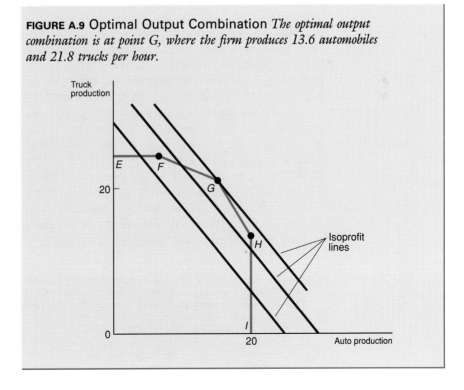

FIGURE A.9 Optimal Output Combination *The optimal output combination is at point G, where the firm produces 13.6 automobiles and 21.8 trucks per hour.*

equation for an isoprofit line is

$$Q_t = \frac{\pi}{250} - \frac{300}{250}Q_a. \qquad [A.16]$$

Obviously, one should find that point in the feasible area, *OEFGHI*, that lies on the highest isoprofit line, that is, the highest black line.

Figure A.9 shows that the optimal solution is at point *G*, where the firm produces 13.6 automobiles and 21.8 trucks per hour. With these output rates, the firm's profit (gross of fixed costs) is $9,547 per hour.[5]

Before leaving this example, it is important to note that this problem is almost exactly the same as the problem we solved with conventional theory in the appendix to Chapter 8. In both cases, the firm, taking the price of each product as given, is faced with the task of deciding how much of each product to produce. A comparison of Figure A.9 with Figure 8.20 (p. 254) shows the similarities quite clearly. In both cases, there are isoprofit lines plotted against a product transformation curve; the isorevenue line in Figure 8.20 is the same as an isoprofit line under the circumstances posited there. However, an important dissimilarity is that in the appendix to Chapter 8, we had to assume that someone handed us a production function; here we assume only that we are given the technological data in Table A.1.

COMPUTATIONAL EFFICIENCY AND THE COMPARISON OF SOLUTIONS AT EXTREME POINTS

Thus far we have emphasized the similarities between the conventional theory of production and production theory based on linear programming. Given that there are so many similarities, one might ask why there is any advantage in the linear programming approach. As we pointed out at the beginning of this Appendix, one important reason why the linear programming approach is used is that powerful computational techniques have been developed to find the numerical solutions to linear programming problems. These computational techniques make use of the following fact: The optimal solution will lie at one

Extreme points of the *extreme points*—or corners—of the feasible area.[6] This rule is consistent with the cases discussed in the previous paragraphs. For example, in Figure A.9, the optimal point, *G*, was an extreme point of the feasible area *OEFGHI;* and in Figure A.6, the optimal point *Y*, was an extreme point of the feasible area *OXYZ*. This fact reduces very greatly the number of points that must be examined to find the optimal solution, since it shows that all one needs to bother with are the extreme points of the feasible area.

5. How can a firm produce 13.6 automobiles per hour? By producing 68 autos every 5 hours. In cases in which the solution must be composed of integers, an extension of linear programming called integer programming must be used. See W. Baumol, *Economic Theory,* Chapter 8. Note that it is easy to find the coordinates of *G* by making Inequalities A.13 and A.14 into equations and solving them simultaneously for Q_a and Q_t.

6. Of course, it sometimes happens that other points are as good (but not better than) any extreme point. See Harvey Wagner, *Principles of Operations Research,* 2d ed. (Englewood Cliffs, N.J.: Prentice-Hall, 1975).

To illustrate, consider Figure A.9. There are six extreme points of the feasible area *OEFGHI*. To find the optimal solution, we need only compute the profit (gross of fixed costs) at each of these points. At the origin O, profit obviously is zero. At E ($Q_a = 0$ and $Q_t = 25$), profit is \$6,250. At $I(Q_a = 20$ and $Q_t = 0$), profit is \$6,000. We must find the coordinates of the other three extreme points before we can compute the level of profit at them. To find the coordinates of F, we must make Inequalities A.12 and A.13 into equations and solve them simultaneously; to find the coordinates of G, we must make Inequalities A.13 and A.14 into equations and solve them simultaneously; and to find the coordinates of H, we must make Inequalities A.11 and A.14 into equations and solve them simultaneously. We find that point F is $Q_a = 8\frac{1}{3}$ and $Q_t = 25$, the result being that profit is \$8,750. Point G is $Q_a = 13.6$ and $Q_t = 21.8$, the result being that profit is \$9,547. Point H is $Q_a = 20$ and $Q_t = 13\frac{1}{3}$, the result being that profit is \$9,333$\frac{1}{3}$. Thus, on the basis of these few computations, we know that point G must be the optimal solution.

In problems where the number of processes and constraints are too large for the graphical analysis used in previous sections, this kind of comparison of extreme point or corner solutions may be employed to find the optimal solution. The *simplex method,* which may be used for this purpose, is a systematic procedure for comparing extreme point or corner solutions. Combined with the speed and capacity of modern computers, it can solve extremely large problems in a very short period of time. There is a large literature on the simplex method, much of it involving a good deal of mathematics.[7] For present purposes, it is only necessary to know of the existence and general nature of this method.

THE DUAL PROBLEM AND SHADOW PRICES

Linear programming can do more than just find an optimal production program, the objective discussed in previous sections of this chapter. It can also find values to be placed on particular resources or inputs. For example, one could carry out the programming problem concerning the production of automobiles and trucks, assuming that the firm had a small amount of additional engine assembly capacity. Then one could compare the maximum profit obtainable with the extra amount of engine assembly capacity with the maximum profit obtainable without it. The increase, if there is an increase, in maximum profit is, of course, a measure of the value of the extra amount of engine assembly capacity.

Although this method of finding the value of an extra unit of a particular input is perfectly correct, it is cumbersome. A very interesting characteristic of linear programming problems is that one can obtain such values without going through this cumbersome procedure. Every linear programming problem has a corresponding problem called its *dual.* (The original problem is called the *primal* problem.) If the primal is a maximization problem, the dual is a minimi-

---

7. For example, see G. Dantzig, *Linear Programming and Extensions* (Princeton, N.J.: Princeton University Press, 1963). In the 1980s, N. Karmarkar of American Telephone and Telegraph's research laboratories suggested an alternative algorithm that results in faster solutions of linear programming problems.

zation problem; if the primal is a minimization problem, the dual is a maximization problem. The solutions to the dual are *shadow prices,* the values we seek.

For example, the shadow price of each type of capacity (in the problem concerning the production of automobiles and trucks) tells us what would happen to the firm's profits if the company were somehow able to increase this type of capacity. Obviously, these shadow prices are of great practical importance. They show which types of capacity are bottlenecks, or effective constraints on output, since capacity that is underutilized receives a zero shadow price. More important, they indicate how much it would be worth to management to expand each type of capacity. A comparison can then be made between the extra profit due to expansion and the extra costs that must be incurred. If the costs are lower than the extra profits, as indicated by the shadow price, the expansion seems desirable. For example, if the firm producing automobiles and trucks can rent an additional 1 percent of engine assembly capacity at $100 an hour and if an extra 1 percent of such capacity would increase profits by $200, it would be well worth it to rent the extra capacity.[8]

APPLICATION OF LINEAR PROGRAMMING IN THE PETROLEUM INDUSTRY

Linear programming has been used in countless ways by many segments of industry and government. To illustrate the sorts of problems it has helped to solve, we present in this section one of its applications in the petroleum industry, which is composed of various phases: exploration, production, refining, and distribution and marketing. An integrated oil firm must explore in order to locate places where oil is most likely to be found. It must drill for oil, and refine it to produce gasoline and other products. It must transport the oil, both to and from the refinery. Finally, the oil and oil products enter the distribution system and are marketed by the firm. The petroleum industry is as large as it is complex. The international oil companies like Exxon, Texaco, and Mobil are among the giants of American industry.

Each phase of the petroleum business is full of unanswered problems and questions. The oil potentialities of a region can be explored in various ways. How should these ways be combined for maximum effectiveness? There are a number of different ways of planning and organizing production in an oil field. Which is best? A modern oil refinery is an extremely complex type of plant. What is the best way of operating it? And what do we mean by *best*? Of course, linear programming has not been able to solve all of these problems, but it has helped to solve some of them. For example, it has been useful in solving the following problem, which obviously is an important one to oil producers.

Consider the production phase of the petroleum industry. Suppose that a firm has a number of oil fields, or reservoirs, which are producing at various rates. The total production of the reservoirs must be adjusted to meet a commitment, such as keeping a pipeline full or a refinery supplied. An outside

8. See R. Dorfman, P. Samuelson, and R. Solow, *Linear Programming and Economic Analysis* (New York: McGraw-Hill, 1958).

source of crude oil also exists. Technological factors require that the production rates do not exceed certain levels. The profit per barrel of crude oil produced is given, as is the number of years the operation is to be run on this basis. The problem is to determine a schedule of production rates so that the profit over the entire period is a maximum.

This can be viewed as a linear programming problem. For simplicity, assume that the firm has only two reservoirs and that the firm is planning for only two years. The results can easily be extended to larger numbers of reservoirs and longer periods of time. Let Q_{11} be the number of barrels of crude oil produced from the first reservoir in the first year, Q_{12} be the number of barrels of crude oil produced from the first reservoir in the second year, Q_{21} be the number of barrels of crude oil produced from the second reservoir in the first year, and Q_{22} be the number of barrels of crude oil produced from the second reservoir in the second year. Let Q_1 be the number of barrels of crude oil purchased from the outside source in the first year, and Q_2 be the corresponding number in the second year.

The objective function is the total profit over the two years, which is

$$\pi = G_{11}Q_{11} + G_{12}Q_{12} + G_{21}Q_{21} + G_{22}Q_{22} + G_1Q_1 + G_2Q_2 \qquad [A.17]$$

where G_{11} is the profit per barrel of crude oil produced from the first reservoir in the first year, G_{12} is the profit per barrel of crude oil produced from the first reservoir in the second year, G_{21} is the profit per barrel of crude oil produced from the second reservoir in the first year, G_{22} is the profit per barrel of crude oil produced from the second reservoir in the second year, G_1 is the profit per barrel of crude oil obtained from the outside source in the first year, and G_2 is the profit per barrel of crude oil obtained from the outside source in the second year.

The constraints are as follows. First, there are certain maximum levels of production. Thus

$$Q_{11} \leq Q_{11}^* \qquad [A.18]$$

$$Q_{12} \leq Q_{12}^* \qquad [A.19]$$

$$Q_{21} \leq Q_{21}^* \qquad [A.20]$$

$$Q_{22} \leq Q_{22}^* \qquad [A.21]$$

where Q_{11}^* is the maximum production level of the first reservoir in the first year, Q_{12}^* is the maximum production level of the first reservoir in the second year, Q_{21}^* is the maximum production level of the second reservoir in the first year, and Q_{22}^* is the maximum production level of the second reservoir in the second year.[9]

Second, the total production from the two reservoirs in each year plus the amount purchased from the outside source must equal the commitment for that

9. See W. Garvin, H. Crandall, J. John, and R. Spellman, "Applications of Linear Programming in the Oil Industry," reprinted in part in E. Mansfield, *Managerial Economics and Operations Research,* 5th ed. This section is based largely on their paper. The model in the text is simplified in various respects to make it more easily comprehensible to students. In particular, the constraints in Inequalities A.18 to A.21 are not the only ones that were actually used. But this should make little difference in this context.

year. That is,

$$Q_{11} + Q_{21} + Q_1 = M_1 \qquad [A.22]$$

$$Q_{12} + Q_{22} + Q_2 = M_2 \qquad [A.23]$$

where M_1 is the commitment for the first year and M_2 the commitment for the second year. Also, $Q_{11}, Q_{12}, Q_{21}, Q_{22}, Q_1$, and Q_2 must be nonnegative.

Using linear programming, this problem can be solved to determine the values of $Q_{11}, Q_{12}, Q_{21}, Q_{22}, Q_1$, and Q_2 that maximize the firm's profits. The Magnolia Petroleum Company and the Arabian American Oil Company have done a considerable amount of work on this problem, using a simple model like that described above and more complicated variants of this model. The results have been useful to these companies and others in the industry.[10]

Summary

1. Linear programming is the most famous of the mathematical programming methods that have come into existence since World War II. It is a technique that allows decision-makers to solve maximization and minimization problems when there are certain constraints that limit what can be done.
2. It is useful to look at production decisions from the programming point of view because, unlike conventional theory, it does not take the production function as being given to the economist before he or she attacks the problem. Also the programming analysis is easier to apply in many respects, and powerful computational techniques are available to obtain solutions.
3. Linear programming views the technology available to the firm as being a finite number of processes, each of which uses inputs in fixed proportions. The firm has a certain amount of each of the inputs at its disposal. Each unit of output resulting from a particular process yields the firm a certain amount of profit; this amount of profit varies from process to process. Knowing the profit to be made from a unit of output from each process and bearing in mind the limited amount of the various inputs at its command, the firm is visualized as attempting to determine the output from each process that will maximize profit.
4. To illustrate the use of linear programming, we discussed a case in which a hypothetical textile firm had to choose which combination of a number of alternative processes to use, given that it has only a limited amount of certain inputs. We solved the problem by graphical techniques. Isoprofit curves were constructed and superimposed on a diagram showing the feasible input combinations, and the point was chosen that, among those that were feasible, was on the highest isoprofit curve. In addition, we considered a variant of this problem in which the firm is no longer constrained by limitations on inputs.
5. Turning to a more complex case, we discussed the problem of a firm that produces more than one product and has various fixed facilities which set limits on the amount of each product that can be produced. The problem is to determine the optimal combination of outputs of the two products. This problem too was solved by graphical means, with isoprofit lines superimposed on a diagram showing feasible output combinations. In addition, in the context of this

10. Ibid. As presented above, the problem is, of course, much simpler than the one dealt with by these companies. (As it stands, it can be solved in an elementary way.) For present purposes, it seemed wise to strip it down to its simplest form.

example, we discussed the fact that the optimal solution of a linear programming problem will lie at one of the extreme points or corners of the feasible area.

6. Every linear programming problem has a corresponding problem called its dual; the original problem is called the primal problem. If the primal is a maximization problem, the dual is a minimization problem; if the primal is a minimization problem, the dual is a maximization problem. In the example concerning the optimal combination of outputs of two products, whereas the primal looked for optimal output rates for the two products, the dual seeks to impute values to the fixed facilities. These imputed values, or shadow prices, are very useful, since they show what would happen to the firm's profits if the company somehow were able to increase each type of capacity.

1. A family is composed of a husband and wife. The husband needs 3,000 calories per day and the wife requires 2,000 calories per day. The doctor says that these calories must be obtained by eating not less than a certain amount of fats and a certain amount of proteins. The family wants to minimize its food bill, but it does not want to violate the doctor's orders. Is this a linear programming problem? If so, what are the objective function and the constraints?

2. Describe various ways in which linear programming might be used in your own university. What are some of the most important problems in applying it to university problems?

3. Suppose that a firm's product transformation curve is as follows:

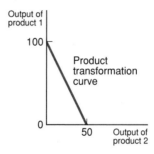

If the price of a unit of product 1 equals the price of a unit of product 2, draw several isorevenue lines in this graph. What is the optimal amount of each product that the firm should produce? Is this a point where an isorevenue line is tangent to the product transformation curve? Is this essentially the same problem as that analyzed in Figure A.9?

4. In the previous question, is the optimal point at an extreme point of the feasible area?

5. In Example A.1, suppose that the firm can use more than 120 hours of machine-time. Under these circumstances, how many units should it produce with process A? process B? process C?

6. Suppose that the wage rate for labor is $7.00 per hour, not $6.00 per hour, as assumed in the problem on p. A9–A10. Which of the three processes (or what combination of them) should be used to produce the 400 batches per week of finished cotton cloth? (The linear programming problem is given in Equations A.7, A.8, and A.9.)

7. In a production process, there are two inputs, machine-hours of finishing capacity and hours of labor. If there are at most 2,000 machine-hours and 200 labor-hours available per week, draw the set of feasible input combinations in a graph.

8. In Example A.1, draw the ray corresponding to process A. Is it parallel to the ray corresponding to process B?

GLOSSARY

GLOSSARY OF TERMS

Alternative cost The value of what particular resources could have produced had they been used in the best alternative way; also designated as opportunity cost.

Arc elasticity of demand If P_1 and Q_1 are the first values of price and quantity demanded, and P_2 and Q_2 are the second set, the arc elasticity equals $-(Q_1 - Q_2)\,(P_1 + P_2) \div (P_1 - P_2)\,(Q_1 + Q_2)$.

Asymmetric information In some markets, all participants do not have the same information. For example, in the market for used cars, sellers frequently have better information regarding the quality of a used car than do prospective buyers.

Average cost Total cost divided by output. It is also called average total cost.

Average fixed cost Total fixed cost divided by output.

Average product Total output divided by the quantity of input.

Average variable cost Total variable cost divided by output.

Beta A measure of the nondiversifiable risk attached to a stock, it shows how sensitive the stock's return is to changes in the return from all available stocks.

Bond yield The interest rate earned on a bond.

Break-even chart A chart showing how both total revenue and total cost vary with changes in the total number of units of a product that is sold. The break-even point is the minimum number that must be sold to avoid loss.

Budget line A line showing all combinations of quantities of good X and good Y the consumer can buy. Its slope equals -1 times the price of good X divided by the price of good Y.

Bundling A marketing technique whereby a firm that sells two products requires customers who buy one of them to buy the other as well.

Capital Equipment, buildings, inventories, raw materials, and other nonhuman producible resources that contribute to the production, marketing, and distribution of goods and services.

Capitalism A type of economic system that depends on the price system to answer the basic economic questions: What is produced? How is it produced? Who gets how much? What should be the rate of economic growth?

Cardinal utility Utility that is measurable in a cardinal sense, like a person's weight or height (which means that the difference between two utilities, i.e., marginal utility, is meaningful). This is in contrast to ordinal utility, which is measurable in only an ordinal sense.

Cartel A form of market structure where there is an open and formal agreement among firms to collude.

Chance fork A fork (sometimes called a juncture or branching point) in a decision tree where chance controls the outcome.

Cobb-Douglas production function A production function where $Q = AL^{\alpha_1}K^{\alpha_2}M^{\alpha_3}$. In this equation, Q is the output rate, L is the quantity of labor, K is the quantity of capital, M is the quantity of raw materials, A, α_1, α_2, and α_3 are constants.

Collusion Agreements by firms with others in their industry with regard to price, output, and other matters.

Complements If goods X and Y are complements, the quantity demanded of X is inversely related to the price of Y.

Constant-cost industry An industry with a horizontal long-run supply curve; its expansion does not result in an increase or decrease in input prices.

Constant returns to scale If the quantities of all inputs are increased by the same percentage, and if as a result output increases by the same percentage, there are constant returns to scale.

Consumer's surplus The maximum amount that the consumer would pay for a particular good or service less the amount that he or she actually pays for it.

Contestable market A market in which entry is absolutely free and exit is absolutely costless. The essence of contestable markets is that they are vulnerable to hit-and-run entry.

Contract curve The locus of points where the marginal rates of substitution are the same for both consumers (in exchange between consumers) or the locus of points where the marginal rates of technical substitution are the same for both producers (in exchange between producers).

Corner solution Case where the budget line reaches the highest achievable indifference curve at a point along an axis. (Analogous cases occur in the theory of production too.)

Cross elasticity of demand The percentage change in the quantity of good X resulting from a 1 percent change in the price of good Y.

Decision fork A fork (sometimes called a juncture or branching point) in a decision tree where the decision-maker is in control of the outcome.

Decreasing-cost industry An industry with a negatively sloped long-run supply curve; its expansion results in a decrease in its average cost.

Decreasing returns to scale If the quantities of all inputs are increased by the same percentage, and if as a result output increases by less than this percentage, there are decreasing returns to scale.

Demand curve A curve showing the amount of a product demanded at each price.

Diversifiable risk Risk that can be avoided by diversification.

Dominant firm In an oligopolistic industry, a single large firm that sets the price, but lets the small firms in the industry sell all they want at that price.

Dominant strategy A strategy that is best for a player regardless of what the other player's strategy may be.

Duopoly A form of market structure where there are two sellers. The Cournot model, among others, is concerned with duopoly.

Economic efficiency A situation where all changes that harm no one and improve the well-being of some people have been carried out. Such a situation is economically efficient (or Pareto-efficient or Pareto-optimal).

Economic profit The difference between a firm's revenues and its costs, where the latter include the returns that could be gotten from the most lucrative alternative use of the firm's resources.

Economic region of production The input combinations where isoquants are negatively sloped. No profit-maximizing firm will operate at a point where the isoquant has a positive slope, since the marginal product of one or the other input must be negative.

Economic resource A scarce resource, which commands a nonzero price.

Economies of scope Economies resulting from the scope rather than the scale of the enterprise. They exist where it is less costly to combine two or more product lines in one firm than to produce them separately.

Endowed wealth The amount that the consumer could consume this year if he or she borrowed against all of next year's receipts.

Engel curve The relationship between the equilibrium quantity purchased of a good and the consumer's level of income. It was named after Ernst Engel, a nineteenth-century German statistician.

Equilibrium A situation where there is no tendency for change. For example, an equilibrium price is a price that can be maintained.

Excess capacity The difference between the minimum-cost output and the actual output in a long-run equilibrium. A famous and controversial conclusion of the theory of monopolistic competition is that firms under this form of market structure will tend to operate with excess capacity.

Expansion path The locus of points where the isoquants corresponding to various outputs are tangent to the isocost curves. (No inputs are fixed.)

Expected monetary value To determine the expected monetary value of a gamble, calculate the sum of the amount of money gained (or lost) if each outcome occurs times the probability of occurrence of the outcome.

Expected profit The long-term average value of profit, that is, the sum of the various possible levels of profit, after each is weighted by its probability of occurrence.

Expected value of perfect information The amount by which the expected monetary value increases as a consequence of the decision-maker's having access to perfect information. It is the maximum amount that the decision-maker should pay to obtain perfect information.

Explicit costs The ordinary expenses of the firm that accountants include, such as payroll costs and payments for raw materials.

External diseconomy An uncompensated cost to one person or firm resulting from the consumption or output of another person or firm.

External economy An uncompensated benefit to one person or firm resulting from the consumption or output of another person or firm.

First-mover advantages The advantages that accrue to the player who makes the first move in a game.

Fixed cost The total cost per period of time of the fixed inputs.

Fixed input A resource used in the production process (such as plant and equipment) whose quantity cannot be changed during the period under consideration.

Free resource A resource that is so abundant that it can be had for a zero price.

General equilibrium analysis An analysis that (in contrast to a partial equilibrium analysis) takes account of the interrelationships among various markets and prices.

Giffen's paradox A situation where the quantity demanded of a good is directly related to its price. This occurs when the substitution effect of a price change is not strong enough to offset an inferior good's income effect.

Implicit costs The alternative costs of using the resources owned by the firm's owner, such as his or her time and capital.

Income-compensated demand curve A curve showing how much of a good the consumer demands at each price, when the consumer's income is adjusted so that, regardless of the price, the original market basket can be purchased.

Income-consumption curve A curve connecting points representing equilibrium market baskets corresponding to all possible levels of the consumer's money income. Curves of this sort can be used to derive Engel curves.

Income effect The change in the quantity demanded of good X due entirely to a change in the consumer's level of satisfaction, all prices being held constant.

Income elasticity of demand The percentage change in quantity demanded resulting from a 1 percent change in consumer income, when prices are held constant.

Increasing-cost industry An industry with a positively sloped long-run supply curve; its expansion results in an increase in input prices.

Increasing returns to scale If the quantities of all inputs are increased by the same percentage, and if as a result output increases by more than this percentage, there are increasing returns to scale.

Indifference curve The locus of points representing market baskets among which the consumer is indifferent.

Inferior good A good where the income effect is such that increases in real income result in decreases in the quantity demanded.

Innovation An invention, when applied for the first time, is called an innovation.

Input Any resource used in the production process.

Interest rate The premium received by the lender one year hence if he or she lends a dollar for a year. If the interest rate equals r, he or she receives $(1 + r)$ dollars a year hence.

Intermediate good A good that is used to produce other goods and services.

Internal rate of return The interest rate that equates the present value of the net cash inflows from an investment project to the project's investment outlay.

Investment The process of creating new capital assets.

Isocost curve A curve showing the combinations of inputs that can be obtained for a fixed total outlay.

Isoprofit curve A curve showing all input combinations that can produce a given level of profit.

Isoquant A curve showing all possible (efficient) combinations of inputs that are capable of producing a certain quantity of output.

Isorevenue line A line showing all combinations of outputs of two commodities that result in the same total revenue.

Kinked demand curve A demand curve facing an oligopolist where there is a kink at the existing price, demand being more elastic for price increases than for price decreases.

Labor Human effort, physical or mental, used to produce goods and services.

Land Natural resources, including both minerals and plots of ground, used to produce goods and services.

Law of diminishing marginal returns According to this law, if equal increments of an input are added (and if the quantities of other inputs are held constant), the resulting increments of product will decrease beyond some point; that is, the marginal product of the input will diminish.

Law of diminishing marginal utility According to this law, as a person consumes more and more of a given commodity (the consumption of other commodities being held constant), the marginal utility of the commodity eventually will tend to decline.

Learning curve Relationship between a good's average cost and the producer's cumulative total output.

Limit pricing A form of pricing where price is set so as to bar entry. A limit price is one that discourages or prevents entry.

Linear programming A mathematical technique that permits decision-makers to solve maximization and minimization problems.

Long run The period of time in which all inputs are variable. The firm can change completely the resources it uses in the long run.

Marginal cost The addition to total cost resulting from the addition of the last unit of output.

Marginal cost pricing A pricing rule whereby firms or government-owned enterprises set price equal to marginal cost.

Marginal expenditure curve A curve showing the additional cost to the firm of increasing its utilization of input X by one unit.

Marginal product The addition to total output due to the addition of the last unit of an input (when the quantity of other inputs is held constant).

Marginal rate of product transformation The negative of the slope of the product transformation curve.

Marginal rate of substitution The number of units of good Y that must be given up if the consumer, after receiving an extra unit of good X, is to maintain a constant level of satisfaction.

Marginal revenue The addition to total revenue due to selling one more unit of the product.

Marginal revenue product The increase in total revenue due to the use of an additional unit of input X. It equals the marginal product of input X times the firm's marginal revenue.

Marginal utility The additional satisfaction (that is, utility) derived from an additional unit of a commodity (when the levels of consumption of all other commodities are held constant).

Market A group of firms and individuals in touch with each other in order to buy or sell some good.

Market demand curve A curve that shows the relationship between a product's price and the quantity of it demanded in the entire market.

Market demand schedule A table that shows the relationship between a product's price and the quantity of it demanded in the entire market.

Market period A period of time during which the quantity that is supplied of a good is fixed.

Market structure Four general types of market structure are perfect competition, monopoly, monopolistic competition, and oligopoly. The structure of a market depends on the number of buyers and sellers, as well as the extent of product differentiation and other factors.

Market supply schedule A table showing the quantity of a good that would be supplied at various prices.

Markup A percentage (or absolute) amount added to a product's estimated average (or marginal) cost to obtain its price; this amount is meant to include costs that cannot be allocated to any specific product and to provide a return on the firm's investment.

Microeconomics The part of economics dealing with the economic behavior of individual units such as consumers, firms, and resource owners (in contrast to macroeconomics, which deals with the behavior of economic aggregates like gross national product).

Minimum efficient size of plant The smallest size of plant where long-run average cost is at or close to its minimum value.

Model A theory based on assumptions that simplify and abstract from reality, from which predictions or conclusions about the real world are deduced.

Money income Income of the consumer measured in actual dollar amounts per period of time.

Monopolistic competition A market structure where there are many sellers of differentiated products, where entry is easy, and where there is no collusion among sellers.

Monopoly A market structure where there is only one seller of a product. Public utilities often are examples.

Monopsony A market structure where there is only a single buyer. A firm that hires all the labor in a company town is an example.

Moral hazard A person's or firm's behavior may change after buying insurance so as to increase the probability of theft, fire, or other loss covered by the insurance.

Multinational firm A firm that invests in other countries, and produces and markets its products abroad.

Multiplant monopoly A monopolist that owns and operates more than one plant, and that must determine the output for each of its plants.

Multiproduct firm A firm that produces more than one product. For example, Du Pont produces a wide variety of chemical, oil, and other products.

Nash equilibrium An equilibrium in game theory where, given that every other player's strategy is what it is, each player has no reason to change his or her own strategy.

Natural monopoly An industry where the average cost of production reaches a minimum at an output rate large enough to satisfy the entire market; thus competition cannot be sustained and one firm becomes the monopolist.

Neumann-Morgenstern utility function A function showing the utility that a decision-maker attaches to each possible outcome of a gamble; it shows the decision-maker's preferences with regard to risk.

Nondiversifiable risk Risk that cannot be reduced by diversification.

Nonprice competition Rivalry among firms based on the use of advertising and other marketing weapons, as well as on the variation in product characteristics due to research and development and styling changes.

Normal goods Goods that experience increases in quantity demanded in response to increases in the consumer's real income.

Oligopoly A market structure where there are only a few sellers of products that can be identical or differentiated. Examples are the markets for computers or petroleum.

Oligopsony A market structure where there are a few buyers.

Opportunity cost The value of what particular resources could have produced if they had been used in the best alternative way; also designated as alternative cost.

Optimal input combination The combination of inputs that is economically efficient or that maximizes profit (that is, is optimal from a profit-maximizing firm's point of view).

Ordinal utility Utility that is measurable in an ordinal sense, which means that a consumer can only rank various market baskets with respect to the satisfaction they give him or her.

Pareto criterion A criterion to determine whether a particular change is an improvement; according to this criterion, a change that harms no one and improves the lot of some people (in their own eyes) is an improvement.

Partial equilibrium analysis An analysis assuming (in contrast to a general equilibrium analysis) that changes in price in a particular market can occur without causing significant changes in price in other markets.

Pecuniary benefits Benefits arising because of changes in relative prices that come about as the economy adjusts to a project (as distinguished from real benefits, which augment society's welfare).

Perfect competition A market structure where there are many sellers of identical products, where no one buyer or seller has control over price, where entry is easy, and where resources can switch readily from one use to another. Examples having many of the characteristics of perfectly competitive markets include many agricultural markets.

Predatory pricing The practice of setting price at a low level in order to drive a rival firm out of business.

Present value rule The rule that a firm should carry out any investment project with a positive present value.

Price ceiling A government-imposed maximum for the price of a particular good. For example, New York City's rent controls impose a ceiling on rents.

Price-consumption curve A curve connecting the various equilibrium points corresponding to market baskets chosen by the consumer at various prices of a commodity.

Price discrimination The practice whereby one buyer is charged more than another buyer for the same product.

Price elastic The demand for a product if its price elasticity of demand exceeds 1.

Price elasticity of demand The percentage change in quantity demanded resulting from a 1 percent change in price (by convention, always expressed as a positive number).

Price elasticity of supply The percentage change in quantity supplied resulting from a 1 percent change in price.

Price floor A government-imposed minimum for the price of a particular good. For example, federal farm programs impose floors for the prices of wheat and corn.

Price inelastic The demand for a product if its price elasticity of demand is less than 1.

Price leader A firm in an oligopolistic industry that sets a price that other firms are willing to follow.

Price system A system whereby each good and service has a price, and which in a purely capitalistic economy carries out the basic functions of an economic system (determining what will be produced, how it will be produced, how much of it each person will get, and what the nation's growth of per capita output will be).

Principal-agent problem The problem that arises because managers or workers may pursue their own objectives, even though this reduces the profits of the owners of the firm. The managers or workers are agents who work for the owners, who are the principals.

Prisoners' dilemma A situation in which two persons (or firms) would both do better to cooperate than not to cooperate, but where each feels it is in his or her interests not to do so; thus each fares worse than if they cooperated.

Private cost The expense incurred by the individual user to obtain the use of a resource.

Probability The proportion of times that a particular outcome occurs over the long run. For example, if a die is thrown many, many times, and if it comes up a 1 on $\frac{1}{6}$ of the times, the probability of its coming up a 1 is $\frac{1}{6}$.

Process A way of using inputs to produce one or more outputs. In linear programming, each process can be described by a set of technical coefficients that shows the amount of each input that is needed to produce one unit of output.

Product transformation curve A curve showing the various combinations of quantities of two products that can be produced with a given amount of resources.

Production function The relationship between the quantities of various inputs used per period of time and the maximum amount of output that can be produced per period of time.

Profit The difference between a firm's revenue and its costs.

Public good A good that is nonrival and nonexclusive. By nonrival, we mean that the marginal cost of providing the good to an additional consumer is zero. By nonexclusive, we mean that people cannot be excluded from consuming the good (whether or not they pay for it).

Quasi-rent A payment to an input in temporarily fixed supply. For example, in the short run, a firm's plant cannot be altered, and the payments to this and other fixed inputs are quasi-rents.

Ray A line that starts from some point and goes off into space. If capital is on one axis, and labor is on the other, a ray from the origin describes all input combinations where the capital-labor ratio is constant.

Reaction curve A curve showing how much one duopolist will produce and sell, depending on how much it thinks the other duopolist will produce and sell.

Real benefits Benefits that augment society's welfare (as distinguished from pecuniary benefits, which arise because of changes in relative prices that come about as the economy adjusts to a project).

Rent The return paid to an input that is fixed in supply.

Ridge lines Lines (on a graph with capital on one axis and labor on the other axis) between which are included all input combinations that would be chosen by a profit-maximizing firm.

Risk A situation where the outcome is not certain, but where the probability of each possible outcome is known or can be estimated.

Saving When a consumer refrains from consuming part of the goods he or she has, this is saving.

Second-degree price discrimination A monopolist charges a different price, depending on how much the consumer purchases, thus increasing its revenue and profit.

Selling expenses The expenses of advertising and distributing a product and of trying to convince potential customers that they should buy it.

Short run A period of time in which some of the firm's inputs (generally its plant and equipment) are fixed in quantity.

Social cost The cost to society of producing a given commodity or taking a particular action. This cost may not equal the private cost.

Static efficiency Efficiency when technology and tastes are fixed. If departures from static efficiency result in a faster rate of technological change and productivity increase, they may lead to a higher level of consumer satisfaction than if the conditions for static efficiency are met.

Strategic move A move that influences the other person's choice in a manner favorable to one's self, by affecting the other person's expectations of how one's self will behave.

Substitutes If goods X and Y are substitutes, the quantity demanded of X is directly related to the price of Y.

Substitution effect The change in the quantity demanded of a good resulting from a price change when the level of satisfaction of the consumer is held constant.

Supply curve A curve that shows how much of a product will be supplied at each level of the product's price.

Target return A desired rate of return that a firm hopes to achieve by means of markup pricing.

Technological change New ways of producing existing products, new designs enabling the production of new products, and new techniques of organization, marketing, and management.

Technology Society's pool of knowledge regarding how goods and services can be produced from a given amount of resources.

Third-degree price discrimination A situation where a monopolist sells a good in more than one market, where the good cannot be transferred from one market and resold in another, and where the monopolist can set different prices in different markets.

Tit for tat A strategy in game theory where each player does on this round what the other player did on the previous round.

Total cost The sum of a firm's total fixed cost and total variable cost.

Total cost function Relationship between a firm's total cost and its output.

Total fixed cost A firm's total expenditure on fixed inputs per period of time.

Total revenue A firm's total dollar sales volume per period of time.

Total utility A number representing the level of satisfaction that a consumer derives from a particular market basket.

Total variable cost A firm's total expenditure on variable inputs per period of time.

Transaction cost The cost of bringing buyers and sellers together, of contracting, and of obtaining information concerning the market.

Transferable emissions permits Permits to generate a certain amount of pollution, limited in number, that are allocated among firms and that can be bought or sold.

Two-part tariff A pricing technique where the consumer pays an initial fee for the right to buy the product as well as a usage fee for each unit of the product that he or she buys.

Tying A marketing technique whereby a firm producing a product that will function only if used in conjunction with another product requires its customers to buy the latter product from it, rather than from alternative suppliers.

Unitary elasticity A price elasticity of demand equal to 1.

Utility A number that represents the level of satisfaction that the consumer derives from a particular market basket is the utility attached by the consumer to this market basket.

Utility-possibility curve A curve showing the maximum utility that one person can achieve, given the utility achieved by another person.

Value of marginal product The marginal product of an input (i.e., the extra output resulting from an extra unit of the input) multiplied by the product's price.

Variable cost The total cost per period of time of the variable inputs.

Variable input A resource used in the production process whose quantity can be changed during the particular period under consideration.

Winner's curse If a number of bids are made for a particular piece of land (or other good or asset), and if the bidders' estimates of the land's value are approximately correct, on the average, the highest bidder is likely to pay more for the land than it is worth, if each bidder bids what he or she thinks the land is worth.

Chapter 1

1) Some of the factors influencing output per employee are the quality of management, the dedication and quality of the employees, the nature and level of the technology used, and the extent and quality of the capital used.

3) (a) The amount of cigarettes bootlegged into a particular state depends on this state's tax rate relative to that of its neighboring states. If a state's tax rate is much higher than that of its neighbors, bootleggers can make money by bringing cigarettes into this state. Also, the amount bootlegged into a particular state depends on the cost of transporting the cigarettes. The higher the cost per mile of transporting a truckload of cigarettes, the smaller the distance it is profitable to take them. (b) No. Florida's loss from tax evasion was over 15 percent of that in all states, which is disproportionately large. Thus its tax rate would be expected to have been higher than that of neighboring states (which in fact is true). (c) Since its loss from tax evasion increased (while that in other states decreased) during 1975–79, one would expect that its tax increased relative to that in neighboring states. In fact, it increased its tax by 3 cents per pack. (d) Yes. The cost of transporting the cigarettes increased.

5) No, because most of the disagreements stem from differences in ethical and political views.

7) No. This is the so-called fallacy of composition.

9) Yes, because the latter statements reflect the value judgments of the economist.

11) The price of medical care will tend to rise if the quantity of medical care demanded exceeds the quantity supplied. You could construct a model to show how Medicare and Medicaid affected the quantity of medical care demanded and the quantity supplied. Models of this sort are taken up in Chapter 2.

Chapter 2

1) (a) According to the economic consultant's demand curve, about 60,000 tickets will be purchased if the price of a ticket is $400; about 70,000 will be purchased if the price is $200. Thus the arc elasticity of demand is

$$\frac{-(70,000 - 60,000)}{(70,000 + 60,000)/2} \div \frac{(200 - 400)}{(200 + 400)/2} = 0.23.$$

This is quite different from Verleger's finding (that the price elasticity is 0.67). (b) Such an increase in price would reduce the *quantity of tickets demanded,* but it would *not* shift the demand curve. In other words, there would be a *movement along* the demand curve from a point corresponding to the old price to a point corresponding to the new price, but no *shift* in the demand curve. (c) Yes, it may shift it to the left, because fewer people will travel between these two cities for vacations and recreation, and because business travel may also be curtailed. (d) No, but it does affect the supply curve, which is shifted to the left.

3) Since the quantity supplied (Q_S) must equal the quantity demanded (Q_D), we have two equations to be solved simultaneously:

$$120 - 3Q_D = 5Q_S$$
$$Q_D = Q_S$$

Letting quantity equal Q, it follows that

$$120 - 3Q = 5Q$$
$$120 = 8Q$$
$$15 = Q.$$

Since $P = 5Q$, it follows that $P = 75$. Thus the equilibrium price is 75 cents and the equilibrium quantity is 15 million pounds per year.

5)

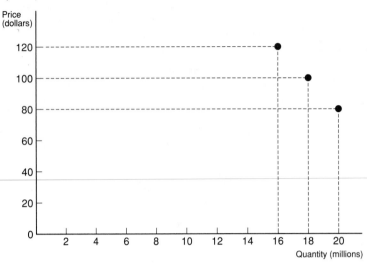

(a) $\eta = -\dfrac{(20 - 18)}{(20 + 18)/2} \div \dfrac{(80 - 100)}{(80 + 100)/2} = 0.47.$

(b) $\eta = -\dfrac{(18 - 16)}{(18 + 16)/2} \div \dfrac{(100 - 120)}{(100 + 120)/2} = 0.65.$

7) $100. Excess demand. Excess supply.

9) With the excise tax, the supply curve is

Price (dollars)	Quantity supplied (millions)
100	14
120	16
140	18
160	19

Thus the equilibrium price of a camera is $120, since at this price the quantity supplied equals the quantity demanded. If the government sets a price ceiling of $100, there will be a shortage of 4 million cameras per year, since the quantity demanded will equal 18 million while the quantity supplied will equal 14 million.

11) From Question 3,

$$P = 120 - 3Q_D$$

or

$$3Q_D = 120 - P$$

$$Q_D = 40 - 1/3\, P.$$

Also, $Q_S = 1/5\ P$. Thus, if $P = 80$, $Q_D = 40 - 80/3 = 13\frac{1}{3}$, and $Q_S = 80/5 = 16$. Consequently, $Q_S - Q_D = 16 - 13\frac{1}{3} = 2\frac{2}{3}$, which means that the resulting surplus equals $2\frac{2}{3}$ million pounds per year. To reduce this surplus, the government could attempt to reduce the amount of cantaloupes produced by farmers or expand the demand for cantaloupes.

Chapter 3

1) $1,000, since the budget line intersects the vertical axis at 20. $Q_A = 20 - 0.5Q_B$, where Q_A is the quantity consumed of good A and Q_B is the quantity consumed of good B. -0.5. It must be $1,000 \div 40$, or $25. 0.5.

3) 1. It does not vary at all, at least in this range. No.

5) Martin will be better off and will consume less bread. Because the $50 gift enables him, despite the price increase, to buy as much bread (and the other good) as he did before the price increase, the new budget line (after the price increase and gift) goes through point A, which corresponds to the old market basket Martin purchased. (See the figure below.) The new equilibrium market basket (point B) is on a higher indifference curve than point A, and contains less bread than point A.

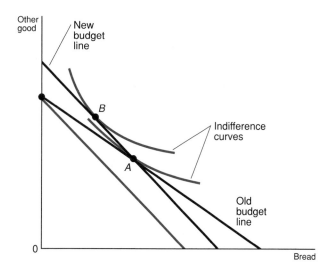

7) No. Los Angeles, because the price of a pear divided by the price of an apple is higher in Los Angeles.

9) He should set the ratio of the marginal utility of good X to its price equal to the ratio of the marginal utility of good Y to its price. If he buys 5 units of good X and 1 unit of good Y, the total amount spent is $1,000, and this condition is met, since for each good this ratio equals 1 util $\div 10$.

Chapter 4

1) (a) According to the diagram, a decrease in the price of good X from P_1 to P_2 results in an increase (from OA to OB) in the amount not spent on good X but spent on all other goods. This means that the consumer's expenditure on good X must have declined with a decrease in price, which implies that the consumer's demand for good X is price inelastic. (Recall p. 25.) (b) If this price-consumption curve were downward sloping, a decrease in the price of good X would result in a decrease in the amount not spent on good X. Thus the consumer's expenditure on good X must have increased with a decrease in price, which implies that the consumer's demand for good X is price elastic. (Recall p. 24.)

3) (a) The loss is the area under the demand curve from 5 to 10 trips, which equals $6 + $4 + $3 + $2 + $1, or $16. (b) Once a family buys the permit, a trip to the lake is free. Thus, if it buys the permit, it will make 10 trips per year, as shown by the demand curve. The maximum amount that each family would pay for these 10 trips is the area under the demand curve from zero to 10 trips, which is $20 + $16 + $12 + $10 + $8 + $6 + $4 + $3 + $2 + $1, or $82. Since the maximum amount exceeds $75, each family would find it worthwhile to buy the permit. (c) The calculations assume that these indifference curves are parallel. That is, if we measure the number of trips along the horizontal axis and the amount of money for all other goods along the vertical axis, the vertical distance between any two indifference curves is assumed to be the same regardless of where along the horizontal axis one measures this distance. (Recall note 8 in Chapter 4.)

5) (a) Yes. (b) If all consumers are maximizing utility (and if the optimal point is a tangency point, not a corner solution), the marginal rate of substitution of telephone calls for newspapers must equal the price of a telephone call divided by the price of a newspaper. (c) Yes, it equals 25 ÷ 25, or 1.

7) Both part (b) and part (c) are true.

9) 3. Price elastic. Decrease.

11) (a) Yes. This tax would increase the price of gasoline relative to the price of the other good. Thus, since the slope of the budget line equals minus one times the price ratio, the slope would be changed by the tax. (b) Yes. This rebate would increase the amount of money that the consumer could spend on gasoline or the other good; in effect, the consumer's money income would increase. Thus, the consumer's budget line would shift upward; that is, its intercept (on both the horizontal and vertical axes) would increase.

Chapter 5

1) (a) A 1 percent increase in the price of electricity would cut electricity consumption by about 1.2 percent, because the price elasticity of demand is 1.2. A 6 percent increase in the price of natural gas would raise electricity consumption by about 1.2 percent, because the cross elasticity of demand is 0.2. Thus, if the price of natural gas were to increase by about 6 percent, this would offset the effect of the increase in electricity's price. (b) Based on the data in the table given on p. 131, a 10 percent increase in income seems to result in about a 1 percent increase in electricity consumption. Thus the income elasticity seems to be about 0.1, not 0.2, as reported by Chapman, Tyrell, and Mount. This discrepancy could be due to the fact that the inhabitants of this suburb regard electricity to be more of a necessity than do all Americans. (c) Both would be expected to be lower in the short run because consumers have less time to adapt to changes in income or price. In fact, Chapman, Tyrell, and Mount found both to be about 0.02 in the short run.

3) (a) There are a considerable number of important substitutes, notably plastics, aluminum, and concrete. For example, buildings and bridges formerly requiring structural steel can now use prestressed concrete. (b) No, because the demand curve for the output of a single firm (Bethlehem) is not the same as the demand curve for the output of the steel industry as a whole. In general, we would expect the demand curve for the output of a single firm to be more price elastic than the industry's demand curve, because the output of other firms in the industry can be substituted for the output of the firm in question. (c) If the demand for a firm's product is inelastic, this means that its price elasticity of demand, η, is less than 1. Based on Equation 5.3, it follows that, if η is less than 1, the firm's marginal revenue must be *negative*. Since marginal revenue is the change in total revenue attributable to the increase of one unit to sales, it follows that a *reduction* in the amount produced and sold by the firm would *increase* total revenue (because price would be raised enough to more than offset the smaller number of units sold). In a case of this sort, the firm could increase its profit by reducing its output (and raising its price). Why? Because profit equals total revenue minus

total cost, and a reduction in output would increase total revenue and reduce total cost (since it would cost less to produce fewer units). Consequently, a reduction in output would increase profit, which means that the firm is not currently maximizing its profit. (d) The cross elasticity of demand is positive because Bethlehem's steel and imported Japanese steel are substitutes.

5) Holding his income constant, the total amount he spends on Geritol is constant too; that is,

$$PQ = I$$

where P is the price of Geritol, Q is the quantity demanded by the consumer, and I is his income. Thus

$$Q = \frac{I}{P}.$$

Since I is held constant, this demand curve is a rectangular hyperbola, and the price elasticity of demand equals 1. Since $Q = I/P$, it follows that a 1 percent increase in I will result in a 1 percent increase in Q, when P is held constant. Thus the income elasticity of demand equals 1. Since Q does not depend on the price of any other good, the cross elasticity of demand equals zero.

7) Substitutes have a positive cross elasticity of demand. Thus cases (b) and (e) are likely to have a positive cross elasticity of demand.

9) It would indicate the extent to which fare increases would decrease subway travel. For example, if demand is price inelastic, fare increases would increase total revenue. Obviously this is an important fact.

11) Other factors—notably the general level of prices and incomes and the quality of the students—have not been held constant. Holding these factors—and the tuition rates at other universities—constant, it is almost surely untrue that large increases in tuition at this university would not cut down on the number of students demanding admission to the university.

13) The Engel curve shows the relationship between money income and the amount consumed of a particular commodity. If this relationship is a straight line through the origin, it follows that the amount consumed of this commodity is *proportional* to the consumer's money income. Thus a 1 percent increase in the consumer's money income results in a 1 percent increase in the amount consumed of this commodity. Consequently, the income elasticity of demand for this commodity equals 1.

Chapter 6

1) The complete table is

Number of units of variable input	Total output	Marginal product	Average product
3	90	Unknown	30
4	110	20	$27\frac{1}{2}$
5	130	20	26
6	135	5	$22\frac{1}{2}$
7	$136\frac{1}{2}$	$1\frac{1}{2}$	$19\frac{1}{2}$

3) Because of the law of diminishing marginal returns, the marginal product begins to decline at some point. If the marginal product exceeds the average product at that point, the marginal product can fall to some extent without reducing the average product. Only when it

falls below the average product will the average product begin to decrease. The marginal product can continue to fall without reducing the total product. Only when it falls below zero will the total product begin to decrease.

5) 1.04 percent.

7) Yes.

9) (a) Yes, since it seems to reduce the amount of grain and protein that must be used to produce 150 pounds of pork. However, this assumes that it has no negative effect on the quality of the pork and that it does not increase the amount of other inputs that must be used. (b) At each quantity of protein, curve B is steeper than curve A. In other words, the absolute value of its slope is greater. Thus the marginal rate of technical substitution of protein for grain is greater when Aureomycin is added than when it is not (when the quantity of protein is held constant).

Chapter 7

1) (a) The marginal cost is the extra cost of an additional flight in 1989. The fuel, wages, and other extra costs are included. (b) No, because some of these costs would be incurred regardless of whether the extra flight occurred. (c) There probably would be additional costs to raise safety levels.

3) The table is as follows:

Total fixed cost (dollars)	Total variable cost (dollars)	Average fixed cost (dollars)	Average variable cost (dollars)
50	0	—	—
50	20	50	20
50	50	25	25
50	70	$16\frac{2}{3}$	$23\frac{1}{3}$
50	85	$12\frac{1}{2}$	$21\frac{1}{4}$
50	100	10	20
50	110	$8\frac{1}{3}$	$18\frac{1}{3}$
50	115	$7\frac{1}{7}$	$16\frac{3}{7}$

Each value of marginal cost would increase by 50 percent.

5) (a) Its fixed cost equaled $182.1 million, because, when $Q = 0$, $C = 182.1$, according to the equation. (b) If U.S. Steel produced 10 million tons of steel, $Q = 10$. Thus $C = 182.1 + 55.73 (10) = 739.4$. This is total cost, not total variable cost. To obtain total variable cost, we subtract the fixed cost, 182.1, from 739.4, the result being $557.3 million. Since 10 million tons were produced, average variable cost was $557.3 million divided by 10 million, or $55.73 per ton. (c) If output increased by 1 ton, the equation indicates that total cost increased by $55.73. Thus marginal cost was $55.73 per ton. (d) No. Beyond some point, as output increased, marginal cost was bound to increase, because of the law of diminishing marginal returns. (See page 207 for further discussion of this point.) (e) This equation is not appropriate for present conditions, because it is based on the input prices and technology of the 1930s, not those of today. (f) No, because it is based on input prices and technology in the United States in the 1930s, not on those in Japan now.

7) (a) No, since no information is given concerning the way in which cost varies with output when capacity is held constant. (b) The steam reforming process using natural gas, since its cost is lowest. (c) Yes, because costs tend to fall as the scale of a plant increases. (d) Yes, the function shifted downward. In the early 1960s, it was not possible to produce ammonia for $16 a ton, as is evident from the graph.

9) 1,000 copies sold.

Chapter 8

1) Suppose that the equilibrium rent and quantity are P and Q respectively. If the rent is reduced by 1 percent, the quantity demanded will increase by 1 percent, which means that it will increase by $.01Q$. At the same time, the quantity supplied will fall by .5 percent, which means that it will fall by $.005Q$. Thus the difference between the quantity supplied and the quantity demanded will equal $.01Q + .005Q$, or $.015Q$. In other words, it will equal 1.5 percent of the equilibrium quantity.

3) (a) No. (b) Firms had to leave the textile industry, so that eventually the profit rate in cotton textiles would increase to the point where it approximated the profit rate in other industries. Also, the industry had to become more concentrated in the South, the exit rate being higher in the North than in the South. (c) Yes.

5) (a) No. This is the cost per acre, not the cost per bushel of corn produced. (b) If Mr. Webster could rent the land that he owns for $110 per acre, the alternative cost of using an acre of land he owns is $110. Thus, based on the concept of alternative cost, the cost of using his own land is the same as that of using rented land. (c) If each acre of land yields 120 bushels of corn, the cost per bushel of corn of fertilizers, herbicides, insecticides, fuel, seed, electricity, and labor equals ($41.84 + 2.76 + 5.50 + 18.00 + 16.50 + 15.00 + 15.00) ÷ 120, or 95.5 cents. Assuming that these inputs (and no others) are variable, average variable cost is 95.5 cents per bushel. Since the price of 80 cents is less than average variable cost, he should not produce any corn (unless, of course, he can somehow reduce his average variable cost by altering his output or by taking some other measures). (d) Since the price of $1.50 per bushel exceeds the average variable cost of 95.5 cents per bushel, he should produce corn, even though the price is less than average total cost.

7) (a) Less. The supply curve will be to the left of the one shown on p. 250. (b) Less. The supply curve will be to the left of the one shown on p. 250. (c) There commonly are substantial errors in estimates of this sort, if they are based on no actual operating experience. Many unanticipated problems can arise in operating new types of plants. (d) Because of the uncertainties cited in part (c), such an investment would clearly be risky. Thus less shale oil is likely to be produced than under riskless conditions.

9) The firm's marginal cost curve is

Output	Marginal cost (dollars)
0 to 1	10
1 to 2	12
2 to 3	13
3 to 4	14
4 to 5	15
5 to 6	16
6 to 7	17

(a) If the price is $13, the firm will produce 2 or 3 units. (b) 3 or 4 units. (c) 4 or 5 units. (d) 5 or 6 units. (e) 6 or 7 units.

11)
$$\eta_S = \frac{(8-7)}{(8+7)/2} \div \frac{(4-3)}{(4+3)/2} = 0.47.$$

13) A difference of about 3.24 percent.

Chapter 9

1) (a) One cannot tell, because the answer depends on the long-run (not the short-run) average cost curve. A firm is a natural monopolist if its long-run average cost reaches a minimum at an output rate that is big enough to satisfy the market at a price that is profitable. (b) Many natural monopolies—for example, telephone companies and electric-power producers—are privately owned, so it is by no means clear that government ownership is implied. (c) 4 million pieces, since this is the point where the average total cost curve intersects the demand curve. (d) First-class-mail, because it earns a profit. With respect to parcels, there is already considerable competition (from United Parcel Service, in particular). (e) More competition might prod the post office to increase its own efficiency.

3) (a) In the early 1950s, IBM seems to have been close to a monopoly, since it sold over 90 percent of the electronic data processing products and services in the United States. But during the 1960s and 1970s, its share of the market fell to about 50 percent and then to about 40 percent, according to its economists. Based on these data, they argued that IBM was not a monopolist. (b) Yes. If a firm has a large share (say 60 percent or more) of the market, and if there is evidence that the firm's dominant position resulted from its own policies (and particularly if some form of abuse can be shown), past experience indicates that it may be challenged under Section 2 of the Sherman Act. (c) Not necessarily. If the firm's large market share has been achieved by its own "superior skill, foresight, and industry," this can be an effective defense. (In fact, this was one of IBM's defenses.) The firm may argue that, if it were broken up, this would result in a slower rate of innovation and less efficiency. (d) One of the most important considerations is the cross elasticity of demand among products. One wants to include products that are closely substitutable (i.e., that have high cross elasticities of demand). (e) The narrower the definition of the market, the larger IBM's share is likely to be. Based on the government's definition, IBM's market share exceeded those shown in the table on p. 292. Clearly, it was consistent with the government's case to show that IBM's market share was high. (f) In 1981, the Justice Department ended the case on the grounds that it was "without merit."

5) The monopolist's total revenue, total cost, and total profit at each level of output are as follows:

Output	Total revenue (dollars)	Total cost (dollars)	Total profit (dollars)
5	40	20	20
6	42	21	21
7	42	22	20
8	40	23	17
9	36	24	12
10	30	30	0

Thus the optimal output is 6, which means that price should be $7.

7) Marginal revenue $= 100 - 2Q$.
Marginal cost $= 60 + 2Q$.
Consequently, $100 - 2Q = 60 + 2Q$
$$40 = 4Q$$
$$10 = Q.$$

That is, you should choose an output of 10 units.

9) $MR_1 = 160 - 16Q_1$
$MR_2 = 80 - 4Q_2$
$MC = 5 + (Q_1 + Q_2)$.

Therefore $160 - 16Q_1 = 5 + Q_1 + Q_2$
$80 - 4Q_2 = 5 + Q_1 + Q_2.$

Or $155 - 17Q_1 = Q_2$
$75 - 5Q_2 = Q_1.$

Thus $155 - 17[75 - 5Q_2] = Q_2$
$155 - 1275 + 85Q_2 = Q_2$
$84Q_2 = 1120$
$Q_2 = 13\frac{1}{3}.$

It should sell $13\frac{1}{3}$ units in the second market, and the price in this market should be $53\frac{1}{3}$.

$$Q_1 = 75 - 5Q_2$$
$$= 75 - 5(1120/84)$$
$$= 75 - \frac{5600}{84}$$
$$= 75 - 66\frac{2}{3}$$
$$= 8\frac{1}{3}.$$

It should sell $8\frac{1}{3}$ units in the first market, and the price in this market should be $93\frac{1}{3}$.

Chapter 10

1) (a) No. Entry does not seem to be free, and exit does not seem to be costless. (b) This shift in the long-run average cost curve occurred as a consequence of technological change. For example, on the closing line, 900 cans could be moved per minute in 1965, whereas about 1,500 cans per minute could be moved in the late 1970's. (c) Certainly, this shift in the long-run average cost curve was one of the factors responsible for the decrease in the number of firms. Because breweries had to get so much bigger, fewer of them were required.

3) Since $Q = 300 - P$, and the demand for the firm's output is $Q - Q_r$, it follows that the firm's demand curve is

$$Q_b = Q - Q_r = (300 - P) - 49P$$
$$= 300 - 50P,$$

or

$$P = 6 - 0.02Q_b.$$

Thus the firm's marginal revenue curve is $MR = 6 - 0.04 \, Q_b$. And since its marginal cost curve is $2.96Q_b$

$$6 - 0.04Q_b = 2.96 \, Q_b$$
$$Q_b = 2.$$

That is, your output level should be 2 million units.

Since $P = 6 - 0.02 \, Q_b$, and $Q_b = 2$, it follows that $P = 6 - 0.02(2) = 5.96$.

That is, the price should be $5.96 per unit.

Since $Q = 300 - P$, and $P = 5.96$, it follows that $Q = 300 - 5.96 = 294.04$.

That is, the industry output is 294.04 million units.

5) Whether or not it costs a great deal to distribute milk in other parts of New York, the competition from Farmland is likely to reduce prices, thus benefiting consumers. New York consumers should be able to buy goods (including milk) produced by workers outside New York.

7) They should set the marginal cost at one firm equal to the marginal cost at each other firm. If firm 1 produces 4 units, firm 2 produces 3 units, and firm 3 produces 4 units, the

marginal cost at each firm equals $30. Thus this seems to be the optimal distribution of output.

9) See pp. 304–6. No; it might, for example, induce consumers to buy the advertiser's product by means of misleading or erroneous claims.

11) (a) No. As shown in panel A in Question 11, the new marginal cost curve (EE') intersects the marginal revenue curve at an output of OQ, which means that the profit-maximizing price is OP_1, not OP_0. Thus, if the firm maximizes profit, it will increase its price to OP_1. (b) Its demand curve now is P_0VD', as shown in panel B in Question 11. In contrast to the situation before Congress acted, the firm now cannot sell anything at a price exceeding OP_0. Its marginal revenue curve now is P_0VR'. Since its demand curve is horizontal for outputs less than OQ_1, so is its marginal revenue curve. Its output now is OQ_1, since this is the output where the marginal revenue curve (P_0VR') intersects the new marginal cost curve (EE').

13) $15. No.

Chapter 11

1) (a) Strategy 2. Strategy I. (b) Strategy II. Strategy 1.

3) (a) Yes. Strategy 1. (b) Yes. Strategy II. (c) Firm C will choose strategy 1, and firm D will choose strategy II.

5) If firm A believes that firm B will produce Q_B units of output per month, its marginal revenue equals

$$100 - 8Q_A - 8Q_B.$$

To maximize its profit firm A will set its marginal revenue equal to its marginal cost, which is $4. Thus

$$100 - 8Q_A - 8Q_B = 4,$$

or

$$Q_A = 12 - Q_B.$$

7) No. One firm often can increase its profit without decreasing its rival's profit by the amount of its profit gain.

9) (a) The payoff matrix is as follows:

Possible strategies for the Miller Company	Possible strategies for the Morgan Company	
	Advertise	Do not advertise
Advertise	Morgan's profit: $2.5 million Miller's profit: $4 million	Morgan's profit: $2 million Miller's profit: $5 million
Do not advertise	Morgan's profit: $2 million Miller's profit: $2 million	Morgan's profit: $2.5 million Miller's profit: $3 million

(b) Miller has a dominant strategy (to advertise), but Morgan does not have a dominant strategy. (c) Yes. Both Miller and Morgan will advertise.

Chapter 12

1) (a) Such a graph is shown in panel A on p. A45. The budget line here is CD. To derive this budget line, note that a physician who devoted every hour in the week to leisure would receive no income from working. That there are 168 hours in a week explains why the budget line passes through point D. If the physician devotes no time to leisure, the amount of income received from working is OC (which equals $168W$, where W is the physician's hourly wage

rate). This explains why the budget line passes through point C. Note that the slope of the budget line equals -1 times the physician's hourly wage rate, because every extra hour devoted to leisure reduces the amount of income received from working by an amount equal to the hourly wage rate. Panel A also shows the physician's indifference curves. Given these indifference curves and the budget line, the physician will maximize utility by choosing OX hours of leisure and by obtaining OY dollars of income from working.

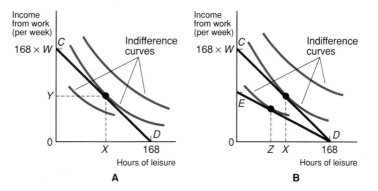

(b) A decrease in the physician's hourly wage rate reduces the amount that he or she can earn if no time is devoted to leisure from OC to OE in panel B. Thus, the budget line is no longer CD, but ED, and the physician will maximize utility by choosing OZ rather than OX hours of leisure. Since he or she is in the backward-bending portion of the supply curve, OZ is less than OX. (c) If the price elasticity of supply for physicians' services is negative, this does not appear to be true.

3) (a) Point B. 1,500 hours per year. (b) None. (c) The relation between income and leisure is now AC. Thus he will choose point D, and work $8,760 - 7,960 = 800$ hours per year. (d) No. It depends on the specific provisions of the negative income tax and on a worker's preferences (as reflected in the indifference curves).

5) No. It should set the marginal product of labor divided by \$5 equal to the marginal product of capital divided by \$6.

7) The value of the marginal product is shown in the following table.

Number of days of labor	Output	Marginal product	Value of marginal product (dollars)
0	0		
		8	40
1	8		
		7	35
2	15		
		6	30
3	21		
		5	25
4	26		
		4	20
5	30		

Thus, if the daily wage of labor is \$30, the firm should hire 2 or 3 days of labor.

9) The wage, P_L, will equal the price of the product, P, times the marginal product of labor, which equals

$$\frac{\delta Q}{\delta L} = 0.8L^{-.2}K^{.2} = \frac{0.8Q}{L}$$

Thus $P_L = \dfrac{0.8Q}{L} \cdot P$, which means that

$$\frac{P_L L}{PQ} = 0.8.$$

Since $P_L \cdot L$ equals the total wages paid by the firm and PQ equals its revenues, this completes the proof.

Chapter 13

1) (a) Based on the theory of monopsony, one might expect school districts that are the only buyers of teachers' services in a particular area to pay less than those that must compete with other school districts in the area. (b) If teachers could move costlessly to school districts outside the county, a school district that was the sole buyer of teacher's services within a county would have much less monopsonistic power, and would be less able to pay lower salaries than is now the case. (c) It will probably tend to increase teacher's salaries, because there will be more competition among school districts for teachers. (d) One major argument is that decentralization allows educational curricula to be tailored more closely to the differences among communities in preferences.

3) 3 or 4 units of labor, because labor's marginal revenue product is $12 when between 3 and 4 units of labor are used. To see this, note that total revenue is $128 when 3 units of labor are used, and $140 when 4 units of labor are used.

5)

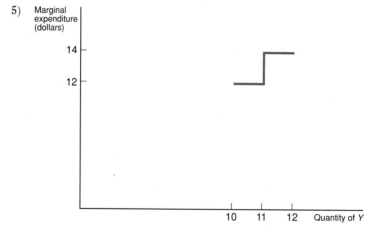

7) The supply curve for labor is shifted to the left, with the result that the price of labor will increase. There may be no effect on the demand curve for labor, unless employers are forced to hire more labor than they otherwise would have.

9) Because union contracts tend to introduce rigidity in wage structures.

11) This law makes it easier for unions to maintain high wages. The general public loses because the cost of federal construction projects is increased.

Chapter 14

1) (a) No, because fuel must be used to produce and transport the corn required to produce the ethanol. (b) Yes. Although the cost of a gallon of ethanol was 35 cents higher (that is, $1.20 minus 85 cents) than a gallon of gasoline, exemption from the federal gasoline tax was worth 40 cents per gallon and exemption from state taxes was often worth at least 40 cents more per gallon. Thus the tax exemptions more than offset the higher cost of production of ethanol. However, some very optimistic forecasts in the late 1970s of gasohol sales were not achieved. Gasohol would never displace regular gasoline completely, because as more and more gasohol is produced, the price of corn would be bid up, and eventually,

despite the tax exemptions, it would no longer be profitable to substitute more gasohol for regular gasoline. (c) Corn prices and the value of corn-producing land tend to rise. A general equilibrium analysis can handle these questions more adequately than a partial equilibrium analysis.

3) The quantity of lemon chicken might be measured along the horizontal axis; the quantity of sweet and sour pork might be measured along the vertical axis. The indifference curves of each person (A_1, A_2, A_3 for Joan; B_1, B_2, B_3 for John) might be inserted, as shown below.

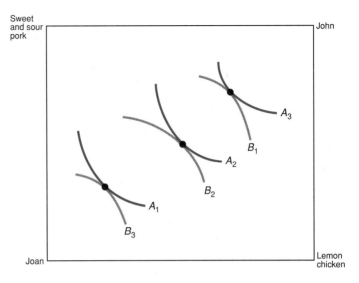

The optimal point would be on the contract curve connecting the dots.

Probably not, since he probably gets satisfaction from her well-being (and in the interest of courtship, one hopes that she feels the same way).

5) Point Y represents your pretrade position.

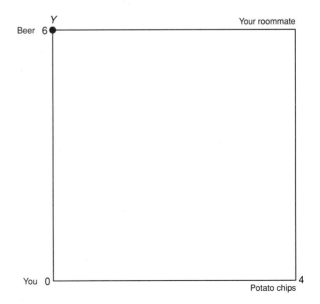

7) This trade would put her on her indifference curve 1, which is a higher indifference curve than that going through point Y. (To identify point Y, see the answer to Question 5.) Thus she should agree to this. This trade would put you on your indifference curve II, which is a higher indifference curve than that going through point Y. Thus the trade will make you better off.

9) (a) Yes. Yes. (b) Probably not. For example, relative to the price of substitutes, the price of this good may have risen. Thus the demand for this good might fall, and there might be a surplus of it.

Chapter 15

1) The output of the paper industry will be OQ_0, since this is the point where the demand and supply curves intersect. To determine the economically efficient output, we construct curve S_1S_1', which shows the marginal *social* cost of producing each level of output. This equals the marginal *private* cost (given by the supply curve) plus the marginal *external* cost of $5 per ton. Assume that a product's price can be regarded as a reasonable measure of the social value of an extra unit of output. Then, since the economically efficient level of output is the one where the marginal social value of an extra unit of output equals its marginal social cost, the efficient level of output must be OQ_1. Why? Because under these assumptions, the demand curve shows the marginal social value of an extra ton of output, and S_1S_1' shows the marginal social cost, so the efficient output level is at the point where the demand curve (showing marginal social value) intersects the S_1S_1' curve (showing marginal social cost).

3) This will result in a malallocation of resources because the marginal rate of technical substitution between any two inputs will *not* be the same for any two firms using water. For example, suppose that a farm (which pays a low water price) pays 10 times as much for an hour of unskilled labor as for 100 cubic feet of water, whereas a steel plant (which pays a high water price) pays 5 times as much for an hour of unskilled labor as for 100 cubic feet of water. Then the farm will choose the quantity of its inputs so that the marginal rate of technical substitution of labor for water is 10, whereas the steel plant will choose its inputs so that the marginal rate of technical substitution is 5 (see Chapter 7). Inputs are not allocated efficiently when marginal rates of technical substitution are unequal in this way. In general, we would expect farms to use too much water and steel mills to use too little. To get a better allocation, the price of water should be equal for all producers—and equal to its marginal cost.

5) No. Because, if the two consumers arrive at any point off the contract curve, they can find a superior point on the contract curve, in the sense that one of them can be made better off without making the other worse off.

7) The plane's landing at that time may delay large commercial jets and impose substantial costs (in terms of delay and inconvenience) on the passengers carried by these commercial aircraft. Increases in the landing fees paid by small private aircraft could help to eliminate such divergences.

9) An important problem is that $50 may mean more to Harry than $100 does to Tom. This makes money, together with the existing distribution of income, a measure of the relative strength of feeling of individuals.

Chapter 16

1) (a) Yes. Projects with benefit-cost ratios exceeding 1 seem worthwhile if the budget is variable. (b) No.

3) The Corps of Engineers included many kinds of benefits that the railroad consultants did not include, such as enhancement of waterfront land values. Also, the Corps of Engineers made a lower estimate of the costs. To some extent, as Prest and Turvey point out, the difference may be "due to the facts that the Corps likes to build canals and that the consultants were retained by the railroads."

5) 7 units of national defense.

7) It is not true that all public goods must be provided by the government. As pointed out in the text, some quantity of public goods may be provided privately, particularly if the number of people in the society is small. But the amount provided privately is likely to be less than the efficient amount.

9) No. According to Parkinson, the bureaucracy tends to grow, regardless of whether there is a decline in the amount of work it must perform.

11) If there is a sufficiently large number of firms and permits, a competitive market for the permits will develop. The price of a permit will tend to equal the marginal cost of reducing pollution by one ton, which will tend to be equalized among firms.

Chapter 17

1) (a) The present value of the costs and benefits is

$$-1.5 - \frac{3}{1.10} + \frac{1}{1.10^2} + \frac{1}{1.10^3} + \frac{1}{1.10^4} + \frac{1}{1.10^5} + \frac{1}{1.10^6} + \frac{1}{1.10^7},$$

which equals $-.27$ billions of dollars. Since the present value is negative, it should not be carried out. (b) If the interest rate is .05, the present value is

$$-1.5 - \frac{3}{1.05} + \frac{1}{1.05^2} + \frac{1}{1.05^3} + \frac{1}{1.05^4} + \frac{1}{1.05^5} + \frac{1}{1.05^6} + \frac{1}{1.05^7},$$

which equals .48 billions of dollars. Since the present value is positive, it should be carried out. (c) Because net costs occur early and net benefits occur late in the life of water projects. (d) The interest rate should be based on the alternative cost of public funds. That is, it should reflect the value of private alternatives forgone by the expenditure of public funds for water projects.

3) (a) The present value (in millions of dollars) was

$$-15 + \frac{2}{1.10} + \frac{2}{1.10^2} + \frac{2}{1.10^3} + \frac{2}{1.10^4} + \frac{2}{1.10^5} + \frac{2}{1.10^6} + \frac{2}{1.10^7} + \frac{2}{1.10^8} + \frac{2}{1.10^9},$$

This is equal to $-15 + 2(.9091 + .8264 + .7513 + .6830 + .6209 + .5645 + .5132 + .4665 + .4241) = -15 + 2(5.7590) = -3.482$ millions of dollars. (b) The present value would be

$$-20 + \frac{2}{1.10} + \frac{2}{1.10^2} + \frac{2}{1.10^3} + \frac{2}{1.10^4} + \frac{2}{1.10^5} + \frac{2}{1.10^6} + \frac{2}{1.10^7} + \frac{2}{1.10^8} + \frac{2}{1.10^9},$$

This is equal to $-20 + 2(.9091 + .8264 + .7513 + .6830 + .6209 + .5645 + .5132 + .4665 + .4241) = -20 + 2(5.7590) = -8.482$ millions of dollars. (c) Yes. Since its present value was negative, the investment was not worthwhile. (It decreased the firm's wealth.) The firm's analysts carried out the above calculations and recommended that the project be turned down.

5) (a) If the interest rate is 10 percent, the present value of the investment is

$$-\$100,000 - \frac{\$100,000}{1.10} - \frac{\$100,000}{(1.10)^2} - \frac{\$100,000}{(1.10)^3} - \frac{\$100,000}{(1.10)^4}$$

$$- \frac{\$100,000}{(1.10)^5} - \frac{\$100,000}{(1.10)^6} + \frac{\$15,000}{(1.10)^7}$$

$$+ \frac{\$15,000}{(1.10)^8} + \frac{\$15,000}{(1.10)^9} + \frac{\$15,000}{(1.10)^{10}}$$

$$+ \frac{\$200,000}{(1.10)^{11}} + \frac{\$700,000}{(1.10)^{12}} + \frac{\$700,000}{(1.10)^{13}}$$

$$+ \frac{\$700,000}{(1.10)^{14}} + \frac{\$700,000}{(1.10)^{15}} + \frac{\$700,000}{(1.10)^{16}}$$

$$+ \frac{\$700,000}{(1.10)^{17}} + \frac{\$700,000}{(1.10)^{18}} + \frac{\$700,000}{(1.10)^{19}}.$$

This is equal to $-$ \$100,000 (1 + .9091 + .8264 + .7513 + .6830 + .6209 + .5645) + \$15,000 (.5132 + .4664 + .4241 + .3855) + \$200,000 (.3505) + \$700,000 (.3186 + .2897 + .2633 + .2394 + .2176 + .1978 + .1799 + .1635), or $-$\$100,000 (5.3552) + \$15,000 (1.7893) + \$200,000 (.3505) + \$700,000 (1.8698). Thus the answer is $-$\$535,520 + \$26,840 + \$70,100 + \$1,308,860 = \$870,280. Since its present value is positive, the investment is worthwhile. It increases the firm's wealth. (b) If the effect on the firm's cash flow is zero in 1987–91, the present value is $-$\$100,000 (5.3552) + \$700,000 (1.8698), or \$773,340. Since it is positive, the investment is still worthwhile.

7) $10 \div 1.08 = 9.26$. $10 \div 1.08 = 9.26$.

9) \$200.

11) A profit-maximizing firm generally will not scrap existing equipment merely because somewhat better equipment is available. The new equipment must be sufficiently better to offset the fact that the old equipment is already paid for, whereas this is not the case for the new. Yes.

Chapter 18

1) (a) No. If the prize for the winner is \$100,000 and the prize for the runner-up is \$32,000, he would be sure to receive \$66,000 if he split. If he did not split, he would be involved in a gamble where the probability of winning \$100,000 would be 0.50 and the probability of winning \$32,000 would be 0.50. The expected monetary value of this gamble is \$66,000. Since a risk lover prefers a less certain outcome over a more certain outcome (when the expected monetary value is equal), he would prefer not to split.* (b) If he splits, he is certain to receive \$66,000; thus the expected utility is 16. If he does not split, the expected utility is 0.50 times the utility of \$100,000 plus 0.50 times the utility of \$32,000; that is; it equals $0.50 \times 19 + 0.50 \times 10 = 14.5$. Since the expected utility of splitting exceeds that of not splitting, he will split. (c) If P is the top-seeded player's probability of winning, his expected utility if he does not split equals $P \times 19 + (1 - P) \times 10$. If he prefers not to split, this expected utility must exceed the expected utility if he splits, which is 16 (as we saw in the answer to part (b)). Thus $P \times 19 + (1 - P) \times 10 > 16$, or $P > 2/3$. In other words, he must have regarded his probability of winning as being greater than 2/3.

3) $.09 + 1.4 (.12 - .09) = .132$. Thus the rate of return is 13.2 percent.

5) 0.5 (\$1 million) + 0.5 ($-$\$2 million) $=$ $-$\$0.5 million.

7) (a) No, since it would have chosen not to purchase it if it were indifferent to risk. (b) No, since it would have chosen not to purchase it if it were risk averse.

9) (a) The utility of zero equals $10 + 2(0) = 10$. The utility of $-$ \$25,000 equals $10 + 2(-25) = -40$. The utility of + \$32,000 equals $10 + 2(32) = 74$. Her expected utility equals $0.5(-40) + 0.5(74) = 17$. (b) Since the expected utility if she makes the investment (17) exceeds the expected utility if she does not make it (10), she should make it.

11) A stock's estimated value of beta can change over time. The assumption that the historical relationship will continue to prevail in the future can be quite wrong.

*We assume for simplicity here and below that all that is of concern to the player is the prize money. Of course, there are lots of other considerations, including the amount of effort put forth, and the possibility that players who split will be caught and punished. Without question, the analysis in this example is highly simplified and incomplete, although of illustrative use.

1) Yes. Food cost is the objective function, and the attainment of the proper amount of calories, fats, and proteins is a series of constraints. Also, there are nonnegativity constraints.

3) The isorevenue lines are drawn below.

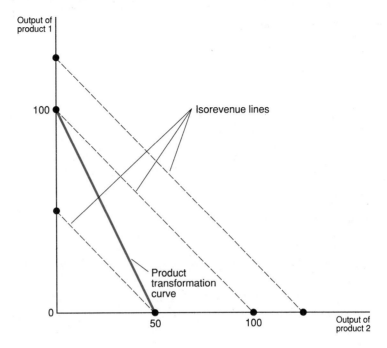

It should produce 100 units of product 1 and none of product 2, since this puts the firm on the highest isorevenue line that is attainable. No. This is a corner solution. There is no point where the isorevenue line is tangent to the product transformation curve in this case. Yes.

5) The cost of making one unit of the good is $8 with process *A,* $7.50 with process *B,* and $7.70 with process *C.* Thus all 100 units should be produced with process *B* since this is the cheapest procedure.

7) The set of feasible input combinations is *ABC* below.

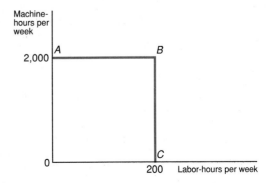

BRIEF ANSWERS TO ANALYTICAL QUESTIONS IN CROSS-CHAPTER CASES

Part Two: The Demand for Airline Travel

1) Business travelers account for a much higher proportion of first class than of excursion travelers. Business travelers may be influenced less than vacation travelers by the level of consumer incomes.

2) Because the price elasticity of demand is greater than 1 between the United States and Europe, but less than 1 between Canada and Europe.

3) Negative. Positive. Positive. Because it indicates whether additional tickets sold will increase revenue.

4) Yes. Increases in these prices tend to reduce air travel. Yes, because increases in their prices tend to reduce air travel.

5) Negative, because air travel from Europe to the United States and ground transportation in the United States probably are complements (although they may not be very strong complements).

Part Three: Optimal Lot Size and Japanese Manufacturing Methods

1) Yes, it reduced the amount of labor time required to set up a press.

2) $5 \times \$100,000 = \$500,000$.

3) 5,000 parts. Because the cost of financing the inventory and the amount of space required to hold the inventory increase as the inventory gets bigger.

4) $5,000 \times \$2 = \$10,000$. $\$500,000 + \$10,000 = \$510,000$.

5) No. The optimal lot size equals $\sqrt{\dfrac{2(\$100,000)50,000}{\$2}} = \sqrt{5 \text{ billion}} = 70,711$.

6) This question is important because firms would like to know whether they should be concerned about relatively small departures from the optimal lot size or whether, so long as the lot size is reasonably close to the optimum, costs are not much higher than if the optimum lot size is adopted. To answer this question, a firm can use the first equation in footnote 1 on p. 214 to determine the total costs if various lot sizes (near the optimum) are used, and compare these costs with the cost with the optimal lot size.

7) How much American firms should invest depends on how much extra profit they will make per year if they reduce their setup costs to the Japanese level. Clearly, beyond some point, it will not pay them to increase further their investment to achieve this goal.

Part Four: The Economics of 1992

1) As pointed out on page 272, a monopoly produces at a point at which the marginal social value of the good exceeds the good's marginal cost. In a static sense, society would be better off if more resources were devoted to the production of the good, as it would be in a competitive market.

2) Yes, the demand curve is changed to P_1AD.

3) Yes, its new output will be at the point where marginal cost equals OP_1.

4) Yes.

5) Profit maximization is only a first approximation. In fact, many firms could reduce their costs to some extent if their managers felt it was necessary. One reason for costs being higher than the minimum level is the principal-agent problem (discussed on pp. 140–41).

6) Politicians like to use government contracts to promote the economic interests of their districts and to promote their own careers. For obvious reasons, the United States govern-

ment would probably feel uncomfortable about relying on other countries (no matter how friendly at present) for key military hardware vital to our defense. Also, there would be intense political pressure to buy from domestic producers.

Part Five: Sex Discrimination and Comparable Worth

1) It is very difficult to determine how many points to give a specific occupation with regard to "mental demands" or to determine the proper weights to apply to various criteria. Moreover, these four criteria are not the only ones that could be used. Such a point system seems largely arbitrary.

2) No.

3) Yes.

4) Yes. Yes. Not if they are displaced by other typists.

5) Because firms have to keep their costs down in order to be competitive with their rivals.

6) No. Efforts should be continued to reduce barriers to entry by women into high-paid occupations like law and medicine. Changes in productivity, due to education and other factors, certainly are important.

Part Six: Effects of Quotas on Steel Imports into the United States

1) There is no entirely satisfactory way to compare the losses of the losers (such as consumers) with the gains of the gainers (such as steel producers).

2) Consumers could pay up to $178,000 to each steelworker who would lose his or her job if the quotas were abandoned, and still be better off than under the quotas. If a steelworker earns less than $178,000, he or she would be better off as well. (Of course, parties other than consumers and steelworkers are involved.)

3) No.

4) One important indicator is whether its costs are no higher than its foreign rivals. However, it frequently is difficult to make accurate comparisons of costs in various countries, and movements in exchange rates can be important.

5) Steel producers and their employees, as well as regions dependent on the steel industry, have favored these quotas. Some reasons for their adoption are given on pp. 485–88.

Part Seven: Aircraft Development and the SST

1) $4.5 billion. (Why? Because 0.4 ($4.5 billion) + 0.6 (−$3 billion) = 0.)

2) $7.5 million. $6.25 million + C if each approach is taken to the point where C dollars have been spent on it and if the cheaper approach is chosen at this point.

3) Yes, because the expected cost will be $6.25 million + $1 million = $7.25 million, which is less than the expected cost ($7.5 million) with a single approach.

4) Because the net benefits are large and negative in the immediate future and positive only in the more distant future. A high interest rate makes the positive net benefits in the more distant future of less significance relative to the negative net benefits in the immediate future.

5) Ideally, it should be based on the alternative cost of public funds.

6) The present value of the investment is $-100 + \dfrac{25}{1.10} + \dfrac{25}{1.10^2} + \dfrac{25}{1.10^3} + \dfrac{25}{1.10^4} +$

$\dfrac{25}{1.10^5} = -100 + 25(.909 + .826 + .751 + .683 + .621) = -100 + 25(3.790) = -5.25$

millions of dollars. Since the present value is negative, the firm should not accept the project.

PHOTOGRAPH CREDITS

INDEX

(continued from front endpaper)